Volu

The
American
Past

A Survey of American History

SIXTH EDITION

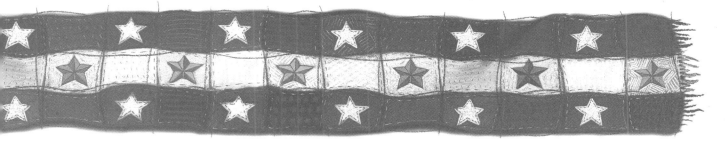

Harcourt College Publishers

Where Learning Comes to Life

TECHNOLOGY

Technology is changing the learning experience, by increasing the power of your textbook and other learning materials; by allowing you to access more information, more quickly; and by bringing a wider array of choices in your course and content information sources.

Harcourt College Publishers has developed the most comprehensive Web sites, e-books, and electronic learning materials on the market to help you use technology to achieve your goals.

PARTNERS IN LEARNING

Harcourt partners with other companies to make technology work for you and to supply the learning resources you want and need. More importantly, Harcourt and its partners provide avenues to help you reduce your research time of numerous information sources.

Harcourt College Publishers and its partners offer increased opportunities to enhance your learning resources and address your learning style. With quick access to chapter-specific Web sites and e-books . . . from interactive study materials to quizzing, testing, and career advice . . . Harcourt and its partners bring learning to life.

Harcourt's partnership with Digital:Convergence™ brings :CRQ™ technology and the :CueCat™ reader to you and allows Harcourt to provide you with a complete and dynamic list of resources designed to help you achieve your learning goals. Just swipe the cue to view a list of Harcourt's partners and Harcourt's print and electronic learning solutions.

http://www.harcourtcollege.com/partners/

Volume I — *to 1877*

The
American
Past

A Survey of American History

SIXTH EDITION

Joseph R. Conlin

Harcourt College Publishers

Fort Worth   Philadelphia   San Diego   New York   Orlando   Austin   San Antonio

Toronto   Montreal   London   Sydney   Tokyo

Publisher	**Earl McPeek**
Executive Editor	**David Tatom**
Market Strategist	**Steve Drummond**
Developmental Editor	**Margaret McAndrew Beasley**
Project Editor	**Laura J. Hanna**
Art Director	**Burl Sloan**
Production Manager	**Linda McMillan**

Cover illustration: Kathleen Kinkopf

ISBN: 0-15-506119-4
Library of Congress Catalog Card Number: 00-104138

Address for Domestic Orders
Harcourt College Publishers, 6277 Sea Harbor Drive, Orlando, FL 32887-6777
800-782-4479

Address for International Orders
International Customer Service
Harcourt, Inc., 6277 Sea Harbor Drive, Orlando, FL 32887-6777
407-345-3800
(fax) 407-345-4060
(e-mail) hbintl@harcourt.com

Address for Editorial Correspondence
Harcourt College Publishers, 301 Commerce Street, Suite 3700, Fort Worth, TX 76102

Web Site Address
http://www.harcourtcollege.com

Harcourt College Publishers will provide complimentary supplements or supplement packages to those adopters qualified under our adoption policy. Please contact your sales representative to learn how you qualify. If as an adopter or potential user you receive supplements you do not need, please return them to your sales representative or send them to: Attn: Returns Department, Troy Warehouse, 465 South Lincoln Drive, Troy, MO 63379.

Printed in the United States of America

1 2 3 4 5 6 7 8 9   032   9 8 7 6 5 4 3 2 1

Harcourt College Publishers

To **L.V.C.**

and the Memory

of **J.R.C.**

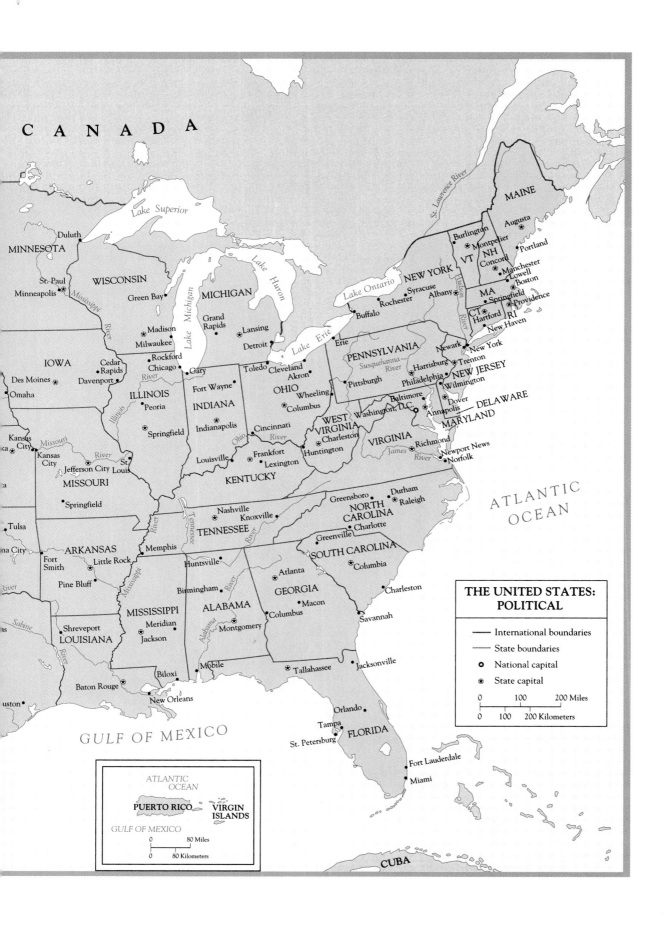

CANADA

MINNESOTA

Duluth

Lake Superior

WISCONSIN

St. Paul
Minneapolis
Mississippi
River

Green Bay

MICHIGAN

Lake Michigan

Lake Huron

Grand
Rapids

Lansing

Madison

Milwaukee

IOWA

Cedar
Rapids

Rockford

Chicago

Detroit

Lake Erie

Erie

Lake Ontario

Buffalo

Rochester

Syracuse

Albany

NEW YORK

St. Lawrence River

MAINE

Augusta

Burlington

Montpelier

VT

NH

Concord

Portland

Manchester
Lowell
Boston

Springfield

Providence

Hartford

RI

New Haven

MA

CT

Hudson River

Des Moines
Omaha

Davenport

Gary

ILLINOIS

Peoria

Fort Wayne

INDIANA

Toledo

Cleveland

Akron

OHIO

Columbus

Wheeling

PENNSYLVANIA

Susquehanna
River

Pittsburgh

Harrisburg

Philadelphia

Trenton

Newark

New York

NEW JERSEY

Wilmington

DELAWARE

Dover

Kansas
City

Missouri
River

Kansas
City

Jefferson City
St.
Louis

Springfield

Indianapolis

Ohio
River

Louisville

Frankfort

Lexington

Cincinnati

Charleston

WEST
VIRGINIA

Baltimore

Washington, D.C.

Annapolis

MARYLAND

MISSOURI

Illinois

KENTUCKY

Huntington

VIRGINIA

Richmond

James
River

Newport News
Norfolk

ATLANTIC
OCEAN

Tulsa

Springfield

Nashville

Knoxville

Tennessee
River

Greensboro

Durham

Raleigh

NORTH
CAROLINA

ARKANSAS

Fort
Smith

Little Rock

Memphis

TENNESSEE

Greenville

Charlotte

Pine Bluff

Mississippi

Huntsville

Birmingham

SOUTH CAROLINA

Columbia

River

MISSISSIPPI

ALABAMA

Atlanta

GEORGIA

Charleston

Shreveport

Meridian

Alabama
River

Macon

Columbus

Savannah

LOUISIANA

Jackson

Montgomery

Sabine
River

Baton Rouge

Biloxi

Mobile

Tallahassee

Jacksonville

uston

New Orleans

GULF OF MEXICO

Orlando

Tampa

St. Petersburg

FLORIDA

Fort Lauderdale

Miami

ATLANTIC
OCEAN

PUERTO RICO

VIRGIN
ISLANDS

GULF OF MEXICO

0   80 Miles
0   80 Kilometers

CUBA

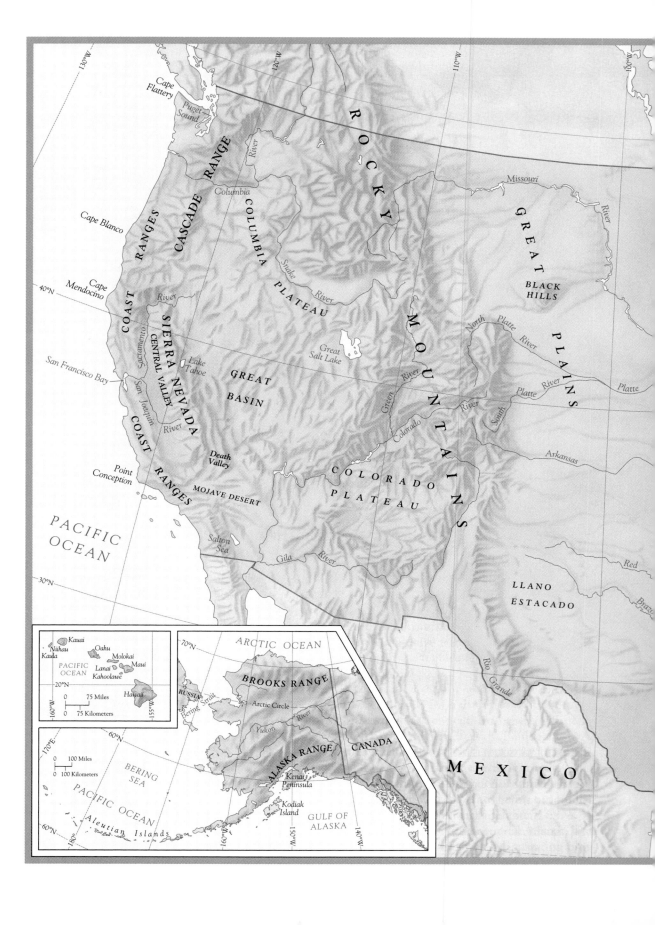

R O C K Y

Cape
Flattery

Puget
Sound

Columbia   River

Cape Blanco

CASCADE RANGE

COAST RANGES

COLUMBIA

Snake   River

PLATEAU

M O U N T A I N S

Missouri

G R E A T

BLACK
HILLS

River

Cape
Mendocino

40°N

River

SIERRA NEVADA

CENTRAL VALLEY

Great
Salt Lake

Great
Salt Lake

Lake
Tahoe

GREAT

BASIN

Green   River

North   Platte   River

P L A I N S

San Francisco Bay

Sacramento

San Joaquin

River

COAST

RANGES

Death
Valley

Colorado   River

South   Platte   River

Platte   River

Platte

Point
Conception

MOJAVE DESERT

C O L O R A D O

Arkansas

PACIFIC
OCEAN

Salton
Sea

P L A T E A U

30°N

Gila   River

LLANO

ESTACADO

Red

Rio

Grande

Brazos

M E X I C O

Kauai
Niihau
Kaula

Oahu
Molokai

PACIFIC
OCEAN

Lanai   Maui
Kahoolawe

20°N

0   75 Miles

Hawaii

0   75 Kilometers

ARCTIC OCEAN

70°N

RUSSIA

BROOKS RANGE

Arctic Circle

River

Bering Strait

Yukon

CANADA

ALASKA RANGE

0   100 Miles

60°N

Kenai
Peninsula

0   100 Kilometers

BERING
SEA

Kodiak
Island

GULF OF
ALASKA

PACIFIC OCEAN

60°N

Aleutian   Islands

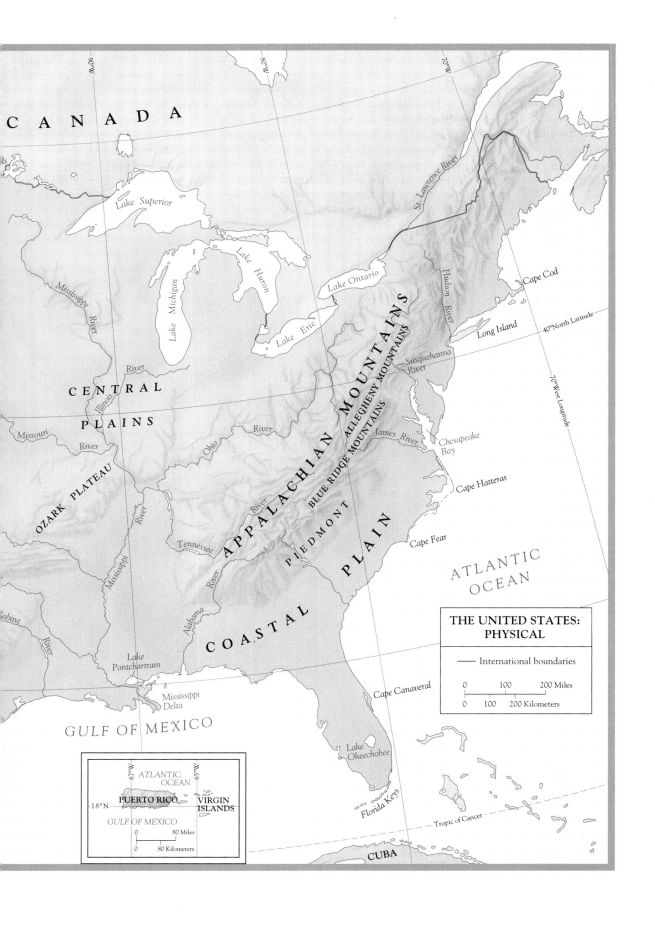

CANADA

Lake Superior

Lake Michigan

Lake Huron

Lake Ontario

Lake Erie

Mississippi River

CENTRAL

PLAINS

River

Illinois

Missouri

River

OZARK PLATEAU

River

Ohio

River

River

APPALACHIAN MOUNTAINS

ALLEGHENY MOUNTAINS

BLUE RIDGE MOUNTAINS

St. Lawrence River

Hudson River

Susquehanna River

Cape Cod

Long Island

40°North Latitude

70°West Longitude

James River

Chesapeake Bay

PIEDMONT

Cape Hatteras

Tennessee

River

Mississippi

Sabine

River

Alabama

River

COASTAL

PLAIN

Cape Fear

ATLANTIC
OCEAN

Cape Canaveral

Lake
Pontchartrain

Mississippi
Delta

GULF OF MEXICO

Lake
Okeechobee

Florida Keys

Tropic of Cancer

CUBA

THE UNITED STATES:
PHYSICAL

—— International boundaries

0   100   200 Miles

0   100   200 Kilometers

67°W

ATLANTIC
OCEAN

65°W

18°N   PUERTO RICO

VIRGIN
ISLANDS

GULF OF MEXICO

0   80 Miles

0   80 Kilometers

PREFACE TO THE SIXTH EDITION

There are many approaches to teaching a survey course in American history. During thirty years in the college classroom teaching principally that course, I have tried a good many of them. My courses have ranged from the prescriptive and highly structured to (when class size allowed it) open-ended seminar. One semester, inspired by a pedagogical fashion of the hour, I tried to teach U.S. History Survey with no reading material except documents—primary sources—no textbook. That lasted one semester. The experiment was a failure. Indeed, one reason I wrote the first edition of *The American Past* was my recognition, after the documents-only experiment, of just how important a textbook is to a successful survey course. I came to think that the quality of the textbook is second only to the quality of the instructor in making the U.S. History Survey a valuable—no, essential—part of undergraduate education.

The reason that the U.S. History Survey course is so important is that all but the very best of students at the most selective universities come to college lacking a foundation in the stuff of American history. A good textbook provides this. The best classroom teachers need that foundation if they are going to build in students an understanding of how human beings have faced the challenges presented them by circumstances of their times and the actions of those other human beings with whom they shared the earth in 1607, 1776, 1925, and 1980.

The textbook that provides this foundation must be, first of all, a book that is actually read. Few of the students in survey courses are budding historians willing to plow through sometimes murky documents (and scholarly prose) in order to master their subject. They are, rather, would-be accountants, ecologists, engineers, nurses, psychologists, retailers, webmasters, and zookeepers who, often enough, are enrolled in the U.S. History Survey only because they are required to do so. Such, often reluctant, students must be wooed, first by the skills and personality of the instructor, and second by the *readability* of their textbook. The book bought and put aside in favor of memorizing a crib sheet off the Internet is worthless to everyone but the individuals who profited from its purchase.

A textbook that is actually read is the kind of textbook I meant to produce in *The American Past*, and the kind of textbook I have meant to improve in revising it. Keeping in mind that my readers are not professional historians, I have painted in broad strokes, avoiding the hyper-specialization that wounds in some textbooks and disturbs so many nonhistorians (and historians!) today. I have tried to clarify difficult concepts and points of interpretation with anecdote, and I have not shunned humorous commentary when the material deserved it.

There is always room for improvement. Each time I have revised this book, I have winced to discover that sections I thought adequate or even good a few years earlier needed basic rehabilitation or even total replacement. Nevertheless, I believe I have been more successful than not in accomplishing my goals, and with each edition moved closer to the unattainable ideal. During the two decades that *The American Past* has been in print, I have received dozens of letters—perhaps close to two hundred—from professors who have assigned the text to their classes. They have pointed out my boners, taken me to task for the slant I put on a particular topic, asked my source for one specific or another, and complimented my book. It has been gratifying that even some of the most annoyed correspondents closed their critical letters with a comment something like, **"My students really like *The American Past*. They actually read it."**

That has been the idea, and remains the guiding principle behind this Sixth Edition.

NEW TO THE SIXTH EDITION

Those familiar with *The American Past* Fifth Edition will find no major structural or organizational changes. The primary focus of this revision was updating, with a secondary emphasis on refining—of scholarship, interpretation, clarity, and pedagogical function. In the process of the revision, every sentence was reconsidered and polished as necessary. Selected notable revisions to specific chapters include: expanded treatment of Native Americans (Chapters 1–3 and 5); new material on politics and political culture (Chapter 15); new information and expanded treatment of Mormons, utopias, and Know Nothings (Chapter 17); new material on American Colonization Society (Chapter 18); more discussion of cavalry and African-American soldiers (Chapter 23); expansion of impeachment section (Chapter 25); expanded discussion of the telephone and Standard Oil (Chapter 27); modified interpretation of Southern Pacific Railroad (Chapter 28); extensive rewriting (Chapter 31); incorporation of new material on Clinton, Whitewater, impeachment proceedings, CBS and Viacom merger, presidential campaign for Election of 2000, and end of the millennium (Chapter 51); in fact, Chapter 51, the final chapter, is virtually new as a whole.

New Features: Chronologies

Based on suggestions from reviewers of the Fifth Edition, a chronology has been added to the end of each chapter. These chronologies outline the major events of the period reflected in each chapter, providing a quick reference for student review.

Thoroughly Updated "For Further Reading" Sections

The annotated bibliographies at the end of each chapter were thoroughly reviewed and include a total of nearly three hundred new entries.

New "How They Lived," "Notable People," and Sidebar Essays

The Sixth Edition includes a wealth of new social, cultural, biographical, and anecdotal material within three different types of boxed essays that have become favorite features of *The American Past* readers. "How They Lived" essays provide students with a snapshot of daily life and issues at a particular time in a particular place. "Notable People" boxes introduce students to figures of interest—some well known and others simply "ordinary" men and women with extraordinary stories. The Sidebar features are a trademark of *The American Past* and offer little gems of information that add life and dimension to the periods and events covered in the narrative.

ACKNOWLEDGMENTS

I have had splendid assistance in preparing this edition by a number of teaching historians who each read and critiqued chapters from the Fifth Edition. Among them: Scott Carter, Shasta College; Linda Cross, Tyler Junior College; Martha Kirchmer, Grand Valley State University; Jack Oden, Enterprise State Junior College; Richard H. Peterson, emeritus, San Diego State University; Nancy L. Rachels, Hillsborough Community College; William Scofield, Yakima Valley Community College; Ronald Story, University of Massachusetts; and Daniel C. Vogt, Jackson State University. I hope I have done their scrutiny justice.

In addition to reviewers commenting on the book as a whole, Donald W. Whisenhunt virtually scoured the entire Fifth Edition line by line looking for cases of poor explication, disputable interpretation, inconsistency, and typographical or factual errors. I particularly hope I have responded adequately to his observations. My thanks as well to Ronald

Story who reviewed the "For Further Reading" sections and provided hundreds of new annotated entries to bring the bibliography up to date.

Once again I have benefited from the professional ministrations of a number of people at Harcourt College Publishers. David Tatom, executive editor, has overseen the development and production of this edition, as he did the Fifth. To Margaret McAndrew Beasley, senior developmental editor, that is, the person on the floor, daily dirtying (or breaking) her fingernails as she prodded me in the right direction, I owe my fullest thanks. I am also grateful to Laura Hanna, the very able senior project editor who, herself, dirtied a few fingernails; Linda McMillan, production manager; Burl Sloan, senior art director; Steve Drummond, executive market strategist (in charge of many operations mysterious to me, yet appreciated all the more for that); and Lili Weiner, resourceful freelance photo researcher for their respective roles in the process. In a sixth edition, a book should not need much editing for clarity and style, and *The American Past* did not. It was assigned, nevertheless and to my delight, a freelance editor of the first order, Charles Naylor, whose eye for inappropriate nuances and lapses of clarity astonished me, and who also brought an extensive knowledge of American history to his task.

The American Past **Web-enhanced Sixth Edition**

Harcourt College Publishers brings *The American Past* to life with quick and easy access to Web-enhanced learning content. The :CueCat™ reader from Digital:Convergence makes it easy! Just a swipe of the :CueCat reader across strategically placed cues within the text immediately takes you to additional, relevant online content and resources. Many of Conlin's trademark "How They Lived" and "Notable People" boxes now include cues.

To see how it works, follow the cue. . .

CONTENTS IN BRIEF

TABLE OF CONTENTS

LIST OF MAPS

LIST OF FEATURE BOXES

Volume I — *to 1877*

The
American
Past

SIXTH EDITION

A Survey of American History

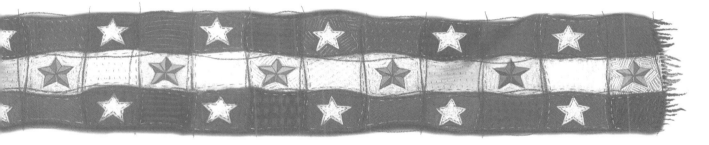

The first known European depiction of Native Americans was printed in Germany between 1497 and 1504.

1

CHAPTER

WHEN WORLDS COLLIDE

America and Europe
Before 10,000 B.C.—A.D. 1550

The greatest event since the creation of the world, excluding the incarnation and death of Him who created it, is the discovery of the Indies.

— Francisco López de Gómara

I feel a wonderful exultation of spirits when I converse with intelligent men who have returned from these regions. It is like an accession of wealth to a miser. Our minds, soiled and debased by the common concerns of life and the vices of society, become elevated and ameliorated by contemplating such glorious events.

—Peter Martyr

Broken spears lie in the roads;
We have torn our hair in our grief.
The houses are roofless now,
And their walls are red with blood. . . .
We are crushed to the ground;
We lie in ruins.
There is nothing but grief and suffering
in Mexico and Tlatelolco.

—Anonymous Aztec poet

The first Americans came from Asia. More than 10,000 years ago, some say as early as 40,000 B.C., wandering Asian hunters picked their way eastward over land that then connected Siberia and Alaska. Before them, no human being had ever stood on soil we call "American."

Many nomadic bands crossed the land bridge. They were pursuing herds of caribou, fleeing from enemies, or just checking out the country, as nomads do. Some may have come by sea in small boats, hugging the shoreline. They stayed. They became colonists in an empty land, and their descendants fanned out to populate two continents in a few thousand years. These first discoverers of America were, of course, the ancestors of the people we call Indians.

DISCOVERY

Historians learn about the past by studying the written word. So, they can tell us nothing of these Paleo-Indians (*old* Indians) who lived, loved, hated, and died before the invention of writing. For the story of human beings before there was writing, we look to archaeologists, linguists, and folklorists, scholars who sift particles of information, like flecks of gold, from the gravel of artifacts—things human beings created—and from language and from tales passed down by one generation to another.

History and Prehistory

The pictures these men and women sketch are fuzzier than the portraits historians draw using written documents. As a Chinese saying has it, "the palest ink is clearer than the best memory." But blurred is better than blank. Without folklore, analysis of language, and archaeology, the American past would not begin until 1492, just over 500 years ago. It was then that Europeans, who scribbled endlessly of their achievements and follies, discovered a "New World" in the Western Hemisphere. Thanks to archaeologists, linguists, and folklorists, we can pencil in a far more ancient heritage.

Diversity

The earliest Paleo-Indians knew nothing of agriculture. When they migrated to North America, there was not a farmer on the planet. Like all human be-ings of that primeval day, the first Americans lived by hunting and gathering, taking from nature the makings of their meals, clothing, and shelter. They were nomads because they had to be. In all but the richest environments, even a small band of people soon exhausts the food that can be hunted and gathered in the neighborhood of their camps.

By the time the mystery of agriculture was first unlocked in the ancient Middle East, about 8000 B.C., the first Americans had lost all significant contact with the peoples of the Eurasian land mass from which they had come. There had been a global warming. Glaciers and the polar ice caps melted so that, worldwide, sea level rose. Salt water submerged the land bridge between Siberia and Alaska (and other low-lying lands and coastlines throughout the world).

Paleo-Indian ways of life diversified rapidly. The Americas were uncrowded, to say the least. Wandering bands found it easy to split up when their numbers grew too large for the range or, no doubt, when headstrong leaders had a falling out. Soon enough, vastness and the diversity of American climates and land forms scattered tribes, isolated them from one another, and created many different cultures and economies.

American Indian languages, for example, once just a handful, multiplied until there were at least 500 of them (some scholars say 1400!). In harsh country, some tribes continued to live precariously into the modern era, seeming to outsiders barely to survive week to week on what they could hunt, snare, gather, and grub. Other peoples farmed, producing the surplus of food that, as in Mesopotamia, Egypt, China, and India, made possible the beginnings of civilization.

The Indians of Meso-America (meaning *between* the Americas, that is, Mexico and South America) invented agriculture. Some nameless hero or heroine among them unlocked the secrets of actively producing food, rather than depending on nature to provide it. Probably, agriculture was invented in only one other part of the world, the hills of the ancient Middle East. Every other people of both hemispheres learned how to farm from others who were already doing so.

Some Indians had mastered only primitive tool making when, after A.D. 1500, they were dazzled (and soon crushed) by European technology. Others perfected handicrafts to a level of refinement unmatched anywhere in Africa, Asia, or Europe. Some peoples left no other mark on the land than the remains of campfires and garbage dumps that, in order to identify today, we need space-age equipment. By way of contrast, the labor force of the mysterious "mound builders" of central North America was sufficiently organized and disciplined that they heaped up massive earthen structures that have survived the ages. One great mound, in the shape of a bird, was seventy feet in height, an edifice as impressive as a Mesopotamian ziggurat. In Ohio, two parallel mound-builder "walls" ran sixty miles from Chillicothe to Newark. Some scholars believe (others deny it) that Cahokia, in Illinois across the Mississippi from the site of St. Louis, had a population of 30,000.

The Indians' closeness to nature over hundreds of generations made them canny in lore based on observation and trial-and-error experiment. For example, the effects of more than 200 medicines in use in the United States today were known in prehistoric America. Given the isolation of the Indians from the process of cultural diffusion — the exchange of ideas and techniques that cross-fertilized the cultures of the "Old World" of Asia, northern Africa, and Europe — their achievements are astonishing.

MESO-AMERICAN CIVILIZATION

In Guatemala, Belize, and southern Mexico, Indian farmers also made the leap that signals the birth of civilization and history. Olmecs and later Toltecs and Mayas farmed so productively that they could support a large, dense, and highly organized society in which many individuals could work at tasks other than agriculture. Just as in the ancient civilizations of the Old World, the Meso-Americans soon developed a system of writing with which they carved records in stone and composed books on processed strips of cactus fiber similar to ancient Egypt's papyrus.

Alas for historians, in the 1500s, a zealous Spanish bishop condemned these writings as full of "superstition and lies of the devil." So effective was his command they be burned that only three Mayan literary works survive. But inscribed rock proved too much for righteous censors. Carved writings are abundant in Meso-America and, in recent decades, experts have learned to read them. They provide us with a chapter of American history that had been given up as forever lost.

City-States

At one time or another, some forty cities dotted Meso-America. Several were home to 20,000 people and twice that many people lived in Dzibilchaltún. Teotihuacán, founded about the time of the birth of Christ some 30 miles northeast of present-day Mexico City, was home by 500 A.D. to 125,000 souls, more than lived in Shakespeare's London a millennium later.

Meso-American cities were governed by an aristocracy of priests and warriors who directed the construction at the center of each city of at least one earth and stone temple in the shape of a pyramid. The pyramid at Chichén Itzá rose 18 modern stories.

The Mayans, the farthest-flung of the Meso-Americans, were superb mathematicians and astronomers, too. They discovered the use of the zero, another breakthrough achieved in only one other world culture, India. They timed the earth's orbit around the sun as accurately as any other astronomers of their day, and applied their findings to a calendar that was as complex as it was accurate.

War and Religion

The rulers of the Mayan cities had immense power. However, they had little interest in the empire-building that obsessed Old World cultures. Each city-state was an independent entity. Not that the Meso-Americans were a peaceful people. They were chronically at war with their neighbors. The Mayan religion compelled war, for its gods (jaguar-like beings, eagles, serpents, and the sun) thirsted for human blood.

In solemn public rituals, Mayan noblewomen made symbolic blood sacrifices by drawing strings of thorns through wounds in their tongues. Their husbands and brothers drew the cruel thongs through the foreskins of their penises. The blood that fell from these wounds was absorbed into strips of paper-like fiber, which were burned, dispatching the sacrifice to the heavens.

Alas, symbolic blood sacrifice did not satisfy the Mayan deities. They also demanded that priests throw young women into pits to die, and drag other victims to the tops of the pyramids where, using stone knives, priests tore their hearts, still beating when the operation was correctly performed, from their breasts. Thus the demand for prisoners of war.

Cultural Cul-de-Sac

Elsewhere in the world, city-states made war in order to conquer and exploit their neighbors. Along with the misery it caused, such imperialism often led to some of the greatest breakthroughs in the evolution of civilization. The blood lust of the Meso-American gods, however, meant that the Mayans and others made war for the unproductive purpose of rounding up victims for sacrifice. They expended vast resources in a direction that, in material and intellectual terms, led nowhere. Their culture did not, in that word so central to the story of western civilization, *progress*. The genius and energy of the civilization, not to mention the lives of so many of its people, were devoted to staying on the right side

of fearsome gods to avoid worse than what the society already had. It was an almost pathologically conservative culture.

So far as the Mayans were concerned, conservatism did not work. By 1500, virtually every Mayan city had been abandoned. The Spaniards who swooped down on Meso-America found the great pyramids already crumbling or vanishing beneath lush tropical vegetation. Most of the Meso-Americans they conquered, including the Mayans, lived in small villages and visited the ruins of the old cities only on religious holidays.

What happened? Some archaeologists think that the Meso-Americans warred themselves into cultural exhaustion. They point to the Olmecs' massive stone heads that were deliberately buried, as if hidden from

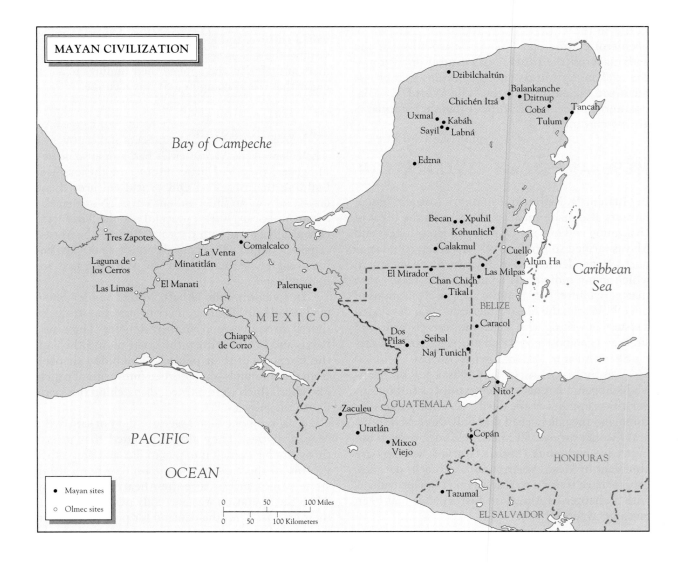

enemies, to be unearthed at a better time that was never to come. Other scholars think that the Meso-American cities were rendered unlivable by soil depletion. In order to support a large urban population, farmers must produce a large surplus of food. But the earth beneath a tropical forest is easily exhausted by intense cultivation, as Brazil is learning today in its denuded jungles. Whatever the explanation, by 1500 Meso-American civilization was thriving only to the north of the old Mayan stronghold, in the fertile Valley of Mexico, in the land of the Aztecs.

The Aztecs

The Aztecs were comparative newcomers to Meso-America, arriving in Mexico from the north during the 1200s. They were a poor and primitive folk by comparison with the Toltecs and other peoples who brought Meso-American civilization to central Mexico. However, like the Turks who overran the sophisticated Arab world, and the Manchus who made China their own, the Aztecs recognized a better way of life when they conquered one. Carving out an enclave on the shores of Lake Texcoco, they embraced Meso-American culture.

Aztec power grew. Although they did not directly rule large alien populations, by 1500 the Aztec presence loomed over Mexico. Tribute — "protection money" — rolled in from as far as both Pacific and Gulf coasts. The Aztecs put this wealth to work

building one of the world's most splendid cities, Tenochtitlán. By 1500, Tenochtitlán covered six square miles and was home to 200,000 people. One plaza, site of a major market, could accommodate 50,000 people exchanging goods that were borne to Tenochtitlán from as far as 800 miles away. Surrounded by Lake Texcoco, the Aztec capital was superbly defended. Three narrow causeways—broken here and there by drawbridges—connected Tenochtitlán to the mainland homes of weaker tribes who lived in fear of the Aztecs.

Blood and Gore

The greatest temple in Tenochtitlán was a pyramid with a base of 210 feet by 240 feet. Two dizzyingly steep staircases climbed to altars 200 feet above the street. These steps were stained black with dried blood for, like the Mayans, the Aztecs practiced human sacrifice. Indeed, Huitzilopochtli, a god who accompanied the Aztecs from the north, demanded 10,000 hearts in an ordinary year. According to Aztec records, in 1478, when Huitzilopochtli was very angry, priests dressed in cloaks of human skin and stinking of gore, for they were forbidden to wash or cut their hair, sent 20,000 volunteers and captives to their doom in just four days. Or so the chronicles say.

Bad years came to the Aztecs all too often during the late 1400s and early 1500s. Omens of all sorts, from natural calamities to wandering female spirits

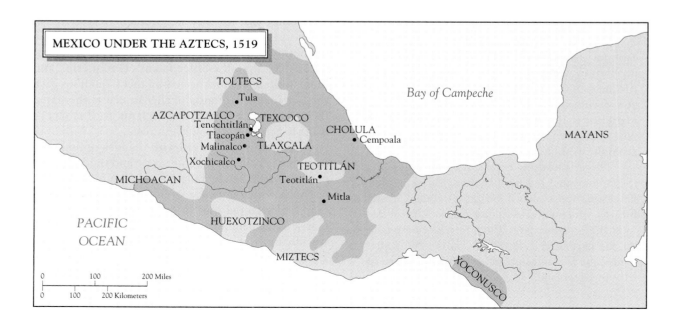

lamenting what was to become of their children, had the Aztecs on edge. None was more nervous than the emperor Moctezuma II, whose reign began in 1502. The Aztec calendar, inherited from the Mayans, also hinted at impending disaster. It has been suggested that, psychologically, the Aztecs were ready prey for enemies who devoted their resources not just to staying on the right side of the gods, but to exploiting the new and the strange wherever they found it.

EUROPE: DRIVEN, DYNAMIC, EXPANSIVE

On October 12, 1492, on an island beach in the Bahamas, a thousand miles east of the Aztec realm, a band of rough, cursing, praying men, mostly Spaniards, waded ashore from three small ships to name their landfall San Salvador, or Holy Savior. Their

---

Many Discoverers

Columbus was not the first outsider to touch on the Americas after the seas drowned the land bridge from Siberia. Aleuts and Inuit (Eskimos), seagoing Arctic hunters, regularly landed in both Asia and North America. Possibly, like the styrofoam Japanese floats that wash up on our Pacific beaches today, Japanese fishermen survived being blown eastward to land in the Americas. Certain themes in Indian art tantalize archaeologists as "Asian."

There are also many tantalizing legends about explorers from abroad. The Olmecs told of black peoples in Central America. Some have seen African features in the famous Olmec heads. A Chinese document of 200 B.C. tells of Hee Li, who visited a land to the east he called Fu-Sang. Irish bards sang of St. Brendan, a monk who lived in a country far to the west of the Emerald Isle.

There is nothing mythical about Norsemen (Scandinavians) led by Thorfinn Karlsefni, Leif Erickson, and a sword-swinging woman named Freydis, who founded a colony in North America—"Vinland"—around A.D. 1000. A lack of hospitality on the part of the skraelings, as the Norsemen named the Vinland Indians, persuaded them to retreat to Greenland.

---

leader was a red-haired Italian about forty years of age. To his Spanish crew he was Cristóbal Colón, to us Christopher Columbus. To the Arawaks, the people of the Bahamas who greeted him, he represented a bizarre world unlike anything they had ever imagined.

Christopher Columbus

Falling to his knees, for his religion was as zealous as any Aztec priest's, Columbus proclaimed San Salvador the possession of the woman who had financed his voyage, Queen Isabella of Castille, and her husband, Ferdinand. They were the first rulers of unified Spain. Columbus noted that the Arawaks were "very gentle, and do not know what it is to be wicked, or to kill others, or to steal." He concluded it would be easy to enslave them! The Spaniards would try. For the moment, however, Columbus inquired of the Arawaks about the location of Japan and China. Those countries, and certainly not the balmy but poor Bahamas, were the places for which he was looking.

The historical development of the America we know begins with Christopher Columbus. Its origins lay not on the pyramids of Mexico, but in the churches, state chambers, and counting houses of western Europe, in a culture that was to impress itself not only upon the Americas, but upon the world.

Motives

Columbus believed that San Salvador was an outlying island of "the Indies," the name Europeans gave to the mysterious, distant East: Cipango (Japan), Cathay (China), the Spice Islands (Indonesia), and India itself. It was for this reason that Columbus gave the original inhabitants of the Americas the name that has stuck to their descendants to this day—indios in Spanish, in English Indians.

Columbus had set sail with the idea of finding a feasible sea route between Europe and the Indies. In part, he was driven by religious belief. A pious Roman Catholic with a mystical streak, Columbus believed God had selected him to carry the gospel of Jesus Christ to the peoples of the Indies. But Columbus had worldly motives, too. He longed for glory and fame. Like the artists, architects, and scholars of the Renaissance, he craved recognition as a great individual.

And Columbus wanted money. He hoped to get rich by doing business with the peoples he discovered. Gold and silver were always in season, of course. Columbus asked the Arawaks about those precious metals right away. Gold and silver could be exchanged for anything anywhere in the world, including the Asian gems and porcelains that Europeans craved, the fine cotton cloth of Syria and the silks of China, and tapestries and carpets that were beyond the craft of European weavers. Then there were the exotic drugs, dyes, perfumes, and particularly the spices of the Indies—cinnamon from Ceylon, Indonesian nutmeg and cloves, Chinese ginger, and peppercorns from India itself—luxuries that made life more pleasant and interesting, something more than a struggle for survival on earth and salvation after death.

A Business with a High Overhead

These goods had trickled into Europe since the days of the Roman Empire. From Marco Polo, a merchant of Venice, and other Europeans who traveled to East Asia and returned during the Middle Ages, Europeans learned that they were abundant there. Crusaders, European knights who conquered and ruled parts of the Levant (present-day Lebanon, Syria, and Israel) for as long as a century, enjoyed firsthand the richer life of the Muslims of the Near East, itself based partly on imports from the Indies.

The crusaders eventually were driven back to Europe by their Muslim enemies. But they continued to covet the goods of the Indies. These were carried by ship through the Indian Ocean and Persian Gulf or borne overland in caravans to the eastern end of the Mediterranean Sea: Constantinople and the Levant. They then found their way to Europe in the vessels of powerful Italian city-states, particularly Venice and Genoa. Wealthy Venetian and Genoese merchants functioned as middlemen, the wholesale distributors who sold the spices and the rest to smaller retailers all over the continent.

By the time the luxuries of the Indies reached the castles of Spain and the market towns of France, they were expensive indeed. The costs of transport alone were prodigious. The pepper that enlivened an English earl's stew may have traveled as far as eight thousand miles on donkey back. Raising costs yet higher, the old trade routes passed through the lands of warlike Central Asian tribes or, if they came by sea, through the haunts of East African pirates. Merchants had either to pay for safe passage, or hire

Zheng He

The sea link between Europe and Asia might easily have been first discovered by the Chinese rather than by the Portuguese. In 1405, Zheng He, the chief eunuch and greatest admiral of the Chinese imperial court, commanded a fleet of 62 five-masted junks and a hundred smaller ships on an expedition exploring the Indian Ocean. He visited both India and the eastern coast of Africa before returning to China.

Zheng He wanted to continue his explorations, which would have taken him around the Cape of Good Hope decades earlier than Vasco da Gama. But the emperor forbade it. Far from encouraging exploration, the emperor proclaimed that Chinese should not even travel abroad. It was not so much that he feared cultural contagion. The Chinese emperor believed, simply, that there was nothing in it for China to seek out other lands. Everything worthwhile was already there.

tough armed men to battle the villains. Either way, another cost was added to the selling price of Eastern goods.

Nobody Likes a Middleman

The traders of the Levant took a handsome profit. They were not in business for the glory of Allah and the service of humanity. The Christian Italians added their commissions, shrugging off accusations that they were gougers. Today, the splendid Renaissance palaces the Italian merchant princes built are an inspiration to the world. In the time of Columbus, the glories of Italy were just as likely to arouse resentment and envy among those consumers whose purchases of Asian goods made their construction possible.

In western Europe, envy of the wealth of the great Italian merchants fathered the dream of finding a new route to the Indies. The prince whose sailors bypassed the Italian middlemen would stop the flow of his country's wealth to Italy. Indeed, such a prince could imagine his subjects displacing the Italians as Europe's wholesalers of Asian products. As for the navigator who found a workable route to the Indies, he could expect a grand reward. Columbus was but one of several Italian sailors who went abroad to Portugal, Spain, England, and France in search of financial backing.

PORTUGAL AND SPAIN: THE VANGUARD OF EXPLORATION

Portugal and Spain led the quest for new trade routes. The map of Europe reveals one reason why these countries should have been in the vanguard. Both face the Atlantic, Portugal entirely so.

But location is not enough to explain the pioneering role of the Portuguese and Spanish. They were the first to challenge the Italian monopoly of the Asian trade because they were Europe's first unified nation-states. They were the first European countries to shake off feudalism—a political system in which power was fragmented, in many hands—and to create in its place a powerful central government. Such a government, unlike a dozen tiny, jealous feudal states, was capable of directing the use of vast resources toward great goals such as world exploration.

Iberian Nationalism

France and England were well along in the process of national unification at the end of the fifteenth century. Both were to be major players in the overseas expansion of European power and culture. But Portugal was already a unified nation in 1400. Its kings had come to the fore by leading long wars to drive out the Moors, Muslim Arabs, and Berbers having roots in what is now Morocco.

Prince Henry, a son of King John I, helped turn Portugal's attention to the Atlantic. Later dubbed Prince Henry the Navigator, he was fascinated by the sea and far-off lands, both known and imagined. He sent more than 30 expeditions along the coast of Africa to buy gold and slaves from black kingdoms west and south of the Sahara. Under his aegis, the Portuguese colonized Madeira, 350 miles off the coast of Africa, and the Azores, Atlantic islands 900 miles west of Portugal.

The remarkable Henry also endowed a kind of "think tank" of exploration at Sagres. Mariners gathered there to share their experiences with mapmakers, scholars who studied ancient travel accounts, and shipbuilders. Together they speculated, sometimes fantastically, often brilliantly, concerning world geography.

Why "America"? Why Not "Columbia"?

Columbus is to blame for the fact that his great discovery was not named for him. He never admitted that he had discovered a "New World" that could take a new name. For him, America was "The Indies."

The man for whom the Americas were named was Amerigo Vespucci, an Italian merchant who accompanied several Spanish expeditions to the coast of South America. Vespucci never claimed to have discovered anything. He merely wrote several descriptive letters in which he stated that the lands he visited were previously unknown. In 1507, a German cartographer, Martin Waldseemüller, the first mapmaker to show the Americas separate from Asia, misconstrued Vespucci's message and named the "New World" for him using the feminine Latin form of his name.

Sagres was also a research and development center. Confronted with contrary winds off Cape Bojador in West Africa, the Portuguese developed a vessel that was to make long ocean voyages possible, the caravel. Caravels could be rigged with the triangular lateen sails of the Mediterranean, which made it possible to beat against the wind, or with the large square sail of northern European vessels which pushed a ship at high speed when the wind was favorable. Caravels also required relatively small crews; they could be provisioned for voyages longer than other vessels could manage. "The best ships in the world and able to sail anywhere," said Luigi da Cadamosto, an Italian in Prince Henry's service.

Portugal's Route to Asia

Prince Henry died in 1460 but his inspiration lived on. Most notably, in 1488 a ship commanded by Bartholomeu Díaz returned to Portugal after reaching the Cape of Good Hope at the foot of the African continent. This was the corner to be turned. There would be clear sailing to the Indies by way of coasting along Africa.

Not for ten years would another Portuguese, Vasco da Gama, actually reach East Africa and the Indian port of Calicut. Portuguese sailors, particularly those led by Alfonso de Albuquerque, then built a commercial empire consisting of small trading posts stretching from West Africa to the Persian Gulf and Macao in China. The single Portuguese holding in the Americas was the consequence of a mishap befalling a navigator bound for Asia by da Gama's route. In 1500, Pedro Cabral was blown westerly off the coast of Africa to land on the eastern bulge of the South American continent. Cabral thereby established Portugal's claim to Brazil.

In the meantime, Portugal's success in tracing the African coast had the effect of killing any interest King John II might have had in "the Enterprise of the Indies," a plan presented to him by Christopher Columbus. Residing in Portugal since 1476, Columbus argued that the best way to East Asia lay not to the south, hugging the African coast, but due west across the Atlantic. John II entertained his scheme for several years, but eventually dismissed him. He called Columbus "a big talker, full of fancy and imagination."

Spain Looks West

So, in 1484, Columbus took his Enterprise to Spain. He found plenty of ridicule there, too. Scholars at the University of Salamanca described his plan as "vain, impracticable, and resting on grounds too weak to merit the support of the government." But Columbus had influential backers too, and the rulers

of Spain, Isabella and Ferdinand, had not failed to notice the Portuguese explorations. They paid Columbus a modest annuity to keep him around, in reserve, as it were.

Only in 1492, however, when Isabella and Ferdinand drove the last Muslim king out of Spain—an obsession in Spanish history—and Columbus threatened to take his project to France, did Isabella decide to finance him. Events then moved with remarkable dispatch. Columbus was commissioned Admiral of the Ocean Sea, an exalted title. He was granted extensive authority over any lands he discovered, and a generous share of any profits he made. The queen and other investors outfitted him with three small ships, two caravels, the *Niña* and the *Pinta*, and a less useful but larger carrack, the *Santa María*. The total cost of the expedition was $14,000, a pittance if Columbus made good on the boast that he would reach the Indies.

Frustrating Discoveries

Columbus never admitted that, instead of one of the 7,448 islands Marco Polo said lay off Asia, he had found a world new to Europeans and Asians. Four times he crossed the Atlantic bearing letters of introduction addressed to the emperors of China and Japan and others with blanks in which he could fill in names. Four times he returned after Indians told him they had never heard of such persons. Four

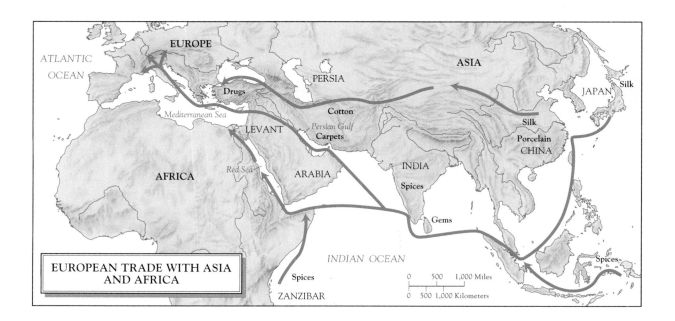

EUROPEAN TRADE WITH ASIA AND AFRICA

A contemporary artist attempts to capture the risks and romance of caravans from the East.

times he told Isabella and Ferdinand that, after just one more voyage he would

> give them as much gold as they need, . . . and I will also give them all the spices and cotton they need, and as for resin which till now has been found only in Greece, and which the traders of Genoa sell at the price they choose, I will bring back as much of it as their Majesties may order.

To the day of his death in 1506, Christopher Columbus insisted that he had reached Asia in 1492. Sustained for a lifetime by a glorious obsession, he could not admit that his discovery pointed toward quite another conclusion.

Indeed, it dawned only slowly on the Spaniards who actually settled on Cuba and Hispaniola (present-day Haiti and the Dominican Republic) that they were living in a "New World," utterly unknown to Europe. When they realized this, many of them cursed Columbus's discovery as an obstacle in the way to Asia. Spanish Cuba and Hispaniola were notorious for bloody quarrels among the frustrated treasure-seekers who settled there.

An expedition of 1513 led by Vasco Núñez de Balboa increased Spanish disappointment in the "New World." Balboa crossed the Isthmus of Panama, discovering that it was only 40 miles at its narrowest point. However, the isthmus festered with disease and, from a peak called Darien, Balboa discovered another great ocean, the Pacific. The implication was obvious: Asia might be far indeed from where the Spaniard stood. In 1519, Ferdinand

The fleet of Ferdinand Magellan, in the strait bearing his name, during the first voyage to circumnavigate the globe, 1519–1522.

Magellan confirmed the suspicion. A Portuguese sailing for Spain with five ships and 265 men, Magellan found a way to the Pacific around the southern tip of South America. He was killed in the Philippines, but one of his vessels, commanded by Juan Sebastián de Elcaño and carrying only eighteen men, struggled back to Europe.

At hideous cost, it was a magnificent achievement—the first voyage around the world. As a way to Asia, however, the Magellan–de Elcaño route was unworkable. Due to powerful adverse winds and currents in the Strait of Magellan, it could take a month or even more just to sail from the Atlantic to the Pacific. (Columbus crossed the entire Atlantic Ocean in just four weeks.) Until the very end of the Age of Sail, the era of the clipper ships, masters winced at the necessity of sailing westward around South America.

A Poor Bargain

International politics also served to disappoint and frustrate the Spanish. In 1493, in order to avoid conflict between Spain and Portugal, the pope of Rome, in *Inter Caetera*, divided all the world's lands not "in the actual possession of any Christian king or prince" between those two nations. The pope's line ran from North to South Pole a hundred leagues west of the Azores. The next year, in the Treaty of Tordesillas, the Portuguese persuaded Isabella and Ferdinand to move the line farther to the west (thus laying the grounds for Portuguese settlement of Brazil after 1500). Wherever the line was drawn, Spain was shut out of all Asia except the Philippines.

Until 1521, the Spanish in the New World thought of Tordesillas as a bad bargain indeed. Their share of the world's non-Christian wealth was profoundly disappointing. Instead of rich rewards such as the Portuguese were reaping in Africa and the Indies, they were masters of steamy, tropical, mosquito-plagued islands where there was neither gold nor spices.

THE SPANISH EMPIRE

Then, in 1519, pretty much the worst of times in Spanish America, an extraordinary soldier, acting on rumors, landed on the coast of Mexico with 508 soldiers, 200 Indians, several Africans, seven small

How They Lived

Locked in a Circle of Time

Nowhere in the world have archaeologists of our era made more exciting finds than in Meso-America. Not so long ago, the Mayans of ancient Mexico and Guatemala were thought to have been as the *conquistadores* of the sixteenth century found them: docile villagers eking out a simple existence by farming in clearings in the jungle. The great pyramids of the Yucatán peninsula, such as at Chichén Itzá were well known—as high as 18 stories, they were hard to miss—but most had been abandoned to the jungle before the Spanish conquest. Until recently, it was assumed that they were religious centers to which the scattered Mayan peasants came on special occasions.

Today, thanks to "high-tech" archaeological digs and the deciphering of Mayan hieroglyphics, we know that between 250 B.C. and A.D. 900, the Mayans supported a magnificent civilization. They lived in cities as large as 6 square miles in area (at El Mirado) with a hinterland of farmland as vast as 50 square miles (at Tikal). Their cities were fortified with moats and walls, and the people built dams and long canals, the purpose of which is not yet understood (there is no need to irrigate in the rainy tropics).

The population of several Mayan city-states rose to 20,000 and at Dzibilchaltún perhaps 40,000. In addition to peasants, there were artisans of all sorts: far-ranging merchants dealing in jade, obsidian, salt, cacao, pottery, feathers, and jaguar pelts; priests who were superb mathematicians and astronomers; and a hereditary nobility, a warrior class as in other early civilizations.

The Mayans had stadiums in which spectators watched ball games of religious significance. In one ceremonial sport, teams of players kept a rubber ball in the air, or careening off walls, using only their hips and buttocks to strike it. In pok-a-tok, perhaps the most difficult ball game ever devised, the court was a hundred yards long with stone walls 30 feet high on either side. Near the top of each wall was mounted a stone ring—vertical like an archery target, not horizontal like a basketball hoop. Using only hips, elbows, and arms, players attempted to knock a ball 6 inches in diameter through a hole in the ring that was barely larger.

Not surprisingly, few goals were scored, but Mayanologists are not sure what that meant for the competitors. One scrap of evidence indicates that the individual who scored a goal was entitled to all the

---

cannon, 16 horses, and war dogs, gigantic mastiffs trained to kill. What this motley party found and did in Mexico brought an end to Spanish grumblings.

Cortés in Mexico

Ruddy, bearded Hernán Cortés had heard rumors of Tenochtitlán and of Aztec riches. He landed at what he named Vera Cruz. After sending word of his arrival

and of his plans back to Cuba, calling for reinforcements, he burned the ships that had brought him to Mexico. It would be conquer or die for his soldiers. There was no third option.

Almost immediately, Cortés was attacked by the coastal Tabascans. With their cannon, horses, and dogs, the Spaniards easily defeated them, losing only two men of their own. The shrewd Cortés then made a generous peace, offering the Tabascans an alliance

clothing worn by the spectators, riches indeed. Some experts think that pok-a-tok was played by captives and the members of the losing team were sacrificed.

The Mayans were only the longest-lasting practitioners of a civilization that originated with the Olmecs and ended two millennia with the destruction of the Aztecs. However, about 600 years before Hernan Cortés landed at Vera Cruz, the civilization of Meso-America appears to have stalled, ceasing to "progress" in the European sense of the word. One of the Mayans' greatest achievements, their complex and ingenious system for marking the passing of time, may provide an insight into why Meso-American civilization stagnated.

Mayan priests were excellent astronomers. They traced the route of Venus more precisely than contemporaries elsewhere in the world. Their solar calendar was nearly perfect, counting 365 days in a year. But because there are virtually no seasons in the tropics, and even the rainy season in Yucatán was wildly erratic and unpredictable, the solar year was of less interest to the Mayans than to makers of calendars elsewhere. One solar cycle did not lead to another, always into the future, as in other civilizations.

Instead, the Mayans devised a variety of other calendars, some still not completely understood. The two most important of these meshed with the solar year, and with one another as the chief means of dating and chronicling events. One was a 13-day cycle, the other, called tzolkin, of 260 days ($20 \times 13 = 260$; the basis of Mayan mathematics was 20 rather than ten). If one imagines the three cycles as wheels meshing with one another, a 13-cog wheel within a 260-cog wheel within a 365-cog wheel, no single alignment of cogs would be repeated for 18,980 days, or 52 years on the button.

The complexity of the calculation illustrates the sophistication of Mayan mathematics. However, the beauty of their cycles within cycles also locked the Mayan mind into a rigidly circular view of time. The Mayans believed that each day was identical in every way to the day 52 years earlier, and 104 years and 156 years earlier, and so on. Each 5,200 years, they believed, the universe was destroyed and created anew. Time passed but mankind did not progress; what might seem to be change was only bringing things back to where they had already been and would be again.

As sophisticated as the Meso-Americans were, their worldview was ill-adapted to cope with the unexpected, with what did not fit in. Hurricanes worried the Mayans more because of their unpredictability than because of their destructiveness. Because their solar year was divided into 18 months of 20 days each, leaving 5 days without a tidy place at the end of the year, the Mayans regarded the 5 leftovers as evil.

How much more paralyzing must it have been for their cultural heirs, the Aztecs, to learn of the arrival of huge seagoing canoes, white-skinned men with hairy faces, suits of iron, horses, and cannons that had thunder within them? There was nothing in the annals of the priests about such an event 52 years past. Meso-America's very cultural foundations constituted a Spanish ally.

against their tribal enemies. He would reprise this procedure—victory in battle, peace, alliance—with every Indian people he confronted on his march to Tenochtitlán. Totonacs, Tlaxcalans, Tolucans, and Cholulans—all joined him against the hated Aztecs.

Aztec religion also served the purposes of the wily Cortés. A legend held that a fair-skinned deity named Quetzalcoatl would one day come from the east to rule Mexico. Moctezuma II feared Cortés to be this god. According to one of his advisors, Moctezuma "enjoyed no sleep, no food. . . . Whatsoever he did, it was as if he were in torment." Reaching Tenochtitlán on November 8, 1519, Cortés was actually welcomed into the city where he quickly made the emperor his hostage.

Aztec nobles soon awoke to the fact that the Spaniards were less than divine. Cortés ordered a stop to human sacrifice, the heart of Aztec belief, and

Cortés and his Indian interpreter, Malinche, lead a group of conquistadores *in this drawing from an Aztec manuscript.*

when the soldiers stumbled on a store of jewels, precious stones, silver and gold, "as if they were monkeys, the Spanish lifted up the gold banners and gold necklaces. . . . Like hungry pigs they craved that gold." With perverse truth, Cortés told Moctezuma, "I and my companions suffer from a disease of the heart which can be cured only with gold."

The Conquest

The Aztecs rebelled and Cortés's men barely managed to fight their way out of Tenochtitlán. Something like half the Spaniards in the city were killed, and as many as 4,000 Tlaxcalans. It was greed that nearly destroyed them. Although their lives were in the balance, the Spaniards insisted on trying to carry eight tons of treasure on their retreat.

But it was the Aztecs, not the invaders, who were doomed by Mexican gold. Cortés gathered new Indian allies and additional Spanish reinforcements. He returned to Tenochtitlán, and conquered the great city brick by brick. About 15,000 people were killed on the final day of the battle, August 13, 1521.

Hernán Cortés won not just a great battle, he won a ready-made empire for Spain. He and his lieutenants simply inserted themselves at the top of Aztec society in place of the nobles they had wiped out. They lived off the labor of the lower classes as the Aztec nobility had done. Rarely has one people been able to set itself up over another with such ease. The already centralized political structure and oppressed condition of the people of Mexico made it possible for the Spaniards to rule with minimal resistance.

The *Conquistadores*

The conquest of Mexico revived Spanish interest in the New World. There was a rush to the Americas as thousands of people of all classes packed into ships to search for their own Mexicos. The young (and some not so young) men called themselves *conquistadores*—conquerors. In little more than a generation they subdued an area several times the size of Europe.

Rarely has history shaped a people for conquest as Spanish history shaped the conquistadors. Because much of Spain is dry, mountainous, or both, agriculture never satisfied the ambitious. Because the Christian Spanish associated trade with the Moors and Jews they despised, the upper classes shunned commerce. The sole worldly role of the *hidalgo*, the Spanish male with pretensions to nobility, was to fight. He was a *caballero*, a knight, a soldier. The bravery and fortitude of the conquistadors under daunting conditions awes us to this day. The other side of their military character, their ruthlessness and cruelty, has also been noted.

The Spanish nation's zealous devotion to Roman Catholicism factored in the extraordinary achievement. Because the national enemy had been of another faith, Spanish nationalism and Roman Catholicism were of a piece. Like their Muslim foes, the Spaniards believed that a war for the purpose of spreading "true religion" was *ipso facto* a holy war. Death in such a war was a guarantee of salvation. It was a value that made for soldiers unafraid to die and, for that, very formidable. The notion that nonbelievers who refused to submit to the one true faith lost their right to mercy also made for the efficiency of ruthlessness.

Such cultural baggage would curse Spain in later centuries. Disdain for agriculture, trade, and other productive work contributed to the nation's impoverishment. In the sixteenth century, however, reckless bravery and religious fanaticism were superbly calculated to conquer a vast New World.

Exploration North and South

After news of Mexican treasure reached him, the Spanish King Charles I (also known as Emperor Charles V) encouraged additional conquests by promising conquistadors the lion's share of the gold and silver they won. (Charles got one-fifth.) He also granted land to his subjects, and *encomiendas*, the legal right to force the Indians who lived on the land

---

Teasers

The Portuguese at Sagres were enticed into their quest for contact with East Asia by a number of documents that had circulated widely in Europe, their messages reaching even the humble in the garbled adaptations of traveling monks and ballad singers.

One was the account of Eldad the Danite, a Jewish scholar of the ninth century who wrote of discovering the ten lost tribes of Israel deep in central Asia. Christian Europeans were not disinterested in this claim, but more important to the cause of inspiring exploration were Eldad's descriptions of the riches of the East.

In the "Letter of Prester John," a Christian king claimed to "reign supreme and to exceed in riches, virtue, and power all creatures who dwell under heaven." His "magnificence dominates the Three Indias," John wrote. He was anxious to contact Christian Europe in order to "wage war against and chastise the enemies of the cross of Christ," the Muslims.

The "Letter" was a hoax. No one fitting Prester John's description of himself dwelled in Asia, and there was in Asia no "sandy sea without water, for the sand moves and swells into waves like the sea," not to mention the red and green lions he mentioned. But the prospect of a Christian friend from whom to buy the goods of the Indies overcame the skepticism of many European merchants and explorers.

The Voyages of Sir Marco Polo also included absurdities, such as snakes wearing eyeglasses and so on. But it was no hoax. Marco Polo, a Venetian, lived in China a dozen years and he insisted that the exquisite Asian porcelains, silks, tapestries, and spices that Europeans coveted could be purchased at a pittance in the city of China's great Khan. Perhaps no single document, more than Polo's *Voyages*, convinced the explorers of the fifteenth century that it was worth it to bet their lives on voyages into the unknown.

---

to work for them. It was not slavery but, in practice, the distinction was a fine one.

Only one conquistador's find rivaled that of Cortés. In 1531, an aging illiterate, Francisco Pizarro, led 106 foot soldiers and 62 horses high into the Andes Mountains of South America. There he found the empire of the Incas, 3,000 miles in extent, united by roads Pizarro called unmatched in Christendom, and rich in gold and silver. As bold as Cortés, Pizarro was also a scoundrel, an artist of deceit and treachery. After holding the Inca emperor Athualpa captive while a rich ransom was gathered, Pizarro had him murdered. He and his men were also peerless soldiers. In one battle, they killed 7,000 Incas.

Few other expeditions brought back much gold and silver, particularly those that ventured north into what is now the United States. Between 1539 and 1542, Hernando de Soto (who had been with Pizarro) explored our Southeast in a fruitless search for riches. De Soto was buried by his soldiers in the Mississippi River. Only half the mourners at the funeral returned to their homes alive.

During the same years, Francisco Coronado trekked extraordinary distances in the Southwest. His quest was for the "Seven Cities of Cíbola" among which, according to an imaginative priest, Fray Marcos de Niza, was "the greatest city in the world . . . larger than the city of Mexico." Coronado's 1,500 men found only dusty villages of adobe brick. "Such were our curses that some hurled at Fray Marcos," wrote one, "that I pray God may protect him from them."

Spanish America

Nevertheless, for more than a century Mexican and Peruvian gold and silver made Spain the richest and most powerful nation of Europe. By 1550, $4.5 million in precious metals were crossing the Atlantic each year, by 1600 $12 million. Not for another fifty years would this river of riches dry to a trickle. American wealth financed the cultural blossoming of Spain as well as huge armies to do the king's bidding. By the end of the 1600s, Spain's empire stretched from Florida to Tierra del Fuego at the foot of South America.

Over so vast an area, economy and society varied immensely. For the most part, however, the ownership of land in Spanish America was concentrated in the hands of a small group of privileged *encomenderos* who lived off the labor of Indians in peonage or black Africans in slavery. Government was centralized in the hands of viceroys (vice kings). The Roman Catholic Church exercised great power,

Discoverer of the United States

What may be Florida appears on a Spanish map dated 1502. However, the first European positively known to explore part of what is now the United States was Juan Ponce de León, who had come to the New World with Columbus in 1493 and led the conquest of Puerto Rico, of which he was governor for three years. Grizzled, tough, and, at 53, rather old for exploration in 1513, he was intrigued by rumors of an island called Bimini where Indians said there was "a particular spring which restores old men to youth"—a fountain of youth.

Ponce de León explored the Atlantic coast of south-central Florida in 1513. However, because he was preoccupied by fierce wars with the Caribs back in Puerto Rico, he was unable to return to Florida with a colonizing expedition for eight years. In 1521, he attempted to establish a Spanish settlement in Florida but, instead of reinvigoration at a fountain, he was wounded in a fight with Indians and died.

often protecting those on the bottom from the greed and cruelty of the upper classes.

The empire flourished. Before more than a handful of other Europeans had slept overnight in the New World, Spain boasted two hundred towns and cities, and two universities in the Western Hemisphere.

The majority of Spain's American subjects were Indians but their fate was not a happy one. It has been estimated that there were at least 5 million inhabitants of Mexico in 1500. In 1600, there were a million Mexican Indians.

The Black Legend

It can seem wonderful that any Native Americans survived. Indeed, the possibility of their extinction was the main point of the hard-hitting Bartolomé de las Casas, a Dominican priest who devoted his life to lobbying the Spanish king for laws protecting the Indians. The Spaniards treated the Indians, De las Casas said, "not as beasts, for beasts are treated properly at times, but like the excrement in a plaza."

An "F" in Geography

An old story has it that Columbus struggled to convince Isabella and her advisors that the earth was round. Not so. The shape of the earth was never an issue in Columbus's long campaign to win financial backing. Only the ignorant and superstitious believed that the world was flat, that a ship could fall off the edge into a void. Isabella and the scholars of Salamanca knew better. The ancients, whom they respected as if they were divinely inspired, said the world was round. Fifteenth-century observers, like Pierre d'Ailly, pointed out that "lunar eclipses caused by the earth's projected shadow [on the moon] appear round" because the earth was a sphere.

The ironic fact of the matter is that, far from a pioneer of science, Columbus was behind the times in his geography. His hopes of reaching the Indies by sailing west were based on a serious underestimation of the size of the globe. Columbus insisted that Japan lay about 2,500 nautical miles west of Spain's Canary Islands. In fact, the distance is about 9,000 miles.

Had Columbus known this, he would have had to abandon his enterprise. No ship of the time could have been provisioned for a voyage of 9,000 miles.

Today, most scholars believe that his scorching description of conquistador cruelty, *A Brief Relation of the Destruction of the Indians*, is overblown. De las Casas was, first and foremost, a propagandist. Nevertheless, his words served as the basis of the *leyenda negra*, the "Black Legend" of Spanish barbarity that remained an article of faith in the English-speaking world for three centuries.

Moreover, the behavior of the *encomenderos* should be viewed in the context of Europe in the sixteenth century. It was an era of chilling indifference to human suffering. For a century, Europeans had seen their population devastated by plague and war. Nor was the callousness a European monopoly—it was Asian, African, Native American too, and it was directed not only toward those of different races. Warfare in Europe during the period and into the seventeenth century meant unmitigated horror for anyone caught in the paths of marauding armies.

The horrors of Meso-American religion have been noted. Africans also devised devilishly ingenious tortures without any tutoring from outside.

Many more Indians died of pick and shovel than at sword point. The Arawaks of the Caribbean, for example, were a physically delicate people who seem to have died off within a few generations under the hard labor to which they were forced. An even more devastating scourge of the native peoples was a weapon Europeans did not even know they possessed: disease. For example, the Indian population of Hispaniola in 1492 was at least 200,000; in 1508, 60,000; in 1514, 14,000. By 1570, only two small native villages survived on the island. Elsewhere the Spanish trod, bringing their diseases, the story was scarcely happier.

THE COLUMBIAN EXCHANGE

The collision of worlds occasioned by Columbus's voyage established a biological pipeline between land masses that had drifted apart about 150 million years before human beings appeared on the earth. Some species had flourished in both worlds: oaks, dogs, deer, mosquitoes, and the virus that causes the common cold. Some species had been well developed by the time of the separation of the continents. Others, such as sea birds and plants producing air and waterborne seeds, navigated the ocean long before the *Santa María*. There were, however, a large number of animals and plants in the Americas that were new to the first Europeans to arrive. And they brought with them species of flora and fauna that were unknown to the Indians.

The Impact on America

Because mammals in Spanish America were generally smaller and less suited for meat and draft than Old World livestock, the Spaniards immediately imported hogs, cattle, and sheep along with European grasses to feed them (plus about 70 percent of what we know as weeds). The arrival of these beasts not only altered the ecology of the New World, the Indians introduced to them soon came to depend on them for survival.

Even those native peoples who escaped Spanish political domination were glad to raid the strangers' flocks and herds as a step toward better living. The magnificent wool-weaving art that is closely identified with the Navajo of the American Southwest was developed when the Navajo domesticated sheep.

The impact of Europe's horse was more dramatic. The people of Mexico were initially terrified by the sight of a mounted man. It reinforced their belief that the Spaniards were gods. Even after the Indians recognized that horses were ordinary beasts, the Spanish equestrian monopoly gave the conquistadors an immense advantage in battle.

Two centuries later, herds of wild horses had migrated north to the Great Plains of North America. There they became the basis of several cultures. The Sioux, Comanche, Pawnee, Apache, Nez Percé, Blackfoot, Crow, and other tribes of the plains, previously agricultural peoples, captured the mustangs and became peerless horsemen independent of European example. Their semi-nomadic way of life was built around the horse and the herds of bison they hunted long before they had any contact with the "white eyes."

Other valuable "green immigrants" from Europe were grains, such as wheat and barley, citrus fruits, and sugar cane. It is difficult to imagine a Caribbean island without cane.

Feeding the World

The American continents contributed few food animals to the world larder. (The turkey and other game birds are noble exceptions.) The plant foods of the New World, by way of contrast, revolutionized European, African, and Asian diet. Maize (Indian corn), an American native, astonished Europeans by the height of its stalks and size of its grains. Cultivation of the crop spread to every continent, increasing the food supply and contributing to the rapid increase in population that has characterized the last five hundred years of human history.

The white potato and the sweet potato, two more Americans, were scarcely less important. The white potato became a major staple in temperate countries from Ireland to northern China. The sweet potato flourished in warmer areas and became a staple in West Africa, where it was introduced by slave traders. Beans, squash and pumpkins, manioc, peppers, and tomatoes are other foods that were unknown in Europe, Africa, and Asia before Columbus sailed the ocean blue.

Many national cuisines depend on foods of American origin, particularly the tomato and the extraordinary variety of chili peppers that have been developed from a Mexican forebear. It has been estimated that of 640 food crops grown in Africa today, all but 50 originated in the Americas. Think of Hungarian paprika. Think of southern Italian reliance on tomatoes. These, as well as tobacco, were contributed to Old World civilization by the New.

New Diseases for Old

The sixteenth century understood the exchange of animals and plants. But people of that day were merely conscious of the most tragic of the intercontinental transactions in microscopic forms of life. Many diseases for which Europeans, Africans, and Asians had developed immunities were unknown to American Indians before 1492. They had been insulated from them by 3,000 miles of open sea. Biologically, the Indians had not learned to live with measles, smallpox, whooping cough, chicken pox, and even mild influenzas.

The effect of these diseases on the Indians was catastrophic. While Europeans and Africans suffered badly enough from the epidemics that swept through the colonies, the Indians died in heartrending numbers. Invisible bacteria and viruses killed far more Native Americans than did Spanish swords or English muskets. Like wild horses out of Mexico, Old World diseases preceded the white advance, brought to isolated Indian villages by individuals who had made contact with the newcomers.

In return, the Indians probably made a gift of venereal disease to Europe and then to Africa and Asia. Medical historians disagree on the origins of syphilis, but we know that it was first identified by physicians in 1493 — in Cadiz, Spain, the port to which Columbus returned after his first voyage. From Spain, syphilis traveled to Naples, where several of Columbus's crewmen are known to have gone. Then it spread like wildfire throughout the world, following the trade routes, exactly where sailors, a notoriously promiscuous lot, would be expected to take it.

Europeans, Africans, and Asians reacted to syphilis as Indians reacted to measles and chicken pox. Symptoms were severe and death came quickly. About 10 million people died of syphilis within fifteen years of Columbus's voyage. Only later did the disease take on the slower-acting form in which we know it today.

CHRONOLOGY

10,000 B.C.	Last Ice Age ends. Sea level rises, covering "land bridge" by which first Americans crossed from Asia
1000 A.D.	Short-lived Viking colony of Vinland in North America
1200s A.D.	Arrival of Aztecs in the Valley of Mexico
1405	Chinese navigator Zheng He reaches eastern coast of Africa
1488	Bartholomeu Díaz sails from Portugal to Cape of Good Hope
1492	Christopher Columbus begins exploration of the "New World" in the Bahamas
1498	Vasco da Gama sails around Africa to Calicut in India
1502–1519	Reign of Moctezuma II in Aztec Mexico
1507	Martin Waldseemüller names Americas after Amerigo Vespucci
1513	Vasco Balboa crosses Panama to discover Pacific Ocean
1519–1521	Hernán Cortés conquers Mexico
1519–1522	Magellan-Del Cano circumnavigate globe
1531	Francisco Pizarro conquers Peru
1539	De Soto and Coronado explore present-day southeastern and southwestern United States

FOR FURTHER READING

On Native Americans before and at the time of Columbus's voyage (a subject to be examined in more detail in subsequent chapters), see Alvin M. Josephy, Jr., *The Indian Heritage of America*, 2nd ed., 1991; Harold E. Driver, *Indians of North America*, 1970; Wilcomb E. Washburn, *The Indian in America*, 1975; Robert F. Spencer and Jesse D. Jennings et al., *The Native Americans: Ethnology and Backgrounds of the North American Indians*, 1977; and Brian Fagan, *Ancient North America: The Archaeology of a Continent*, 1991.

There is as yet no single book bringing together the exciting research of recent decades on Meso-American civilization in the pre-Columbian period. However, on the subject of Mayan art and religion, see Linda Sechele and Mary Ellen Miller, *The Blood of Kings*, 1986. Carroll L. Riley et al., *Man across the Sea: Problems of Pre-Columbian Contact*, 1971, deals with pre-Columbian America from the other sides of the Atlantic and Pacific. Also see David B. Quinn, *North America from Earliest Discovery to First Settlements: The Norse Voyages to 1612*, 1977.

For Europe during the Age of Discovery, see J. H. Parry, *The Age of Reconnaissance*, 1963; J. H. Elliott, *The Old World and the New*, 1970; and Fernand Braudel, *Capitalism and Medieval Life*, 1973. Charles R. Boxer, *The Portuguese Seaborne Empire*, 1969, is the standard work on Portugal overseas. On the many explorations in the Americas, two works by Samuel Eliot Morison are classics and, for that reason, well worth a read despite many persuasive revisions of Morison's view: his biography of Columbus, *Admiral of the Ocean Sea*, 1942,

and *The European Discovery of America*, 2 vols., 1971, 1974. A later work is William D. Phillips, Jr., and Carla Rahn Phillips, *The Worlds of Christopher Columbus*, 1992. Kirkpatrick Sale, *The Conquest of Paradise*, 1990, was written to mark the 500th anniversary of the Columbian discovery. It depicts Columbus as an ass when he is not a fiend, which is silly. But the book also is exhaustively researched, pleasantly written, and filled with fascinating information. A more recent work is David E. Stannard, *American Holocaust: The Conquest of the New World*, 1992.

Students interested in Spanish conquests cannot do better than with a history in the grand old literary tradition of the nineteenth century: William H. Prescott, *History of the Conquest of Mexico*, 1873. See also the biographical study, William W. Johnson, *Cortes*, 1975. Leon Lopez-Portilla, *The Broken Spears*, 1962, tells of the conquest of Mexico from the Aztec point of view.

Standard works in English on early Spanish America are Clarence H. Haring, *The Spanish Empire in America*, 1947; Charles Gibson, *Spain in America*, 1966; Carl Sauer, *The Early Spanish Main*, 1966; and especially James Lockhart and Stuart B. Schwartz, *Early Latin America*, 1983. The author who revealed the significance of the distinct biotic systems of the Old World and New is Alfred E. Crosby; see his *The Columbian Exchange: Biological and Cultural Consequences of 1492*, 1972, and *Ecological Imperialism: The Biological Expansion of Europe*, 1986. See also William Cronon, *Changes on the Land*, 1983, for a superb example of the "new" environmental history.

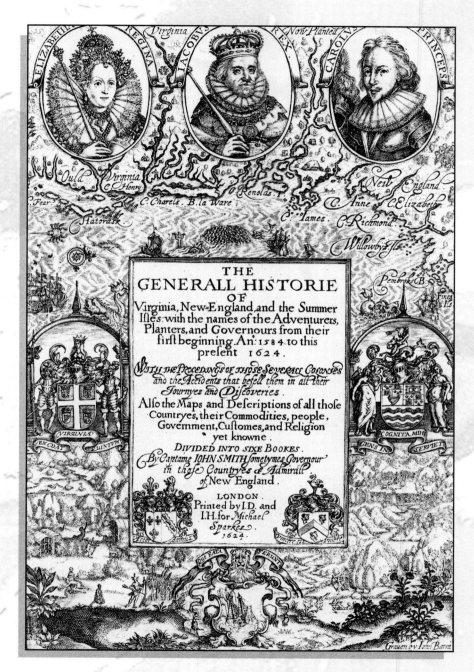

The frontispiece of Captain John Smith's General History of Virginia, *1624, written in part to encourage English men and women to settle in Virginia.*

2
CHAPTER

ENGLAND IN AMERICA
The Struggle to Plant a Colony
1550–1624

I, JAMES, by the Grace of God, King of England, Scotland, France, and Ireland, Defender of the Faith, &c. WHEREAS our loving and well-disposed Subjects, Sir Thomas Gates . . . and divers others of our loving Subjects, have been humble Suitors unto us, that We would vouchsafe unto them our Licence, to make Habitation, Plantation, and to deduce a Colony of sundry of our People into that part of America, commonly called VIRGINIA . . . .

— *First Charter of Virginia*

Where every wind that rises blows perfume,
And every breath of air is like an incense.

— *Francis Beaumont and John Fletcher*

I your Child am in a most heavy Case by reason of the nature of the Country is such that it Causeth much sickness, and the scurvy and the bloody flux, and divers other diseases, which maketh the body very poor, and Weak. . . . We are in great danger, for our Plantation is very weak, by reason of the death, and sickness. . . . I have nothing to Comfort me, nor there is nothing to be gotten here but sickness, and death.

— *Richard Frethorne*

England's king in 1492, Henry VII, passed up a chance to have Christopher Columbus claim the Americas for him. Henry failed to act when Columbus, then despairing in Spain, sent his brother to Henry, proposing that the "Enterprise of the Indies" be an English project. Even so, England's claim to a piece of the Americas was almost as old as Spain's. In 1497, Henry VII sent John Cabot, another Italian sailor with big ideas, across the Atlantic to find a sea route to Asia. Cabot touched on Newfoundland and Nova Scotia, claiming them and adjacent properties for Henry VII.

The French crown showed little interest in overseas exploration until 1523, when one of King Francis I's privateers (in effect, pirates the King protected) captured a Spanish ship carrying Aztec gold. The next year, his curiosity aroused by so pretty a cargo, Francis sent his Italian navigator, Giovanni Verrazano, across the ocean. Verrazano claimed much of what is now the east coast of North America for France.

When the pope scolded Francis I, reminding him that, in *Inter Caetera*, he had divided the world's non-Christian real estate between Portugal and Spain, Francis dipped his pen in sarcasm. He asked to examine the section of Adam's will that gave the pope the right to bestow such a gift.

ENGLAND'S PROBLEMS

Adam's will or no, Spain enjoyed a near monopoly in the Americas for a century. (For a time, even Portugal and, therefore, Brazil, was a Spanish possession.) It was not that other nations were indifferent to the riches of the New World. It was, simply, that through most of the 1500s—Spain's *siglo de oro* or "golden century"—no other European country was up to challenging Spanish might.

During the second half of the century, the Dutch were fighting to win their independence from Spain. France was convulsed by religious hatreds and civil wars to determine which great duke would be king. And in England, the Tudor dynasty Henry VII founded was vexed by the miscarriages of a queen, a momentous royal divorce, short reigns, and religious tensions. Only toward the end of the sixteenth century, under Elizabeth I, the last and greatest of the Tudor monarchs, did the English challenge Spain for a piece of America.

The Protestant Reformation

The sixteenth century was a time of religious turmoil in Europe, the era of the Protestant Reformation. During the same years that Cortés was shattering the civilization of the Aztecs, a German monk, Martin Luther, was shattering the unity of European Christendom. While Coronado was looking for the Cities of Cíbola in the deserts of the Southwest, and De Soto was wandering the Mississippi Valley, a French lawyer named John Calvin was laying the foundations of a dynamic religious faith that would profoundly influence American history.

In 1517, in the Saxon city of Wittenberg, Martin Luther posted a paper bearing 95 "theses," or subjects for debate, to a church door. He attacked several doctrines and practices of the Roman Catholic church as corrupt or outright false. Called to account by the Holy Roman Emperor Charles V (who was also king of Spain as Charles I), Luther denied the authority of the pope to determine true religion. The only infallible source of God's word, Luther declared, was the Holy Bible.

In a remarkably short time, Scandinavia and parts of Germany, Hungary, Poland, and the Netherlands fell in behind the passionate monk. Many ordinary folk had long been disgusted by a moral laxity that was all too common among priests of the Roman Catholic church. Some princes and princelings were attracted to Luther's protestantism for less edifying reasons. If they broke with Rome, they could seize church lands, something between a fourth and a third of Europe. Thus, just when the riches of the Americas began to flow into western Europe, much of northern and central Europe was permanently lost to Roman Catholicism. A large minority of the French also embraced Protestant doctrines, as did many Scots.

In Spain, however, the powerful monarchs stood by the pope of Rome and called on the Spanish Inquisition, a religious court designed to ferret out Muslims and Jews, to persecute suspected Protestants before the new faith could gain a foothold. It never did. In England, Henry VIII, crowned king in 1509, condemned Lutheran beliefs in a scholarly book, *Defense of the Seven Sacraments*. In gratitude for his loyal service, the pope honored Henry as "Defender of the Faith."

The Church of England

The title proved to be high irony for in 1527 Henry himself cut England's ties to Rome. He had little quarrel with Catholic doctrine and ritual. Henry's motivation was his belief that he must end his marriage to a Spanish princess, Catherine of Aragon who, after a history of babies dead in womb or cradle, was at the end of her childbearing years. Catherine's daughter, Mary, was healthy. But these were days when monarchs joined their soldiers on the battlefield. Henry believed that, for his young dynasty to survive a foreign or domestic threat, he must have a son. And then there was Cupid. Henry fell in love with a comely young flirt of the court, Anne Boleyn, who wanted a wedding ring, not a mistress's pillow.

Popes inclined to be sympathetic when kings had problems of this sort. They had granted royal divorces on grounds flimsier than those Henry set before Pope Clement VII. (Henry said he had sinned because Catherine was the widow of his brother. He had a biblical verse to back him up.) However, Pope Clement feared the wrath of the Holy Roman Emperor Charles V, who happened to be Catherine of Aragon's nephew, more than he wanted to oblige Henry VIII. He refused to annul the king's marriage, whereupon Henry had Parliament declare papal authority invalid in England. The king, according to the Act of Supremacy, was now head of the Christian church in England.

Like the German princes, Henry confiscated the rich lands owned by monasteries and nunneries in England. The monks and nuns he sent packing. The estates on which they had lived Henry sold to ambitious subjects for whom owning land meant prestige. Thus did a clever king fill his treasury, scatter his enemies, and create a class of well-to-do landowners whose social station depended on the health of the Tudor dynasty. History might rank Henry VIII as one of the jewels of the age of monarchy were it not for a gluttony that turned him into a physical grotesque, and a rapacity that carried him through six wives, two of whom he divorced and two of whom he executed.

A Changing Church

Henry VIII made few changes in religious doctrine and church structure. His "reformation" had few consequences for the daily lives and Sunday worship of

Handsome in youth, Henry VIII cut a splendid figure in his prime.

the English people. But, as many people in power have discovered before and since, tinkering with an established order, however delicately, often liberates a spirit of debate and an impulse to innovate that can become revolutionary. That is what happened in England.

A true Protestantism germinated in the Church of England during the reign of Edward VI, Henry VIII's only son. Alas for the religious reformers who called the shots during Edward's reign, the king was sickly and died in 1553, just sixteen years of age. Worse for Protestant leaders, Edward's successor was his older half-sister, Mary Tudor, the daughter of Catherine of Aragon. Mary was a zealous Catholic who had seethed for two decades over her mother's humiliation. Now queen, she married her cousin, Prince Philip of Spain, who also was devoted to the Roman religion. Then, Mary alarmed even Philip by the ardor with which she rooted out Protestants in her court. Mary also persecuted, as best sixteenth-century methods allowed, Protestants among ordinary people. Three hundred were executed, earning the queen the unflattering nickname of "Bloody Mary."

Had Mary been a better politician, lived a long life, and borne a child to succeed her, England might well have been eased back into the Catholic Church. The Protestants of Poland and most of Hungary were reconverted to the church by persuasion and persecution. However, like brother Edward, Mary was destined to sit on the throne for a very short time. She died in 1558, childless.

In the meantime, many English Protestants had fled to live in exile in Geneva, the home of the most radical of the Protestant reformers, John Calvin. Returning home after Mary's death, they became known as Puritans because they spoke of "purifying" the Church of England of Catholic beliefs and practices. These included such things as statues in churches, the use of incense in religious services, and the authority of bishops. The Bible was the only religious authority for the Puritans and they found justification for none of these things in the good book.

THE ELIZABETHAN AGE

England's ruler after Bloody Mary was one of the shrewdest politicians ever to wear a crown. Elizabeth I, Henry VIII's daughter by Anne Boleyn, was a survivor. To have been alive and kicking in 1558, she had to be wily. Her father beheaded her mother as an adulteress when Elizabeth was three. When she was fourteen, the English church embraced Protestantism under Edward VI and the official sentiments of the royal court took an anti-Spanish turn. Elizabeth went along. When she was twenty, England proceeded back to Rome under Mary and became an ally, virtually a client state of Spain. Elizabeth went along. Now queen at twenty-five, she was well practiced in the art of concealing her heart. She knew how to cajole the schemers who crowded the royal court, pushing wildly differing views of religious truth and foreign policy. She also knew how to bide time.

Queen Elizabeth I ensured her subjects viewed her as a glorious national leader with pomp and ceremony.

Thus, when King Philip II rushed to England to propose marriage to her, Elizabeth waffled. To wed his Most Catholic Majesty, the scourge of the Reformation, would surely set English Protestants to plotting against her. To humiliate Philip by rejecting him abruptly, however, might plunge Elizabeth into a war with Spain for which England was not prepared. Coyly flirtatious when circumstances demanded, regally aloof when it served her purposes, Elizabeth seemed to say yes to Philip's suit, then no, then maybe. In fact, she said nothing at all. She wore Philip down (he found a wife in France), and had her way. She won time in which to determine in which direction lay the most auspicious prospects.

The Sea Dogs

Elizabeth's policy toward the New World was also devious. During the first two decades of her reign, an official state of peace with Spain meant that she recognized Philip's claim to all the Americas. By the late 1570s, however, Elizabeth first tolerated, then quietly encouraged a restless, swashbuckling fraternity of Spaniard-hating sea captains who meant to chip away at Philip's empire.

The most daring of these "sea dogs" (the name comes from a shark common in English waters) was a slave trader who aspired to more respectable work, Francis Drake. In 1577, this remarkable sailor set sail in the *Golden Hind*, rounded South America by the Strait of Magellan, and attacked undefended Spanish ports on the Pacific. No ship of any nation save Spain had ever plied these waters. Ports like Valparaíso in Chile and Callao in Peru were hardly fortified.

The pickings were easy but, Drake reckoned correctly, Spanish warships awaited him in the Atlantic. Instead of returning the way he had come, Drake sailed north to California, careened the *Golden Hind* on a beach, scraped the barnacles from her hull, recaulked her oaken planks with rope and pitch, and struck west across the Pacific. Drake's expedition was only the second, after that of Magellan and De Elcaño, to circumnavigate the globe.

In the same years, another sea dog (and ex-slave trader), Martin Frobisher, sailed three times to Newfoundland looking for a likely site to plant a colony and find gold. There was no settlement, and the thousand tons of "gold ore" Frobisher returned to England with turned out to be worthless arctic rock. In 1578, Elizabeth quietly licensed two half brothers, Humphrey Gilbert and Walter Raleigh, to establish an English settlement in any land "not in the actual possession of any Christian prince."

In winking at the operations of the sea dogs, Elizabeth was playing her usual game. While appearing to acquiesce in Spain's monopoly in the New World, she was in fact challenging it. Although Philip II claimed all of North America for Spain, the northernmost outpost in his actual possession was a lonely fort at St. Augustine in Florida, founded in 1565 on the site of an Indian village and a short-lived French colony the Spanish had destroyed.

But Elizabeth's game with Philip II was nearly up. The "Spanish party" at her court had withered away (although there was a Spanish spy with Frobisher). Protestants who wanted to singe Philip's beard were ascendant. Then, in 1580, Drake returned to England, his ship so stuffed with Spanish treasure that it listed dangerously, at risk of capsizing. The profit on the voyage was 4,700 percent. Coveting her royal share of the loot and knowing that Philip's patience was exhausted anyway, Elizabeth boarded the *Golden Hind* and knighted Drake.

Sir Francis Drake (ca. 1540–1596), English privateer, commanded the second-ever expedition to circumnavigate the globe.

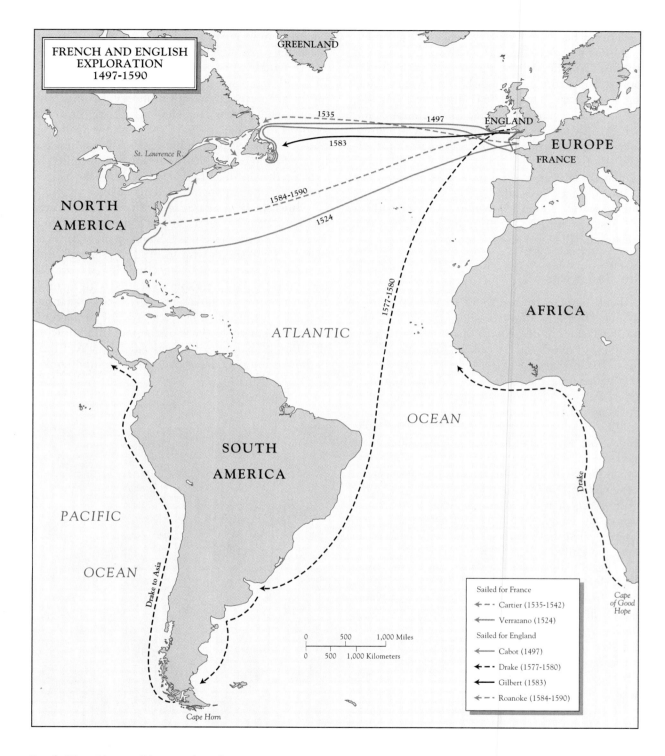

FRENCH AND ENGLISH
EXPLORATION
1497-1590

GREENLAND

1535   1497   ENGLAND

1583

EUROPE

FRANCE

St. Lawrence R.

NORTH
AMERICA

1584-1590

1524

1577-1580

AFRICA

ATLANTIC

OCEAN

SOUTH
AMERICA

PACIFIC

OCEAN

Drake to Asia

Drake

Cape
of Good
Hope

0   500   1,000 Miles

0   500   1,000 Kilometers

Sailed for France
- ◄- - Cartier (1535-1542)
- ◄—— Verrazano (1524)

Sailed for England
- ◄—— Cabot (1497)
- ◄- - Drake (1577-1580)
- ◄—— Gilbert (1583)
- ◄- - Roanoke (1584-1590)

Cape Horn

Bad Weather, Worse Luck

In the meantime, Gilbert and Raleigh failed in their attempts to plant a colony in North America. In 1578, foul weather foiled them. In 1583, Gilbert actually built an outpost in Newfoundland but the descent of the northern winter persuaded him to flee south where his two ships were caught in a storm. Bold old dog to the end, Gilbert's last recorded words, called across the waves, were "We are as near to heaven by sea as by land."

The Lost Colony

The next year, scouts in Raleigh's employ recommended the shores of Chesapeake Bay as the best site for an English colony. The climate was mild, the soil good, and the great bay seemed far enough from St. Augustine to be safe from Spanish attack. Knowing how to flatter the right people, Raleigh named the country Virginia after Elizabeth, the "Virgin Queen" (she never married). In 1587, he shipped 91 men, 17 women, and 9 children to settle it.

Strong winds blew the expedition south to Roanoke Island in what is now North Carolina. The sandy, wooded island was not nearly so well located as any number of sites on the Chesapeake. Still, Roanoke might have been England's first successful American colony, and North Carolina called "Virginia," had it not been three long years before the settlers were resupplied. When Raleigh's agents finally returned to the Carolina coast in 1590, they found Roanoke's buildings abandoned. The word "CROATOAN," and nothing else, was carved on one of them in "fayre Capitall letters."

This was a good sign. Governor John White — whose granddaughter, Virginia Dare, the first English child born in North America, was among the missing — had instructed the colonists that, if they left, they were to leave the name of their destination. If they were forced to leave, they were to punctuate their message with a cross. There was no cross at Roanoke so White concluded the colony had voluntarily removed to Croatan Island near Cape Hatteras. Sailing there, White's entourage wandered the woods, discharging muskets and singing English songs to assure any who might be hiding that they were not Spaniards looking for blood. To no avail — there was no trace of the Roanokers on Croatan.

What happened? Some historians suggest that the settlers, finding themselves unable to survive on Roanoke, joined with the Lumbee Indians who then frequented Croatan. A century later, after the Lumbees had relocated to the interior of North Carolina, some members of the tribe were observed to be fair-skinned and blue-eyed, with a number of English words in their language.

BEGINNINGS OF EMPIRE

In part, Raleigh was late in resupplying Roanoke because of the financial problems for which he had a genius. It was not easy to convince tightfisted Eliza-

Sir Walter Raleigh (ca. 1553–1618), unsuccessful colonizer.

bethan merchants to invest money in enterprises "without sure, certayne, and present gayne." More important, in 1588 and 1589, Englishmen of wealth and power were preoccupied with a mortal threat to the nation itself. Philip II of Spain, now enraged by Drake and other sea dogs, had assembled a fleet of 130 ships with which to invade England.

The Spanish Armada

The Spanish (or "Invincible") Armada of 1588 was a disaster. Designed to transport 30,000 troops, its large galleons, galleasses, and galleys, built for the Mediterranean Sea, were awkward on the swells of the North Atlantic. The Armada was outmaneuvered in the English Channel by small but quick English pinnaces. Holing up in the harbor of Calais in France, the Armada was savaged by fire ships, old vessels the English lathered with tar, stuffed with gunpowder, and sailed aflame and unmanned, rudders lashed, amidst the Spanish fleet.

The next year, trying to return home by rounding the British Isles to the north, the Armada was beset by Arctic storms. Only half of Philip's ships made it back to Spain, only a third of his soldiers.

HOW THEY LIVED

Common Seamen

They were little people by today's standards. Few of the seamen who sailed the seas of the world were taller than five and a half feet. But they were as tough as the oaken decks they walked, for they could not have otherwise survived to adulthood in the fifteenth and sixteenth centuries. Diseases that are now merely a nuisance carried off those children who were weak and sickly in the Age of Discovery.

Common seamen were often little more than children themselves: young teenagers or men in their early twenties. Reaching adulthood did not guarantee a long life, however. The odds were that a person who survived the childhood diseases of the sixteenth century would die before the age of 35. The odds were even worse for the men who went to sea.

Ships were frequently wrecked when their wooden hulls faced the might and fury of the Atlantic. The rules governing ships meeting at sea were those of the jungle: do what you are strong enough to do. The men on a Spanish vessel were prepared to battle every Portuguese, Dutch, French, English, or freebooting pirate ship they encountered. Spanish ships sailing from the Americas were especially attractive prey—who knew what treasures might be stored in their leaky hulls?—and defeat in battle meant death, or enslavement. Vasco da Gama once poured boiling oil on the belly of a prisoner in order to extract information from him.

If the sixteenth-century sailor survived the assaults from other ships, he then faced hazards on his own vessel. He might be killed by one of his own crewmates in a fight over a trivial matter. Or he might be executed for a petty offense as an object lesson to his fellows. Discipline on the high seas consisted of quick, harsh punishment for the slightest transgressions. These were usually flogging, keelhauling (dragging a man under water the length of the hull where, if he was not drowned, his body was shredded and broken by barnacles), or hanging from the yardarm. After a mutiny against him, Magellan decapitated one ringleader, quartered another alive, and marooned a third on a desert island. When he pardoned the rest, they were so grateful that they became Magellan's most loyal followers.

Finally, the common seaman not only continued to risk the diseases that plagued people on land, but he also ran a higher risk of scurvy. Scurvy is a vitamin C deficiency and was a very common disease in the centuries before our own. The disease can be reversed by a crash diet of fresh fruits and vegetables. The island of Curaçao in the Caribbean got its name—curaçao is the Portuguese word for "cure"—when Columbus left several men nearly dead from scurvy there, later returning to find them fit and strong. They had fed on fresh fruits in his absence.

At sea, however, the men's daily diet did not contain fresh fruit and consisted of about one pound of

---

The Elizabethans may be excused for suggesting that God had lined up on their side. They called the storms that finished off the Armada "the Protestant Wind." They told themselves that "God himselfe hath stricken the stroke, and ye have but looked on."

Spain did not collapse. Far from it: gold and silver from the Americas continued to top $12 million a year to the end of Philip's reign. Nevertheless, the sea dogs had demonstrated that Spain was less than invincible. As the *siglo de oro* drew to a close, England, France, and the Netherlands were ready to chance creating their own American empires.

Promoters

If the sea dogs showed the English that they could challenge Spain, some Elizabethan landlubbers promoted the idea that the English *should* establish American colonies. The most energetic of them was Richard Hakluyt, a bookish but by no means parochial minister of the Church of England. Hakluyt rummaged incessantly through the libraries of Oxford and London, collecting and publishing hundreds of explorers' reports on the geography, resources, and recommendations of the Americas. He published his first collection of documents in 1582,

salt beef, one and a half pounds of biscuit, two and a half pints of water, and one and a quarter pints of wine. The captain's larder served him and his officers scarcely better, although there might be onions, garlic, and dried fruits in it.

Sixteenth-century sailors worked with their muscles as few people do today. They loaded cargoes of a hundred tons with only the help of a winch or a windlass. At sea they hauled, only with the aid of ropes, heavy canvas 50 feet up and down the masts. Merely holding the ship on course in peaceful seas was heavy work. The crude tiller pitted the seaman's strength directly against the forces of wind and ocean currents. Every ship leaked and had to be pumped by hand regularly, and constantly during storms.

On long voyages the ship had to be serviced and refitted regularly. When this was wanted, the ship was sailed onto a beach where it was "careened," turned on its side, and the barnacles covering its hull were scraped off. Then the hull was recaulked with pitch and tar. If the captain decided that the sails needed to be rearranged, the seamen virtually rebuilt the ship above deck. Even when such special tasks were not needed, the crew was kept hopping every moment, repairing sails and lines, and scrubbing the decks with vinegar and salt water. Boredom was far more dangerous than overwork.

Why did someone choose such a life? The first answer is that *choose* is the wrong word. Most sailors were born and raised in seaports. They were literally bred to the life. Occupation, like social status, was not something about which a person of the sixteenth century had much choice. What else could a young man of Cádiz or Seville (or Le Havre or Bristol) do to make his way through life?

Then too, some portion of the crews of the sixteenth century were forced onto the ships. The crew for Columbus's momentous voyage, for example, was put together in part by drafting convicts. For several centuries to come, shorthanded captains made up their crews by waylaying ("shanghaiing") young men.

Finally, for all its dangers and discomforts, the sea offered a remote but alluring chance for social and economic advancement. While some of the great captains of the era were, like Magellan, born into the upper classes, others, like Columbus, worked their way up. Columbus first shipped out as a boy, perhaps only ten years old, and was illiterate until he was thirty. Yet he became the adviser of royalty and, for what the title was worth, Admiral of the Ocean Sea. Quite a number of the *conquistadores*, who first came to the New World as common seamen, lived to become wealthy landowners.

Of course, such success stories tell us of only a tiny fraction of the whole. For most sailors, life was brutal and short. But, in the sixteenth century, these seamen, brutal or not, were the agents of the great adventure that revolutionized the world.

---

just after Drake's return on the *Golden Hind*. Hakluyt's massive masterwork, *The Principal Navigations, Voyages, Traffiques, and Discoveries of the English Nation*, came out between 1598 and 1600, after the English ceased to fear a Spanish invasion.

In his books and in countless conversations with men of capital, Hakluyt argued that investment in American colonies would infallibly produce a profit, add to England's glory, and "enlarge the glory of the gospel." He lived until 1616, long enough to be as good as his sales pitch: he was a shareholder in the first permanent English settlement in America.

Sir Walter Raleigh, who also endlessly promoted colonization, survived until 1618, but he was not so lucky. After a lifetime sinking his and others' money in failed American projects, the dashing soldier, poet, and personal favorite of Elizabeth ran afoul of her successor, James I. Raleigh spent the last 13 years of his life imprisoned in the Tower of London, harmlessly writing books of history.

Other writers contributed to the promotional campaign. Like advertisers of every era, they played down the dangers and risks, inflated the prospects, and simply lied through their teeth. Virginia rivaled "Tyrus for colours, Balsan for woods, Persia for oils, Arabia for spices, Spain for silks, Narcis for shipping, the Netherlands for fish, Pomona for fruit and by tillage, Babylon for corn, besides the abundance of mulberries, minerals, rubies, pearls, gems, grapes, deer."

Hard Economic Facts

Naturally, the boosters held out the possibility that English conquistadors too might stumble on gold and silver mines as the Spanish had, or find the passage to Asia that the Spanish had not. Some of them imagined outposts in America from which sea dogs would sally forth to seize Spanish ships and raid Spanish ports. Hakluyt showed that the North American continent provided dozens of likely harbors and coves for such enterprises. Even in the Caribbean, the overextended Spaniards had already abandoned islands which the English, Dutch, and French would later make their own.

But an economy could not be built on a foundation of piracy. Moreover, expensive as the Spanish found it to be—20 warships to defend a treasure fleet of 20 merchantmen—it was possible to protect the most valuable cargoes against high seas raiders. Even in the "golden age" of piracy, buccaneers usually had to content themselves with prizes that barely qualified as grand larceny.

Rather more persuasive to sober men of capital, there were signs by 1600 that Spain's American gold and silver mines were as much a curse as a blessing. It was true that Spain's fabulous American wealth enabled grandees at home to purchase whatever they desired, from a style of life that was the envy of Europe to huge armies that terrorized the continent. It was also true, however, that the men of the Spanish ruling class assumed that their matchless bravery and sense of honor were quite enough on which to base a national economy.

Philip II was not fooled. Taciturn, hardworking, and ascetic in his personal habits, invariably dressed in black, Philip thought in the longest of terms, eternity. (He kept his parents' coffins in his suite of rooms as a reminder of his mortality.) Philip knew that the mines of Mexico and Peru had bottoms. The gold and silver would run out. Therefore, he tried to enforce measures that would provide for his beloved Spain when the easy money was gone. He failed. Philip's subjects spent and spent on their luxuries. Philip himself spent and spent on his wars and fleets, all together ensuring that one day Spain would be one of the poorest in Europe.

Easy Come, Easy Go

Instead of putting American gold and silver to work to improve Spanish agriculture, Spain purchased much of its food abroad, impoverishing its own farmers. Fisheries were neglected in favor of buying from others. Philip II's attempts to encourage the manufacture of textiles, leather, and iron goods at home were thwarted by the cheaper costs of imports. Even the bulk of the dreaded Spanish army spoke German or Italian. Spain paid to have its warships built abroad rather than protect the prosperity of its own shipyards.

The result was that gold and silver dribbled out of Spain as steadily as they poured in. American riches ended up in countries with no mines but with a canny merchant class and enterprising manufacturers. Other nations did the final count of the Spanish doubloons. They included enemies of Spain quite glad to make whatever the Spanish would buy and to transport whatever the Spanish would ship. Even the hated Drake had little trouble finding Spanish buyers for slaves he had purchased in Africa or stolen from other Spaniards.

Every transaction left Spain poorer and its enemies richer. England and Holland, Spain's bitterest foes, actually fought wars with each other to determine which would have the edge in bleeding the Spanish of their loot. In the Treaty of Utrecht in 1713, England took as the spoils of victory not only the odd island but the *asiento de negros*, a license to sell 4,000 Africans into slavery in the Spanish colonies each year. Trade rivaled the vanities of dynasties as a justification for war.

Surplus Population

Another circumstance encouraging interest in colonies was the widespread anxiety that there were just too many Englishmen and women. The population of England had in fact soared during the 1500s, probably because of a decline in the incidence of mortal disease. But food production and opportunities for employment had not kept pace with this population explosion. The real wages (purchasing power) of the lower classes declined steadily during the reign of Good Queen Bess.

Some believed that the "enclosure movement" was at fault. That is, raising sheep was more profitable than farming land in small plots. Therefore, wealthy landowners and villagers who owned land in

Theodore DeBry's engraving presents a cut-away depiction of a Mexican gold mine.

common sometimes converted their separate little fields into large pastures which they *enclosed* with hedges that served as fences. Tending sheep called for a fraction of the labor force that tilling the land did. Consequently, villagers who lost their rights to farm the land were sent packing.

These surplus people wandered the countryside where their struggle to survive worried villagers and gentry alike. They begged, they stole, and they waylaid travelers on lonely stretches of road. At best they looked like a menace in their "rags and tags." The refugees also congregated in cities where they formed a large, half-starved, and seemingly permanent underclass that, like the poor of many ages, was

a source of disease, crime, and disorder. "Yea many thousands of idle persons," Richard Hakluyt wrote, "having no way to be set on work . . . often fall to pilfering and thieving and other lewdness, whereby all the prisons of the land are daily pestered and stuffed full of them."

One response to England's population problem was a chilling criminal code. In the seventeenth and eighteenth centuries, a wretch could be hanged for the pettiest of thefts, of as little as filching a rabbit from a gentleman's hutch. When the poor were so numerous as to worry the ruling class, it was easy to believe that only the constant threat of the gallows kept them from running amok and ruining everything.

Or, the pestering poor could be sent abroad. To Hakluyt and others, colonies were safety valves. People who were economically superfluous and socially dangerous at home could, by the alchemy of a sea voyage, become valuable, happy consumers of English goods and the gatherers of the raw materials that England needed. "The fry of the wandering beggars of England," Hakluyt wrote, "that grow up idly, and hurtful and burdenous to this realm, may there be unladen, better bred up, and may people waste countries to the home and foreign benefit, and to their own more happy state."

Indeed, the desperation of people who still lived on the land in huts of "stickes and turfes" rendered many Englishmen and women glad to go overseas. As for those who found the idea unattractive, the "Bloody Code" served nicely as an inducement.

North America was better than the noose. During the first century and a half of English settlement in the New World, it has been estimated that about one colonist in ten (about 50,000 total) was a convict.

Private Enterprise

The financing and organization of colonies were carried out by private companies that were forerunners of the modern corporation. These merchant-adventurer companies ("adventurer" refers to the adventuring or risking of capital) had developed in response to the expense and risks involved in overseas trading expeditions.

It was neither cheap nor a sure thing to send a ship packed with trade goods out to sea where pirates, warships of hostile nations, and nature's storms and shoals were waiting. Instead of gambling an entire fortune on a single ship's luck, investors preferred to join with others and divide both the risks and the anticipated profits into shares. If a ship owned by such a company went down, individual shareholders lost money, but they were not necessarily ruined; they owned shares of other ships. Adventurers of capital covered themselves at home, too. Typically, they secured charters from the Crown granting them a monopoly over the importation and sale of the goods they intended to buy.

The Muscovy Company, founded in 1555, was such a chartered monopoly. Its shareholders had government sanction to import furs and forest products from Russia. No English merchant outside the company was permitted in the business. The most famous and longest lasting of the trading companies was the East India Company, founded in 1600. It would actually govern large parts of India for a century and a half.

Companies Founding Colonies

When King James I was persuaded to approve of English outposts in North America, he chartered private companies to do the job. In 1606, he authorized the Virginia Company of Plymouth to establish a settlement on the coast of North America between 38° and 45° north latitude. The Virginia Company of London had the same rights between 34° and 41°.

The tracts overlapped but the two groups were forbidden to set up within a hundred miles of one another. The buffer zone was designed to avoid rivalries that, in the Spanish West Indies, had sometimes turned violent. The hundred-mile zone also put a premium on being first to found a colony, thus

NOVA BRITANNIA.

OFFERING MOST

Excellent fruites by Planting in VIRGINIA.

Exciting all such as be well affected to further the same.

LONDON
Printed for SAMVEL MACHAM, and are to be sold at his Shop in Pauls Church-yard, at the Signe of the Bul-head.
1 6 0 9.

Frontispiece of a book encouraging emigration to Virginia.

hurrying the two companies along. First come had pick of site.

JAMESTOWN, VIRGINIA

The Plymouth Company was first at sea. Soon after winning its charter, the Plymouth investors sent an expedition to the mouth of Maine's Kennebec River. Like Humphrey Gilbert in Newfoundland, however, the settlers found the northerly climate uncongenial. They scurried home within a few months.

The First Families of Virginia

The London Company had better luck in Raleigh's Virginia, if 15 years of suffering and wholesale death may be called "better luck." In May 1607, Captain Christopher Newport brought three ships into Chesapeake Bay and landed his passengers on a peninsula on the James River (named for the king). Newport had Roanoke on his mind. He would select no island that could be surrounded by ships, but he made sure to pick a peninsular site that could be defended from native peoples almost as easily as an island. Captain John Smith, a soldier assigned to remain in Virginia, called Newport's choice "a verie fit place for the erecting of a great citie."

This was nonsense. Jamestown, as the fortified village was called after the king, sat on low-lying land. All around was brackish, malarial swamp poorly suited to crops. Two centuries later, when Jamestown ceased to serve as a center of government, just about everyone living there moved out.

Jamestown's dim agricultural prospects were not overly important to Newport or Smith. The first English settlers of Virginia were not expected to be self-supporting, growing their own food. Their assignment was to look for gold and to buy goods from the local Indians that would turn a profit back in England. And, preposterously, several Polish glassmakers among them, refugees from the Protestant Polish Brethren, were to set up a workshop in which to practice their trade. The first Virginians arrived in their new home with some illusions.

The Problem of Survival

They found mere survival to be a struggle. Raw wilderness proved to be too demanding for the English. They had no experience as forest foragers. They could not compete as hunters and gatherers

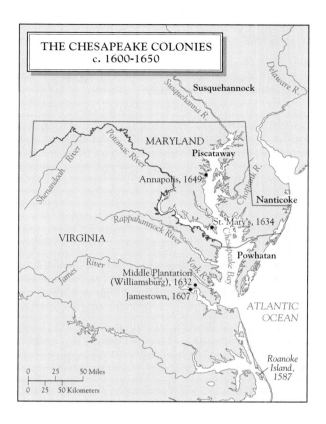

THE CHESAPEAKE COLONIES
c. 1600-1650

with the native Powhatan Indians for whom extracting their living from nature was at the heart of their culture. Hunting and gathering provided perhaps two-thirds of the food of the Indians of the Chesapeake. Hunger, as John Smith would write, "forced many to flee for reliefe to the Savage Enemy."

It may be that, at about 40,000 in 1607, the Native American population of the Chesapeake region had reached a level at which the Indians were suffering shortages in winter. (In Algonkian, the language of the native tribes, Virginia was Tsenahkommaka, "densely populated land.") The sudden introduction of 200 new residents may have been just too much for Virginia. Once the Jamestowners' numbers declined to a few dozen, they did hang on. If they survived on such as oysters and snakes and mushrooms, that is what foraging is all about.

There were soldiers like John Smith among them. Smith had a distinguished battle record. The Virginians might have lived by raiding Indian farms, and they tried. But the Indians, loosely allied in what the English called the Powhatan Confederacy, held the preponderance of power in the region and would continue to hold it for more than a decade. Had the

Powhatans been determined to wipe out the new-comers, they could easily have done so. Jamestown may have survived destruction in war largely because, along with food, annual relief ships brought trade goods the Indians learned to covet.

Finally, there was disease. Malaria, dysentery, typhoid fever, scurvy, and simple, enervating apathy took a devastating toll. In 1607, 144 Englishmen landed at Jamestown. The next year, 38 were still alive. In 1608 and 1609, 500 new colonists arrived. By 1610, only 60 survived.

Unpermissive Society

John Smith, who rivaled Raleigh as both stylist and self-publicist, credited his military discipline with saving the colony in these years. Indeed, his no-nonsense control of the colony—he executed one settler for eating his wife—probably did avert complete disintegration. But Smith was far from beloved by the first Virginians. His successor as governor, George Percy, called him "an Ambitious unworthy and vayneglorious Fellowe."

Thomas West, Baron de la Warr, named governor in 1610, is also credited with preserving Jamestown by instituting a rigorous discipline aimed at making the colony self-sufficient in food. The settlers were marched to work in the fields as if they were soldiers. Troublemakers and the merely idle were dealt with swiftly and harshly. De la Warr and his successors, Thomas Dale and Thomas Gates, prescribed the death penalty for dozens of offenses, including individual trade with the Indians. They actually executed people for little more than laziness and whipped them for throwing washwater into the streets or carrying out "the necessities of nature" within a quarter mile of the fort. Under their authoritarian rule, fields were expanded, better shelters built, and the settlement expanded along the James River.

Still, mortality remained high. Between 1610 and 1618, 3,000 new settlers arrived. In 1619, the population of Virginia was 1,000. Between 1619 and 1623, 4,000 settlers arrived. In 1624, the population of Virginia was 1,300.

The "Stinking Custom"

If the Virginians had not found a way to make money, their backers would surely have given up on them, returning them to England or leaving them to assimilate into the Powhatan tribes. But they did find

profit growing tobacco, a native American plant that Columbus had brought back to Europe on his first voyage to the New World.

The first European smoker, Rodrigo de Jerez, was with Columbus. Jerez was jailed by the Spanish Inquisition for seven years because of his bad habit, but he was the wave of the future. Slowly, inexorably, the practice of "drinking" tobacco smoke spread throughout Europe. James I, who found smoking "Lothsome" and forbade it in his presence, could not stop it. Nor could the sultan of Turkey, who threatened to execute puffers.

The lure of the exotic—the trendy—is always potent among the leisured classes, and some European physicians seized on tobacco as a miracle drug—"the holy, healing herb," "a sovereign remedy to all diseases"—prescribing it liberally to their patients. Throughout the 1500s, the Spanish were pleased to meet Europe's demand from their West Indian plantations.

One tobacco addict was John Rolfe, a Virginian usually remembered for his marriage to Pocahontas, an alliance that helped keep the peace in Virginia for several years. Like other Englishmen, Rolfe found the local tobacco "poore and weak and of a byting taste." Securing tobacco seed from Trinidad, Rolfe experimented with it in his garden in 1612. In 1614, he had more than enough for his own pipe and shipped four barrels packed with it back to England. The reception was sensational. In 1617, Virginia exported 10 tons of the golden leaf at a profit of three shillings a pound! In 1618, the shipment was 25 tons; and in 1628, 250 tons. The price tobacco brought explains this amazing growth. Ordinary tobacco brought $17 in the early seventeenth century, the finest grades the equivalent of $100 a pound.

The Tobacco Boom

Immigrants with the scent of smoke in their nostrils hurried across the Atlantic. The very streets of Jamestown were planted in the crop. A colony recently in trouble because there was no food now neglected food production for the cultivation of a leaf to be burnt. Authorities feared losing control, one lamenting that the settlers' "greediness after great quantities of tobacco causeth them after five or six years continually to remove and therefore neither build good homes, fence their grounds, or plant any orchards."

In 1632, the Virginia Assembly feared that other basic tasks would not be performed for the lure of the soothing blue smoke. In "An Acte for Tradesmen to Worke on Theire Trades," the Assembly declared

> The necessitie of the present state of the country requiringe, It is thought fitt, that all gunsmiths and naylers, brickmakers, carpenters, joyners, sawyers and turners, be compelled to worke at theire trades and not suffered to plant tobacco or corne or doe any other worke in the grounde.

Who Shall Till the Fields?

An industrious individual could tend a thousand tobacco plants plus four acres of maize, beans, and squash—enough to support a household of five people. It did not require a gift for higher mathematics to calculate what the income from 10,000 or 50,000 tobacco plants would buy.

The land for growing tobacco was rich, seemingly endless, and for sale at a pittance. The problem was labor. Who would work for another in a country that offered so extraordinary an opportunity to get rich? The Jamestowners enslaved Indians. However, unlike the Indians of Mexico, the natives of Virginia were unfamiliar with intensive, disciplined labor, and resisted it. Moreover, they had the bad habit of disappearing into a forest which, to them, was no howling wilderness but an accommodating home.

In 1619, a Dutch ship tied up at Jamestown and paid for the tobacco it took aboard with "20 and odd Negroes," probably seized as a prize from a slave trader bound for the Spanish West Indies. Soon, human cargoes from Africa would arrive regularly in Virginia (see Chapter 5). Not until after 1700, however, would enslaved blacks comprise a majority of the workforce. During the seventeenth century, ambitious Virginians made the transition from toiling farmer to comfortable planter by importing white servants from England.

The Headright System

Under the "headright system," introduced by the London Company to encourage settlement in Virginia in 1618, each head of a household who came to the colony received 50 acres of land for every person whose Atlantic passage he paid. Thus, a family of five could secure 250 acres upon disembarking.

People with cash to spare could amass even larger estates instantly by recruiting servants from among the impoverished masses of England. In

Thank You for Not Smoking

Both James I (r. 1603–1625) and his son, Charles I (r. 1625–1649) disapproved of tobacco. James called it "a custom loathesome to the eye, harmful to the brain, dangerous to the lungs, and in the black stinking fume thereof, nearest resembling the Stygian smoke of the pit that is bottomless." That was in 1604, before there was an English colony, let alone a colony flourishing by growing tobacco.

However, as late as 1631, when Virginia was booming because of the leaf, Charles I ordered the Earl of Carlisle to limit tobacco cultivation on his estate because of "the great abuse of tobacco to the enervation of the body and of courage." Several years later, the governor of Virginia was chided because "the King has long expected some better fruit from the colony than smoke and tobacco."

Nevertheless, neither father nor son was willing to pay in order to stifle the habit. When James I's 4,000 percent hike in the tobacco tax resulted in a reduction of imports—and of the duties his regime collected on tobacco—he consented to cut the tax down to a payable level.

Curiously, what was to become a second center to tobacco production, Turkey, was also an early hotbed of anti-tobacco zealots. One sultan threatened to decapitate smokers. He was no more able to head off the nicotine habit than James I. Ibrahim Pechevi observed that "the fetid and nauseating smoke of tobaco was brought . . . [to Turkey] by English infidels, . . . pleasure-seekers and sensualists who became addicted, and soon even those who were not pleasure-seekers began to use it."

return for their transportation to Virginia, these people signed contracts binding themselves to labor for their master without pay for a number of years, usually seven. Thus was Virginia peopled, thus the tobacco grown.

The Massacre of 1622

For fifteen years the English coexisted with the native peoples of the Powhatan Confederacy. Many held the Indians in contempt as savage and degraded, if not subhuman. They compared them to the "savage Irish," whom the English detested. So, red and white skirmished often enough, but few battles were serious. The aged head of the several tribes, whom the English also called Powhatan, did not view the tiny enclave of pale-skinned foreigners as much of a threat, and he was fascinated by the goods that the newcomers offered him in trade, from firearms to woven cloth, pots, pans, and mirrors. In 1614, when John Rolfe married Powhatan's daughter, Pocahontas, something of a détente was inaugurated.

Then Pocahontas died while visiting England, and shortly thereafter, Powhatan joined her. He was succeeded as chief by his brother, Opechancanough, an altogether different sort. Opechancanough had nearly been killed by John Smith in 1609 and he recognized what many Indians after him were to learn, always too late: the once little, once half-starved white enclaves with interesting things to sell grew in size and strength, and pushed hungrily into Indians' ancestral lands.

In March 1622, Opechancanough tried to turn back the tide. He entered Jamestown with warriors as if to talk or trade. Suddenly, his men attacked. They killed the founding father of the tobacco business, John Rolfe, and 346 others, about a third of Virginia's white population. At Martin's Hundred, seven miles from Jamestown, 58 were murdered and 20 women taken as hostages.

It was not enough. The survivors regrouped, bandaged their wounds, refused Opechancanough's offer to trade the women for peace, and retaliated with their superior weapons, sorely punishing the Powhatans. Other Indians were tricked into a peace parley at which perhaps 200 were poisoned. Indeed, the Virginians called for a kind of genocide, "a perpetuall warre without peace or truce [to] roote out from being any longer a people, so cursed a nation, ungratefull to all benefitte, and incapable of all goodnesse." By 1625, it is estimated, the numbers of the Powhatans were reduced from 40,000 to 5,000. (Nevertheless, one of the women captured at Martin's Hundred was not ransomed until 1630.)

After one last Indian offensive in 1644, the Powhatans were decimated yet further and driven far into the interior. In 1669, 2,000 were counted. By 1685, the culture was apparently extinct. The pattern of white–Indian relations that would be repeated in America for more than two and a half centuries had been drawn in the mud of Jamestown.

A Royal Colony

Virginia survived the massacre of 1622 but it wrote an end to the London Company. Although some

Pocahontas in the dress of an English lady. She did not survive her visit to London but died of disease, as did many Native Americans who ventured to Europe.

planters and merchants were getting rich from tobacco, the company itself never recorded a profit. Citing this failure and the massacre as excuses, James I revoked the company's corporate charter in 1624 and took direct control of Virginia. The House of Burgesses, a legislative assembly of 22 members elected by landowners and established in 1619, continued to function. But the king appointed a governor with the power to veto their actions.

Virginia was, thus, the first English colony, the first colony in which there was significant self-government, and the first royal colony, under the direct rule of the Crown.

OTHER BEGINNINGS

By 1622, the Englishmen and women in Virginia were not the only Europeans establishing footholds on lands that were to become part of the United States. Before the seventeenth century was ten years old, both the Spanish and the French had registered their presence on lands to become part of the American nation.

French America

In 1562, a French adventurer named Jean Ribault tried to launch a colony, Charlesfort, near what is

Pocahontas

Not long after landing in Virginia, John Smith was taken prisoner by the Powhatan Indians. According to Smith—and never has there been a man more willing to make up stories for the edification of his readers—he was seconds away from having his skull crushed by war clubs when Powhatan's 12-year-old daughter, Matoaka, also known as Pocahontas, "the playful one," begged Powhatan to spare Smith's life.

Pocahontas was indeed playful. She often visited Jamestown where, naked, she turned cartwheels in the muddy tracks that passed for streets there. In 1614, Pocahontas became a Christian and married John Rolfe just as he was in the process of fathering the American tobacco business. She also bore a son by Rolfe, but both parents died when he was just a lad. Pocahontas died in 1617 while on a visit to England, where she caused a sensation. Rolfe was killed by her relatives, the Powhatans, in the great massacre of 1622.

now Port Royal, South Carolina. Like Roanoke, it simply evaporated. Two years later, René Goulaine de Ladonnière took 300 colonists to Florida, close by the spot where Ponce de León began his explorations. The settlers were Huguenots, French Protestants who were fleeing persecution at home. Like the English sea dogs, they were interested in using an American outpost as a base from which to raid Spanish treasure ships.

As at Jamestown, Fort Caroline was plagued by Indian hostility and the refusal of the aristocrats among the colonists to work with their hands. However, it was destroyed in 1565 only when attacked by a Spanish expedition led by Pedro Menéndez de Avilés. Florida's history did not have a pretty beginning. When Menéndez discovered that the French he defeated were Protestants, he had them hacked to death.

France's interest in North America then shifted north, to far from the centers of Spanish power. In 1608, an extraordinary sailor, Samuel de Champlain (he made 12 voyages to the New World) founded Quebec on a site on the St. Lawrence River that was claimed for France in 1535.

The next year, in company with Huron Indian friends, Champlain was exploring the lake in New York and Vermont that bears his name when he stumbled on a party of Iroquois, old enemies of the Hurons. At their request, Champlain's men turned their muskets on the Iroquois. It was that people's introduction to European military technology and the beginning of long intertribal wars in which the French and English would play major roles.

New France grew very slowly. Quebec city was something of a religious and cultural center. A college was founded there in 1635, a year before Massachusetts' Harvard, as well as an Ursuline convent school for Indian girls. But no cash crop grew along the St. Lawrence. Mostly, Quebec was a trading post where Indians exchanged hides and furs for European manufactures: decorative trinkets, blankets, other textiles, iron tools and implements, guns, and brandy. Quebec was also a launch site for exploration. French explorers and priests penetrated what is now the central United States while the English clung to their narrow belt on the Atlantic seaboard.

Hispanic Origins

In 1565, shortly before destroying the French Huguenot colony of Fort Caroline, Pedro Menéndez de Avilés established St. Augustine on a peninsula between the Matanzas and San Sebastian Rivers. In 1586, Sir Francis Drake sacked the town, but St. Augustine recovered. By 42 years, it is the oldest European settlement in what is now the United States.

In 1602, Sebastian Vizcaino claimed Monterey in what is now California for Spain, although the site was only developed much later. In 1609, two years after the founding of Jamestown, a party of Spaniards walked the banks of the Rio Grande almost to its source in the Sangre de Cristo Mountains of New Mexico. There they founded Santa Fe, from which traders tapped the numerous Indians of the country for furs, hides, and small quantities of precious metals.

Today, Santa Fe is the oldest seat of government in the United States (St. Augustine was administered from Cuba). But by 1609, the Spanish empire had long since reached the limits of its capacity to expand. Along with the Hudson's Bay settlements, Santa Fe remained the remotest of European outposts in North America, isolated by colossal distance from the imperial and cultural center of Mexico. Like the French in Canada, the Spanish in Santa Fe would not contribute to American culture as dominant forces, but only in their responses to the great English experiment in settlement that had its beginnings in Virginia.

CHRONOLOGY

1497	John Cabot establishes English claims in North America
1517	Martin Luther inaugurates Protestant Reformation in Wittenberg, Germany
1524	Giovanni Verrazano establishes French claims in North America
1558	Elizabeth I crowned queen of England
1577–1580	Francis Drake circumnavigates globe
1578	Elizabeth I authorizes Humphrey Gilbert and Walter Raleigh to plant colony in North America
1582	Richard Hakluyt publishes his first promotion of the idea of American colonization
1587	Lost Colony of Roanoke, North Carolina
1588	Spanish Armada defeated by English seamanship and violent weather
1603	Elizabeth I dies; James I king of England
1606	James I charters two companies to found colonies
1607	Jamestown, Virginia, founded
1608	French found Quebec in Canada
1609	Spanish found Santa Fe in present-day New Mexico
1617	First significant shipment of Virginia tobacco sold in England
1618	"Headright system" established to promote populating of Virginia
1619	First Africans in English America arrive at Jamestown
1622	One-third of Virginia colonists killed in raid by Powhatan Indians

FOR FURTHER READING

The English leapt into the forefront of European civilization during the sixteenth century and were soon to be Europe's most expansive power. Literature laying bare the basis of these developments is too vast to allow for more than skimming here. G. R. Elton, *England under the Tudors*, 1974, is a good introduction to the era. On the English religious context, see Patrick Collinson, *The Elizabethan Puritan Movement*, 1967.

For social and "mental" background, we have Peter Laslett, *The World We Have Lost: England Before the Industrial Age*, 3rd ed., 1984. Specifically related to interest in North America is Carl Bridenbaugh, *Vexed and Troubled Englishmen*, 1968, A. L. Rowse, *Elizabethans and America*, 1959, and Keith Wrightson, *English Society, 1580–1680*, 1982. Dealing with important incidents are Garrett Mattingly, *The Armada*, 1959, and Thomas E. Roche, *The Golden Hind*, 1973. See also these biographies: Paul Johnson, *Elizabeth I*, 1974; P. L. Barbour, *The Three Worlds of Captain John Smith*, 1964; Stephen J. Greenblatt, *Sir Walter Raleigh*, 1973; and James A. Williamson, *Sir Francis Drake*, 1975.

On Roanoke, see Karen Ordahl Kupperman, *Roanoke: The Abandoned Colony*, 1984, and David B. Quinn, *Set Fair for Roanoke*, 1985. On Virginia, see Carl Bridenbaugh, *Jamestown, 1544–1699*, 1980; Alden Vaughan, *Captain John Smith and the Founding of Virginia*, 1975; and Edmund S. Morgan, *American Slavery, American Freedom*, 1975. On the displaced Indians of the country, see Gary Nash, *Red, White, and Black*, 1982; Thad W. Tate and David W. Ammerman, eds., *The Chesapeake in the Seventeenth Century*, 1979; the relevant chapters of James Axtell's books, *The European and the Indian*, 1981, *The Invasion Within: The Contest of Cultures in Colonial America*, 1985, and *After Columbus: Essays in the Ethnohistory of Colonial North America*, 1988; and Peter Wood et al., *Powhatan's Mantle: Indians in the Colonial Southeast*, 1989. See also Bernard W. Sheehan, *Savagism and Civility: Indians and Englishmen in Colonial Virginia*, 1980; and James Merrell, *The Indians' New World: Catawbas and Their Neighbors from European Contact through the Era of Removal*, 1989.

General works that also will be of use in connection with subsequent chapters are Charles M. Andrews, *The Colonial Period of American History*, 1934–1938, an old chestnut much corrected but still valuable; Daniel Boorstin, *The Americans: The Colonial Experience*, 1958; Wesley F. Craven, *The Southern Colonies in the Seventeenth Century*, 1949; Jack P. Greene and J. R. Pole, eds., *Colonial British America*, 1984; Curtis E. Nettels, *The Roots of American Civilization*, 1938; John E. Pomfret with Floyd Shumway, *Founding the American Colonies*, 1970; and Clarence Ver Steeg, *The Formative Years*, 1964.

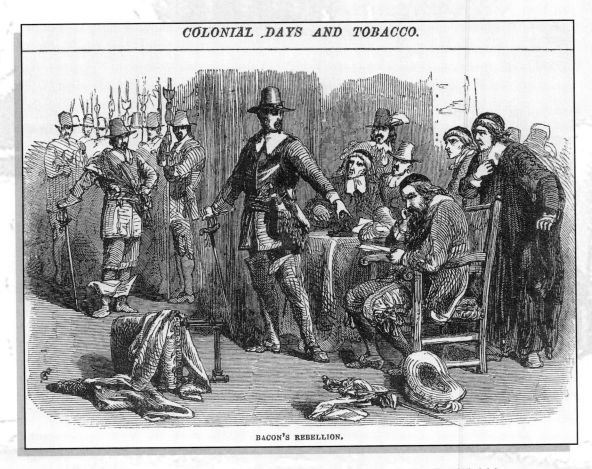

COLONIAL DAYS AND TOBACCO.

BACON'S REBELLION.

For a short time, rebel leader Nathaniel Bacon controlled Jamestown and humiliated Virginia's longtime governor, Sir William Berkeley.

3
CHAPTER

PURITANS AND PROPRIETORS

Colonial America

1620–1732

We must be knit together in this work as one man; we must entertain each other in brotherly affection; we must be willing to abridge ourselves of our superfluities for the supply of others' necessities; we must uphold a familiar commerce together in all meekness, gentleness, patience and liberality; we must delight in each other, make other's conditions our own, rejoice together, mourn together, labor and suffer together.

— John Winthrop

They differ from us in the manner of praying, for they winke when they pray because they thinke themselves so perfect in the highe way to heaven that they can find it blindfold.

— Thomas Morton

In 1608, the year Quebec was founded, about 125 men and women left the village of Scrooby in the English Midlands. They made their way to the port of Hull and took ship to Holland, where they settled in the "fair and beautifull citie" of Leiden.

They were quiet in their travels because they were breaking the law. England forbade its subjects to travel abroad without permission. The Scrooby villagers were willing to risk detection and prosecution because they had suffered persecution for their religious beliefs. They were members of a small sect called "Separatists" because they believed that Christians who were "saved"—elected by God for salvation—should worship only in the company of other such "saints," separate from those who were damned. This belief earned them the hostility of the Church of England, to which all Englishmen and women were required to belong, and of the Crown, which was closely allied to the church.

The Separatists are better known to history as the Pilgrims. Their leader for a generation, William Bradford, called them that because they did a good deal of wandering, as if on a pilgrimage, in search of a place where they would not be persecuted for their faith.

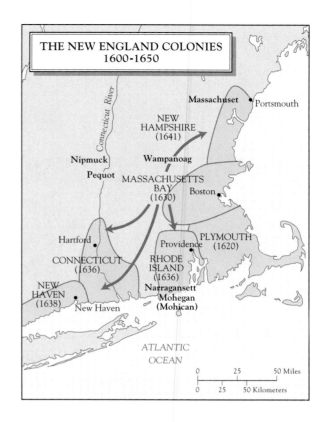

NEW ENGLAND COLONIES

Leiden was not that home. The Pilgrims were not persecuted there; the Dutch were a tolerant folk. The fact was, the atmosphere of Leiden was a bit too free and easy for the straitlaced Pilgrims. They fretted that their children were absorbing a casual attitude toward parental authority, "getting the reins off their necks," juvenile misbehavior with which the Dutch were associated. At the very least, they were, like the children of immigrants before and since, becoming as much Dutch as English. The Pilgrims might have yearned for a home where their religious beliefs were unfettered. They were also stolidly English, as ethnocentric as any Chinese, Ghanian, or Powhatan Indian. Any number of Dutch ways offended them.

Plymouth Plantation

The success of Virginia, such as it was by 1620, helped provide a solution to the Pilgrim dilemma. Profits gained from growing tobacco on the Chesapeake rekindled the enthusiasm of the Plymouth branch of the Virginia Company for developing a settlement across the Atlantic.

The trouble was that Jamestown's newfound prosperity meant that most English emigrants headed in the direction of Virginia. The Plymouth Company had difficulty finding settlers for an entirely new colonial venture at least a hundred miles to the north of Virginia, which the company charter required. Then, Sir Edwin Sandys, a major shareholder in the company, hit on a solution. He won the consent of James I not to molest the Separatists for their religion if they moved to North America. It was an easy concession for a king interested in expanding England's young empire.

In 1620, some of the exiles returned to England just long enough to board two small ships, the *Mayflower* and the *Speedwell*, but the *Speedwell* leaked too much and immediately hastened back to port. The *Mayflower* was itself none too seaworthy, but it survived a rough passage that was longer than that of Christopher Columbus a century earlier.

When the *Mayflower* arrived, just over 100 colonists disembarked at the southern end of Massachusetts Bay. They built the Plymouth colony on the site of Pawtuxet, an Indian village that had been wiped out in an epidemic several years earlier. The fact that their settlement was ready-made, with fields ready to

The Forgotten Colony

Many English settlements in North America are rarely remembered because they were abandoned or absorbed by those that survived. For example, hundreds of English fishermen set up base camps on the shores of Newfoundland, Nova Scotia, and New England to which they returned year after year. Some evolved into villages that survive today. One of the most interesting forgotten colonies was "Merrymount," located near what is now Quincy, Massachusetts, a few miles from Plymouth.

In 1623, a curious character named Thomas Morton arrived at Plymouth in a servant ship commanded by Captain Wollaston. The captain disliked the area and left for Virginia with most of his servants. He apparently intended to send for the rest, but Morton led a peaceful rebellion among them, persuading those who remained (in the words of Plymouth Governor Bradford) to join in a colony where they would be "free from service, and . . . trade, plante, & live togeather as equalls."

Morton presided over a riotous style of life that infuriated the austere Puritans. Like many pioneers after them, the Merrymounters were frequently drunk, and they "set up a May-pole, drinking and dancing aboute it many days togeather, inviting the Indean women, for their consorts, dancing and frisking togither, (like so many fairies, or furies rather), and worse practices."

Worst of all, Morton seems to have stolen the Indian trade from Plymouth—firearms for furs and hides. This worried Governor Bradford because the Indians were better hunters than the whites "by reason of ther swiftnes of foote, & nimblnes of body" and because the firearms could be turned against his own people.

He resolved to break up the colony and sent Captain Miles Standish and a few other men to arrest Morton. There was no battle because, according to Bradford, Morton and his friends were too drunk to shoot. The only casualty was a Merrymounter who staggered into a sword and split his nose.

Morton was put on an uninhabited island to await the next ship bound for England. There, the Indians brought him food and liquor. He managed to slip away, returning on his own to England, where he denounced the Pilgrims in words as impassioned as Bradford's. Neither he nor Plymouth was punished, however, and Morton later returned to America to lead a quieter life. It is interesting to reflect on how differently New England might have developed had Morton's taste for the "high life" and anarchic attitude toward government and social class taken hold, as it might well have done. Morton seems to have been prospering, and Bradford tells us that when "the scume of the countrie, or any discontents" heard that Morton forbade the holding of servants, they "would flock to him from all places."

---

plant, the Pilgrims regarded as a sign that God approved of their mission. He had "cleared" the land of others so that his saints might dwell there. Nevertheless, the first winter in America was as terrible as Virginia's starving times. Half the Pilgrims died of malnutrition or disease before the spring of 1621.

Then another positive sign, "a special instrument sent of God," an English-speaking Indian named Squanto, wandered into the village. A native of Pawtuxet, Squanto had been kidnapped in 1615 and taken to England. When he finally managed to get back to North America, he discovered ragged Plymouth where his native village had stood. Squanto adopted the Pilgrims as his tribe and proved an invaluable member of the community. He guided the newcomers about the country, taught them native methods of fishing and cultivation, and, according to Governor

William Bradford, asked for prayers so that "he might goe to the Englishmen's God in Heaven."

Self-Government

Squanto was a better citizen than many of the people who arrived on the *Mayflower*. Even before landing, Separatist elders such as Bradford, William Brewster, and the colony's military officer, Captain Miles Standish, grew nervous that, once ashore, the "strangers" among them—that is, the non-Separatists—would defy their authority. Several strangers had said as much aboard ship. What was worse, the grumblers could claim legal justification for going their own way. The site chosen for Plymouth lay outside the tract of land assigned to the Pilgrims in their royal charter. Therefore, the legal authority the charter vested in the leaders of the expedition was shaky enough to justify worry. The Pilgrims needed the Crown's goodwill as well as the Lord's.

In order to assert their authority, 41 of the settlers signed the Mayflower Compact. The document began by asserting the party's enduring loyalty to "our dread Sovereign Lord King James," the standard opening for documents of all kinds. Then, the signers bound the settlers together in a "Civil Body Politik" for the purpose of enacting and enforcing laws.

The Mayflower Compact is memorable because of its implicit principle, that a government's authority derives from the consent of those who are governed. King James got his ceremonial due. However, the signers of the compact, who were a majority of the adult males, stated that the authority to make laws in the colony was also based on the fact that the inhabitants consented to be subject to those laws.

By seventeenth-century standards, early Plymouth was a rather democratic place. Almost every male head of household was a shareholder in the company and could, therefore, vote to elect the governor. (William Bradford held the post for thirty years.) Important questions were resolved by majority vote. Only as the years passed did the percentage in the population of freemen, or eligible voters, decline.

Subsistence Economy

Plymouth was also autonomous for most practical purposes. The Crown interfered little in the colony's affairs. This was a consequence of the fact that the Pilgrims never came up with a money-making commodity like John Rolfe's tobacco plants and, therefore, failed to attract the attention of influential Englishmen back home. Furs purchased from the Indians provided some cash to buy goods from English merchants. Fishing for cod off the coast also helped. Still, Plymouth remained largely a community of subsistence farmers. The Pilgrims raised enough food to live. Indeed, after the first terrible winter, they thrived. But none got rich tilling New England's rocky soil.

The dearth of profits discouraged investors in England, and by 1627 they were ready to cut their losses. They agreed to sell their shares in the Plymouth Company to the settlers. Although it took 15 years to complete the transaction, the sale had the effect of transferring control of "Plimouth Plantation" to those who lived there. Plymouth remained a self-governing commonwealth until 1691, when it was absorbed into its younger but much larger neighbor, Massachusetts Bay.

Massachusetts Bay

Virtual self-government was half accidental in Plymouth. Had a Pilgrim plowman turned up a gold mine in his cornfield—or developed a profitable staple crop such as tobacco or sugar—the English investors and the king would have seized on the colony. Plymouth's very lack of natural riches assured its autonomy. In the most important colony of New England, by way of contrast, self-government was in large part the consequence of well-laid plans.

Puritan Names

So dedicated to the Bible were some Puritans that they named their children from the Bible, not only after the great figures of the scriptures such as *Adam, Noah, Moses, Deborah, Judith*, but after obscure characters that may have rung as discordantly in Puritan ears as the names of people today named by "hippie" parents.

Others went quite as far as any hippie couple of the 1960s, making a statement with an infant's name. There was the famous divine, *Increase Mather*, named for the biblical injunction, "Increase, multiply, and subdue the earth." New England records have revealed no one named *Multiply* or *Subdue*, but there is a *Fight the Good Fight of Faith Wilson, Be Courteous Cole*, and a *Kill-Sin Pemble*. Other bizarre first names discovered by scholars include *The Lord is Near, Fear-Not, Flee Fornication*, and *Job-Raked-Out-of-the-Ashes*. A couple named Cheeseman believed their infant was going to die during childbirth and, not knowing the child's sex, baptized it *Creature*. Creature Cheeseman fooled the midwives and lived a long life with her unusual moniker.

Not too much should be made of such names. A statistical study has shown that only 4 percent of Puritans were saddled with them. A boy was likelier than today to be named John, Samuel, or just plain Bill. Fully half the females in the study of baptisms were called by one of only three solid English names: *Sarah, Elizabeth, and Mary.*

There were no starving times in Massachusetts Bay, established in 1630 some 40 miles up the coast from Plymouth. The founders of the Bay Colony thoroughly planned the details of their great migration before they weighed anchor in England. Supplies were abundant, and more than a thousand people formed the first wave of settlement. Within a few months, Massachusetts was home to seven towns.

By design, the settlers formed a fair cross section of English society. They were of both sexes, more or less balanced in numbers, and of all ages and social classes up to the rank of lady and gentleman. There were skilled artisans and professionals among them, most notably well-educated ministers of God. Only nobles were missing from the mix.

The founders of Massachusetts Bay intended to create, quite literally, a *New* England that would duplicate the society they knew at home. In only one particular did the settlers of Massachusetts reject old country ways. Although they considered themselves members of the Church of England, they abhorred the church's practices in 1630. Their New England would be a truly godly commonwealth such as the world had not known since the days of the apostles.

In order to ensure that they had the autonomy to create and shape such a Zion, the settlers brought with them the charter of the Massachusetts Bay Company, the legal justification of their right to self-

The seal of the colony of Massachusetts Bay (1676).

government. Shareholders in the company who chose to stay in England sold out to those who were going to America. There would be no company directors back home to question decisions made on site in Massachusetts.

Puritan Religious Beliefs

These cautious, prudent, even conniving people — calculating every contingency — were the Puritans. Their religion was Calvinistic. Like the Separatists, they were disciples of the French lawyer and Protestant theologian John Calvin, who believed that human nature was inherently depraved, and that men and women bore the guilt and burden of Adam and Eve's original sin within their breasts. In the words of the Massachusetts poet Anne Bradstreet, man was a "lump of wretchedness, of sin and sorrow."

If God were just, and nothing more, every such "lump" would be damned to hell for eternity. Since God was all good, there was nothing that sin-stained men and women could do to earn salvation. From so corrupt a source, no act of charity, no act of faith, no sacrifice, no performance of a ritual could possibly merit divine approval.

Was there then no hope? In fact there was, and in the Puritans' hope for the next world lies the key

Increasing and Multiplying

Nearly half the settlers of Plymouth died during the first winter on Massachusetts Bay. Just two of the survivors, however, more than made up for the loss within their own lifetimes. John Alden and Priscilla Mullins arrived on the *Mayflower* and married soon thereafter (the wedding was immortalized and romanticized two centuries later by Henry Wadsworth Longfellow).

The Aldens both lived into their eighties. They had 12 children of whom 10 survived to adulthood. Eight of the Aldens married and, together, had at least 68 children, more than died in Plymouth in 1620–1621. Alden's and Mullins's great-grandchildren, a few of whom they lived to know, numbered 400, four times the original population of the colony.

to understanding the kind of society they built in this one. God was not merely just. He was also infinitely loving. He granted the gift of grace to some, to the "elect," his "Saints." They believed they did not deserve this amazing gift, for Saints were by nature just as sinful and corrupt as the damned souls who surrounded them. God's love alone was the reason they were predestined to join him in paradise. The Saints had nothing to do with their election.

In return for the gift of grace, the elect bound themselves to a covenant (or contract) with God. They were to enforce divine law in the community in which they lived. If they failed to keep their part of the bargain, if they tolerated sin within the community, God would punish them as severely as he had punished his chosen people of an earlier epoch, the ancient Hebrews, when they countenanced wrongdoing.

An Errand in the Wilderness

It is not quite correct, therefore, to say that the Puritans came to America in order to worship as they pleased. First of all, the Puritans were a powerful minority in England. Most Puritans worshiped pretty much as they pleased on the fens of Lincolnshire and the moors of the North. One of their most respected preachers, John Cotton, had been the pastor of St. Botolph's in old Boston, which was said to be the largest parish church in England. Cotton was no wild-haired creature of the fringe, hiding in a hedge from persecutors.

It is more accurate to say that the Puritans came to America because they were not at all pleased with the way non-Puritans were worshiping in England. Like the Pilgrims after their disillusionment with the Dutch, they wanted to remove themselves from "the multitude of irreligious, lascivious, and popish persons" in England. Their "errand in the wilderness" of Massachusetts was to *purify* the Church of England of the Roman Catholic practices to which the Anglican establishment clung. These included the authority of bishops, sacramental services patterned on the Catholic mass, and so on. Thus the name Puritans.

To Puritans, the English church was violating the covenant. The church was guilty of blasphemy, a most grievous violation of God's covenant with the nation and therefore deserving of severe punishment. "I am verily persuaded," wrote John Winthrop, the leader of the Massachusetts Puritans, "God will bring some heavy affliction upon this land."

In Massachusetts, Winthrop and the Puritans believed, they would be spared God's wrath because there they would honor the covenant. For years, some Puritan leaders harbored the comforting illusion that England would look across the Atlantic at them, see by their shining example the errors of its ways, and invite the Puritan fathers home in triumph to escort England back to godly ways. "We shall be as a citty on a hill," Winthrop wrote hopefully, a beacon of inspiration to the godly everywhere.

Commonwealth

The Puritans believed in community, that individuals should support one another in life's spiritual quest, and in its material concerns, too. In the godly commonwealth, in Winthrop's words, "every man might have need of [every] other, and from hence they might be knit more nearly together in the bond of brotherly affection."

There was little room for individualism in such a community. The Puritans enforced a strict code of moral and social behavior on everyone, saint and sinner alike. The Puritan belief that God punished the community that left sinners to their evil ways, and not just the sinners themselves, explains why the Puritans were swift and harsh with what are today called "victimless crimes," or acts not regarded as crimes at all.

"Hypocrites"?

"We are decendid," wrote the humorist Artemus Ward in 1872, "from the Puritans, who nobly fled from a land of despitism to a land of freedim, where they could not only enjoy their own religion, but prevent everybody else from enjoyin' his."

Witty? Yes. But it is wrong to imply that the Puritans were hypocrites because they persecuted religious practices other than their own. They came to America because they disapproved of the religious practices of the dominant Church of England. They never claimed that, in Massachusetts, they would tolerate those or other forms of worship they regarded as sinful. Intolerant? Yes. But the Puritans were not hypocritical. They were consistent in their attempts to suppress other forms of worship.

For example, when in 1656 a girl named Tryal Pore confessed to a Massachusetts court that she was guilty of fornication, she said that "by this my sinn I have not only done what I can to Poull Judgement from the Lord on my selve but allso upon the place where I live." She was not the only one liable for her lapse.

The same sense of community moved Puritans to point out to their neighbors that they might be committing sins. Judge Samuel Sewall of Massachusetts was not thought to be a busybody—in the disagreeable connotation we give the word—when he visited a wig-wearing relative to tell him that his hairpiece was sinful. Sewall was seen as looking after his kinsman's soul and the well-being of the community alike. The man liked his wig too well to give it up, but he did not tell Sewall to mind his own business. He argued only as to whether wearing a wig really was a sin.

Blue Laws

The law books of Massachusetts and other New England colonies were filled with regulations that, in the late twentieth century, would be considered outrageous or ridiculous. God commanded that the sabbath be devoted to him. Therefore, the Puritans forbade, on Sundays, activities that on another day might be perfectly in order: working; playing games, such as was the custom in England; "idle chatter"; singing; whistling; breaking into a run; and "walking in a garden." Some things were permitted in private but not in public. For instance, married couples were forbidden to embrace or kiss in public. A sea captain, returning home after a long voyage, kissed his wife on the threshold of their cottage and was fined.

Other minor offenders—a woman who was a "scold," for example, given to nagging in public—spent a few hours in the stocks or pillory on market day. This intriguing mode of punishment humiliated offenders by subjecting them to the ridicule of passersby, as did the ducking stool, a seat on the end of a lever that, with the offender on it, was lowered repeatedly into a pond to the merriment of onlookers. Serious crimes, such as wife-beating, were punished with a public flogging.

The Puritans should not be thought unduly harsh; other non-Puritan colonies had similar laws. Indeed, in one particular, Massachusetts was far more liberal than other English communities. In the then emerging "bloody code," non-Puritan Englishmen executed convicts for dozens of crimes, including poaching a rabbit. Because the Bible was the Puritans' guide in matters of crime, they reserved capital punishment only for those offenses that were punished by death in the Bible: murder, treason, witchcraft, incest, homosexuality, and bestiality.

Leviticus 20:15

And if a man lie with a beast, he shall surely be put to death: and ye shall slay the beast.

In 1642, Thomas Granger of Plymouth suffered the supreme penalty for violating the Puritans' Old Testament law. He was "detected of buggery" with a mare, a cow, goats, sheep, and a turkey. "I forbear perticulers," Governor William Bradford wrote. "A very sade spectakle it was. For first the mare, and then ye cowe, and ye rest of ye lesser cattle, were kild before his face, according to ye law, Levit: 20.15. And then he himself was executed."

A brank—a device made of iron used for the punishment of scolds, gossips, and liars in early Massachusetts.

HOW THEY LIVED

How the Puritans Worshiped

Early in the morning on Sunday, Thursday, and on special days of humiliation and thanksgiving, even before the sun rose in winter, the Puritan family bundled up in heavy woolen clothing and furs and walked to the meetinghouse. Few people skipped worship services, even during a blizzard. There was a fine for absenteeism, and if the weather could be withering, the distance to be traveled was short. Most New Englanders lived in villages, their houses clustered together with the meetinghouse near the center.

They went to a *meetinghouse*, not to a church. To call the simple, unpainted clapboard structure a church would have been "popish," and the Puritans shunned every emblem that hinted of the Church of Rome. In the meetinghouse, there were no statues or other decorations, such as adorned Catholic and Anglican churches. The building was a place of preaching and worship, not an object for beautification. A weather-cock rather than a cross sat atop the steeple, and was a good Calvinist symbol. It reminded the congregation that even St. Peter had sinned by denying that he knew Christ before the cock crowed three times after the Romans had seized the Lord. The sinfulness of humanity was a theme on which the Puritans con-stantly dwelled. In their churchyards, the tomb-stones were carved with death's heads—skulls.

Inside the meetinghouse in winter, it was little warmer than the snow-swept fields that surrounded the village. There may have been a fireplace, but the heat had little effect on those sitting more than ten feet from the flames. The congregation bundled in envelopes made of fur—*not* sleeping bags; there was a fine for nodding off!—and people rested their feet on brass or iron foot warmers that contained coals brought from home. In towns that prohibited the use of foot warmers—since they were a fire hazard—worshipers brought to meeting a large, well-trained dog to lie at their feet.

The women sat on the left side of the meeting-house with their daughters. The men sat on the right side, but boys who were apt to be mischievous were placed around the pulpit where a churchwarden could lash out at fidgety ones with a switch. He prob-ably had his work cut out often enough, for the ser-vice went on and on, sermons alone running at least an hour and a half and sometimes three hours. If a sermon was shorter, there might well be gossip about the preacher's lack of zeal. And lest anyone wonder how long the sermon was lasting, an hourglass sat

Adultery was also a capital crime in Massachu-setts, but few of the countless offenders seem to have hanged for it. In 1695, a law of Salem, Massa-chusetts, punished adulterers by requiring them to sew an "A" cut from cloth on their everyday gar-ments. Although the psychological implications of this sentence provided the inspiration for Nathaniel Hawthorne's great novel *The Scarlet Letter*, written a century and a half later, the punishment was actu-ally a softening of traditional practice. Offenders previously had been branded with a hot iron: "T" for thief, "A" for adulterer, and so on.

The Puritans also believed that social class and social distinctions were divinely decreed. "Some must be rich, some poore," said John Winthrop, not some *are* rich, some poor. It was therefore a crime for people of lesser class to ape the fashions of their betters. In Connecticut, an offshoot of Massachu-setts in 1675, 38 women were arrested for dressing in silk. Obviously, the offenders could afford their finery, but their social standing in the community did not warrant their wearing it. Other laws forbade people of modest station to wear silver buckles on their shoes. Such adornments were fit only for mag-istrates and ministers.

A Well-Ordered Society

Between 1630 and 1640, 21,000 Englishmen and women settled in New England. Most were farmers who depended largely on the labor of their families. Indentured servants were few in Massachusetts com-

conspicuously on the preacher's pulpit; when the sand ran down, the hourglass was turned by the man who kept watch over the boys. Many people took notes—some out of piety; some, no doubt, to keep themselves awake.

Although the Puritans forbade organs in their meetinghouses (organs were not mentioned in the scriptures), they loved to sing psalms, at home as well as at service. The *Bay Psalm Book*, from which they sang, was written with accuracy rather than poetry in mind.

The psalms, which are so beautiful in the King James version of the Bible, sounded awkward and strained in Puritan voices. For example, in the Puritans' translation, the magnificent and touching Psalm 137 is barely comprehensible:

> The rivers on of Babylon, there when we did sit
>   downe;
> Yes even then we mourned, when we remembered
>   Sion.
> Our harp we did hang it amid upon the willow tree,
> Because there they thus away led in captivitie,
> Required of us a song, thus asks mirth; us waste
>   who laid
> Sing us among a Sion's song unto us then they said.

Morning services ended around noon, and the family returned home for a meal that had been prepared the previous day. Like observant Jews, the Puritans took the sabbath very seriously. There would be no work and certainly no play or sports, as in the Anglican England they had fled. Even conversation was spare on Sunday. It was no more proper to talk about workaday matters and tasks than to perform them. At most, a pious family discussed the morning's sermon and other religious topics. In the afternoon, the family returned to the meetinghouse to hear secular announcements and another sermon and to sing psalms. Sunday was a day of rest only in one sense of the word!

The solemnity of the Puritan sabbath and the earnestness with which the pious approached life did not mean that family life was without affection, laughter, and homely enjoyment. It was partly because of their love for their children that, in the Half-way Covenant of 1657, the Massachusetts Puritans eased the requirements of church membership and, according to some historians, fatally diluted the vitality of that remarkable people's religion.

pared to Virginia and other colonies, and slaves brought over from Africa were exotic until the final decades of the colonial period.

By retaining close control over settlements, the Puritans were able to construct a village society more like the one they knew in the old country than took root elsewhere in English America. Arriving groups were allotted land for towns of between 50 and 100 families. There was a church (called a meetinghouse) at the center, of course, with the congregation itself governing most of its affairs. Each family was granted fields for tillage, a woodlot for fuel, and the right to keep animals on the village common. Social status in old England determined just how much a family received.

When newcomers settled too far from the town center to find church and common convenient, the township's lands were divided into communities independent of one another. When townships without spare land grew crowded, people moved west and north not as individuals but as members of a new community given authority to establish a new town.

Such firm social control enabled the Puritans to found schools and create one of the most literate populations in the world. So well-planned and organized was their colony that Boston was building seaworthy ships just two years after it was a "howling wilderness." So quickly was New England populated that the Puritans had a college to train ministers, Harvard in Cambridge, Massachusetts, as early as 1636. The colony was as well ordered as New France, but the order was not impressed by a military governor sent from Europe; it came from within.

THE EXPANSION OF NEW ENGLAND

Not everyone remained within the boundaries of Massachusets. Puritan insistence that everyone in the community conform to God's law, as the elite defined it, played a large part in the expansion of New England beyond the Bay Colony. Religion was a major factor in the founding of the Rhode Island, Connecticut, New Haven, and New Hampshire colonies.

Troublesome Roger Williams

Rhode Island and Providence Plantations, still the long official name of the smallest state, was founded by a brilliant, zealous, and rather cranky Puritan divine named Roger Williams. Arriving in Massachusetts in 1631, he quarreled with John Winthrop and the colony's other overseers almost before he was comfortable in his new bed, for Williams was the strictest sort of Puritan. His demanding conscience, as rigorous with himself as with others, eventually led to his banishment from Massachusetts Bay.

Williams agreed with the mainstream Massachusetts Puritans that the vast majority of people were damned, that only a few were saved. But just who were the elect? The Massachusetts Puritans had highly refined procedures for determining who were "visible saints" and, therefore, who was eligible for church membership and the right to vote. Williams said that no person could be sure of anyone's election but his own. To underscore his point, he said that although he prayed with his wife, he did not even know if she was truly saved. Only she and God did.

Williams was, in a word, the ultimate separatist. And he concluded from his beliefs that religion and government—church and state—should be entirely separate. If no one could determine who was saved, there must be no religious test, such as Massachusetts enforced, to determine the right to vote and otherwise participate in civil affairs.

Because church members were a minority in Massachusetts, this point of view threatened Puritan control of the commonwealth, the very reason the Puritans had come to America. If the damned majority were to make laws to suit their unregenerate selves, the Lord's covenant would soon lie in tatters and God would "surely break out in wrath" against the colony.

Rhode Island: "The Sewer of New England"

Roger Williams also made enemies in Massachusetts by challenging the validity of the royal charter on which Puritan control of the colony was legally based. New England had been occupied when the English arrived, Williams pointed out, and the Indians' right to the land was as good as that of anyone. The king of England had no right to give it away; it was not his. Only by purchasing land from the natives could newcomers justly take possession of it.

In fact, the Massachusetts Puritans usually paid the Indians for the land they settled, although the integrity of their bargaining practices may have been questionable. Nevertheless, when Williams assailed the charter the Puritans used to assure their control of Massachusetts, he touched the same tender nerve he had bruised in calling for the separation of church and state.

By 1635, Winthrop and his party had enough. Williams was ordered to return to England. Instead, he escaped into the forest, wintered with the Narra-

Roger Williams, who founded Rhode Island after being banished from Massachusetts Bay in 1635, believed in separation of church and state.

God's Hand

The early Puritans saw God's hand at work in the most ordinary occurrences. When the Rev. Cotton Mather's small daughter fell into a fire and severely burned herself, Mather in painful anguish wrote in his journal: "Alas, for my sins the just God throws my child into the fire."

gansett Indians, and in 1636, established a farm and township, Providence, on land purchased from that then numerous tribe.

Roger Williams may have believed in his heart that the king of England had no right to give away Indian land. But he was also a prudent man who knew how to play the world's games. In 1644, he sailed to London where he secured a charter for his colony. The Puritans of Massachusetts, staking so much on the sanctity of their own royal charter, would not dare to violate Rhode Island's.

Before 1644, the Puritans could have rooted out Williams and his followers with little difficulty. But, with Williams beyond the boundaries of Massachusetts, the worst Puritan fears were allayed: the Bay Colony would not suffer for the blasphemous doctrines he preached. In an ironic way, Rhode Island was indispensable to Massachusetts. It was a place to which they could banish the dissenters they found noxious. They called it the "sewer of New England."

Anne Hutchinson

In 1638, another Massachusetts dissenter was dispatched to the shores of Narragansett Bay. Like Williams, Anne Hutchinson was a devout Puritan. Taking seriously the admonition that saints should study the word of God, she invited people to her home after services to discuss the sermon they had just heard. Hutchinson's own observations were often critical and sometimes acidic. When her informal meetings grew in popularity, they raised the hackles of preachers who were wounded by her sharp intelligence and formidable wit.

They shook their heads that a woman should dabble in subtle theology. "You have stept out of your place," Winthrop told Hutchinson, "you have

rather bine a Husband than a Wife and a preacher than a Hearer." The governor expressed his fear that women jeopardized their mental balance by pondering theological questions too deeply.

Still, had Hutchinson's offense been no greater than crowing, she might have gotten off with a scolding. She had influential supporters as well as powerful critics. But Hutchinson believed that the Holy Spirit directly instructed some persons, such as herself, to speak out. This tenet, like those of Williams, challenged Puritan control of Massachusetts. If the Holy Spirit directly tutored some people, what they said was not "subject to controll of the rule of the Word or of the State."

Known as Antinomianism, Hutchinson's doctrine pointed logically, like Williams' separatism, to the separation of church and state. Like Williams, she was banished to Rhode Island. Later, she emigrated to New York where, in 1643, she was killed by Indians.

Anne Hutchinson handled herself brilliantly when called before the governors of Massachusetts. Her "unwomanlike" behavior contributed to her downfall.

New Hampshire and Connecticut

New Hampshire's first settlers were followers of Anne Hutchinson who moved north from Massachusetts with a minister, John Wheelright. However, the colony never developed Rhode Island's reputation for eccentricity. New Hampshire was peopled largely by conventional Puritans looking for better lands than they could find in Massachusetts.

The rich bottomlands of the Connecticut River valley also played a major part in the peopling of Connecticut colony. However, personality conflicts and religious bickering also motivated the Reverend Thomas Hooker and his followers to move there in 1636 whence they founded Hartford. In England, Hooker had been even more prominent than John Cotton. In Massachusetts, he was unwilling to play second fiddle to anyone.

The migration to Connecticut caused a conflict with the Pequots, the most powerful Indian tribe of lower New England. In May 1637, after a Pequot raid on the Connecticut village of Wethersfield, the Massachusetts and Plymouth colonies sent a combined force that, by night, surrounded and set fire to the largest of the tribe's villages. As the Pequots fled the flames, the New Englanders shot and killed more than 400 of them, women and children as well as men. After a few smaller actions, the Pequots were for all practical purposes exterminated.

During the Pequot War, Theophilus Eaton and John Davenport, ministers who worried that Massachusetts was too soft on moral offenders, settled at New Haven on Long Island Sound. New Haven was the strictest of the Puritan commonwealths and its strictures influenced Connecticut, into which it was incorporated in 1662. One Connecticut law provided that "If any Childe or Children above fifteen years old, and of sufficient understanding, shall Curse or Smite their natural Father or Mother, he or they shall be put to death, unless it can be sufficiently testified, that the Parents have been unchristianly negligent in the education of such Children."

ROYAL AND PROPRIETARY COLONIES

Except for New Hampshire, the New England colonies were corporate colonies. Their constitutions, derived from commercial charters of incorporation, provided for broad powers of self-government.

Corporate colonies acknowledged the sovereignty of the king, but even this was largely a symbolic gesture. In practice, the New England colonies were self-governing commonwealths responsible to those having the right to vote according to the colonial charter.

Virginia was a corporate colony until 1624, when James I took it over. Then, as a royal colony, Virginia was ruled directly by the king through an appointed governor. Royal colonies had elected assemblies with extensive powers over the treasury, but the royal governor could veto any law these assemblies enacted. By the time of the American Revolution in 1776, nine of the thirteen colonies were royal colonies.

Feudal Lords

Proprietary colonies had yet another structure of government. Ironically, for a system that worked quite well in the New World, the principle underlying the proprietary system was antiquated, dating to the Middle Ages. The proprietors—wealthy gentlemen and nobles who were favorites of the king—became in effect feudal lords over the American land

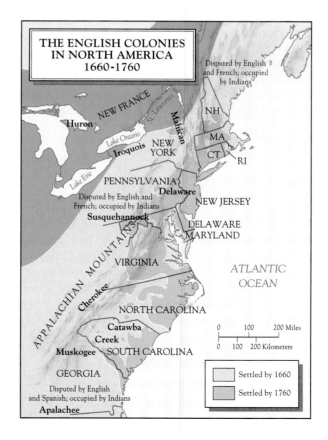

THE ENGLISH COLONIES IN NORTH AMERICA 1660-1760

granted to them. Their rights and privileges were defined as similar to those that were held by the bishop of Durham in the Middle Ages. The bishop, who had been the king's vassal in the far north of England, was allowed greater power than most nobles because he commanded the first line of defense against the Scots.

Making Money

Even the proprietors' method of making money out of their colonies was feudal, although, once again, it worked. Like the London Company and later the king in Virginia, they encouraged people to settle on their lands by granting headrights: so many acres per head (the amount varied from colony to colony) to every person who came or for each person whose transportation a settler paid.

In return, landowners were required to pay the proprietor an annual quitrent. This was not rent in our sense of the word. The settlers owned the land; they were not tenants. The quitrent principle dated from the time when the feudal system was breaking up in England (around 1300) and landowners commuted, or changed, their tenants' obligations to work for them into an annual cash payment. People who held land in "free and common socage" were "quit" of their old obligations to serve their lord as a soldier, to shear sheep, to repair the castle moat, or whatever the lord of the land required.

Colonial quitrents were almost always small: the idea was to get people to come to America, not to bleed them for doing so. For example, for each acre freeholders in Maryland held, they paid an annual quitrent of two pence worth of tobacco. The quitrent for each hundred acres in New York was a bushel of wheat. In Georgia, the quitrent was two shillings per fifty acres.

But for the proprietor of a vast domain, thousands of such pittances added up to a handsome income while the quitrents that the lord proprietors owed the king were purely symbolic: two arrowheads a year for Maryland; two beaver pelts a year for Pennsylvania.

Maryland: Refuge for Catholics

While making money was a major motive of every proprietor, some had other agendas as well. Maryland, chartered in 1631 and formally settled in 1634, was intended by its proprietors, George Calvert and his son Cecilius, the first and second Lords Baltimore, to be a refuge for their coreligionists, English Catholics. The Calverts favored Catholics in making land grants, and they invited priests to the colony.

Comparatively few Catholics took the Calverts up on their offer and they were a minority of Maryland's population from the beginning. (In 1640, there were only about 600 Marylanders total.) Because they were often the richest planters, Catholics were the targets of social resentment as well as religious suspicion. In 1649, Cecilius Calvert feared for their future and approved the Act of Toleration. It provided that "noe person or persons whatsoever within this province . . . professing to believe in Jesus Christ, shall from henceforth bee any waies troubled, Molested or discountenanced for or in respect of his or her religion."

It was hardly complete toleration: Jews were not welcome, as they were in Rhode Island and in the Dutch colony of New Amsterdam. But, protecting Catholics as it did, the act was too much for Maryland's Protestant majority. They revolted in 1654 and repealed it, inflicting double taxation and other disabilities on Roman Catholics.

Maryland's Catholics were too well established to be chased out. The colony remained a center of American Catholicism, and in 1808 the first bishop appointed in the United States was seated in Baltimore.

New Netherland and New Sweden

In 1624, a Dutch trading company established New Netherland between the two English settlements that then existed, Virginia and Plymouth. The town of New Amsterdam, at the tip of Manhattan Island, defended what the Dutch hoped would be a prosperous farming and fur-trading colony strung along the Hudson River.

Curiously, because the Dutch were a progressive people at home, they tried to populate New Netherland by means of an absurdly archaic plan. The company granted huge patroonships, vast tracts of land, to any worthy who settled 50 families—people to be beholden to their patroon—in the colony. Only one such domain actually succeeded, 700,000-acre Van Rensselaerwyck, south of Fort Orange in present-day Albany, New York.

As buyers of furs and deer hides from the Indians, however, the Dutch were successful enough to think in terms of expanding their little empire. In

1655, ships from New Amsterdam sailed south to the Delaware River where they took over New Sweden, a short string of tiny riverfront settlements of Swedes and Finns. New Sweden was founded in 1638 by Peter Minuit, a Dutchman who had also been the first director-general of New Netherland. It was Minuit who purchased Manhattan Island from the Manhattan Indians for the equivalent of $24.

New York: An English Conquest

What was fair for the Dutch was fair for the English, particularly after the ill-tempered governor, Peter Stuyvesant, arrived in New Netherland in 1647. His nastiness and tyrannical ways angered virtually everyone in the colony. As a result, a British fleet commanded by the lord high admiral, the duke of York, seized New Netherland in 1664 without firing a shot, because Stuyvesant could not organize a force to defend the colony.

The duke's brother, King Charles I, promptly gave the prize to him as a proprietary colony and New Netherland was renamed New York after him.

Double Dutch

The Dutch of New Netherland coined the word Yankee, or, rather Jan Kies. It was a collective personification of a none-too-admired group. The New Netherlanders, called New Englanders Jan Kies, just as World War II soldiers called their German enemies "Jerries" and our soldiers in Vietnam called the Vietcong "Charlies."

The English retaliated with a host of insulting uses of the word Dutch. A one-sided deal was a "Dutch bargain," a potluck dinner a "Dutch lunch." (Young men and women still speak of "going Dutch" if each is to pay his or her share of the costs of a date.) "Dutch courage" was strong liquor; a "Dutch nightingale" was a frog; and a "Dutch widow" was a prostitute.

One of the few more-or-less cordial uses of the adjective is in "Dutch Uncle," which means a firm but kindly disciplinarian, but it dates from a later era. In the seventeenth century, the English and Dutch were fierce rivals and not likely to speak fondly of one another.

The city of New Amsterdam also took his name. When the duke became King James II in 1685, New York became a royal colony.

Loathed at home, the duke of York was popular in his colony. He ratified the Dutch land grants and tolerated the Dutch Reformed Church and use of the Dutch language. Indeed, Dutch men and women continued to emigrate to New York throughout the colonial period. The duke also encouraged English settlement, so that when Holland briefly recaptured New York in 1673, it was already as much English as Dutch.

Tolerance and cosmopolitanism characterized life in New York. As early as 1643, the French Jesuit priest, Isaac Jogues, heard 18 languages on the streets of New Amsterdam. Other Dutch contributions to American culture survive in some foods (cole slaw), numerous place names, and folklore. It has been suggested that the American inclination to coddle children is of Dutch origin. Certainly the Puritans in New England thought the New Yorkers were too indulgent, and several of the Dutch words that have been adopted into English seem to bear them out. The word "hooky" is of Dutch derivation, as is "hanky-panky," and that unsounded but eloquent child's word that is spoken by putting one's thumb to one's nose, wiggling the fingers, and running away.

The Quakers

In 1681, King Charles II gave a large tract of land, including the present states of Pennsylvania and Delaware and parts of New Jersey, to William Penn, the son of a man to whom the king owed £16,000. Unlike other recipients of land grants, Penn was no courtier stroking the king's vanity, but a member of an unpopular religious sect, the Society of Friends, or, as they were called because they trembled with emotion at their religious services, "Quakers."

The Quakers were figures of scorn, amusement, and some anxiety in England. George Fox, the founder of the sect, wandered about preaching in village squares. Conventional people thought of him and his followers much as later generations would think of "Holy Rollers" or "Hare Krishnas."

The Quakers worried people in authority because they preached an absolute Christian pacifism. Members were forbidden to take up arms, even in self-defense. Seventeenth-century armies were not made

Political Correctness in Early Maryland

The contemporary university is not unique in forbidding people to use words that may offend someone. Lord Calvert's Act of Toleration provided a whipping for "Persons reproaching any other within the Province by the Name or Denomination of Heretic, Schismatic, Idolater, Puritan, Independent, Presbyterian, Popish Priest, Jesuit, Jesuited Papist, Lutheran, Calvinist, Anabaptist, Brownist, Antinomian, Barrowist, Round-Head, Separatist, or any other Name or Term, in a reproachful Manner, relating to matters of Religion."

up of draftees, but pacifism was still a challenging doctrine in a time when war was considered a normal state of human affairs.

The Quakers also disturbed the establishment because they taught that every individual had the light of God within, a teaching similar to Ann Hutchinson's. Consequently, Christians had no need of priests, ministers, and bishops. In their early years, the Quakers also challenged the legitimacy of civil authority and social class. When they were haled before magistrates, Quakers refused to remove their hats and to take oaths. Telling the truth was the individual's responsibility to God, they said, and none of the civil authority's business.

The Quakers dramatized their belief in the equality of all people before God by addressing everyone, including nobles and the king himself, in the familiar thee, thy, and thou forms of the second person singular pronoun. This seems merely quaint today, but in the seventeenth century it was highly insulting to address a social superior or even a stranger in that way.

Finally, believing that all people were equal before God, Quaker women were as active as the men in preaching and testifying. This affronted the popular feeling that women should not play a role in public life, least of all in religious matters. It is not difficult to imagine Anne Hutchinson, had she survived, becoming a Quaker. In fact, one of her followers, Mary Dyer, was twice condemned to the gallows in Massachusetts for preaching Quaker doctrine. She escaped death only because she was the wife of a Rhode Island official.

William Penn's "Holy Experiment"

William Penn was the Quakers' savior. Whereas most Quakers were of the lower classes, he was an educated and wealthy gentleman. Penn used his prestige to moderate some of the Quakers' more extravagant practices, and he gave them a refuge. Like other proprietors, he saw his Pennsylvania ("Penn's Woods") as a means of making money. But he also envisioned it as a "Holy Experiment." All people who believed in "One Almighty and Eternal God" were welcome. Because the Quakers believed in an "Inner Light," they would not impose their faith on any person.

Consequently, Pennsylvania thrived from the start. Pietists from the German Rhineland and from Switzerland, whose ideas resembled those of the Quakers, settled there in great numbers. They developed the fertile rolling land of southeastern Pennsylvania into model farms. Their descendants survive, many still observing some seventeenth-century customs, as the Pennsylvania Dutch of Lancaster and York counties.

Along with Charleston, South Carolina, Philadelphia was a planned city. The streets of the "greene countrie towne" were laid out on a gridiron, making

This charcoal sketch by Francis Place is the only known authentic likeness of William Penn.

possible a tidiness that even the well-ordered Puritans had been unable to command of Boston. Philadelphia became the largest and most prosperous city in English North America, at least in part because of the Quakers' enlightened policies. At the time of the American Revolution, it was "the second city of the British empire," smaller only than London in the English-speaking world.

The Quakers maintained control of the Pennsylvania assembly until after the age of religious fanaticism had passed. Unlike Maryland, therefore, Pennsylvania remained a refuge for persecuted sects, and was the most cosmopolitan of the English colonies. New Jersey and Delaware developed as separate proprietary colonies. However, they too were heavily populated by Quakers and practiced many of the same policies as Pennsylvania. Indeed, western New Jersey can claim to be the first Quaker colony, preexisting Pennsylvania.

The Carolinas: Another Feudal Experiment

The proprietors of the Carolina Grant of 1663 (named after Charles II, *Carolus* in Latin) were a consortium of eight powerful gentlemen and nobles. In 1669, they attempted to fasten to their grant a social structure that was more fantastic than the patroonship plan for New Netherland. Their scheme was outlined in The Fundamental Constitutions of Carolina, the brainchild of Anthony Ashley Cooper, one of the most active of the proprietors. Its 120 detailed articles were actually written by his secretary, the political philosopher John Locke, whose primary place in history is as a defender of principles of political liberty. It is difficult to realize that in the Fundamental Constitutions he created a blueprint for a society that was as rigidly structured as the feudal patroonship system of New York.

The Carolina grant was divided into square counties, in each of which the proprietors ("seigneurs") owned 96,000 acres. Other contrived ranks of nobility called "caciques" (an Indian title) and "landgraves" would have smaller but still vast tracts. The work would be done by humble "leetmen" and even humbler African slaves, over whom their owners were guaranteed "absolute power and authority."

Some historians think that this fantastic system was simply a promotional device designed to excite English land buyers with the promise of puffed-up titles. Certainly it was unworkable. A city might be laid out in squares, but not a country shaped by rivers, creeks, hills, swamps, and mountains. The mere abundance of land meant that development would be free and open, not a subject of strict regulation. Although the Fundamental Constitutions remained technically in effect for several decades, the document had little to do with the actual development of the Carolinas.

One Carolina Becomes Two

Geography shaped the colony. The vastly different environments of the northern and southern parts of the Carolina grant dictated that settlements there would develop in significantly different ways.

In the north, most settlers were small farmers who drifted down from Virginia and planted tobacco, as they had done at home. Centered on Albemarle Sound, northern Carolina was poor, rather democratic of mood, and independent. It was quite isolated even from Virginia by the "Great Dismal Swamp." In 1677, a Virginian named John Culpeper led a rebellion in northern Carolina that briefly defied all outside authority.

In the southern part of the grant, the proprietors and early settlers from Barbados (an English sugar-growing island) founded Charleston on the coast where the Ashley and Cooper rivers flowed into the Atlantic. At first, southern Carolina was a trading colony, tapping the interior as far as present-day Alabama for furs and hides, and converting the vast pine forests into timber and naval stores. By 1700, however, the outline of a plantation system similar to that of tidewater Virginia took shape.

Probably from their African slaves, the planters learned how to grow rice, a lucrative export crop. The easily flooded lowlands along the rivers were ideally suited to its cultivation. Cotton, used in manufacturing fine textiles, found favorable conditions on the sandy sea islands that fringed the coast. Indigo, a plant that produced a coveted blue dye, was later added to the list of Carolina products that were sold profitably abroad. Indigo was invaluable because it was cultivated and harvested when rice was not in season, providing work for laborers year-round.

All of southern Carolina's crops lent themselves to being worked on large tracts of land by gangs of laborers, and by 1700, half of the 5,000 people in southern Carolina were slaves. This was by far the highest proportion of Africans in the population of any mainland colony.

The slaves' owners dominated southern Carolina society to an extent that even the tobacco grandees of Virginia and Maryland might have envied. Because the low country that produced their wealth was so unhealthy, however, this small elite took to keeping town houses in Charleston, which was open to the sea and its breezes. There they spent at least the malarial summer months and in some cases the better part of the year.

The result was an urban, cultured, and cosmopolitan society that was obnoxious to the small farmers of northern Carolina. In 1712, recognizing the different social bases of the northern and southern settlements, the proprietors granted the two Carolinas separate assemblies and governors. When they sold their holdings to the king in 1729, he wisely confirmed them as separate royal colonies: North Carolina and South Carolina.

Georgia: A Philanthropic Experiment

Georgia was the last of the 13 colonies to be founded. It was chartered in 1732, with Savannah actually established the next year. The Crown's interest in this afterthought of a settlement was as a military buffer state protecting valuable South Carolina against the Spanish in Florida. Although Spain had recognized England's right to its colonies in 1676, ten years later an armed force destroyed a small English settlement on the Florida side of the boundary. During an English–Spanish war between 1702 and 1713, Charleston was threatened.

In Colonel James Oglethorpe, Parliament found the perfect man to develop a fortress colony. Oglethorpe was an experienced and successful soldier. He was also a philanthropist who was troubled by the misery of the English poor. At that time, a person could be imprisoned for debt and not released until his obligation was paid—a somewhat self-defeating provision since a man in jail could hardly earn money for his creditors.

Oglethorpe and others conceived of Georgia (named for the king) as a place to which such unfortunates might go to begin anew. They received the colony as a "trust." That is, they were to make no profit from it. Landholdings were to be small, only 50 acres, both to discourage land speculators and to encourage the formation of a compact, easily mobilized defense force. Slavery was forbidden. Oglethorpe did not want to see the development of an elite such as dominated South Carolina. He also

Health Food

The staples of the New England diet were corn (maize), in porridges and baked; whole grain wheat bread; apples in the form of vinegar and cider as well as cooked and eaten off the tree; maple syrup or molasses for a sweetener; and fair quantities of meat.

In the twentieth century, when some health food devotees discovered that, compared to southerners, seventeenth- and eighteenth-century New Englanders had a stunningly long life expectancy—except for high infant mortality and the deaths of young women in childbirth, it was almost as long as American life expectancy is today—they fastened on the whole grains, apple vinegar, and unrefined sweeteners of the colonial New Englanders as the secret to their longevity.

There are other explanations of the long life span in colonial New England, but one school of health food devotees bases its diet on the ancient staples.

prohibited alcohol, believing that drunkenness was a major source of crime and poverty in England.

In all, the trustees sent about 1,800 debtors and paupers to Georgia, and about 1,000 people came on their own. Unfortunately, among the latter were some slave owners from South Carolina. Oglethorpe, although inclined to be a tyrant, was unable either to keep them out or to keep other Georgians away from the bottle. He returned to England disgusted, and in 1752 the trustees returned control of the colony to the king, one year earlier than their charter required.

The experiment in social engineering was a failure, as others had been. The natural character of the region, and the opportunities it offered, determined how it developed. Although sparsely populated at the time of independence, Georgia became a slavery-based agricultural colony much like South Carolina.

Other English Colonies

With the founding of Georgia, the 13 colonies that were to become the original United States were marked on the maps of North America, and recorded in the books of the Board of Trade, the agency that administered the colonies for the Crown. It should be noted, however, that England was active elsewhere in the Western Hemisphere. In fact, several English possessions still loosely tied to Great Britain are older than most of the settlements that became part of the United States.

English-speaking Belize, in Central America, dates from the early 1600s, although, as a haven of pirates, it was hardly an official colony. Bermuda, a group of islands east of Georgia, was settled in 1609 when Sir George Somers, bound for Virginia, was shipwrecked there. (This incident was the inspiration of William Shakespeare's play *The Tempest*.) Tobago, a tiny island off the coast of Venezuela, was seized by English adventurers in 1616, four years before Plymouth was founded. Nearby Barbados, where many early South Carolinians originated, dates from 1627. (Local tradition insists that English settlement in Barbados dates from 1605, two years before Jamestown.)

In 1621, Sir William Alexander received a charter to found English colonies in Acadia, present-day Nova Scotia. However, the French controlled most of that rugged land until 1713. In 1655, an English fleet under Admiral William Penn, the father of the founder of Pennsylvania, seized Jamaica from Spain. Several continuously occupied trading posts on Hudson Bay, which was claimed for England by a Dutch navigator, Henry Hudson, were planted in the 1670s. The Bahamas, where Columbus first saw the New World, have been British since about that time.

Tropical islands where sugar cane grew were the most lucrative colonies from the Crown's point of view. To ordinary folk interested in actually settling in the New World, the 13 mainland colonies beckoned more seductively. There society was remarkably free, and the economy offered the greatest opportunities in the world.

CHRONOLOGY

1608	"Separatists" flee Scrooby, England, for Leiden, Holland
1620	Separatists found Plymouth Colony
1623	Short-lived colony at Merrymount near Plymouth
1624	Virginia becomes a royal colony Dutch found New Netherland colony
1630	Massachusetts Bay Colony founded
1630–1640	"Great Migration" of Puritans to Massachusetts Bay
1631	Maryland colony chartered
1635	Roger Williams founds Rhode Island
1636	Connecticut colony founded
1637	New England militias massacre Pequot Indians New Haven colony founded
1662	New Haven incorporated into Connecticut
1663	Carolina colonies created
1664	English seize New Netherland from Dutch
1681	Pennsylvania colony chartered
1732	Georgia colony founded

FOR FURTHER READING

The books cited in the final paragraph of "For Further Reading" in Chapter 2 also are relevant, in part, to this chapter. On Plymouth, students surely should begin with the history written by the colony's great governor, William Bradford, *History of Plimoth Plantation*, (numerous editions), and then enhance their understanding with George Langdon, *Pilgrim Colony: A History of New Plymouth, 1620–1691*, 1966. On Massachusetts Bay, see (with some wariness) James Truslow Adams, *The Founding of New England*, 1930, and the less literary but also less tendentious George L. Haskin, *Law and Authority in Early Massachusetts*, 1960; Mary J. Jones, Congregational Commonwealth, 1968; Darrett Rutman, *Winthrop's Boston: Portrait of a Puritan Town, 1630–1649*, 1965; Virginia De John Anderson, New England's *Generation: The Great Migration and the Formation of Society and Culture in the Seventeenth Century*, 1991; and the titles by James Axtell cited in "For Further Reading" in Chapter 2.

Our appreciation of the Puritans owes largely to the work of two unambivalently great American historians, Perry Miller and the profession's reigning dean, Edmund S. Morgan. Students interested in the subject will read all their works, beginning with Miller's *The New England Mind*, 1939-1953, and *Errand into the Wilderness*, 1964; and *Morgan's Visible Saints*, 1963, *The Puritan Dilemma: The Story of John Winthrop*, 1958, *The Puritan Family*, 1966; and Roger Williams: *The Church and the State*, 1967. On Anne Hutchinson, see Emery Battis, *Saints and Sectarians: Anne Hutchinson and the Antinomian Controversy in Massachusetts*, 1962.

In recent decades, special studies of Puritan society and culture by other scholars have been numerous and worthy. The briefest of samplings would include Sacvan Bercovitch, *The American Jeremiad*, 1978; Andrew Delbanco, *The Puritan Ordeal*, 1989; John Demos, *A Little Commonwealth: Family Life in Plymouth Colony*, 1970; Philip Greven, Jr., *Four Generations: Population, Land, and Family in Colonial Andover*, 1970; Kenneth Lockridge, *A New England Town*, 1971; Sumner Chilton Powell, *Puritan Village*, 1963; David Stannard, *The Puritan Way of Death*, 1977; Michael Walzer, *The Revolution of the Saints*, 1965; and Larzer Ziff, *Puritanism in Old and New England*, 1973. Important recent studies are Laurel Thatcher Ulrich, *Good Wives: Image and Reality in the Lives of Women in Northern New England*, 1982; and Carla Gardiner Pestana, *Quakers and the Baptists in Colonial Massachusetts*, 1991.

On the middle colonies, see Thomas J. Wertenbaker, *The Founding of American Civilization: The Middle Colonies*, 1938; Edwin B. Bronner, *William Penn's "Holy Experiment,"* 1962; Gary Nash, *Quakers and Politics: Pennsylvania, 1681–1726*, 1971; Michael Kammen, *Colonial New York*, 1975; Robert C. Ritchie, *The Duke's Province*, 1977; Joyce D. Goodfriend, *Before the Melting Pot: Society and Culture in Colonial New York City*, 1991; and J. E. Pomfret, *The Province of East and West New Jersey*, 1956.

For the later southern colonies, see William S. Powell, *Colonial North Carolina*, 1973; Eugene Sirmans, *Colonial South Carolina*, 1966; Phinizy Spalding, *Oglethorpe in America*, 1977, for Georgia; and James R. Perry, *Foundation of a Society on Virginia's Eastern Shore*, 1990.

Philadelphia, William Penn's "greene countrie towne," was at least orderly and tidy.

4
CHAPTER

COLONIAL SOCIETY

English Legacies, American Facts of Life

It doth often trouble me to thinke that in this bussines we are all to learne and none to teach.

—Robert Cushman

And those that came were resolved to be Englishmen,
Gone to the world's end but English every one,
And they ate the white corn kernels parched in the sun
And they knew it not but they'd not be English again.

—Stephen Vincent Benét

There is a nod of truth in the old adage that the British Empire was created in a fit of absentmindedness. True, the approval of the Crown, in the form of a charter, was the essential first step for anyone interested in founding a colony. However, unlike the case in Spanish America or in New France, neither the English king nor Parliament played an active role in setting up a single settlement. From the frontier farms outside Portsmouth, New Hampshire, to the stockade around Savannah, Georgia, every English colony in North America was funded and promoted in what today would be called "the private sector."

The creators of the American colonies were investors looking to make money. They were religious dissenters looking for a sanctuary, or a place to shape the world according to their beliefs. They were courtiers making the most of the king's favor. And in the belated case of Georgia, they were visionary philanthropists who thought they could make a corner of the world a better place for the wretched refuse of English society.

So insouciant was the Crown toward its American real estate—in the law, it all started out as royal property—that the boundaries drawn for colonies were often vague and overlapping, breezy strokes of a quill pen on maps in London that caused endless bickering on the actual ground.

And yet, the absentminded empire grew. By 1702, when Queen Anne ascended the throne, 300,000 of her subjects made their homes in an English North American empire that stretched, however thinly in most places, a thousand miles north to south.

TRADE LAWS

Parliament first took an interest in formulating a coherent colonial policy during the Interregnum of the 1650s, the decade after Puritan revolutionaries had beheaded Charles I and ruled without a king. His son, Charles II, returned to reign in 1660 and he confirmed most of these enactments. Charles II also created a Committee for Trade and Plantations, later known as the Board of Trade, to advise the Crown on colonial affairs. As the name implies, commerce between the colonies and the mother country was the subject in which the Crown was most interested. As Charles himself said in 1668, "The thing that is nearest the heart of the nation is trade."

Mercantilism

The economic philosophy underlying English colonial policy is now known as mercantilism. Its principles were systematized in 1630 in Thomas Mun's *England's Treasure by Foreign Trade*, although, in fact, the English, French, Dutch, and even the Spanish (unsuccessfully) had acted according to mercantilistic ideas for a century and more.

The object of mercantilism was to increase a nation's wealth in gold and silver—the wealth of all the realm's subjects, not merely the royal treasury. The key to success was a favorable balance of trade. That is, the people of the nation must sell goods abroad that were more costly than the goods they bought from other countries.

Thus the name *mercantilism*, because overseas merchants were of peculiar value to the mercantilist nation. (*Mercator* is Latin for merchant.) If a ship's master of Bristol carried a cargo of Flemish cloth to the Spanish colony of Cuba and Cuban sugar back to France, the gold and silver coin he charged the shippers for his services enriched England at the expense of three rival nations. Mercantilist policy was, therefore, to encourage England's merchants in every way possible.

Manufacturing was another activity dear to the mercantilist heart. Long before 1600, the English learned that it was economic lunacy to ship raw wool to the Low Countries, and to buy it back in the form of woven cloth. The manufactured cloth cost considerably more than the wool that went into it. The difference represented coin drained out of the realm. The Crown, therefore, had forbidden the export of raw wool and, through subsidies and favors, encouraged the sheep raisers, carders, spinners, dyers, and weavers of wool whose skills added value to the sheep's fleece. Mercantilists urged the Crown to favor all manufacturers with such regulations.

The Colonial Connection

In the best of all possible mercantilistic worlds, England would be completely self-sufficient. The nation would produce everything its people needed and buy nothing abroad. Were that ideal achieved, the gold and silver from trade and sales abroad would roll in, while none would leave.

In the real world, such self-sufficiency was out of the question. An island nation in a northerly latitude, England imported any number of tropical

A tobacco planter and tobacco "factor" from England oversee the loading of the weed in hogsheads.

products. The English people produced little wine, but drank a good deal of it: wine was imported from France, Portugal, and the Rhineland. England consumed large quantities of furs in the manufacture of clothing and felt. These were imported from Muscovy, as Russia was known. As a maritime nation, England consumed timber and naval stores (tar, pitch, and fiber for rope) in quantities far beyond the productive capacity of the country's depleted forests. Forest products too had to be imported from Muscovy and Scandinavia.

In practice, then, the object of mercantilism was to minimize imports that cost money and maximize exports and the trade that brought money in. It was at this point that mercantilists became promoters of colonies.

First, colonies reduced England's dependence on foreign countries. By gaining control of the forests of North America, seemingly limitless and teeming with beaver, mink, and other fur-bearing animals, England could stop the flow of gold and silver to Scandinavians and Russians. By occupying islands in the tropics, some seized from Spain, the English could produce their own sugar and stop paying money to Spaniards for it. And by settling loyal subjects overseas, the Crown would create exclusive and dependable markets for English manufacturers. The colonists themselves would have to scare up the coin, as best they could, with which they purchased these goods.

The Navigation Acts

These principles were put into practice in the Navigation Acts of 1660–1663. The laws minced no words in defining the purpose of the American colonies as the enrichment of the mother country. The prosperity of the colonies was a consideration. However, when the economic interests of colonials clashed with those of the mother country, the latter were what counted. Colonies were tributaries, not partners.

Thus, the Navigation Acts stipulated that all colonial trade be carried in vessels built and owned by English or colonial merchants. These ships were to be manned by crews in which at least three seamen in four were English or colonials. Not even niggardly seamen's wages were to be paid to foreigners who would take their earnings home with them.

Next, the Navigation Acts required that European goods intended for sale in the colonies be carried first to certain English ports called entrepôts (places from which goods are distributed). There they were to be monitored and only then shipped to America. The purpose of this law was to ensure a precise record of colonial trade, to collect taxes on it, and to see to it that English merchants and port laborers benefited from every colonial transaction.

Important trade goods were covered by this provision. For example, wealthy colonists had a taste for claret and other French wines. But they could not receive them directly from France. First the bottles and casks had to pass through the entrepôts. This raised the cost, of course; that was the idea. The premium that colonial drinkers paid for their wines went into English purses.

The Navigation Acts also dealt with colonial exports, designating some of them as "enumerated articles." These could be shipped only to an English port, even if they were destined for sale on the continent of Europe. Once again, the object was to guarantee that part of the profit on colonial transactions went to English merchants. Moreover, taxes on the enumerated articles were an important source of revenue. Charles II collected £100,000 a year from the tax on tobacco alone.

The enumerated articles included most colonial products that could be sold for cash on the world market: molasses, furs and hides, naval stores, rice, cotton, and tobacco. Foodstuffs—grain, livestock, salted fish, and lumber not suited to shipbuilding—were not enumerated. They could be shipped directly to foreign ports.

THE SOUTHERN COLONIES

Imperial trade law was uniform; the Navigation Acts applied to every colony from Massachusetts to Barbados. However, the disparate topography, climate, and social structure of England's far-flung provinces meant that the acts affected colonials in sharply different ways.

Already by 1700, North Americans thought in terms of New England colonies, Middle Colonies, and the South. New England was made up of New Hampshire, Massachusetts, Rhode Island, and Connecticut (Maine was a part of Massachusetts, Vermont securely under Indian control). To the south and west lay the Middle Colonies: New York, New Jersey, Pennsylvania, and Delaware. The South included Maryland, Virginia, North Carolina, South Carolina, and after 1732, Georgia (Florida was Spanish).

With good reason, English merchants smiled contentedly when they thought of the southern colonies. They produced, next to sugar, the most profitable of the enumerated articles—tobacco. Like the sugar islands of the West Indies, the southern colonies were home to a large, bonded labor force of white servants and black slaves for whom cheap clothing, shoes, and tools had to be purchased in En-

gland. And living off the labor of these workers by 1700 was an increasingly rich and extravagant master class that coveted every luxury that ever merchant thought to load on sailing ship.

Tobacco: Blessing and Curse

The tobacco plant grew in England; it is almost as adaptable to diverse climates and soils as maize. But English farmers were not permitted to grow it. So long as all Virginia and Maryland leaf was brought into the country to pass through customs, merchants and the Crown profited directly from every pipe that was lit in country home and hovel.

By the 1660s, however, Maryland's and Virginia's monopoly on England's smoking habit was not enough to ensure prosperity in those colonies. The wholesale price of tobacco (the price at which the planters sold) collapsed from two pence halfpenny a pound to a halfpenny. The Chesapeake planters had

The first published illustration of the tobacco plant appeared as a woodcut in Stirpium Adversia Nova, *a botanical study published in 1570.*

The Tobacco God

When Edward Seymour was asked to support the creation of a college in Virginia because the ministers trained there would save souls, he replied, "Souls! Damn your souls! Make tobacco!"

expanded their acreage so quickly that their markets were no longer able to absorb production.

From the planter's point of view, the solution to the problem of falling prices was obvious. The Dutch served markets that the English could not, and they lacked an adequate source of tobacco. However, the Navigation Acts prohibited the planters from selling to England's chief commercial rival. Planters complained in memorials to the Crown. "If the Hollanders must not trade to Virginia, how shall the planters dispose of their tobacco? . . . The tobacco will not vend in England, the Hollanders will not fetch it from England." (The Dutch were mercantilists, too, loathe to enrich English merchants by buying from them.) "What must become thereof?"

Smuggling

One thing that became thereof was a cavalier attitude toward English trade laws. Planters and shippers evaded the Navigation Acts or they simply ignored them.

Thus, merchantmen collected cargoes of tobacco at the plantations, then called at a colonial port. Although having no business there, simply by dropping anchor they fulfilled the letter of the law that all enumerated articles be shipped to an imperial port before it was carried elsewhere. The Crown acted to end this practice in 1673 by providing for the collection of a "plantation duty" on tobacco in colonial as well as British ports.

Outright smuggling was a common colonial vocation. Dutch traders arriving at Virginia and Maryland wharves had little difficulty persuading distressed planters to sell them their leaf. Such brazen defiance

When tobacco was a boom crop, it was planted right up to the steps of the planter's house.

of imperial law was not difficult, thanks to the topography of the Chesapeake region.

The Tidewater

The Chesapeake is a huge estuary fed by numerous smaller ones. Among hundreds of briny creeks and inlets, the larger rivers that empty into the great bay — the Potomac, the Rappahannock, the James, the Choptank — are broad, slow-moving streams. They were deep enough for the small seagoing vessels of the seventeenth and eighteenth centuries to sail for as many miles inland as high tide pushed salt water. Ships and even large schooners might careen in river mire when the tide ebbed, but twice a day the sea dependably returned to float them and their profitable cargoes back to Europe.

The land washed by this salt water, a series of peninsulas called necks, was known as "the tidewater." It was the first part of the tobacco colonies to

be settled, and it became home to an elite that dominated Virginia and Maryland society.

Although their descendants did not like to admit it, few tidewater aristocrats were well-to-do when they settled in America. Few Britons of high station and wealth emigrated to a land where the life expectancy was 40 years of age. Nor, however, were many tidewater aristocrats descended from the dregs of English society: convicts, beggars, destitute farm laborers. Most of the men and women of the "First Families of Virginia" were from families of artisans, petty merchants, or yeomen — the middling sort. They brought enough capital with them to develop plantations, sometimes of considerable size, but their social pretensions were possible only because of the boom in tobacco.

Some Virginians of modest origins did benefit from the tobacco boom. In 1629, seven members of the Virginia assembly — by definition the colony's elite — had been indentured servants only five years earlier. There were even black taxpayers, that is,

This fanciful eighteenth-century tidewater plantation was a complete community in itself.

The Oyster War

In 1632, when King Charles I drew the boundary between Virginia and Maryland, he did not, as was customary, set it at the *thalweg*, or deepest part of the Chesapeake Bay, but at the high-water mark on the Virginia side. This gave Maryland oystermen the right to harvest oysters up to the very shores of the Old Dominion. Virginia oystermen were not delighted with this state of affairs, and they periodically engaged in a shooting war that killed at least 50 men. Disputes between Virginia and Maryland watermen were to play a part in the writing of the American Constitution in 1787. The war raged off and on throughout the nineteenth century, with boats sunk and blood spilled. The last known fatality was in 1959. Today, oystermen on the Chesapeake are forbidden to carry firearms.

property owners. This was social mobility pushed by gale force winds, but it did not last.

Depression at the End of the World

The chances of going from rags to riches in the tobacco colonies dwindled in the later 1600s. Indeed, making a merely decent living became difficult for all but the wealthiest planters. The collapse in the price of tobacco bankrupted hundreds of small farmers so that larger planters, who were less vulnerable to the downturn, picked up small holdings and became even more powerful. Social advancement for blacks was almost absolutely at an end.

After 1660, even comparatively well-off immigrants to Virginia were forced to trek into the backcountry if they wished to build estates. There in the Piedmont, or foothills of the Appalachians, they found hundreds of hardscrabble frontiersmen. Some had been recently dispossessed in the tidewater. Others were freed servants without land, unmarried, boisterous young men who survived by doing casual work for wages. There were a few blacks in the region, but not many. Free but destitute African Americans were more likely to find a bearable life among Indians than lower-class whites. In 1676, differences between these westerners and the tidewater planters burst into a miniature civil war, ragtag and improvised, but plenty nasty.

East–West Conflict

The royal governor of Virginia in 1676 was Sir William Berkeley. In the colony for more than 30 years — a long time for an English gentleman — he did quite well for himself. Berkeley was a major landowner (he was also one of the proprietors of the Carolinas) and the social doyen as well as the political leader of the tidewater planters.

He and his friends supplemented their earnings from tobacco by carrying on a prosperous trade with the Indians. In return for furs and deerskins, they provided manufactured goods, especially woven blankets, iron products ranging from pots to traps, and rum. When the bottom dropped out of tobacco prices in the 1660s, this business loomed larger in their accounts. It also provided the Berkeley group with good reason to cultivate a working relationship with the tribes that supplied them.

Settlers in the Piedmont, by way of contrast, looked on Indians as obstacles and enemies. As they expanded their fields, they encroached on the hunting grounds of the Susquehannocks and other Algonkian and Iroquoian-speaking peoples, including some tribes that had already been forced off lands in the tidewater where they had lived before colonization. Inevitably, there were bloody clashes. The Indians complained to Berkeley of white marauders. The settlers of the Piedmont complained of hit-and-run raids on their farms. Berkeley and his associates, their trading interests caught in the middle, tried to resolve the conflict by building a system of defensive stockades along the line of white settlement.

The plan did not win over the Piedmont whites. The forts were so far apart that Indian raiders, especially the aggressive Susquehannocks, could easily slip between them, wreak havoc, and retreat. More important, like frontier settlers for two centuries to come, Virginia's backcountry pioneers did not think in terms of holding a line. Ever increasing in numbers, they were an expansive people. They meant to clear the land of the natives, not to share it with them.

Bacon's Rebellion

Tempers flamed. When the death toll of backcountry whites climbed to more than a hundred, and kidnappings of women and children increased, the Piedmont planters took matters into their own hands. Nathaniel

HOW THEY LIVED

How They Crossed the Ocean

European sailors in the African or Asian trade found their way by the ancient and honorable way of keeping the coastline in sight. They sailed like the pilot of a small airplane flies his craft, by what is seen following interstate highways from charted town to charted town. The seamen needed more than their eyes only when adverse winds blew them out of sight of land, or when they dashed from the east coast of Africa to India. For such eventualities, they depended on the compass, the prototype of which Europeans had received from the East in ancient times. Have you been blown westerly off the coast of Africa as Pedro Cabral was? Sail due east. Where else?

Deepwater sailors of the American colonial era, whose entire voyage was out of sight of land, depended on the compass and the astrolabe. By the seventeenth century, the ship's compass consisted of a round brass bowl marked with thirty-two directions. In the center of the circle, a magnetized needle was delicately balanced. The compass was positioned within sight of the helmsman and mounted on pivots so that it remained level despite the pitching and rolling of the vessel.

The astrolabe, perfected in Portugal in the century before Columbus, enabled navigators to measure the angle between the sun or, at night, the North Star (the Southern Cross below the Equator) and the horizon. From this information, ships' masters could determine their latitude, that is, the distance of their position from the equator and from the poles. Using an astrolabe, a sailor knew on which east-west line his ship was sailing.

So, an English captain seeking to make a landfall at Cape Cod, which he knew was located at about 42 degrees north latitude, sailed in a southerly direction out of England until his ship arrived at 42 degrees. Then, using his compass, he sailed due west. It was simple—so long as winds and currents were cooperative.

What sailors could not determine with any accuracy before the mid-eighteenth century was longitude—their positions on the imaginary arcs than run north-south from pole to pole. On an east-west voyage such as across the Atlantic between the colonies and the Mother Country, navigators had no more than a reckoner's notion of how far they had sailed from their port of departure and, therefore, how far they were from their destination.

Bacon, an immigrant of some means, set himself up as the commander of a force that decimated the Oconeechee tribe. The Oconeechees had not been involved in attacks on whites and had even expressed some interest in an alliance with the white Virginians against the Susquehannocks. No matter; they were Indians. Bacon crushed them and then turned his "army" toward the colonial capital of Jamestown.

Angry words with Berkeley led the governor to arrest Bacon as a rebel but he was forced to release him when his supporters demonstrated that they were quite capable of taking over the little town. After a period of uneasy stalemate between tidewater and Piedmont, Bacon returned to Jamestown and blustered that he would hang the governor. Berkeley took him seriously enough to flee across the Chesapeake to the eastern shore. For several months, Nathaniel Bacon and his frontier rebels governed Virginia.

Legacy of Suspicion

It will never be known how the English authorities would have dealt with this first American rebellion. In October 1676, Nathaniel Bacon fell ill and, like so many Virginians, died before his time. (He was 29.) Bacon must have been a compelling figure. Without his leadership, the rebels quickly lost heart and scattered into the forests. Berkeley returned, rounded up several dozen, and hanged them.

However, the governor never regained his preeminence. Charles II was disgusted by Berkeley's vindictiveness; he remarked that "the old fool has hanged more men in that naked country than I have done for the murder of my father." Berkeley was recalled to England where he died within a few months.

The suspicion and ill feeling between tidewater and Piedmont endured for more than a century. The

They had some rude instruments for determining speed, which is what longitude measures on an east-west voyage. The log line was a rope knotted every forty-eight feet with a wood float, a log, tied to the end. It was thrown overboard. Measuring minutes with a sandglass or hourglass, the captain counted the number of knots that passed over the stern in a given period of time. Since the log was not blown, as the ship was, wind speed could thus be ascertained.

However, ships were rarely blessed with a wind they could ride in a straight line to Cape Cod or anywhere else. Moreover, the logline did not take account of the action of ocean currents, which could radically increase or decrease a ship's progress: The log was in the grip of currents, just as the ship was.

The problem of longitude was complicated by patriotism. The British measured it from St. Paul's Cathedral in London, the Dutch from Amsterdam, the Spanish from the Isle of Hierro, and the French from Paris. (The French insisted on being further ornery by numbering longitudinal lines easterly rather than to the west.)

Beginning in the mid-eighteenth century, the problem of determining longitude was resolved. In 1752, a German astronomer, Tobias Mayer, devised a set of tables and a mathematical formula for determining longitude from the position of the moon. The method is not very practical. Even a skilled mathematician needed four hours to complete the calculation, a block of time available to few ships' masters. In 1767, the Royal Observatory at Greenwich, England (which was to replace St. Paul, Hierro Island, Paris, and Amsterdam as 0 degrees longitude), issued the *Mariner's Almanac*, a volume of tables that increased the speed of nautical calculations.

But not until the invention, by Larcum Kendall, of a highly accurate clock, the chronometer, was longitude mastered. Set at the beginning of a voyage at Greenwich mean time, it enabled a navigator to know the time "back home" wherever he was in the world, compare it with the time aboard his ship (determined from the position of the sun), and thus establish his position on the globe. Captain James Cook, the peerless explorer of the seas, was the first to use a chronometer on his second voyage of exploration in 1772.

tidewater aristocracy continued to dominate Virginia's economy, government, and culture, and the people of the backcountry continued to resent them.

A Land without Cities

The great planters' domination of Virginia and Maryland was so thoroughgoing because, short of rebellion by an underclass, there existed no other social group able to compete with them. There was no urban middle class of merchants, bankers, and manufacturers in Virginia or Maryland because no centers of commerce, no cities, developed in the tobacco colonies.

One Marylander attributed this curiosity to the appetite of land for growing tobacco. "Tobacco," he wrote, "requires us to abhor communities or townships. . . . A planter cannot carry on his affairs without considerable elbow room." Moreover, because the Potomac and James and York and Nanticoke and Choptank rivers were navigable so far inland, ships from Europe tied up at the private wharves of the great tidewater plantations. They did not need a port in which to drop anchor.

The planters sold their tobacco and received the goods that they had ordered the previous year in their own backyards. The small farmers whose lands did not front on tidewater depended on the great planters' facilities for their trade. Such people were unlikely to mount a resistance to planter power.

Roll out the Barrel

They were exhilarating days in the naked land when the merchantmen arrived. Servants and slaves rolled great hogsheads of tobacco to the dock, enjoying the expansive hospitality of the master. Farmers, backcountry planters and their families, and Indians gathered to dance, drink, race on foot and horseback, and shoot targets. For women, who lived a far more isolated life than their menfolk, the arrival of a tobacco factor (agent) was a rare opportunity to enjoy company.

Everyone discussed the news that the shipmasters brought with them about European battles and the machinations of the kings they had left behind. Some received letters from old country associates. The sailors enlivened the carnival with their giddiness at being ashore after weeks at sea, and they spent their wages on games and drink and the favors of women.

A People Who Lived on Imports

Most important was the receipt of the manufactured goods on which the isolated colonists depended in order to live in something like a European style. A single ship might be loaded with spades, shovels, axes, and saws; and household items such as kettles, pots, pans, sieves, funnels, pewter tankards, and tableware. There were oddments such as buttons, needles, thread, pins, and ribbons. There were textiles for both the planter families' fine clothing and rough wraps for servants and slaves; shoes and boots; bricks, nails, and paint; goods to trade with the Indians (which would include all of the above plus trinkets, mirrors, and the like); and firearms, shot, and gunpowder. And for the very wealthy few there were luxuries: silver candlesticks, chests and other fine furniture, wine, brandy, spices, books, and perhaps even violins and harpsichords with which to grace a parlor and enliven an evening.

All the business affairs that were carried out in cities elsewhere were transacted at the great plantations for a week or two each year. When the ships departed for London, Plymouth, Bristol, or perhaps Amsterdam, they took not only tobacco but also Virginia and Maryland's banks, factories, and commercial apparatus. The middle class of the tobacco colonies lived across the Atlantic. Virginia and Maryland's shops were afloat. Indeed, tobacco was money on the Chesapeake. Clergymen's fees were paid in leaf. It cost two hundred pounds of tobacco to get married, four hundred to be buried.

Even the capitals of the tobacco colonies, Jamestown (Williamsburg after 1699) and Annapolis, were ghost towns when the legislative assemblies were not in session. County seats were clusters of buildings at the crossings of trails. Small farmers lived isolated from one another by forests. There were churches, but not many public houses—inns and taverns—worth mentioning. Travelers depended on an invitation to a private home, humble or grand, in which to shelter from the night.

A Life of Elegance

By the end of the seventeenth century, the great planters of Virginia and Maryland were creating a gracious style of life patterned after that of the country gentry back home. They copied as best they could the manners, fashions, and quirks of English squires and their wives. When tobacco was returning a good price, they built fine houses in the style of English manors and furnished them with good furniture. They stocked their cellars with port and Madeira wine, hock from the Rhineland, and claret from France, which they generously poured for one another at dinners, parties, balls, and simple visits that marked the origins of "southern hospitality."

Some tidewater families educated their sons at Oxford, Cambridge, or the Inns of Court (the law schools of Great Britain). Or if they feared the effects of English miasmas on innocent American bodies (smallpox, a deadly scourge in Europe, did not spread so easily in rural America), they schooled their heirs at the College of William and Mary. The college was founded at Williamsburg in 1693 and staffed by Oxford and Cambridge graduates.

And yet, the grandeur of the great planters' social and cultural life must not be overstated. William Byrd of Westover (one of the richest of them—he owned 179,000 acres when he died in 1744), was very well-educated, and he preferred living in London. When his first wife, Lucy Park, died, Byrd returned to England to find the daughter of a wealthy nobleman to replace her. However, when he pressed his suit, he learned that his would-be bride was to have an annual income equal to Byrd's entire fortune! Her father scornfully rejected Byrd as too poor. William Byrd looks like a duke in his portraits. But the fact remains that even the richest tobacco planters were poor relations of the English upper classes.

A Habit of Debt

Like many poor relations with pretensions, the planters were almost constantly in debt. When the profits from tobacco dropped, or even disappeared, the Virginians and Marylanders found it difficult to break the pleasant habits of consumption. They continued to order the luxuries from England that enhanced their lives. To pay for them, they mortgaged future crops—at a discount, of course—to the merchants who delivered the goods. It was not unusual that, by the time the tobacco went into the ground in spring, the imported products it was to pay for had already been purchased and, in the case of wine, had already been consumed.

Planter debt gratified mercantilists. It meant more money in the form of interest and discounts flowing from colony to mother country. In time, chronic indebtedness would make anti-British rebels of almost the entire tidewater aristocracy. During the lifetimes of first-generation gentlemen like William Byrd, however, England stood not as an enemy but as a mother country—loved, admired, and imitated.

The Carolinas

The social structure of South Carolina was similar to that of Virginia and Maryland but the rhythms of life were quite different. The cash crops there were rice and, by the mid-1700s, indigo, a plant that produced a precious blue pigment for dying cloth. Indigo was developed as a crop by Eliza Lucas Pinckney on her father's Wappoo plantation.

Rice and indigo nicely complemented one another. They required intensive labor at different times of the year, so South Carolina slaves produced wealth for the planter class 12 months a year.

However, the low-lying rice plantations were extremely unhealthy. Flooded for parts of the growing season, rice fields were breeding grounds for mosquitoes and mosquito-borne diseases—malaria and the dreaded yellow fever. Consequently, while the slaves were left to fend as best they might, the South Carolina planters spent much of the year in airy Charleston, open to the sea, leaving the management of their plantations to hired overseers.

By congregating in a real city, South Carolina's elite was all the more conscious of its privileged position, all the more united in its determination to preserve it. No colony (or state) was dominated by so small an aristocracy as ran South Carolina for over 200 years.

North Carolina was an exception within the South. Although tobacco was grown there, the colony was largely a society of small farmers with few servants and slaves. Quite unlike its neighbor to the south, North Carolina was never the province of a tiny elite.

THE NEW ENGLAND COLONIES

New England was peopled by immigrants similar in background to those Englishmen and women who went south. However, the Puritan heritage continued to shape New England society long after the generation of Winthrop and Cotton died out and their zeal faded. Just as important in explaining New England's way of life was geography. The land and the climate decreed an economy for Connecticut, Rhode Island, Massachusetts, and New Hampshire that was quite different from that in the Chesapeake colonies and the Carolinas.

Geography and Society

The preeminent facts of life in New England were the cold climate, short growing season, and the demanding rocky character of the soil.

Winter and summer, temperatures in New England could be 20° to 30° F cooler than in Virginia. The subtropical diseases of the South were unknown in Massachusetts and the other New England colonies. On average, New Englanders lived ten years longer than southerners. Rather more striking, twice as many children survived infancy in Massachusetts than in Virginia.

The result was a large number of extended families, in fact, the world's first society in which men and women could expect to know their grandparents. The New England emphasis on "well-ordered households" was reinforced by the climate with which the Puritans' God presented them.

In its soil, New England was less blessed. Geologically, New England is a huge glacial moraine. It was there that the continental glaciers of the last ice age halted their advance. When they receded, they left behind the boulders and gravel that they had scooped from the earth on their trip from the Arctic.

Before the farmers of New England could plow straight furrows, they had to clear thousands of rocks from every acre, breaking up the big boulders and piling the lot in the endless stone fences of the region that are so picturesque to those of us who did not have to build them. This back-breaking toil went on for decades, for each year's frozen winter heaved more boulders to the surface of the earth.

The intensive labor required to clear and plant the land reinforced the Puritans' ideological commitment to a society of small family farms. The demanding New England countryside could and did

The earliest known view of the busy Charleston, South Carolina, harbor.

produce food for a fairly dense population. But there were no plantations, no big commercial farms. Families grew their own sustenance and, at most, a small surplus for sale in the towns and cities.

The Need for Coin

Few products of New England's soil could be sold in old England. The crops that New Englanders produced in no plenitude were much the same as those that flourished in abundance in the mother country: grain, squash, beans, orchard nuts and fruits (particularly apples), livestock of all sorts, and perishable vegetables.

Consequently, English mercantilists took less interest in New England than in the South and the West Indies. Indeed, English shipbuilders, merchants, and fishermen resented the competition of the New Englanders. Boston was sending ships down the ways before 1640. The shipwright's craft flourished in every town with a protected harbor.

Whaling, a calling that New Englanders would eventually dominate, began as early as 1649. Nantucket Island and New Bedford, Massachusetts, became synonymous with whalers. Fishermen sailed out of Portsmouth, Marblehead, New London, and dozens of towns to harvest more than their fair share of the codfish of the North Atlantic. In every port of the world open to commerce, the nickname "Yankee trader" came to signify shrewdness at business with a hint that the Yankee was a thief. Newport, Rhode Island, was a center of the African slave trade, another pursuit that English shippers would have preferred to reserve for themselves.

The New Englanders had no choice but to compete. It took money—gold and silver coin—to purchase English manufactures, and the country produced no cash crop. Only through fishing and trade could the Yankees solve their balance-of-payments problem.

Yankee Traders

A few New England traders plied three-legged routes to accumulate money. For example, a ship might call in West Africa, purchase captives, and transport them to the West Indies where they were exchanged for molasses made from sugar cane. The molasses was returned to New England, where it was distilled into rum. Resuming the cycle, the rum went to West Africa as one of the goods exchanged for slaves. Not only did shippers in this triangular trade profit from each exchange of cargoes, but the colonies improved their balance of payments by manufacturing cheap molasses into higher-priced rum. It was homegrown mercantilism!

There were also other "triangles." New Englanders carried provisions from the Middle Colonies to the West Indies; sugar and molasses from there to England; and English manufactures back home. Or, reversing direction, they might carry tobacco from Maryland and Virginia to England; manufactures to the West Indies; and molasses back home or slaves to the southern colonies. Only a very few ships were involved in triangular trading at one time. Many more plied a leg or two of these routes when opportunity offered or necessity required. The facts of economic life in New England demanded ingenuity, improvisation, and opportunism.

Even more numerous merchantmen were involved in the coastal trade, transporting a variety of goods from one colonial port to another. Thus the large number of shipwrecks off places like Cape Hatteras and Cape Fear in North Carolina: transatlantic ships did not sail those waters; coastal merchantmen did.

An Independent Spirit

To many English mercantilists, the Yankees were no better than common smugglers. Indeed, the most pious Puritan and Quaker shipmasters saw no sin in dodging British trade laws. Because their charters

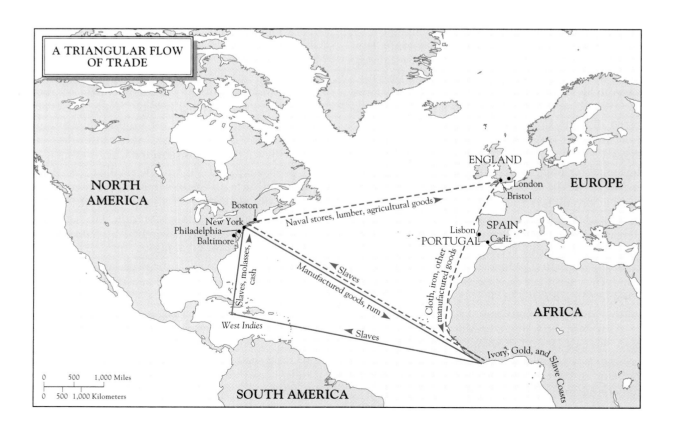

gave them such extensive powers of self-government, the corporate colonies of Massachusetts, Plymouth, Rhode Island, and Connecticut functioned much like independent commonwealths. They acknowledged the king. Technically, the Puritans claimed that they were members of the Church of England. But these proved to be but polite formalities in a century when two English kings were dethroned, one of them decapitated, and it took a month for a ship to cross the Atlantic carrying new laws.

During the years when Oliver Cromwell ruled England as virtual dictator (1649-1658), the New England colonies disregarded almost every directive that he and Parliament issued. In 1652, Massachusetts even minted its own money, the "Pine Tree Shilling," thus assuming a right reserved to sovereign rulers since antiquity.

Nor did Massachusetts retreat when Charles II became king in 1660. The colony continued to strike the shilling, to evade royal instructions, and to protect smugglers and even pirates. Charles was forced to sue to have the Massachusetts charter revoked. In 1684, he won his case.

The Dominion of New England

The next year, a new king, James II, combined all the New England colonies into a single Dominion of New England. (New York and New Jersey were later added.) He abolished all local assemblies within the dominion and gave what amounted to a viceroy's power to his appointed governor, Sir Edmund Andros.

Andros never had a chance. Not only was he detested in New England, but James II's reign was short-lived. In 1688, the king was forced to flee the country in the Glorious Revolution. The news was the signal for popular uprisings in several colonies. In Maryland, John Coode seized power from the Catholic proprietors whom he assumed had fled England with the Catholic James II. In New York, a German named Jacob Leisler gained effective control, claiming that he acted in the name of the new English sovereigns, William and Mary. In New England, the merchant elite, so briefly out of power, simply resumed acting as it always had—independently. Andros prudently put to sea.

However, the Calverts of Maryland had not supported James II, and they and the Penn family in Pennsylvania regained their proprietary rights under William and Mary. In New York, Leisler became overconfident by the ease with which he had taken control. Rashly, he ordered a volley fired at arriving

troops who really did act in the name of William and Mary. He was hanged.

As for New England, William and Mary knew better than to revive the hated dominion, but they had no intention of allowing Massachusetts to return to its semi-independent status. They restored the charters of Connecticut and Rhode Island (where there had been little tumult), but they made Massachusetts, with Plymouth incorporated into it, a royal colony. After 1691, the governor of the Bay Colony was no longer elected but was appointed by the Crown.

This was no easy pill for latter-day Puritans to swallow. They had regarded their mission in America as divinely mandated. They expected to be at odds with the Crown. But for God to allow the Crown to take control of the "citty on a hill" from his chosen people, permanently to all appearances, was a mighty blow to their morale.

The Devil in Massachusetts

It has been suggested that the suffering in New England caused by King Philip's War (see Chapter 5) and the loss of the charter with its guarantee of self-government, help account for the remarkable hysteria that convulsed parts of Massachusetts beginning in January 1692—the Salem witchcraft scare. That is, covenant theology taught that when the saints committed or tolerated sin within their community, God punished the community as well as the guilty individuals. The loss of the charter was harsh punishment indeed. Boston preacher Cotton Mather called the era the "Woeful Decade." Only some very terrible sin could account for God's toleration of such a disaster. In January 1692, some latter-day Puritans believed they had discovered what that sin was.

Two young girls of Salem, a village north of Boston, fell ill with fits of screaming and crawling about while making odd throaty sounds. Their physician found no earthly affliction. He reckoned that the girls had been bewitched by Satan or by Satan's sworn servants, witches.

Few were shocked and fewer laughed at the mention of witchcraft. Most seventeenth-century Europeans and Americans believed that people could strike a bargain with Satan by which they traded their souls for the power of black magic. Witchcraft was mentioned in the Bible along with the admonition "thou shalt not suffer a witch to live." Since the Middle Ages, thousands of people had been executed for worshiping Satan, or for having sexual intercourse with imps called *incubi* and *succubi*. Others had suffered lesser penalties for practicing minor magic—a fine for causing a neighbor's cow to go dry, for example. Just the year before the suspected outbreak of sorcery in Salem, a witch had been hanged in Boston. No doubt the incident weighed on the minds of the unstable young ladies who found themselves the center of attention in Salem.

Hysteria

They were also agitated by the spooky tales of a slave, Tituba, who had come from the West Indies where the cultish practices we know as voodoo were well developed to the home of the Reverend Samuel Parish. In any case, once the word witch was spoken, the girls began to accuse easy targets of enchanting them, the kind of people who had few friends to defend them. Tituba, a black, was of course an outcast and an easy target. Another witch was an impoverished hag who may have been senile and did not half understand the charges against her. There was also

an 88-year-old man notorious as a crank, and an unabashed adulterer.

Soon, better-established people were named as witches. Most of them had been on the wrong side of a political battle. They had opposed the appointment of the Reverend Parish to the Salem pulpit and, no doubt, had had unpleasant things said about them in the Parish household. Parish's supporters were prominent among the persecutors.

However, such petty animosities cannot account for the fact that some of Massachusetts' most distinguished men, including the great preacher Cotton Mather and respected judge Samuel Sewall, participated in the witch-hunt. Nevertheless, after the accused turned from the weak and the eccentric to the prominent and powerful, the authorities brought the hysteria to an end. In the meantime, 139 people had been accused, 114 were charged, and 19 were hanged. One man was pressed to death—a plank was laid on him and stones heaped on it—because he refused to plead either innocent or guilty. (To plead

"Accusation of a Witch" at Salem, a painting by Elias C. Larrabee.

not guilty and then to be convicted meant that the accused forfeited his property.) He was a tough character; his final words were, "Put on more weight."

Aftermath

Although a witch would be executed in Scotland as late as the era of the American Revolution, the Salem hysteria was the last mass witchcraft scare in the western world. It should be added, however, that many people involved in the accusations and persecutions later admitted that they were wrong and publicly asked forgiveness of God and their community, accepting punishment for their sin. They did not admit that they were wrong in believing in witchcraft, but they did take responsibility for falsely accusing innocent people or, in the case of Judge Samuel Sewall, for having accepted inadequate evidence in reaching his decisions.

THE MIDDLE COLONIES

Not every person of the late seventeenth century believed in witchcraft. At the height of the Salem hysteria, when William Penn was asked if there might not also be witches in Pennsylvania, he replied sarcastically that people were quite free to fly about on broomsticks within the boundaries of his colony.

The liberality of the laws of the Middle Colonies, particularly those guaranteeing religious toleration and easy access to land, ensured that New York and the Quaker colonies of Pennsylvania, New Jersey, and Delaware would be contented, placid provinces. Between the time of Leisler's Rebellion in New York in 1689, and a dispute between Quakers and non-Quakers in Pennsylvania in the mid-1700s, the Middle Colonies grew faster than either New England or the South.

Balanced Economies

Except for the Hudson Valley of New York, where a few Dutch patroonships survived into the eighteenth century, great estates were rare in the Middle Colonies. As in New England, the agricultural pattern was a patchwork of small, family farms tilled by the landowners themselves with comparatively few servants and slaves. Unlike that of New England, the climate of the Middle Colonies provided a long growing season, and the soils in the alluvial valleys of the

Hudson, Delaware, Schuylkill, and Susquehanna rivers were deep and rich. The farmers of the Middle Colonies were also blessed in that they could grow the same crops they grew in Europe, using much the same methods. They did not have to develop new economic strategies as in New England and the South.

The Middle Colonies also produced a large surplus of grain and livestock. Pennsylvania earned the nickname "breadbasket of the colonies." Delaware, New Jersey, and New York were scarcely less productive.

Because foodstuffs (with the exception of rice) were not enumerated under the Navigation Acts, the products of the Middle Colonies could be sold wherever the sellers could find a market. A canny merchant class in the cities of Philadelphia and New York soon found one. They shipped grain and meat animals on the hoof to the sugar islands of the West Indies, where a small master class forced huge gangs of black slaves to grow cane and little else. The Middle Colonies found a comfortable niche for themselves within the imperial system. They were neither overdependent on the mother country nor constantly in competition and at odds with British policies.

The merchants of Philadelphia and New York governed those cities as though they were personal property. However, because landowning farmers (and therefore voters) were so numerous in the Middle Colonies, merchants were not able to dominate the elected assemblies as planters dominated them in the South. Neither agricultural nor commercial interests were completely in charge. Instead, they cooperated to counterbalance the power of the proprietor's appointed governor in Pennsylvania and of the royal governors in Delaware, New Jersey, and New York.

Liberal Institutions

New Jersey and Delaware practiced toleration on the same Quaker grounds as Pennsylvania. In New York, the Church of England was established but laws proscribing other forms of worship were rarely enforced. For a time, a Roman Catholic, Thomas Dongan, served as governor of New York; a Jewish synagogue established under Dutch rule in 1654 continued to flourish unimpeded.

Indeed, once the Puritan grip on Massachusetts was broken, religious toleration was the rule in all the colonies. America was a young country in need of people. Whatever the law said, there were few serious attempts to discourage immigration. Few questions were asked about an individual's personal beliefs.

Until about 1700, most colonists either had been born in England or had English-born parents. There were a few third-generation families in Virginia and Maryland, more in New England. And there was some diversity, too: a handful of Jews in Rhode Island, New York, and South Carolina; and a contingent of French Protestants in South Carolina who had fled persecution at home.

Among Europeans, however, the most important non-English group was made up of Germans who congregated in Lancaster and York counties, Pennsylvania, just to the west of Philadelphia. Many of these refugees from persecution and chronic warfare were members of pietistic religious sects with beliefs much like those of the Quakers. William Penn and his heirs actively recruited the Amish and Mennonite sectarians for his Holy Experiment. They were hardworking, productive, utterly untroublesome, and they loyally supported the English brethren who had provided them a refuge.

Non-English minorities suffered little discrimination because of their origins, religion, and language, either. By no means, however, was America the land of opportunity for everyone. Equality and liberty were not extended to the two large groups of colonial people not of the Caucasian race.

CHRONOLOGY

1630	Publication of Thomas Mun's *England's Treasure by Foreign Trade*
1660	Charles II crowned king of England after a decade of rule by Lord Protector, Oliver Cromwell
1660–1663	Parliament enacts the Navigation Acts defining the colonies' economic relationship to the Mother Country
1673	Parliament's "plantation duty" aims at reducing smuggling in the colonies
1676	Bacon's Rebellion in Virginia
1685	James I is king; he attempts to consolidate colonial administration in the Dominion of New England
1688	James I is overthrown; rebellions in Maryland and New York.
1691	Massachusetts proclaimed a royal colony
1692	Witchcraft hysteria in Salem, Massachusetts

FOR FURTHER READING

Again, consult the final paragraph of "For Further Reading" in Chapter 2 for general works dealing with colonial America and, concerning the development of the colonies, the titles listed under "For Further Reading" in Chapter 3. In addition, see Lewis C. Gray, *History of Agriculture in the United States to 1860*, 1933, and, as a corrective in some particulars, Howard S. Russell, *A Long, Deep Furrow: Three Centuries of Farming in New England*, 1976.

On social and cultural developments, see James A. Henretta, *The Evolution of American Society, 1700–1815*, 1973; Thomas J. Wertenbaker, *The Planters of Colonial Virginia*, 1927; Louis B. Wright, *Cultural Life of the American Colonies, 1607–1763*, 1957, and *The First Gentlemen of Virginia*, 1940; and Carl Bridenbaugh, *Myths and Realities: Societies of the Colonial South*, 1963. The standard work on Bacon's Rebellion is Wilcomb E. Washburn, *The Governor and the Rebel*, 1957. A recent study with an economic orientation is Lois Green Carr, *Robert Cole's World: Agriculture and Society in Early Maryland*, 1990.

Witchcraft in Salem and elsewhere in colonial America is the subject of enduring controversy. Once the standard explanation and still provocative is Marion G. Starkey, *The Devil in Massachusetts*, 1969. Books adding new dimensions to the topic include Paul Boyer and Stephen Nissenbaum, *Salem Possessed*, 1974; John Demos, *Entertaining Satan: Witchcraft and the Culture of Early New England*, 1982; Carol Karlsen, *The Devil in the Shape of a Woman*, 1987; and Richard Godbeer, *The Devil's Dominion: Magic and Religion in Early New England*, 1992.

The trustees of the Georgia colony receive a delegation of native Georgians in London, 1734.

5
CHAPTER

OTHER AMERICANS
The Indians, French, and Africans
of Colonial North America

Why will you take by force what you may obtain by love? Why will you destroy us who supply you with food? What can you get by war? We are unarmed, and willing to give you what you ask, if you come in a friendly manner.

— *Chief Powhatan*

It is true that this country has twice the population of New France, but the people there are astonishingly cowardly, completely undisciplined, and without any experience in war. The smallest Indian party has always made them flee. . . . It is not at all like that in Canada. . . . The Canadians are brave, much inured to war, and untiring in travel. Two thousand of them will at all times and in all places thrash the people of New England.

— *Officer, Troupes de la Marine*

Oh, ye nominal Christians!, might not an African ask you, learned you this from your God, . . . Do unto all men as you would men should do unto you? Is it not enough that we are torn from our country and friends to toil for your luxury and lust of gain? Must every tender feeling be likewise sacrificed to your avarice? Are the dearest friends and relations, now rendered more dear by their separation from their kindred, still to be parted from each other, and thus prevented from cheering the gloom of slavery with the small comfort of being together and mingling their sufferings and sorrows?

— *Olaudah Equiano*

When the colonies were mentioned to a British gentleman in the age of Queen Anne, he might think of precious national possessions, daily enriching his nation and adding to her glory. Or he might picture ragged gaggles of his countrymen gone too far abroad for their own good. At a time when London was a sophisticated metropolis, rustic colonials were easy targets of ridicule.

Britons of the poor and middling sort would have looked differently on North America. The fact that they emigrated steadily to the colonies (378,000 English went to the Western Hemisphere during the 1600s) tells us that many ordinary people thought America a land of opportunity that was preferable to the old country.

There were other perspectives from which the colonies were observed. To West Africans, America was a dread mysterious place to which people were taken in chains, never to return. To the French, the British colonies were a threat to their own American empire in the Great Lakes Basin and the Mississippi Valley. The British were rivals in a hot competition for primacy in the wilderness of the North American interior.

And then there was the perspective of those for whom North America was neither new nor a wilderness, but the home of their ancestors and their gods, the Indians.

THE INDIANS OF NORTH AMERICA

The most striking characteristic of the Native American world was diversity. Indeed, American prehistory is a lesson in just how rapidly cultures diversify when population is small and the land vast, when people of differing beliefs and practices are not in constant, intimate contact with one another. Although all Indians probably were descended from culturally similar bands of Asians, and shared a comparatively small gene pool, they divided and divided again into a kaleidoscope of linguistic and cultural groups, and even of distinct physical types.

Cultural Diversity

Native American political systems ran the gamut from would-be totalitarianism (the Natchez Indians) to the absence of the idea of government among some peoples of the North American high desert (especially in what is now Nevada). Socially, there were caste systems so complicated that tribes supported genealogical specialists as the only means to keep track of who was who (in the southeastern United States). Other tribes were egalitarian and democratic.

There were tribes in which the men virtually ignored the existence of every woman but their wives, others in which women spoke a significantly different language from that of the men. Yet other tribes were matrilineal, tracing an individual's descent through the female line, and some relied on councils of women to make important tribal decisions (the Iroquois). The variety of social relationships among the Indians at the time the whites arrived was as broad as it was in Europe.

Manners and morals varied widely. The Cherokee considered it rude to address another person directly. Yahis each gave themselves a name which they never told another person. Tribes of the Great Plains tolerated homosexuals. Others found homosexual practice as abominable as the Puritans did. Sexual activity generally was unregulated in some parts of the continent while some tribes whipped and shaved the heads of unfaithful women. In the Northeast, rape was the only crime punishable by death and the warriors

The Hurons inspired awe and respect but also fear and horror in the European author of this image.

of many tribes of that region were bound to strict sexual continence when they were on the warpath.

Some Indians were warlike and aggressive, renowned for their cruelty toward enemies. Archaeologists recently discovered the site of a village near Crow Creek, South Dakota, where, in the fourteenth century, some 500 men, women, and children were captured and massacred. Every tribe in the Northeast (and Europeans too) feared the Mohawks because they scalped their victims, sometimes alive. Other Indians were gentle folk, principled pacifists who had survived by finding secluded nooks of the continent in which to shelter. Many of the tribes of California, with whom whites became acquainted only later, did not resist violent interlopers, but submitted, bewildered at the turn fate had taken.

Many Indians were genuine monotheists who worshiped a single Manitou, or "Great Spirit." Others were fetishists. They concerned themselves with supernatural powers in stones, trees, bugs, and birds, and consulted magicians to cope with otherworldly powers.

Economy, Ecology, and Language

Some Indians shaped the environment to the extent their technology allowed. For instance, there was intense cultivation and a quasi-urban way of life among the Pueblo Indians of New Mexico and Arizona, while the Indians of southern New England methodically burned the underbrush in their hunting grounds, creating park-like forests in which grasses and herbaceous plants thrived, luring moose, deer, rabbits, and other game.

In California, by way of contrast, whole peoples left scarcely a footprint in the sand, grubbing out a subsistence on little but acorns, a few roots and berries, and the odd small animal they snared. In the Pacific Northwest, food was so abundant that some tribes expressed a disdain for material goods such as we associate with only very rich and wasteful economies. Periodically, families which had accumulated great stores of food and other possessions gave them away at festivals called potlatches, and even destroyed their goods. Just about the only generalization that may confidently be made about the Indians of the United States is that, in the end, they were all to be subordinated by the Europeans who began to arrive when Ponce de León set foot on a Florida beach.

The diversity of Native American cultures may best be illustrated by the Indian languages. There are only obscure (and arguable) relationships between any North American tongue and the contemporary language of any Asian people. Among the Indians themselves, the linguistic differences were greater than they were in Europe. In one corner of North Carolina, several small tribes living within ten miles of one another for at least a century could not communicate except by sign language.

During the colonial period, the Indians of both Americas spoke at least 500 mutually unintelligible tongues. There were 50 language *families* in North America as a whole. However, the process of linguistic fragmentation may have come to a halt on the Eastern seaboard at the time the English first settled it. There were only three significant language groups in the territory staked out for themselves by the people of the 13 English colonies.

Tribal Names

The most common name each American tribe had for itself translates into English as "the people" or "the human beings." Tribes referred to other people, members of different tribes, in terms that were usually unflattering, something like "the beasts" or "the other things."

In some cases, like *Kiowa*, we designate contemporary tribes with the names tribal members gave themselves. In other cases, when white people first learned of a tribe's existence from a neighboring people hostile to that tribe, we adopted that people's negative designation. For example, *Sioux* is Ojibwa (Chippewa) for "Snake." *Mohawk* is Narragansett for "blood sucker." *Apache* is Zuni for "enemy."

Then there are names given tribes by Europeans from their own languages: *Pueblo* from the Spanish for those Southwestern tribes who lived in villages, or *pueblos; Nez Percé* from the French, "pierced nose," after a cosmetic custom of that tribe; *Delaware* from the English, for the homeland of the Lenni Lenape that the English had already renamed after an English investor in the New World.

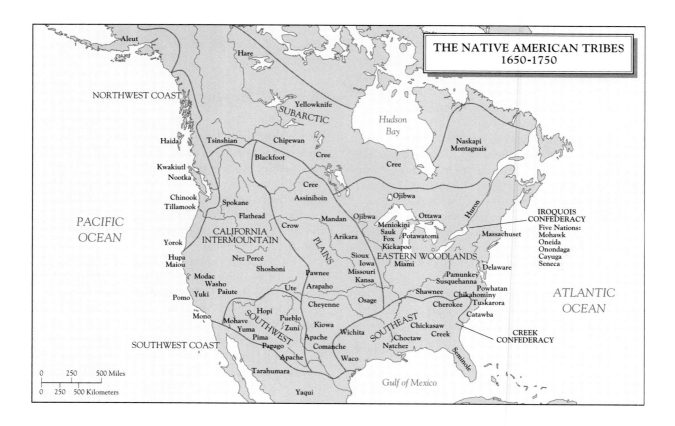

THE NATIVE AMERICAN TRIBES 1650-1750

THE INDIANS OF THE EASTERN WOODLANDS

Algonkians (Algonquins to the French) occupied the coast from New England through the Chesapeake Bay to parts of interior New York and Pennsylvania. Tribes in this group included the Mohegans (or Mohicans), Narragansett, Abnaki, Lenni Lenape (Delawares), Pequots, Ojibwas (Chippewas), and Powhatans. Algonkian speakers were the peoples with whom the English first made contact in both Virginia and Massachusetts and whom, by taking their lands, they made their enemies. The colonists also expropriated a number of Algonkian words (in addition to Algonkian place names) into their and our own language. A few are *hickory, hominy, moccasin, succotash, tomahawk, totem, wigwam,* and *woodchuck.*

The second major linguistic group of the Eastern Woodlands was the Iroquoian. The Iroquois occupied a large wedge-shaped territory, running from the eastern Great Lakes through New York and into Pennsylvania. The Conestogas and Eries were Iroquoian-speaking, as were the powerful Hurons who lived along the St. Lawrence River in New

France, what is now Canada. But the most important Iroquois so far as the English were concerned were five tribes that had joined together in a confederation under the legendary figure Hiawatha a generation earlier than the founding of Plymouth colony.

The Five Nations of the Iroquois Confederacy, founded about 1570 to keep the peace among them, were the Cayugas, Mohawks, Oneidas, Onondagas, and Senecas. Farther south, separated from the main group by Algonkian territory, were the Tuscarora of inland Virginia and North Carolina. During the 1710s they were defeated by colonial forces from South Carolina and trekked north to become the sixth nation of the Iroquois Confederacy.

The earliest southern colonists had less contact with the third major linguistic group of the Eastern Woodlands, the Muskohegan. These tribes included the Apalachee, Chickasaw, Choctaw, Creek, Natchez, and Seminole. These socially sophisticated tribes lived in what are now the southeastern states of Georgia, Alabama, Mississippi, and Tennessee. Few English settlers penetrated this country until late in the seventeenth century, when South Carolinians developed a slave, fur, and deerskin trade there. In Florida, however, Spanish incur-

Languages: Fragmentation and Loss

Fragmentation was the natural tendency of language before the modern era. Until language is written down and rules of expression are devised, and when there is no pressing need to communicate day to day with more than a few associates, language changes very rapidly. Thus, in the vast, thinly populated world of the North American Indians, with bands constantly breaking up into smaller groups, distinct tongues developed and multiplied at an astonishing rate.

The phenomenon has been observed firsthand in a part of the world that, only recently, has been heavily touched by Western civilization: New Guinea. Although not so vast as North America, New Guinea is divided by nearly impenetrable mountains and rivers into innumerable, isolated tribal areas. Some 1500 languages are still spoken there, one-sixth the world's total. Diversity is an understatement. One language, Rotokas, has the fewest basic units of sound of any language in the world, 13. Another, Yele, has more than any other language, 96. There is a simple language with a vocabulary of but a few hundred words. Another has 68 ways to make a singular noun plural.

Today, the languages of New Guinea are disappearing at a rate that alarms linguists. This too is a natural process in worlds that grow smaller culturally, like the Roman, Arabic, or Chinese empires in ancient times, contemporary New Guinea, the Americas after Columbus, or, indeed, worldwide in our own technologically shrunken earth. With military or cultural dominance, a common means of communication can and does develop.

Thus, 500 North American Indian languages when Europeans arrived have been reduced to 150 today. Only a few of those are robust. Some have been saved only because of the haste with which historically conscious Indians, linguists, and missionaries have recorded them. As of 1994, just thirteen people spoke Chimaheuvi and six people could converse in Wintu. Only one person spoke the language of California's Coast Miwok.

Hunters Who Farmed

The economy of the three Eastern Woodlands groups was similar. Agriculture was built around the "three sisters": maize (corn), beans, and squash. They were planted together in small hills cobbled together by means of a spade roughed out of stone or wood (North American Indians had no metallurgy).

In addition to being the staple grain, maize provided the stalks on which beans could climb. Pumpkins and other squash covered the roots of both plants with their foliage, preserving moisture and providing food. Here and there, peas, cabbages, and melons were cultivated, as well as, by most tribes, tobacco.

Farmland was cleared by slash-and-burn, a method that suited the Eastern Woodlands Indians, who were primarily hunters and gatherers. Well-adapted to an environment in which land was abundant and labor scarce, slash-and-burn was eagerly adopted by the waves of white pioneers in the densely forested eastern third of the country.

A ring of bark was stripped from around the trunks of the mostly deciduous trees, thus killing them. When the last foliage fell, admitting sunlight to the forest floor, the women (who were the chief farmers in the East) burned the underbrush. In these ghost forests, they planted their crops. There were no plows or beasts of burden among the eastern tribes. Dogs and turkeys were the only domesticated animals.

So casual a method of cultivation did not in itself provide sufficient food. Every tribe looked more to forest than to field for its survival, depending primarily on hunting, fishing, trapping, and gathering edible plants. Thus each tribe competed with its neighbors for hunting grounds.

The Eastern Indians valued their weapons, tools, and household goods. They thought of them as exclusive personal property, much as Europeans did. But, hunting and gathering do not require constant occupation or exclusive control of a specific tract of land. Consequently, the European concept of real estate—private, exclusive ownership of land—was alien to the Eastern tribes. The land was God's. People used it and competed to use it, often violently. But no one "owned" it. When a New Englander commented that the Indians "do but run over the grass, as do also the foxes and wild beasts," an Indian might well have shrugged, "Yes. So what?"

At best, foraging for food makes for a precarious livelihood. The Eastern Indians' communities were inclined to be small and scattered so that no individual

sions and the spread of European diseases were already decimating small tribes that would, in time, virtually disappear: the Timucuans, Calusa, Aeis, and Jaega.

Clearing the land by the "slash and burn" method was copied from the Indians by white pioneers in the Eastern Woodlands.

tribe put too much of a strain on the hunting grounds in the vicinity. The Powhatans, whom the first Virginians encountered, gathered in villages of 500 people, a sizable number, during the summer. But in winter they split up into smaller groups. European-style agriculture made larger concentrations of population possible. But the Indians benefited from the newcomers' innovations for only a very short time.

CONFRONTATION

To the Eastern Woodlands Indians, the earliest English colonies were curious appendages on the edge of the universe. The continent was the Indians' world; the Atlantic was an abyss. The pale-faced people who came across it were seen as members of new tribes—soon more numerous than any other tribe, to be sure, and peculiar in more ways than in the color of their skins. Nevertheless, for many decades, the whites were just another people with

whom to fight, to trade, and to compete for the means of living. England and Europe? They were just words, the names of the places from which the whites received the goods that the Indians so desired.

Two Different Worlds

The experience of the Native Americans who first confronted English settlers was rather different than that of Indians who knew the Spanish. There were not so many of them, first of all. Possibly as few as 150,000 Indians lived in those parts of the continent the English penetrated during their first century in America. More Aztecs lived in Tenochtitlán alone when Cortés first laid eyes on the city.

And yet, and despite the loose political organization of most of the Indians of the Eastern Woodlands, the English had a much harder time of dominating the natives than the Spanish did in Mexico and Peru. In large part, this was due to the fact that the English took little interest in conquering, living among, governing, and "Europeanizing" the Native Americans, as the Spaniards did in their part of the New World.

Some Indians were enslaved to work on plantations. In 1708, Indians captured or purchased from tribes in southern Carolina numbered 1,400, 14 percent of the colony's population. At least one Indian was a slave in New Bedford, Massachusetts, at the time of the Revolution, for he ran away to the British, leaving his master a taunting note. But Indians escaped too easily in a country that was, after all, their home. Imported white servants and black slaves (for whom masters paid twice the price of an Indian) were more dependable laborers.

The character of the English emigration also served to keep Indians and Europeans in different worlds. Unlike New Spain, which was conquered by soldiers, New England was settled by families with men and women coming in roughly equal numbers. Even in the South by the time of Queen Anne, the English population was approaching sexual parity. Men found little need to look among the natives for wives. One scholar has found only three Indian-white marriages recorded in Virginia during the colony's first century, including John Rolfe and Pocahontas. With marriage within the race easy, it was feasible in English America to define miscegenation as disreputable. There was plenty of it outside marriage, of course, but the colonials consigned "half-breeds" to the Indians, thus maintaining the first American color line.

The Iroquois, allied to the English, were considered savages by the French. In fact, the Iroquois were a politically sophisticated people who survived while other tribes of the Eastern Woodlands disappeared.

In fact, most whites who chose to consort with Indians also chose to live with their spouse's people, where adherence to tribe and clan determined status, not skin color. So did some whites (usually women and children) who were kidnapped by Indians specifically for the purpose of replacing tribal members who had died or been killed. A New Yorker commented incredulously in 1699 that he could not "persuade the People that had been taken Prisoners by the French Indians, to leave the Indian Manner of living."

Land Hunger

The goal of English colonization was to replicate, as closely as possible, the way of life the settlers knew back home. Indians had no place in such little Englands. The object was to get land from them, push-

ing them peacefully or forcefully outside the pale of white settlement.

Like the Spanish, conscientious colonials devised moral and legal justifications for taking Indian land. The Pilgrims justified their occupation of Plymouth on the grounds that no one was there when they arrived. John Cotton of Massachusetts elaborated on this rationale, adding "just war" as a means of securing title to land.

Roger Williams, the Dutch, and the Pennsylvania Quakers bought the land they wanted. Their view of these transactions, however, differed sharply from that of the Indians. To Europeans, purchase meant exclusive use of the land as, indeed, intensive agriculture required. The Indian sellers often believed they were agreeing to share their slice of the Manitou's earth with the newcomers. Thus could Staten Island be "sold" to the Dutch three times over. To the Dutch, their multiple purchase proved the Indians were dishonest business people. From the Indian point of view, three different tribes were accepting the Hollanders.

Moreover, "chiefs" with whom the Europeans dealt did not possess the sovereign power to dispose of land that the newcomers assumed they had. And many Indians must have been simply bewildered by European dealings. Jasper Danckhaerts wrote of a transaction in New York in 1679: "The Indians hate the precipitancy of comprehension and judgmen [of the whites], the excited chatterings, . . . the haste and rashness to do something, whereby a mess is often made of one's good intentions."

Other colonials lacked both patience and good intentions. They shot, took, and shrugged. Possession by right of conquest was not a universally approved principle in the seventeenth century, but it had a long pedigree and some compelling recommendations.

Bringers of Baubles

The Indians' first reaction to the English was curiosity. Few in the Eastern Woodlands were as flabbergasted by the sight of whites as the Arawaks had been. The fleeting visits of European explorers and fishermen, and gossip among tribes, had informed most Eastern peoples of the existence of the white-skinned strangers before they confronted them face to face.

The earliest English settlements posed no threat and the colonists did offer goods that were highly desirable to a Stone Age people. There were the famous baubles: glass beads, ribbons, trinkets, and mirrors. New to Indians, they were accorded the high price of any rarity. It was with such goods that Peter Minuit purchased Manhattan Island in 1626. A novelty brimming with tragedy, but coveted nonetheless, was liquor, usually rum. Some Eastern tribes made a weak corn beer but nothing so potent as distilled alcohol. From the first, the Indians took with tragic zest to "firewater." It devastated many tribes both physically and morally.

Much more important to a people who smelted no metals were the European commodities that improved their standard of living: brass and iron vessels; tools (spades, hatchets); woven blankets (which were much warmer than hides) and other textiles; and firearms, which allowed the Indians to hunt more efficiently and get a leg up on old tribal enemies.

In return for such goods, the Indians provided foodstuffs to the earliest settlers. When the English became agriculturally self-sufficient, they supplied furs and hides for the European market.

The Fur and Hide Trade

In the decline and destruction of the Eastern Woodlands tribes, furs and hides played a far greater role than liquor, or even the military superiority of the English. The English (and Dutch and French) appetite for animal skins resulted in the destruction of the ecology of which the Eastern Indians had been a part for centuries.

Before the whites arrived, the Woodlands tribes killed only those moose, deer, beaver, and other animals that they needed for food, clothing, and ceremonial. Why do otherwise? Because the Indians were so few, their needs probably had little impact on the wildlife population. Their harvests of game may have had a healthy effect on wildlife by preventing overpopulation and disease.

But Europeans could not get enough American skins and pelts. The upper classes back home coveted the lush furs of the beaver, otter, and weasel. Both furs and deerskin were made into felt, which was pressed into hats and dozens of other useful goods. In order to increase production, and buy more European goods, the tribes rapidly exterminated the valuable creatures in their ancestral hunting grounds.

It does not take very long to destroy a species when hunting is relentless and systematic. In only a couple of generations, nineteenth-century Americans would annihilate a population of passenger pigeons that previously darkened the skies. The nearly total destruction of the North American bison after the construction of the transcontinental railroad took only ten years! Thus it happened in the Eastern Woodlands, as Indians and the odd white hunter and trapper set out after deer and beaver.

Unlike the case of the passenger pigeon, very much like the case of the bison, the destruction of the animals of the eastern forests meant the destruction of a way of life.

A New Kind of Warfare

The demands of the fur traders also introduced a new kind of warfare to the world of the Indians. Not that war was new to them. On the contrary, enmity toward other tribes was an integral part of Iroquois and Algonkian culture. But traditional Indian warfare was largely a ritualistic demonstration of individual bravery. A young man gained as much glory

English Legalism

English colonists—in New England at least—were as legalistic as the Spanish in justifying the taking of land from the Indians. However, the Puritans based the legality of their seizures not on a royal proclamation like Spain's *requerimiento*, but on the Bible. In 1630, John Cotton spelled out the three ways in which "God makes room for a people." First, in a just, unprovoked war, which God would bless (Psalm 44:2 "Thou didst drive out the heathen before them"), the victors had the right to the land they conquered. Second, newcomers had the right to purchase land or accept it as a gift "as Abraham did obtaine the field of Machpelah" or as the Pharaoh gave the land of Goshen "unto the sons of Jacob." Third—and here was legalistic loophole-making at its best, "when hee makes a Countrey though not altogether void of inhabitants, yet voyd in that place where they [the newcomers] reside . . . there is liberty for the sonne of Adam or Noah to come and inhabite, though they neither buy it, nor aske their leaves." In other words, given the fact that most of North America was uncultivated forest, it was fair game.

in "counting coup," giving an enemy a sound rap, as in taking his life. Women and children were not typically killed in these military actions, although they were often kidnapped.

Once part of an intercontinental economy, however, the Indians embraced a different concept of warfare. No longer was the main object glory, retribution, or thievery, but the exploitation of other tribes' hunting grounds and, if necessary, the total elimination of the competition.

The colonists tacitly encouraged this small-scale genocide by providing the weapons that made it possible. They also helped to spread the practice of scalping, which had been peculiar to the Mohawks, as a means of measuring a tribe's efficiency. In 1721, Pennsylvania paid $140 for an Algonkian warrior's scalp and $50 for a squaw's. And to make the purpose of the bounty unmistakable, a live prisoner was worth a paltry $30.

The gory practice of scalping eventually spread over much of the continent. Because tribes involved in the fur trade penetrated the West long before the whites dared to do so, Indians in the interior were introduced to European trade goods, European diseases, and the report of English and French muskets long before they saw their first paleface.

King Philip's War

The most destructive wars, however, were between the Indians and the ever-expanding English population. The immediate causes of the many conflicts varied, but the results for the Native Americans were as predictable as the setting of the sun: military defeat, heavy casualties, loss of land, and cultural demoralization.

In New England, the Indians' last realistic opportunity to stem the advance of the colonials was King Philip's War. It began in 1675 when Plymouth colony hanged three Wampanoags for murdering a Christian member of their tribe, Sassamon. The Wampanoag chief, Metacomet (called "King Philip" by the New Englanders) was already smoldering with fury at the undercutting of his tribe's culture and because of personal grievances. Metacomet had been fined for plotting against Plymouth colony. He regarded the executions as a violation of Wampanoag sovereignty.

Metacomet persuaded two other powerful chiefs, Pomham and Canonchet of the Nipmuck and Narragansett, to join him in an attack on Plymouth and Massachusetts towns. Through most of 1675, the Indians were successful on every front. Fifty-two of 90 New England towns were attacked; 12 were wiped off the map. A tenth of the New Englanders of military age were killed or captured.

The next year, the tide turned. King Philip's armies ran short of provisions and were troubled by internal disagreements. Most of the "praying Indians" of New England (Christian Indians, about a fourth of the native population) allied themselves with the whites. Several tribes of "wild Indians," including the Pequots and Mohicans, either joined with the New Englanders or declared neutrality. In an attack on the Narragansetts, 2,000 of 3,000 Indians were killed. King Philip's head was mounted on a stake in Plymouth as a reminder of the conflict, Canonchet's in Hartford, Connecticut.

Contempt and Respect

The colonials both respected the Indians and held them in contempt. Simply because the native peoples were different, they appalled settlers who had less than an anthropologist's appreciation of cultural diversity. Indian practices ranging from their treatment of captives to personal hygiene were lumped under the rubric "savage." Often, settlers would emphasize their distaste for the Indians by comparing them to the Irish, who were despised in the old country for their perceived lack of civilization.

By way of contrast, colonials envied some aspects of Indian culture. Even Benjamin Franklin, the Pennsylvanian who became in his lifetime a patron saint of hard work, squirreling away money, and bourgeois virtues in general, betrayed a certain wistfulness when he wrote of the Indians: "Having few artificial wants, they have abundance of leisure for improvement by conversation. Our laborious manner of life, compared with theirs, they esteem slavish and base."

Indians regarded the whites with a mixture of awe and disdain. Few Native Americans, if any at all, turned their backs on the trade goods the colonials offered. However, as Franklin observed, the nonmaterial benefits of European civilization were often lost on them. In 1744, according to Franklin, Virginia invited the Iroquois to send six boys to be educated at the College of William and Mary. The Indians replied that they had had bad luck with lads that had been educated at New England colleges. "When they came back to us, they were bad runners, ignorant of every means of living in the woods, unable to bear either cold or hunger, knew neither how to build a cabin, take a deer, or kill an enemy . . . ; they were totally good for nothing."

However, the whites meant well and Franklin's Iroquois appreciated it: "If the gentlemen of Virginia will send us a dozen of their sons, we will take great care of their education, instruct them in all we know, and make men of them."

THE FRENCH IN NORTH AMERICA

Anglo-Indian relations were complicated by the presence of another European people in North America. In 1608, just a year after Jamestown was settled, Samuel de Champlain planted the white banner of France's Bourbon kings on the banks of the St. Lawrence River. He built one fort at Quebec and another at Port Royal in Nova Scotia. (Montreal was not founded until 1642, on the site of an Indian stockade.)

Grand Empire, Few People

Driven by the same impulses as the English Crown, determined to keep pace with their rivals in North America, the Bourbons were disappointed by the reluctance of their subjects to emigrate across the Atlantic. For farmers, which most Frenchmen and women were, the problem was the climate and soil of New France. The soil of Nova Scotia and the St. Lawrence basin was even less inviting than New England's and the winters were worse. Censuses of the immigrant population of Canada showed a high proportion of people who had been urban tradesmen or laborers in the old country, not peasants. About two-thirds of those who came to Canada returned to France, contributing to the anti-Canadian prejudice back home.

Bourbon religious intolerance also served to defeat the object of populating New France. Louis XIV (reigned 1643–1715) forced the Huguenots, Protestants much like the English Puritans, to leave France. But they were forbidden to emigrate to New France where, like the Puritans they resembled, they might well have chosen to go.

The French crown stridently sought to encourage emigration by Catholics. Indentured servants had to serve only three years, opposed to as many as seven years in the English colonies, and they received land when their term of service was up. The French kings forced emigration by people they deemed expendable at home. Entire villages of poor and rugged Bretons were uprooted and shipped to Quebec. Soldiers stationed in North American forts were ordered to remain when their term of service was complete. Prostitutes from the streets of Paris and French seaports (the *filles du roi* , the king's daughters) were rounded up and dispatched to be their wives—as were orphan girls and the respectable daughters of peasants who got into tax trouble.

But New France just would not grow. By 1713, after a century of settlement, the French population in North America was 25,000, about the same number of people as lived in the single English colony of Pennsylvania, which was less than 40 years old. As the great nineteenth-century historian Francis Parkman wrote, "France built its best colony on a principle of exclusion and failed; England reversed the principle, and succeeded."

French Expansion

Still, the boldness of the French Canadians almost made up for the poverty of their numbers. French traders, trappers, and priests fanned out in the north woods surrounding the Great Lakes while the English huddled within a few miles of ocean breakers. These coureurs de bois (not quite translatable as "runners of the woods") adapted more than halfway to the way of life by which the Indians flourished in the forests.

In traveling through the Indians' forests, consorting with and marrying native women, and adopting Indian dress (with a few of their own affectations), the coureurs de bois renounced their European heritage in a way that was incomprehensible to the English. When a governor of Virginia reached the crest of the Appalachians, he celebrated by setting a table with pressed linen, fine china, and silver, and by pouring three kinds of wine into crystal glasses. When a Frenchman broke new ground much deeper in the interior, he was more likely to roast a slab of meat and eat it with his hands while hunkering in the dust.

Spurred on by the tales of the coureurs de bois, intrepid French explorers charted what is now the central third of the United States. In 1673, Louis Joliet, an explorer, and Jacques Marquette, a Jesuit priest, navigated the Mississippi to the mouth of the Arkansas River. They turned back when Indians told them of other whites to the south, which Marquette and Joliet correctly reckoned to be Spaniards on the Gulf of Mexico.

In 1682, Robert Cavelier, the Sieur de La Salle, did reach the mouth of the Mississippi. (The "Father of Waters" had never been discovered from the Gulf of Mexico because, at the end of its journey, the great river divides into hundreds of muddy channels lazing their way through forbidding swamps.) In 1699, Pierre le Moyne, the Sieur d'Iberville, began the series of settlements on the gulf that became New Orleans, Mobile, and the hub of the second French province in North America, Louisiana.

It was a flimsy empire by English standards, a string of lonely log forts and trading posts in the wilderness: Kaskaskia and Cahokia in the Illinois country; St. Louis, where the Missouri flows into the Mississippi; dots on a map connected by lakes, rivers, creeks, and portages (a word that Americans learned from the Canadians, meaning a place canoes had to be carried from one waterway to another).

But the French had one big edge on their English rivals. Most of the Algonkian-speaking people, plus the Hurons, an Iroquois-speaking tribe independent of the Confederation—a large majority of the Indians of the northeastern forests—were allies of the French and the sworn enemies of the English.

Contrasting Ways of Life

The French were able to maintain better relations with these tribes for several reasons, none more important than the paucity of their numbers that Louis XIV so regretted. In remaining so few, the French did not threaten the natives with inundation as the growing English settlements did.

Second in importance, while the English way of life clashed head-on with Indian use of the land, French economic interests in North America seemed only to benefit the tribes. Both English and French wanted to trade European goods for furs and hides. But whereas New France was little more than trading posts and trappers, the English colonies were primarily agricultural settlements. The French glided quietly through the forests, like the Indians and the deer themselves. The English chopped the forests down. Each acre of land put under cultivation meant one acre less in the hunting and gathering economy.

Moreover, intensive agriculture required exclusive use of land, and the very concept of owning the earth was foreign to the Indians. "Sell the land?" said the nineteenth-century chief Tecumseh, echoing many before him. "Why not sell the air, the clouds, the great sea?" The French could accommodate themselves to this philosophy; the English could not.

The Role of Religion

The difference in religion between the Roman Catholic French and the Protestant English, particularly the Puritans of New England, also affected their respective relations with the tribes. Like every Christian people in the Americas, both English and French partly justified their presence in terms of winning the Indians to true faith. The intention to do so was mentioned more or less sincerely in every colonial charter. A few pious Englishmen, such as Roger Williams and John Eliot, the "Apostle of the Indians," who devoted his life to preaching among the tribes of the upper Connecticut Valley, took the mission seriously. Dartmouth College in Hanover, New Hampshire, originated as a school for Indians. When the College of William and Mary was established in Virginia in 1693, provision was made for Indian education.

It was not difficult, however, for the English colonists to lose interest in saving the souls of savages. The Anglican and Puritan religions were both highly nationalistic and ethnocentric. That is, the colonists' religious beliefs were intimately wrapped up with their own English customs, prejudices, language, moral codes, manners, and even the kind of clothes they wore.

The Puritans, moreover, looked upon salvation, and therefore church membership, as a gift given to very few of their own culture. Foreigners were scorned not only because, in the case of the Spanish and French, they were Roman Catholic, but because their customs were different. Indians, with ways of doing things far more bizarre than those of other Europeans, were infinitely further beyond the pale.

The French had their fair share of cultural prejudices. However, their Roman Catholic church held that everyone should belong to it. (The word catholic means "universal.") The church was built on accommodating religious beliefs to a welter of cultures as far distant and as exotic as those in Japan and China. When French priests preached to Indians, therefore, they emphasized the similarities between Indian tradition and Catholic practice. By way of contrast, English Protestant preachers seemed always to be talking about practices the Indians had to give up.

The priests of New France had another advantage over the Protestants in the competition for Native American loyalties. The ornate Roman Catholic ritual—the mystery of the Mass and other ceremonies, the vividly decorated statues—appealed to the Indians' aesthetic sense. The Puritans remained a people of the word. Bible study and long, learned sermons were the foundations of Protestant worship services. Both were foreign to Indian culture.

The Five Nations

Despite these handicaps, the English won Indian allies, and very valuable ones at that. Ancient hatreds among the native peoples, dating back to long before the arrival of Europeans, put the Iroquois Confederation, the Five Nations, squarely on the side of the English.

It is not clear how long the Cayugas, Mohawks, Oneidas, Onondagas, and Senecas had been warring with the Algonkians and their fellow Iroquois, the Hurons. In 1609, however, when Samuel de Champlain, in company with a group of Hurons, opened fire on a party of Mohawks, the balanced match-up tipped decisively in favor of the allies of the French. Over the next several decades, the Algonkians and the Hurons exploited their French friends and gunpowder to wear down the Five Nations. The hardships and fears of this period guaranteed that when the Iroquois themselves made contacts with Europeans—first the Dutch in Fort Orange and then the English, who replaced them in Albany—they had a generation's worth of scores to settle.

Settle them they did. With their own firearms and white allies, the Iroquois took the offensive against the Algonkians, Hurons, and French with a frightening vengeance. Their cruelties shocked a people who, having perpetrated a few themselves, might have been inured to them. The Iroquois slowly burned and even ate captives who were still alive, chewing off fingers and toes one by one. They dined on husbands before the eyes of their wives and

While Iroquois dwelled in longhouses, most Algonkian Indians constructed individual family lodges of saplings and hides. (The "teepee" was found only farther west.)

mothers in front of their children. The coureurs de bois so feared the Five Nations that they added as many as a thousand miles to their trek to the trapping grounds in the Illinois country rather than take the chance of running into a party of Cayugas, Oneidas, or Senecas.

AMERICANS FROM AFRICA

To Europeans who came to the colonies to farm, the Indians were as much an impediment to progress as the massive oaks and maples of the forests were. The land had to be cleared of both trees and people before agriculture could thrive. Colonists came to view the people of the third race of North America, by way of contrast, as valuable and eventually essential to economic development. These were people of the Negro race, mostly from around the Gulf of Guinea in West Africa, who were imported to America against their will in order to solve the commercial farmer's problem of getting things done in a country where land was limitless, but backs to bend over it were few.

Slavery in the Western Hemisphere

There may have been crewmen of African origin with Columbus. Estevan the Moor, who explored around the Gulf of Mexico, and who accompanied Coronado, may have been of Negro descent. (The Spanish did not always distinguish between Berbers and Arabs of the Mediterranean, and black Africans from below the Sahara.)

In any case, blacks had resided in the Americas for a century before an Englishman or woman did. By the mid-1500s, they were the backbone of the labor force in the West Indies, on the Spanish Main, and in Portuguese Brazil. Some of these people, particularly those of mixed race, were free subjects of the Spanish kings. A few exceptional individuals rose from slavery to prosper as craftsmen, sailors, landowners, and even as priests of the church. The vast majority, however, were slaves—the personal property of other people in accordance with laws that had their origins in Roman times.

The English also needed cheap, dependable labor, particularly in the tobacco colonies. But they did not turn immediately to slavery to solve their problem. Unlike the Spanish and Portuguese, the English lacked a tradition of holding people in bondage for life. English society had developed as a frontier

holding of the Roman Empire, not one of Rome's oldest provinces, and thus was comparatively uninfluenced by the Roman imperial heritage in which slavery was accepted as a fact of life. Even the medieval institution of serfdom, which bound families to a piece of land—if the land were sold, the right to the serf's services went with it—had died out in England centuries before North America was colonized.

Nor did the English, like the Spanish and Portuguese, have a history of trade and war with the darker-skinned peoples of Africa, which resulted in large numbers of enslaved (and free) black captives in Spain and Portugal. There was not, in England, a frame of mind that made it possible for a Las Casas to suggest the use of slaves to bring in the crops in the New World. In fact, as late as 1620, when a Gambian merchant offered slaves to an English shipmaster as payment for his trade goods, the captain replied indignantly that "we were a people who did not deal in any such commodities, neither did wee buy or sell one another, or any that had our owne shapes." The African was amazed and said that the other white men who came to his country wanted nothing but slaves. The English captain answered that "they were another kinde of people different from us."

Had this goodly Englishman's principles prevailed, North America would have been spared its greatest historical tragedy, the enslavement of Africans and their descendants on the basis of their race. However, just a year before the curious incident on the Gambia River—and a year before the *Mayflower* anchored at Plymouth, Massachusetts—the history of black Americans had begun as part of an institution with which the English were familiar: indentured servitude.

New Uses for an Old Institution

During the first century of colonization, the English settlers solved their labor problem by adapting to America an institution by which, back home, skills involving long training and practice were passed from generation to generation, and by which communities provided for the raising of orphans and illegitimate children.

In England, boys were trained to be blacksmiths, coopers (barrelmakers), bakers, wheelwrights, clerks, printers, or whatever by binding them to a master of the craft. For a period of seven years—often from age 14 to age 21—the master was entitled to the apprentice's complete obedience and to the use of the

HOW THEY LIVED

Enslavement

There must have been many girls named Akueke and Matefi among the Africans who were brought to the tobacco colonies as slaves. Akueke and Matefi were common Ibo names, and the Ibo people of what is now Nigeria were favorite targets of the slave traders. The Hausas and Yorubas raided their villages up the Niger River. So did the Ashantis, who built an empire on making slaves of other tribes, and white men from Europe and the American colonies.

Akueke and Matefi were likely captured at night. Slave traders wrote of calling peacefully on the mud-walled compounds by day, trading openly, and then swooping down on the same village under cover of darkness. Darkness and the brutal clamor of the raid heightened the nightmare of enslavement, and therefore for the defenselessness of captives, something that twentieth century secret police forces have understood explicitly. Mostly the traders took men, but teenage girls—healthy and young enough to have a long life of childbearing ahead of them—were also desirable merchandise. Older men and women, however, could not withstand the rigors of the "middle passage" across the Atlantic and were either left behind or clubbed to death by rough men in an ugly business.

The captives were marched quickly toward the sea in "coffles," tied or chained together to prevent daring or desperate individuals from making a break for the bush or mangrove swamps of coastal West Africa. If the raiders feared an attack in retaliation, there was no delay on behalf of people ill, injured, or exhausted. They were cut out of the coffles and, as likely as not, killed on the spot.

At one of the many mouths of the Niger, the Volta, the Sassandra, or any of the dozens of southward-flowing rivers of the region, the girls were put into a stockade called a "factory." There they might stay for weeks, fed on yams, millet, and possibly some meat and fish if their captors worried about the health of their slaves. If there had not been whites in the party that captured her, they soon made their appearance. At the African end, the trade took place at or near the mouths of rivers where Portuguese, Spanish, Dutch, French, English, or American ships could anchor close to shore.

Akueke and Matefi would only half understand the transactions that took place after the buyers felt their muscles and looked at their teeth, as if they were horses. They were sold for (in 1700) about £5 in iron bars, cloth, rum, guns, and other tools such as kettles and axes. To the captives, the experience was terrifying. They had been wrenched out of familiar surroundings and a static, reassuring life in which their fate was prescribed by laws and traditions, into a world of dizzying uncertainty. They probably knew of people who had been kidnapped like them, but had little idea what happened to them. They simply disappeared.

Some historians have compared the experience of enslavement to the treatment of Jews in Nazi Germany: a midnight call by the Gestapo, weeks of being shunted about like livestock, every moment living in fear of death and at the constant cruel mercies of all-

boy's labor in return for housing, board, clothing, and teaching the lad the mysteries of the master's trade. Ideally, master, apprentice, and society benefited.

Similarly, communities provided for orphans, girls as well as boys, by binding them to householders as servants. In return for the labor of the child (no craft was involved in this kind of arrangement) the family that took in an orphan assumed the community's financial responsibility to care for the helpless waif.

Apprentices and servants were not free. The law gave their masters the same broad authority over them that parents legally held over their children. This included the right to administer pretty harsh corporal punishment for wrongdoing. At the same time, apprentices and servants were not slaves. Their persons were not the property of their masters. They retained certain individual rights their masters were legally bound to respect, and the term of their servitude was spelled out in a legal document. The day came when the apprentice and the maidservant walked off as free as anyone of their class. In theory, once again, everyone benefited: the householder got a servant; the orphan was raised to adulthood; and the community was spared the cost of caring for a child.

powerful captors, all leading to a bewildered sense of unreality and helplessness. In one sense, the Africans' lot was better than that of the Jews. Their masters wanted to keep them alive; the Jews in Germany were scheduled for deliberate extermination.

The ship on which new slaves were shipped across the Atlantic was possibly, by the eighteenth century, specially constructed for the purpose. "Shipped" is the appropriate word. Akueke and Matefi and their unlucky companions were packed side by side on their backs on decks like shelves, one deck only two feet above the other. They were chained, wrist to wrist and ankle to ankle. Instead of providing reasonable conditions under which the whole cargo might survive, most slave traders packed their holds tightly with the maximum number of people that would fit, absorbing the losses of the high mortality that resulted. If a ship made the crossing with only 5 percent or 10 percent breakage, that is, one of ten or one in twenty dead, it was considered a grand success. But the traders could absorb as much as a one in three loss and still make a profit. The girls who cost £5 in West Africa sold for £25 or £30 in Virginia.

A contagious disease or simple bad luck with weather—calm or storm—could send scurvy or dysentery sweeping through the holds. Every morning, the crew's first task was to check through the slaves in order to cut out the dead and dump their bodies overboard. If the weather was especially bad or the captain or crew merely nervous about mutiny, the Africans would rarely be allowed on deck (and then only in small groups). The stench and filth in the hold—from sweat, vomit, urine, and feces—can hardly be imagined. Numerous people simply cracked, killing themselves or others in fits of insanity.

Young girls were liable to the sexual abuse of the sailors. It depended largely on the character of the captain. He might be so hardened by the trade that he allowed his men (and perhaps himself) full rein. Many did. However—rather more difficult to understand—many English and New Englander slave traders were pious, morally strict Calvinists or Quakers who would punish such sins with a lashing. The unholy and horrible business of shipping humans as if they were cattle was not recognized as morally wrong. They were "captives" and enslavement was justified on that basis. The author of that greatest of hymns, *Amazing Grace*, was a slave trader who repudiated his part in the commerce only after he resigned from it.

Arrival in Virginia or South Carolina (or New York or Massachusetts) was practically a deliverance for the Africans. There were horrors yet to be undergone—the sale at market, the less dramatic but emotionally devastating experience of settling into a new, altogether foreign way of life, and the hard forced labor for which they had been seized. But anything was for the better after the nightmarish "middle passage" across the ocean. This—the fact that any life was to be preferred to the horrors of enslavement and shipment—may explain why rebellion was so rare among "first generation" American slaves. In a tragic sense, they were glad to have arrived.

Indentured Servants

Colonial planters and farmers who needed laborers adapted this familiar institution in the form of indentured servitude. For an outlay of from £6 to £30, which paid the cost of transatlantic passage, and the fee of a contractor who signed up servants in England, a colonist secured the services of a bound worker for between four and seven years. (The price of a servant, and the length of time served, were set by the law of supply and demand. Cost and term depended upon just how badly American masters needed field hands, and how many English men and women were willing to sign an indenture, as the document was called.)

The system worked. Well into the 1700s, indentured servants brought in the bulk of America's cash crops, particularly in the plantation regions of the southern colonies. During the colonial period, a majority of immigrants to America probably stepped from the ship in bondage. The proportion of servants in the population was highest in the South. Because more than 80 percent of the servants were men—by custom, English women were

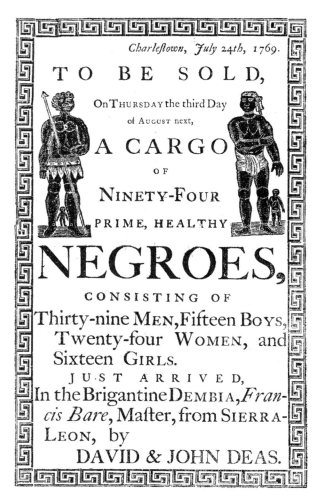

Charlestown, July 24th, 1769.

TO BE SOLD,

On THURSDAY the third Day
of AUGUST next,

A CARGO

OF

NINETY-FOUR

PRIME, HEALTHY

NEGROES,

CONSISTING OF

Thirty-nine MEN, Fifteen BOYS,
Twenty-four WOMEN, and
Sixteen GIRLS.

JUST ARRIVED,
In the Brigantine DEMBIA, *Francis Bare*, Master, from SIERRA-
LEON, by

DAVID & JOHN DEAS.

Poster announcing the sale of Africans as slaves, 1769.

Before the *Mayflower*

Most indentured servants were British: English, Scots, Welsh, and Irish. As early as 1619, however, a Dutch vessel sailed into the Chesapeake Bay and displayed to the settlers about twenty black Africans whom the Dutch had probably captured from a slave ship bound for the Spanish West Indies. The Virginians bought them, and continued to buy blacks throughout the 1600s.

The members of at least one generation of African Americans were servants rather than slaves. One of the blacks brought into Jamestown in 1619 took the name Anthony Johnson and became a prosperous farmer with several white servants bound to him. As early as 1650, there was a small, free black population in the Chesapeake colonies. The only plausible explanation of this fact is that, like white servants, the first blacks in English America were freed after a number of years in bondage. Also by 1650, however, the assemblies of Virginia and Maryland were enacting laws stating that black servants would, in the future, serve *durante vita* ("for life"). This fatal, tragic turn in law and custom was due to changing economic and social circumstances in the colonies, to problems inherent in the institution of indentured servitude, and to the peculiar vulnerability of the first Americans of African descent.

Declining Death Rate, Collapsing Prices

A black slave serving *durante vita* cost considerably more than a white servant bound to labor for his master for as few as four years. The difference in price could amount to several tons of tobacco. Transportation costs from Africa were higher than for servants brought from Britain. And, unlike in the case of white servants, who were signed to their indentures at no cost, slave traders had to pay in West Africa for their human cargoes.

On the face of it, the African slave was the better bargain. His master could work him for a lifetime. In fact, during most of the first century of settlement, the cheaper white servant was the better buy. Because of malaria, typhoid fever, yellow fever, and other contagious diseases ranging from smallpox to influenza, everyone coming to the Chesapeake colonies faced poor prospects of living a long life. Life expectancy for male immigrants to Maryland was 43. Governor

less likely to work in the fields—there was little natural increase of population among the lower classes. (Not until black slaves replaced white indentured servants would Virginia's population stabilize.)

A majority of servants signed their indentures voluntarily. They were more than willing to trade several years of wretched lives for the chance of a fresh start. However, the practice of filling the hold of a servant ship by kidnapping boys or careless adults in English seaports was common enough. It was unwise to drink too heavily in a tavern near the harbor on the night a servant ship was scheduled to weigh anchor. In addition, English courts sentenced criminals—guilty of petty or vicious crimes—to "transportation" to the colonies where they joined the ranks of indentured servants.

Indentures

The word indenture refers to a notch, a literal indentation in the paper on which the contract between a master and a person being bound into servitude was written. Most servants were illiterate and could understand the contract terms only if a third party read it to them. To protect them against fraud, one copy of the contract was placed atop its duplicate before signing and then snipped with a few notches, or "indentures." In any contract dispute, the indentures had to match.

The following contract of 1659 between "Richard Smyth of Virginia, planter, and Margaret Williams of Bristol, spinster" (an unmarried woman), was typical:

Witnesseth that the said Margaret doth hereby covenant, promise, and grant to and with the said Richard, his executors and assigns [the master could sell her services to another], from the day of the date hereof, until her first and next arrival at Virginia, and after, for and during the term of four years, to serve in such service and employment as the said Richard or his assigns shall there employ her, according to the custom of the country in the like kind. In consideration whereof the said master doth hereby covenant and grant to and with the said servant to pay for her passing [her transportation to Virginia], and to find and allow her meat, drink, apparel, and lodging, with other necessaries during the said term; and at the end of the said term to pay unto her one axe, one hoe, double apparel [two suits of clothes], fifty acres of land, one year's provision, according to the custom of the country.

Berkeley of Virginia estimated that, during the 1660s, four out of five indentured servants in that colony died within a few years of arriving.

So, it did not matter much that, in the law, a planter owned an African for life. African slave and Irish servant alike were apt to be dead within two years of purchase. The best buy in such circumstances was the laborer whose purchase price was the lowest. Term of service was a theoretical abstraction. So long as tobacco prices were high, the best business decision was to get your workers as cheaply as you could and get the most tobacco out of them before you laid them in their graves.

Beginning in the 1660s, however, the price of tobacco declined. By the end of the century, the death rate declined, too. By 1700, planters were presented with an incentive to save on the annual cost of their labor force rather than just initial outlay. Now that Virginians and Marylanders were living longer, it made sense to buy workers who served longer. Moreover, blacks seemed more resistant to some of the diseases that toppled whites in the South's semitropical climate. Finally, as Bacon's Rebellion illustrated so dramatically, white servants and former servants could be troublesome people.

The Servant Problem

The violence of the Bacon episode was exceptional. At the best of times, however, colonial courts were jammed with cases of masters complaining about their servants' insolence, negligence, and laziness; about stolen food and drink, rowdy parties, and pregnancies among the women, which exempted them from work for as long as a year.

More serious was the runaway problem. Throughout the colonies, including the most settled parts of the tidewater, America was a forest. Farms and plantations were mere gaps in a wilderness. In Virginia and Maryland, the grandest plantations were separated from one another by belts of virgin hardwood or second-growth "pineys" (old fields gone to scrub). There were few towns. Roads were narrow tracks; many of them were not wide enough for two horsemen to pass without bumping.

Many servants found it easy to run away, hide, and elude capture. Planters' letters were filled with complaints of missing workers and lost investments. The recapture and return of runaways seems to have been the major activity of some county sheriffs, the only law enforcement officials in rural areas. Officials in cities like Baltimore and Philadelphia were flooded with descriptions of runaways, although, with hundreds of recent immigrants walking the streets of coastal cities, they probably caught very few. Punishment was harsh—a whipping and extra time in service. Nevertheless, the opportunities of freedom and the odds of success tempted many.

The most famous runaway was Benjamin Franklin. In 1723, at the age of 17, he walked out on his brother, to whom he was bound, and traveled from Boston to Philadelphia. Any number of people suspected him for what he was, a fugitive servant, but no one turned him in to the authorities.

The Badge of Race

In the ease with which a white runaway could blend into a crowd, and in the reluctance of many colonials to turn in people they suspected of being servants, lies another reason planters turned from white indentured servants to black slaves as their workforce. A black's color was a badge. An escaped slave could not blend easily into the crowds milling in the seaport towns. If it was assumed that a Negro was a slave unless he or she could prove otherwise, the workforce was that much more controllable.

In 1670, there were only 2,000 blacks in Virginia, more than half of them slaves under a law passed in that year. After 1700, when the institution was universally accepted, the slave population grew rapidly until, by the time of the Revolution, there were about 500,000 slaves in the 13 colonies, 450,000 in the South. A British officer observed, "They sell the servants here as they do their horses, and advertise them as they do their beef and oatmeal."

THE SLAVE TRADE

This demand for black labor completely changed the English and colonial attitude toward trading in "any that had our owne shapes." Not only did ships from England and New England, especially Newport, Rhode Island, sail annually to West Africa to capture or purchase slaves, but the British actually pursued a policy of expanding their share of the trade. In 1713, British diplomats demanded of and won from Spain the *asiento de negros,* or right to supply blacks to the Spanish colonies. Trade in human beings became an integral part of the mercantilist system and a profitable leg of colonial trading tours.

First Rebellion

The first recorded rebellion of Africans scheduled to become Americans was in 1730 when 96 captives aboard the *Little George* took control of the ship and forced the crew to pilot it back to their homeland.

Collaboration in Atrocity

The African slave trade was a sordid business in which Africans collaborated with European and American merchants. At first, African chiefs seem to have sold only their criminals and members of enemy tribes to the white-skinned strangers. As the European demand grew and the profits soared, some aggressive tribes began to build their economies on raids inland in search of fresh sources of supply. The economy of the Ashanti Confederation of West Africa rested more than casually on the commerce in slaves. When the transatlantic slave trade was abolished early in the 1800s, Ashanti prosperity collapsed.

For the most part, the whites anchored their ships off the coast or fortified themselves in stockades on islands like Gorée, off Dakar, or at the mouths of rivers. There they offered iron bars, steel knives, brass, glass bottles, kettles, bells, cloth, guns, powder, liquor, and tobacco in return for human merchandise. Occasionally, a European or American joined their African partners or ventured inland themselves. A trader of 1787 explained how the business worked: "In the daytime we called at the villages we passed, and purchased our slaves fairly; but in the night we . . . broke into the villages and, rushing into the huts of the inhabitants, seized men, women, and children promiscuously."

The cruelest part of the trade was the sea crossing, which was called the "middle passage" because it was flanked by overland marches at either end. Rather than providing the most healthful circumstances possible for their valuable cargo and keeping mortality low, the traders crammed the slaves in layers of low decks "like herrings in a barrel."

If only one in twenty captives died, the voyage was considered an extraordinary success. If one in five died, by no means unusual, the profits were still considerable. A slave who cost £5–10 in Africa in 1700 sold in the New World for a minimum of £25. The Portuguese, who were said to be more humane than the English and New England traders, called their slave ships *tumbeiros* ("coffins"). Only as the eighteenth century progressed did mortality decline. By the late 1700s, ship's masters reported that proportionally more slaves survived than crewmen—of whom one in five in the Guinea trade would not complete a voyage. By way of contrast, deaths at sea on the North Atlantic routes were one in every hundred.

Captives in West Africa awaiting sale as slaves to European or American whites.

West African Roots

The Portuguese took most of their slaves in the southwestern part of Africa (Angola) and even on the east coast (Mozambique). English and American traders concentrated on the lands bordering the Gulf of Guinea, present-day Gambia, Senegal, Liberia, Ivory Coast, Ghana, Togo, Benin, and Nigeria.

Sellers Need Buyers

Ottobah Cuguano, who was enslaved on the Gold Coast in 1770, later wrote his recollections of the experience.

I must own, to the shame of my own countrymen, that I was first kidnapped and betrayed by some of my own complexion, who were the first cause of my exile and slavery; but if there were no buyers there would be no sellers.

Much of the coastline was mangrove swamp, but approximately a hundred miles inland the country pitched upward and provided a living that was rich enough to support a large population and a sophisticated culture. Until profits from the slave trade enabled the Ashanti Empire to extend its sway over a vast area in the late seventeenth century, there were few large domains in West Africa. It was a region of numerous tribes speaking many languages and following a variety of customs.

Most West Africans were polytheists who worshiped a complicated hierarchy of gods and spirits. Many tribes venerated the spirits of dead ancestors, and sacrifice was central to most religions. Islam and Christianity had made some headway, but since they were the faiths of the slavers, not very much.

West Africa was no Eden. The people who lived there had to be skilled agriculturists. Ironically, their range and skills increased as slave traders introduced new crops: maize, cassava, peanuts, sweet potatoes, and rice. The fact that intensive farming was a bulwark of West African culture helps to explain why

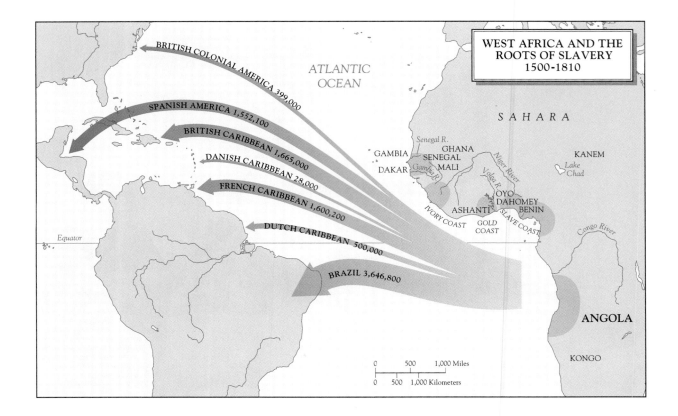

WEST AFRICA AND THE
ROOTS OF SLAVERY
1500-1810

ATLANTIC
OCEAN

SAHARA

BRITISH COLONIAL AMERICA 399,000

SPANISH AMERICA 1,552,100

BRITISH CARIBBEAN 1,665,000

DANISH CARIBBEAN 28,000

FRENCH CARIBBEAN 1,600,200

DUTCH CARIBBEAN 500,000

BRAZIL 3,646,800

Equator

Senegal R.
GAMBIA
DAKAR
Gambia R.
GHANA
SENEGAL
MALI
Niger River
Volta R.
OYO
ASHANTI
DAHOMEY
BENIN
IVORY COAST
GOLD COAST
SLAVE COAST
KANEM
Lake Chad
Congo River
ANGOLA
KONGO

0   500   1,000 Miles
0   500   1,000 Kilometers

they were more appealing to American planters than Indians were. In addition to rice cultivation, which Africans almost certainly introduced to the Carolinas, they utilized the heavy hoe, which was the mainstay of chopping weeds in the fertile southern soil.

The Vulnerability of a Disunited People

There was no such person as a typical captive. Males might be princes, priests, or criminals. Most likely, however, they were ordinary farmers who had the bad luck to cross the path of a raiding party. Most female slaves also came from the ordinary classes. Their status in Africa depended on the tribe to which they belonged. In most, women did a major part of the heavy labor. In other tribes, such as the Ashanti, descent was traced in the maternal line, and women were accorded high status.

Like the American Indians, the Africans were no technological match for Europeans. Superior weaponry and attractive trade goods made it possible for most slave traders to have their way. Also, as among

the Indians, ancestral hatreds among African tribes made it easy for outsiders to manipulate the superior numbers of the natives. Not only was one tribe happy to sell its neighbors to the white men for profit, but the divisions among the blacks were exploited to make them more manageable. "The safest way," wrote William Smith, who took part in an expedition of 1748, "is to trade with the different Nations, on either side of the River, and having some of every sort on board, there will be no more likelihood of their succeeding in a Plot, than of finishing the tower of Babel."

Once in the colonies, these diverse peoples adopted English as the only feasible means of communication among themselves. In time, they also found in their masters' Protestant religion, albeit with a great deal of emphasis on the stories of the ancient Hebrews' captivities and deliverance, a solace in their misery. For the most part, however, they were shut out of the mainstream of American development for more than three centuries after the first African stepped nervously from the gangplank of the Dutch ship to the soil of Virginia.

CHRONOLOGY

Before 10,000 B.C.	Wandering Asians into North America, first populating the continent
c. 1570	Five linguistically related tribes in the area of New York State form the Iroquois Confederacy
1608	Samuel de Champlain founds New France at the site of Quebec
1609	Champlain and Huron allies open fire on Mohawks on shores of Lake Champlain
1626	Acting for the New Netherland Company, Peter Minuit purchases Manhattan Island from Indians
1630	Puritan minister John Cotton devises justifications for taking Indian land
1673	Louis Joliet, Jacques Marquette, and Indians explore Mississippi River from Wisconsin to mouth of Arkansas River.
1675–1676	King Philip's War in New England Sieur de la Salle reaches mouth of Mississippi
1699	Sieur d'Iberville founds New Orleans
1710s	Defeat of Tuscaroras by South Carolina and their migration north
1713	Britain forces Spain to grant British sale traders the *asiento de negros*
1730	African captives aboard the *Little George* take control of ship and force its return to Africa

FOR FURTHER READING

On the Indians of North America, see Alvin M. Josephy, *The Indian Heritage of America*, 1968; Harold E. Driver, *Indians of North America*, 1970; Wilcomb E. Washburn, *The Indian in America*, 1975; *Cambridge History of the Natives of the World. vol. 3, North America*, 1993; and Robert F. Spencer and Jesse Jennings, et al., *The Native Americans: Ethnology and Background of the North American Indians*, 1977.

James Axtell is the leading historian of Native Americans in the colonial period; see his *The European and the Indian*, 1981, *The Invasion Within: The Contest of Cultures in Colonial America*, 1985, and *After Columbus: Essays in the Ethnohistory of Colonial North America*, 1988. Also see Gary Nash, *Red, White, and Black*, 1982, and Neal Salisbury, *Manitou and Providence: Indians, Europeans, and the Making of New England*, 1982. Also of special interest are Richard Slotkin, *Regeneration through Violence*, 1973; Alden Vaughan, *New England Frontier: Puritans and Indians, 1620–1675*, 1965; and on the most powerful of the Indian presences, Daniel K. Richter, *The Ordeal of the Longhouse: The Peoples of the Iroquois League in the Era of European Colonization*, 1992.

A series of books by nineteenth-century historian Francis Parkman remains fine reading about French North America: *The Pioneers of France in the New World*, 1865, *The Jesuits in North America*, 1867, *The Old Regime in Canada*, 1874, *Count Frontenac and New France*, 1877, and *LaSalle and the Discovery of the Great West*, 1879. A fine single-volume history of the subject is William J. Eccles, *France in America*, 1972. Also see Eccles, *The Canadian Frontier, 1534–1760*, 1969; Raphael N. Hamilton, *Marquette's Explorations*, 1970; Joseph P. Donnelly, *Jacques Marquette, S. J.*, 1968; and Samuel Eliot Morison, *Samuel B. Champlain: Father of New France*, 1972. A sophisticated exploration of cultural and political interaction is Richard White, *The Middle Ground: Indians, Empires, and Republics in the Great Lakes Region*, 1991.

On indentured servitude and the evolution of African slavery in English America, see David W. Galenson, *White Servitude in Colonial America*, 1981, and Edmund S. Morgan, *American Slavery, American Freedom*, 1975. Winthrop D. Jordan presents a widely acknowledged thesis concerning the background of white racism in *White over Black*, 1968. Philip D. Curtin, *The Atlantic Slave Trade*, 1969, is still the definitive work on that subject. An invaluable overview is David B. Davis, *The Problem of Slavery in Western Culture*, 1966. Studies of Southern society and slavery include Timothy Silver, *A New Face on the Countryside: Indians, Colonists, and Slaves in the South Atlantic Forests, 1500–1800*, 1990; and Mechal Sobel, *The World They Made Together: Black and White Values in Eighteenth-Century Virginia*, 1987. Among the best special studies are G. W. Mullin, *Flight and Rebellion*, 1972; T. H. Breen, *Tobacco Culture*, 1985; and T. H. Breen and Stephen Innes, *"Myne Owne Ground," Race and Freedom on Virginia's Eastern Shore*, 1980.

General James Wolfe, informed of his victory at Quebec as he lay dying on the battlefield, 1759.

6
CHAPTER

BRITISH AMERICA
The Colonies at the Equinox

God hath sifted a nation that he might send choice grain into this wilderness.

— *William Stoughton*

Sir, they are a race of convicts, and ought to be thankful for anything we allow them short of hanging.

—*Samuel Johnson*

In 1706, a male child was born into the household of a Boston tallowmaker, an artisan who made candles and soap from the fat of cattle and sheep. There would not have been much excitement about the arrival of Benjamin Franklin: he was the tenth child in the family.

Large families were common in the colonies. The typical wife, who married in her early twenties, several years younger than women in Britain, bore six to eight. By the eighteenth century, a majority of them were surviving to be adults. Big families were economic assets in the colonial economy, not luxuries. Children consumed little and the necessities of life—food, clothing, and shelter—were abundant and cheap. There was plenty of work to do in the households of farmers, artisans, and shopkeepers, and they began at a tender age. A child of five or six could feed chickens, gather eggs, and run errands, sweep a floor. By adolescence, boys and girls were contributing more to a household's economy than they took from it.

Benjamin Franklin went to work in his father's business at the age of ten. Two years later he was bound as an apprentice to his half brother, a printer. They did not get along, and Ben ran away to Philadelphia. But he had learned the mysteries of the trade, which, in the eighteenth century, involved writing as well as setting the words of others in type.

Franklin's pen was nimble. He learned to imitate the elegant style of the fashionable English essayists Joseph Addison and Richard Steele.

No one faulted him for lack of originality. No colonial said, as Noah Webster and Ralph Waldo Emerson would say a century later, that Americans should create a distinctively American literature from a distinctively American language. Bostonians (and New Yorkers, Philadelphians, and Baltimoreans) were happy to be colonials. They were pleased to be the overseas subjects of a realm that they believed the most beneficent on earth, "a mighty empire in numbers little inferior to the greatest in Europe, and in felicity to none." They gladly took their customs and culture, as well as their laws and the manufactured goods they consumed, from the mother country.

During Ben Franklin's long life (he lived until 1790), British North America flowered. Indeed, the colonies fruited, outgrowing their dependent status and mentality. Franklin himself did not miss a turn

---

Poor Richard

Benjamin Franklin first won fame among Americans as the publisher of *Poor Richard's Almanack*, which he began to publish annually in 1732. In addition to providing the useful information that is the staple of almanacs—phases of the moon, dates of holidays, and so on—Franklin charmed readers with his rendition of homilies praising thrift, frugal living, hard work, and other "bourgeois virtues" which have, ever since, been an important part of American culture. Among his advice:

Leisure is the time for doing something useful.

A ploughman on his legs is higher than a gentleman on his horse.

Handle your tools without mittens.

Time is money.

Benjamin Franklin (1706–1790) was as comfortable with princes as with artisans. He could discuss Enlightenment science, politics, or the price of movable type. He wrote banalities but also keen satire. There was no American—or European—quite like him in the eighteenth century.

on that long road. Was there an American population explosion during the 1700s? Franklin capitalized on it, financing his apprentices in print shops all over the colonies. Was the population growing less English? Franklin knew what that meant; he lived in the colony with the most diverse population (and he did not like it). Did the colonies become a factor in international affairs as European wars took on a worldwide character? Franklin espoused an aggressive foreign policy and several times went to Europe as a lobbyist on behalf of colonial interests.

He became the best-known American of his time, respected at home, lionized in Europe. He founded libraries, learned societies, the first American hospital, and the first trained fire department. Devoted to social improvement, he was a scientist, a wit, and a celebrity who charmed countesses and ragamuffins alike. There was scarcely a major event or trend in the eighteenth century in which Franklin did not figure. He devised a scheme to unite the colonies as early as 1754, the Albany Plan of Union, a scheme that drew from the Iroquois Confederacy as well as traditional sources. He signed the Declaration of Independence and the Constitution. Slavery, which during his lifetime quietly evolved from a minor aspect of colonial life into a matter of grave concern, did not escape Franklin's notice. The last public act of his life was to petition the American government to abolish the institution.

SOCIETY AND ECONOMY

Between 1700 and 1776, the population of the colonies increased tenfold, from about 250,000 people to 2.5 million. Unlike in the previous century, natural increase accounted for much of this astonishing growth. Both family size and life expectancy at birth were greater in North America than on any other continent. Surveys of rural New England graveyards show that with the exception of infants and women dying in first childbirth, life expectancy could be as high as it is today with all of our precautions and medicine. The New England male who survived his first five years, and the female who bore children easily or never married, both stood a good chance of surviving into their sixties and seventies.

The colonies were also flooded with immigrants, perhaps 350,000 newcomers between 1700 and the War for Independence. The majority, but by no means all, were English.

Immigration from Germany

Germans and German-speaking Swiss and Austrians responded enthusiastically to William Penn's invitation that they take up farms in Pennsylvania. By the 1750s they were so numerous in Philadelphia, Lancaster, and York counties that Benjamin Franklin, who called the settlers "the most stupid of their nation," was alarmed. They will "Germanize us instead of [us] Anglifying them," Franklin wrote, "and will never adopt our Language or Customs." Germans represented a third of Pennsylvania's population and, in 1776, it was seriously proposed that German, not English, should be the official language of the newly

The Pennsylvania Dutch

The people known today as "the Pennsylvania Dutch" are not of Dutch origin, but are descended from German speakers of southern Germany and Switzerland. They got their name from their own word for German, *Deutsch;* indeed, until the First World War, many Americans referred to Germans as "Dutchmen."

The Pennsylvania Dutch are sometimes known as the "Plain People" because, followers of an early Protestant reformer (who was Dutch), Menno Simons, they practiced a simple, frugal austerity in their daily lives. As times changed—very rapidly—they became plainer, clinging to seventeenth-century dress and technology. The strictest, known as the Amish, do not even use electricity in their homes.

Today, there are about 20 Mennonite and Amish sects, about 600 congregations and some 95,000 adherents living in tight-knit communities all over the United States. However, about 75 percent of the "Pennsylvania Dutch" live in Pennsylvania, Ohio, and Indiana, with Lancaster and York Counties, Pennsylvania, remaining their capital. Although they speak English (with a few quirks), their religious services are held in archaic German. Families are large, averaging seven children, with 22 percent of couples having ten or more. This fecundity helps make up for the fact that, each year, about 12 percent of young Pennsylvania Dutch men and women abandon the rigorous life of their ancestors.

independent state. The Declaration of Independence was set into type in a German-American newspaper, *Wöchentliche Philadelphische Staatsnote* before it was printed in English.

Many of the German immigrants were members of the plain-living Moravian, Amish, Mennonite, and Hutterite sects. Like the Quakers, they were pacifists and, having little interest in politics, they passively supported their benefactors. No doubt, their bloc voting annoyed Franklin, a member of Pennsylvania's anti-Quaker faction, as much as did the sounds of the German language on the streets of Philadelphia.

The Scotch-Irish

Even more numerous than the Germans (and more greatly despised) were the Scotch-Irish. These people were descendants of Protestant Scots whom James I had settled in northern Ireland to counterbalance the Catholic Irish. By the early 1700s, they lost favor with the Crown and suffered from steep increases in rent and from parliamentary acts that undercut the weaving industry, on which many depended for their livelihood. About 4,000 Scotch-Irish a year gave up on the Emerald Isle and emigrated to the colonies, "huddled together like brutes without regard to age or sex or sense of decency."

They were a combative people back home, ready with cudgels and pikes to fight the Catholic Irish (and one another), and they did not mellow in American air. James Logan, a Quaker and the agent of the Penn family in Philadelphia, wrote to England in consternation: "I must own, from my experience in the land office, that the settlement of five families from Ireland gives me more trouble than fifty of any other people."

The Scotch-Irish wanted land. To acquire it they moved to the backcountry in Virginia and the Carolinas as well as to western Pennsylvania. There they confronted potent Indian tribes with whom Quakers like Logan tried to have amicable relations. On this issue, these obstreperous frontiersmen helped drive the Quakers from public life.

The Retirement of the Quakers

As often as not, Scotch-Irish frontiersmen took Indian policy into their own hands. Far from the capital of Philadelphia, they attacked the tribes for good reason and bad. Franklin's anti-Quaker party gener-

ally supported them in the colonial assembly and, when Britain and France were at war, so did the Crown, for most western tribes were at least casual allies of the French in Canada.

The dominant Quakers were sincere in their pacifism. But they were not immune to the advantages of political power nor oblivious to the conditions of retaining it during wartime. They accommodated the Crown by such contrivances as voting money "for the king's use," laying on royal shoulders the sin of spending it on guns and soldiers. Another act of the Pennsylvania assembly provided money for "grain"—a word that could be construed to mean gunpowder as well as wheat.

The aggressiveness of the Scotch-Irish presented the Quakers with a more difficult problem. If they clung to their principle that government should be responsive to popular wishes, they would be parties to frontier carnage, a mockery of their pacifism. If they insisted on peace and fair dealings with the Indians, they would deny the demands of the majority of Pennsylvanians, a mockery of their democratic inclinations.

By the end of the 1750s, most Quaker officeholders gave up wrestling with their consciences and

An early edition of the Philadelphia Zeitung. *The lead story is about a peace treaty between Persia and the Turkish Empire.*

retired from public life. Thus they preserved their personal scruples (and prospered mightily in trade) while the backcountry settlers, Franklin's party, and the Crown had the opportunity to practice the aggressive policies that they desired.

Well-Ordered Families

Whatever their national origin or religion, colonials assumed that the family was the basic social and economic institution. Early Puritan laws requiring all people, including bachelors, spinsters (unmarried women), infants, and the elderly to live within a household were long gone. But the practice survived: the "loner" was looked upon with suspicion.

The family, not the individual, was vested with political identity. Only the heads of property-owning households voted, no matter that there might be several adult males living in the same home. Property laws, inherited from England, were designed to maintain the family as the basic economic unit. For example, Virginia, Maryland, and South Carolina enacted laws of primogeniture and entail. Primogeniture required that an estate of land be bequeathed as a unit to the eldest son of the deceased, or if there were no male heir, to his first daughter. Entail meant that a property could not be divided and sold. To sell an estate, one was required to sell it intact.

The purpose of these laws was to preserve the economic power and privileges of the wealthy. If a tobacco planter with a thousand acres and 30 slaves, enough to support a household in grand style, were free to divide his estate among four or five children, the result would be four or five households of middling size. If each of these properties were subdivided in the next generation, the result would be a community of struggling subsistence farmers where once there had been a grandee.

A class of people conscious of their social position wanted no such leveling. And the colonial rich, especially in the cities, grew richer during the eighteenth century. In 1700, the richest tenth of Philadelphia's population owned about 40 percent of the city's wealth. By 1774, the richest tenth owned 55 percent.

Social Mobility

Primogeniture did not mean that propertied people were insensitive to the fortunes of their daughters and younger sons. They could provide for them by bequeathing them money (*personal* as opposed to *real* property) or by giving them land not part of an entailed estate. As in England, second sons might be educated to the ministry or another profession, which maintained their social standing without breaking up the family property, or they might serve in the military.

George Washington is a case in point. His older brother, Lawrence, inherited the family lands. He helped George train as a soldier and surveyor (which meant land speculator) in the hope he would found his own family. Washington also kept an eye peeled for an heiress or wealthy widow to marry, which he eventually found in Martha Custis.

Daughters of the middle and upper classes were provided with dowries in order to attract husbands of means, or, at least, of the same social class. The woman who came into property as a daughter without brothers or as the widow of a man who had no direct male descendants—as did Martha Custis Washington—was likely to be deluged with proposals not many days after her husband's funeral. The woman who wished to control her property required a strong will to resist the pressure inflicted on her.

On the other hand, through a shrewd marriage to a well-to-do man, a widow could ensure her children's wealth and social position. Mary Horsmanden had two husbands and was far more the founder of several prominent Virginia families, including the Carters and Byrds, than either of her husbands were. Frances Culpeper successively married three colonial governors. Lucy Higginson also had three husbands and was the matriarch of several generations of Virginians.

Women's Rights

Unmarried women could own property in their own right, thus enjoying the status of head of the household. (In New Jersey, such women could vote.) Married women, however, lost control of the property they brought to marriage. The legal principle of coverture held that, in law, "husband and wife are one and that one the husband."

A husband had the use of his wife's land and money, though the married woman's economic welfare was guaranteed by laws reserving for her at least a third of her husband's property when he died.

Although the colonial woman's status was markedly inferior to that of men, she enjoyed a more favorable situation than her cousins in Europe. In most colonies, husbands were not permitted to beat their wives. At least one man in Massachusetts was fined because he referred to his wife as "a servant"; that is, he demeaned her. Visitors from Europe commented on the deference colonial men paid women, and the protections women were provided by custom and law. In former old Puritan colonies, a woman could sue for divorce on the grounds of adultery, bigamy, desertion, impotence, incest, or absence for a period of seven years.

The Lower Orders

Laws pertaining to property and customs restraining behavior toward women were relevant only to the middle and upper classes. To people of the lower orders, scraping out an existence took precedence.

In the countryside, poor farmers and wage workers without property were a potential source of disorder as in the days of Bacon's Rebellion. In the seaports, a marginal class of unskilled workers, roustabouts, ex-servants, sailors on leave, and derelicts congregated in disreputable quarters of the towns.

There was enough casual work to be done to keep them alive, but not enough compensation to generate a sense of belonging to the community or respect for conventional morals. Illegitimate births were common. As many as a third of all births occurred outside marriage or in less than nine months after the wedding.

The colonial poor were sometimes racially mixed, thereby earning the further contempt of their

The Childbearing Sex

Favorable as American women's situation may have been compared to their European sisters, nothing in North America could ameliorate the physical ravages of almost constant childbearing. The case of the second Mrs. Michael Wigglesworth is a sobering illustration.

Michael Wigglesworth, a widower, was at age 48 disturbingly frail, bearing "great bodly infirmities" and appearing to be a man past 60 years of age—ancient in the colonies. Nevertheless, he married his maidservant of just 20 years.

After bearing six children in rapid succession, she died at age 28. Michael Wigglesworth lived into his seventies.

betters. "The crowd" they formed was kept under control by strict laws and inconsistent but no-nonsense law enforcement. Nevertheless, the crowd made its presence and wishes known in occasional "bread riots." And the lower classes were to play a major part in the tumult that preceded the American Revolution. As with subordinate peoples before and since, riot was the most accessible means of political expression, for they did not vote. Only about 20 percent of colonial adult males had that right.

Slave Rebellions

The lowliest of the lowly were the slaves. They were not numerous north of the Mason-Dixon line, the boundary between Pennsylvania and Maryland surveyed in 1769. Slaves were only 8 percent of the population in Pennsylvania, 3 percent in Massachusetts. As early as the 1750s, Quakers John Woolman of New Jersey and Anthony Benezet of Pennsylvania condemned slavery as intrinsically immoral. (Benezet also wrote pamphlets on behalf of women and Indians.)

In the southern colonies, by way of contrast, slavery grew in importance in the eighteenth century. The number of blacks in Virginia, most of whom were slaves, grew from about 4,000 in 1700 to 42,000 in 1743, and to more than 200,000 at the time of the American Revolution. In a few Virginia counties and in much of South Carolina, blacks outnumbered whites.

Now and then, slaves rebelled. In 1739, about 20 blacks from the Stono plantation near Charleston seized guns, killed several planter families, and put out a call for an uprising. About 150 slaves joined them and "with Colours displayed, and two Drums beating," they began to march toward Florida where, they had learned through the remarkable African-American grapevine, the Spanish would grant them freedom.

Most were captured within a week but some managed to reach St. Augustine and settled to the north of the town in the fortified village of Santa Teresa de Mose. They swore to "shed their last drop of blood in defense of the Great Crown of Spain, and to be the most cruel enemies of the English." The threat—or at least the attraction that Santa Teresa might hold out to other slaves—was great enough that, the next year, General Oglethorpe of Georgia attacked the village, a sad errand for a man who had hoped to keep slavery out of Georgia.

The Stono uprising aroused anxieties as far north as New York. In the summer of 1741, thirty-one blacks and four whites were executed there for plotting a rebellion. It is not clear that anything was actually afoot.

WORLD WARS, COLONIAL WARS

The fabulous growth of the 13 mainland colonies during the eighteenth century, coupled with the physical isolation from the mother country, ensured that so expansive and ever more confident a people as the Americans could not remain the tail on the British imperial lion. This is not to say that American independence was inevitable. However, some independence of interests and action surely was.

The colonists demonstrated this clearly between 1689 and 1763 when the mother country was involved in a series of worldwide wars. The Americans participated, or withheld participation, according to what they perceived to be their interests, as opposed to those of Great Britain.

Another Kind of War

The European wars of 1689–1763 were also world wars because Britain and France were both possessed of far-flung empires. The conflicts raged not only in Europe and North America, but also in the Caribbean, in South America, in India, and wherever ships flying belligerent flags met on the high seas.

There the resemblance to twentieth century wars ends. In the late seventeenth and the eighteenth centuries, war was considered an extension of diplomacy, the concern of rulers rather than of ordinary people. Wars were fought frankly to win, or to defend, territory or trade from rivals, or to avenge what one prince regarded as the insult of another. There was no clash of ideologies, no claim that one social, economic, or political system was engaged in a life-or-death struggle with another.

Armies were made up of professional soldiers, rough men for whom fighting was a means of making a living. Soldiers thought not at all that they were defending or furthering an abstract ideal. If they were attached to anything, it was to the person of their commander, who saw to it that they were paid.

What did ordinary farmers, artisans, and shopkeepers have to do with such a business? As little as they could. At best, war meant heavier taxation. At worst, people were unlucky enough to make their homes where armies fought or marched. Then they suffered, no matter whose flag the fighting men were waving.

Otherwise, ordinary people went on as in peacetime. Because princes neither expected, sought, nor won popular support for their wars, it was not a matter of treason in the modern sense of the word when, as in the world wars of 1689 to 1763, many Americans simply sat out the conflict or even continued trading with the French enemy.

Indigo and Slavery

Indigofera tinctoria was the source of a brilliant, coveted, and expensive blue dye. By the eighteenth century, it was grown on a small scale in Montserrat and other islands of the West Indies. During the early 1740s, the plant was introduced into South Carolina by Eliza Lucas, the daughter of a West Indian planter who also owned land in South Carolina. Eliza was well-educated in England, almost unheard of for a woman of any social class, and her extraordinary father then entrusted her with the management of a South Carolina plantation.

In 1745, she married another rich planter, Charles Pinckney, but already she had imported West Indian slaves who knew how to grow and process *Indigofera tinctoria*, thus creating another cash crop for South Carolina.

Indigo brought a high price and a subsidy from Britain. It grew on high ground which rice growers had theretofore considered wasteland. Moreover, its growing season was precisely the opposite of that of rice, allowing planters owning huge workforces to keep their slaves busy the year around.

Thus, Eliza Lucas Pinckney's experiments made slaves doubly valuable in South Carolina, contributing to the fact that, a generation later, while Virginia's tobacco growers seriously considered abandoning slavery, South Carolina's slaveholders were hard-liners on the question. The South Carolina delegation to the Second Continental Congress insisted that a backhanded slap at slavery in the Declaration of Independence be deleted before they would sign.

NOTABLE PEOPLE

William Byrd (1674–1744)

William Byrd of Westover was born in Virginia in 1674. He had the good luck to come into his maturity just as the plantation aristocracy was entering its golden age. Indeed, the historian Louis B. Wright called Byrd "the Great American Gentleman" because his life epitomized the elegance and culture of his class. In his famous portrait, Byrd looks more like a duke than a rude colonial.

Byrd loved the social whirl of London. He was educated in Holland and in England, at the Inns of Court, and, rather remarkable for the time, made several trips back to the mother country as a lobbyist for the Virginia colony. He appears to have been a bit bored by the quiet life of the New World.

Like most planters, Byrd chased after riches. During one long sojourn in London, he tried unsuccessfully to find a wealthy wife. One nobleman rejected Byrd's request to marry his daughter by sneering that her annual income was more than the Virginian's entire fortune. There was a big difference between being rich in England and rich in America.

And yet, few English owned the empire in land that Byrd amassed. He inherited 26,231 acres in 1704 and possessed 179,000 acres when he died in 1744. Most of this was wilderness, a speculation on the future, but huge tracts were planted in tobacco and food crops. William Byrd presided over a small kingdom of servants and slaves.

How did such a grandee spend his day? He awakened with the sun but stayed in bed to eat a small breakfast brought by a servant. Much more bookish than most planters, Byrd read for an hour or two in one of the six languages he knew (Hebrew, Greek, Latin, French, Dutch, and English). When he rose, he did some calisthenics ("I danced my dance"). Then his day varied according to circumstances and the season.

Byrd would often have guests to entertain. In a country with few towns and fewer inns, a gentleman like Byrd provided hospitality for travelers. Ordinary people were treated as such; they were provided some sort of roof and simple food for a day or two. Gentlemen and ladies, however, stayed in the plantation house and were feted at banquet-sized meals for as long as they chose. Living in isolation, cultured and sociable people like Byrd craved company. On a plantation that produced more than enough food for master and servant, the expense of wholesale entertainment was hardly noticed.

When there were no guests (and Byrd was not visiting someone else), there was plenty of work to be done. Although a grand gentleman did not labor in the fields, he was no idler. Managing thousands of acres and hundreds of people required nearly constant attention. A plantation was a delicately integrated community that was involved in the cultivating, processing, and storing of food, some manufacturing, blacksmith

King William's War, 1689–1697

The wars began when William of Orange, the sour-tempered ruler of the Netherlands, became king of England in 1689. William cared about colonies and even English domestic politics only to the extent that they affected his animosity toward the king of France, Louis XIV. William's life was dedicated to preventing the expansion of France.

William was a superb soldier. He had wrestled Louis XIV to the mat with the limited resources of the Dutch and a few German princelings. He could not wait to turn the greater wealth and power of

England on his foe. In 1689, he got his chance when Louis XIV claimed the right to take possession of a valuable state on the Rhine River.

Few Americans cared who ruled the Rhineland or who became archbishop of Cologne (another matter over which Louis and William squabbled). Unconsciously, but with a certain elegance, they proclaimed their disdain for the war by ignoring Europe's name for the conflict, the War of the League of Augsburg. In America, the war was called King William's War, as though it had been foisted on the colonies.

In North America, French, Algonkians, and Hurons struck the first blow in the winter of

work, and barrelmaking, for example. Other planters of Byrd's class took greater interest than he did in account books and the mechanics of agriculture. But no one responsible for such an operation could escape endless duties.

Indeed, William Byrd had to oversee many of the household functions that usually kept the planter's wife busy from daybreak to long after dark. His first wife, Lucy Park, was a poor housekeeper. She and Byrd frequently quarreled about her management of the kitchen and larder, and he complained to his diary when he had to supervise the bottling of wine.

Byrd regularly rode and boated to Williamsburg. A gentleman in his position had interests to protect, and he was, at various times, a member of the House of Burgesses and the Governor's Council. In the capital, he roomed at a tavern. During the afternoon and early evening he conducted business, after which he and his cronies regularly got drunk. Every morning he vowed to break out of the cycle but only occasionally kept his word. There were few diversions in the sleepy town but dining, drinking, and chatting.

Byrd was something of a roué, but, oddly, otherwise practiced strict moderation. Virginia's abundance produced such a variety of fine foods that meals were huge, delicious, and long. Through most of his life, however, Byrd shunned gluttony. He practiced a strict regimen designed by a fashionable Scottish physician,

George Cheyne, who made a handsome living by prescribing "fad diets" to the wealthy of London and of the resort city of Bath. Byrd adopted two of these regimens: the "milk diet" and the recommendation that a person eat only one dish at a meal. Thus, while his dinner companions were stuffing themselves with as many as seven or eight kinds of meat (the typical fare at a wealthy house), Byrd ate only one. Like a contemporary "Weight Watcher," he kept a written record of every morsel he consumed.

Life in London, in Williamsburg, and at Westover was comfortable, but no Virginian was ever far from the outdoors. In 1728, Byrd helped command an expedition that surveyed the dividing line between Virginia and North Carolina, a route which took him into the Great Dismal Swamp. There, without complaint, he slept on the sodden ground and lived off game like any pioneer. He described the expedition and the way of life of the occasional settler the surveyors met. He told of people ailing with malaria and other diseases, drinking themselves to death with cheap, sometimes poisonous rum, and scraping hour by hour for their food. It is difficult to imagine a more striking contrast with his own lot in life, but, while witty in depicting these early-day "poor whites," Byrd was never surprised. The grandest of the great American gentlemen were not insulated from the harsher realities of life.

1689–1690 with a series of raids on frontier settlements in New York, New Hampshire, and Maine (then part of Massachusetts). These were not great battles on the European pattern. Although often led by French officers, they were Indian-style attacks in which a few dozen warriors hit without warning at isolated farms in the forest, killing or capturing the settlers and burning houses and fields. The French called it *petite guerre* ("little war") and viewed the raids as harassment and as a warning.

Petite guerre worked. Each successful raid moved the unmarked boundary between New France and New England deeper into lands that the

colonials considered their own. More aggravating to the New England commercial elite were assaults on their merchant and fishing vessels by French ships out of Port Royal in Acadia (Nova Scotia). In 1690, an expedition from Massachusetts captured the French base but in vain. By the terms of the Peace of Ryswick in 1697, the fortress was returned to France. The English armies had not fared well in the European theater, and the peacemakers gave up Port Royal in order to limit concessions to France at home. The New Englanders were reminded that their interests were subordinate to those of England in Europe, as interpreted, in this case, by a Dutchman.

Queen Anne's War, 1702–1713

The French took North America more seriously. While King William's War was still in progress, they began to build a chain of forts in the backcountry. During the brief peace of 1697 to 1702, the Gulf of Mexico and Illinois country settlements were sketched in on French maps. Then, in 1700, the king of Spain died without an heir, and Louis XIV moved to place his grandson on the throne of the declining, but still rich empire. Austria, where a dynasty related to the dead Spanish king still ruled, joined England to support another claimant.

Again, the colonists named the war after the reigning British sovereign, Queen Anne, but this time European dynastic squabbles were of more than casual interest to colonials in the far north and south. The same dynasty ruling both Spain and France meant the union of neighbors who previously had sniped at each other. This time around, southerners, who had taken no part in King William's War, were in the thick of things.

Like the New Englanders, South Carolinians competed with the Spanish and French in the fur and hide trade. Beaver pelts were not so lush in the warm southern climate, but there were deer and bison, important sources of leather. The South Carolinian network of Indian contacts extended beyond the Mississippi River, well into territory that the French thought of as their own. However, the Carolinians had some formidable Indian enemies in what is now Georgia, Alabama, and Mississippi. Slave-catching expeditions among the Creek and Cherokee peoples kept the southwestern frontier in a state of chronic *petite guerre.*

In the North, the French and their Indian allies were more audacious than before, wiping out the substantial town of Deerfield, Massachusetts, in 1704. Once again, however, the New Englanders captured Port Royal. This time, at the Peace of Utrecht in 1713, the British kept it and the whole of Acadia. The war had gone well for England in Europe, and the French were forced to retire to Cape Breton Island and build a new and stronger Atlantic fortress, Louisbourg.

In the south, the treaty resolved few difficulties for the simple reason that the European nations did not hold the ultimate power there. The Creeks and Cherokees were numerous, confident, and proud peoples, less dependent on Europeans than were the Algonkians and Hurons of the north. They had but-

A French and Indian raid wiped out the town of Deerfield, Massachusetts, in 1704.

tressed the strength of their numbers by selectively adopting the ways of the whites. They took easily to European agricultural techniques and even to the use of slave labor (although many blacks became members of the nations). They would not finally fall before white expansion for more than a century after Queen Anne's War.

In the Middle Colonies, there were no difficulties to be resolved by the negotiators of the Peace of Utrecht. Virginia, Maryland, Delaware, New Jersey, and Pennsylvania had not taken part in Queen Anne's War. New York actually issued a formal declaration of neutrality and continued to trade with French Canada during the years in which the New England colonists were the victims of bloody raids.

THE LONG PEACE, 1713–1739

During the 26 years after 1713, North America was at peace. These were also generally prosperous years for the colonies. While tobacco never sold for the bonanza prices of the mid-1600s, it returned a handsome enough profit to large planters. Rice, naval stores, and hides and furs were lucrative, as were the

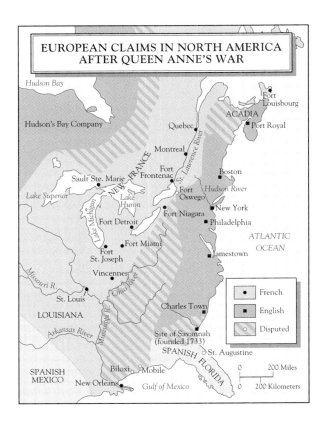

EUROPEAN CLAIMS IN NORTH AMERICA
AFTER QUEEN ANNE'S WAR

various overseas trade routes plied by the merchant ships of New England and the Middle Colonies. In troubled times to come, colonists with historical memories would look back on the long peace as a golden age.

Salutary Neglect

The vision of a golden age was wrapped up in a parcel with the colonial policy of the first British prime minister, Robert Walpole. By disposition an easygoing fellow who fancied his daily outsized bottle of port wine and idle gossip with other comfortable gentlemen, Walpole believed that the best way to govern a country or an empire during good times was to govern as little as possible. Action only disturbed what was working quite well on its own.

Walpole's policy came to be called "salutary neglect." If the colonists were content, bustling, and prosperous, he believed, thus enriching the English merchant class as it was their duty to do, it was salutary—healthful—not to disturb things.

For the most part, therefore, Walpole winked at colonial violations of the Navigation Acts. Only when

interest groups that suffered from his inaction complained did he appear to take some notice. Even then Walpole's strategy was splendidly neglectful. He would ask Parliament to satisfy complaints and immediately forget about its enactments. For example, in 1732, London hatmakers complained that the growth of that industry in the northern colonies was hurting their business in North America. Walpole obliged the British hatters by saddling colonial hatmakers with various restrictions. They were not to sell their wares outside the boundaries of their own colonies, nor to train blacks in the craft. London's hatters were happy. American hatmakers ignored the law. Colonial officials enforced it now and then, but not much.

The Molasses Act

The Molasses Act of 1733 was enacted in response to the complaints of sugar planters from the British West Indies that Americans were buying molasses from French islands, where it was cheaper. They pointed out that the principles of mercantilism entitled them to a monopoly of the huge molasses market in New England, just as the tobacco growers of Virginia and Maryland had a monopoly in the sale of that product. (Rum, distilled from blackstrap molasses, was the common man's liquor in the colonies and was also valuable in the slave trade.) Therefore, they demanded that Walpole place a tax on foreign molasses.

Such a law was bound to rile the New Englanders. They were accustomed to filling the holds of their ships with the cheaper French molasses. Walpole solved the problem by approving the Molasses Act of 1733, and promptly forgot about it. The West Indian planters were placated but not particularly helped; New England shipsmasters were as content to buy French molasses illegally as legally. The bootleg product was either smuggled into Boston and other ports or provided with false invoices stating that the cargo came from Jamaica or Barbados, British islands. Colonial customs officers were not fooled by the phony documents. But they could be bribed, and if a penny or so on each barrel made them happy, too, that was the idea of salutary neglect.

Another law that was ignored in the interests of prosperity and calm was passed in 1750 at the behest of English ironmakers, who wanted a monopoly of the colonial market in iron goods. The act forbade colonists to engage in most forms of iron manufacture.

But not only did colonial forges continue to operate with impunity, several colonial governments actually subsidized the iron industry within their borders. Salutary neglect was a wonderful way to run an empire—as long as there was no war and times were good.

Political Autonomy

An unintended consequence of Walpole's easygoing colonial policy was the steady erosion of the mother country's political control over her American daughters. In part, the seizure of the governors' powers by colonial assemblies merely reflected what was going on in England at the same time. During the eighteenth century, Parliament assumed governmental functions formerly exercised by the kings and queens. In the colonies, elected assemblies took powers from the governors, who were appointed by either the monarch or proprietors.

The key to this important shift in the structure of government was the English political principle that the people, through their elected representatives, must consent to all tax legislation. In England, Parliament held the power of the purse; all money bills had to be approved by the House of Commons. In the colonies, the elected assemblies—whether called the House of Burgesses or the House of Delegates or whatever—owned this important prerogative.

Theoretically, the governor of a colony could veto any budget bill that he did not like. But to do so was risky. An assembly that was determined to have its way could retaliate by denying the governor the funds that he needed in order to operate his office and even his personal household—that is, they "starved him into compliance" as a hungry royal governor of New York phrased it in 1741.

Men on the Move, Men in the Middle

The power of the purse was a formidable weapon. Few men who served as governors in America were excessively wealthy before they took the job. Englishmen who were rich enough to maintain themselves opulently in London did not choose to live in Hartford, Charleston, or Savannah. Most of the royal and proprietary governors were men on the make. To make money in the colonies, they had to get along with powerful colonials, the men who were elected to seats in the assemblies.

Of course, it was possible for a colonial governor to get along too well with influential Americans, to yield too much to them, and thus earn the displeasure of the Crown or proprietor. But during the era of salutary neglect, it came easily for governors to be cooperative. As long as the quitrents flowed back to England, a governor was doing the important part of his job.

Religious Developments

Religious developments also reflected Britain's policy of neglect. Whereas toleration had been the rule in the colonies after the collapse of Puritan power in New England in the 1690s, religious regimentation virtually disappeared during the Walpole era.

Except in Rhode Island and Pennsylvania, every colonial was required to contribute to the support of the legally established church. In some colonies, members of other denominations were not allowed to vote, serve on juries, or exercise other civil rights. For example, Catholics were penalized in Maryland.

But rarely did authorities interfere with worship. In this atmosphere, one of the peculiarities of American society to this day took root: the bewildering multiplicity of religious denominations. By midcentury, it was not uncommon for modest villages to support two or three meetinghouses close enough to one another that the congregations might have harmonized their hymns and psalms. During the 1740s, religions divided along yet finer lines, and another distinctly American institution, the revival, was born.

The Great Awakening

The first American revival, the Great Awakening, broke out almost simultaneously in several colonies. The towering figure of the movement was the Reverend Jonathan Edwards of Northampton, Massachusetts. At the age of 17 he was stunned by an emotional conversion experience, "a direct intuitive apprehension of God in all his glory," and he never forgot it. In 1734, Edwards began to preach sermons emphasizing the sinfulness of humanity, the torment everyone deserved to suffer in hell, and the doctrine of salvation only through the grace of God. "The God who holds you over the pit of hell," Edwards preached in his most famous sermon, "much as one holds a spider or some loathsome insect over the fire, abhors you, and is dreadfully provoked."

This was good Calvinist doctrine. In one sense, Edwards was simply preaching the old-time religion of early Massachusetts. However, whereas the Puritans closely scrutinized the claims of every man and

SINNERS

In the Hands of an

Angry GOD.

A SERMON

Preached at *Enfield*, *July* 8th 1 7 4 1.

At a Time of great Awakenings ; and attended with remarkable Impreſſions on many of the Hearers.

By *Jonathan Edwards*, A.M.

Paſtor of the Church of CHRIST in *Northampton.*

Amos ix. 2, 3. *Though they dig into Hell, thence ſhall mine Hand take them ; though they climb up to Heaven, thence will I bring them down. And though they hide themſelves in the Top of Carmel, I will ſearch and take them out thence ; and though they be hid from my Sight in the Bottom of the Sea, thence I will command the Serpent, and he ſhall bite them.*

B O S T O N : Printed and Sold by S. KNEELAND and T. GREEN. in Queen-Street over againſt the Priſon, 1 7 4 1.

The sermons of Jonathan Edwards helped fuel the Great Awakening.

woman who said they had been saved, Edwards was inclined to admit to the fold everyone who displayed the physical, highly emotional signs of being visited by the Holy Spirit that he himself had known.

Revivals were aimed at stimulating this trauma of salvation. People broke down weeping, fainting, frothing at the mouth, shrieking, and rolling about the floors. Many had to be restrained lest they injure themselves. Edwards himself took care not to inspire false conversions. He studiously refrained from theatrical arm-waving and dancing about. It was said that he stared at the bellpull at the entrance to his church rather than incite ungodly hysteria with dramatics.

Other revivalists had less integrity. Demagogic preachers tore their clothes and rolled their eyes like lunatics, pranced and danced about pulpit or platform, and whooped and hollered. They devised a large bag of psychological tricks to arouse their audiences to a state of high excitement, which became virtually the purpose of revivals and a feature of them to this day.

A Groping for Equality

The Great Awakening affected all social classes, but revivalism appealed most to ordinary people, especially the poorest, least privileged people. And how it appealed to them! Just between 1740 and 1742, when the population of New England was 300,000, 50,000 people joined a church for the first time.

The intense emotion of the revival meeting offered a moment's release from the struggle to survive on the margins of society. The assurance of happiness in the hereafter compensated for deprivation in the here and now. The emphasis on the equality of all men and women before God—there was no "elect" closed to all but a minority —rendered society's disdain for the unsuccessful more bearable.

Equality was the message of the farthest ranging of the Awakening's ministers, English-born George Whitefield. Traveling tirelessly throughout the colonies—he made seven trips to America—Whitefield often preached 60 hours in a week. During one 78-day period, he delivered more than a hundred *lengthy* sermons. His voice was "an excellent piece of music," Benjamin Franklin said. No doubt, but, like Edwards', Whitefield's themes reeked of hell's sulphur.

The teachings of the Great Awakening about salvation were similar to those of Anne Hutchinson a hundred years earlier. The college education of traditional ministers counted for nothing compared to the preacher with the hand of God on him. However, while the civil authority was ready and able to clamp down on Hutchinson, the freer atmosphere of the eighteenth century permitted the revivalist message to burn over the colonies.

Oddly, given the antiintellectual bias of revivalism, the Great Awakening led to the foundation of a number of "New Light" colleges. On the grounds that the established institutions of learning, such as Harvard and Yale, were dominated by "dry husks," the College of New Jersey (Princeton) was founded in 1796—Jonathan Edwards was its third president— and Dartmouth in New Hampshire in 1769. Other

George Whitefield's booming voice, legendary even during his lifetime, enabled him to preach outside to throngs hundreds of times larger than in this portrayal.

new colleges, such as Brown in Rhode Island, King's College (Columbia) in New York, and Queen's College (Rutgers) in New Jersey, were founded by the "Old Lights" to defend against the new preaching, which they regarded as ignorant and a threat to the established order.

Of all the colonial-era colleges and universities, only the University of Pennsylvania, chartered at Benjamin Franklin's urging in 1751, was without a religious affiliation.

Age of Enlightenment

While Americans of modest means were turning to emotional religion, Franklin and much of the educated upper class embraced the worldview of the European Enlightenment, the belief that human reason by itself, without any revelation from the heavens, could unlock the secrets of the universe and guide the improvement, even the perfection, of humanity and society.

The origins of eighteenth-century rationalism lay in the discoveries of the English scientist Sir Isaac Newton, especially those published in his *Principia Mathematica* (1687) and *Opticks* (1704). In these highly technical and difficult books, Newton showed that forces as mysterious as those that determined the paths of the planets and the properties of light and color worked according to laws that could be reduced to mathematical equations.

Although Newton was a physicist and mathematician (and his personal religion was rather mystical), the impact of the rationalism he taught was felt in practically every field of human knowledge and art—the pure sciences, economics, music, politics, and religion.

The order and symmetry that Newton found in the universe were translated into architecture by strict laws of proportion and in literature into inflexible classical rules of style and structure. Baroque music explored the multitudinous variations that could be played on simple combinations of notes.

Rationalist philosophers likened the universe to a clock—intricate, but understandable when dismantled and its parts examined rationally. God, according to Deism, as the rationalists called their religious belief, did not intervene in the world of nature. Rather, like a clockmaker, he had set the natural world in motion according to laws that human beings could discover and understand, whence he retired to allow his creatures to exercise their precious reason. The educated members of the last generation of colonial Americans were to some degree partisans of this rationalism.

THE WARS RESUME

In 1739, Great Britain went to war with Spain. For a year, this conflict was known as the War of Jenkins' Ear because Parliament was said to have been enraged when a shipmaster named Robert Jenkins arrived in London with his ear in a box. It had, Jenkins said, been separated from his head by savage Spanish customs officials.

Georgians, South Carolinians, and Virginians were involved in the earliest fighting, but not out of sympathy for the disfigured Jenkins. As they expanded into the interior, they increasingly clashed with the Spanish. Colonial southerners were the majority of the force that assaulted the African-American fortress of Santa Teresa de Mose in 1740 and, the next year, a disastrous attack on the port of Cartagena in Colombia. Of the 1,500 who set out, only 600 escaped the cutlasses of the Spanish, the incompetence of the British commanders, and the tropical diseases endemic on the Spanish Main.

One survivor was Lawrence Washington, the elder brother of nine-year-old George Washington. Not so bitter as many of his fellows, Lawrence named his estate Mount Vernon, after his commander, Admiral Edward Vernon.

King George's War, 1740–1748

By the time Lawrence returned to Virginia, the great powers of Europe were again on the march. The eight-year conflict that began in 1740 is known in world history as the War of the Austrian Succession. For the colonists once again, it did not matter much who wore the crown of the remote Austrian Empire. They called their theater of the conflict King George's War.

Petite guerre flickered once more on the frontiers of New England, this time extending into New York. But there was no repetition of the Deerfield disaster. Much better prepared than previously, a force of 4,000 men, mostly from Massachusetts, besieged the great French fortress at Louisbourg. On June 17, 1745, the French commander surrendered.

This was a glorious victory. Louisbourg had been considered impregnable, "the Gibraltar of North America." As the base from which French privateers operated, the fortress was a curse looming over New England merchants and fishermen. But the American celebration was short-lived. Under the terms of the Treaty of Aix-la-Chapelle, Louisbourg was returned to the French. The British had lost Madras in India to a French-led army and traded Louisbourg for its return. Once again, imperial interests took precedence over those of the colonies.

Parliament reimbursed Massachusetts for the expense of the campaign, but this did not make up for the 500 men who lost their lives on Cape Breton Island, nor for the fact that French raiders were restored to their sanctuary. The protest was mild. The colonists were loyal British subjects. But the nullification of the greatest military victory that Americans had won to date rankled in many breasts.

Struggle for a Continent

The world war that broke out in 1756 was somewhat different from those that preceded it. There was a diplomatic revolution in Europe, with Austria, previously England's ally, joining forces with France. England then formed an alliance with its old enemy, Prussia. To the colonists, it made no difference who killed whom in the Old World, or which European prince got money from Great Britain to fight. In North America, it was still the English and the colonists versus France and its Indian allies.

For the first time, the Middle Colonies participated in the struggle. (It was during this war that the Quakers turned over the government of Pennsylvania to the pro-war party.) And once again, the colonists had their own name for the conflict. What became known as the Seven Years' War in Europe was called the French and Indian War in America.

This time, Britain would not return North American fortresses for territory on the other side of the globe. From the beginning, the Crown made it clear that a major object of the war was to drive France out of North America for all time.

Despite their usual success at *petite guerre,* the French were in a perilous situation. There were only about 50,000 whites in all of French-claimed territory, compared with 1.2 million in the 13 English colonies plus Nova Scotia. The French still claimed the goodwill of the majority of Indians in the region, but even this advantage was partially nullified by the efficiency and fierceness of the pro-British Iroquois.

For the first time since the long series of wars began, the largest English colony, Virginia, took a serious interest in the fighting. The Virginians were beginning to look beyond the Appalachian Mountains and north of the Ohio River to lands that were dominated by Algonkian Indians. This country was particularly attractive to the wealthy tobacco planters who dominated the Old Dominion because a combination of exhausted soil and a glut in the international tobacco market was undercutting their income. They saw speculation in Ohio Valley real estate as the likeliest means of restoring their fortunes.

Humiliation on the Frontier

With the heart of New France thinly populated, the French had few hopes of settling the Ohio Valley. But the country was of vital interest to French trappers and France's Indian allies. As early as 1753, in order to placate them, the French began to lay out a string of forts in what is now western Pennsylvania.

Robert Dinwiddie, the governor of Virginia, responded by sending 22-year-old George Washington to inform the French that they were trespassing on Virginian soil. Accompanied by 150 men, Washington was also instructed to construct a fort where the Allegheny and Monongahela rivers join to form the Ohio (the site of present-day Pittsburgh).

Washington never got that far. Attacked by the French, he built Fort Necessity, little more than a log palisade, and was handily defeated by the French in an almost bloodless battle. The French seized the conjunction of rivers and built Fort Duquesne. Washington was released, and he returned to Virginia to accept a commission under the command of General Edward Braddock. Again, things went poorly. In 1755, Braddock, an arrogant, stubborn, and unimaginative soldier, was roundly defeated and killed in the Pennsylvania forests.

The rout of Braddock's forces left the American frontier vulnerable to raiding fiercer than any since the destruction of Deerfield. The French were also

winning in Europe and India. For the British, it was a dismal hour.

Germ Warfare and Refugees

For those at the mercy of the British, it was even worse. Both General Braddock and the supreme commander of British forces in North America, Sir Jeffrey Amherst, employed a primitive form of germ warfare against the Indians. They saw to it that blankets used by smallpox victims fell into the natives' hands.

In Nova Scotia, the British feared that the French farmers and fishermen who were the majority in the province would rise in rebellion against the stronghold at Halifax. To forestall such a revolt, they launched a mass deportation. Thousands of Acadians—*Acadie* was the French name for Nova Scotia—were forced aboard ship and dispersed throughout the other English colonies from Massachusetts to Georgia and the West Indies. A few managed to make their way back home overland. Others found a haven in the French territory of Louisiana where their descendants still form a distinct ethnic and cultural group in the state of Louisiana, the Cajuns. (The word is a corruption of *Acadiens.*)

Pitt and Wolfe

When it appeared the French would win the war, perhaps regaining all of Nova Scotia, two men appeared on the scene to change the course of North American history. William Pitt became prime minister of Great Britain in 1757, and he selected the young General James Wolfe to join Sir Jeffrey Amherst's army in North America. Pitt turned the war around by generously paying Prussia to fight the French and Austrians in Europe, while he concentrated British power across the Atlantic. Wolfe engineered one of the most daring attacks on a city in military history.

A nervous, frail-looking young man, brittle in his intensity, Wolfe looked at French Canada as a woodsman eyed a tree. He saw Quebec City was the root structure that supported the whole. The St. Lawrence, Ohio, and Mississippi rivers were but trunks and branches. It was all very well to snip and hack at leaves here and there, as Wolfe pictured *petite guerre* and even the capture of Louisbourg. The secret to a total victory over French Canada was to strike at the source of its life.

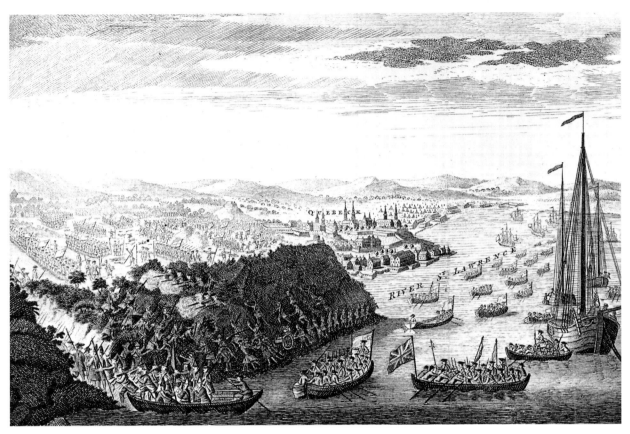

William Pitt, the British prime minister, assigned General James Wolfe the task of capturing the French city of Quebec. Wolfe launched a bold surprise attack, and his troops captured the city.

The theory was easier than its practical application. Quebec stood atop a steep, rocky cliff. On September 12, 1759, after leading several futile frontal attacks on this natural fortress (which lulled the French commander, Louis de Montcalm, into overconfidence), Wolfe quietly led 4,000 troops up a steep, narrow trail under cover of night. When the sun rose over the Plains of Abraham, a broad prairie on the undefended landward side of Quebec, Montcalm saw a scarlet-coated army in full battle formation.

The Glorious Victory

Wolfe's gambit was risky. He had no avenue of retreat. If the battle did not end in total triumph (and few military victories were total in the eighteenth century), Wolfe's whole army would have been in danger of capture. Luckily, Louis de Montcalm was

so unnerved by Wolfe's daring that, despite his superior position and artillery, he joined battle with little preparation. After a single close-range exchange of musket fire, Montcalm lost his life and with it the French empire in America. Wolfe did not live to savor his triumph. He too died on the battlefield, only 32 years of age.

The war in Europe dragged on until 1763, but as far as the colonists were concerned, it was over at Quebec. In the Peace of Paris, the British redrew the map of North America. Great Britain took Florida from Spain as well as Canada from France. In order to compensate Spain for the loss of Florida, France handed over Louisiana (the central third of what is now the United States) to the Spanish.

The year 1763 saw the first British Empire in full bloom. Britain had elected to find its future outside the European continent and had succeeded on every front. Or so it seemed.

CHRONOLOGY

1689–1697	King William's War (War of the League of Augsburg)
1700s	Substantial immigration of German pietists and Scotch-Irish
1702–1713	Queen Anne's War (War of the Spanish Succession)
1704	Deerfield Massacre
1733	Molasses Act
1734	Jonathan Edwards begins revivalist preaching in Massachusetts
1739	Stono Rebellion of slaves in South Carolina
1740–1748	King George's War (War of the Austrian Succession)
1741	Thirty-one blacks and four whites hanged in New York for plotting rebellion
1754	Albany Plan of Union proposed
1754–1763	French and Indian War (Seven Years' War)
1759	James Wolfe's capture of Quebec signals Britain's triumph over France in New World

FOR FURTHER READING

Basic works on relations with the mother country include Daniel Boorstin, *The Americans: The Colonial Experience*, 1958; Ian R. Christie, *Crisis of Empire*, 1966; Richard Hofstadter, *America in 1750*, 1971; Leonard W. Labaree, *Royal Government in America*, 1930; James Henretta, *Salutary Neglect*, 1972; and Stephen Webb, *The Governors-General*, 1979. Absolutely essential is Bernard Bailyn, *The Origins of American Politics*, 1968. Also consult the early pages of John C. Miller, *Origins of the American Revolution*, 1957, and Edmund S. Morgan, *The Birth of the Republic*, 1956.

On the Anglo-French wars, the great Francis Parkman is again a classic historian of the first order in his *A Half Century of Conflict*, 1892, and *Montcalm and Wolfe*, 1884. Then move on to Howard H. Peckham, *The Colonial Wars, 1689–1762*, 1964; Douglas E. Leach, *Arms for Empire: A Military History of the British Colonies in North America*, 1973; and Fred Anderson, *A People's Army: Massachusetts Soldiers and Society in the Seven Years' War*, 1984. On the Indian role in the conflicts, see Francis Jennings, *Empire of Fortune*, 1990, and *The Ambiguous Iroquois Empire*, 1984; James Merrell, *Beyond the Covenant Chain: The Iroquois and Their Neighbors*, 1987; and Howard H. Peckham, *Pontiac and the Indian Uprising*, 1947.

On cultural developments, see Louis B. Wright, *The Cultural Life of the American Colonies*, 1957; Alan Heimert and Perry Miller, eds., *The Great Awakening*, 1967; Perry Miller, *Jonathan Edwards*, 1958; Henry F. May, *The Enlightenment in America*, 1976; Benjamin Franklin's autobiography, various editions; and Esmond Wright, *Franklin of Philadelphia*, 1986. Two important recent studies are Richard D. Brown, *Knowledge Is Power: The Diffusion of Information in Early America*, 1991; and Frank Lambert, *"Pedlars in Divinity": George Whitefield and the Transatlantic Revivals*, 1994.

Colonial social history has been a field of busy endeavor in recent years. Much of this work is to be found in scholarly journals, but see James Axtell, *The School upon a Hill*, 1974; James T. Lemon, *The Best Poor Man's Country*, 1972; James G. Leyburn, *The Scotch-Irish*, 1962; Robert W. Wells, *The Population of the British Colonies in America before 1776*, 1975; and Richard L. Bushman, *The Refinement of America: Persons, Houses, Cities*, 1992.

An official entrusted with selling stamped paper is tortured in effigy. Some fared worse.

7
CHAPTER

YEARS OF TUMULT

The Quarrel with Great Britain

1763–1770

Westward the course of empire takes its way;
The first four acts already past,
A fifth shall close the drama with the day:
Time's noblest offspring is the last.

— *George Berkeley*

My lord, I don't know whether the neighbourhood of the French to our North American colonies was not the greatest security for their dependence on the mother country, which I feel will be slighted by them when the apprehension of the French is removed.

—*The Duke of Bedford*

An idea, strange as it is visionary, has entered into the minds of the generality of mankind, that empire is traveling westward; and every one is looking forward with eager and impatient expectation to that destined moment, when America is to give law to the rest of the world. But if ever an idea was illusory and fallacious, I will venture to predict, that this will be so.

—*Andrew Burnaby*

In 1763, church bells pealed throughout the colonies to celebrate Britain's triumph in the Seven Years' War. In 1776, a scant 13 years later, the 13 colonies declared their independence and took up arms against the mother country. Contemplating this remarkable turn of events, Oliver Wolcott of Connecticut wondered what had gone wrong. "So strong had been the Attachment" of Americans to Great Britain in 1763, he wrote, that "the Abilities of a Child might have governed this Country."

Wolcott blamed the breakup on British folly, incompetence, and tyranny. He had a point about folly and incompetence. Blunder after stupidity atop miscalculation told the story of British colonial policy between 1763 and 1776. But it would be a mistake, given the education in tyranny that the twentieth century has provided us, to take seriously Wolcott's third explanation of the American Revolution. Far from oppressed by tyrants, colonial Americans may have been the world's freest people between 1763 and 1776.

What transformed contented men like Wolcott into rebels was a change in British colonial administration from the salutary neglect of the Walpole era to an attempt—a botched attempt—at imperial control. What made it possible for colonials to translate their worry into anger and rebellion was the self-confidence born of the colonies' extraordinary growth during the eighteenth century.

THE PROBLEMS OF EMPIRE

General Wolfe's capture of Quebec put Canada into British hands. However, before the peace negotiators sat down in Paris, there was some question as to whether or not Britain would keep Wolfe's gift. Some influential men proposed that, like Port Royal and Louisbourg after earlier wars, Quebec and Canada be returned to France. Instead, Britain would take as the fruits of her victory the French West Indian islands of Martinique and Guadeloupe.

One Side of the Story

A land of endless forests was not so grand an imperial prize, the argument went. The Indians of Canada and the trans-Appalachian West—former French allies—were numerous, powerful, and hostile to the British. As for the *habitants* along the St. Lawrence River, what could they be except trouble? Britain had recently deported Frenchmen and women from Nova Scotia for fear of rebellion. What sense did it make, just a few years after that scare, to take 50,000 French Canadians into the empire?

Sugar-producing islands, by way of contrast, could be managed by small military garrisons. The handful of French planters that dominated Guadeloupe and Martinique cared less about the color of the flag that flew over their harbors than about the price for which they sold their crop. And that crop could be sold at a profit throughout the world.

There was yet another consideration. By 1763, the 13 Atlantic colonies constituted a substantial country in themselves. Was it not possible that the colonials had remained loyal Britons only out of fear of French and Indian attack? Remove that threat from their backyard, as the acquisition of Canada would do, and the Americans would no longer need British naval and military protection, nor be grateful for it. They might unite, in the words of a Swedish observer, Peter Kalm, and "shake off the yoke of the English monarchy."

All That Red on the Map!

These arguments did not carry the day. British property owners were weary of war. They had paid monstrously large taxes to fight it. And if Canada remained French, another North American conflict was inevitable. Influential colonials like Governor William Shirley of Massachusetts and the ubiquitous Ben Franklin, who was then in England as an agent of Pennsylvania, spoke lyrically of the potential of the vast Canadian landmass.

Such lobbyists found allies in the sugar planters of the British West Indies. This small but influential group of men feared that raising the Union Jack over Martinique and Guadeloupe would glut the imperial sugar market, driving down the price of their commodity. British sugar planters also relished the idea of adding 50,000 sweet-toothed French Canadians, formerly served by the French West Indies, to the list of customers reserved to them by mercantilist laws.

And, in the end, few influential Britons seriously doubted the loyalty of the Americans. In 1763, it was difficult for them to imagine that anyone who had a choice in the matter would choose to be anything but British.

Les Canadiens

The French Canadians could imagine otherwise. For one thing, they were Roman Catholics, pious communicants of a faith that was disliked and discriminated against in eighteenth-century Britain. Catholics were generally unmolested in the 13 colonies. But there was a big difference between tolerating a small, quiet, and largely genteel Roman Catholic minority in Maryland or New York, and coming to terms with a sprawling province in which almost everyone, Indians included, was a Catholic. To Protestants, particularly the descendants of the Puritans who were Quebec's closest neighbors, Catholicism meant superstition, blasphemy, and oppression.

Nor was the precedent of Englishmen governing foreigners encouraging. For two centuries, Catholic Ireland had been an English province. Avaricious conquerors (including several men who had been interested in American land) had been guilty of unspeakable atrocities in creating their estates and reducing the Irish to submission and poverty. Their descendants, the Anglo-Irish gentry, looked on the Irish as lazy, superstitious, and barbaric, not to mention prone to intermittent rebellion.

As in Ireland, however, the British held the military trump card in Canada. Moreover, the Quebecois had no experience with representative government, and no inclination to bombard the Crown with protests and supplications such as the assemblies of the 13 colonies did. The Estates General, once the French equivalent of Parliament, had not met since 1614, 150 years earlier. At home, the Bourbon king was an absolute monarch and his governors in New France, always military men, had commanded Canada as if the colony were a regiment. To the *habitants*, taking orders from officers in red uniforms was not much different in day-to-day terms from command by Frenchmen in blue and buff. Their country had been defeated in war and they knew it. The British could hope for a breathing spell as they searched for a formula by which to govern the new province.

Pontiac's Conspiracy

The Indians who were allied to the French presented a more urgent problem. Unlike the French army, the warriors of the Ohio River basin had not been decisively defeated in battle; they had difficulty believing that their French friends were finished. The Treaty of Paris might proclaim them subjects of King George III. In reality, they were securely in possession of the forests west of the Appalachians. Almost immediately, the British blundered in dealing with them.

General Sir Jeffrey Amherst, entrusted with this task, looked on Indians as "wretched people" whose proper condition was subjection. As soon as the Treaty of Paris was on the books, he informed the western tribes that they would no longer regularly receive the "gifts" of European goods they were accustomed to getting from the French: blankets, iron and brass tools and vessels, firearms, and liquor.

In retaliation, a resourceful Ottawa chieftain named Pontiac attacked the British fort at Detroit and was soon joined on a thousand-mile front by 18 tribes. Detroit and Fort Pitt (Pittsburgh) held off Pontiac's forces, but the other ten western forts were overrun and 2,000 people were killed in Virginia and Pennsylvania — more than were lost in any battle of the French and Indian War. British regulars and some colonial forces regrouped and defeated Pontiac at Bushy Run near Pittsburgh. But they had only stung the Indians, not destroyed their power.

The Proclamation of 1763

Amherst restored the gift-giving and informed the Crown of the problem. In October 1763, in order to let tempers cool, an imaginary line was drawn on the Appalachian divide, between the sources of the rivers that emptied into the Atlantic and those that flowed into the Ohio–Mississippi River system. The Crown proclaimed, "We do strictly forbid, on pain of our displeasure, all our loving subjects from making any purchases or settlements whatever" west of the line. A few plucky frontiersmen who had already pushed into the closed zone were forced to return east, and there was a freeze on land sales in the trans-Appalachian region.

No one considered the Proclamation Line as anything more than what one land speculator, George Washington, called "a temporary expedient to quiet the minds of the Indians." Too many Virginia planters and influential British politicos dreamed of riches from Ohio valley real estate to consider the freeze permanent. Indeed, two newly appointed superintendents of Indian affairs immediately began to purchase territory from the western tribes. The southern part of the line was redrawn within a few months, and, regularly over the

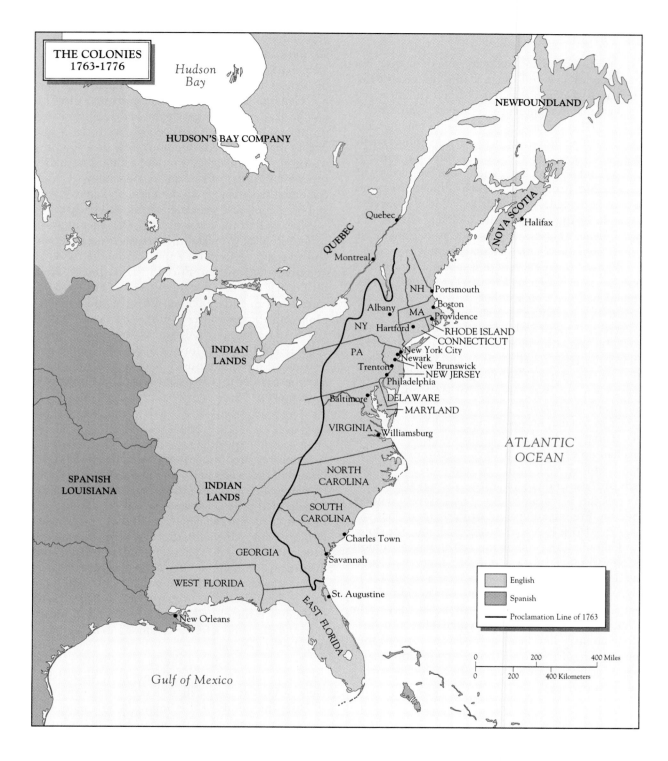

next decade, trans-Appalachian lands were opened to speculation and settlement.

But Americans were already an impatient people, and the West was the place to which many looked for their fortunes. By interfering even temporarily with expansion, the British touched a tender nerve. Protest was quiet. Few colonials were so foolish as to belittle the power of the Indians after the devastation wreaked by Pontiac's warriors. Later, however, Americans would remember the Proclamation of 1763 as an early example of King George III's campaign to throttle their "liberties."

The Redcoats

In the wake of Pontiac's rebellion, General Amherst asked Parliament for a permanent American garrison of 5,000 to 6,000 troops. The soldiers would be stationed in Canada and in a dozen frontier forts along the Great Lakes and the Ohio River. Parliament responded by voting Amherst 10,000 soldiers, thereby sending more than twice as many troops to North America as had been stationed there during the years of the French menace.

A few years later, when many of these soldiers were billeted in coastal cities in order to police riotous colonial crowds, they became the "hated redcoats" and the "lobsters." When the force first began to arrive, however, the Americans' biggest concern was the expense of maintaining them—£200,000 a year. The Quartering Act of 1765 charged the cost of the troops' shelter, food, and drink to the colony in which they were posted. Indeed, one of Parliament's motives in doubling Amherst's request was to pension off the veterans of the French and Indian War at colonial expense. The men had some reward coming to them, and the English have never liked to keep large standing armies at home during peacetime. Unhappily, Parliament ignored the fact that Britain's loyal colonial subjects had also inherited this tradition. Another point of friction had, imperceptibly, been created.

Reorganizing the Empire

The flurry of activity in the wake of the war was a signal that the men who governed Great Britain were taking a new, keener interest in colonial affairs. Some sort of change was sorely needed. Counting Canada, the West Indies, and British Honduras, 20 colonies in the Western Hemisphere now flew the British flag. If each were to go merrily its own way, pretty much governing itself, as the 13 "ancient provinces" of North America were accustomed to doing, the result would be chaos.

During and immediately after the French and Indian War, "the king in Parliament" methodically scrapped the policy of salutary neglect and tried to create in its stead a centrally administered empire.

Money

Before the war, Parliament was content that the colonies were profitable to British land speculators, manufacturers, and merchants. Prewar governments had not been overly concerned that the administration of the colonies was a net cost to the Exchequer. Until the French and Indian War, governing the colonies had cost, on average, £70,000 a year, while colonial trade annually pumped as much as £2 million into British counting houses and manorial treasuries.

By 1764, however, the cost of colonial government had risen to £350,000 a year and Parliament was in serious financial difficulties. Prime Minister William Pitt had laid heavy taxes on the British in order to win the war. And he had borrowed wherever and whatever he could. A national debt of £130 million had England teetering on the edge of bankruptcy.

Cost cutting was a possibility. The British government was shot through with graft and top-heavy with officials who lived off public funds without doing anything in particular. But these were the very people whose job it was to solve the financial problem. They were no more inclined to economize at their own expense than university officials are inclined to cut their expenditures and pensions in the interest of the institution. Parliament preferred to look for more money with which to pay the bills.

More taxes at home were out of the question. Each year, British landowners paid 20 percent of their income into the Exchequer, a crushing burden in an agricultural society. Other taxes were also high. When Parliament tried to increase a small tax on cider, the daily drink of southwestern England, there were riots.

The Villain Grenville

The task of finding revenue fell to George Grenville, who became prime minister in 1763. Grenville was a talented individual and an expert on fiscal matters. If the reforms he introduced had succeeded, history might well record him as a major architect of the British Empire. Instead, he is a passing figure in the British history books and, in American tradition, a villain.

HOW THEY LIVED

At Home among the Iroquois

In the middle of the eighteenth century, the Iroquois Confederacy, consisting of the Cayuga, Seneca, Onondaga, Oneida, and Mohawk tribes, numbered about 15,000 people and securely controlled most of what is now New York State and much of western Pennsylvania. Iroquois hunters and war parties ranged even farther, covering a million square miles, as far west as the Mississippi River and as far north as Hudson Bay.

The hunters and warriors were men, of course. Men also traveled to carry out the intricate and constant diplomatic negotiations that the confederacy depended on for its stability and to deal with non-Iroquois peoples, including the English and French. "It is not an exaggeration," Anthony F. C. Wallace wrote in the standard history of the Senecas, "to say that the full-time business of an Iroquois man was travel."

Because Iroquois men were so often gone, Iroquois women played a peculiarly important, even central role in Iroquois culture, society and governance. They stayed home in more or less fixed towns. They raised the corn that was the staple of the Iroquois diet. They cared for the children in the secure village, instilling Iroquois values into them, including, for Iroquois boys, a masculine ideal of imperviousness to hardship and pain. They kept the long-houses in repair and maintained order in the towns, governing by social pressure—reputation was extremely important to the Iroquois—rather than by force. Finally, with their husbands absent so much of the time, the women effectively decided whose children they would bear. Descent, therefore, was traced through the maternal line.

A typical Iroquois town consisted of about 12 to 40 longhouses in each of which dwelt 50 or 60 members of a clan. The clan (whose animal symbol was carved above the door of the longhouse and painted red) included its eldest female member, who was head of the house, and her sisters, daughters, granddaughters, immature male children, and sons-in-law. Because of a strict incest taboo, an Iroquois male left the clan into which he had been born and became a member of his wife's clan. Indeed, because marital relationships were fragile and transitory, an Iroquois man might drift from clan to clan throughout his life, making his bed where a woman would have him. At any given time, he was obligated to defend the honor of his wife's clan. For example, if a member of her clan was killed and the matriarch insisted that revenge be taken, a warrior was required to do so, even if it was against the clan into which he had been born.

In addition to the authority to declare war between clans (which was not frequent and was gov-

---

Among his abilities, Grenville brought a fatal limitation to his task. Like too many English politicians of the era, he knew little about Americans and did not see a good reason for learning more. He had a vision of worldwide British power, but he contemplated it through the half-closed eyes of the complacent upper class. To Grenville, Americans were half-civilized louts whose opinions were not worthy of consideration. He would have smiled at Samuel Johnson's famous quip, "I am willing to love all mankind, except an American."

Grenville knew that Americans paid few taxes. Using somewhat distorted figures, he calculated that the average English taxpayer paid an annual tax of 26 shillings, while a British subject living in Massachusetts paid one shilling a year and the average Virginian only five pence (less than half a shilling). And yet, the colonials had gained the most from the French and Indian War, the cause of the debt that loomed over England. Colonials should, therefore, Grenville concluded, do their part to pay off that debt and, in the future, shoulder the expenses of running their colonies.

Few Americans openly denied that they had an obligation to do more than they did in the past. Unfortunately, even if the 13 assemblies had been willing to vote Grenville enough money to satisfy him, they did not get the chance to do so. Instead of requesting grants of funds, as Walpole and Pitt had

erned by a complex set of rules), the elder women of the Iroquois selected each of the 49 delegates of the confederacy when death created a vacancy. They also participated, albeit more quietly than the orating men, in community decision making.

The system worked quite well. Iroquois lands remained secure because the mobile men were such effective warriors and home life was placid and orderly. A Quaker wrote that the Senecas

> appear to be naturally as well calculated for social and rational enjoyment, as any people. They frequently visit each other in their houses, and spend much of their time in friendly intercourse. They are also mild and hospitable, not only among themselves, but to strangers, and good-natured in the extreme, except when their natures are perverted by the inflammatory influence of spirituous liquors.

Alcohol was a serious problem. A good sale of pelts and hides to the whites inevitably led to the purchase of rum and wholesale drunkenness among men, women, and children. Although this was the most tragic element introduced into Iroquois life by the arrival of whites, it was not the only one. Contact with Europeans, into its fifth generation by the middle of the eighteenth century, also meant guns and metal tools ranging from scissors, knives, awls, kettles, and other household goods, to hatchets and axes. The latter influenced Iroquois building methods: by the mid-1700s longhouses were made less often in the traditional way—sheets of elm bark lashed to bent saplings—and increasingly of logs.

Another interesting consequence of the mixing of cultures was the increased tendency of Iroquois to abandon living by clan in the longhouses and to cluster in single-family log cabins. The white presence probably made for a more intensive agriculture by the end of the colonial era. Not only was game scarcer because of overtrapping, but European tools made it possible for the Seneca alone to produce as many as a million bushels of corn a year by 1750. During the American Revolution, a patriot general destroyed 60,000 bushels in one pro-British Iroquois village. It is difficult to imagine such a crop resulting from traditional slash-and-burn cultivation.

The appearance of the Iroquois also changed. European calico shirts, linen breechcloths, and woolen blankets characterized the Indians whom the Americans of the eighteenth century knew. Nevertheless, the Iroquois continued to shun Christian missionaries, and they "made obscene gestures" when anyone suggested that the white settlers' way of life was superior to their own.

done, Grenville treated the financial crisis as part and parcel of his administrative reforms.

The Sugar Act of 1764

Grenville's first move was to overhaul the ineffective Molasses Act of 1733. Its sixpence-per-gallon tax on molasses imported into the colonies from non-British sources was so high that American merchants felt morally justified in ignoring it. Instead of paying the duty, they paid bribes of a penny or so per gallon to customs collectors. If they were arrested as smugglers, they could count on juries of their neighbors to acquit them regardless of the evidence—and then join them at the nearest inn for a dram of rum, the principal product made from molasses.

Grenville's Sugar Act of 1764 struck at both the revenue problem and the problem of enforcing import duties. It enlarged the customs service and transferred the task of enforcing the import tax from local courts to a new system of vice-admiralty courts that would try violators without juries. Grenville also cut the molasses duty to threepence per gallon. He calculated that dealers would pay the lower rate rather than run the risk of conviction in courts they could not control. Also in 1764, Grenville levied duties on imported wines, silks, tropical foods, and other luxury goods.

George Grenville (1712–1770) was an estimable figure in British politics and government. Unfortunately, his plans for the empire took colonial sensibilities into little consideration.

The First Protest

In New England, where molasses was a major item of trade, protest was loud and fierce. The Boston town meeting declared that the city would import no British goods of any kind until Parliament repealed the obnoxious tax. Other cities, including New York, followed suit. Even "the young Gentlemen of Yale College" announced that they would not "make use of any foreign spirituous liquors" until Grenville backed down from his importunity. This painful sacrifice was eased by the fact that limitless quantities of domestic beer, cider, and fiery New England rum were still available for their academic revels.

Grenville was unmoved by the hubbub. He assumed that the Americans simply did not want to pay any taxes, that they wanted to enjoy the benefits of being a part of the British Empire at no cost. No doubt he was the better part of correct. Importers of molasses, sippers of Madeira, and wearers of silk wanted the best bargains they could get. To this extent, the Sugar Act protest was sheer self-interest.

The Rights of British Subjects

Nonetheless, there were two worthy principles at stake, and a colonial frame of mind was evolving in which a worthy principle was sacred.

As a tax designed to keep French molasses out of the empire, the Molasses Act of 1733 had regulated trade. According to colonists like Daniel Dulany of Maryland, who wrote a widely distributed pamphlet about the Sugar Act, this was perfectly legitimate. Parliament had the right to regulate trade for the good of the empire. But the Sugar Act of 1764 was not designed to keep foreign molasses out of the empire. Indeed, so far as Grenville was concerned, the more foreign molasses the colonies imported legally, the better. His goal was to raise money. The official title of the Sugar Act was the American Revenue Act.

It was Grenville's announced goal—revenue—that raised the ticklish constitutional question. It was a "sacred right" of British subjects that they consented to the taxes levied on them. To Whigs, members of one of the two great political factions in Great Britain, the very meaning of their history was the struggle against the monarchy to win such rights. By 1764, Parliament had almost total control of money matters in Great Britain. However, Americans were not represented in Parliament. They had their own "little parliaments," their elected assemblies. According to the Sugar Act protesters, only these bodies could tax them. This arrangement had, in fact, been the unofficial custom for 150 years.

Many Americans interested in political matters were "Whiggish" in temper. Like the British Whigs, they believed that constant vigilance was necessary to protect the liberties that had been so hard-won. The merest hint of an attempt to curtail those liberties in a law such as the Sugar Act, and colonial Whigs were inclined to panic.

Trial by Jury

Just as important was the right of a British subject to be tried for a crime before a jury of his peers, or social equals. This right, dating back to the Magna Carta of 1215, British and colonial Whigs believed, set them apart from (and made them superior to) the French, Spanish, Poles, Chinese, Hottentots, and what have you of the world. By denying colonials this ancient right, as the vice-admiralty courts did,

But Grenville did not stop with the Sugar Act. In 1765, he announced a new bill to raise money in America by means of a tax that could not easily be ducked because those who did not pay it suffered immediately from the act of noncompliance.

THE STAMP ACT CRISIS

The English people had been paying a stamp tax since 1694. In order to be legal, documents such as wills, bills of sale, various licenses, deeds, insurance policies, and other contracts had to be inscribed on paper that was embossed with a government stamp. Purchase of the paper, therefore, constituted payment of a tax. Evasion was not feasible. A marriage certificate that was not inscribed on the stamped paper was not legitimate. A contract written on ordinary paper was not enforceable.

The Stamp Act of 1765

Grenville's Stamp Act of 1765 went somewhat further than the English law. It required that in addition to colonial legal documents, all newspapers, pamphlets, handbills, and even playing cards were to be printed on the embossed government paper. The

Tempers flash and canes and swords are brandished at a town meeting. The behavior could be mocked, but the right to participate actively in government was one New Englanders valued and meant to keep.

George Grenville was tampering with the essence of British liberties.

It is impossible to say what would have happened if Grenville's program had ended with the Sugar Act. The Americans were noisy, and some of their language was inflammatory. But there was no violence. The Sugar Act protest began and ended with an annoying but perfectly legal boycott of imports. To the extent that colonial resentment of the act was a matter of greed, the protest might well have died out. The duties of 1764 seriously affected only wealthy consumers and a small number of shippers and distillers. When, in 1766, the molasses duty was reduced to a penny (the level of the traditional bribe), protest ceased although "the principle of the thing" remained quite intact.

> ### *Stamps*
>
> What we call a stamp is, by eighteenth-century standards, a misnomer. The adhesive-backed evidence that postage has been paid on a letter was invented only in 1834 (the perforations in 1854) and, when it was, the speakers of no other European language chose "stamp" to name the ingenious device. To them, and to colonial Americans, a stamp was something impressed *on* or stamped *into* paper, not something attached to it. Eighteenth-century stamping was what we would call embossing.
>
> Thus, the stamp that caused all the excitement in 1765 was an embossment, pressed into the paper to be used for licenses, newspapers, and so on by a press. Few Americans ever saw the Stamp Act stamps. Save for a little in Georgia, none of the embossed paper was ever sold.

cost varied from a halfpenny on a handbill to £1 for a liquor license, quite a sum in both cases.

Enforcement of the law was entrusted to the unpopular vice-admiralty courts. However, Grenville tried to gain colonial favor by providing that all money raised under the Stamp Act would be used solely in "defending, protecting, and securing the colonies." Not a farthing would go back to England to retire the debt or for any other purpose.

American sensibilities were not soothed. On the contrary, the stipulation that revenues from the Stamp Act were to be raised and spent entirely within the colonies led a Quaker grandee of Pennsylvania and Delaware, John Dickinson, to devise a detailed constitutional distinction between legitimate external taxes, duties on trade between the colonies and other places, and unacceptable internal taxes, duties collected within the colonies.

The Stamp Act was plainly internal, Dickinson said, a direct tax on the people by a body in which they were not represented, Parliament. Clearly, only a colonial assembly could enact such a tax within its boundaries. (Massachusetts had, in fact, experimented with a stamp act in 1755.)

Grenville had no ear for Dickinson's argument. In his administrative scheme, Parliament was the supreme governing authority for the entire empire. Most members of Parliament agreed with him. A dull

Various stamps (embossments on paper) such as those shown above led to rioting throughout the colonies in 1765.

debate addressed few of the issues that were to explode in the colonies and the House of Commons voted 204 to 49 to enact the tax. Many prominent Americans also failed to see a problem in the Stamp Act. Richard Henry Lee of Virginia, who would introduce the independence resolution in 1776, applied for a job as a stamp tax collector in 1765.

A Stupid Law

Constitutional niceties aside, the Stamp Act was politically stupid. Its burden fell most heavily on just those people who were best able to stir up a fuss. Newspaper editors, with their influence on public opinion, were hard hit. Advertisements, a newspaper's bread and butter, were taxed two shillings, and every edition had to be printed on stamped paper. Printers, who profited by putting out broadsides (posters used for announcing goods for sale and public meetings—including protest meetings!), saw their business taxed at every turn of the press.

Lawyers, then as now the single largest group in colonial public office, and persuaders by profession, had to pay a tax on every document with which they dealt. Tavern keepers, saddled with more expensive licenses by the new law, were key figures in every town and neighborhood. Their inns and ordinaries were the gathering places where, over rum, brandy, coffee, or tea, locals read newspapers and discussed affairs.

What was worse for Grenville, most of these groups were concentrated in cities, where they could easily meet with one another, cooperate, and have an impact out of proportion to their numbers. It was one thing to upset such groups one at a time, as the Sugar Act had riled shippers and distillers without significantly injuring anyone else. The Stamp Act hit all of these key elements of the colonial population. Possibly to everyone's surprise, they won the support of large numbers of ordinary working people.

Riot

Parliament approved the Stamp Act in February 1765. It was scheduled to go into effect in November. As soon as the news reached the colonies, however, they erupted in anger. Local organizations called Sons of Liberty (a phrase used to describe Americans by one of their Whiggish parliamentary friends, Isaac Barré) condemned the law and called for a boycott of British goods.

Some of the Sons took violent action. When the stamped paper was delivered to warehouses in port cities, mobs broke in and lit bonfires. Men who accepted jobs as stamp masters were shunned, hanged in effigy, or roughed up. A popular if brutal method of punishing tax collectors was to daub them, sometimes naked, with hot tar, roll them in chicken feathers, and carry them, straddling a fence rail, about town.

One official in Maryland was forced to flee for his life to New York. That was a mistake, because the New York Sons of Liberty were the most militant of all. They located the Marylander and forced him to write a letter of resignation. Led by Isaac Sears, the captain of a merchant vessel, the New Yorkers frightened their own lieutenant governor (another future revolutionary named Cadwallader Colden) so that he went into hiding. When they could not find Colden, they burned his carriages. In Boston, the crowd looted and burned the homes of several officials of the Crown.

Rowdies are seldom popular, but the Stamp Act rioters were. When one governor was asked why he did not call out the militia to restore order, he pointed out that it would mean putting pikes and

The Funny "S"

In documents of the Revolutionary era, including early printings of the Declaration of Independence, the letter *s* is often written ∫. It is not an *f*; note that the character has only half a crossbar, if that; and it is pronounced with a hiss as surely as the esses in sassy.

The "funny" ∫ originated in German handwriting and was adopted by printers in the old German printed alphabet known as Gothic. Its use was reinforced in England because the movable type used by early English printers was imported from Germany, the home of printing.

Use of ∫ was governed by strict rules. It was a lowercase letter, never a capital at the beginning of a proper noun or sentence; the familiar *S* served that purpose then as now. The ∫ appeared only at the beginning or in the middle of a word, never at the end. Thus, *business* was *bu∫ine∫s* and *sassiness* was *∫a∫∫ine∫s*. The use of this form of *s* died out in the United States during the early nineteenth century.

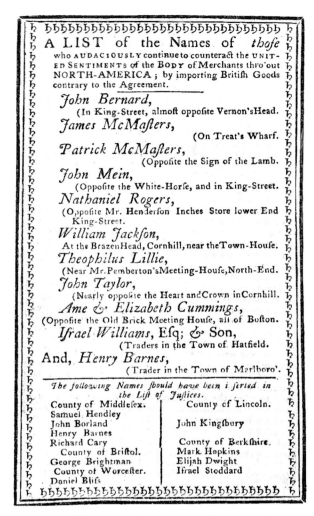

A 1770 broadside encouraging a boycott of merchants importing British goods.

muskets into the hands of the very people who were wreaking havoc. The British had expected protests. Isaac Barré had warned of resistance. But everyone was caught short by what seemed to be the whole American people on a rampage.

The Stamp Act Congress

Among those surprised were prominent and wealthy colonials who hated the Stamp Act but shuddered at the sound of shouts in the streets. Mobs are beasts that take on a life of their own, moving easily from one target to another and the colonial crowd had as many grievances against its social betters in the colonies as against Parliament. In October 1765, in an attempt to channel and control the protest, 37

delegates from nine colonies assembled in New York City, in the Stamp Act Congress.

Although the Congress was the brainchild of one of the most volatile agitators, James Otis of Massachusetts, the 14 resolutions and the "Declaration of Rights and Grievances" the delegates adopted were largely the work of conservative men like John Dickinson. The Stamp Act Congress criticized the Stamp Act, Sugar Act, and other parliamentary policies while the delegates prominently and tactfully made it clear they acknowledged "all due subordination" to the Crown.

THE BRITISH CONSTITUTION

What did "all due subordination" mean? Loyalty to the king? Unquestionably. Just about everyone in eighteenth-century Britain and the colonies agreed on the importance of the monarch as the symbol which unified the British people wherever they dwelled. *Lèse-majesté* — "injuring the king" — was the gravest of political crimes, punishable by hanging, often followed by disembowelment and quartering—harnessing four horses to each of the traitor's limbs and cracking the whip.

On other rather basic questions of governance, however, Britons and colonials disagreed. Fundamental disagreement was possible because, while the British constitution included a few hallowed written documents, like the Magna Carta of 1215 and the Bill of Rights of 1689, it was largely unwritten. Most of the principles and practices of British government had evolved over the centuries through tradition, actual usage, and acceptance over time.

What Is Representation? The Colonial Case

Colonial protesters said that Parliament had no right to tax them because they were not represented in Parliament; colonials did not vote for members of the British Parliament. Their own assemblies, which they elected, were their little parliaments. They alone were empowered to tax them.

The colonial case is easy for us to understand for it is the governing principle of representation in the United States today. In order for an individual to be represented in government, he or she must be entitled to vote for a city council member, county supervisor, state legislator, representative, or senator. The senators from Kentucky are not considered representatives of Iowa farmers. Only those senators for whom those farmers voted do so. Reforms of voting laws throughout United States history—extending the vote to people who did not own property, to blacks, and to women—have been based on this concept of representation: one must be able to vote in order to be represented.

James Otis spoke for this way of thinking at the Stamp Act Congress of 1765 when he suggested that Parliament end the dispute by allowing the colonists to elect members of Parliament. His proposal was not popular. Indeed, Otis's colleagues of the Stamp Act Congress virtually ignored him. They did not want to send representatives to Parliament. They wanted Parliament to recognize the authority of their own assemblies over them, at least in matters of taxation.

Grenville might well have confounded the colonial protest by acting favorably on the Otis proposal, because colonial members of Parliament would be too few to affect policy. He did not do so because he and other members of Parliament, including many who were sympathetic to the colonials, believed that the Americans were already represented in Parliament.

Virtual Representation: The British Case

By the lights of the eighteenth century, they were correct. The British concept of representation differed (and differs) from our own. For example, it was (and is) not necessary that a member of the British Parliament reside in the electoral district that sends him or her to the House of Commons. While it is unlikely to happen in our own time, a member of Parliament may never set foot in the district from which he or she is elected. Districts are for the sake of convenience in balloting, but each member of Parliament is regarded as virtually representing the entire nation. As Edmund Burke, a friend of the Americans, put it to his own constituents in the city of Bristol during the dispute with the colonies, "You choose a member . . . but when you have chosen him, he is not a member of Bristol, but he is a member of Parliament."

The colonials practiced virtual representation in their own elections. Washington and other Virginians were elected to the House of Burgesses from counties in which they did not reside. Often, would-be burgesses stood for seats in more than one county

at a time so that they were covered in the event they were defeated in one election. Few objected to this practice. It was assumed that those who were elected would act with the interests of all Virginians in mind.

The colonists also practiced virtual representation when they restricted the suffrage to free, white, adult male heads of household who owned property in land or money. The number of actual voters in colonial elections amounted to a small proportion of the inhabitants in every colony. Nevertheless, the colonists considered poor white men, all women and children, and even, in a queer way, African-American slaves, to be virtually represented. The assumption was that elected assembly members acted on behalf of all, not just on behalf of the few freeholders who voted for them.

This was precisely the position Parliament took when the colonials complained that they were not represented in Parliament: the colonists were virtually represented in that ancient body.

BRITISH POLICIES AND POLICYMAKERS

The Stamp Act crisis was not resolved by adding up debaters' points. Few political battles are. If the protesters' constitutional argument was flimsy, they were a powerful and articulate group in every colony with support among all social classes. None of them spoke of independence or, after the riots, of rebellion. But they were adamant that Americans were not subjects of Parliament. They took their "rights as British subjects," as they interpreted them, quite seriously.

Poor Leadership

Some members of Parliament appreciated the colonial position and supported the Americans. William Pitt, then the Earl of Chatham, rejoiced "that America has resisted. Three millions of people so dead to all the feelings of liberty," he said, "so voluntarily to submit to be slaves, would have been fit instruments to make slaves of the rest." Americans returned the compliment and idolized Pitt.

Edmund Burke, the father of traditional conservatism, also saw the colonists as the defenders of British tradition and the Grenville group as dangerous innovators. At the other extreme, English radicals like John Wilkes egged on the colonial protesters because he saw them as natural allies in his agitations on behalf of a free press, and in opposition to George III.

Unfortunately for the empire, except for a brief spell in 1766 and 1767 when the Marquis of Rockingham and Lord Chatham headed ministries, these men did not make colonial policy. For the most part, the leaders of Parliament were unable to see beyond constitutional fine points and their snobbish disdain for colonial rustics. This narrow-mindedness was one consequence of the way English politics functioned during the reign of King George III.

Members of Parliament used party names like Whig and Tory, but these were not political parties in the modern sense of the word. Parliament was a collection of half a dozen or more shifting factions. Some, such as Burke's Old Whigs, ever on the watch for violations of traditional liberties, were drawn together by agreement on a principle. Most parliamentary factions, however, were alliances of convenience, cliques of men who supported one another because they were related by blood or marriage, or for the purpose of serving their own immediate interests.

There was money to be made in politics, not only in outright graft (which was not rare), but also through the distribution of public offices and government favors. Colonials played this game too. One way for an American speculative venture to gain parliamentary approval was to cut in a parliamentary clique as stockholders. Benjamin Franklin named one land company after Robert Walpole, and may be said to have profited when he was named postmaster-general for the colonies, the highest imperial post to which any American rose.

King George III

A new wrinkle was added after 1760, when George III ascended the British throne at the age of 22. His two predecessors had used the royal favors at their disposal to reward military heroes, to support musicians and artists, or simply to keep congenial companions hanging around the palace. The first two Georges were German. George I could not even speak English, and George II, who could, preferred French. Coming from the small state of Hanover, they were delighted merely to have the large royal income of Great Britain at their disposal. Neither took much interest in domestic matters. It was a situation much to the liking of Whigs.

George III, by way of contrast, was raised an Englishman. His mother had urged him to "be a king," and he meant to play a part in government. The days when an English monarch could issue decrees were long gone. But George could and did use the patronage he controlled to create a parliamentary faction beholden to him. This group was known as the "king's friends."

The king's friends were no more venal than other parliamentary factions. Nor was George III evil, as the Americans would come to depict him. He could not have been a tyrant had he wished to be. Indeed, several times during his first ten years as king and politician, George III used his influence to support conciliation with the colonies, and he won American favor. There would be plenty of statues of him to be toppled when American opinion shifted.

But George III was not intelligent, and he was vain and stubborn. The king was uneasy with politicians whose abilities exceeded his own, and with those who failed or refused to flatter him. By keeping such men out of office, and raising up mediocrities and sycophants, he denied power to those who best understood the American situation.

What was worse, the king was emotionally unstable. (Eventually he went insane.) He even dismissed *flunkies* on slight pretexts, and his colonial policy was inconsistent. The effect was to worsen relations between Britain and its colonies and to embolden the more radical American agitators.

Mixed Victory

Thus, George Grenville, a hard-liner who insisted that the army could have solved the colonial problem in 1765, was dismissed in July 1765 over an unrelated matter. Early the next year, during the short ministry of Lord Rockingham, Chatham moved to repeal the Stamp Act, and it was done. The colonial celebrations were so noisy that few paid much attention to the fact that king and Parliament had not yielded an inch on principle. Parliament also passed a Declaratory Act, which stated that Parliament "had, hath, and of right ought to have, full power and authority to make laws and statutes of sufficient force and validity to bind the colonies and people of America, subjects of the Crown of Great Britain, in all cases whatsoever."

Not only did the Declaratory Act deny the Americans' claims for their own assemblies, but

Statues of George III, erected only a few years earlier, were toppled by patriotic mobs in the excitement of independence.

the wording was lifted from a law of 1719 that made Ireland completely subject to Great Britain. Whiggish colonials had good reason to wonder if their rights as British subjects were being restored or if they were being reduced to the unenviable status of the despised Irish. At the time, however, few did. Chatham succeeded Rockingham as prime minister, and he ignored the Declaratory Act with the panache of Robert Walpole. Chatham also eliminated another aggravation when he reduced the duty on molasses from threepence to a penny per gallon. The colonial protesters were Georgian politicians, too. What mattered a piece of paper when a good friend held power?

Then, in one of those accidents that change the course of events, Chatham was taken ill and ceased to play an active part in the government. From the perspective of the colonists, the man who stepped into the vacuum was as bad a piece of luck as George Grenville had been.

Champagne Charley and the Townshend Duties

Charles Townshend was no more evil a fellow than Grenville or King George. In fact, he was rather too convivial and charming, winning the nickname "Champagne Charley" because of his penchant for arriving at the House of Commons giggling and unsteady on his feet. (In fairness to Townshend, Parliament met in the evening and, on a given night, any number of members were at less than their best.)

Townshend was chancellor of the Exchequer, a post equivalent to our secretary of the Treasury, and he hoped to be prime minister. To win the prize, Townshend planned to cut taxes at home and to make up in the colonies for the loss of revenues. He studied the Americans' distinctions between external taxes for regulating trade and internal taxes for raising money and designed a series of duties that were undeniably external in form. The Townshend Duties

A teapot—made in England for export to the colonies—commemorating the repeal of the Stamp Act of 1766.

were imposed on paper, paint, lead, glass, and tea imported by the colonies.

It was an odd combination of goods. Although none of the taxed goods were produced in the colonies in any quantity, all of them except tea could be made there. In failing to appreciate that the controversy was not an academic debate, Townshend invited a boycott, and he got it. Trade between England and America fell off by 25 percent and then by 50 percent. Townshend had predicted that his duties would bring in £40,000 annually. The actual take was £13,000 in 1768 and under £3,000 the next year, hardly enough to operate a few frontier forts.

There was little violence. The boycott was organized by merchants, wealthy men who were still nervous about the Stamp Act riots. But it worked. English merchants felt the pinch and flooded Parliament with petitions for repeal. They pointed out that if Townshend had answered the colonial distinction between internal and external taxes, he had also penalized goods that English manufacturers and merchants shipped abroad! In 1770, with the exception of the threepence-per-pound tax on tea, Parliament repealed the Townshend Duties. The tea tax was kept in the spirit of the Declaratory Act. It was Parliament's statement that Parliament retained the right to tax the colonies.

CHRONOLOGY

1760	George III crowned king
1763	Treaty of Paris ends French and Indian War
	Pontiac's Rebellion
	Proclamation of 1763
1764	Sugar Act
1765	Quartering Act
	Stamp Act
	Stamp Act Congress
1766	Declaratory Act
1767	Townshend Duties
1770	Townshend Duties Repealed

FOR FURTHER READING

Among a vast number of general histories of the events leading up to the American Revolution, and differing radically in their explanations and focus, are J. R. Alden, *A History of the American Revolution,* 1969; Bernard Bailyn, *The Ideological Origins of the American Revolution,* 2nd ed., 1992; Jack P. Greene, *The Reinterpretation of the American Revolution,* 1968; Merrill Jensen, *The Founding of a Nation,* 1968; Robert Middlekauff, *The Glorious Cause: The American Revolution, 1763–1789,* 1982; and Alfred T. Young, *The American Revolution: A Radical Interpretation,* 1976. These may be supplemented and in some cases corrected by Gordon W. Wood, *The Radicalism of the American Revolution,* 1991; Marc Egnal, *A Mighty Empire: The Origins of the American Revolution,* 1988; and especially Edward Countryman, *The American Revolution,* 1985.

Valuable special studies include Carl Bridenbaugh, *Seat of Empire: Eighteenth-Century Williamsburg,* 1950; John Brook, *King George III,* 1972; Edmund S. and Helen Morgan, *Prologue to Revolution: The Stamp Act Crisis,* 1953; Lewis B. Namier, *England in the Age of the American Revolution,* 1930; Arthur M. Schlesinger, Jr., *The Colonial Merchants and the American Revolution, 1763–1776,* 1951; Charles S. Sydnor, *Gentleman Freeholders,* 1952; and John W. Tyler, *Smugglers and Patriots: Boston Merchants and the Advent of the American Revolution,* 1986. On Pontiac's uprising, see Howard H. Peckham, *Pontiac and the Indian Uprising,* 1947; Wilbur R. Jacobs, *Wilderness Politics and Indian Gifts,* 1966; and, edited by Jacobs, *Dispossessing the American Indian: Indians and Whites on the Colonial Frontier,* 1985.

The Bloody Massacre, *an engraving by agitator Paul Revere, designed to inflame anti-British feelings in the colonies.*

8

RIOT TO REBELLION

The Road to Independence

1770–1776

He has dissolved Representative Houses repeatedly, for opposing with manly firmness his invasions on the rights of the People. . . . He has obstructed the Administration of Justice, by refusing his Assent to Laws for establishing Judiciary Powers. . . . He has kept among us, in times of peace, Standing Armies without the consent of our legislatures. . . . He has abdicated Government here, by declaring us out of his Protection, and waging War against us. . . . He has plundered our seas, ravaged our Coasts, burnt our towns, and destroyed the lives of our people.

—The Declaration of Independence

In this arduous Contest I can have no other Object but to protect the true Interests of all My Subjects. No People ever enjoyed more Happiness, or lived under a milder Government, than those now revolted Provinces. . . . My Desire is to restore to them the Blessings of Law and Liberty, equally enjoyed by every British Subject, which they have fatally and desperately exchanged for the Calamities of War, and the arbitrary Tyranny of their Chiefs.

—George III

Nothing was settled by the repeal of the Townshend Duties. Neither Parliament nor colonial protesters yielded an inch on the principle at stake: Did Parliament have the right to tax the American colonies? So long as Parliament did not test the Declaratory Act, Americans ignored its existence. Anti-British protests were few and muted. Parliament did not test its declaration for three years after 1770. Relieved to see an end to the confrontation, British ministries sympathetic to the Americans avoided provocations.

In fact, tensions began to ease before March 1770 when the Townshend Acts were scrapped. A door-to-door survey revealed that a majority of households in New York was willing to buy all the taxed items except tea (which they could get more cheaply from Dutch smugglers). Beginning in early 1770, imports into the New England colonies, the most obstreperous of the provinces, increased from a low of £330,000 to £1.2 million, more than ever before. Total colonial exports rose from £1.7 million in 1770 to £4.5 million in 1772. As perhaps most people usually do, Americans wanted calm—business as usual—a resumption of daily life unaggravated by the folderol of politics and the fancies of philosophy.

STORMS WITHIN THE LULL

Still, several incidents between 1770 and 1773 indicated that not all was harmony in British North America. On the streets of Boston, a bloody brawl between workingmen and British soldiers dramatized a simmering hostility toward the large numbers of redcoats stationed in the colonies. In North Carolina, frontier settlers took up arms against the elite of the eastern counties who governed the colony. In Rhode Island, farmers shielded smugglers who burned a British patrol boat.

The Boston Massacre

On March 5, 1770, the day the Townshend Duties were repealed, the weather in Boston was frigid. The streets were icy, and heaps of gritty snow blocked the cobbled gutters. No doubt aggravated by the severity of the winter, which brought unemployment as well as discomfort, some men and boys exchanged words with British soldiers who were patrolling the streets. From a handful of hecklers there grew a crowd, many cursing and throwing snowballs at the redcoats. A few dared them to use their muskets.

When, on King Street, the mob pressed close, backing the soldiers against a wall, they fired. Five in the crowd, including a boy and a black seaman named Crispus Attucks, fell dead. Boston, scarcely more than a town of 15,000, was shocked. A few men who had been active in the Stamp Act crisis tried to revive anti-British feelings. Silversmith Paul Revere prepared (some say plagiarized) an engraving that depicted soldiers aggressively attacking innocent people. Samuel Adams, a former brewer, circulated prints of the picture of the "Boston Massacre." Joseph Warren, a physician, embroidered passionately on the theme. "Take heed, ye orphan babes," he told a public meeting, "lest, whilst your streaming eyes are fixed upon the ghastly corpse, your feet slide on the stones bespattered with your fathers' brains." Rabble-rousing, to be sure, but with an eloquence not to be heard from demagogues today.

The agitation failed to bear fruit. Most people seemed to blame the incident on the mob. John Adams, cousin of Samuel and a friend of Warren, agreed to represent the accused soldiers in court. John Adams was nobody's stooge, least of all for the British. He was opinionated to the point of self-righteousness and a strident critic of British policies. Indeed, in arguing the redcoats' innocence in the law, Adams roundly criticized the practice of stationing professional soldiers in cities like Boston. "Soldiers quartered in a populous town will always occasion two mobs where they prevent one," he said. "They are wretched conservators of the peace." Nevertheless, Adams argued that British policy and an unsavory mob, not the indicted redcoats, bore the blame for the violent deaths on March 5. The jury agreed, acquitting all of the defendants save two and sentencing them only to branding on the thumb, a slap on the wrist by eighteenth-century standards.

The Hated Redcoats

The significance of the Boston Massacre, and the Battle of Golden Hill in New York in January—in which soldiers and citizens drew blood during a major riot—was that most colonials let them pass.

They lost interest overnight, as Americans of the late twentieth century moved on from one sensational "trial of the century" to another every eighteen months or so. Still, such clashes and a hundred less notable confrontations exposed a sore spot in colonial city life. As John Adams allowed in his address to the Boston jury, colonials simply did not like the scarlet-uniformed soldiers in their midst. Taxpayers resented paying for their keep. And ordinary working people disliked rubbing shoulders with men who commanded little respect.

The soldier of the era was not, like the soldier of today, the boy next door in uniform defending the nation and its ideals. Eighteenth-century soldiers were rough and lusty young men seined from the sewers of society. Some were convicted criminals who were in the army because it was offered to them as an alternative to prison or worse. Others joined the army in order to dodge arrest. Some, guilty of no crime, were pressed into service simply because they were unable to support themselves.

Civilians feared and despised them. The soldiers' own officers, drawn from the gentry, looked down on them: *scum* was the word that leapt first to mind when an eighteenth-century officer described the men he commanded. Soldiers had few rights and were brutally punished for infractions. If not slaves, they suffered a kind of bondage. There was little feeling among them of selfless service to king and country or of commitment to some abstract national ideal. In America, they were further alienated by the fact that few colonials signed up. The "lobsters" (a name reflecting the color of British uniforms) were almost all from Great Britain.

A Dangerous Relationship

So long as the soldiers lived in frontier forts or in isolated bases such as Castle Island in Boston harbor, conflict with civilians was minimal. However, after the Stamp Act riots, the Crown stationed large detachments within coastal cities and towns. Some 4,000 redcoats were camping on Boston Common at the time of the massacre. Others, under the terms of the Quartering Act of 1765, were billeted in vacant buildings and taverns.

Such quartering brought the tightly knit and suspicious redcoats into intimate daily contact with working-class colonials. They were young men and some found girlfriends, stirring up resentment on that primeval count. Others coarsely accosted young women who had brothers and fathers. When off duty, they competed with local men and boys for casual work. There had been a fistfight over jobs at a rope factory in Boston just a few days before the massacre. Redcoats also passed idle hours in inns and taverns where colonials also gathered.

Colonial inns and taverns were not merely hostels in which transients supped and bedded down. They were a focal point of urban social life. The colonial tavern was the neighborhood meeting place, more like a contemporary English pub, perhaps, than a modern American bar. Local workingmen popped in throughout the day for a cup of tea or coffee and, in the evening, for a shot of rum, a mug of mulled cider, a pipe of tobacco, and a chat with friends about work and politics. With time on their hands, unemployed men and those between jobs, such as seamen, spent even more time at "the ordinary," as these taverns were called. The intrusion of uniformed foreigners into such intimate places, rough men laughing loudly and carrying on by themselves, kept resentments up even when, as between 1770 and 1773, relations with Great Britain were generally good.

Street People

The redcoats had more to do with the anti-British feelings of lower-class colonials than Parliamentary taxation did. Poor people worried about the next day's meal, not about the price of a bottle of the best Madeira wine or the fine points of the British Constitution. And such people were central to the protest that was to boil over into rebellion and revolution. Workingmen, the unemployed, boisterous street boys and apprentices, and the disreputable fringe elements of colonial society did the dirty work in the Stamp Act crisis. They were the ones who fought the soldiers in the streets and who were killed in the Boston Massacre.

They had little to lose as a consequence of rash action. The street people were themselves often social outcasts by virtue of class, occupation, or race. Seamen, suspect because they came and went, and belonging to no community, were prominent in the riotous crowds. (Crispus Attucks was a sailor out of work. John Adams described the mob on King Street as "Negroes and mulattoes, Irish teagues and outlandish jack-tars.") And yet, the revolution he was to

Inns and taverns were places where colonists dined, socialized, and exchanged opinions.

join with enthusiasm owed much to the boldness of this motley crowd.

Demon Rum

It is worth noting the role of alcohol in the agitation. The soldiers were a bibulous lot. It was standard military practice to pass around strong drink before battle, and the royal governor of New York dissolved the colonial assembly in 1766 when its members refused to provide the redcoats with their accustomed ration of five pints of beer or four ounces of rum a day, enough for a buzz and its possible consequences.

Americans were a hard-drinking folk, too, and the lower classes, with more to forget, were the thirstiest of all. Many signal episodes on the road to independence seem to have been carried out by men in their cups. "The minds of the freeholders were inflamed," wrote an observer of the Stamp Act protest in South Carolina, "by many a hearty damn . . . over bottles, bowls, and glasses." The crowd that precipitated the Boston Massacre had come out of

the taverns. The Sons of Liberty, who ignited the last phase of the revolutionary movement with the Boston Tea Party of 1773, assembled over a barrel of rum.

Upper-class protest leaders had mixed feelings about this kind of support. They were more than willing to exploit an angry, perhaps inebriated crowd, by stirring up resentment of British policies and by winking at abuses of the law. John Adams, so scornful of the massacre mob, called the men at the Boston Tea Party "so bold, so daring, so intrepid." But they also worried about "the rabble." They counted on the crowd fading away after having played its historic role.

But the masses did not disappear. British concessions did nothing to remedy their grievances. The redcoats continued to jostle them in the streets and to intrude on their lives. Their elemental economic problems were untouched by lighter taxation and parliamentary expressions of good will. They remained anonymous, producing few leaders quoted in newspapers. But they continued to be fertile ground for agitation.

The Regulators

Conflict between colonial classes was, as it had been during the seventeenth century, clearer in the countryside. In the backcountry of South Carolina, between 1767 and 1769, frontiersmen rebelled against the refusal of the colonial assembly, which was dominated by Charleston planters, to set up county governments in the West. They proclaimed their own counties to which they paid taxes that were legally to go to Charleston. The rebels called themselves Regulators because they said they would regulate their own affairs.

In North Carolina, a similar dispute led to actual battle. A band of westerners rode east to demonstrate their resentment of the colony's penny-pinching policies. They were met and defeated by a smaller but better-trained militia at the Battle of Alamance. Only nine men were killed and six were later hanged for rebellion, but the modesty of the clash did not sweeten the bitterness in the backcountry.

Shared Prejudice

Some historians suggest that the British missed a splendid opportunity to win colonial support when they failed to exploit the hostility between western farmers and the eastern elites. To some extent, British imperial interests coincided with the demands of the frontiersmen: the Regulators wanted more government, not less, and their chief complaint was that not enough tax money was spent on maintaining law and order in their foothills homeland.

By wooing the backcountry farmers with policies that favored them, the British might have gained powerful allies in their disputes with the wealthy southern planters. Indeed, during the Revolution, many Regulators fought on the British side, while others pushed beyond the Appalachians in order to remain neutral.

The British did not win more backwoods support than they did because their contempt for the lower classes was as keen as that of the colonial elite. It was impossible for a British gentleman to regard the poor people of the frontier and the city streets as anything other than a rabble. The American rebellion was not to be the last time quarreling factions of a social elite failed to take the discrete interests and power of the masses into consideration.

The *Gaspée*

In June 1772, a British schooner patrolling the Narragansett Bay in Rhode Island, the *Gaspée*, spied a vessel suspected of smuggling and sailed after it toward Providence. About seven miles from the port, the *Gaspée* ran aground. That night, men from eight boats boarded the schooner, roughly set the crew ashore, and burned it to the waterline.

Because the *Gaspée* was a royal vessel, this was an act of rebellion. The authorities believed they knew who the ringleader of the gang was, a merchant named John Brown, a veteran of several run-ins with customs collectors. However, neither a £500 reward nor the fact that Rhode Island's elected governor took part in the inquest persuaded anyone to provide evidence. The Commission of Inquiry finally disbanded angrily only in June 1773. By that time, the three-year lull in British–American relations was drawing to a close.

THE MARCH TOWARD WAR

The quiet years ended in the spring of 1773, when Parliament once again enacted a law that angered the Americans. This time, however, instead of spontaneous protests under the control of no one in particular, resistance to British policy was aroused and organized by a number of able, deliberate men.

They might almost be described as professional agitators. Some of them were orators who articulated resentments of the British. Others were organizers, people willing to devote their time to shaping anger into rebellion. There can be no revolutions without such revolutionaries. Men like James Otis of Massachusetts and Patrick Henry of Virginia made the difference between spontaneous incidents like the burning of the *Gaspée* and calculated provocations like the Boston Tea Party.

James Otis

James Otis was a hot-tempered Boston lawyer who had been a prosecutor for the hated vice-admiralty courts. His contribution to the agitation of the 1760s may have had as much to do with personal political disappointments as with commitment to a principle.

Rebellious Rhode Islanders burn the British patrol boat Gaspée *in Narragansett Bay, 1772.*

Whatever the case, his was an exciting presence. He could whip up passions to the fighting point like few of his contemporaries. In 1761, Otis led Boston's fight against "writs of assistance." The writs were general search warrants that enabled customs collectors to enter any property to search for smuggled goods. Arguing the case, Otis appealed to the cause of the rights of British subjects, apparently coining the phrase "taxation without representation is tyranny." John Adams later said that "then and there the child Independence was born."

Curiously, Otis grew more temperate while men like John Adams grew more militant. By the time the spirit of revolution matured, Otis was no longer among its leaders. Tragically, he lived out his final years intermittently insane as the result of a brawl with a British official. In a horrible moment that seemed to symbolize his career, he was killed by a bolt of lightning in 1783.

Patrick Henry

Patrick Henry was his counterpart in the South. Not a deep thinker, Henry was a red-haired, sharp-tongued, Scotch-Irish shopkeeper who educated himself to become one of Virginia's most successful trial lawyers. He caused a furor in 1767 when, only 27 years old, he denounced George III as a tyrant because the king reversed a law that had been passed by the Virginia House of Burgesses.

Two years later, Henry gained attention throughout North America during the Stamp Act crisis. Although only the more moderate of the resolutions he introduced were actually passed by the House of Burgesses, all of them were published throughout the colonies under his name. Henry became even more famous for a speech he delivered to the burgesses. "Caesar had his Brutus," he was quoted as shouting, "Charles I his Cromwell, and George

Patrick Henry declaiming "Give me liberty or give me death" in a patriotic painting done long after the event. An eyewitness to the speech reported a somewhat less heroic scene.

were fundamental to his dislike of British rule. He was obsessed with the concept of republican virtue such as educated people of the eighteenth century attributed to the ancient Greeks and Romans. (He said that Boston should be a "Christian Sparta.") Political power, he believed, was legitimate only when exercised by men who lived austerely and were ever vigilant to preserve liberty.

Adams's scorn for luxury and fear of tyranny put him at the forefront of every major protest in Boston. He led the battle against the Sugar Act, the Stamp Act, and the Townshend Duties. Unlike other agitators, however, Samuel Adams was no orator. He was nervous at the podium, trembling and stumbling over his words. Nor was he so impetuous as Otis and Henry. Adams was an organizer, the man who handled the undramatic but essential work that transforms anger into protest, and protest into politics. He served as a link between wealthy critics of British policy such as the merchant John Hancock and the Sons of Liberty, drawn from the artisan class, whom he neither feared nor disdained.

Samuel Adams may have been thinking in terms of independence as early as the mid-1760s. However, perhaps because of his failure to create a fuss over the Boston Massacre, he was generally quiet until the winter of 1773. Then, Parliament presented him with a revolutionary's opportunity.

III may profit by their example." Referring offhandedly to the execution of rulers was heady stuff; Henry was shouted down with cries of "Treason." Legend has him replying, "If this be treason, make the most of it."

Relentless in his attacks on the Crown (and on the tidewater planters), Patrick Henry spearheaded the final drive toward independence by calling for the establishment of an army in May 1775 with the famous words "Give me liberty or give me death."

Samuel Adams

More thoughtful and deliberate than Otis and Henry was Samuel Adams of Massachusetts. A brewer as a young man, a tax collector between 1756 and 1764, Adams thereafter devoted himself to the dual career of moral censor and professional anti-British agitator. Indeed, to Samuel Adams, morality and virtue

Fatal Turn: The Tea Act

In May 1773, Parliament enacted the law that led directly to the American Revolution. Ironically, the Tea Act of 1773 was not designed to wring money out of the colonies. Its primary purpose was to bail out the East India Company, a private commercial concern involved in trade with Asia.

The East India Company was invaluable to the Crown. In return for a monopoly of the Indian trade, the company carried out many governmental and military functions on the subcontinent. (The Hudson's Bay Company did much the same in the wilderness north of Canada.) In 1773, however, the company was teetering on the edge of bankruptcy as a result of mismanagement and bad luck. Among other problems, much of its capital was tied up in some 17 million pounds of tea in London warehouses for which no buyers could be found. Early in 1773, East India shares plummeted in value from £280 to £160.

To prevent financial disaster (in which some members of Parliament would have shared), company officials proposed that they be allowed to sell their tea directly in the American colonies. Because the tea was, in effect, being dumped, it would actually be cheaper than the smuggled Dutch tea that had become fashionable in America since the enactment of the Townshend Duties. To sweeten the Americans' cup further, the company's directors asked that all British taxes on tea be repealed.

The prime minister, Frederick, Lord North, met the company nine-tenths of the way. His Tea Act eliminated all taxes except the Townshend levy of threepence on the pound. North, a favorite of George III, saw a chance to succeed where Grenville and Townshend had failed. Even with the tax, Tea Act tea was a bargain. It would cost colonials money to uphold their principle of no taxation without representation. Like his predecessors, Lord North believed that colonial protest was about nothing but greed.

The Tea Parties

North guessed wrong. When a dozen East India Company ships carrying 1,700 chests of tea sailed into American ports, they were greeted by the angriest defiance of British authority since 1765. The Americans would not be bought. Tea Act tea may have been cheap, but the precedent of granting a monopoly on sales in the colonies to a private company was dangerous. If the Tea Act succeeded, any number of parliamentary regulations might follow.

The company managed to land its tea in Charleston where it was hastily locked up in a warehouse lest an angry crowd get to it. In New York and Philadelphia, royal authorities ordered the ships to return to England for fear of riots. In Annapolis, Maryland, a tea ship was burned. But it was a milder action in Boston that triggered the crisis.

The American-born governor of Massachusetts, Thomas Hutchinson, would not permit the tea ships to depart Boston. Instead, while sparks flew at public meetings throughout the town, he hatched a plan to seize the tea for nonpayment of a port tax. This would enable him to get the tea ashore and under the authority not of a vulnerable private company but of the royal governor.

It was a clever scheme, but Samuel Adams was cleverer. On December 16, 1773, the day before Hutchinson could legally seize the tea, Adams presided over a protest meeting attended by a third of the population of Boston. With such immense support, some 60 Sons of Liberty slipped out of the meetinghouse, dressed up as Mohawk Indians, and boarded the East India Company ships. To the cheers of the crowd, they dumped 342 chests of tea worth £10,000 into Boston harbor.

The Indian costumes were a stroke of political genius. In addition to disguising the perpetrators, they lent an act of gross vandalism the air of a prank, the "Boston Tea Party." Samuel Adams and other protest leaders knew that Britain could not let the incident pass, and they probably gambled that Parliament would overreact. Parliament did. Instead of trying to root out the individual vandals and treat the incident as a criminal matter, Lord North decided to punish Boston and the whole colony of Massachusetts.

The Intolerable Acts

With Lord North's party, the king's friends, in control of Parliament, the Coercive Acts of 1774—which the Americans called the Intolerable Acts—sailed through both Commons and Lords. The act first closed the port of Boston until such time as the city (not the individual culprits) paid for the spoiled tea. Second, the new governor (an army general, Thomas Gage) was empowered to transfer out of the colony the trials of soldiers or other British officials accused of killing protesters. This seemed to be an

The Morning After

If the men of Boston who dumped the tea into Boston harbor were in their cups, a few at least suffered no hangovers. One participant remembered what he did on the morning after:

The next morning, after we had cleared the ships of the tea, it was discovered that very considerable quantities of it were floating upon the surface of the water, and to prevent the possibility of any of its being saved for use, a number of small boats were manned by sailors and citizens, who rowed them into those parts of the harbor wherever the tea was visible, and by beating it with oars and paddles so thoroughly drenched it as to render its entire destruction inevitable.

open invitation to the redcoats to shoot. Third, the entire structure of government in Massachusetts was overhauled, with elected bodies losing powers to the king's appointed officials. Fourth, a new Quartering Act further aggravated civilian–soldier relations to the breaking point. It authorized the army to house redcoats in occupied private homes!

Lord North hoped that by coming down hard on Massachusetts, he would isolate the Bay Colony, which, with its Puritan heritage, had never been popular in North America, and issue a warning to protesters elsewhere. Instead, the Coercive Acts proved to be intolerable everywhere. Several cities shipped food to paralyzed Boston. More ominous than charity, when Massachusetts called for a continental congress to meet in Philadelphia in order to discuss a united response, every colony except Georgia sent delegates.

Salt in the Wound

Although it was not designed as one of the Coercive Acts, the Quebec Act of 1774 also angered colonists by officially recognizing the French language and Catholic religion in the province of Quebec. It also extended the boundaries of the province into the Ohio River Valley. Finally, the Quebec Act failed to provide for an elective assembly in French Canada.

There were a number of good reasons for the Quebec Act. Many historians have regarded it as a rare example of enlightened imperial government. Instead of oppressing its French subjects, the Crown respected and protected their institutions. As for the absence of an elected assembly, there never had been one in New France.

Nevertheless, to English-speaking colonial Protestants whose own elected assemblies were under attack, the religious and political provisions of the Quebec Act were alarming. Nor were land-hungry farmers and speculators pleased to hear that western reserves they regarded as their own had been assigned to the French province.

THE REVOLUTION BEGINS

The Intolerable Acts and the Quebec Act mark an important turning point on the road to revolution. Before 1774, confrontations between Americans and the mother country were scattered, episodic, and local. Except for the Committees of Correspon-

dence, which several colonies set up to exchange news and opinions via the mails, almost every effort to get the 13 colonies to act in concert was initiated by the British and scuttled by the resistance of one colony or another. Now, while most of the delegates to the Continental Congress who trickled into Philadelphia during the summer of 1774 continued to speak of their loyalty to George III, the fact that they were meeting together pointed unmistakably to the possibility of a serious break.

The Delegates

The delegates to the congress arrived in Philadelphia in early September and began their discussions on the fifth of the month. Some of them, such as Benjamin Franklin, were quite well-known. Others, such as Samuel Adams and Patrick Henry, had become notorious only recently. Most were gentlemen of only local renown, and, since each of the colonies had closer relations with England than with any other American province, few of the 56 delegates had ever met. The delegates themselves were different in many ways — in temperament, in their sentiments toward Great Britain, and in their opinions as to what should or could be done.

But they got along remarkably well. Ironically, the heritage they were soon to rebel against gave them something in common. They were all gentlemen in the English mold — merchants, planters, and professionals, particularly lawyers. They prized education and civility. They knew how to keep debates decorous and impersonal. In the evening, they recessed to a round of festive dinners and parties with Philadelphia high society. George Washington rarely

---

Longing for the Good Old Days

Not until 1776 did more than a few colonials think of Great Britain's actions as meriting a fight for independence. On the contrary, most of them thought that the solution to the crisis was to go backward — to relations as they existed before 1763. Benjamin Franklin's advice was to "*repeal* the laws, *renounce* the right, *recall* the troops, *refund* the money, and *return* to the old method of requisition."

dined in his own rooms. John Adams gushed in letters to his wife, Abigail, about the lavishness of the meals. Only his cousin Samuel, nurturing his ideals of Roman republican frugality, shunned the social whirl. He quickly won the reputation of being a Gradgrind.

Defining the Issues

The delegates also worked together so smoothly because most of them were uncertain about what to do. All were angry, even those who would later remain loyal to Britain, and they were determined to settle their squabble with Parliament. The congress adopted a defiant set of declarations called the Suffolk Resolves, which were rushed to Philadelphia from Boston (Suffolk County), by the rebellious silversmith who publicized the Boston Massacre, Paul Revere. The resolutions stated that the Intolerable Acts were completely invalid, and called for a boycott of trade with Britain if the obnoxious laws were not repealed.

But the congress also insisted on loyalty to the Crown. The delegates agreed to British regulation of colonial trade, and they almost adopted a conciliatory plan designed by Joseph Galloway of Pennsylvania just a few days before they voted for the hardline Suffolk resolutions. At their parties and dinners they self-consciously lifted their glasses to the health of the king and queen. The idea of rebellion was still repugnant.

Unhappily, George III did not share their mood. He, too, was determined to stand firm, and, assuming that he wielded overwhelming power, he was more than willing to use force. "Blows must decide whether they are to be subject to the country or independent," George told Lord North at a time when no colonial leader had publicly mentioned the possibility of independence or violent resistance.

Learning of the king's intransigence, the delegates to the congress could no longer ignore the likely consequence of their convention. One of their last actions before adjourning was to call on Americans to organize and train local military units.

Colonial Soldiers

Little encouragement was needed. In the Massachusetts countryside; tempers were already aflame. When a British spy, sent out from Boston to get a feel for the mood of the people, asked an old farmer why, at his age, he was cleaning his gun, the old man replied that "there was a flock of redcoats in Boston, which he expected would be here soon; he meant to try and hit some of them." Did his neighbors feel the way he did? Yes, most of them. "There was one Tory house in sight," the old man said, "and he wished it was in flames."

Younger men oiled their guns and met on village greens to elect officers and drill. Practically every adult male was armed in rural America, for guns were as much tools as axes were. Farm families still hunted for some of their food, and the day when they had to protect themselves from the Indians and the French was not long gone.

The Americans were said to be excellent marksmen. Their rifles were generally more accurate than the redcoats' muskets, and powder and shot were too expensive to waste. But the colonists were not soldiers. They had shunned British attempts to recruit them, and General Wolfe had called his American militia "the dirtiest, most contemptible cowardly dogs you can conceive." Considering the nature of eighteenth-century warfare, however, this was almost a compliment.

How Wars Were Fought

Like so many endeavors of educated people in the Age of Enlightenment, eighteenth-century warfare was highly structured. In battle, two armies in close formation maneuvered to face one another from the best possible position, usually high ground. After an exchange of artillery, soon to be the key to battle, but not yet fully appreciated, the attacking army closed the gap to the oddly cheerful music of fife and drum (or bagpipes if the soldiers were Scots). The armies exchanged musket fire in volleys. The men pointed rather than aimed their weapons, and the army that stood its ground amidst the horror of smoke, noise, and companions dropping to the sod—in other words, the army that maintained good order and clockwork discipline—defeated the one that panicked, broke ranks, and fled.

The key to winning such battles was long, hard, and tedious training according to manuals written by French and Prussian tacticians. These drills (and a dram of rum or gin before battle) were designed to make a machine of thousands of individual human beings. Marksmanship counted for little. Individual

These watercolors of Revolutionary soldiers are crude but frankly grant the place of blacks in eighteenth-century America. Later, when slavery was reinvigorated, the participation of blacks in major historical events was usually forgotten.

initiative was a curse, to be exorcised by brutal discipline. The goal was nothing less than unnatural behavior on a grand scale: not fleeing from a terrifying experience.

Lexington and Concord

And so, when General Gage decided to seize rebel supplies at Concord, Massachusetts, 21 miles from Boston, he did not worry about the minutemen, plain farmers pledged to be ready to fight at a minute's notice. How could such play-soldiers trouble one of Europe's finest armies? On April 19, 1775, he sent 700 troops to seize the munitions and, if possible, to arrest Samuel Adams and John Hancock, who were thought to be hiding in the area.

The Americans were warned by the midnight ride of Paul Revere, and by William Dawes, and Samuel Prescott of Lexington, who actually got

farther than Revere, bringing the news to crossroads and village commons that "the British are coming." When British Major John Pitcairn arrived at Lexington, he discovered 70 nervous farmers drawn up in a semblance of battle formation. Their fate seemed to confirm British confidence.

The Americans were frightened and confused at the sight of the solid ranks of tough, grim men who outnumbered them ten to one. They stood around uncertainly, murmuring among themselves. Pitcairn twice ordered them to disperse. Then a shot was fired.

No one knows who started the battle, a colonial hothead who was determined to force the issue or a British soldier blundering as George III and Lord North had blundered. In the end it did not matter. In London, on the same day as the Battle of Lexington, Parliament was passing another Intolerable Act, which banned Massachusetts fishermen from the Grand Banks of Newfoundland. When Americans heard of that law, which was designed to finish off the already crippled New England economy, it would surely have set off armed rebellion.

Major Pitcairn's men easily cleared Lexington green and marched on to Concord. There, however, a larger group of Americans met them at a bridge. Surprised and alarmed by the extent of resistance, Major Pitcairn ordered a retreat to Boston. All the way, minutemen sniped at the British soldiers from behind trees and stone fences, inflicting serious casualties. When the redcoats reached the city, more than 250 of the expedition were dead or wounded. The minutemen, elated by their success, set up camp outside Boston.

The Bottom Line

The sincerity of Paul Revere's patriotism, indeed, its zeal, cannot be questioned. Nonetheless, there were bills to be paid. When Revere was released by the British (he was arrested before completing his midnight ride), he billed the revolutionary government of Massachusetts for his costs in rousing every Middlesex village and farm. In writing the poem that immortalized Revere, Henry Wadsworth Longfellow neglected to mention the expense account.

NOTABLE PEOPLE

Two Blacks of the Revolutionary Era

Samuel Johnson, who was recognized during his own lifetime as one of the greatest figures of English literature, did not like Americans. Among their own unpleasant traits, Dr. Johnson said, they were shameless hypocrites. "Why is it," he wrote in 1775, "that we hear the loudest yelps for liberty among the drivers of negroes?" His point, of course, was painfully apparent to many of the people who subscribed to the phrase "all men are created equal," and then held one American in five in bondage for life.

Proslavery whites simply ignored the sentiments of the Declaration of Independence. Others, who disliked slavery, lived with the contradiction by consoling themselves that blacks were intellectually and morally inferior to whites, and so could not fulfill the duties of a citizen in a republic. In order to hold to this rationalization, however, they had to ignore the example of two remarkable individuals.

Phillis Wheatley (1755?–1784) was born in West Africa, probably in what is now Senegal. She was kidnapped when eight years of age by slavers bound for Boston. There, despite the girl's frail appearance, a successful tailor and merchant, John Wheatley, purchased her as a personal maid for his wife.

Phillis, as the Wheatleys named her, was lucky in her master and mistress. Had she been sold to work on a farm or plantation, her intelligence and charm would have gone unnoticed, as the abilities of other blacks were ignored. The Wheatleys recognized the girl's brilliance and treated her as they did their own children, providing her an education as well as decent food, clothing, and lodging. Wheatley was a prodigy, mastering the English language within

16 months and astonishing visitors by reading and explaining the meaning of the most difficult sections of the Bible, Greek myths, and the poetry of Alexander Pope and Thomas Gray, then the most admired of the English poets.

At the age of 13, Phillis wrote her first poem, an ode "To the University of Cambridge in New England" (Harvard), and in the next years a salute to King George III (still immensely popular in America) and a eulogy to George Whitefield, the founder of American Methodism, a faith Phillis adopted.

In 1772 or 1773, John Wheatley freed the young woman, not an uncommon practice in Massachusetts during the decade of the Revolution, and helped pay her passage to England, where she hoped to recover her health and to meet the countess of Huntingdon, a Methodist noblewoman with whom she had corresponded. With the countess's help, Phillis published a book of her *Poems on Various Subjects, Religious and Moral,* but she soon returned to Boston when she heard that Mrs. Wheatley was dying.

In 1775, with the Revolution about to explode, Phillis wrote a letter to George Washington, who responded, expressing his interest in meeting her (they never met). Like many Virginia slaveowners, Washington worried about the wisdom and morality of slavery, and he might have looked on Wheatley as evidence that blacks were indeed capable of great attainments.

In 1778, Phillis alienated the Wheatley heirs by marrying John Peters, a free black who apparently was quite intelligent and was a writer of some ability. Peters, however, was a ne'er-do-well and a deserter. He stole a manuscript that Phillis was preparing for publi-

Bunker Hill

Soon 16,000 Americans surrounded the city. In England, Edmund Burke pleaded with Parliament to evacuate Boston and allow tempers to cool. As usual, the most thoughtful politician of the age was ignored. Lord North dispatched another 1,000 troops to Boston, along with three more generals—Henry Clinton, John "Gentleman Johnny" Burgoyne, and William Howe.

They argued Gage out of his reluctance to take provocative action, and Howe agreed to occupy high ground on a peninsula across the Charles River. The day before he moved, the Americans took the peninsula, including Bunker Hill and, nearer to Boston, Breed's Hill. When Howe's men took to their boats, 1,600 armed colonials were dug in on the summit of Breed's Hill.

Howe sent 2,000 crack troops up the slopes but, at first, no one returned their shots. Then, when the

cation, lost it, and was jailed for bad debts. After bearing three children, all of whom were stillborn or died in infancy, Phillis Wheatley died in poverty in 1784.

Benjamin Banneker (1731–1806), who is known as the black Benjamin Franklin because of the breadth of his interests and the fact that he published a popular almanac, was the son of a free black mother and a slave father who, when Benjamin was still a child, prospered as a planter in Maryland. The elder Banneker educated his son at a Quaker school near Baltimore, one of very few in the colonies that accepted blacks as students.

As a young man, Benjamin farmed his father's lands, which he inherited, but his heart was not in the life. Neighbors remembered him as detached and dreamy, given to eccentric dress and habits. On clear nights, Banneker lay outside on a blanket, studying the stars. In free moments during the day, he studied bees, on which he wrote a treatise, and worked difficult mathematical problems, at which he was a genius. Banneker constructed a wooden clock (said by some to be the first clock made wholly in North America) and was locally famed as an astronomer. His reputation spread in 1789, when he accurately predicted a solar eclipse. This led to the publication of *Banneker's Almanac* (1792–1802), a successor to *Poor Richard's* in popularity, and to a correspondence with Thomas Jefferson, who secured from President Washington a position for Banneker on the commission that surveyed the District of Columbia.

Banneker was a natural scientist; politics were of no great interest to him. As a Quaker, he was a pacifist during the Revolutionary War. In 1791, he wrote a letter to Jefferson, which has since become famous, in which he offered his own example of proof that blacks were capable of citizenship and should be granted it:

> I apprehend that you will embrace every opportunity to eradicate that train of absurd and false ideas and opinions, which so generally prevail with respect to us [black people]; and that your sentiments are concurrent with mine which are: that one universal Father hath given being to us all; that He not only made us all of one flesh, but that He hath also without partisanship afforded us all with the same faculties and that, however variable we may be in society or religion, however diversified in situation or color, we are all the same family and stand in the same relation to Him.

Banneker knew that only the most extraordinary individuals, such as Wheatley and himself, could hope to break through the prejudice against blacks. He hoped that political leaders like Jefferson would see in their accomplishments evidence that, given the opportunities of freedom, all blacks could earn places in society commensurate with their abilities. The existence of a Banneker did trouble Jefferson, who wanted to believe that blacks were not the intellectual and moral equals of whites and therefore were not entitled to the rights stated in his Declaration of Independence. Habit, self-interest (Jefferson's social position was built on slave ownership), and the death of the astronomer in 1806, when Jefferson was president, allowed him to suppress his doubts.

Americans could "see the whites of their eyes" (in other words, when they could aim rather than just point), they let loose a murderous volley. The redcoats staggered and retreated. Again Howe advanced his troops, and again they were thrown back. Now, however, the British correctly calculated that the Americans were short of ammunition. Reinforcing his badly mauled front line with fresh men, Howe took Breed's Hill with bayonets.

The British had won, or had they? Hearing that 200 men had been killed and 1,000 wounded, General Clinton remarked that too many such "victories" would destroy the British capacity to fight. Clinton was right. The misnamed Battle of Bunker Hill was an American strategic triumph. The British gained nothing, for the colonial militia simply fell back, maintaining their circle around Boston, while revolutionaries secured their control of the New England countryside.

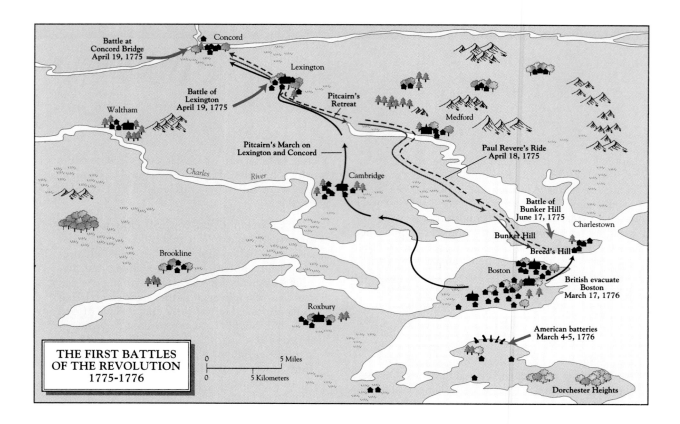

Battle at
Concord Bridge
April 19, 1775

Concord

Lexington

Battle of
Lexington
April 19, 1775

Pitcairn's Retreat

Waltham

Medford

Pitcairn's March on
Lexington and Concord

Charles River

Cambridge

Paul Revere's Ride
April 18, 1775

Battle of
Bunker Hill
June 17, 1775

Charlestown

Bunker Hill

Breed's Hill

Boston

British evacuate
Boston
March 17, 1776

Brookline

Roxbury

American batteries
March 4-5, 1776

THE FIRST BATTLES
OF THE REVOLUTION
1775-1776

0   5 Miles

0   5 Kilometers

Dorchester Heights

Ticonderoga

Rebel morale had another boost in the spring of
1775. Soon after Lexington and Concord, a would-
be revolutionary government, the Massachusetts
Committee of Safety, instructed Benedict Arnold,
scion of a wealthy Connecticut family and a proven
soldier, to raise an army and attack Fort Ticonderoga, a small former French outpost on Lake
Champlain in New York. Before he started, Arnold
learned that a group of backwoodsmen from what is
now Vermont, a kind of guerrilla group calling themselves the Green Mountain Boys, were preparing to
march on the same fort behind an eccentric land
speculator named Ethan Allen.

Arnold caught up with the Green Mountain
Boys, but he was unable to get the headstrong Allen
to recognize his authority. Quarreling all the way to
the remote fort, the two shut up just long enough to
capture Ticonderoga on May 10. When the British
detachment, having heard nothing of Lexington and
Concord, asked in whose name they were supposed
to surrender, Allen allegedly replied, "in the name of
the great Jehovah and the Continental Congress."

Striking and memorable as the words are, since Allen
was an aggressive atheist, he was unlikely to have in-
voked Jehovah.

Over the next days, the Arnold–Allen group captured several other small forts. They were not big
battles. They were hardly battles at all by European
standards. The British garrisons were caught entirely
by surprise. But along with Bunker Hill, these triumphs established that a war had begun, forcing
Americans to take sides. Nowhere was the psychological impact greater than in Philadelphia, where the
Second Continental Congress was already in session.

The Second Continental Congress

The delegates to the Second Continental Congress
were less cautious than those to the first. Some conservatives, such as Joseph Galloway, were no longer
present. Their places were taken by militants like
young Thomas Jefferson, a Virginian who had written several scorching anti-British polemics.

Even if the men who gathered in Philadelphia in
May 1775 were more cautious, events would have

forced them to take drastic steps. Open armed rebellion was now a reality, and if the congress was to retain the authority that Ethan Allen ostensibly bestowed on it, the delegates had to catch up with the New Englanders. In order to do so, they sent George Washington, silently eloquent in military uniform, to take command of the troops around Boston. The delegates mulled over the news of Bunker Hill, Ticonderoga, an unsuccessful attack on Canada led by Arnold, and the defeat of Governor Dinsmore of Virginia by Virginians and North Carolinians at the end of 1775. Even where there was no bloodshed, royal authority was disintegrating as governors fled to the safety of British warships and self-appointed rebel committees took over government functions. Only in isolated Georgia did a decisive royal governor hold fast to real authority. But even he could not prevent three Georgia delegates from making their way to Philadelphia.

The congress still shied away from independence. Its "Declaration of the Cause and Necessity of Taking up Arms" in July 1775 insisted that the rebels sought only their rights as British subjects. But the inconsistency of shooting at George III's soldiers while swearing undying love for the king was preying on the minds of all. Throughout the autumn of 1775, more and more voices were raised for independence. With Lord North refusing to propose any kind of compromise, the congress held back only because of a thread of sentiment—the commitment of virtually all of western civilization to the principle of monarchy, and lingering affection for the person of George III.

LETTING GO

The man who snipped the thread was not an American, but an Englishman, 38 years of age in 1775, and only recently arrived in the colonies, Thomas Paine. Benjamin Franklin sponsored Paine's emigration. Perhaps because both men were of the artisan class—Paine was a corsetmaker—Franklin saw beyond Paine's history of failures in business, "loathesome" personal appearance, and vainglorious opinion of his own talents.

Common Sense

Paine was an insufferable egotist, but his talents as a rouser of protest merited considerable self-esteem. In January 1776, he published a pamphlet

that ranks with Luther's 95 theses and the *Communist Manifesto* as works of few words that changed the course of history. In *Common Sense*, Paine argued that it was foolish to risk everything for the purpose of British approval, and he shredded the Americans' sentimental attachment to King George III and to the very idea of monarchy. George was a tyrant, Paine said, a "Royal Brute." All kings were vile.

With a genius for propaganda that would produce many stirring calls on behalf of democracy and individual liberty over the next 20 years, Paine made converts by the thousands. Within a year, a land with a population of 2.5 million bought 150,000 copies of the pamphlet. (Within a decade, a half million copies

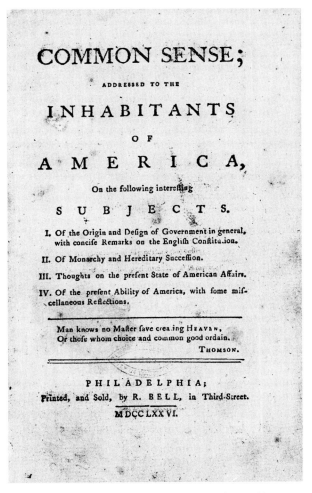

The title page of Thomas Paine's Common Sense. *His pamphlet was so widely distributed that almost every "inhabitant of North America" must have at least skimmed a copy.*

Rousing Revolution

O! ye that love mankind! Ye that dare oppose not only the tyranny but the tyrant, stand forth! Every spot of the Old World is overrun with oppression. Freedom hath been hunted around the globe. Asia and Africa have long expelled her. Europe regards her as a stranger and England hath given her warning to depart. O! receive the fugitive and prepare in time an asylum for mankind.

—Thomas Paine

were printed.) Every American who could read must have at least skimmed it. Paine boasted that it was "the greatest sale that any performance ever had since the use of letters."

Paine's depiction of the king seemed to come to life with every new dispatch from London. George III refused even to listen to American suggestions for peace, and he backed Lord North's plan to hire German mercenaries to crush the rebellion. As the spring of 1776 wore on, colony after colony formally nullified the king's authority within its boundaries. Others, borrowing phrases from Tom Paine, instructed their delegates in Philadelphia to vote for independence.

Independence

On June 7, Richard Henry Lee of Virginia introduced the resolution that "these United Colonies are, and of right ought to be, free and independent states." For three weeks the delegates debated and privately argued the issue. New England and the southern colonies were solidly for the resolution; the Middle Colonies were reluctant and divided. New York never did vote for independence, but Pennsylvania, the large, prosperous, strategically located "keystone" of the colonies, gave in. The pacifistic John Dickinson, a Quaker, and the troubled conservative Robert Morris agreed to absent themselves so that the deadlock in the delegation could be broken in favor of the resolution. (Both men later supported the patriot cause.)

Delaware swung to the side of independence when delegate Caesar Rodney galloped full tilt from Dover to Philadelphia, casting the deciding vote in his delegation. On July 2, these maneuvers concluded, the congress broke America's legal ties with England. "The second day of July 1776," an excited John Adams wrote home, "will be the most memorable epoch in the history of America." He was two days off. The "Glorious Fourth" became the national holiday when, on that day, the congress gathered to adopt its official statement to Americans and to the world of why it chose to dissolve the political bands that tied America to Great Britain.

The Declaration of Independence

Officially, the Declaration of Independence was the work of a committee consisting of Thomas Jefferson, Roger Sherman of Connecticut, John Adams, Benjamin Franklin, and Robert Livingston of New York. In fact, appreciating better than we do today that a committee cannot write anything readable, the actual composition of the document was assigned to Jefferson because of his "peculiar felicity of style." The young Virginian, red-haired, lanky, almost as careless of his personal appearance as Thomas Paine, holed up in his rooms and in two weeks emerged with a masterpiece. Franklin and Adams changed a few words, and the congress made some alterations,

Writing the Declaration

Thomas Jefferson did not try to be original in writing the Declaration of Independence, but to call on ideas that were in the air so that the American cause would be immediately accepted. His famous statement of the natural rights of man, for example, was taken from a speech that Samuel Adams made in Boston in November 1772: "Among the natural rights of the colonists are these: first, a right to life; secondly, a right to liberty; thirdly, to property; together with the right to support and defend them in the best manner they can." Beyond that, he drew from philosophical ideas well known to educated people in the colonies, Great Britain, and elsewhere in Europe.

the most important of which was to delete an attack on the institution of slavery.

Then, on July 4, the signing began. John Hancock, the president of the congress, wrote his name in flamboyant outsized script so that King George would not need his spectacles in order to read it. Hancock was risking little. Along with Samuel Adams, he already had a price on his head. Many of the others who affixed their names, some only months later, were taking a bolder step for they were unknown to the king and his advisers.

King George bore the brunt of Jefferson's attack. He was blamed for practically everything that was wrong in the colonies but the weather and the worms in the corn. The personalization of the attack was quite improper on one level, of course. King George was beholden to Parliament for every colonial policy he tried to enforce. He needed parliamentary support to raise an army. But the propaganda worked. Like

Common Sense, Jefferson's essay focused American anger on a visible and vulnerable scapegoat.

Universal Human Rights

The declaration is not remembered for its catalog of George III's high crimes and misdemeanors. It is one of the great political documents in history because, in his introductory sentences, Jefferson penned one of the most stirring statements of the rights of human beings that has been written to this day. He did not speak only of the rights of American colonials. He put the case for independence in terms of the rights of all human beings: "We hold these truths to be self-evident, that all men are created equal, that they are endowed by their Creator with certain unalienable Rights, that among these are Life, Liberty and the pursuit of Happiness." And he codified the principles that government drew its authority only

The signing of the Declaration of Independence, depicted as more formal and structured than it actually was.

Anonymous Author

For a quarter century after the Declaration of Independence was written, few people knew that Thomas Jefferson was its author. Only in 1800, when Jefferson was a candidate for the presidency, was his authorship made public and celebrated by Jefferson's supporters.

from the consent of the people to be governed, and that when the people withdrew that consent, they had the right to rebel.

Wording would be borrowed from the Declaration of Independence over the two centuries that have elapsed since its signing by many peoples asserting their right to independence from others, from the republics of Central and South America early in the 1800s to the Vietnamese on September 2, 1945. In the United States, groups demanding their human rights—from blacks to feminists to labor unions—have based their demands on their inalienable rights. In the summer of 1776, however, Americans thought less of the declaration's remote future than the necessity of confirming its pretensions on the battlefield.

CHRONOLOGY

1770   Boston Massacre

1772   *Gaspée* Burned

1773   Tea Act
       Boston Tea Party

1774   Coercive (Intolerable) Acts
       Quebec Act
       First Continental Congress

1775   Armed confrontations at Lexington, Concord, Bunker Hill, Ticonderoga
       Second Continental Congress
       Congress sends Washington to Boston to take command of troops

1776   Declaration of Independence

FOR FURTHER READING

Most of the books listed in the first paragraph of "For Further Reading" in Chapter 7 also deal with events following 1770. In addition, see David Ammerman, *In the Common Cause*, 1974; Carl Becker, *The Declaration of Independence*, 1922; Edmond S. Morgan, *Inventing the People: The Rise of Popular Sovereignty in England and America*, 1988; Robert A. Gross, *The Minutemen and Their World*, 1976; Don Higginbotham, *The War for American Independence*, 1971; Pauline Maier, *From Resistance to Rebellion*, 1972; John Shy, *Toward Lexington: The Role of the British Army on the Coming of the Revolution*, 1965; Morton White, *The Philosophy of the American Revolution*, 1978; Garry Wills, *Inventing America: Jefferson's Declaration of Independence*, 1978; Gordon S. Wood, *The Creation of the American Republic, 1776–1787*, 1969; and Hiller B. Zobel, *The Boston Massacre*, 1970.

Valuable biographies include Bernard Bailyn, *The Ordeal of Thomas Hutchinson*, 1974; Richard R. Beeman, *Patrick Henry: A Biography*, 1974; Eric Foner, *Tom Paine and Revolutionary America*, 1976; Noel B. Gerson, *The Grand Incendiary: A Biography of Samuel Adams*, 1973; Pauline Maier, *The Old Revolutionaries: Political Lives in the Age of Samuel Adams*, 1980; David Hackett Fischer, *Paul Revere's Ride*, 1994; Michael Bellesisles, *Revolutionary Outlaws: Ethan Allen and the Struggle for Independence*, 1993; and Milton E. Flower, *John Dickinson: Conservative Revolutionary*, 1983.

British General John Burgoyne surrenders to Horatio Gates at Saratoga, New York, in 1777. It was the most important American victory of the war until the climactic fight at Yorktown.

9
CHAPTER

WAR FOR INDEPENDENCE

Winning the Revolution

1776–1781

The history of our Revolution will be one continual lie from one end to the other. The essence of the whole will be that Dr. Franklin's electrical rod smote the earth and out sprang George Washington. That Franklin electrified him with his rod—and thenceforward these two constructed all the policy, negotiations, legislatures, and war.

— John Adams

By the rude bridge that arched the flood,
Their flag to April's breeze unfurled,
Here once the embattled farmers stood,
And fired the shot heard round the world.

— Ralph Waldo Emerson

The signers of the Declaration of Independence pledged their lives, their fortunes, and their sacred honor to the cause of independence. This was no empty vow. Had George III won the quick victory he expected to win, the men of the Second Continental Congress would have been punished severely, possibly hanged. The noose had been the fate of rebels in Ireland and would be again. The Americans called themselves patriots, but from where the king sat, they were traitors.

THE IMBALANCE OF POWER

Looked at without benefit of hindsight, patriot chances of success were not, in 1776, very bright. Despite the military and moral victories of the preceding year, the patriots had challenged Europe's premier power and one of its finest armies. And they did not even have a majority of Americans behind them.

The Numbers

After the fighting around Boston in 1775, Lord North's military advisor, Lord George Germain, assembled an army of 32,000 which was dispatched to join the redcoats already in America. They sailed in a flotilla of more than 400 ships. It was Britain's largest military endeavor to that date. In addition to British regulars, Germain contracted in January 1776 to hire 18,000 (later 30,000) mercenaries from several petty German princes who supported themselves by training and renting out crack soldiers. Many, from the principalities of Hesse, earned the Germans the name Hessians. By hiring them, Britain internationalized the civil conflict even before Thomas Jefferson made his appeal to "the opinions of mankind." During much of the war, the British had 50,000 troops ready for battle.

Against this massive force, the Americans could field only hastily organized militia made up of farm boys, restless apprentices, and city laborers. "To place any dependence on them," George Washington wrote, "is assuredly resting on a broken staff." Terms of enlistment in the militia were short, often geared to the demands of agriculture. At harvest time—and with winter coming on—whole armies evaporated. Nevertheless, militiamen played a key role in the Revolution. They maintained patriot authority in those areas the British did not occupy.

The Continental Congress created its own army, but Washington himself was never to have more than 18,500 of these "continentals" ready at one time. On several occasions, his command dwindled to a mere 5,000. Still, those who served impressed foreign observers for their commitment to the cause of independence and their willingness to endure setbacks and sometimes terrible hardship. Some 4,400 patriot soldiers were killed in battle, perhaps 20,000 more died of illness, disease, and prison. About 16 percent of able-bodied American males served in one or another part of the military.

The patriot navy was, as a whole, little more than a joke. George Washington paid for the first American warship, the *Hannah*, a schooner with only four guns, out of his own pocket. The Continental Congress eventually appropriated funds to build 13 frigates, one for each state, but they fared poorly against what was the finest and largest navy in the world. Of the eleven frigates actually built, one was destroyed in battle, seven were captured, two were scuttled in order to avoid capture, and one was accidentally set afire by its crew. Not the sort of record about which military marches are written.

The Loyalists

Moreover, the patriots could not always rely on the support of the civilian population. John Adams probably overshot the mark when he estimated that a third of the white population was Tory, loyal to the king. Nevertheless, in March 1776, when General William Howe evacuated Boston, a city of just 15,000 people and notorious for its anti-British sentiment, a thousand Americans went with him. When Howe moved his headquarters to New York in September, he was received more as a liberator than as a conqueror. At the end of the war, as many as 100,000 Americans (1 in 30) left their native home for England, the West Indies, and Canada, particularly Nova Scotia.

Most northern Anglicans were Loyalists. So were some rich merchants with close commercial ties to England and, in the South, backcountry farmers who had been Regulators. Imperial officials naturally supported the Crown, as did some very rich South Carolina and Georgia planters who feared that the social disruptions that accompany war would lead to slave uprisings.

Indeed, the British won some support among slaves by promising freedom in return for military

General William Howe, the first commander of the British troops sent to suppress the revolution.

service. As many as 5,000 blacks served in the American forces, too. Indians were likewise divided in their choice of sides. After first declaring neutrality, the Iroquois Confederacy split wide open on the issue of the war. The Oneidas and Tuscaroras supported the patriots. The Senecas, Cayugas, and Mohawks were persuaded by a high-ranking brother and sister, Joseph and Mary Brant—she was the widow of a British Indian Commissioner—that their lands would be safer if the British prevailed. The Revolution thus wrote the end of the longest-lasting confederacy among North American Indians.

Far more numerous than active Tories were people who were indifferent to the conflict. Adams said they comprised a third of the population and

The Fears of a Loyalist

The Reverend Mather Byles (1706–1788) was an oddity, a Massachusetts Congregational minister who opposed the Revolution. In a sermon of 1776 he expressed his fears of democracy: "Which is better, to be ruled by one tyrant three thousand miles away, or by three thousand tyrants not a mile away?"

Francis Hopkinson of New Jersey vilified them as cynical opportunists willing to hop either way, depending on which side was winning in the neighborhood. In a poem about a metaphorical war between birds and beasts, Hopkinson wrote that there were

'Mongst us too many, like the Bat,
Inclin'd to do this side or that
As in'trest leads—or wait to see
Which party will the stronger be.

He was too harsh, as zealots usually are. As in every era, many Americans, perhaps a majority, wished only to be left alone. Most of the "bats" were neither heroes nor villains, just ordinary folk who failed to see what all the palaver and battling had to do with them.

Patriot Chances

Despite the handicaps, the patriot cause was far from doomed. The rebels were fighting a defensive war in their homeland. As many twentieth-century "wars of liberation" have shown, such conflicts bestow great advantages on the rebels. Militarily, the patriots did not have to destroy or even decisively defeat the British. Rebels on their own ground need only to hold on and hold out until weariness, demoralization, and dissent take their toll on the enemy.

An army attempting to suppress a rebellion, by way of contrast, must wipe out the enemy force and then occupy and pacify the entire country. The patriots' loyal parliamentary friend, Edmund Burke, tried to point out the difficulty of doing this in 1775. "The use of force alone is but temporary," he said. "It may subdue for a moment; but it does not remove the necessity of subduing again; and a nation is not governed which is perpetually to be conquered."

The British were never able to wipe out patriot military resistance. The redcoats occupied most port cities through most of the war. As late as 1780, they captured Charleston. But only one American in twenty lived in the seaports. The countryside remained under patriot control or, at least, beyond the capacity of the British to control it. The huge British garrison had to be provisioned from abroad. Even grain for horses was carried by ship from England and Ireland. At one point, British commanders thought they would have to import hay!

Pro-American sentiment was strong in England. Influential members of Parliament such as Burke and the Marquis of Rockingham sniped at Lord North's ministry throughout the war. John Wilkes, radical and disreputable but claiming the support of a small groups of politicos, was pro-patriot. These men believed that the Americans were more right than wrong.

The Americans also had reason to hope for foreign intervention. Since 1763, the major powers of Europe had been uneasy with Great Britain's preeminence. In Spanish Louisiana, Governor Bernardo de Gálvez provided arms to the Americans from the start. France, so recently humiliated in North America, India, and Europe, was even more helpful. In May 1776, the French government began to funnel money and arms to the rebels through a secret agent, Pierre de Beaumarchais. Over the next two years, the Americans depended on France for 80 percent of their gunpowder.

War Crimes

Soldiers and Native Americans on both sides were guilty of acts that, today, we would call atrocities. Colonel Henry Hamilton, the British commander of the fort at Detroit, was nicknamed the "hair-buyer" because he paid Indian allies for patriot scalps, whether of men, women, or children. In 1776, Cherokees devastated the Virginia and Carolina frontiers, leading to a reprisal by South Carolina militiamen who destroyed Cherokee towns and the year's entire crop.

In July 1778, a British-led force of Loyalists and Indians scourged Pennsylvania's Wyoming Valley and, in November, a similar group swept through Cherry Valley, just 50 miles from Albany, New York. On November 11, 40 patriots were massacred after they had surrendered.

At King's Mountain in 1780, American troops did the same thing, firing on British soldiers trying to surrender. In the same year, Virginia and North Carolina militia burned 1,000 Cherokee villages and destroyed 50,000 bushels of corn, not bothering to count the fatalities. In March 1782, Pennsylvania militia murdered 96 Indians of the Delaware nation who were trying to stay out of the conflict.

Most, but not all, of the baldest atrocities were the work of militia, guerrillas, or Indians. Many probably had less to do with empire and independence than with that ageless opportunity of wartime: it is an excellent time to settle old scores.

Business and Pleasure in Paris

In September 1776, the Continental Congress sent Benjamin Franklin, 70 years old but far from creaky, to join other American diplomats in Paris to work for a French alliance. Franklin was a social sensation in France. The aristocracy, in the final years of its glitter, was enamored of him. The bewigged and powdered ladies and lords of Louis XVI's court were in the throes of a "noble savage" craze. The gist of the fad, based on the writings of Jean Jacques Rousseau, was that primitives such as their own peasants and the rustic Americans led happy, wholesome lives because of their closeness to nature.

Queen Marie Antoinette built a model peasant village at Versailles, where she and her ladies-in-waiting dressed like milkmaids, tended well-scrubbed cows, and giggled along behind flocks of perfumed geese. Well aware of this nonsense, Franklin (who preferred the high life) made a point of appearing at court wearing homespun wool clothing, no wig on his bald head, and rimless bifocal spectacles (which he had invented) on his unpowdered nose.

French high society loved the show, but the foreign minister, Charles, Count Vergennes, was more demanding. Secret shipments of arms were one thing. Before Vergennes would commit the French army and navy to open war with Britain, he wanted evidence that the rebels were more than rioters who would disperse after a good snort of gunpowder. In 1776 and the first half of 1777, Franklin was unable to provide Vergennes much encouragement.

"THE TIMES THAT TRY MEN'S SOULS"

General Howe, who took command of British forces in the colonies after the Battle of Bunker Hill, was equally deliberate. A meticulous planner, he moved only when sure of the consequences, preferring to err on the side of caution.

Early in 1776, caution dictated that he evacuate Boston. A Massachusetts general, Henry Knox, had arrived outside the city with 43 cannon and 16 big mortars from Fort Ticonderoga, 60 tons of artillery moved through frozen Massachusetts, a feat by which he won Washington's lasting friendship. Washington positioned the guns on Dorchester Heights, high ground to the south of Boston. With a

The Battle for New York

On July 2, 1776, the same day that Congress voted for independence, Howe landed 10,000 men on Staten Island, just south of New York City. Within seven weeks, he tripled his numbers and moved to Long Island, where Washington's smaller force had hurriedly dug in. The American position was untenable. Washington had to fight on ground laced by navigable waterways that gave the edge to the force with naval power. Washington had a few fishermen from Massachusetts to ferry his soldiers about. Howe could call on a fleet of more than 200 ships, commanded by his brother, Admiral Lord Richard Howe.

Benjamin Franklin donned no powdered wig or finery when he mixed with French aristocrats. He knew perfectly how to exploit their infatuation with the notion that Americans were "noble savages."

never-friendly population restive under the threat of a bombardment, Howe decided to relocate his headquarters by sea to New York, where Loyalists were more numerous. Washington would have no choice but to follow him and fight on ground more favorable to the British.

The Cincinnati

Lucius Quinctius Cincinnatus was an early Roman who was twice appointed dictator of the Republic in order to defeat invaders. Each time Cincinnatus was victorious but, instead of using his vast powers to entrench himself as a tyrant, he returned to his farm, a private citizen. It is not surprising that educated Americans of the Revolutionary era, who were steeped in classical lore, thought of George Washington as their Cincinnatus.

In 1784, veteran officers of the Continental Army formed the Society of the Cincinnati. The organization was controversial from the start. It was semisecret and membership was hereditary, passed down by officers to their first-born sons, who passed it to their first-born sons. In other words, the society preserved the aristocratic principle of primogeniture that was then being abolished in American legal codes. Thomas Jefferson thought the society represented a "nascent nobility" and most of its members seem indeed to have favored electing a president for life. During the troubled 1790s, rumors of a military coup led by the Cincinnati periodically worried the Jeffersonians.

However, the charter members grew long in the teeth without biting, the principle of primogeniture was abandoned so that all male descendants of Revolutionary officers might belong, and the society evolved into an organization "devoted to the principles of the Revolution, the preservation of history and the diffusion of historical knowledge." As such it exists today.

NOTABLE PEOPLE

Daniel Boone (1734–1820)

Stephen Vincent Benét's poetry celebrated America. In *John Brown's Body* and *Western Star*, his homages ran to more than a hundred pages of often moving verse. And yet, his finest poem about America may be his shortest:

> When Daniel Boone goes by, at night,
> The phantom deer arise
> And all lost, wild America
> Is burning in their eyes.

The name of Daniel Boone is probably known to as many schoolchildren as any figure in American history. It evokes an image more vivid than the Gilbert Stuart portrait of Washington: a long, lank woodlands frontiersman in fringed buckskin and coonskin cap, striped tail dangling languidly on "Dan'l's" neck as he crouches behind a hickory with his Kentucky Long Rifle, poised to "cill a b'ar"—or a skulking Shawnee.

The Boone of legend is an *American* hero, simultaneously delving into the mystery of the wilderness and devoted to it, moving on when he needed more "elbow room"—when he could see the smoke rising from his nearest neighbor's fire.

The kernel of truth is there—Boone was superb in the woods and doubtless happiest there—but the rest of the grain is bogus or, at best, very dubious. If Boone ever wore a coonskin cap, it was *in extremis*, when Indians had stolen his wilderness gear, including the broad-brimmed beaver felt hat he preferred. Theft, not murder (as both legend-makers and sentimentalists would have it), was his and the Shawnees' chief crime against one another.

"D. Boon" was not particularly long, just five feet, eight inches tall by his son's recounting. Far from fleeing those who followed him west, his most notable accomplishment was to build a road to encourage others to come. The idea was to have buyers for land he thought he owned.

If Boone was an American type, his patriotism was less than hysterical. He thought seriously of locating in Spanish Florida as a young man, was court-martialed as a Tory during the Revolution (he was acquitted, but the facts remain not quite conclusive), and left the United States for Spanish Missouri in 1799, not because he craved solitude, but because he was embittered with his treatment under the Stars and Stripes. One thinks more of Stephen Austin and Brigham Young than of James K. Polk.

Daniel Boone was born in 1734 near Reading, Pennsylvania, to a family of Quaker inclinations but casual commitments. The family was neither rich nor destitute, and emigrated to "the West" of the era, western North Carolina.

In 1755, at 21 years of age, Boone was a teamster with the disastrous Braddock campaign in western Pennsylvania. He may have made the acquaintance of young George Washington, but comrades much more important to his future were Thomas Walker, who had discovered the Cumberland Gap through the Appalachians in 1750, and a frontier roustabout, John Finley, who had hunted in the trans-Appalachian forests and canebrakes the Iroquois called Kentucky.

On August 27, the Howes almost surrounded Washington at the Battle of Long Island, but the Americans slipped away to fortifications at Brooklyn Heights, across the East River from Manhattan. Again Howe's redcoats and Hessians punished the 5,000 rebels, but, in one night, Washington managed to sneak the bulk of his army to Manhattan. Howe pursued him, capturing 3,000 American troops at Fort Washington and forcing General Nathaniel Greene to abandon Fort Lee, across the Hudson River in New Jersey. Once again Washington and his bedraggled army escaped within hours of capture, first north to White Plains and, when nearly surrounded there, across the Hudson River into New Jersey. His New England oarsmen were toiling every bit as hard as his foot soldiers.

Fox and Hounds

General Howe was having a jolly good time. The New York campaign reminded him of the British gentry's favorite sport, the fox hunt. When the

Hardly obsessed with Kentucky, Boone was not to rediscover the Cumberland Gap for himself for 12 years, and then only because Finley showed up on his doorstep with the idea. He was by no means, as legend-maker Timothy Flint would call him in 1847, "the first white man of the West."

In 1769, Boone finally traced the Gap. He really was the first white man to locate the "Warrior's Path," which Shawnee and Cherokee hunters used to move through Kentucky. Ironically, few Indians actually lived on "the dark and bloody ground." The Cherokee and Shawnee uneasily shared Kentucky as a hunting ground. The land's lack of a native population was a major reason that men like Boone found it attractive for settlement. Boone's employer in 1775, Richard Henderson of the Transylvania Company, scrupulously paid the Cherokee for rights to it.

In 1775, with 30 skilled axemen, Boone supervised the construction of the Wilderness Road, which was, in fact, a trace. Only in 1796 was it widened to accommodate wagons. It was over this trail that he led the first permanent settlers into Kentucky. George Caleb Bingham was right to pick the moment Boone's party emerged into the sun of Kentucky to immortalize him in oils.

Boone was a major in the Virginia militia during the Revolution, but he was also accused of collaboration with the British and their Shawnee allies. Still, as early as 1784, when Boone was 50, the legend was building. A book promoting Kentucky by John Filson included an "autobiographical" sketch allegedly by Boone.

During the confederation years, Boone supported himself by hunting and hoped to make a bigger killing as a land speculator. Unfortunately, just as he lost thousands of buckskins to Indians, he lost just about every title dispute in which he was involved to another kind of pilferer. By the 1790s, he was virtually landless in the country, now a state, which he had done so much to develop.

It is tempting to remember Boone for his morality as a land speculator, a rarer distinction than being a pioneer. What he did not lose in court he sold in order to compensate associates for whose losses he felt responsible. But he was bitter, too. When he went to Spanish Missouri in 1799, it was in part to get out of the United States.

The flag followed him four years later and, again, men sharper at finagling before the bar separated most of his land from him. Again, he sold to pay off debts, claiming that, in 1815, his assets totaled 50 cents. A creditor from Kentucky who descended upon him at his son's farmstead near Defiance, Missouri, was told, "You have come a great distance to suck a bull and, I reckon, you will have to go home dry."

Boone died in 1820, not sitting up facing west, as the mythmakers told it, but in bed. Three years later, his fame was such that Byron devoted a few stanzas of *Don Juan* to him.

> Of the great names which in our faces stare,
> The General Boone, back-woodsman
>   of Kentucky,
> Was happiest amongst mortals anywhere.

Americans were on the run north of New York City, he infuriated the dignified and self-conscious Washington by sounding the traditional bugle call of the chase.

In truth, Washington's army was as desperate as a fox dodging hounds. Washington had to flee across New Jersey without a fight. When he crossed the Delaware River into Pennsylvania, his men were demoralized and ready to desert. In Philadelphia, one day's march to the south, Congress panicked and fled to Baltimore, effectively leaving the Virginian in command of what was left of the Revolution.

"These are the times that try men's souls," Thomas Paine wrote in desperation. "The summer soldier and the sunshine patriot will, in this crisis, shrink from the service of his country." About 3,000 rebels in British-occupied New York and New Jersey took an oath of allegiance to the Crown. The Revolution was in danger of being snuffed out not six months after the signatures on the Declaration of Independence had been blotted dry.

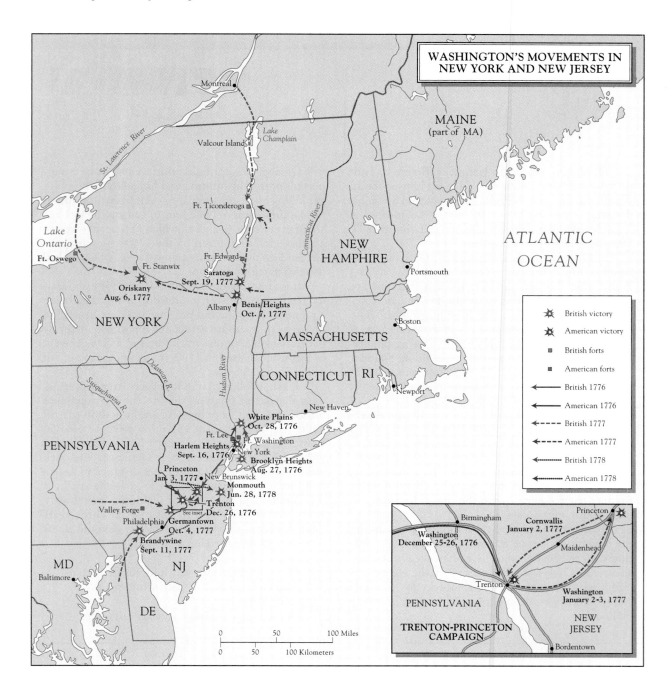

WASHINGTON'S MOVEMENTS IN NEW YORK AND NEW JERSEY

Montreal

MAINE
(part of MA)

St. Lawrence River

Valcour Island

Lake Champlain

Ft. Ticonderoga

Lake Ontario

Ft. Oswego

Ft. Stanwix

Ft. Edward

NEW HAMPHIRE

ATLANTIC OCEAN

Oriskany
Aug. 6, 1777

Saratoga
Sept. 19, 1777

Portsmouth

Connecticut River

NEW YORK

Albany

Benis Heights
Oct. 7, 1777

MASSACHUSETTS

Boston

Delaware R.

Susquehanna R.

Hudson River

CONNECTICUT   RI

Newport

PENNSYLVANIA

White Plains
Oct. 28, 1776

New Haven

Ft. Lee   Ft. Washington

Harlem Heights
Sept. 16, 1776

New York

Princeton
Jan. 3, 1777

New Brunswick

Brooklyn Heights
Aug. 27, 1776

Monmouth
Jun. 28, 1778

Valley Forge

See inset

Trenton
Dec. 26, 1776

Philadelphia   Germantown
Oct. 4, 1777

Brandywine
Sept. 11, 1777

MD

Baltimore

NJ

DE

✸	British victory
✸	American victory
■	British forts
■	American forts
←	British 1776
←	American 1776
←- -	British 1777
←- -	American 1777
←····	British 1778
←····	American 1778

0   50   100 Miles
0   50   100 Kilometers

TRENTON-PRINCETON CAMPAIGN

Birmingham

Princeton

Cornwallis
January 2, 1777

Washington
December 25-26, 1776

Maidenhead

Trenton

Washington
January 2-3, 1777

PENNSYLVANIA

NEW JERSEY

Bordentown

But William Howe soldiered by the book, and the book said that an army went into winter quarters when the snow fell. Howe settled into New York, where his mistress and a lively round of dinners and parties beckoned. He recalled the hounds from Washington's heels, leaving small garrisons of Hessians to guard Trenton and Princeton.

Crossing the Delaware

George Washington was no more an innovator than Howe. Had his army not been near disintegration, he also might have followed the book into winter quarters. But his army needed a boost, a big one. On Christmas night, 1776, Washington's fishermen rowed the army across the Delaware into New

The Battle of Princeton, *by William Mercer. The surprised British forces had the upper hand until George Washington arrived with his main force and routed them.*

Jersey, the boats dodging ice floes and, in the fog, one another. The troops quickly marched nine miles to Trenton, the most isolated British outpost. At dawn, they caught the Hessians in their bedrolls and, none the better for their holiday celebrations. Washington captured almost the entire garrison of 900, while sustaining only five American casualties.

An annoyed Howe sent two forces to battle Washington before the Americans could press close enough to New York to ruin his holidays. Washington wisely avoided a fight with General Charles Cornwallis and, on January 3, 1777, defeated another small garrison at Princeton. Cornwallis withdrew to New Brunswick, within range of reinforcements from New York but far enough from the city to soothe Howe's nerves. Washington set up his winter quarters at Morristown on the Delaware.

Washington had saved the patriot cause. His offensive across the Delaware provided a needed boost to patriot morale. Still, the victories at Trenton and Princeton did not significantly affect Howe's posi-

tion or strategy. His army was intact and snug in New York, while another force amassed in Canada. The British had the initiative.

The Northern Strategy

Howe's initial plan to win the war, conveyed by letter to Lord Germain in London, was to march north up the Hudson River and join forces with another British army moving south out of Montreal. This pincers movement would isolate New England from the rest of the colonies. With the support of the Royal Navy, the British could subdue Massachusetts from the west. If the occupation of New England did not discourage the rebels south of New York, the army could then turn in that direction.

Germain was persuaded, but not so much by Howe as by General John Burgoyne, who had returned to England from Boston. Burgoyne, a playwright and bon vivant popular in London society, was given command of an army in Montreal which

Military Music

Drum, fife, and trumpet were an essential part of eighteenth-century armies. Boys 12 to 16 beating snare drums set the cadence for soldiers on the march. With his men stepping off 96 paces of 30 inches each per minute, a commander knew that he was moving three miles in fifty minutes, allowing ten minutes each hour for a breather and a drink.

The fifers tootled both to entertain the men and to communicate orders: the "Pioneers' March" was the signal for road-clearing crews to get started ahead of the infantry. "Roast Beef" meant it was time to eat (although roast beef was seldom on the menu for Americans). Fife and drum were essential in battle. The men could hear them above the roar of firearms, but not necessarily an officer's voice.

Cavalry also used music for communication, but kettle drums instead of snare drums, so as not to be confused with infantry, and a valveless trumpet instead of fife because, requiring only one hand to play instead of two, it could be played on horseback.

Drummer boys were in the thick of battle and quite as apt to be killed as other soldiers. At 16 years of age, they generally graduated to the army. A few of them, grown too old for fighting, or hobbled by a wound, returned to the fife and drum corps as drum majors.

numbered 8,000 troops and was armed with more than 100 cannon. It was Burgoyne's big chance for glory, a fact that annoyed Howe. Thanks to Burgoyne's personal lobbying in London, he and not Howe would get credit for the conquest of New England.

Howe was therefore receptive to the pleas of Loyalists such as Joseph Galloway to move south rather than north. Galloway, a Pennsylvanian, persuaded the general that taking Philadelphia would knock the Middle Colonies out of the war, a victory that would exceed in esteem anything Burgoyne managed.

The Watershed Campaign of 1777

In the summer of 1777, leaving 3,000 men in New York under General Henry Clinton, Howe moved by sea into Pennsylvania. Washington followed once again and, once again, on September 11, was defeated at Brandywine Creek, southwest of Philadelphia. On September 26, after another victory at Paoli, Howe occupied Philadelphia. On October 4, Washington counterattacked at the suburb of Germantown. While coming close to victory, he was finally repulsed—again. The Americans had to fall back to winter quarters at Valley Forge. Howe was comfortably ensconced in the largest city in the colonies, which was also, in theory, the capital of the United States.

Howe had his glory but it was soon tarnished by news from upper New York. In June, while Howe was putting to sea, General Burgoyne left Montreal. The first part of the long trek went well. The old Indian trail to Lake Champlain was broad and secure. The lake itself provided a fast highway 125 miles into New York. Fort Ticonderoga, at the foot of the lake, fell without a fight.

Then, however, the wilderness began to take its toll. Burgoyne's heavy artillery and the provisions needed to supply 8,000 troops (and 2,000 camp followers) could be moved only slowly on a trail meant for moccasins. Burgoyne's personal baggage alone was immense, filling 30 carts with a living and dining suite fit for the toast of London: heavy beds and tables, linens, fine china, crystal, silverware, wine, and brandy. Small groups of patriots felled large trees across the road, creating a far more difficult job of

Despair at Valley Forge

The winter of 1777–1778 was extremely difficult for Washington's army. Inadequately fed, clothed, and sheltered at Valley Forge, while the British enjoyed comfortable quarters in Philadelphia, many fell to the depths of despair. Albigence Waldo, a surgeon with Connecticut troops, wrote this entry in his journal on December 14, 1777:

Poor food—hard lodging—cold weather—fatigue—nasty cloathes—nasty cookery—vomit half my time—smoaked out of my senses—the Devil's in't—I can't endure it—Why are we sent here to starve and freeze?—What sweet felicities have I left at home: A charming wife—pretty children—good beds—good food—good cookery—all agreeable—all harmonious! Here all confusion—smoke and cold—hunger and filthyness—a pox on my bad luck!

after yet another damaging battle, the patriots accepted the surrender of some 5,700 soldiers. The Battle of Saratoga was the most important event of the year, perhaps of the war. With it, New England was lost to the British. Except for Newport, Rhode Island, which they held only by tying down an army and fleet, the British never again secured a foothold north of New York City.

THE TIDE TURNS

In Paris, Saratoga was exactly the news for which Benjamin Franklin and his colleagues were waiting. The victory allayed Vergennes's doubts about patriot chances of winning. The rout of an army of 8,000 crack redcoats and German mercenaries was no skirmish, even by French military standards.

Nor by British standards. When Lord North heard of the battle, he wrote to Franklin that King George was willing to end the war on the basis of the terms demanded by Americans up to July 1776. That is, the Intolerable Acts and every other obnoxious law enacted between 1763 and 1775 would be repealed.

George Washington at Verplanck's Point, *by John Trumbull (1790).*

clearance for British axemen. During one three-week spell, Burgoyne's army moved less than a mile a day.

Then Gentleman Johnny learned that reinforcements he had expected to arrive via the Mohawk River had been turned back by Benedict Arnold; and then, that thousands of Iroquois, demoralized by patriot destruction of their food supply, had abandoned the British cause. Next, a Hessian raiding party sent east to seize supplies in Bennington, Vermont, was wiped out by local militia. In a series of skirmishes around Saratoga, another fort, Burgoyne lost hundreds more men.

Knowing by now that Howe was en route to Philadelphia, Burgoyne should have given up the expedition and backtracked to the safety of Canada. The intended attack on New England was out of the question. Even if he reached New York, he would accomplish little. He could not occupy the ground he had traversed. Nevertheless, Burgoyne sat tight, ordered his wines and sauces, and waited for help from General Clinton in New York.

Burgoyne's blunder was a godsend to the Americans under General Horatio Gates. On October 17,

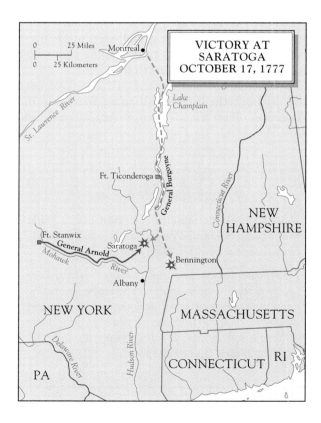

Great Britain would concede colonial control of internal affairs in return for loyalty to the king.

This attractive offer amounted to an American victory. Essentially, Lord North had proposed to reorganize the empire as a commonwealth of autonomous dominions, the status Britain was to accord to Canada, Australia, and New Zealand in the nineteenth century. But victory is a tonic. After Saratoga, American blood was up. By the end of 1777, American animosity toward the mother country had intensified. In New Jersey, British and Hessian troops had been brutal, bullying farmers, raping women and girls. The old rallying cry, the "rights of British subjects," had lost its magic. The French offer of a formal military alliance was more attractive than returning, however autonomously, to the British Empire.

Foreign Friends

On December 17, 1777, Vergennes formally recognized the United States as an independent nation. In February 1778, he concluded a treaty of alliance, to go into effect if France and Britain went to war (which they did in June 1778). The agreement provided for close commercial ties between France and the United States and stated that if the United States conquered Canada, France would assert no claims to its former colony. France's reward at the peace table would be in the British West Indies.

The Revolutionary War could not have been won without the French alliance. Not only did "America's oldest friend" pour money and men into the fray, but France also provided a fleet to make up for the Americans' nearly total lack of sea power. Although Americans relished the one-on-one victories over British warships by such captains as John Paul Jones ("I have not yet begun to fight") and John Barry (no particularly memorable sayings), the American coastline was, without French help, at the mercy of the Royal Navy.

France's diplomatic influence was also critical to the American cause. Spain sent Bernardo de Gálvez into British Florida, where he quickly occupied every fort. Vergennes averted a war brewing between Prussia and Austria that would have tied down French troops in Europe (a traditional British objective). He persuaded both of those countries, as well as Russia, to declare their neutrality in the American conflict. Vergennes's diplomatic maneuvers denied England an ally against the Americans and paved the way for informal assistance to the patriots from all over Europe. Next to France, the Netherlands was the most valuable ally.

Mercenaries for Liberty

In addition, the chronic warfare of eighteenth-century Europe had created a class of military professionals who, during times of peace, were unhappily unemployed. Gentlemen and aristocrats of this stripe, hungry for a commission with a salary attached, poured into the infant United States. There was plenty of deadwood in the bunch. But others were able men who were motivated by more than money. Some sympathized with the principles of liberty expressed in the Declaration of Independence.

John Barry was an Irishman, John Paul Jones, Scottish. Another idealist was Marie Joseph, the Marquis de Lafayette, a 19-year-old aristocrat (the British called him "the boy") who proved an excellent field commander and a close personal friend to Washington. Lafayette was no dilettante, dabbling in fashionable notions. After returning to France, he worked for social and political liberalization until his death in 1834.

Equally idealistic was Casimir Pulaski, a Polish noble who had fought for his country's independence from Russia. Recruited in Paris by Benjamin Franklin, Pulaski was a romantic figure, a cavalry commander in gaudy uniform and waxed mustache. He was killed leading a charge at the Battle of Savannah late in the

---

A Vision of the Future

John Adams understood that circumstances made him a politician and a revolutionary. But he envisioned another kind of future for his country:

I must study politics and war, that my sons may have liberty to study mathematics and philosophy, geography, natural history and naval architecture, navigation, commerce, and agriculture, in order to give their children a right to study painting, poetry, music, architecture, statuary, tapestry and porcelain.

war. Johann Kalb, a Bavarian who took the title Baron de Kalb when he went to America (then as now, titles wore well in the United States), also lost his life during the war, at the Battle of Camden.

Jean Baptiste, the Comte de Rochambeau, who had secured arms for the Americans, arrived in Newport, Rhode Island, in 1780 and was to play a major role in the final victorious American battle at Yorktown, Virginia, the next year. Possibly more valuable to the revolutionary cause than combat officers were support specialists like Thaddeus Kosciusko, an engineer who was expert in building fortifications, a military field in which few Americans were trained. Kosciusko returned to Europe to fight for the independence of Poland, where he became a national hero.

Friedrich Wilhelm von Steuben, a Prussian who also dubbed himself a baron, apparently without justification, was an expert in drill. He is credited with supervising the training program that turned Washington's soldiers from a ragtag crowd into a well-disciplined army at Valley Forge during the winter of 1777–1778.

The War Drags On

Steuben worked his wonders just in time. Washington lost 2,500 men to disease, exposure, and desertion during the winter at Valley Forge and, by the spring of 1778, it was obvious that the war would go on for years. The Americans could not hope to force the issue against the British. Their strategy was to hold on, fighting battles only when conditions were auspicious. Lord Germain and General Clinton (who took over from Howe in May 1778) planned to strangle the American economy through a naval blockade and to concentrate their major military effort in the South.

Beginning with the occupation of Savannah, Georgia, in December 1778, the redcoats won a series of victories in the South, but they could not break the stalemate. For each British victory, the Americans won another, or, in losing ground, the rebels cost the British so heavily that they had to return to the coast, to within reach of supply ships flying the Union Jack.

The war wore heavily on the American side, too. Prices of necessities soared. Imports were available only at exorbitant costs. On the frontier, British-backed Indians ravaged newly settled areas in Pennsylvania's Wyoming Valley and Cherry Val-

ley in New York. When Congress failed to pay and provision troops during 1780 and 1781, mutinies erupted on the Connecticut, Pennsylvania, and New Jersey lines.

Then, in September 1780, Washington learned that Benedict Arnold, commander of the fortress at West Point, had agreed to sell the fort and his services to the British for £20,000. Disgruntled at what he considered shabby treatment by Congress, Arnold was also deeply in debt. He calculated that the British would eventually win, and so accepted a commission along with pensions for his wife and children. It was an expensive proposition, but the British believed that the defection of one of the Revolution's few heroes would demoralize the rebels.

It helped. The campaign of 1781 opened with American hopes lower than they had been since the Battle of Trenton. Washington was idle outside New York. The most active British army, led by Lord Cornwallis, lost a battle at Cowpens, South Carolina, but then repeatedly pummeled Nathaniel Greene the width of North Carolina. Cornwallis then joined with several other commanders (including Benedict Arnold) to amass 7,500 men in Virginia.

Washington Seizes an Opportunity

But Charles Cornwallis had problems. Anywhere far from navigable water was dangerous ground for the British troops. So, on August 1, 1781, Cornwallis set up what he regarded as a routine encampment at Yorktown, Virginia, a little town on the same neck of land where the first permanent English settlement in America was founded. Cornwallis then requested supplies and further orders from General Clinton in New York. When Clinton dawdled, Washington sensed an opportunity for a decisive blow.

In mid-August, Washington learned that a French admiral, Count François de Grasse, was sailing from the West Indies to the Chesapeake Bay with 3,000 French troops aboard 25 warships. Although he had just completed plans for an assault on New York, Washington recognized the better prospect in Virginia. Maneuvering around New York City so that Clinton would sit tight, he raced across New Jersey. In September, he joined his troops to those of Lafayette, Rochambeau, Steuben, and de Grasse. This combined army of 17,000 outnumbered Cornwallis's 8,000, almost the first time in the war that the rebels enjoyed numerical superiority.

Washington and "The Boy," his devoted aide Lafayette, at winter quarters, Valley Forge, Pennsylvania.

Yorktown

Cornwallis did not panic. His men were well dug in, and he expected to move them out by sea and resume the war of attrition elsewhere. But between September 5 and 10, de Grasse sent the British evacuation fleet sailing off empty to New York. Cornwallis fought a futile defense. On October 17, he asked for terms, and on October 19, he faced the inevitable and surrendered.

He gave up, but without grace. As if to provide one last symbol of the British arrogance that had driven the Americans to rebellion, Cornwallis tried to surrender to the French rather than the upstart colonial, Washington. Rochambeau, the ranking French officer, refused. Then, at the surrender ceremonies, Cornwallis refused to hand his sword personally to Washington, as military etiquette required. Instead, he sent an inferior officer to the American camp

with his blade. Washington refused to receive him, nodding that the symbol of capitulation should be given to General Benjamin Lincoln, whom the British had humiliated at Charleston at the beginning of the southern campaign. It may also have been designed as a jibe that a British band played the hymn, "The World Turn'd Upside Down." No doubt, however, many American soldiers hummed along merrily to the tune.

The Treaty of Paris

The British could have fought on. They still had 44,000 troops in North America. But no one had the stomach for it. In February 1782, the House of Commons voted against continuing the war, and Lord North resigned. He was succeeded by the Marquis of Rockingham, the Whig peer who had moved to repeal the Stamp Act in 1766.

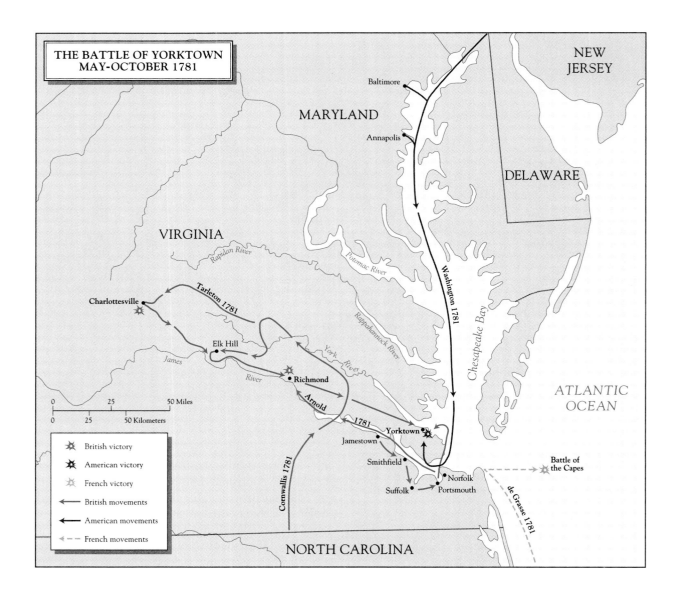

The Treaty of Paris was not finally signed until September 1783. The delay was due in part to the fact that, once the war was won, the Americans and the French grew increasingly suspicious of one another. Fearing betrayal, each ally tried to betray the other first. The Americans won the game. They agreed with the British on independence, a boundary between the United States and Canada, American fishing rights off Newfoundland and Nova Scotia, and a promise that Congress would urge the states not to molest Loyalists or seize Loyalist property.

George III was as unsporting about independence as Cornwallis had been about surrender at Yorktown. He wrote of his former colonies that "knavery seems to be so much the striking feature of its inhabitants that it may not in the end be an evil that they become aliens to this Kingdom."

The "Father of His Country"

George Washington was no knave. But he was in many ways an unlikely candidate to be accorded the honor, "father of his country," and to be heaped with adulation throughout Europe. In every particular by which greatness is usually measured, Washington comes up short. He lacked originality and boldness.

The British army surrenders to American troops in Yorktown, Virginia, October 19, 1781.

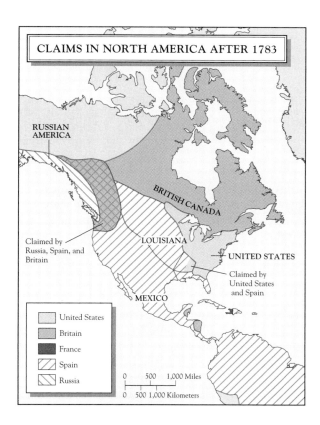

CLAIMS IN NORTH AMERICA AFTER 1783

RUSSIAN AMERICA

BRITISH CANADA

LOUISIANA

UNITED STATES

Claimed by Russia, Spain, and Britain

Claimed by United States and Spain

MEXICO

United States
Britain
France
Spain
Russia

0   500   1,000 Miles
0   500 1,000 Kilometers

He was no thinker, and seems to have read few books. He contributed nothing to the rich literature of colonial protest. His personality was subdued, quiet, dull. He excited no one.

Nor was Washington a successful field commander. His expeditions during the French and Indian War were fiascoes. In the early years of the Revolution, he won a few small battles while his defeats were legion. Most of his seven years in command were spent in retreat or wary watchfulness, a step ahead of annihilation. Any number of American commanders—Gates, Greene, Arnold!—excelled him as a tactician. His strategy until Yorktown amounted to responding to British actions.

And yet, it would be difficult to overstate Washington's contribution to the establishment of the American republic. It was in successful retreat that his military contribution to independence lay. He kept an army in the field against overwhelming odds. Washington survived in the face of repeated defeats, superior British forces, inadequate provisions, disease, poor shelter for his men during two severe winters, poor support from the Continental Congress, and even a cabal against him.

In order to explain his achievement, it is necessary to fall back on the intangibles that transfixed most of his contemporaries. Radicals like Samuel Adams, instinctive conservatives like Alexander Hamilton, intellectuals like Thomas Jefferson, warriors like Israel Putnam, cultivated European aristocrats like the Marquis de Lafayette—all idolized and deferred to the Virginian. Washington's aristocratic bearing, integrity, sense of dignity, and aloofness from petty squabbles set him a head taller than the best of his contemporaries, just as his height of six feet two inches made him a physical giant of the time. Despite his setbacks and lack of flash, he held the revolutionary cause together by that vague, indefinable quality known as "character." If the very notion rings a little sappy today, the dishonor is not to the era of the American Revolution.

CHRONOLOGY

1776   British victories in battles around New York
       American victory at Trenton

1777   American victory at Princeton
       American victory at Saratoga
       France recognizes American independence

1778   Massacres in Wyoming Valley, Pennsylvania, and Cherry Valley, New York
       Mutinies on Connecticut, Pennsylvania, and New Jersey lines

1781   American and French victory at Yorktown

1782   Parliament votes to end war

1783   Treaty of Paris ends War for Independence

FOR FURTHER READING

Again, students are referred to "For Further Reading" in Chapter 7. Other important general works dealing with the Revolutionary War are Samuel F. Bemis, *The Diplomacy of the American Revolution*, 1935; Don Higginbotham, *The War of American Independence: Military Attitudes, Policies, and Practice*, 1971; J. Franklin Jameson, *The American Revolution Considered as a Social Movement*, 1926; and Cathy D. Matson and Peter S. Onuf, *Union of Interests: Political and Economic Thought in Revolutionary America*, 1990.

Also see Robert M. Calhoon, *The Loyalists in Revolutionary America*, 1973; H. J. Henderson, *Party Politics in the Continental Congress*, 1974; Richard B. Morris, *The Peacemakers*, 1965; Mary Beth Norton, *Liberty's Daughters*, 1980; Charles Royster, *A Revolutionary People at War*, 1979; John Shy, *A People Numerous and Armed*, 1976; and Paul H. Smith, *Loyalists and Redcoats*, 1964. Useful studies of particular groups include Steven Rosswurm, *Arms, Country, and Class: The Philadelphia Militia and the "Lower Sort" in the Era of the American Revolution*, 1987; Sylvia R. Frey, *Water from the Rock: Black Resistance in a Revolutionary Age*, 1991; Charles Patrick Neimeyer, *America Goes to War: A Social History of the Continental Army*, 1996; and Linda K. Kerber, *Women of the Republic: Intellect and Ideology in Revolutionary America*, 1980.

Two classic biographies of George Washington are James T. Flexner, *George Washington in the American Revolution*, 1968, and Douglas S. Freeman, *George Washington*, 1948, 1957.

Election day, here in Philadelphia, was a major public holiday in the early United States.

10
CHAPTER

INVENTING A COUNTRY

American Constitutions

1781–1789

North America itself appears to be in a very distracted and broken condition. . . . The different States are at variance among themselves, disputing territories, removing boundaries, and contesting other questions of property! They are not less divided about the quantum and mode of taxation. . . . These, and many other important questions, agitate them exceedingly. . . .

Such are the blessed fruits of American Independency! Oh ye Northern Americans! How fatal has that chimera, that false light . . . been to you! . . . Generations yet unborn will lament your folly, and curse your false policy and base ingratitude to your parent country.

—European Magazine and London Review

Without some alteration in our political creed, the superstructure we have been seven years raising at the expense of so much blood and treasure, must fall. We are fast verging to anarchy and confusion.

— *George Washington*

Our affairs seem to lead to some crisis, some revolution — something that I cannot foresee or conjecture. I am uneasy and apprehensive, more so than during the war. . . . We are going and doing wrong, and therefore I look forward to evils and calamities.

—*John Jay*

The American Revolution was not the first war for independence. People subject to others have risen in rebellion since the dawn of civilization. The history of empires is also a history of uprisings against imperial control.

The American Revolution was novel in the fact that Americans had to invent their country and their sense of nationhood from scratch. They were not a people, like the Dutch, whom the vagaries of inheritance had made subject to another people, the Spanish. They were not a people who were conquered and ruled by foreigners as, for example, the Aztecs, or the Chinese under the Mongols. Most Americans were British, ethnically and culturally. Moreover, the 13 colonies—states now—had no institutional links with one another before the Revolution. Their only political links had bound them to the mother country.

Consequently, a sense of American nationhood was slow to take shape. The frame of government the patriots forged during the Revolution, the Articles of Confederation, was not much more than an alliance of independent states with a common problem: 50,000 redcoats determined to subjugate them. Only in 1787, more than a decade after the Declaration of Independence and six years after Yorktown, did "We the people of the United States"—something of a contrivance even at that date—venture to ordain "a more perfect union." The fruit of their labors was the Constitution that remains today the basic law of the nation.

THE REVOLUTION ON PAPER

The constitutions of 11 of the 13 states were drawn up in the midst of the war against Britain. Not surprisingly, these frames of government consciously and specifically reflected the anti-British sentiments of the rebels.

Black and White and Read All Over

The most obvious break with the British past was the fact that the first American constitutions were written down and comprehensive, covering every contingency that their authors could foresee. The unwritten British constitution had served that nation well enough, and it does so to this day. But the lack of a definition of Parliament's powers in black and white was central to American grievances with the mother country. The patriots believed that Parliament violated unwritten tradition in trying to tax them but they could not prove it without resorting to force of arms. Written constitutions could be violated, too, of course. However, as Thomas Jefferson wrote, "they furnish a text to which those who are watchful may again rally and recall the people."

Notably, the two states that still had written corporate charters at the time of the Revolution, Connecticut and Rhode Island, merely adjusted the wording of these old documents. Their colonial charters continued to serve as their state constitutions until 1818 in Connecticut, and 1842 in Rhode Island.

Limiting Power, Striking Down Privilege

The new state constitutions were written not by legislative assemblies but by conventions elected especially for that purpose. They were then ratified by a popular election and could be altered only by a similar procedure, *not* by the legislature. The American tradition that sovereignty (ultimate government power) rested with the people was thereby institutionalized at the time of the Revolution.

New Hampshire's Slaves Petition for Freedom

On November 12, 1779, 19 of New Hampshire's 150 black slaves petitioned the state House of Representatives for freedom on the basis of the ideals of liberty that the patriots were asserting. The petition concluded:

Your humble slaves most devoutly pray for the sake of injured liberty, for the sake of justice, humanity and the rights of mankind, for the honor of religion and by all that is dear, that your honors would graciously interpose in our behalf, and enact such laws and regulations, as you in your wisdom think proper, whereby we may regain our liberty and be ranked in the class of free agents, and that the name of slave may not more be heard in a land gloriously contending for the sweets of freedom.

The petition was firmly within the spirit of the Declaration of Independence, but it was rejected by the New Hampshire legislature.

Reaction to British rule took other constitutional forms. Because the patriots resented the old office-holding elite, they guarded against creating their own by requiring that most officials stand for election annually. As well, many state constitutions (and the Articles of Confederation) limited the number of years a person elected to office might serve in that office.

The authors of the state constitutions feared executive power most of all. The royal governors had been George III's representatives in the colonies. They remained staunch Tories when the war broke out. In order to preclude the development of centers of power independent of elected assemblies, the new state governors were allowed little real power. They were largely administrative or ceremonial figures, symbolic heads of state. In Pennsylvania, which in 1776 adopted the most radical constitution of all the new states, there was no governor at all. Nor was there a single executive in the government created by the articles.

Other old resentments surfaced in the movement to separate church and state. Except in New England, the Anglican church had been the established church, supported by taxes and allowed other privileges. For that reason among others, the Anglican clergy had been pro-British. Everywhere, patriots disestablished the Church of England, transforming it into a private denomination like all others. Thomas Jefferson wrote the Virginia ordinance that struck down the privileges of the Anglican church. So important was the issue to him, he regarded authoring the law as one of the major accomplishments of his life.

A Democratic Drift

In every new state, the right to vote was extended to more people than had enjoyed it under the Crown. In Georgia, Pennsylvania, and Vermont (a "state" in fact if not yet in name), every adult male taxpayer could vote. In most of the other states, the property qualification was lowered so that few free white males were excluded. Women who met other qualifications could vote in New Jersey, while in some states, for example, North Carolina, free blacks who met other tests were enfranchised. In 1777, New York joined Rhode Island in granting full citizenship to Jews.

There were limits to this democratic trend. Roman Catholics were not allowed to vote in North Carolina until 1835; Pennsylvania required office-holders to be Christian. In a majority of the states, a voter could not necessarily stand for office. More strict property qualifications for officeholding were

common, and the higher the office, the greater the wealth that was required of a candidate. The patriots may have been radical by European standards, but they clung to the eighteenth-century's belief that property gave a person a greater stake in society and therefore better qualified him to govern it. John Adams staunchly opposed allowing men without property to vote in Massachusetts.

Bills of Rights

Eight states listed rights that were guaranteed to each citizen in their constitutions, beginning with Virginia's in 1776. After the vice-admiralty courts, the quartering acts, and arbitrary actions by the British army, the patriots were determined that there be no vagueness on the question of a person's liberties. Most of the rights later listed in the first ten amendments to the United States Constitution were defined in one or another of the state bills of rights that were written during the 1770s: freedom from cruel punishment; the right of counsel and trial by jury; the right to remain silent during one's own trial; and so on.

Liberty's Limits: Sex and Race

In 1777, when the air was thick with talk of expanding personal liberties, Abigail Adams wrote to her husband, John, who was engaged in writing the Articles

Fomenting Rebellion

Abigail and John Adams were touchingly affectionate with each other, and, much rarer, they discussed the momentous issues of the Revolutionary era. Abigail was twitting John when she made her famous appeal for the rights of women in 1777, but it would be a mistake to think that her challenge was nothing more than a joke:

In the new code of laws . . . I desire you would remember the ladies and be more generous and more favorable to them than your ancestors. Do not put such unlimited power into the hands of husbands. Remember, all men would be tyrants if they could. If particular care and attention is not paid to the ladies, we are determined to foment a rebellion, and will not hold ourselves bound to any laws in which we have no choice or representation.

of Confederation, to make a plea for the rights of women. But the time was not ripe for redefining the subordinate civil status of women. Indeed, New Jersey would rescind its enfranchisement of women in 1807 because an increasing number of women were taking advantage of their right to vote in that state.

By way of contrast, blacks in the northern states, where slavery was of little economic value, won some victories because of the Revolution's expansion of liberties. Quasi-independent Vermont abolished slavery in 1777. Pennsylvania followed suit in 1780. A few years later, Elizabeth Freeman of Massachusetts, whose slave name was Mumber, sued for her freedom on the basis of the Massachusetts constitution, which stated that "all men are born free and equal." The courts agreed and forbade slavery in the Bay State. Rhode Island and Connecticut gradually phased the institution out by forbidding the enslavement of any person after a date set by law. That is, no person born or entering the state after that date could be enslaved.

In the South, as the British Tory Samuel Johnson trenchantly remarked, "the loudest yelps for liberty" were heard "among the drivers of negroes." Many southern patriots were troubled by the hypocrisy inherent in owning slaves, Thomas Jefferson foremost among them. However, economic necessity, fear of the social upheaval abolition of slavery might mean, and the racism a century of slavery fostered were more powerful than revolutionary ideals.

ETHNIC GROUPS OF THE CONFEDERATION PERIOD

Legend:
- Jewish
- African
- Dutch
- English
- French
- German
- Native American
- Scotch-Irish
- Spanish

Three New Jersey women exercise the franchise. Their daughters would lose the right to vote early in the nineteenth century.

The belief that race was an elemental condition of humanity extended even to those who hoped to transcend it. In Virginia, Patrick Henry tried to extend the state's liberties to Indians by means of racial amalgamation. In 1784, he proposed that the House of Burgesses pay a bounty of £10 to each free white person who married an Indian and £5 for each child born of such unions. Another distinguished Virginian, John Marshall, later commented that the bill "would have been advantageous to this country." He added: "Our prejudices, however, opposed themselves to our interests, and operated too powerfully for them." It is a timeless commentary on the costs of racism.

AMERICA UNDER THE ARTICLES OF CONFEDERATION

The constitution the patriots wrote to coordinate the affairs of all 13 states—the Articles of Confederation—reflected the same fears and ideals as the constitutions of the new states.

Basic Principles

Drafted during the heady years 1776 and 1777, the Articles of Confederation provided for no president, nor any other independent executive. Congress was the only organ of government. Members were elected annually and could serve only three years out of every six. That is, a man elected to Congress three years in a row was ineligible to stand for election until he sat out three years. Or, a delegate could serve every other year indefinitely. The object of this provision was to prevent the emergence of a class of professional officeholders who regarded public office and its prerogatives as their personal property.

Under the Articles, the United States of America was explicitly *not* a nation. It was "a firm league of friendship," little more. New Hampshire, New Jersey, North Carolina, and the rest explicitly retained their "sovereignty, freedom, and independence." The United States was a confederation of equals. In Congress, for example, delegates did not vote as individuals. They assembled as members of their state delegation, took a vote, and the state then cast a single vote. The state, not members of Congress, was representative.

Divided Authority

Congress was authorized to wage war and make peace, to maintain an army and a navy, and to supervise diplomatic relations with foreign countries and the Indian nations. Congress was also entrusted with maintaining a post office and setting uniform weights and measures, and had the power to coin money, issue paper money, and to borrow money at home or abroad.

Having granted these powers to Congress, however, the Articles of Confederation also permitted the states to coin money, to ignore the standards of measurement Congress might establish, and individually—as states—to make trade treaties with other countries. Under the Articles, an individual state could even, "with the consent of Congress," declare war on a foreign power. Nor was Congress empowered to regulate trade among the various states. It was "constitutional," in other words, for Delaware to be at war with a foreign power that had a trade agreement with neighboring New Jersey. In fact, New York actually did take military action against Connecticut smugglers during the Confederation period.

Successes against All Odds

The weakness of the ties that bound the states under the Articles was not the consequence of incompetence, indecision, or awkward compromise. Weakness was deliberately written into the Articles because of the revolutionary generation's aversion to strong central government. It was a strong, central government against which the patriots were in rebellion when they penned the document.

Nor was the Confederation government an unmitigated disaster. On the contrary, it was under the Articles that the Americans warred on and defeated Europe's premier military power. For 11 years of war and peace, a far-flung country of (by 1787) more than 3.5 million people survived as 13 "sovereign, free, and independent" states.

By the end of the Confederation era, Congress had created a bureaucracy to administer the day-to-day affairs of the government. States did contribute, albeit reluctantly sometimes, to the Confederation treasury. And Congress solved a problem that could

easily have plunged the North Americans into an ugly interstate conflict.

The Western Lands

The treasure that threatened to divide the states was the one that attracted most immigrants to America—land, specifically the land beyond the Appalachians that Great Britain had closed to settlement in 1763. The question was: Who held title to the vast acreage between the mountains and the Mississippi River?

Colonial charters were the source of the uncertainty. They had been drawn with little knowledge of North American geography; boundaries of individual colonies overlapped; the result was a snarl of conflicts thicker than forest underbrush. Virginia claimed that its boundaries fanned out like a funnel at the mountains, encompassing virtually the whole trans-Appalachian region. Because its charter was the most ancient, Virginia insisted it held precedence over other charters written later.

Connecticut agreed that New York's and Pennsylvania's charters (written later than Connecticut's) modified its own western claims. Nevertheless, Connecticut claimed a "western reserve" beyond those states in what is now Ohio. Massachusetts, New York, North Carolina, South Carolina, and Georgia also had claims overlapping those of other states.

These disputes were complicated by the fears of the six states with no charter claims to western lands: New Hampshire, Rhode Island, New Jersey, Pennsylvania, Delaware, and Maryland. Quite reasonably, leaders of those states worried that the landed states would be able to finance themselves indefinitely by selling trans-Appalachian farms, while they, states without western lands, would drive their citizens out with high property taxes. On these grounds, Maryland refused to sign the Articles of Confederation until 1781.

The solution was obvious. John Dickinson suggested it as early as 1776. But it was not easy to effect. The landed states would have to grant their western territories to the Confederation government, so that all states could share in the wealth.

Fortunately, Virginians—with the most to lose—had good reasons to cede their state's lands to Congress. Virginians played a prominent role in the Confederation government, and they did not want to see it fall apart. Moreover, many Virginians

very thought caused men of property to shudder. They yearned for a reliable currency that would be valid in every state. Only a strong central government could guarantee such a currency.

Congress was unable even to maintain the value of the bonds and certificates it had issued during the Revolution. Tellingly, 40 of the 55 men who were to draft the Constitution owned some of the depreciated Continental currency and notes. They were badly stung as long as the government was unable to collect taxes and meet its financial obligations.

Diplomatic Vulnerability

Squabbles among the states made it difficult for Confederation diplomats to negotiate with other nations. France, the indispensable ally in war, would lend no money in peace because the Americans failed to make good on earlier loans. Nor was credit the only problem. Virtually every European country regarded the United States as a collection of weak principalities, like Indian tribes or the petty states of Germany that occasionally formed "a firm league of friend-ship" but, more often, could be played off against one another.

In 1784, a shrewd Spanish diplomat, Diego de Gardoqui, played on the commercial interests of the northern states in an effort to split the country in two. He offered to open Spanish trade to American ships (which meant northern ships) if Congress would give up its insistence on the right of Americans to ship their goods down the Mississippi River for 25 years.

The northern states cared little about the Mississippi. Their delegations tried to ram the treaty through Congress. Had the Gardoqui Treaty been effected, the southern states would have had little choice but to go their own way, fulfilling the predictions of even friendly Europeans that the former colonies would remain weak and divided, for the Mississippi was a vital artery to the tens of thousands of Virginians and North Carolinians who had moved to what are now Kentucky and Tennessee.

In the far north, England schemed to detach Vermont from the United States. By custom an extension of New York but also claimed by New Hampshire, the isolated Green Mountain country actually functioned as an independent commonwealth under the leadership of Ethan and Levi Allen, two Revolutionary veterans who trusted no one but each other, and kept their backs to the wall even then. The Allens attempted to make a treaty with the British that would have tied the area more closely to Canada than to the Confederation, and Congress was powerless to stop them. Only because the British failed to act quickly did the venture fall through. Certainly the Confederation government was in no position to force an issue. By 1784, the Continental Army had shrunk to 700 men, dispersed in garrisons of 25 to 50.

Wounded Pride

Britain's condescension was insulting and infuriating. The former mother country refused to turn over a string of Great Lakes forts that were American under the terms of the Treaty of Paris. Nor did the British send a minister (ambassador) to America. A British diplomat joked that it would be too expensive to outfit 13 men with homes and the other accouterments of ministerial office. In London, the American minister to Great Britain, John Adams, was ridiculed when he attempted to act with the dignity of a national legate.

It was the same elsewhere. A world-traveling American sea captain said that the United States was regarded "in the same light, by foreign nations, as a well-behaved negro is in a gentleman's family," that is, as an inferior, scarcely to be noticed. Even the venal Barbary states of northern Africa looked down on Americans. These little principalities lived by piracy, collecting tribute from nations whose ships traded in the Mediterranean. When American ships lost the protection that the British annually purchased for vessels flying the Union Jack, they were sunk or captured. The bey of Algiers sold American crews into slavery, and Congress was unable either to ransom them or to launch a punitive expedition. It was a sorry state of affairs for the young men of the Revolution who dreamed of national greatness.

Social Butterfly

George Washington was, of course, the "star" of the Constitutional Convention. In 128 days in Philadelphia, he rode every morning at five o'clock, dined out 110 times, attended 69 afternoon teas, went out in the evening on 20 occasions to attend lectures, concerts, and plays, had his portrait painted four times, and went fishing at least once.

Calls for Change

It was a minor problem in domestic waters that actually launched the movement to overhaul American government. In March 1785, a small group of men from Maryland and Virginia gathered at Mount Vernon, George Washington's home on the Potomac River, to discuss the conflicting claims of Maryland and Virginia fishermen over rights to fish in the Chesapeake Bay. They were unable to draw a boundary between the two states' fisheries. They did, however, conclude that the Chesapeake problem was only one in a tangle of disputes among the states, and between the states and the Confederation government. They invited all 13 states to send delegates to a meeting the next year in Annapolis, Maryland, to discuss what might be done.

Only five states responded, so decisive action was out of the question. Undiscouraged, Washington's former aide-de-camp, Alexander Hamilton of New York, persuaded the small group to assemble once again, this time in centrally located Philadelphia. They should prepare, Hamilton told them, to discuss all the "defects in the System of the Federal Government."

Hamilton and some other delegates, such as James Madison of Virginia, had more than an academic debate in mind. They intended to plump for replacing the Articles of Confederation with a completely new frame of government. Rumors about their plan spread quickly and met less than resounding approval. Patrick Henry, Madison's rival in Virginia politics, said that he "smelled a rat" and refused to attend. Rhode Island sent no delegates at all. Since the days of Roger Williams, Rhode Islanders had smelled a rat in any hint that their independence of action, which the Articles of Confederation nicely guaranteed, might be harnessed.

Elsewhere, discontent with the Confederation was rife, particularly when, in the winter of 1786–1787, a wave of protests among farmers in western and central Massachusetts turned into armed rebellion.

The Shays Rebellion

Farmers in western Massachusetts resented the fact that the state's tax laws, enacted by the merchants of Boston and other seaports, favored trade at the expense of agriculture. In 1786, many farmers assembled in conventions at which they demanded that their property taxes be reduced. To make up for the loss of revenue, they called for the abolition of aristocratic branches of the government in Boston.

In several towns, angry crowds surrounded courthouses, harassed lawyers and judges whom they considered to be unproductive parasites, and forcibly prevented the collection of debts. Then, in September, a Revolutionary War veteran named Daniel Shays led as many as 2,000 armed men against the Springfield arsenal. Shays's rebellion collapsed in December, but the bitterness of the Shaysites did not sweeten.

Shays and his followers did not regard themselves as a dangerous social force. They believed that they were carrying on the spirit and struggle of the Revolution against a privileged elite. Then minister to France, Thomas Jefferson agreed with them. "A little rebellion now and then is a good thing," he wrote to a friend. "The tree of liberty must be refreshed from time to time with the blood of patriots and tyrants."

The men who were preparing to gather in Philadelphia in 1787 had another opinion: it was not the pine tree of liberty that needed attention; it was the ailing oak of social peace, stability, and order. George Washington, for one, was deeply troubled by the news of Shays's Rebellion. Four years earlier, he had squelched a group of army officers with a military coup on their minds. He was no more tolerant of the Shaysites. Society could not tolerate its members taking up arms whenever they felt aggrieved. Washington and others believed that such disorder was the natural consequence of excessive democracy.

THE AMERICAN CONSTITUTION

For 200 years the American Constitution has been hailed with a reverence that can only be described as religious. Patriots, politicians, moralists, and historians—Americans and foreigners alike—have bowed

Back Home Again in Chersonesus

In time, the Northwest Territory became the states of Ohio, Indiana, Illinois, Michigan, Wisconsin, and part of Minnesota. If Thomas Jefferson had had his way, the states of the Old Northwest would have been called Assenisipia, Chersonesus, Macropotamia, Metropotamia, Pelisipia, and Polypotamia. We can thank those Americans who preferred Indian names to Greek ones that Jefferson lost that battle.

in awe before a legal document that could survive for more than two centuries during which technology, ideology, revolution, imperialism, and war have turned the world upside down. William E. Gladstone, prime minister of Great Britain in the midst of this tumultuous historical period, was neither alone nor excessive when he called the American Constitution "the most wonderful work ever struck off at a given time by the brain and purpose of man."

"Demigods"

The men who struck it off in the summer of 1787—the "founding fathers"—have been heaped with praise, and depicted as wise, selfless individuals who peered into their nation's future and designed for it a timeless gift. The Constitution was "intended to

endure for ages to come," Chief Justice John Marshall proclaimed in 1819. On the floor of the Senate in 1850, a critical year for the union of states that the Constitution had created, he was echoed by Henry Clay of Kentucky. "The Constitution of the United States," Clay said, "was not made merely for the generation that then existed but for posterity—unlimited, undefined, and endless, perpetual posterity."

In truth, the Constitution has been a remarkably successful basic law, and the generation of political leaders who wrote and debated it was rich in talent and wisdom. But the founding fathers were not demigods, as Thomas Jefferson feared Americans would make them out to be. They were decidedly human, with prosaic faults and, among their ideals, very immediate purposes to serve.

Although Shays's Rebellion began as fistfights and riots, it frightened some of the country's most thoughtful leaders.

NOTABLE PEOPLE

James Madison (1751–1836)

"Every person seems to acknowledge his greatness," a delegate to the Constitutional Convention wrote of James Madison of Montpelier Plantation, Virginia. "He blends together the profound politician, with the Scholar. In the management of every great question he evidently took the lead in the Convention, and tho' he cannot be called an Orator, he is a most agreeable, eloquent, and convincing Speaker."

Students of political science since Madison's time have been even more generous. They have called his *Federalist Papers* one of the masterpieces of political theory. Certainly Madison is America's most impressive political thinker. Alexander Hamilton, his collaborator on the *Federalist Papers,* was not so thoughtful. Thomas Jefferson, Madison's political idol and patron, was a sloganeer by comparison. John C. Calhoun, Madison's illegitimate heir, conceived during a lapse of discretion, was more ingenious, but carping and contrived next to the master.

James Madison was the eldest of ten children born into a comfortable family of planters that had, perhaps, declined from better days. He was tutored at home and then well educated at the College of New Jersey, as Princeton was then known. He probably planned to become a minister. He spent an extra year at Princeton to study languages, theology, and ethics.

The Revolution changed any such plans. Only 25 years of age in 1776, Madison was caught up in the ferment in Virginia and took the lead in fighting for the disestablishment of his own Anglican church in the new state. Whether because he felt himself too weak and sickly for the soldier's life—Madison was tiny in stature and a lifelong hypochondriac who did not "expect a long or healthy life"—or, like Jefferson, because he disdained the military, he spent the war years in civil office. He was a member of the Virginia governor's council and, after 1780, a member of Congress.

His projects in Congress were unexceptionable and, except perhaps in private discourse, he displayed little of the profundity that was to impress the Convention of 1787. It appears that only during the era of the Confederation, which Madison feared would disintegrate at any moment—like his health—did he take up the historical and philosophical study of government. At his frequent request, Thomas Jefferson, serving as minister to France, bought and sent him books about government.

At the Convention of 1787, Madison seems to have spoken even less than implied in the earlier quotation. The voluminous notes he took on the proceedings (in violation of convention rules) must have consumed much of his time. But he lobbied assiduously on behalf of the dominance of the large states in the new republic and for a centralized, powerful national government.

Madison accepted the compromises that were necessary to win the support of the small states, but

The Constitutional Convention

The convention in Philadelphia at which the document was actually written began on May 25, 1787. After only a few days, the 55 delegates from 12 states agreed that revision of the Articles of Confederation was not enough. Indeed, they had little choice but to start from scratch. It was easier to effect a coup d'état, to create a new government without regard to the procedures of the one that existed, than to amend the Articles of Confederation. Amendment required that every state agree to the change and Rhode Island had made it quite clear that the state opposed any revision.

The Constitutional Convention met in secret from first to last. For four months the delegates bolted the doors and sealed the windows of the Pennsylvania State House (later to be called Independence Hall), a demigod-like sacrifice in the humid Philadelphia summer. In addition, every

he was not happy about them. Morose, as he often was, he was convinced that the new government was too weak and that "local mischiefs" would split the thirteen states into three countries, New England, a Middle States confederacy, and the South.

A streak of melancholy and misgivings about his abilities ran through Madison's life, reflecting his hypochondria. But if he suffered from depression, the attacks were sporadic. He was as often self-confident as trembling. His private conversation was witty and animated. He wooed and won as his wife a vivacious Philadelphia beauty, Dolley Madison, and brought elegance and flair to Washington's fusty, masculine, whiskey-and-playing-cards society. And despite his chronic groaning, he lived to be 85 years of age.

Although he was a nationalist, Madison was also a devout Virginian. He continued to serve the interests of his state even when Virginia's House of Delegates neglected to pay his salary. (Madison was one of the penurious patriots Haym Salomon bailed out during the war years.)

His devotion to Virginia and to that less-steady nationalist, Jefferson, also helps to account for the great aberration in a career dedicated to strengthening the United States government, Madison's Virginia Resolutions of 1798. This proclamation and Jefferson's Kentucky Resolutions stopped just shy of saying that if an individual state judged an act of Congress in conflict with the Constitution, that state could declare that act null and void within its borders.

Surely Madison, who dissected the most delicate of political organisms in the *Federalist Papers*, under-stood what "local mischiefs" so ham-handed a doctrine could loose. He lived to see it done in 1828 when John C. Calhoun explicitly formulated the implications of the Kentucky and Virginia Resolutions in his *South Carolina Exposition and Protest.* Calhoun's doctrine of Nullification provided the justification and procedure for the secession of the southern states in 1860 and 1861. Secession from Madison's Union was a state's final recourse when the other states overturned one state's nullification.

Madison referred to Calhoun only indirectly when he wrote, "Let the open enemy of [Union] be regarded as a Pandora with her box opened, and the disguised one as the serpent creeping with his deadly wiles into paradise."

He was also troubled by the positive enthusiasm with which, in his old age, the South defended slavery. Like other Virginians of his generation, Madison regarded slavery as a "dreadful calamity." He took up the study of law during the 1780s so as to have a profession in which he had to "depend as little as possible on the labor of slaves." He supported the work of societies that encouraged the freeing of slaves by transporting free blacks to West Africa. Not long before his death, he told Harriet Martineau, the English author of a book about American society, that everything negative ever written about slavery was valid. His was the tragedy of a founder of the Union who lived too long into the era of sectional division.

member swore not to discuss the proceedings with outsiders. George Washington, who presided, was furious when a delegate misplaced a sheet of notes.

There was nothing sinister in the secrecy. The purpose of the convention was common knowledge. The delegates sequestered themselves because they knew they were performing a historic act, and should proceed with the utmost caution and calm. As James Wilson, a Pennsylvania delegate, said, "America now presents the first instance of a people assembled to weigh deliberately and calmly, and to decide leisurely and peaceably, upon the form of government by which they will bind themselves, and their posterity." No small business that never had a nation been founded so methodically. The delegates wished to voice their frankest opinions without fear of affecting their political careers back home.

Moreover, they knew there would be opposition to their constitution. Wilson said that "the people" were assembled in Independence Hall. The document

The "Founding Fathers" at the Constitutional Convention in Philadelphia, 1787.

that the convention produced begins with the words "We the People of the United States." But in fact, the men who drew up the Constitution represented just one political tendency. They wanted their platform to be complete before they had to defend it against their critics.

The Delegates

The job was finished in September 1787. After a hard-drinking celebration, the delegates scattered north and south to lobby for their states' approval of their document. They were a formidable lot to sally forth on such an errand. By virtue of wealth and education they were influential people back home. Of the fifty-five, only two, Roger Sherman of Connecticut, who had been a cobbler as a young man, and Alexander Hamilton, the bastard child of a feckless Scottish merchant, could be said to have been weaned on anything less glittering than a silver spoon.

Lifetimes spent in justifying independence and creating state governments made most of the dele-

gates keen students of political philosophy. During the years preceding the convention, James Madison augmented his own library with 200 books ordered from Europe. Just as important was the delegates' practical experience: 7 had been state governors; 39 had sat in the Continental Congress.

The founding fathers were young. Only nine signers of the Declaration of Independence were among them (and three of them refused to sign the Constitution). Only Benjamin Franklin, 81 years old in 1787, was truly antique. The other founding fathers averaged just over 40 years of age and the two leading spirits of the meeting were only 36 (James Madison) and 32 (Alexander Hamilton). Ten delegates were less than 35 years of age, one just 26. Such men had been just old enough in 1776 to play a minor role in the war. They had been children at the time of the Stamp Act crisis; they were heirs of the Revolution, not makers of it.

The comparative youth of the founding fathers is of some importance in understanding the nature of the Constitution they wrote. Most delegates did not have the habit of thinking as colonials impressed in their minds. They did not grow to full maturity thinking of themselves as Virginians or New Yorkers before they decided to become Americans. Their vision of the United States was forged in the crucible of a national struggle, "these United States" versus a foreign power.

More often than their more provincial forebears, these young men moved freely and often from one state to another. In the Continental Army (a third of the delegates had been soldiers, mostly junior officers) and in the Confederation Congress, they met and mixed easily with men from other states and from Europe. They thought in terms of a continent rather than of coastal enclaves that looked back to a mother country for an identity. They wanted the United States to take its place in the world as an equal among nations. Thus were they chagrined at the weakness of the Confederation government.

A Conservative Movement

Youth does not, as we are sometimes accustomed to think, equate with radicalism. The men who drew up the Constitution were conservatives in the classic meaning of the word. They did not believe with Jefferson (then in France) that human nature was

---

Conservatives

In identifying men such as Washington, Hamilton, and Adams as conservatives, it is important not to confuse their political philosophy with that of the "conservatives" of the late twentieth century. Classical conservatives like these three founding fathers were suspicious of human nature and therefore inclined to cling to tried and true institutions rather than to experiment. Unlike conservatives of today, they believed that a strong central government that was active in the economic life of the nation was desirable and essential. They had no more tolerance for unbridled economic freedom than for excess of political freedom.

Present-day conservatives, by way of contrast, want a minimum of government interference in the economy. Implicitly, they say that in economic life human nature should not be closely supervised.

Alexander Hamilton on Democracy

All communities divide themselves into the few and the many. The first are the rich and the wellborn, the other the mass of the people. . . . The people are turbulent and changing; they seldom judge or determine right. Give therefore to the first class a distinct, permanent share in the government. They will check the unsteadiness of the second, and as they cannot receive any advantage by change, they therefore will ever maintain good government.

---

essentially good and eternally malleable, that people and human society were perfectible if left free. In fact, the founding fathers feared the darker side of human nature. Free of institutional restraints and given power, such traditional conservatives believed, selfish individuals were quick to trample on the rights of others. To conservatives, democracy and liberty did not go hand in hand. On the contrary, people left to their own selfish devices would destroy liberty.

The most pessimistic and therefore the most conservative of the lot was Alexander Hamilton. Sent to King's College in New York by friends who recognized his talents, Hamilton never returned to the West Indies, where he was born. He served George Washington as aide-de-camp during the Revolutionary War and impressed his superior with his intelligence and perhaps also with his conservatism, for Hamilton had no sympathy with democratic ideas. A few years after the adoption of the Constitution, he would listen to Thomas Jefferson expound on the wisdom and virtue inherent in the people and snap back angrily, "Your people, sir, are a great beast."

Had Hamilton been an Englishman, he would have defended those institutions that conservatives believed helped to control the passions of the people: the ceremonial monarchy, the privileged aristocracy, the established church, education in tradition, and the centuries-old accretion of law and custom that is the British constitution. In fact, Hamilton was an unabashed admirer of English culture and government. Like Edmund Burke, he thought of the American Revolution as a conservative movement. In rebelling, the Americans had defended tradition against a reckless Parliament.

Alexander Hamilton (1755–1804), advocate of a strong central government.

In the Constitution, Hamilton wanted to recapture as much of tradition as he could. He suggested that president and senators be elected for life, thus creating a kind of monarch and aristocracy, but he was unable to sway his fellow delegates. As much as many of them may have harbored similar sentiments, they also understood that most people would not accept such backsliding toward the old order. What the majority of delegates did approve, and Hamilton accepted, was a system of government that expressed democratic yearnings but placed effective checks on them. The government they created was a mixed government, a balance of the three principles: the democratical (power in the hands of the many); the aristocratical (power in the hands of a few); and the monocratical (power in the hands of one).

Mixed Government

The chief exponent of mixed government, John Adams, did not attend the Constitutional Convention. In 1787, Adams was serving unhappily as minister to Great Britain. Before going abroad, however, Adams had stamped his ideas about government on the Massachusetts state constitution against which the Shaysites had rebelled. It provided for a strong governor, a voice for the wealthy in the state senate, and a voice for the people in the state assembly.

James Madison pushed for a similar structure for the new national government, and he had his way. The basic principle of the American Constitution is a complex network of checks and balances.

Checks, Limits, and Balances

The House of Representatives was "democratical." Representatives were elected frequently (every two years) by a broad electorate—all free, white, adult males in many states. The Senate and the Supreme Court reflected Adams's "aristocratical" principle. Senators were elected infrequently (every six years) by state legislatures. Senators were insulated from the democratic crowd by both the length of their terms and a buffer of state legislators. However, because state legislatures were elected by the same broad electorate that chose the House of Representatives, senators were not completely independent of the popular will.

The Supreme Court was. Justices were appointed by the president, but, once confirmed by the Senate and seated, they were immune to his influence. Justices served for life and could be removed only by a difficult impeachment process.

The "monocratical" principle was established in the presidency, the most dramatic break with the government of the Confederation. The president alone represented the whole nation, but he owed his power neither to the people nor to Congress. He was put into office by an electoral college that played no other role than selecting the president.

An intricate system of checks and balances tied together the three branches of government. Only Congress could make law, and both democratic House and aristocratic Senate had to agree to the last syllable. The president could veto an act of Congress if he judged it adverse to the national interest. However, Congress could override his veto by a two-thirds majority of both houses.

Judging according to these laws was the job of the judiciary, with the Supreme Court being the final court of appeal. In time (it was not written into the Constitution), the Supreme Court claimed a legislative role of its own in the principle of judicial review; that is, in judging according to the law, the Supreme Court also interpreted the law. Implicit in this process was the power to declare a law unconstitutional. This proved to be a mighty power because, while there are checks on the court, they are indirect and difficult to exercise.

Finally, the Constitution can be amended, although the process for doing so was deliberately made difficult. An amendment may be proposed in one of two ways: two-thirds of the states' legislatures can petition Congress to summon a national constitutional convention for that purpose. Or, and this is the only method by which the Constitution has in fact been amended, Congress can submit proposals to the states. If three-fourths of the states ratify a proposed amendment, it becomes part of the Constitution.

The Federal Relationship

Another network of checks and balances defined the relationship between the central government and the states. Under the Articles of Confederation, the United States was not a nation. The Articles created a confederation of independent states that retained virtually all the powers possessed by sovereign nations. The powers of the Confederation government itself were severely limited.

Under the Constitution, the balance shifted, with preponderant and decisive powers going to the federal government at the expense of the states. The states were not reduced to mere administrative divisions, like the counties of England or the provinces of France. Nationalistic sentiments may have been riding high in 1787, but local interests and jealousies were far from dead. If the Constitution were to win popular support, the states had to be accommodated.

Small states like New Jersey and Connecticut were particularly sensitive. If they were not to be bullied and even absorbed by their larger, wealthier neighbors, delegates from the small states insisted, they must be accorded fundamental protections. These they received in the decision that states rather than population would be represented in the Senate. That is, each state elected two senators, no matter what its population. Virginia, the largest, was ten times as populous as Rhode Island, but had the same number of senators. Without this great compromise, which was accomplished after a tense debate in July 1787, the Constitution would not have been completed and union not achieved without coercion.

The Constitution and Slavery

The difference between North and South also was recognized in convention compromises, particularly in the matter of America's 700,000 slaves. By 1787, the institution of slavery was dead or dying in all the states north of Maryland and Delaware. Indeed, with the exception of the delegates from South Carolina, few of the founding fathers from the South looked favorably on slavery. Tellingly, the unpleasant word "slave" does not appear in the Constitution, as if the framers were embarrassed that such an institution existed in a country consecrated to liberty.

Instead, in a provision that prohibited Congress from abolishing the African slave trade for 20 years (Article I, Section 9), slaves are referred to obliquely as "such Persons as any of the States now existing find proper to admit." Elsewhere in the document, slaves are designated "all other persons." This euphemism was also used in the three-fifths compromise by which slaves and indentured servants were counted as three-fifths of a person for purposes of taxation and apportioning representation in the House of Representatives.

RATIFYING THE CONSTITUTION

The Constitution provided that it would go into effect when nine of the thirteen states ratified it. Three did so almost immediately, Delaware and Connecticut almost unanimously, Pennsylvania in a manner that dramatized the widespread opposition to the new government and the determination of the supporters of the Constitution to have their way.

Federalist Shenanigans

People who favored the Constitution called themselves Federalists. This was something of a misnomer, since the Federalists sought to replace a federated government with a more centralized one. In Pennsylvania, the Federalists managed ratification only by physically forcing two Anti-Federalist members of the state convention to remain in their seats when they tried to leave. This rather irregular maneuver guaranteed a quorum so that the Federalists could cast a legal pro-Constitution vote.

It was only the first of a series of manipulations that has led some historians to speculate that a majority of Americans preferred the old Articles to the

And a Partridge in a Pear Tree

Two days before the founding fathers signed the Constitution, most of them and some other celebrants gathered at the City Tavern for a party in honor of George Washington. There were only 55 guests, yet they consumed 7 bowls of punch, 8 bottles of cider, 8 bottles of whiskey, 12 bottles of beer, 22 bottles of port wine, 54 bottles of madeira, and 60 bottles of claret.

Constitution. In Massachusetts, ratification was voted in February 1788 by the narrow margin of 187 to 168, and then only because several Anti-Federalist delegates voted against their announced position. Anti-Federalists also claimed that the midwinter date prevented many Anti-Federalist western farmers from getting to the polls.

In June 1788, Edmund Randolph of Virginia, an Anti-Federalist, changed his vote and took a coterie of followers with him. Even so, the Federalist victory in Virginia was by a vote of only 89 to 79. A switch of five or six people would have reversed the verdict of the largest state, and that, in turn, would have kept New York in the Anti-Federalist camp.

In New York, a large Anti-Federalist majority was elected to the ratifying convention. After voting at first to reject the Constitution, they reversed their decision when news of Virginia's approval reached them. Even then, the vote was a razor-thin 30 to 27 and the New Yorkers saddled ratification with the proviso that a convention be called to amend the Constitution. It never was. Technically, New York's vote was negative.

The Anti-Federalists

North Carolina was decisively Anti-Federalist. The state ratified the Constitution reluctantly and not until November 1789, eight months after the new government began to function. Rhode Island held out even longer, until May 1790. Rhode Island became the thirteenth state to accept the Constitution only when Congress threatened to pass a tariff that would have kept its goods out of the other twelve states.

Today, now that the Constitution has worked successfully for 213 years, it would be easy to ignore the Anti-Federalists of 1787 and 1788 as a collection of nonconstructive reactionaries and cranks. In fact, the reasons why many Anti-Federalists preferred the old Articles of Confederation were firmly within the tradition of the Revolution.

Among the Anti-Federalists were fiery old patriots who feared that centralized power was an invitation to tyranny. Samuel Adams, still padding about Boston shaking his head at moral decadence, opposed the new government until Massachusetts Federalists, needing the old lion's support, agreed to press for a national bill of rights.

In Virginia, legendary Patrick Henry battled James Madison around the state. Some of Henry's arguments against the Constitution were rather bizarre. At one point he concluded that the Constitution was an invitation to the pope to set up court in the United States, a most extraordinary bit of textual exegesis.

But Henry and other Anti-Federalists also argued that free republican institutions could survive only in small countries such as Switzerland and ancient Greece, and they had the weight of historical evidence on their side. Their favorite example was the Roman Republic which, when it grew into an empire, also grew despotic. Would the same thing happen to a unitary, centrally governed United States? Many Anti-Federalists sincerely believed that it would.

Answering such objections was the Federalists' most difficult task. Madison, Hamilton, and John Jay of New York took it upon themselves to do so in 85 essays under the name the *Federalist Papers*, still a basic textbook of political philosophy. They argued that a powerful United States would guarantee liberty. These ingenious essays, however, were less important to the triumph of the Federalists than their agreement to add a bill of rights to their Constitution.

The Bill of Rights

The Constitutional Convention dedicated little time to debating the rights of citizens under the new government. The concern of the delegates was strengthening government, not putting limits on the powers that it was to exercise over individuals. The delegates, including even Hamilton, were not necessarily opposed to guaranteeing the civil liberties of citizens. They assumed that these were accounted for in the lists of rights most states included in their basic law.

Because the Constitution made the national government superior to those of the states, however,

Anti-Federalists such as Samuel Adams and Edmund Randolph agreed to drop their opposition to the new government only when the various rights that had been adopted by the states since 1776 were guaranteed on a national level.

The first ten amendments to the Constitution were ratified in 1791. The First Amendment guaranteed the freedoms of religion, speech, the press, and peaceable assembly. The Second Amendment guaranteed the right to bear arms. The Third and Fourth Amendments guaranteed security against the quartering of troops in private homes (then still a sore issue among Americans) and against unreasonable search and seizure.

The famous Fifth Amendment is a guarantee against being tried twice for the same crime and, in effect, against torture, it is the basis of the citizen's right to refuse to testify in a trial in which he or she is a defendant. The Sixth Amendment also pertains to trials, ensuring the right to a speedy trial and the right to face accusers (no secret witnesses). The Seventh and Eighth Amendments likewise protect the rights of a person who is accused of committing a crime.

The Ninth and Tenth Amendments are catchalls. They state that the omission of a right from the Constitution does not mean that the right does not exist, and that any powers not explicitly granted to the federal government are reserved to the states. The elegantly handwritten Constitution of the United States was signed by the Constitutional Convention on September 17, 1787, and ratified by the required number of states (nine) by June 21, 1788.

CHRONOLOGY

1776	Virginia first state to write Bill of Rights into state constitution
1777	New York grants full citizenship to Jews
1781	Virginia first state to cede western lands to Congress
1785	Congress adopts rectangular survey for western lands
1787	Northwest Ordinance enacted Constitutional Convention meets in Philadelphia
1787–1788	Eleven of thirteen states ratify Constitution
1791	Bill of Rights ratified

FOR FURTHER READING

The era of the Confederation and the writing of the American Constitution are, unsurprisingly, a field of tumultuous controversy among historians, as is the interpretation of the American Revolution. The cause of much of the dispute is Charles A. Beard, *An Economic Interpretation of the Constitution of the United States*, 1913. Discredited as much of Beard's explanation of the Constitution is, it is an excellent starting point for reading about this era. Also see a yet older work, John Fiske, *The Critical Period of American History, 1783–1789*, 1883.

More recent works revising these once-influential books include Merrill Jensen, *The Articles of Confederation*, 1940, and *The New Nation*, 1950; Jackson T. Main, *The Antifederalists*, 1961, and *Political Parties before the Constitution*, 1973; Frederick W. Marks, *Independence on Trial*, 1973; Forrest MacDonald, *We the People: Economic Origins of the Constitution*, 1958; Andrew C.

McLaughlin, *The Confederation and the Constitution*, 1962; J. N. Rakove, *The Beginnings of National Politics*, 1979; and David P. Szatmary, *Shays' Rebellion: The Making of an Agrarian Insurrection*, 1980. For an overview, see Gordon S. Wood, *The Creation of the American Republic*, 1969. The finest recent book on understanding the Constitution is Garry Wills, *Interpreting America: The Federalist*, 1978; but see also Donald S. Lutz, *Origins of American Constitutionalism*, 1988; and Willi Paul Adams, *The First American Constitutions: Republican Ideology and the Making of the State Constitutions*, 1980.

Useful biographies of the men Thomas Jefferson called "demi-gods" include: Irving Brant, *James Madison the Nationalist*, 1948; Jacob E. Cook, *Alexander Hamilton*, 1982; James T. Flexner, *George Washington and the New Nation*, 1970; John C. Miller, *Alexander Hamilton: Portrait in Paradox*, 1959; and John Ferling, *John Adams*, 1992.

George Washington was first sworn in as president in New York City. He set the precedent for public inauguration.

11
CHAPTER

WE THE PEOPLE

Putting the Constitution to Work

1789–1800

The father of his country.

—Francis Bailey

His memory will be adored while liberty shall have votaries, his name will triumph over time and will in future ages assume its just station among the most celebrated worthies of the world.

—Thomas Jefferson

The character and services of this gentleman are sufficient to put all those men called kings to shame.

—Thomas Paine

First in war, first in peace, first in the hearts of his countrymen.

—Henry Lee

America has furnished to the world the character of Washington. And if our American institutions had done nothing else, that alone would have entitled them to the respect of mankind.

—Daniel Webster

During the debate over the Constitution, one question never arose: who would be the first president of the United States? Revolutionary battlefields had produced many heroes but one figure towered over the rest, just as he had commanded them—George Washington. True to script, the electoral college voted unanimously to install Washington in what was, at the time, an office unique in the world. He took the presidential oath on April 30, 1789, and the new republic was launched.

THE FIRST PRESIDENCY

Washington possessed qualities that were nigh indispensable to the launching of a government designed from scratch. He was committed to the republican ideal. Dignity and a sense of duty were the foundations of his personality. He was sensitive to the fact that he was one of his era's major historical figures, idolized in Europe as well as at home. He also knew that he set a precedent each time he signed a bill into law or greeted a guest at dinner. "I walk on untrodden ground," he wrote.

Setting Precedents

It is fortunate that Washington was a republican. Lionized as he was after the Revolution, he could likely have been crowned a king. Some members of the Order of Cincinnatus, an organization of Revolutionary War officers, wanted to do just that. Then, it was suggested that Washington be addressed as "Your Elective Majesty." But he rebuffed hints of crowns and elevated titles, settling for "Mr. President" as adequate.

Not that Mr. President was self-effacing, or "just one of the boys." Washington was fussy about the dignity of the office he held. He thought "Mr. President" too plain. He lived surrounded by servants in livery and powdered wigs, and he drove about New York (the first national capital under the Constitution) in a splendid carriage drawn by matched cream-colored horses. He looked and acted like the prince of a small European state, far from regal but decidedly aloof. His dignity, wrote Abigail Adams, "forbids familiarity." When, on a bet that he would not dare to do it, New York statesman Gouverneur Morris slapped Washington on the back, the president stared him down with such icy disdain that Morris retreated stammering from the room. They were never quite cordial again. Morris said it was the costliest bet he had ever won.

In being as much monument as man, Washington won respect abroad. No European statesmen feared the United States. Neither did any of them mistake George Washington for a head-scratching bumpkin who had had a bit of luck on a battlefield.

The Cabinet

Washington was as able a head of government as he was a dignified head of state. He was accustomed to wielding authority as a great planter and soldier, of course. A rarer quality among leaders was his awareness of his own limitations and his recognition of his need of advice. Far from resentful of brighter people (as was, for instance, George III), Washington conscripted the men he believed to be the country's best to serve as his advisors. The chief of these, supervising the workaday operations of the government, were five "Heads of Departments" or "secretaries" soon known collectively as the cabinet.

In creating the first cabinet, Washington tried to balance political tendencies and sectional sensitivities. From Virginia came Attorney General Edmund

The Vice Presidency

The vice president's only constitutional function is to preside over the Senate, and on the very rare occasions a vote is tied, to cast the deciding ballot. No ambitious politician has ever been happy in the post. John Adams called it "the most insignificant office that ever the invention of man contrived." When Theodore Roosevelt was nominated for the job in 1900, he feared that his political career had come to an end. John Nance Garner, vice president between 1933 and 1941, said the job wasn't "worth a pitcher of warm spit." Finley Peter Dunne, who wrote a popular newspaper column in Irish-American dialect around the turn of the twentieth century, summed it up: "Th' prisidincy is th' highest office in th' gift iv th' people. Th' vice-presidincy is th' next highest an' the lowest. It isn't a crime exactly. Ye can't be sint to jail f-r it, but it's a kind iv a disgrace."

Randolph and Secretary of State Thomas Jefferson. By naming Randolph, an opponent of the Constitution until the last moment, Washington extended a hand of reconciliation to the Anti-Federalists. Jefferson, by virtue of his agrarian book of 1785, *Notes on the State of Virginia*, was recognized as a spokesman for farmers who were suspicious of the nondemocratic features of the new government.

To balance the southerners, Washington named General Henry Knox of Massachusetts as secretary of war. Knox was a wartime crony of the president; he had wrestled the cannon to Boston that enabled Washington to drive the British from that city. More important, as the chief military official under the Confederation, Knox represented continuity from old government to new. Samuel Osgood of Massachusetts, the postmaster-general, was a former Anti-Federalist like Randolph.

Dynamic Alexander Hamilton of New York was Washington's secretary of the treasury. Partly because his conservative political instincts were in tune with the president's, partly because the most urgent challenges facing the new government were financial, Hamilton's power soon proved to be second only to Washington's.

Hamilton's Goals and Policies

To pay the government's running expenses, Hamilton asked Congress to enact a 5 percent tariff on imports. The duty was low, not enough to impede sales of foreign goods in the United States. However, the government needed short-term credit to keep its books balanced, and the 5 percent tariff would not provide the money needed in a crisis. In an emergency—war was the most obvious to come to mind—the government

George Washington and the first "cabinet," a body for which the Constitution did not provide.

would have to borrow hugely. Therefore, Hamilton set out to establish a good credit rating for the nation.

This was no easy chore. The Confederation Congress was grievously remiss in paying its debts, some $12 million owed to foreign banks and governments plus $44 million borrowed from American citizens. The new government's borrowing power was hamstrung by the old government's weakness and neglect.

The First Debate

Hamilton proposed to wipe the slate clean by funding the entire Confederation-era debt at face value. That is, by trading new bonds for the old ones—restructuring the debt, we might say—the Constitutional government would immediately demonstrate its fiscal reliability. Few in Congress objected to repaying foreign creditors in full. The United States was a cash-poor country. Big future loans would have to be floated abroad. Foreign lenders had to be ac-commodated. But Hamilton's insistence on paying American creditors in full led to a serious debate.

Why? Speculation and the bad odor in which many people held speculators. Most of the domestic debt dated to the war years when, moved as much by patriotic fervor as by mercenary motives, thousands of Americans bought government bonds. As the years passed and the Confederation Congress failed to redeem these debts, many lenders lost hope and sold their claims to speculators at big discounts. By 1789, most of this public paper was in the strongboxes of financial adventurers.

Nor had all of them been so very adventurous. As James Madison explained to Congress in opposing the funding bill, some speculators, advised in advance of what Hamilton would propose, had scoured rural villages and towns, buying up all the old government debts they could find, sometimes at a few cents on the dollar. In our parlance, they had traded on "insider information."

Should Congress reward such chicanery? Madison said no. Instead, he proposed to pay the face value of the debts plus 4 percent annual interest to original lenders who still held the old bonds. Speculators who bought public paper at bargain rates were to receive half the face value of their notes, with the remainder going to the original lenders.

Madison's argument was morally appealing. He proposed to reward those people who had stepped forward during the times that tried men's souls, and not conniving speculators. Hamilton replied that morality was beside the point. The issue was the new government's credit, stability, and prosperity: the future. By rewarding capitalists, the funding bill would encourage them to be lenders in days to come. The wealthy classes—the key to a government's stability in Hamilton's view—would be wedded to the success of the new government.

These practical arguments, not to mention the fact that several dozen congressmen stood to profit personally from the funding bill, carried the day. The old debt was funded.

Assumption

Hamilton next proposed that the federal government assume responsibility for debts contracted by the state governments. By paying back loans that some states had ignored for a decade, the federal government would further strengthen its good credit. Indeed, assumption would enhance the prestige of the

---

Almighty Dollar

The word *dollar* derives from the German *Taler*. The first silver coin by that name was the *Joachimstaler*, minted in what is now Czechoslovakia in the sixteenth century. The Dutch called similar coins *daler* and our spelling of the word comes from the Spanish, who then governed the Netherlands.

But why, in 1785, should the infant United States have adopted the Spanish dollar rather than the British pound sterling as its basic monetary unit? In part, the decision was just one of many anti-British actions during the 1780s. (The ever-patriotic Thomas Jefferson first suggested the dollar.) More to the point, there were more Spanish dollars circulating in the infant United States than British pounds. Coin had flowed from the colonies to Britain, but Americans enjoyed a favorable balance of trade with Spain and the Spanish colonies; silver dollars flowed in and accumulated.

Nevertheless, Americans, like other peoples, accepted any gold or silver coin offered to them. As late as the California Gold Rush of 1849, many businesses in San Francisco quoted their prices in pounds, shillings, and pence.

federal government *vis à vis* that of the states, a project dear to the hearts of nationalists like Hamilton.

Again, James Madison led the opposition. He pointed out that some states, such as his own Virginia, had retired much of their debt. By way of contrast, other states had been lax in repaying lenders or, as in the case of Massachusetts, still had big debts despite responsible fiscal practices. If the federal government assumed the obligations of all the states, the citizens of some of them would, in effect, pay twice. They had retired their own states' debts by paying state taxes. Now, by paying federal taxes, they would pay part of the debt run up in other states. Was this fair? Enough congressmen, particularly southerners, thought not. The assumption bill was defeated in the House of Representatives by a vote of 31 to 29.

Hamilton was determined that so close a vote would not scuttle his plan. Knowing that Virginians wanted the permanent national capital in the South, Hamilton worked out a deal with Thomas Jefferson, James Madison's political ally. If Jefferson used his influence to allow the assumption bill to pass, Hamilton would deliver the votes of enough northern congressmen to move the capital south. Thus, in a kind of political horse trade, was selected the site of Federal City, later renamed Washington, D.C., in woodland and worn-out tobacco fields on the banks of the Potomac River. On its second round in Congress, Hamilton's assumption bill passed 34 to 28.

The Bank of the United States

The third pillar of Hamilton's fiscal program was the Bank of the United States (B.U.S.), a central financial institution in which all government monies would be deposited. With such vast resources at its disposal, the B.U.S. would be invested with immense power over other banks and the nation's finances in general. The B.U.S. was not, however, a government agency. While the president would appoint five of the twenty-five directors who made bank policy, the remaining twenty were to be elected by shareholders, once again Hamilton's men of capital.

This time, Hamilton had nothing to trade to Jefferson in return for his support, and the secretary of state had had his fill of the marriage of government and capital. When the bank bill passed Congress, Jefferson urged President Washington to veto it. He argued that Congress had overstepped its constitutional powers. Nothing in the document gave the government the power to create such an institution.

Bucks and Quarters

The word *buck*, as slang for dollar, dates to the eighteenth century when the hide of a deer, or buckskin, was commonly used as a medium of exchange. By the time of the revolution, a buckskin's value was about that of a Spanish dollar.

Although the American dollar was officially divided into 100 cents, in popular usage, and soon enough in actual coinage, it was also divided into quarters. This apparently queer practice also dates back to the importance of Spanish coins in North America. Spanish dollars were divided into eight *reales*. In order to make change, they (and Portuguese *joes*) were actually sawed into eight pie-shaped pieces Thus, not only the American quarter coin but the now-dying custom of calling a quarter "two bits," and half a dollar "four bits."

Washington was impressed by Jefferson's reasoning. But Hamilton won the day by arguing that nothing in the Constitution specifically prohibited Congress from chartering a national bank. Therefore, such an action was justified under Article I, Section 8, which authorized Congress "to make all laws which shall be necessary and proper for carrying into execution," among other things, the regulation of commerce, which the B.U.S. would certainly do, and to "provide for . . . the general welfare," which in the estimation of men like Hamilton and Washington, the bank would also do.

Interpreting the Constitution

In the bank debate, Jefferson and Hamilton formulated fundamentally different theories of constitutional interpretation. Jefferson's "strict construction" of the Constitution held that if the document did not spell out a governmental power in black and white, it did not exist. Hamilton's "broad construction" held that Article I, Section 8 permitted Congress to exercise any and all legislative powers that were not specifically prohibited elsewhere in the Constitution. Both positions were plausible, honest. They were also incompatible. By the close of Washington's presidency, the two visions of the nation's highest law would contribute to the emergence of opposing political parties.

Hamilton Spurned

The B.U.S. was the last hurrah in Hamilton's campaign to shape the economy of the republic. He failed to build the fourth pillar of his edifice when Congress rejected the "Report on Manufactures" he submitted in December 1791. In this report, Hamilton argued that Congress should promote industry to augment the nation's well-established agricultural and commercial base. His means of doing so was the time-honored device of the protective tariff. By slapping high duties on, for example, British cloth and shoes, Congress could price those imports out of the American market. This would encourage investors to build textile mills and shoe factories in the United States, creating jobs and new founts of wealth.

Farmers were inclined to oppose a protective tariff, particularly southern planters with numerous slaves to clothe and shod. Agriculturalists were consumers of manufactured goods and Hamilton's tariff meant higher prices. Farmers also feared that the European nations that suffered from high American tariffs on manufactured goods would retaliate by enacting high tariffs on American agricultural produce. Some overseas traders also opposed Hamilton's tariff. Many of them lived by carrying British cloth, shoes, and iron goods across the Atlantic. The temporary coalition was too much for even Hamilton's deft political touch. The tariff remained low, just enough to pay the government's expenses.

Clouds on the Horizon

Washington was reelected without opposition in 1792 and his second term, like the first, was, on balance, a success. He managed to carry out most of the policies he felt strongly about, and to establish sensible precedents for his successors to imitate. Most important, he presided over the establishment of a stable government for 4 million people and (on the map, at least) 900,000 square miles of territory.

The United States of America, so recently a gaggle of small ex-colonies, was a going concern when, in 1797, the sixty-five-year-old father of his country returned to the plantation home where he had spent so little of his life.

Washington's success was not unblemished. In his farewell message, published in September 1796, Washington warned the country about four ongoing and related problems he was unable to resolve.

First, Washington urged his countrymen—virtually begged them—not to line themselves up in political parties. Washington regarded parties as combinations of selfish men who were willing to sacrifice the common good in order to benefit their own narrow interests.

Second, he admonished Americans to "discountenance irregular opposition" to the authority of their government. That is, they should voice their opposition to policies they disliked peacefully through legal channels, rather than resort to resistance and rebellion.

Third, he regretfully identified the beginnings of sectionalism in the United States. He feared that too many Americans pledged allegiance to North or South rather than to the republic as a whole. Division along sectional lines, fraught with the potential for civil war, must be nipped before it bloomed and sapped the energy of the organism.

Finally, Washington warned against "the insidious wiles of foreign influence," the attempts by European diplomats to entangle the United States in their chronic, wasteful wars. Honor alliances already in effect, Washington said, but make no new permanent commitments to other countries.

Washington's False Teeth

George Washington's false teeth were not, as an old saw has it, wooden teeth. They were, however, painful to wear and influenced more than the fact that in his many portraits, Washington is never smiling. In life, he rarely did.

By the time he was elected president, Washington had only one natural tooth in his head, a bicuspid. His false teeth, uppers and lowers hinged at the rear, were made of other human teeth anchored in ivory. They served to do little more than fill out Washington's face and provide a semblance of dentition when Washington did speak or smile. With nothing to hold his teeth in place, Washington avoided oratory. (He may well have been an excellent speaker; his writing is superb: clear and eloquent.) Of course, he could eat little in public and, at any time, only food that had been finely cut or mashed.

Washington the Villain

Although no one dared oppose him in the election of 1792, Washington was not universally worshiped. Indeed, the invective heaped on him by editor Benjamin Bache (who was Benjamin Franklin's nephew) exceeds anything to be found in newspapers today. In December 1796, Bache wrote, "If ever a nation was debauched by a man, the American nation has been debauched by Washington." When Washington turned over the presidency to John Adams in March 1797, Bache exulted, "If ever there were a period for rejoicing, it is this moment. Every heart, in unison with the freedom and happiness of the people, ought to beat high in exultation, that the name of Washington ceases from this day to give a currency to political iniquity and to legalize corruption." In another place, Bache warned, "The American people, Sir, will look to death the man who assumes the character of a usurper."

Even Thomas Paine, who had worshiped Washington, wrote privately to him that "the world will be puzzled to decide whether . . . you have abandoned good principles, or whether you ever had any."

TROUBLES ABROAD

The most troublesome problems facing the Washington administration were in the area of foreign policy, and they would continue to vex and frustrate his successors in the presidency. This should not be surprising. As colonials, Americans had entrusted relations with other nations to the mother country. In no other arena of statecraft were the founding fathers so poorly educated. Moreover, the 1790s were a time when the cleverest of European diplomats were confounded. The old order, which they understood, was being turned upside down.

Revolution in France

In 1789, France exploded in a revolution that, within a few years, pushed far beyond what Americans had done. At first rebelling against the extravagance and excesses of the monarchy, the French revolutionaries

soon set about redesigning their society from bottom to top.

Americans rejoiced almost unanimously at the events of 1789. Had not the Declaration of Independence spoken of the inalienable rights of all people? Now their ally in the struggle against Great Britain was joining them as a land where liberty flourished. It became fashionable for Americans to festoon their hats with a cockade of red, white, and blue—the badge of the French revolutionaries. When Lafayette sent Washington the key to the Bastille, the gloomy fortress where the French kings had imprisoned political dissidents, the president displayed it proudly to his guests. Nor were most Americans perturbed when the revolution turned against the institutions of monarchy and aristocracy. Had not the Americans themselves renounced kingship and forbidden citizens to accept titles of nobility?

Then, however, the French Revolution moved beyond liberty to the ideals of equality and fraternity. Conservatives like Washington and Hamilton could not be comfortable with talk of wiping out social distinctions and privileges, of putting the rudest, most ignorant day laborer on a par with people like themselves. Gouverneur Morris, minister in France, put it another way. The French, he wrote, "have taken Genius instead of Reason For Their Guide, adopted Experiment instead of Experience, and wander in the dark because They prefer Lightning To Light." Even Thomas Jefferson, pro-French and given to exuberant celebration of tumult and uprisings, worried that the French were moving too far, too fast. He doubted that a people accustomed to an all-powerful monarchy could create overnight a free republic like the United States.

Terror and Reason

But found a republic the French did, and in January 1793, as Washington's first term of office was ending, King Louis XVI was beheaded. His queen, Marie Antoinette, mounted the scaffold within the year. During the Reign of Terror that followed, French radicals, known as Jacobins, guillotined or drowned thousands of nobles and political rivals. The blood and gore that flowed in France was quite as unnerving to Europeans (and many Americans) as the Holocaust was to be in the mid-twentieth century.

The virtual dictator of France for a year, Maximilien Robespierre, launched a campaign to wipe out religion. He converted Paris's cathedral of Notre Dame into a "Temple of Reason" where paunchy politicians and perfumed actresses performed rituals that struck many as ridiculous, others as blasphemous.

Few Americans thought fondly of the Catholic church. However, Robespierre attacked all revealed religion. American preachers shuddered when they heard Americans admiring his campaign. William Cobbett, an Englishman living in the United States, observed with distaste that crowds of city people guillotined dummies of Louis XVI "twenty or thirty times every day during one whole winter and part of the summer." He also reported fistfights between gangs of pro-English "Anglomen" and pro-French "cutthroats."

Choosing Sides

Cobbett was observing a point of conflict that contributed to the birth of the political parties that Washington warned against. Americans who supported the French inclined to favor an expanded democracy and the curtailment of social distinctions at home. Working people in the cities, small and middling farmers, and many wealthy southern planters who resented the favors that Hamilton's financial program lavished on merchants and capitalists, turned increasingly to Thomas Jefferson as their spokesman and began to call themselves "Jefferson Republicans." Jefferson, who left Washington's cabinet in 1793, was troubled by the bloodletting in France, but gladly accepted the leadership of the coalescing movement.

Conservatives such as Washington, Hamilton, and Vice President John Adams, calling themselves Federalists, were neither enamored of democracy, which they equated with mob rule, nor hostile to clear social distinctions, which they regarded as a buttress of social stability. Until 1793, they were content to attack the principles of the French Revolution on a philosophical level. Then, Great Britain declared war on France. Under the terms of the alliance of 1778, it appeared that the United States was obligated to join France in the fight.

The reasons for staying out of the war were more than philosophical. The Royal Navy was supreme on the Atlantic, and Washington rightly feared that full-scale war would prove too heavy a burden for the young government. Then Alexander Hamilton found the legal loophole that kept the United States out. He argued that the treaty of 1778 was invalid on two counts: it had been contracted with the French monarchy, which no longer existed; and it provided that the United States must help France only if Great Britain were the aggressor, which, with some justification, the British denied being.

Washington announced that the United States would be neutral, "impartial toward the belligerent powers." This might have averted crisis had it not been for the arrival in Charleston in April 1793 of the French minister, Edmond Charles Genêt, or, as this preposterous character styled himself, Citizen Genêt.

Citizen Genêt

Genêt was young, bombastic, and as subtle as flags and fireworks. Soon after stepping ashore, he began to commission American shipmasters as privateers, armed raiders under contract to France to seize British ships. Within a short time, a dozen of these raiders brought eighty British merchant vessels into American ports, where Genêt presided over trials at which he awarded the prizes to the captors. Genêt also attended dozens of dinners held in his honor, at which he spoke as though he were the governor of a French colony.

By the time Genêt presented his credentials to the president, Washington was livid. Genêt's lack of diplomatic etiquette was bad enough to a man who would not be slapped on the back. Much worse, Genêt's privateers promised to drag the United States into a war with Britain that the president had determined to sit out. Washington received the Frenchman coldly and ordered him to subdue his politicking and to cease bringing British prizes into American ports.

Genêt bowed, retired, and continued to appear at dinners and demonstrations, adding jibes at the president to his speeches. When he directly defied Washington by recommissioning a captured British vessel, the *Little Sarah*, as a privateer, Washington ordered him to return to France.

This was bad news. Genêt was a member of a political faction that had been ousted back home and the Reign of Terror was in full swing. To return to France meant a rendezvous with Madame la Guillotine. Suddenly abject, Genêt asked Washington for asylum, and the president granted it. Most remarkably, Genêt quieted down, married into the wealthy

"Citizen" Genêt defied and infuriated President Washington, then sought his protection.

Clinton family of New York, and lived a long, contented life as a gentleman farmer in the Hudson River Valley.

A British Threat

But the threat of war was far from dead. The British kept it boiling by proclaiming that they would fight the war at sea under the Rule of 1756. This British policy asserted that the ships of neutral countries could not trade in ports from which they had been excluded before the war began.

The targets of this proclamation were American overseas merchants who were shipping provisions to the French West Indies: Martinique, Guadeloupe, and Saint Domingue (present-day Haiti). Before the war, American ships were excluded from this trade by French law. Only after the war began did the French open the West Indies to American merchants.

Carrying grain, livestock, and other foodstuffs, merchants from New England, New York, and Pennsylvania reaped bonanza profits. Shipmasters who had struggled with hard times for decades moved their families from apartments in their ware-

houses to elegant town houses built in the architectural style we admire as Federal period. They hosted grand levees and balls and sponsored a sparkling social whirl in the coastal cities. They also expanded their fleets until the American merchant marine was as large as that of the British.

The British did not want the Americans in the war but British merchants had cause for concern. Would Britain defeat the French in Europe only to discover that their overseas trade had been filched by upstart Yankees? The enforcement of the Rule of 1756 was an attempt to prevent such a development. During 1793 and 1794, British warships seized 600 American vessels, about half of them in West Indian waters, a few within sight of American shores.

American shipowners were not delighted, but neither were they unduly disturbed. Overseas trade was a high-risk enterprise in the best of times. The wartime business with the West Indies was so lucrative that they were able to absorb the losses. Moreover, in New England, the upper classes were generally

Citizen Genêt

The French revolutionaries hated the symbols of inequality as much as the reality of it. They tried to eliminate all titles, not only those of nobility (duke, countess, and marquis), but also *Monsieur* and *Madame*, forms of address that were then reserved for gentlemen and ladies. During the early stages of the French Revolution, it was declared that everyone was to be addressed as *Citoyen* and *Citoyenne*, or "Citizen" and "Citizeness." King Louis XVI was brought to trial as "Citizen Capet," and when Edmond Genêt arrived in the United States as minister, he called himself Citizen Genêt. His Jeffersonian friends briefly adopted the custom, referring to one another as "Citizen."

The Russian revolutionaries of 1917 did much the same thing when they abolished traditional Russian forms of address in favor of *Tovarich*, or "Comrade." In countries like the United States and Britain, the problem has been resolved by upgrading everyone to the level of "Mr." and "Mrs."— titles that previously were reserved to members of the gentry.

sympathetic to the British. Wealthy merchants were inclined to wink at British depredations in the interest of seeing the diabolical French atheists go down in defeat.

Impressment

The pro-French party, on the other hand, was not averse to picking a fight with England. Jeffersonian propagandists, such as former seaman, erstwhile poet, and vituperative newspaper editor Philip Freneau, railed against the British seizures of American ships as an affront to national honor. Seamen and their families had a more personal grievance, the Royal Navy's interpretation of the ancient practice of impressment.

Britain (and other seafaring nations) empowered the captains of warships to replace seamen who died or deserted by means of an impromptu draft. If a ship were in port, its press-gangs roamed the streets of town forcing likely young men into service. At sea, men-of-war ordered merchant vessels to heave to—the proverbial shot across the bow—and press-gangs boarded them. Impressment was highly unpopular. News of a press-gang in an English town sent young men scurrying into cellars or fleeing to the countryside. Seamen on a signaled merchantman feigned crippled legs or idiocy. Few men with a choice between merchant service and the Royal Navy, with its brutal discipline, opted for king and country.

If British seamen hated impressment, Americans were infuriated when warships flying the Union Jack took crewmen from their own ships. Britain claimed the right to impress only British subjects from American ships, but there were plenty of these, for conditions and pay were superior in the American merchant marine. The issue was further complicated by conflicting definitions of citizenship. Britain claimed that British birth made a person a lifelong British subject. The United States insisted that an immigrant became a naturalized American citizen after five years of residence in the United States. Many seamen were caught in the middle, exacerbating the sensitive issue of national independence.

Jay's Treaty: Peace at a Price

In April 1794, faced with a growing clamor for war, Washington sent the chief justice of the Supreme Court, John Jay, to England to appeal for peace. This alone was enough to raise the hackles of the anglophobic Jeffersonians, especially when the news trickled back that Jay was gaily hobnobbing in London society and had kissed the hand of the queen.

That fuss was nothing compared with the reception given the treaty that Jay brought home. The British made a few concessions. They agreed to evacuate the western forts that were declared American in 1783. Britain also agreed to compensate American shipowners for vessels seized in the West Indies and to allow some trade with British possessions. In return, the Americans pledged not to discriminate against British shipping and to pay debts owed to British subjects from before the Revolution.

Not a word was said about impressment, the issue most charged with emotion. Like Hamilton's fiscal policy, Jay's Treaty could be interpreted as benefiting only wealthy merchants. As for the British evacuation of the western forts, the fulfillment of a promise that had been made and broken a decade earlier hardly soothed the wounded pride of Republican patriots.

Party Conflict

Protest swept the country. When Washington submitted Jay's Treaty to the Senate for ratification, he was attacked personally for the first time, and not gently. Jay resigned from the Supreme Court and joked uneasily that he could travel the length of the country by the light of the effigies of him that were burned by furious Republicans. Crowds shouted: "Damn John Jay! Damn everyone that won't put lights in his windows and sit up all night damning John Jay!"

It was, to say the least, an expression of party spirit, for Washington, Adams, Hamilton, and other Federalists did not damn John Jay. They believed that however imperfect his treaty, he had done the country a service by preserving the peace. They did not yet call themselves a party. With Washington in power, the Federalists dared not embrace open factionalism. But the lines between two political parties, already penciled in, were drawn a bit more clearly.

Pinckney's Treaty

A happier consequence of Jay's Treaty was an advantageous agreement with Spain. The Spanish too had been warring with revolutionary France but, by the end of 1794, Spain wanted out of the conflict. France, then fighting practically the whole of Europe, was willing to come to terms. But the Spanish feared that the reconciled British and Americans might join together to invade their province of Louisiana. Not two years earlier, in fact, Citizen Genêt had proposed such an enterprise to pro-French Americans.

To placate the United States, Spanish ministers met with diplomat Thomas Pinckney and acquiesced in practically every demand that the Americans had made on them since 1783. In Pinckney's Treaty (officially the Treaty of San Lorenzo), Spain agreed to the American version of the boundary between the United States and Louisiana; to open the Mississippi River to American navigation (the Spanish owned the western bank); and to grant Americans the "right of deposit" in New Orleans. That is, Americans were empowered to store their exports (mostly foodstuffs and timber) in New Orleans, and to carry on commercial transactions in the city.

These concessions were of vital importance to the westerners, the more than 100,000 people who, by 1795, had settled in Kentucky (admitted to the Union in 1792) and Tennessee (admitted 1796), and the several thousand who lived in what is now Ohio.

WESTERN PROBLEMS

Life on the frontier contrasted sharply with the comfort and security of the thirteen coastal states. The killing labor needed to wrench a farm out of forest combined with infectious disease and malnutrition to generate a death rate west of the Appalachians as high as it had been in seventeenth-century Virginia and Maryland. Isolation from the eastern states meant that manufactured commodities were expensive, when they were available at all. The ways of the people reflected their hardships. Outsiders saw them as dangerously violent, "still more depraved than in Virginia," which, apparently, was saying something. "Like dogs and bears, they use their teeth and feet, with the most savage ferocity, upon one another." And upon the numerous Indians who lived between the Appalachians and the Mississippi, who were happy to respond in kind.

Dark and Bloody Ground

Today, when we conjure up images of Indian wars, we are apt to think of the Great Plains in the later nineteenth century. Here were the dramatic battles of pulp novel and film, the Seventh Cavalry in dusty blue uniforms battling mounted warriors of Sioux and Comanche in the wide-open spaces. In fact, the confrontations of the late eighteenth century between Americans and the tribes of the forested Ohio valley—Miamis, Shawnees, Ottawas, Ojibwas (Chippewas), Sauks, and Foxes—were far fiercer and bloodier than these better-known Indian wars.

For one thing, the tribes of the Eastern Woodlands were more numerous than the Plains Indians. By the 1790s, they were capable of fighting massive pitched battles in the dense forests of the region. George A. Custer's column at the endlessly celebrated battle of the Little Big Horn in 1876 numbered 265 men. In Ohio in 1794, General "Mad Anthony" Wayne led an army ten times that number. Because of the large numbers of casualties in Kentucky, Indians and white pioneers alike called the place "the dark and bloody ground."

President Washington was eager to clear the Ohio Valley of Indians. Not only was it a matter of national pride that the federal government actually

THE FEDERALIST TREATIES

VERMONT (1791)
Fort Dutchman's Point
Fort Pointe-au-Fer
Fort Oswegatchie
Fort Michilimackinac
Fort Oswego
NH
Fort Niagara
MA
CT
NY
RI
Fort Detroit
PA
NJ
MD DE
VA
ATLANTIC OCEAN
KENTUCKY (1792)
NC
TENNESSEE (1796)
SC
GA
PINCKNEY TREATY LINE
Gulf of Mexico
Mississippi River

0   200   400 Miles
0   200   400 Kilometers

New states

Accession under Pinckney Treaty

British forts evacuated under Jay Treaty

HOW THEY LIVED

How They Tamed the Forest

The end of hostilities after the Battle of Yorktown led to the rapid settlement of western Pennsylvania, a land of ridges, rolling hills, and mixed hardwood and conifer forests. The American victory meant that the Proclamation of 1763, which forbade white settlement west of the Appalachians, was null and void. More important, when the fort at Pittsburgh was transferred from the redcoats to the Continental soldiers in their blue and buff, the power of the Indians of the region, who were British allies, was sharply reduced.

Perhaps the social disruptions that accompany every war also played a part in populating western Pennsylvania. In raising its armies, the revolution wrenched thousands of young men from their homes and accustomed ways of life at a critical time in their lives. As young adults, they faced decisions about the future. When the war was over, many veterans found it impossible to return home and take up life where they had left off. In the United States, such people could head west, to a frontier as unsettled as themselves. During the 1780s (and for half a century to come), the West was centered in what is, geographically, the Eastern Woodlands.

The author of an article about the Pennsylvania frontier that appeared in *The Columbian Magazine* for November 1786 did not mention the recently concluded war. But "the first settler in the woods," whom the author describes as a kind of social misfit, sounds very much like a Revolutionary War veteran: the pioneer was "generally a man who has outlived his credit of fortune in the cultivated parts of the State." Not a very good citizen, he was an anarchic, irreligious, and hard-drinking individual who "cannot bear to surren-der up a single natural right for all the benefits of government."

The pioneer moved on when too many people began to crowd into his neck of the woods—when he could hear the barking of his nearest neighbor's dog or see the curl of smoke from his nearest neighbor's fire. He sold out to a settler who improved the primitive farm and who, in turn, made way for the solid citizen whose habits obviously relieved the author of the *Columbian* article. In the third wave came the "settler who is commonly a man of property and good character."

"The third and last species of settler" meant the end of the log-cabin frontier literally as well as figuratively, for the newcomer built a solid house and barn of quarry stone. At last there could be schools, churches, law and order—a civilized town. The writer for the *Columbian* left no doubt as to where his hopes for the country lay. Nevertheless, he granted the obvious: that neither the third nor the second phase of settlement was possible without the pioneers who had been willing to face the hardships of the log cabin in return for freedom and independence.

Pioneers opening up forest land tried to arrive at their destination in April when winter's snows had melted, but the overarching trees were not yet in full foliage. Their first task was to build a cabin and stable in order to be sheltered by the third week of May, when, in Pennsylvania, the year's crop of corn, beans, and squash had to be planted. The pioneers' fields were not pretty; they were not really fields. The pioneers adopted the Indian method of cultivation, killing the great oaks and maples by girding their bark about two or three feet from the ground and

govern all its territories, but many wealthy planters, of whom Washington was one, were deeply involved in land speculation in the Northwest Territory. They owned thousands of acres of virgin forest that they found difficult to sell to settlers so long as the Miamis and Shawnees maintained independence of action.

In 1790, Washington sent Josiah Harmer to find and defeat the Miamis and Shawnees under the war chieftain Little Turtle. Poorly supplied, wracked by dysentery and malaria, and handicapped by unfamiliarity with the country, Harmer and his men were decimated near the site of present-day Fort Wayne, Indiana. The next year, a better-prepared expedition under Arthur St. Clair met the same fate, with 600 soldiers killed.

The Miamis and Shawnees, with their loose ties to the British in Canada, remained supreme in the

planting wherever sun shone through the bare branches. In the rich organic soil, created by the fallen leaves and toppled trees of centuries, even this primitive agriculture produced a crop of 40 to 50 bushels an acre, harvested in October.

Cattle and horses—generally bony, unhealthy beasts—were allowed to roam, at most hobbled by the length of rope or leather thong that tied together two legs. There were few predators in the forests that would attack such large animals, and the frontier family with the most casual work habits had little time for tending livestock.

Most families also owned hogs. They too ran loose and were hunted rather than rounded up when pork was needed. Indeed, with the forests teeming with game, meat shortage was less of a problem than keeping the domestic and wild animals out of the cornfields.

Toward this end, the log-cabin pioneer built a rude zigzag fence. It was a marvelous adaptation to the conditions of the forest frontier—abundant wood and land, scarce labor. Logs could be split into rails using an axe, wedges, and a maul, and the zigzag pattern required no post holes. The zigzag was not a very good fence. The rails were toppled by hungry hogs and easily leapt by deer. But it sufficed, and sufficient was the talisman of the family struggling against the wilderness.

The log cabin was another adaptation to forest conditions. Again, only a few tools were required to build one. With their axes, the pioneers easily felled small trees, hewed (squared) them if they chose, and cut the notches that made it possible to build a cabin wall without upright timbers. In all but the rudest

cabins—and many were but three-sided structures that faced an open fire—the only task requiring more than a single man's and woman's labor was raising the roof beam, itself a log. For this job, other frontier families were called on to help, and the event became a social occasion. Even the sniffy author of the *Columbian* article, who had little good to say about the pioneer, was moved to admire the cooperation involved in performing such tasks "without any other pay than the pleasures which usually attend a country frolic." The roofing itself consisted of split rails or a thatch of rye straw.

Not only did the log cabin go up quickly, but it was a strong house. Its walls were thick and almost invulnerable to arrowhead, musket ball, or fire. (To burn a log cabin, it was necessary to set fire to the roof.) Finally, if the logs were well chinked with moss and mud, they provided better insulation against cold than sawn clapboards did.

The sturdiness of the well-built log cabin was attested to by the fact that the people who came in the second wave of settlement purchased the pioneer log cabin, added on to it, laid floor boards, and shingled the roof. Otherwise they found the pioneer's dwelling quite serviceable. Even the third settler, the permanently fixed farmer, often found a use for the cabin as a hog shed or corn crib after building a stone house.

By the middle of the nineteenth century, the log cabin entered American folklore as a symbol of the opportunity the nation provided its citizens. A man who was born in a log cabin could hope to rise, as Abraham Lincoln had done and James A. Garfield would do, to the highest office in the land.

Northwest Territory until August 1794, when General Wayne defeated them at the Battle of Fallen Timbers near Toledo. (The trees on the battlefield had been leveled by a tornado.) Wayne's victory would have won more friends for Washington among westerners than it did if the president had not also dispatched an army against farmers in western Pennsylvania to collect a tax on their whiskey.

Pioneers and Whiskey

The men and women of the frontier were heavy drinkers. They started their days with an "eye-opener," a "flem-cutter," and a third pull as an "antiformatic." A jug sat on shop counters; every general store doubled as a saloon. Men and women alike swigged corn and rye whiskey like wine with their meals and like water with their work. Preachers refreshed themselves with the concoction during sermons. The image of the hillbilly asleep next to his jug of moonshine was not invented by cartoonists. Future President William Henry Harrison said that he "saw more drunk men in forty-eight hours succeeding my arrival in Cincinnati than I had in my previous life."

One explanation of the pervasiveness of the jug was the prominence of the Scotch-Irish on the frontier. Whiskey was the potable of the Celtic fringe. Another is that breweries demanded a technology beyond the capabilities of primitive communities while distillation was simple. Then there was disease. Settlers on the woodlands frontier suffered miserably from the alternating chills and fevers of malaria, which they called the "ague." The first medicine for which they reached was alcohol.

As well, the isolation of western life promoted heavy drinking. Travelers on the Ohio valley frontier invariably recorded conversations with men, and especially women, who commented mournfully on the lack of company. Whiskey was a companion, not loquacious but not demanding either.

Finally, whiskey was cheap. The corn from which the drink was made was easy to grow, even in slashed and burned forest. When a farm was a few years old, pioneers turned to wheat and rye, which also made a tolerable mash. Fuel for distillation was costless. Many family farmers kept a small still percolating day and night, turning out raw white whiskey, while commercial distillers established large operations on major waterways throughout the Ohio Valley.

Of Whiskey and Rebellion

Whiskey was also a cash crop. The westerners could not ship their grain until the Mississippi River, into which the Ohio flows, was opened to American trade in 1795. The cost of transporting a low-value bulk commodity like grain over the Appalachians was prohibitive. A pack horse could carry 200 pounds, about four bushels of grain. Four bushels, minus what the horse consumed on the road, did not sell for enough to pay for the journey.

However, a horse could carry the equivalent of 24 bushels if it had been converted into liquor. A gallon of whiskey sold for 25 cents or more, which provided a profit. But it was small. Hamilton's excise tax of 1791 (seven cents on the gallon!) wiped the profit out. Just as Daniel Shays's men

had done in Massachusetts in 1786, the Pennsylvania farmers roughed up tax collectors and rioted in river towns.

Washington and Hamilton, who had been alarmed by the Shaysite disorder, recognized a peerless opportunity to demonstrate the contrast between the weakness of the old Confederation and the authority of the new government. The president himself set out at the head of 15,000 troops to suppress the rebellion, though he left the expedition when the rebels scattered. But Hamilton, who had a yen for military glory, pushed on and arrested a few men who were tried, convicted of treason, and sentenced to death. Washington pardoned them, calling them mental defectives. Perhaps they were; perhaps it was just Washington's way of showing his contempt for the rebels and demonstrating that, among his other virtues, he did not thirst for blood.

In one sense, the suppression of the Whiskey Rebellion was a farce. An army as large as the one that had defeated the British—and far larger than the army at Fallen Timbers—was organized to crush a rebellion that its commander could not even find. But the political significance of the episode was profound. The Federalist Hamilton was delighted to assert the national government's right to enforce order in a state with troops raised in other states. The resentment of the westerners, however, ensured that when political parties emerged full-blown, the people of the frontier would not vote for Federalists.

FEDERALISTS VERSUS REPUBLICANS

By the summer of 1796, when Washington announced that he would retire and warned Americans against forming political parties, two parties existed in everything but name. On every controversy that arose during Washington's presidency, Americans not only disagreed, they also divided along much the same lines.

Party Lines

The Federalists supported Hamilton's financial policy; they feared the French Revolution as a fount of atheism and social disorder; they were friendly to England; they accepted Jay's Treaty; and they

Angry westerners tar and feather an excise officer during the Whiskey Rebellion of 1794.

believed that the national government should act decisively and powerfully to maintain internal order, as Washington had done in western Pennsylvania.

Vice President John Adams and Alexander Hamilton were the chief spokesmen for the Federalist group, which also included John Jay, the wealthy Pinckneys of South Carolina, and—because no matter what he said about parties, he agreed with the policies of the Federalists—George Washington himself. Wealthy people were inclined to be Federalists. In the North (especially New England), where money had been made in trade and speculation, the urban rich were almost unanimously Federalists.

The Jefferson Republicans opposed Hamilton's financial policies. Farmers (and some great planters) believed that they paid the taxes that financed funding and assumption while benefiting little from those policies. Republicans were friendly to the ideals of the French Revolution, although not all were comfortable with its excesses, such as the Reign of Terror. Republicans were generally suspicious of England, as both the former oppressor and, in the West, the ally of the Indians. The Republicans despised Jay's Treaty. Jefferson was in the midst of a personal cold war with the British that would last until the day he died. With an affection for democratic values that the Federalists spurned, the Republicans worried about an overly powerful national government quick to use soldiers against protesters such as the Whiskey Rebels.

Election of 1796

Thomas Jefferson was the Republican candidate for president in 1796. Officially, Vice President John Adams of Massachusetts was the Federalists' man, and diplomat Thomas Pinckney of South Carolina

Mrs. Gilbert Yates, in a portrait by Gilbert Stuart, the elegant and self-assured epitome of an upper-class federalist period lady.

was the Federalist vice-presidential candidate. However, the powerful and mischievous Alexander Hamilton designed a scheme to manipulate the electoral college and put Pinckney in Adams's place. Whereas Pinckney was a loyal ally, Hamilton did not personally like Adams and he knew he would have little influence with him.

In 1796, presidential electors did not vote separately for president and vice president. Each elector wrote two names on his ballot. The candidate with the largest number of votes was named president, the candidate with the second largest vote became vice president. Because nine states then empowered their legislatures to select members of the electoral college (popular elections were held in only six states), Hamilton was able to persuade some Federalist politicians in the South to cast one of their two votes for Pinckney, but the other—that should have gone to Adams—to some other person with no chance of winning. He hoped that enough southern Republicans would vote for Pinckney out of sectional loyalty to give him a larger total than Adams.

The plan might have worked if Adams's supporters in New England had not caught wind of it. They retaliated by withholding votes from Pinckney. The upshot was that Adams won, but Pinckney

did not finish second. Thomas Jefferson did. The president was the titular leader of one of the two political parties; the vice president was the actual leader of the other. Then, as now, the vice presidency was not a powerful office. But if the 61-year-old John Adams had died in office, his chief political rival, instead of a member of his own party, would have taken his place.

"His Rotundity"

After 200 years, it is easy to admire John Adams. He was a moderate at heart who acted according to stern and steadfast principles and, in the end, for the good of his country as he saw that good. He could be humorous. When whisperers said that he had sent General Pinckney to London to procure four trollops for his and Adams's use, he responded, "I do declare upon my honor, General Pinckney has cheated me out of my two." His relationship with his wife, Abigail, had a curiously modern ring to it. He sought her advice on everything, and often took it. "The President would not dare to make a nomination without her approbation," an opponent said. Adams was "always honest and often great," in Benjamin Franklin's words.

However, it is easier to admire Adams at a distance. He was also, as Franklin added, "sometimes mad." Impossibly vain and peevish, with a furious temper and a bottomless capacity for intolerance, Adams could be absurdly pompous. When wits sniggered at his short, dumpy physique ("His Rotundity," they whispered) and gossiped about his wife, Adams cut himself off, almost a hermit. He spent astonishingly little time in the national capital, Philadelphia, until the last year of his presidency. During his four years as president, he passed one day in four at the Adams home in Quincy, Massachusetts. (By comparison, Washington was absent fewer than one day in eight.) Adams's absence and his inheritance of Washington's last cabinet, which was as bumbling a group as the first had been brilliant, and which reported every bit of business to Hamilton, made the president a man with only half a party behind him.

Another War Scare

Like Washington in his second term, Adams was preoccupied with the threat of war, this time with France as the enemy. Angered by Jay's Treaty, the French government ordered its navy and privateers to treat American ships as fair game. By the time

John Adams (1735–1826), second U.S. president.

Adams took the oath of office, 300 American vessels had been seized. Moreover, the French defined American sailors captured off British ships (many of whom had been pressed involuntarily into service) as pirates who could legally be hanged. In Paris, the French threatened to arrest the American minister, Charles Cotesworth Pinckney. In the United States, the French minister, Pierre Adet, railed publicly against Adams almost as intemperately as Genêt had assailed Washington.

Hamilton's supporters, the "High Federalists" who had reacted calmly to British seizures of American ships, demanded war with France. Determined to keep the peace, Adams dispatched to Paris two special ministers, John Marshall and Elbridge Gerry, to join Pinckney in asking for negotiations.

The X,Y,Z Affair

The three diplomats were shunned. Weeks passed, and they could not get near the French foreign minister, a randy and charming rogue, Charles Maurice de Talleyrand. Finally, Talleyrand sent word through three henchmen, identified in code as X, Y, and Z, that the foreign minister would be delighted to talk to the Americans if they agreed in advance to a loan of $12 million and a personal gift to Talleyrand of $250,000.

Bribes were routine in diplomacy; but the amount Talleyrand demanded was excessive, and the tempers of the Americans were worn thin from waiting and humiliation. "Not a sixpence," Pinckney snapped, and the Americans walked out. Back in the United States, Pinckney's reply was dressed up (and changed into American currency) as "millions for defense but not one cent for tribute."

The High Federalists celebrated the news of Talleyrand's insult. Hamilton pressured Adams to mobilize an army of 10,000 men, and Washington agreed to become its titular commander on the condition that Hamilton be second in command. Not only did this mean Hamilton would jump rank over a number of Revolutionary War officers, but it humiliated Adams and caused him to worry about a military coup.

Adams was more comfortable with the navy. He came from a maritime state, and sea power posed no threat to domestic order. (A country cannot be subdued from a ship.) Moreover, while it was difficult to say where France and America might fight on land, an undeclared war already raged on the seas. Adams authorized the construction of 40 frigates and lesser warships, a huge jump from the three naval vessels inherited from Washington.

Repression of Dissent

Jefferson's Republicans remained generally pro-French. They trumpeted loudly and widely against all preparations for war. They were egged on by French diplomats and by a group of Irishmen who had fled to America after the failure of a rebellion against England. Both Adams's Federalists and Hamilton's High Federalists responded to this protest with a series of laws called the Alien and Sedition Acts of 1798.

One act extended the period of residence required for American citizenship from five to fourteen years. This was a tacit admission that most newcomers to the United States supported the Republicans. A second Alien Act allowed the president to deport any foreigner whom he deemed "dangerous to the peace and safety of the United States." A third gave the government authority to move expeditiously against enemy aliens at home. The

A Federalist political cartoon attacking France after the X,Y,Z Affair, 1798.

Alien Acts were scheduled to expire shortly after Adams's term expired in 1801; they were unmistakably aimed at the Jeffersonian Republicans.

The Sedition Act

Although some foreigners fled the country for fear of arrest, the Alien Acts were not enforced. But the Sedition Act was. This law called for stiff fines and prison sentences for persons who published statements that held the United States government in "contempt or disrepute." Twenty-five cases were brought to trial, and ten people were convicted. Two Jefferson men in Newark, New Jersey, were imprisoned under the act when John Adams was saluted in the city by a volley of gunfire. One of them said, "There goes the president and they are shooting at his ass." The other responded, "I don't care if they fire through his ass." A court presided over by George Washington's nephew, Bushrod Washington, ruled that these were seditious words exciting resistance to lawful government.

Other prosecutions under the Sedition Act were not so comical. In an effort to crush the political opposition, Federalists convicted four important Republican newspaper editors for the same crime. Thomas Jefferson, at his home, Monticello, received alarmed and angry letters from his supporters in every part of the country.

The Virginia and Kentucky Resolutions

Reading them, Jefferson and his chief advisor, James Madison, became convinced that the Alien and Sedition Acts were unconstitutional. The Federalist Congress, they believed, had not merely adopted obnoxious laws, but it had overstepped the powers vested in it by the Constitution. In particular, Congress had violated the Bill of Rights. But who was to declare when Congress (and the president who signed an act) had acted unconstitutionally? The answer Jefferson and Madison gave was to haunt American history for half a century and contribute to the tragic Civil War of 1861 to 1865.

In the Virginia and Kentucky Resolutions, adopted in the legislatures of those states in 1798 and 1799, Madison and Jefferson wrote that the federal government was a voluntary compact of sovereign states. Congress, therefore, was the creation of the states. When Congress enacted a law that a state deemed to be unconstitutional, that state had the right to nullify the law within its boundaries. Acting on this principle, the Virginia and Kentucky legislatures declared that the Alien and Sedition Acts did not apply in those states.

In effect, the Virginia and Kentucky Resolutions marked a return to the supremacy of states which, under the Articles of Confederation, none had denied. In doing so, they challenged the supremacy of the federal government which, presumably, the Constitution was written to establish. Nothing came of this challenge in 1799. No other state assembly adopted the Virginia and Kentucky Resolutions. The death of George Washington in December 1799 briefly calmed political tempers and, as the election of 1800 drew nearer, it became increasingly obvious that instead of helping the Federalists, the Alien and Sedition Acts were so unpopular that they improved the chances of a Republican victory.

The Bizarre Election of 1800

As it happened, Jefferson's victory over Adams in 1800 was nearly as tight as Adams's victory over Jefferson in 1796, and it was marked by an electoral college confusion with far more calamitous implications. Jefferson won 73 electoral votes to Adams's 65. The only significant change in the political alignment of the states was the switch of New York from the Federalist to the Jefferson Republican column. This neat trick—with 19 electoral votes, New York was the third biggest prize in presidential elections—was the handiwork of a man who was Hamilton's rival for control of the state and his equal in political scheming.

Aaron Burr, only 44 years old, clever and creative, was the Republican vice-presidential candidate who swung New York into the Republican column. However, because none of the 73 Republican electors dropped Burr's name from his ballot so that Burr would finish in second place, the official count showed the New Yorker tied with Jefferson.

The Constitution provided (and still provides) that when no candidate wins a majority of votes in the electoral college, the House of Representatives, voting by states, not by individuals, chooses the president. In 1800, this gave the Federalists the balance of power. The votes of nine states were required for election.

The Republicans, who dutifully voted for Jefferson, controlled only eight state delegations in the House.

A Vote for Stability

When the first ballot was taken, Jefferson received eight votes to Burr's six; two states were evenly divided. The Federalists voted mainly for Burr, some because they believed that Jefferson was a dangerous radical, others because they hoped to throw their Republican rivals into disarray. To his credit, Burr refused to urge on his supporters. At the same time, he did not instruct his few Republican supporters or Federalist friends to vote for Jefferson. He remained in seclusion.

After 35 deadlocked ballots, a Delaware Federalist, James A. Bayard, fearing that the crisis would destroy the national government his party had toiled to build, announced that he would change his vote to Jefferson on the next ballot. In the end, he did not have to do so. Hamilton's agents had contacted Jefferson and extracted vague commitments that he would continue Federalist foreign policy and maintain the Hamiltonian financial apparatus. Just as important, Hamilton despised Burr. If Burr became president, Hamilton said, he would form an administration of "the rogues of all parties to overrule the good men." He conceded that Jefferson had at least a "pretension to character."

It was not much of a compliment, but it was enough. Hamilton pressured a few Federalist congressmen from key states to abstain. This enabled Jefferson to be elected on the thirty-sixth ballot on February 17, 1801.

Recognition of Political Parties

The original method of selecting the president was based on the premise that electors dedicated to the health of the republic would select the best man to be president, and the second best to be vice president. It worked only so long as George Washington was on the scene. The election of 1796 showed that party politicians were willing to manipulate the electoral process to serve factional ends. The election of 1800 demonstrated that parties were permanent fixtures of the American political process.

This meant that the original procedure of electing the president was no longer workable. In 1804, the Twelfth Amendment provided that, henceforth, electors would vote separately for president and vice president—the system that survives today. George Washington was first sworn in as president in New York City. He set the precedent for public inauguration.

CHRONOLOGY

1789	Constitutional government commences
	Revolution in France
1789–1791	Congress enacts most of Hamilton's Financial Program
1791	Congress rejects Hamilton's protective tariff
1793	Louis XVI beheaded in France
	Reign of Terror in France
1793–1794	Edmond Genêt defies Washington by commisioning privateers for France in United States
	British warships seize 600 American merchantmen
1794	Battle of Fallen Timbers
	Whiskey Rebellion
	Jay's Treaty
1795	Pinckney's Treaty
1797	John Adams becomes president
1797–1798	X,Y,Z Affair
1798	Alien and Sedition Acts
1798–1799	Virginia and Kentucky Resolutions
1800	Thomas Jefferson elected president

FOR FURTHER READING

Although a generation old, still the best overview of the Federalist period is John C. Miller, *The Federalist Era*, 1960. Also see, however, Jacob E. Cooke, "The Federalist Age: A Reappraisal" in Gerald N. Grob, *American History: Retrospect and Prospect*, 1971; the appropriate chapters of John R. Howe, *From the Revolution through the Age of Jackson*, 1973; and Stanley Elkins and Eric McKitrick, *The Age of Federalism: The Early American Republic, 1788–1800*, 1993.

The person of George Washington loomed over the 1790s, so that biographies of him cited in previous chapters remain basic reading. In addition, see Marcus Cunliffe, *Man and Monument*, 1958; James T. Flexner, *George Washington: Anguish and Farewell*, 1972; Forrest MacDonald, *The Presidency of George Washington*, 1974; Edmund S. Morgan, *The Genius of George Washington*, 1980; and Garry Wills, *Cincinatus: George Washington and the Enlightenment*, 1984.

On the Adams presidency, particularly on the election of 1796, see Stephen G. Kurtz, *The Presidency of John Adams*, 1957, and Ralph Brown Adams, *The Presidency of John Adams*, 1975; also Manning Dauer, *The Adams Federalists*, 1953; J. R. Howe, *The Changing Political Thought of John Adams*, 1966; and Peter Show, *The Character of John Adams*, 1976. Adams took his intelligent wife's views more seri-ously than most presidents have done: see Lynne Withey, *Dearest Friend: A Life of Abigail Adams*, 1981.

The emergence of political parties in America is treated (with quite different interpretations) in William D. Chambers, *Political Parties in a New Nation*, 1962; Joseph Charles, *The Origins of the American Party System*, 1956; and Richard Hofstadter, *The Idea of a Party System*, 1969. Providing special insights into the Jeffersonians are Daniel Boorstin, *The Lost World of Thomas Jefferson*, 1948; Noble Cunningham, *The Jeffersonian Republicans*, 1957; and Merrill Peterson, *Thomas Jefferson and the New Nation*, 1970. On Jefferson's great rival, see Jacob E. Cook, *Alexander Hamilton*, 1982, and John C. Miller, *Alexander Hamilton: Portrait in Paradox*, 1959.

Sources for specific episodes of the 1790s include Harry Ammon, *The Genêt Mission*, 1973; Daniel G. Lang, *Foreign Policy in the Early Republic*, 1985; Thomas P. Slaughter, *The Whiskey Rebellion: Frontier Epilogue to the American Revolution*, 1986. Gerald A. Combs, *The Jay Treaty*, 1970; Samuel F. Bemis, *Jay's Treaty*, 1923, and *Pinckney's Treaty*, 1926; Leonard W. Levy, *Legacy of Suppression: Freedom of Speech in Early America*, 1960; and James M. Smith, *Freedom's Fetters: The Alien and Sedition Laws and American Civil Liberties*, 1956.

Thomas Jefferson's splendid home, Monticello, which he himself designed.

12
CHAPTER

THE AGE OF JEFFERSON

Expansion and Frustration

1800–1815

Eaten to a honeycomb with ambition, yet weak, confused, uninformed, and ignorant.

— *John Adams*

You and I ought not to die before we have explained ourselves to each other.

— *John Adams*

The immortality of Thomas Jefferson does not lie in any one of his achievements, or in the series of his achievements, but in his attitude toward mankind.

— *Woodrow Wilson*

Since the days when Jefferson expounded his code of political philosophy, the whole world has become his pupil.

— *Michael MacWhite*

In April 1962, President John F. Kennedy played host to an assembly of Nobel Prize winners. He greeted them by saying, "This is the most extraordinary collection of talent, of human knowledge, that has been gathered at the White House, with the possible exception of when Thomas Jefferson dined here alone."

It was more than a witty remark. Few people—and precious few of them politicians—have been so broadly learned and versatile in their skills as was Thomas Jefferson, the tall, slightly stooped man with graying red hair who took the presidential oath of office in March 1801.

THE SAGE OF MONTICELLO

Jefferson was the author of the nation's birth certificate, the Declaration of Independence. He was governor of Virginia during the revolution and minister to France under the Articles of Confederation. He was the first secretary of state, the second vice president, and a shrewd political strategist who created the party that made him president in 1801.

Jack of All Trades

But Jefferson was more than a politician. He was a philosopher, happy when he could sit quietly in his study and think. He read and spoke several European languages and studied Indian tongues. No other president wrote better English than he did. His prose was precise in its vocabulary and mellifluous in its rhythms—and he wrote more than any two presidents. The definitive edition of his works and letters fills 20 volumes, and the project is complete only for his pre-presidential career. Few who wrote to Jefferson received a formula letter in reply.

Jefferson founded the University of Virginia, designing its curriculum and its buildings. He designed his own home, Monticello, and (anonymously) entered the competition among architects to design the president's mansion—the White House.

He dabbled in natural science. He invented the dumbwaiter, the swivel chair, and perhaps decimal coinage. While he inveighed against the industrial revolution, he built a nail factory on his plantation. He was a gourmet who may have introduced pasta to the United States. He spent up to $2,800 a year on wines for his table and up to $50 in a day on groceries when a turkey could be bought for

seventy-five cents. He employed a French chef, possibly the first American to do so. He even once risked arrest to smuggle a strain of rice he fancied out of northern Italy.

Mixed Reviews

Jefferson was no demigod, as he said the men who wrote the Constitution were. His vision of the future was shallow compared to Hamilton's; he could be as narrow-minded and peevish as John Adams, and as vindictive. He was no orator, partly out of shyness, partly because he was intensely self-conscious of a lisp.

Nor was he universally admired. Adams envied his popularity and rarely missed an opportunity to snipe at his reputation. Hamilton thought him softheaded and frivolous. Other Federalists believed that he was an immoral voluptuary and a dangerous radical. During the presidential campaign of 1800, the *Connecticut Courant* warned that Mad Tom's election would mean "your dwellings in flames, hoary hairs bathed in blood, female chastity violated, children writhing on the pike and the halberd." Not yet exhausted, the editor continued, "murder, rape, adul-

---

"Natural Aristocracy"

Thomas Jefferson believed in the democratic principle that, on balance, the mass of people would choose to do the correct thing. He found arguments to the contrary unconvincing, because if "man can not be trusted with the government of himself, can he, then, be trusted with the government of others?" Federalists like John Adams disagreed. They believed that the people in a mass were a danger to the liberties of others and themselves. Government should be trusted to those with the leisure, education, and virtue to practice it intelligently. (Hamilton, of course, thought that the people were "a great beast.")

In the end, however, Jefferson and Adams were not so far apart. By "all men are created equal," Jefferson did not mean that all possessed equal talents. In a long correspondence with John Adams, when both were retired from politics, he agreed entirely with his old enemy that there was "a natural aristocracy among men. The grounds of this are virtue and talent"—inborn faculties.

tery, and incest will be openly taught and practiced" in a Jeffersonian America. More phlegmatic anti-Jeffersonians contented themselves with the widely whispered tale that one of Jefferson's slaves, Sally Hemmings, was his concubine who bore his children.

JEFFERSON AS PRESIDENT

Jefferson was not oblivious to his critics and he knew he owed his election to some Federalists in the House of Representatives. In his eloquent inaugural address, he attempted to woo to his party those Federalists who were not "devoted to monarchy" by saying that "every difference of opinion is not a difference in principle. We have called by different names brethren of the same principle. We are all republicans, we are all federalists." Privately, he wrote of "honest and well-intentioned" Federalists.

Continuities

To a degree, the new president acted on his hint of trans-partisanship. He quietly abandoned some of his prepresidential positions and adopted Federalist policies that, as leader of the opposition, he had condemned. Nothing more was heard from him or his secretary of state, James Madison, about the doctrine of nullification they had put forward in the Kentucky

Thomas Jefferson, a portrait by Charles Fevret de Saint-Mermin.

Tom and Sally

The story that Thomas Jefferson and his slave, Sally Hemmings, were lovers, was circulated during the election campaign of 1800 and remains a subject of historical debate today. Until the 1990s, evidence on both sides of the argument was circumstantial or traditional. Visitors to Jefferson's home at Monticello during Jefferson's lifetime observed that several of Sally Hemmings's children were red-haired (Jefferson had red hair) and resembled the president. Sally Hemmings never spoke publicly in the matter but any number of her descendants insisted that Jefferson was their ancestor too. In 1998, Hemmings's descendants applied (unsuccessfully) for admission to a society of Jefferson descendants.

Critics of the Jefferson–Hemmings connection argue that Jefferson's views on race, miscegenation, and his general sense of propriety precluded such an alliance. They conjectured that one or two of Jefferson's nephews, who lacked their uncle's scruples and were also red-haired, fathered Sally's children.

Then, also in 1998, DNA tests concluded that Jefferson was the father of one of Sally Hemming's children, although not of others. Most historians who had argued against the Jefferson–Hemmings relationship admitted they had been mistaken. A few did not: the DNA tests allowed just enough of a margin of error that the debate, less noticed, goes on.

and Virginia Resolutions. Jefferson allowed parts of Hamilton's financial program to work for him, including the Bank of the United States, which he had called unconstitutional. He appointed as secretary of the treasury the Swiss-born Albert Gallatin, who proved to be as responsible a money-manager as his Federalist predecessors.

Republican Simplicity

Jefferson brought a new style to the presidency. He sincerely disliked the arch formality that characterized the social presence of Washington and Adams. Instead of exchanging bows with visitors, he shook hands. He abolished the presidential levees (regularly scheduled, highly structured receptions). Much to the annoyance of some officials and diplomats, he paid scant heed to the rules of protocol that assigned a rank of dignity, a chair at the table, a precisely fixed position in a procession to every senator, representative, judge, cabinet member, and minister from abroad. Not even at state dinners were seats assigned; guests scrambled for places that they believed suited their dignity. Indeed, Jefferson preferred small parties at which he wore bedroom slippers and served the meal himself. One of his favorite dishes was a macaroni and cheese, which he probably introduced to America, too.

Jefferson's taste for "republican simplicity" was made easier by the move of the capital, the summer before his inauguration, from sophisticated Philadelphia to Federal City, Washington, D.C. Washington was no city at all in 1800, but a bizarre hodgepodge of half-completed public buildings, ramshackle boardinghouses, stables, vast tracts of wooded wilderness, swamps, and precious few private homes.

Abigail Adams had done her laundry in the "ballroom" of the White House. Jefferson spent the night before he was inaugurated in a drafty rooming house, taking his breakfast with other boarders. For years, there would be no place in Washington for congressmen's families. Social life was masculine and on the raw side: smoky card games, heavy drinking, even brawls and gunfights. Strangers got lost trying to find their way from the president's mansion to the Capitol, not in a warren of alleys but on muddy trails cut through forest and brush.

Making Changes

Jefferson's innovations were not exclusively stylistic. He pardoned the people who were still imprisoned under the Sedition Act (all of them were his support-

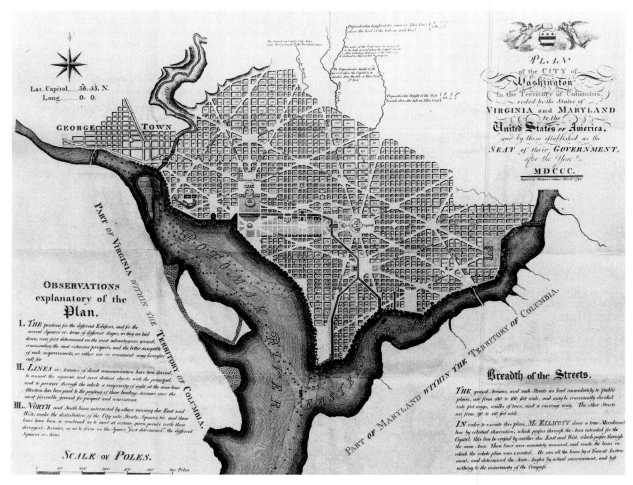

Plan for the construction of Washington, D.C., 1792. The first president to live in the city was John Adams, who moved there from Philadelphia in 1800.

ers, of course). He restored the five-year residency requirement for citizenship, and replaced Federalist officeholders with Republicans. He and Gallatin slashed government expenditures, the army's budget from $4 million to $2 million, the navy's from $3.5 million to $1 million, and put forth a plan to retire the national debt by 1817. Within a few years, the debt was reduced from $83 million to $57 million.

But these actions did not constitute a "Revolution of 1800," as Jefferson called his election. Indeed, the only innovation in governance during Jefferson's presidency that qualified as revolutionary was effected by one of the president's bitterest enemies (although his distant cousin), the Federalist chief justice of the Supreme Court, John Marshall.

Marbury v. Madison

On the day before John Adams turned the White House over to Jefferson, he hurriedly appointed 42 Federalists to the bench. Federal judges served for life, so Adams was securing long-term employment for loyal supporters. In addition, he wanted to ensure that the judiciary, which was independent of both the presidency and Congress (also under Republican control in 1801) would remain a bastion of Federalist principles.

Adams was setting a precedent. The appointment of "midnight judges" would become standard operating procedure for outgoing presidents whose party was defeated at the polls. Like incoming presidents who would follow him, Jefferson could only sit and steam to contemplate the salaries that were lost to his own Republicans.

One exception was the case of William Marbury. Thanks to the inefficiency and oversight that would also become a feature of American government, the document that entitled Marbury to his job was not delivered before March 4, when Jefferson took the oath of office. On the face of it, Adams's dereliction was immaterial. According to the Judiciary Act of 1789, the secretary of state—James Madison as of March 4, 1801—was obligated to deliver Marbury's commission. When Madison refused to do so, Marbury sued for a writ of *mandamus*, a court order that means "we compel" a government official to perform the prescribed duties of his office.

By 1803, the case was before the Supreme Court. As it would continue to be for more than 30 years, the court was then dominated by Chief Justice John Marshall. The force of his personality was such,

---

Party Time

John Adams was not impressed by Jefferson's well-publicized preference for an informal social life. He wrote: "I held levees once a week, that all my time might not be wasted by idle visits. Jefferson's whole eight years was a levee."

---

his willingness to do the lion's share of the court's work so eager, and his legal mind was so acute, that Marshall almost always had his way with the other justices. In his ruling in the case of *Marbury v. Madison*, he scolded Madison for unseemly behavior. However, instead of mandating the secretary to deliver Marbury's commission, Marshall ruled that a section of the law under which Marbury had sued was unconstitutional. Congress, Marshall said, had no constitutional right to give the federal courts the powers the Judiciary Act of 1789 accorded it.

The Doctrine of Judicial Review

Marbury v. Madison was a coup. By sacrificing the paycheck of one Federalist politico and canceling part of one Federalist law, Marshall asserted the Supreme Court's right to decide which acts of Congress were constitutional, and which unconstitutional and therefore void. He decreed that the Supreme Court not only judged cases according to the law, but the court judged the validity of the law itself.

Nothing in the Constitution explicitly vested the court with this substantial power. Jefferson and Madison had tried to claim it for the state legislatures in the Virginia and Kentucky Resolutions. And John Marshall did not quite win it for the Supreme Court. It would require usage to make judicial review an unquestioned part of American government. But Marshall laid sound foundations for the principle.

Just to rub a little salt in Jeffersonian wounds, Marshall ruled at the same session that the Republicans' Circuit Court Act of 1802 could remain on the books because the Supreme Court (John Marshall) had decided it was constitutional.

Retaliation

Jefferson was helpless to fight the battle on high ground. Instead, he approved of a campaign of machination and low blows against the Federalist judiciary.

HOW THEY LIVED

Giving Birth

A woman who married during the Federalist or Jeffersonian era could expect to be pregnant about seven times during her life—if she did not die as a young woman, in childbirth or otherwise. During the 1790s, there were almost 300 live births for every 1,000 women between the ages of 15 and 44—more than one woman in four delivered each year—as compared with 84 pregnancies for each 1,000 women in 1970. Pregnancy, childbirth, and the nursing of infants were a far more important part of a woman's existence in 1790 than they were in the late twentieth century. Indeed, giving birth to children was generally considered to be the chief reason for a woman's existence.

Almost every child was delivered at home. The few hospitals that existed were reserved for the seriously ill or injured, and childbirth was eminently normal. Most children were delivered by female midwives (the word midwife means "*with* a woman") and in the company of the mother-to-be's own mother, sisters, neighbors, friends, and even older daughters. Historian Catherine M. Scholten has shown that childbirth was a communal event, the climactic shared experience of women. Except during the early stages of labor, when the husband might be called in to pray with or comfort his wife, men were usually excluded.

The midwife might have served an apprenticeship, or she might have slipped into the job as a consequence of accidentally getting "catched" in a number of childbirths and therefore developing a reputation as someone who knew what to do. In any event, while midwifery lacked the formal recognition in the United States that it had in England, it was very definitely a profession. The tombstone of one Boston woman says that she "by the Blessing of God has brought into this world above 3,000 Children."

In part, the presence of other women was a practical matter. Water had to be heated, and linens washed. In the event of a prolonged labor, food had to be prepared. Because in the eighteenth century few women gave birth lying on their backs in bed but, instead, squatting or standing, the mother depended on other women for physical support. Moreover, it was common practice for a recent mother to remain in bed for at least four weeks after childbirth. Her friends performed her household duties during this final phase of confinement.

But the attendants also served important cultural, social, and psychological purposes. By their presence and the exclusion of men, they emphasized the uniquely feminine character of the suffering involved in childbirth at a time when liquor was the only anesthetic available. The pains of bearing children were still generally thought of as God's punishment for the sin of Eve. By their presence—because they too had undergone childbirth or could expect to do so—the attendants were sharing in the travail.

Moreover, as Scholten discovered, they cheered the mother-to-be by distracting her with gossip, comparing her labor with more difficult labors they had

---

First, the Republicans impeached and removed from office a Federalist judge in New Hampshire, John Pickering. That was easy; Pickering was given to drunken tirades in court, and was probably insane. Jefferson's men then inched closer to Marshall by impeaching Supreme Court justice Samuel Chase.

Chase was an inferior jurist, grossly prejudiced in his rulings, overtly political, sometimes asinine. But the Senate refused to find him guilty of the "high crimes and misdemeanors" that are the constitutional grounds for impeachment. Like other presidents unhappy with the Supreme Court, Jefferson had no choice but to wait until seats fell vacant. Eventually, he was able to name justices, but John Marshall remained in Washington long after Jefferson was gone.

THE LOUISIANA PURCHASE

If Marshall added a twist to the Constitution, Jefferson gave it a mighty wrench in the most important action of his first term, the purchase of Louisiana from France for $15 million. The Louisiana of 1803 was not merely the present-day state of that name. As a colony,

witnessed (or suffered), and even making her laugh by telling bawdy jokes.

Already in the 1790s, however, the supervision of childbirth was being taken away from women by male physicians who had been trained in obstetrics. This trend began in England during the 1740s and 1750s, when Dr. William Smellie was appalled by the incompetence of many midwives. "We ought to be ashamed of ourselves," he told physicians, "for the little improvement we have made in so many centuries." Smellie invented the forceps used for assisting difficult births.

The development of obstetrics as a branch of medicine also reflected society's general drift away from literally interpreted religion. In 1804, Peter Miller, a student at the University of Pennsylvania, then home of the country's best medical school, wrote that the dangers of pregnancy and the death of so many infants involved enough sorrow for women. It was absurd to cling to the belief that the moment of birth should also be a travail. Dr. William Dewees, a pioneer of medical obstetrics in the United States, asked, "Why should the female alone incur the penalty of God?"

In the cities and particularly among the upper and middle classes, male physicians supplanted female midwives in a surprisingly short period of time. In Boston and Philadelphia (and probably in other large cities) during the Federalist period, physicians were called into childbirth cases only when there were serious difficulties. By the 1820s, doctors virtually monopolized the delivery of children in urban areas.

The survival rate among both mothers and newborns improved with the triumph of medical obstetrics. (Although the significant advance took place only later in the nineteenth century, when the Hungarian Ignaz Semmelweiss and the English surgeon Joseph Lister discovered that "childbirth fever" [puerperal fever] was caused by the failure of most physicians even to wash their hands.) However, the triumph was not entirely progressive. The demands of a sexual modesty that was in fact prudery, which was strongest among the upper and middle classes, forced doctors to ask questions of "a delicate nature"—just about all questions about childbirth—through another woman. It was an unwieldy procedure at best, and in emergencies it was potentially dangerous.

In addition, the birth had to be carried out under covers, with the physician working entirely by touch. Indeed, even such an awkward process offended some people. In *Letters to Ladies, Detailing Important Information Concerning Themselves and Infants*, published in 1817, Dr. Thomas Ewell told of a husband who "very solemnly . . . declared to the doctor, he would demolish him if he touched or looked at his wife." Finally, as is common with scientific advances, there was a human cost. Transforming childbirth from a communal event into a private medical operation destroyed an important social relationship among women.

Louisiana included the better part of the 13 states that, today, lie between the Mississippi River and the Rocky Mountains, some 828,000 square miles. Louisiana cost $15 million, less than three cents an acre. Its purchase was the greatest real estate bargain of all time.

Sugar and Foodstuffs

So grand a deal was imaginable only because the French emperor, Napoleon Bonaparte, first toyed with the idea of reasserting French power in North America and then abandoned the project. His scheme was inspired by the value, but also the vulnerability, of France's possessions in the West Indies: the islands of Martinique, Guadeloupe, and Haiti.

These colonies were producers of sugar and coffee, both lucrative commodities in the world market. They were grown on French-owned plantations by gangs of black slaves worked as hard and treated as badly as any in the world. The blacks grew little but sugar and coffee. Food production was neglected, so grain and meat to feed the population had to be imported, mostly from the United States and Louisiana, then under the Spanish flag.

Napoleon's plan was to force Spain, a client state, to return Louisiana to France. There were only about 50,000 people of European descent in Louisiana but the endless lands bordering the Mississippi River invited development. With Louisiana, Napoleon could feed the people of his sugar islands from within a revived French empire in America. In 1800, by the secret Treaty of San Ildefonso, Napoleon regained Louisiana.

Vital Interest

On Napoleon's orders, even before the terms of San Ildefonso were revealed, the Spanish revoked the right of deposit that was guaranteed to U.S. citizens in Pinckney's Treaty—the right of Americans to store and trade their products in New Orleans. The response in some quarters was near panic. The free navigation of the Mississippi River was absolutely vital to the 400,000 Americans who lived beyond the Appalachians in Ohio, Kentucky, and Tennessee. Each year they rafted 20,000 tons of produce down the Mississippi, the only practical way they could market it. To westerners, in James Madison's words, the great waterway was "the Hudson, the Delaware, the Potomac, and all the navigable rivers of the Atlantic formed into one stream." As Jefferson put it, "There is on the globe one single spot, the possessor of which is our natural and habitual enemy. It is New Orleans," the city that controlled the mouth of the Mississippi.

War with France seemed likely and Congress voted funds to call up 80,000 state militiamen. But any attack on New Orleans would require a naval blockade of the port, as well as an overland assault, and Jefferson was in the process of eviscerating the American navy. The British, sworn enemies of Napoleon, would gladly help but such an alliance was repugnant to a president who had written the Declaration of Independence.

An Offer Not to Be Refused

Fortunately for Jefferson, there was an alternative to war. He instructed his minister in France, Robert R. Livingston, to offer Napoleon $2 million for a tract of land on the lower Mississippi where the Americans might build their own port. (Congress had voted him that sum.) In January 1803, impatient that no news had arrived from France, Jefferson sent James Monroe to Paris to offer as much as $10 million (a sum

that had appeared in no congressional appropriation) for New Orleans and West Florida—the present-day Mississippi and Alabama gulf coast.

When Monroe arrived, he was stunned to learn that, a few days earlier, the French foreign minister, Charles Maurice de Talleyrand of the X,Y,Z Affair, had offered all of Louisiana to Livingston for $15 million.

This remarkable turnabout had little to do with American wants and needs. Louisiana had become worthless to Napoleon. Rebels in Haiti, France's most valuable West Indian colony, had battered a crack French army commanded by General Charles Leclerc. Some 30,000 French troops were killed or incapacitated in battle and from tropical fever. "Damn sugar," Napoleon said on hearing of the debacle, "Damn coffee. Damn colonies! Damn niggers!," for his army had been defeated by slaves and Haitian freemen of color.

Constitutional Niceties

The Louisiana deal was quickly sealed despite the fact that it was without constitutional sanction. The founding fathers had made no provision for purchasing territory nor, as was required by the terms of the sale, for immediately conferring U.S. citizenship on the people of Louisiana. But it was far too great an opportunity to be rejected.

Girl Guide

Sacagawea, the Shoshone guide and interpreter who guided Lewis and Clark over much of their route, is usually depicted in paintings and sculpture as a woman. In fact, she was by any definition, a mere girl. Sacagawea was born in what is now Idaho, the daughter of a Shoshone chief. She was kidnapped and adopted by a band of Hidatsa about 1798. Her name means "Bird Woman" in Hidatsa, not Shoshone. Later, a French trapper, Toussaint Charbonneau, bought her from the Hidatsas as his wife. When Lewis and Clark hired Charbonneau and Sacagawea as translators during the winter of 1805–1805, Sacagawea was nursing a newborn infant, Jean Baptiste Charbonneau, whom she carried with her throughout the great trek. All the evidence indicates she was twelve years old.

Some Federalists called Jefferson a hypocrite for abandoning his strict constructionist theory of the Constitution. Jefferson—one hopes with some sheepishness—wrote that "what is practicable must often control what is pure theory." He instructed his supporters in Congress that "the less we say about constitutional difficulties respecting Louisiana the better." Even members of Jefferson's party far more zealous in their strict constructionism, like John Randolph and John Taylor, held their tongues.

The Magnificent Journey

The acquisition of Louisiana aroused Jefferson's life-long interest in natural science and in the still mysterious interior of the continent. Even before the Senate ratified the Louisiana Purchase, he persuaded Congress to appropriate $2,500 to finance an expedition across the continent for the purposes of looking for a feasible overland trade route (the "Northwest Passage" again), and to gather scientific data.

Jefferson entrusted the mission to Virginia neighbor, Meriwether Lewis, and William Clark, Lewis's friend and former commanding officer. He

The Northwest Passage

The dream of finding a "Northwest Passage" to Asia never did die. When President Thomas Jefferson sent Meriwether Lewis and William Clark across North America in 1804, there was still a wan hope that a workable passage to the Pacific was possible. Throughout the nineteenth century, intrepid sailors attempted to trace an all-water route around the top of North America. Several expeditions spent years locked in polar ice. When, in 1958, the nuclear submarine *Nautilus* circled the continent by cruising under the ice of the North Pole, commentators implied that there was a Northwest Passage after all.

must have yearned to go himself, for he attended to the most picayune details of preparation, even listing in his own hand the provisions that the explorers should carry with them.

The actual trek exceeded anything ventured by conquistadors or voyageurs. Lewis, Clark, and a

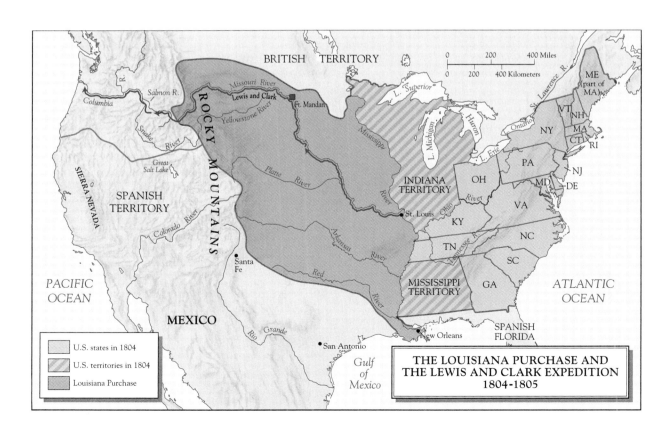

THE LOUISIANA PURCHASE AND
THE LEWIS AND CLARK EXPEDITION
1804-1805

motley crew of 40 rowed, poled, and pulled their skiffs up the Missouri to the river's spectacular falls (present-day Great Falls, Montana). After portaging 16 miles, they enlisted the help of the Mandan, Shoshone, Nez Percé, and other tribes to find a tributary of the Columbia River. Following the great drainage, they reached the Pacific on November 15, 1805. There they spent four and a half months, during which time, as latter-day residents of Oregon and Washington will readily appreciate, it rained every day but 12.

National Heroes

Lewis and Clark arrived back in St. Louis in September 1806. Not only was their trip a prodigious feat of exploration, but they collected a large body of information about the plant and animal life of the continent. Less welcome was the intelligence that there was no easy route to the Pacific.

Lewis and Clark were among the last Americans to confront Indians untouched by Western civilization. Their experience is instructive. While there were a few uneasy moments with the Sioux and Shoshone, on the trip west the explorers engaged in nothing resembling a battle with the dozens of tribes they met. (They did kill two members of the Blackfoot tribe on their return east.) Almost all the native peoples of the interior were curious, hospitable, and helpful. York, Clark's black slave (freed at the end of the expedition) was a source of endless fascination among the Indians because of his dark skin. The Shoshone, with whom the expedition could communicate through a young woman who joined the expedition, Sacajawea, gave key advice toward finding the Pacific, which they themselves had never seen. The tribes of the Northwest coast, of course, had long dealt with American and European seamen, whalers, and fur traders. One of their favorite expressions, Lewis and Clark discovered, was "son of a pitch." An Indian woman who

York, the sole African American on the Lewis and Clark expedition, was a source of fascination to Western Indian tribes.

lived near the mouth of the Columbia River had "Jonathan Bowman" tattooed on her leg.

Jefferson thought that the country traversed by Lewis and Clark would provide land for Americans for a thousand generations. He was mistaken; the lands of the Louisiana Purchase and beyond were settled by 1890. But the West served Jefferson's Republican party very well. Ohio became the seventeenth state in 1803 and, voting Republican like Kentucky and Tennessee, contributed to Jefferson's easy reelection the next year. The Federalists carried only 14 electoral votes, those of Connecticut and Delaware. The nationalists had become the provincials and Mad Tom's Republicans the national party.

The Further Adventures of Aaron Burr

The Louisiana Purchase also figured in the bizarre career of Aaron Burr. His fortunes tumbled downhill immediately after his election as vice president in 1801 when Jefferson (somewhat unfairly) concluded that Burr had schemed to steal the presidency. Jefferson gave Burr no more to do than John Adams had given Jefferson and he denied the master politician access to the federal patronage (appointive offices with which to reward political allies, government contracts to benefit supporters). Burr found—as his successors would—that the vice-presidency provided him with no power and little busywork.

Some evidence indicates that Burr plotted with a group of New England Federalists called the Essex Junto to detach New York and New England from the United States. If true, the plan depended on Burr winning the election for governor of New York in 1804, when Jefferson dropped him from the national ticket. However, Burr was defeated, in part because of Alexander Hamilton's militant opposition, including some scurrilous writings that Hamilton did not sign. Their exchanges grew even more bitter and personal after Burr's defeat and he challenged Hamilton to a duel.

Hamilton disapproved of dueling. His son had been killed in one. But the feud was beyond shrugging off and, on July 11, 1804, the two men and their seconds rowed across the Hudson River to Weehawken, high on the New Jersey Palisades. They fired at one another from 20 paces. Hamilton's bullet went astray; some said he deliberately shot high. Burr's pierced Hamilton's liver and lodged in his spine. He died the next day.

The first secretary of the treasury was never a beloved man, but his eminence was vast. Hamilton's death shocked the nation. Burr was indicted for murder in both New York and New Jersey and had to flee to the South, while friends ironed out the legal difficulties. Still vice president, Burr returned to Washington, but his political career was finished. Not yet 50 years of age, energetic, and possessed of a keen imagination, he turned his gaze toward the West.

The Burr Conspiracy

There, Burr met amidst great secrecy with James Wilkinson, the territorial governor of Louisiana and a character so devious that, by comparison, Burr resembles George Washington. He met with other prominent westerners, including Andrew Jackson of Tennessee, and even the head of the Ursuline convent

Aaron Burr, master politician, vice president, adventurer.

in New Orleans. Burr's oddest associate was one Harman Blennerhasset, an Irish refugee who lived opulently on an island in the Ohio River. Enamored of Burr's plans (whatever they were), Blennerhasset financed the construction of a flotilla of 13 flatboats, including a fabulously outfitted barge for Burr with glass windows, a fireplace, a promenade deck, and a wine "cellar." With 60 men, they meandered down the Ohio and the Mississippi.

Burr and Blennerhasset were accused variously of planning to invade Spanish Mexico or to spark a secession of the western states and territories from the United States. Or both, depending on what circumstances allowed and whose word is to be believed. Jefferson was prepared to believe the worst. When Wilkinson accused Burr of plotting treason, Jefferson had the New Yorker arrested and returned to Richmond, where he was tried before Chief Justice John Marshall.

Marshall was apt to snipe at anything dear to Jefferson's heart and he insisted on defining treason in the strictest of terms. However, there was no need to rig the trial. The prosecution's case was sloppy; few accusations were corroborated; and the unsavory

Wilkinson was a weak reed on which to support a prosecution. Nothing of substance was proved against Burr and he was acquitted. The most significant event in the trial was Marshall's issue of a subpoena to Jefferson. The president refused to appear, citing the independence of the executive branch (which he had denigrated before his election).

Burr moved abroad for a few years before returning to New York, though one more scandal was to pepper his remarkable career. During divorce proceedings, his second wife titillated New Yorkers by claiming (quite absurdly) to have been the only woman in the world to have slept with both George Washington and Napoleon Bonaparte.

FOREIGN WOES

Like Washington and Adams, Jefferson found foreign affairs more frustrating than domestic policy. Indeed, Jefferson helped to set himself up for failure when he allowed the Adams navy to dwindle. He soon learned that a nation with vital interests in international trade had to be able to protect its international traders with more than sermons and moralistic edicts.

The Barbary Pirates

One trouble spot was the Mediterranean, where the economy of the Barbary (Berber) states of Morocco, Algiers, Tunis, and Tripoli was based in part on piracy and extorting a kind of protection money from seafaring nations. So fearsome and efficient were the Barbary corsairs that even mighty Britain paid annual tribute to various beys and pashas. It was

---

Tribute to the Pasha

The annual payment to the pasha of Tripoli, which Jefferson attempted to cancel in 1801, consisted of $40,000 in gold and silver, $12,000 in Spanish money, and an odd assortment of diamond rings, watches, and fine cloth and brocade. The rulers of the Barbary states sincerely thought of these as gifts of friendship rather than as extortion. For example, in 1806 the bey of Tunis, who also received tribute, sent Jefferson a gift of four Arabian horses.

cheaper to buy safe passage for merchant ships in the Mediterranean than to make war on elusive and resilient foes. Before Jefferson became president, the United States paid, too. Through the 1790s, the price of flying the American flag in Barbary waters cost about $2 million.

The indignity of it rankled on Jefferson, so when the pasha of Tripoli seized the crew of an American ship and demanded ransom, Jefferson ordered a punitive expedition to, in the words of the Marine Corps hymn, "the shores of Tripoli." Despite four years of intermittent naval bombardment and a daring amphibious attack led by Stephen Decatur, the issue could not be forced. In 1805, Jefferson gave up and paid Tripoli $60,000 in return for the release of captive Americans, a transaction that was not immortalized in song. Barbary Coast piracy and slave trading continued for another decade until Decatur returned to North Africa, the British unleashed the Royal Navy in the Mediterranean, and France began to establish imperial control over North Africa.

Europe at War

Far more serious a foreign threat than the Barbary states was the war between France and England that broke out shortly after the purchase of Louisiana. Jefferson was gladly neutral, of course, and, at first, American shipowners were delighted to reap profits by trading with both sides. Especially lucrative was the reexport business, West Indian products brought to the United States and then shipped to Europe under the neutral American flag. In two years, the reexport business quadrupled in value from $13 million to $60 million.

Then, in 1805, the Anglo-French war took a critical turn. At the Battle of Trafalgar, Lord Horatio Nelson destroyed the French fleet, thus establishing a British supremacy on the high seas that would last for a hundred years. Retaliating on land, Napoleon defeated the armies of Austria, Prussia, and Russia in rapid succession. France was supreme on the continent of Europe.

The bombardment of Tripoli, one of the repeated American attempts during 1801–1805 to subdue the Barbary states.

Caught in the Middle Again

The British and French then settled down into economic warfare, each aiming to ruin the other by crippling its trade. The British issued the Orders in Council, forbidding neutrals to trade in Europe unless their ships first called at a British port to purchase a license. New England merchants, who inclined to be pro-British, could have lived with the orders. However, Napoleon retaliated with the Berlin and Milan decrees of 1806 and 1807, enacting what he called the Continental System: any neutral vessels that observed the Orders in Council would be seized by the French.

American merchants were caught in the middle. Within a year the British seized 1,000 American ships and the French about 500. Even then, the profits that poured in from successful voyages more than compensated for the losses. One Massachusetts senator calculated that if a shipowner sent three vessels out and two were seized—dead losses—the profits from the third left him a richer man than he had been. Statistics bear him out. In 1807, at the height of the commerce raiding, Massachusetts merchants earned $15 million in freight charges alone.

Impressment Again

Perplexing as the crisis was—immensely profitable humiliation—it was complicated by a renewal of the impressment problem of the 1790s. Chronically short of sailors, British naval captains once again began to board American merchantmen and draft crewmen whom, they insisted, were British subjects. There were plenty of such men on American vessels. Conditions under the American flag were much better than on British ships, the pay sometimes three times as much. As many as 10,000 men of British birth may have been working on American ships among a total of 42,000 merchant seamen.

The trouble was, many of them had become American citizens, a transfer of allegiance British captains did not recognize. Yet other men impressed into the Royal Navy were American by birth. About 10,000 bona fide citizens of the United States (by American standards) were forced into the Royal Navy during the Napoleonic wars. Some 4,000 were released as soon as they reached a British port but, at sea, arrogant or merely desperate naval officers were grabbing more.

The impressment crisis came to a head in June 1807, when, within swimming distance of the Virginia shore, HMS *Leopard*, with 50 guns, ordered the lesser American frigate *Chesapeake* to stand by for boarding. The American captain refused and the *Leopard* fired three broadsides, killing several sailors. A British press gang then boarded the crippled *Chesapeake* and removed four men, including two American-born black men who had once served in the Royal Navy.

The patriotic uproar was deafening. The *Chesapeake* was no merchantman taking a chance on a commercial expedition, but a naval vessel in American waters! Jefferson had to act. He chose what he called "peaceable coercion."

The Embargo

Under the Embargo Act of 1807, American ships in port were forbidden to leave. Foreign vessels were sent to sea in ballast (carrying boulders or other worthless bulk in their hulls). All imports and exports were prohibited. The embargo was total economic war, designed to force the British, who also benefited from American trade, to respect American claims.

For Jefferson, who had seen economic boycott bring Parliament around during his revolutionary youth, embargo was a logical course of action. In 1807, the British were at odds not with their own colonies but with a foreign enemy they feared was sworn to destroy their nation. However, a good many Americans suffered from the embargo, too. Staple farmers lost their foreign markets, their livelihood. The ports of New England languished as ships rode at anchor, generating no profit and rotting. The Federalist party, badly maimed in the election of 1804, began to make a comeback behind a new generation of leaders.

By the end of 1808, Congress had had enough. The embargo had actually cost the American economy three times the price of a war. It was repealed and Jefferson signed the bill. He had already decided to retire after two terms and did not bequeath his handpicked successor the burden of his policy.

Little Jemmy Applejohn

The president elected in 1808, James Madison, had been Jefferson's doggedly faithful disciple and friend for 15 years. A profound student of political philosophy, Madison believed in both Jefferson's exaltation of farmers as the country's most valuable citizens and the nationalism that had made him an active proponent of the Constitution.

He was not, however, particularly cut out to be a head of state. Short and slight, he encouraged a

His face was pinched and sour, leading writer Washington Irving to quip that "Little Jemmy" looked like a "withered applejohn," that is, an apple that had been dried. But he had his charms. He won the hand of a vivacious and fashionably buxom widow, Dolley Payne Todd, who added a sparkle to Washington society that was lacking in the presidency of the widower Jefferson.

Non-Intercourse and Macon's Bill No. 2

Madison was particularly ill-suited to handle the international crisis that confounded Jefferson: "too timid" in the words of critic Fisher Ames, "wholly unfit for the Storms of War," according to his supporter, Henry Clay. Madison's first attempt to resolve the conflict over trade, the Non-Intercourse Act, opened trade with all nations except England and France. It provided that the United States would resume trading with whichever of the two belligerents agreed to respect the rights of American shipping. David Erskine, the pro-American British minister to Washington, negotiated a favorable treaty, and Madison renewed trade with Britain. Then, back in London, the British Foreign Office repudiated the agreement. Madison was humiliated.

In May 1810, the Republicans tried a new twist. Under Macon's Bill No. 2, they reopened commerce with both England and France, with the condition that as soon as either agreed to American terms, the United States would cut off trade with the other. In other words, the United States would take its licks at

physical image of weakness by complaining incessantly of aches, pains, and assorted ailments. (His constitution was sound enough: Madison lived on, sniffling, moaning, and groaning until he was 85.)

sea for the present, and then collaborate with the belligerent power that ceased administering them.

So bizarre a policy was asking for trouble from a trickster like Napoleon. With no intention of denying French captains the pleasure of taking American prizes, he revoked the Continental System. Madison, as Macon's Bill No. 2 required him to do, terminated trade with Britain.

Macon's Bill No. 2 actually worked. On June 16, 1812, with Napoleon invading Russia, the British canceled their Orders in Council. But it was too late. The British foreign minister, Robert Viscount Castlereagh, had given no advance hint of his intentions. On June 18, 1812, with the good news of diplomatic victory just catching the winds out of England, Madison bowed to pressure at home and asked the Congress for a declaration of war.

THE WAR OF 1812

On the face of it, the War of 1812, like the attack on Tripoli, was fought to defend the rights of American shipping on the high seas. However, mercantile New England was largely hostile to the war and the Federalist party, representing the commercial capitalist class, was entirely so. The demands for war came from Jefferson Republicans representing agricultural regions, most of them a goodly distance from salt water.

The War Hawks

In New England and New York, antiwar Federalists, some sufficiently angry to threaten secession from the United States, won election to Congress in numbers unprecedented since 1800. The mercantile states of New England, New York, and New Jersey voted 34 to 14 against declaring war. Not a single Federalist congressman voted for war. When the war ground on, antiwar Federalists actually met, in the Hartford Convention, and called for the liquidation of the union.

The backing for "Mr. Madison's War," as New Englanders disdainfully called it, came entirely from the Jefferson Republican party and largely from the South and the West. A noisy, belligerent claque of young congressmen known as "War Hawks," including Henry Clay, Felix Grundy, and John C. Calhoun, gave Madison the votes and encouragement he needed to get his declaration approved. Pennsylva-

nia, the South, and the West voted 65 to 15 in favor of the declaration of war.

In part, the grievances of these agricultural regions were economic: farmers who lived by exporting their crops suffered quite as much from British depredations at sea as merchants did. As a whole, the American merchant class never ceased to make money, even when the British were most active in seizing their ships. However, when a farmer's crop went unsold, it rotted, a total loss.

Perhaps more important, the War Hawks were generally young, with the cocky belligerence of youth, and extremely nationalistic. They were anglophobes, an inheritance of the revolution. Their outrage at the injuries and indignities heaped on their country by arrogant Britain was genuine and profound. Added to wounded pride, the western War Hawks resented Britain's continued aid to the Indians of the Northwest Territory, with whom their constituents were chronically in conflict. They wanted to break the back of Indian military power. The more exuberant of the War Hawks spoke of invading, conquering, and annexing Canada, the Indians' safe sanctuary.

On to Canada!

The War Hawks had reason to believe that Canada was easy pickings. Many Americans had settled in upper Canada, the rich lands north of Lake Ontario. Many Canadians openly preferred the American political system to their colonial status under Great Britain. Militarily, the situation looked to be bright. With the war against Napoleon in Europe nearing its climax, the British had left a mere 2,200 professional soldiers in North America. To defend Canada, they depended on a confederacy of Indian

---

Anchors Aweigh

So oblivious were the War Hawks to the maritime issues for which, ostensibly they wanted war with Britain, that the Congress, which they dominated, actually cut expenditures on the United States Navy. So unready was the navy for a sea war that President Madison briefly but seriously considered contracting the services of the navy of Portugal.

tribes led by a remarkable Shawnee chief, Tecumseh. But, late in 1811, before Mr. Madison's war was declared, Tecumseh's considerable force was shattered by William Henry Harrison, the territorial governor of Indiana. Jefferson thought he foresaw "the final expulsion of England from the American continent."

"Panther Lying in Wait"

Tecumseh (Shawnee for "Panther Lying in Wait") had a reputation as a warrior dating back to the Indians' victories over Josiah Harmer and Arthur St. Clair in the early 1790s. In 1798, he formed a friendship with an Ohio settler, James Galloway, lived with his family, and studied Galloway's library of 300 books. In 1808, Tecumseh proposed to Galloway's daughter, Rebecca, and she agreed to marriage, but only on condition that Tecumseh abandon Indian ways and live like an American settler.

Tecumseh was not hostile to the civilization of the whites; far from it. Few white settlers in Indiana

could have claimed an education better than his. But a revival of Indian culture was sweeping through the tribes of the Great Lakes basin when Rebecca Galloway set her terms. The movement, partly religious, partly political, was inspired by Tecumseh's brother, a one-eyed reformed drunkard, Tenskwatawa or "The Prophet." Tenskwatawa preached that Indians must reject white ways, particularly alcohol, and return to their ancestral traditions. Firearms and Christianity were the only elements of white culture that Tenskwatawa found appealing.

The Prophet also called for an end to tribal hostilities and urged all the native peoples to join him at Tippecanoe, a town built where a creek of that name flowed into the Wabash River. There, Tecumseh soon rose to be the confederacy's military leader. Governor Harrison respected and feared Tecumseh. He called the chief "one of those uncommon geniuses who spring up occasionally to produce revolutions and overturn the established order of things." In November 1811, when Tecumseh was absent, he swooped down on Tippecanoe and destroyed it. In August 1812, when a three-pronged attack on Canada began, the Indians were reeling.

A Battle of Bunglers

For all their advantages, the American campaign was a fiasco on almost every front. On the Niagara River, New York militia refused to advance and delayed their return home only long enough to watch a quarrel between two American commanders escalate into a duel (which the Canadians from across the river also enjoyed). Surprised at American ineffectiveness, the Canadians counterattacked and captured Detroit, while their Indian allies destroyed the stockade at Chicago, then called Fort Dearborn.

The Northwest would have been laid wide open to further Canadian and Indian advance had it not been for the seamanship of Captain Oliver Hazard Perry. On September 10, 1813, although outgunned by the Canadian–British flotilla, he secured control of Lake Erie for the Americans. Receiving his famous message, "We have met the enemy and they are ours," William Henry Harrison then led 4,500 men toward York (Toronto), the capital of upper Canada.

The British proved as inept as the Americans and, according to Tecumseh, cowards. He told the commanding British general, "We must compare our father's conduct to a fat dog that carries its tail upon its

back, but when afrightened drops it between its legs and runs off." Harrison defeated the British–Indian force at the Battle of the Thames (Tecumseh was killed), and burned the public buildings in the city.

In the meantime, the British invaded New York via the route John Burgoyne followed during the War for Independence. They were stopped by Captain Thomas Macdonough, only 30 years of age, at the Battle of Lake Champlain. While Americans won few victories on land, and those largely symbolic, American naval forces on both the lakes and the ocean won most of their encounters.

Nevertheless, the British revenged the burning of York when, in August 1814, they launched a daring amphibious raid on Washington, D.C. The troops burned the Capitol and the White House and British officers claimed that they ate a dinner, still warm, that had been set for James and Dolley Madi-

The death of the great Tecumseh at the Battle of the Thames.

son. In fact, the president escaped capture narrowly when, at a battle he drove out to view, the American army fled without fighting. To Dolley, however, goes the credit of bundling up and saving many of the nation's charter documents, including the earliest copies of the Declaration of Independence and the Constitution.

New Orleans

The British did not want the American war. But when Napoleon abdicated in the spring of 1814, freeing a large army for American service, they combined the beginning of peace talks at Ghent in Belgium with a plan to seize lower Louisiana from the United States. An army of about 8,000 excellent troops was dispatched under General Sir Edward Pakenham to attack New Orleans. What augured to be a disaster for the Americans turned out to be a most amazing vic-

tory, the salvaging of the War Hawks' battered morale, and the making of a most remarkable national hero, Andrew Jackson of Tennessee.

A self-taught lawyer, slave-owning planter, land-speculator, Indian-fighter, and duelist, Andrew Jackson assembled a force of 2,000 Kentucky and Tennessee volunteers, New Orleans businessmen, two battalions of free blacks, some Choctaw Indians, and artillerymen in the employ of the pirate-businessman Jean Lafitte. Jackson threw up earthworks five miles south of Louisiana's great port, the Mississippi River on his right, an impenetrable mangrove swamp on his left. In front of the gimcrack defenses was an open field.

Too confident, Pakenham sent his men through the morning fog on a frontal assault. Lafitte's cannoneers raked them with grapeshot and, when the redcoats were 200 yards from the earthworks, riflemen opened up with "a leaden torrent no man on

During the War of 1812, the British captured and burned Washington, D.C.

earth could face." More than 2,000 redcoats fell dead. Troops that had helped topple Napoleon broke and ran. Miraculously, only seven Americans were killed, four of them when they ran after the retreating British. (After the battle, Jackson hanged as many American soldiers for desertion as were killed during it.)

The Treaty of Ghent, which restored British-American relations to what they had been before the war, was actually signed before the Battle of New Orleans was fought. Nevertheless, the news of the astonishing victory had an electrifying effect. Such a glorious end to an ill-advised, unnecessary, and calamitous war seemed a reaffirmation of the nation's splendid destiny. When, within three years, Jackson crushed the powerful Creek tribe in the Southeast and Stephen Decatur returned to the Barbary Coast to sting the Algerians, Americans could feel that they had taken a prominent place in a world where armed might was one of the measures of greatness.

According to another of those measures, a nation's sway over vast territory, the United States was already capturing the attention of Europe. Unlike the nations of Europe, however, which expanded piecemeal at the expense of neighbors by annexing new provinces after victorious wars, the American people simply moved west into land they regarded as empty, theirs by the grace of God bestowed upon a people he had chosen for his own.

CHRONOLOGY

1801	Thomas Jefferson becomes president
1803	In *Marbury* v. *Madison*, Supreme Court establishes principle of judicial review
1804–1806	Lewis and Clark Expedition Britain and France wage economic war

1807	Embargo James Madison becomes president Non-Intercourse Act	1813	Tecumseh killed at Battle of Thames
1810	Macon's Bill No. 2	1814	British burn Washington
1812	U.S. Declares war on Great Britain	1815	Battle of New Orleans Treaty of Ghent

FOR FURTHER READING

A classic that exemplifies the best of history writing in the nineteenth century and provides an excellent overview of the Jefferson–Madison years is Henry Adams, *History of the United States during the Administration of Thomas Jefferson and James Madison* (1889–1891). For twentieth-century scholarship, see Marshall Smelser, *The Democratic Republic, 1801–1815*, 1968. On Jefferson, see Daniel Boorstin, *The Lost World of Thomas Jefferson*, 1948; Noble Cunningham, *The Jeffersonian Republicans*, 1957, and *The Jeffersonian Republicans in Power*, 1973; and Dumas Malone, *Jefferson the President: First Term, 1801–1809*, 1970, and *Jefferson the President: Second Term*, 1809–1813, 1974. Controversial but superb reading are Fawn Brodie, *Thomas Jefferson: An Intimate Biography*, 1974; and Joseph Ellis, *American Sphinx*, 1997. Also see Richard E. Ellis, *The Jeffersonian Crisis: Courts and Politics in the Young Republic*, 1971; and Lance Banning, *The Jeffersonian Persuasion: Evolution of a Party Ideology*, 1978.

Alexander Deconde, *The Affairs of Louisiana*, 1976, treats the great purchase in detail. The standard work on the Lewis and Clark expedition is now Stephen Ambrose, *Undaunted Courage: Meriwether Lewis, Thomas Jefferson, and the Opening of the American West*, 1996. But students also should go to the horse's mouth, Bernard DeVoto, ed., *The Journals of Lewis and Clark*, 1953. Jefferson's problems with John Marshall are treated in Richard Ellis, *The Jeffersonians and the Judiciary*, 1971. For Marshall himself, see R. K. Faulkner, *The Jurisprudence of John Marshall*, 1968, and Leonard Baker, *John Marshall: A Life in Law*, 1974. For that other great nemesis of "Mad Tom," see Nathan Schachner, *Aaron Burr*, 1984. On the milieu in which these characters moved, see James S. Young, *The Washington Community, 1801–1828*, 1966. For a significant urban constituency, see Howard B. Rock, *Artisans of the New Republic: The Tradesmen of New York City in the Age of Jefferson*, 1979.

James Madison is the subject of a number of studies, including Irving Brant, *The Fourth President: A Life of James Madison*, 1970, and Ralph Ketcham, *James Madison*, 1971. On problems of "Jemmy Applejohn's" administration, see James M. Banner, *To the Hartford Convention*, 1970; Linda K. Kerber, *Federalists in Dissent*, 1970; and Bradford Perkins, *Prologue to War: England and the United States, 1805–1812*, 1961. Reginald Horsman remains our chief resource on the War of 1812 in his *Causes of the War of 1812*, 1962, and *The War of 1812*, 1969, but also essential is Donald P. Hickey, *The War of 1812: A Forgotten Conflict*, 1989.

SOUTH WATER STREET.

CHICAGO. 1834.

Chicago in 1834, scarcely more than a village.

13
CHAPTER

BEYOND THE APPALACHIAN RIDGE

The West in the Early Nineteenth Century

When I reflect that all this grand portion of our Union, instead of being in a state of nature, is now more or less covered with villages, farms and towns, . . . that hundreds of steamboats are gliding to and fro over the whole length of the majestic river, . . . When I remember that these extraordinary changes have all taken place in the short period of twenty years, I pause, wonder, and although I know it all to be fact, can scarcely believe its reality.

— *John J. Audubon*

From the moment a European settlement is formed in the neighborhood of the territory occupied by Indians, the beasts of the chase take the alarm. Thousands of savages, wandering in the forests, . . . did not disturb them; but as soon as the continuous sounds of European labor are heard in their neighborhood, they begin to flee away, and retire to the West. . . . I have been assured that the effect of the approach of the Whites is often felt at two hundred leagues' distance from their frontier. Their influence is thus exerted over tribes whose name is unknown to them; and who suffer the evils of usurpation long before they are acquainted with the authors of their distress.

— *Alexis de Tocqueville*

The Appalachian Mountains, a series of parallel ridges, rise in Maine and angle southwesterly into Georgia and Alabama. Known as the Catskills, the Poconos, the Alleghenies, and the Blue Ridge at various points, they divide the springs that rise into creeks and rivers that flow into the Atlantic from those that feed the great Mississippi River system.

The Appalachians are not high as mountains go, but they were a formidable obstacle in the eighteenth century. Few natural passes traverse them, and most of those are but narrow gaps. In 1763, the British chose the Appalachian divide as a reasonable boundary between land which colonials might develop and land reserved for the Indian nations.

Independence erased the line of 1763 from the map, but not the wrinkles from the earth. In 1790, the first federal census takers counted only a few thousand intrepid pioneers living west of the mountains. The white and black population of the United States remained concentrated in the 13 original states, looking to the Atlantic Ocean as their portal to the world.

THE FIRST AMERICAN WEST

The Battle of Fallen Timbers, Pinckney's Treaty, and Jefferson's obsession with the mouth of the Mississippi signaled a shift in orientation. By 1830, fully a quarter of the American population dwelled west of the Appalachians. Only a minority of these westerners were born in the Mississippi Valley. Their values were shaped by the experience of cutting ties back east, packing up possessions, and striking off to where land was cheap and therefore, as Americans saw it, the future lay. Opportunity was synonymous with land in the minds of most Americans and, therefore, with "the West."

"The West" would continue to loom large over the American economy and society for the rest of the nineteenth century, and it grips the American imagination to this day. Indeed, in a sense, the American West became as much an idea as a physical place. "The West is but another name for The Wild," wrote Henry David Thoreau. In the United States, the word frontier took on a meaning scarcely known

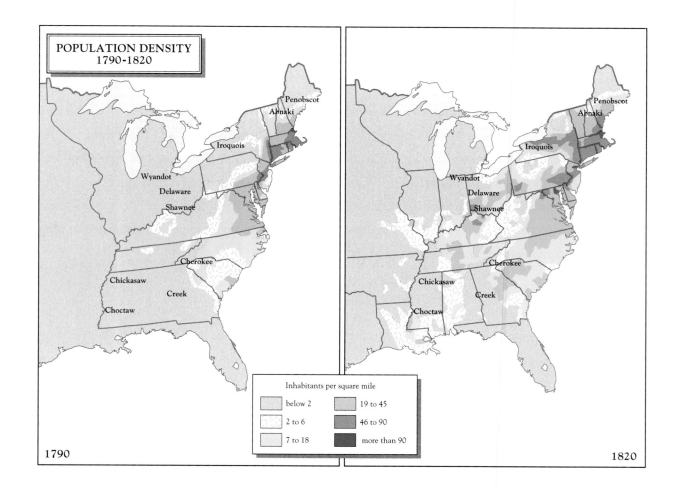

POPULATION DENSITY 1790-1820

Inhabitants per square mile

below 2	19 to 45
2 to 6	46 to 90
7 to 18	more than 90

1790

1820

Abraham Lincoln and Jefferson Davis

Both Abraham Lincoln and Jefferson Davis—opposing presidents during the Civil War—were born in log cabins on the Kentucky frontier. Lincoln's parents migrated there from Virginia in 1782, Davis's from Virginia in 1793. The two men were born within a year of each other—Davis in 1808, Lincoln in 1809.

In 1810, like many restless Kentuckians, the Davis family moved southwest to the rich cotton lands of Mississippi, where they became one of the richest slave-owning families in the state. Other Kentuckians went northwest, and Lincoln's father, a ne'er-do-well named Tom Lincoln, was among them. When Abraham was seven, his family moved to Indiana and, when he was eleven, to Illinois. There, in Salem and Springfield, he became a successful attorney.

Perhaps because Lincoln realized that it was only a quirk of fate—the direction that their families had chosen when, with so many Americans, they "moved on"—that had made Davis the slave owner and himself the antislavery politician, he refused to take a self-righteous attitude toward southern slave owners. "They are just what we would be in their situation," he said.

in European usage. To Europeans, the frontier was a boundary between nations. To Americans, the word came to mean the broader zone where settlement and civilized institutions petered out, and wilderness and savagery began their sway. In Europe, frontiers moved in fits when victorious nations annexed the land of others. In North America, the frontier was in constant motion, ceaselessly shifting as restless men and women pushed towards the setting sun.

Prodigious Growth

During the first decades of the nineteenth century, the American frontier moved bullishly beyond the Appalachian ridge. Between 1800 and 1820, the population of present-day Mississippi grew from 8,000 to 75,000. Alabama, with about 1,000 whites and blacks in 1800, was home to 128,000 in 1820, not counting large Indian nations.

The states north of the Ohio River were populated even more rapidly. In 1800, there were 45,000 white people in Ohio. Ten years later, the population was 230,000. By 1820, trans-Appalachian Ohio was the fifth largest state in the Union. By 1840, there were 1.5 million Ohioans. Only New York, Pennsylvania, and Virginia had larger populations. Ohio was home to more people than Finland, Norway, or Denmark.

Between 1800 and 1840, the population of Indiana grew from almost nil to 685,856; Illinois, from a few hundred whites to 476,183. In 1800, Michigan consisted of one wretched lakefront fort inherited from the French and British. In the 1830s, New Englanders flocked as thickly as passenger pigeons to Michigan's "oak openings," small fertile prairies amidst hardwood forests. By that time, the Mississippi River itself had ceased to lie beyond the frontier. Missouri, on the west bank, was a ten-year-old state, and home to an economy gearing up to support emigration farther west.

People on the Move

The existence of land for the taking is not enough to explain this extraordinary, incessant movement of people. Russia was blessed with even more land than the United States, and a larger, far poorer population; but its "East"—Siberia—attracted few Russians until the government virtually dragooned people into going. As a people, Americans seemed inherently restless, as agitated as the "painters" (panthers) that they chased deeper into the woods and swamps. To Europeans, and sometimes to themselves, Americans seemed incapable of putting down roots.

Ohio, the Forty-Eighth State

Government was so informal during the age of Jefferson that Congress admitted members from Ohio without officially admitting the state to the Union. The boundaries of what was thought to be the seventeenth state were approved and Ohio's congressmen took their seats on March 1, 1803. However, the vote to admit Ohio had not been taken. The oversight was rectified only 150 years later when Congress voted to admit the forty-eighth state on August 7, 1953. No one proposed the cancellation of all legislation in which Ohio's representative comprised the winning margin, or the nullification of all laws signed by Ohio's five presidents.

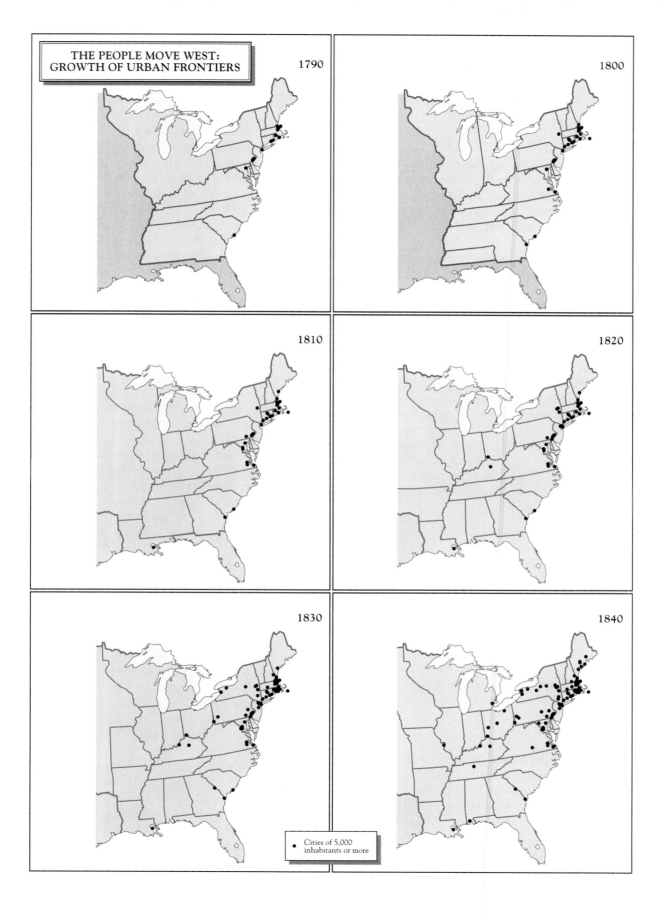

THE PEOPLE MOVE WEST:
GROWTH OF URBAN FRONTIERS

1790

1800

1810

1820

1830

1840

• Cities of 5,000
  inhabitants or more

The young couple saying their marriage vows and promptly clambering aboard a wagon to head west was as familiar a scene in New England as stone fences meandering between cornfields. During the first decades of the century, Virginians headed across the mountains as rapidly as a high birthrate could replace them. In central and western Pennsylvania, site of a major wagon road west, the economy was closely tied to emigration. Inns and the stables of horse traders dotted the highway. A small Pennsylvania valley gave its name to the Conestoga wagon its people manufactured, a high-slung, heavy-wheeled vehicle designed for travel where there were no roads.

"In the United States," marveled Alexis de Tocqueville, the most singular of tourists, "a man builds a house in which to spend his old age, and he sells it before the roof is on." An Englishman looking over lands in the Ohio Valley reported that if he admired the improvements a recent settler had made on his property, the man was likely to propose selling everything on the spot so that he could begin again farther west. Americans joked that in the spring, the chickens crossed their legs so that they could be tied up for the next push west.

PATTERNS OF SETTLEMENT

Some of these pilgrims were simply antisocial, the "eye-gougers" and "frontier scum" of legend and reality. Others were as respectable as the King James Bible and wanted as much company as they could persuade to follow them. Some meant to create the same way of life they knew back east, only better, with more land between their home and that of their neighbor.

Yet others were developers—a profession still with us and sometimes still honored—dreamers, schemers, and promoters of new Edens, Romes, Manchesters, and Lexingtons. Indeed, the men who, like Abraham Lincoln's father, Tom, made a business of clearing a few acres and building a cabin to sell to a newcomer, were developers of a sort. Rather more important were those who bought large tracts of land, trumpeted its glories, and sold subdivisions at a profit.

Town boosters named streets before a tree was felled in imagined intersections. Some of them were merchants or even manufacturers who planned to stay and prosper as the country grew. Others were professional boomers who made their bundle and

Michigan Bound

As they sang of military victories and political candidates, Americans also sang of the experience of going west. There were dozens of songs about every destination that promised a better life. This one celebrated Michigan:

Come all ye Yankee farmers who wish to change your lot,
Who've spunk enough to travel beyond your native spot,
And leave behind the village where Pa and Ma do stay,
Come follow me and settle in Mich-i-gan-i-ay.

moved on, as rootless as hunters and trappers, never investing another thought in their creation and momentary domicile.

Squatters and Soldiers

The pioneer easiest to remember is the snaggle-toothed frontiersman in a ragged buckskin shirt and coontail cap, wresting the forest from the Indians and fields from the forest, and grunting to his wan, washed-out wife in filthy bonnet and smock, corncob pipe clenched in her teeth. An appalling sight, no doubt, many were, but James Madison was unfair to lump such people together as "evil-disposed persons." Most were just dirt poor. They tamed many an acre so that handsomer descendants could deny they ever existed. And, depending on hunting for a good deal of the sustenance, just like the Indians they hated, they had to move on, just like the Indians, when development destroyed game.

The military was the cutting edge on some frontiers. Soldiers posted in the West to keep an eye on Indians had to be fed, clothed, and entertained. Shopkeepers, saloon keepers, and log cabin prostitutes clustered around such lonely military installations. The security the fort provided encouraged trappers, hunters, and others who tramped the woods to congregate there in winter and during times of Indian trouble. Their needs stimulated the growth of a mercantile economy before there was much tillage in the neighborhood. Detroit and other towns gathered about old French and English outposts developed in such a way.

Settlers from Connecticut enter their state's "Western Reserve" in what is now Ohio.

The Urban Frontier

In other parts of the West, cities actually came first. Only after a fairly advanced, if not necessarily refined, urban life had evolved did the hinterland fill in with farmers to provision the town. In such places, there never was a subsistence agriculture. The first farmers in such regions found a market ready-made and a broad range of suppliers and services welcoming them to town. They skipped the "three sisters" agriculture of the Indians and buckskin pioneers, and started out as growers of wheat.

Places like Cincinnati, Louisville, Lexington, and Nashville were true, if small, cities before agriculture was well developed in the surrounding country. Occupying good locations at which river-farers could tie up their keelboats and rafts, these cities served as jumping-off points for emigrants. When the cotton lands of the lower Mississippi Valley began to boom, sending out calls for provisions for their slaves, the citizens of such river ports responded with shipments of grain and livestock. Cincinnati, "the Queen City of the West," became famous for its slaughterhouses and packing plants when, not many miles away, the great hardwood forests blocked the sun from the earth and lonely men and women battled malnutrition and malaria.

In 1815, when there were no more than fifteen steam engines in the whole of France, a nation of 20 million people, half-tamed Kentucky boasted six steam mills that turned out cloth and even paper. Before the War of 1812, St. Louis had a steam mill that was six stories high. Like medieval burghers determined to outdo the cathedral of the next nearest city, Cincinnati built a mill that was nine stories high. Pittsburgh and Lexington, towns of 5,000 and 8,000 respectively, actually manufactured steam engines. Such places were no mere clearings in the wilderness where men bit off one another's ears.

Speculation as a Way of Life

Rapid development encouraged heated financial speculation. Many people went to Ohio or Michigan or Alabama neither to farm, run a shop, pack pork, nor invest in factories. They were speculators, men

Frontier Violence

The Mississippi and Ohio Valley frontier's reputation for violence may be overstated. Few people knew the country better than the great naturalist, John J. Audubon, who wandered the West collecting specimens of birds and animals and painting and describing them. In 1812, Audubon was saved from frontier murderers when an Indian warned him of the plans to rob and kill him and, fortuitously, two other travelers stumbled into the cabin where he was spending an uneasy night.

However, Audubon wrote, "During upwards of twenty-five years, when my wanderings extended to all parts of our country, this was the only time at which my life was in danger from my fellow-creatures. Indeed, so little risk do travelers run in the United States that no one born there dreams of any [violence] to be encountered on the road." Audubon noted that the plotters who thought to kill him were not Americans.

with some capital and plenty of plans to grow rich by the timeless, if risky, game of buying land cheap and selling it dear. Some were sharpers by anyone's definition, interested in little but lining their pockets. Others supervised orderly development which was far preferable to the semi-savage disorder of the squatter. Moreover, in a country where growth was the essence of life, almost everyone with a few dollars to spare, or able to borrow them, was attracted to the inevitability of rising values.

The speculative mentality made the price at which the government disposed of its land (all western land, except for a few old French grants, was government land) a matter of considerable political interest. Under an ordinance of 1785, the federal government offered tracts of 640 acres at a minimum price of $1 an acre—cash.

Farmers protested that 640 acres were more than a family could work, and $640 far more than ordinary folk could raise. From the old Federalist point of view, the complaint was irrelevant. The land would be developed by the inevitable demand for it by a growing population. Administrative efficiency and the Federalist inclination to favor men of capital dictated that the government be a wholesaler, disposing of the land in large chunks and leaving the retailing of small farms to the private sector.

Jeffersonian Land Policy

By way of contrast, Jefferson's Republicans believed in disposing of land in such a way as to favor the people who actually settled on it with plow and mule. The Jeffersonian idealization of the independent, small family farmer mandated a liberal land policy: "the price of land is the thermometer of liberty—men are freest where lands are cheapest." In 1804, a Jeffersonian Congress authorized the sale of tracts as small as 160 acres. The minimum price was $2 an acre but a buyer needed a down payment of only $80, and could pay the balance of $240 over four years.

The Land Act of 1804 made the government a retailer and a very obliging one. However, it neither shut out sharpers nor satisfied poor farmers. Introducing credit purchase actually benefited speculators because, unlike conservative emigrants wary of debt, speculators had no compunctions about borrowing heavily and making down payments on as much land as possible. The idea was to sell to later comers before the second installment came due.

Feeding such speculation, often irresponsible "wildcat banks" sprang up all over the West. On printing presses carted over the mountains, they churned out paper money with which speculators paid the government land office and counted on a rise in values to make good their notes. For a while after the War of 1812, the wildcat banks did quite well.

The Long Rifle

The gun that won the trans-Appalachian West was the Kentucky long rifle. It had a 44-inch barrel and enough maple or walnut stock to make it the height of an average man. It weighed, on average, only about eight pounds, however, and was a muzzle loader. To load it, the butt was placed on the ground, a charge of coarse black powder was poured down the muzzle into the breech, and a ball wrapped in greased linen or a leather patch was rammed home. (The patch was to seal the compression of the explosion and to ensure that the bullet "took" the rifling, the spiraling grooves that gave it spin and therefore accuracy.) Even in the most practiced hands, the long rifle sometimes misfired. Our phrase "flash in the pan" came from the all-too-common phenomenon of a charge that flashed without hurtling the ball on its way.

Land sales soared. In 1815, the government sold about 1 million acres; in 1819, more than 5 million.

Much of it went for more than the government minimum price; before land was let go at $2 an acre, it was offered at auction. This practice also favored speculators. Settlers with small purses found themselves priced out of the market by those who did not care how much borrowed money they handed across the counter at the Land Office. Someone, surely, perhaps another sanguine speculator, would soon be willing to go a higher price. Some government lands in the cotton belt sold for more than $100 an acre—on paper.

Of Booms and Busts

The speculative boom in western lands depended, as do all speculations, on greed and the human species' marvelous capacity for self-delusion. Speculations are built on the principle of the "greater fool": one person pays an irrationally high price for a commodity—land or stocks or gold or, in seventeenth-century Holland, tulip bulbs—on the assumption that there is a "greater fool" coming around the corner willing to pay even more. A great deal of money has been made in speculations.

A great deal of money has been lost in speculations, too. For when the supply of potential buyers runs dry, and some speculators conclude that prices have peaked and can only decline, the result is often a crash. It takes but a few big plungers selling to get out of the market for prices to plummet. Because speculators deal in borrowed money, any significant drop in values causes a panic to sell so that, at least, some loans may be repaid. Indeed, if the lenders—the bankers—are the first to decide that values are going down, they can start the panic by calling in their loans, thus forcing speculators to sell at whatever prices they can get.

The Panic of 1819

This is what happened in 1819. The directors of the Bank of the United States, a cautious and conservative group of gentlemen, began to worry about the freewheeling practices of the western banks and called in the money those banks owed to the Bank of the United States. Having lent out their resources to speculators, the wildcat banks called in their loans to avoid bankruptcy. When the speculators—no greater fools being on the horizon—were unable to sell land and pay their debts, the whole paper structure came tumbling down. Speculators, as rich in

---

Western Rhetoric

The following introduction was made to a small group of land speculators just before an auction for the sale of public lands:

My name, sir, is Simeon Cragin. I own fourteen claims, and if any man jump one of them, I will shoot him down at once, sir. I am a gentleman, sir, and a scholar. I was educated at Bangor, have been in the United States Army, and served my country faithfully. I am the discoverer of the Wopsey, can ride a grizzly bear, or whip any human that ever crossed the Mississippi, and if you dare to jump one of my claims, die you must.

---

acres as Charlemagne, could not meet their installment payments. The wildcat banks folded by the dozens, leaving those thrifty souls who had deposited money in them broke. The B.U.S. lost money, worthless bank notes went to the outhouse, and the land reverted to government ownership.

In 1820, chastised by the panic, Congress abolished credit purchases and tried to dispose of the lands that reverted to the government by reducing the minimum tract for sale to 80 acres, and the minimum price per acre to $1.25. With financial recovery, the speculators were back. In the meantime, westerners on the bottom had devised various ways of dealing with them and other problems of living beyond the mountains.

PROBLEMS AND PROGRAMS

Squatters were emigrants to the West who began to develop farms on the public domain before they bought the land on which they stood. Such improved property was particularly attractive to speculators, since a cabin and a cleared field substantially increased the land's value. When the government surveyors and land office arrived, many squatters saw their claims "jumped." The home they had built on government land was purchased at auction by a newly arrived slicker with a wad of borrowed bank notes in his purse.

In some areas, like Old World artisans threatened by machines, the squatters combated these speculators by vigilante action. They banded together into land clubs and promised physical reprisals against anyone bidding on a member's land. Not infrequently, they made good on their threats, and such ructions have made for many a thrilling book and film. But speculators could hire strong-armed help more than a match for farmers, and the law was, after all, on their side. In the end, squatters turned to the lawmakers to fight their battles.

"Old Bullion" Benton

One spokesman for western settlers was Thomas Hart Benton, known as "Old Bullion" because he distrusted paper money issued by banks. Gold bullion was the only money for him. Born in North Carolina, Benton first entered politics in Tennessee, and was among the earliest American settlers in Missouri. Although well-read in the classics and supremely eloquent, Benton knew how to turn on the boisterous bluff that appealed to rough-hewn westerners. "I never quarrel, sir," he told an opponent in a debate. "But sometimes I fight, sir; and when I fight, sir, a funeral follows, sir."

Elected senator from Missouri shortly after the Panic of 1819, Benton inveighed at every turn against bankers, paper money, and land speculators. He fought consistently throughout his long career for a land policy that would shut all three out of the West.

Benton's pet project was preemption, or, as it was popularly called, squatter's rights. Preemption provided that the man who actually settled on and improved land before the government officially offered it for sale would be permitted to purchase it at the minimum price. He would not be required to bid at an auction against speculators.

Another Benton program was graduation: land that remained unsold after auction would be offered at one-half the government minimum, and after a passage of time, at one-quarter. In a word, the price of the land was graduated downward in order to increase the number of people able to afford it. Eventually, Benton hoped, land that went unsold would be given away to people willing to settle it.

Benton's sentiments were soundly Jeffersonian. He favored those who tilled the soil, "the bone and sinew of the republic" in Jefferson's words, over financial interests associated with Alexander Hamilton and, in Benton's era, the Whig party.

Sectional Tensions

Opposition to liberal land policy was particularly strong east of the Appalachian ridge. The means by which public land was disposed of in Illinois or Missouri was of keen interest to people who lived on the oldest streets of Plymouth and on the James River neck of Virginia. To them, the western lands were a national resource—their wealth as well as that of westerners—a fount from which the government's expenses were to be paid. They feared that if the national domain was sold off as quickly and as cheaply as Benton and others wished, the old states would lose population and their property taxes would increase to make good the loss.

Northern factory owners feared that if emigrating to the West was too easy and cheap, their supply of laborers would shrink. The workers that remained, being in short supply, would demand higher wages.

Well-to-do southern planters, increasingly dependent on slave labor, feared that disposing of western lands too cheaply would force the federal government to depend more heavily upon the tariff—import duties—to finance its operations. As consumers of the cheap British cloth, shoes, and other products that would be larded with new duties, they preferred to finance the government through land sales. Land policy, whether it was to be closely monitored or liberal, was an issue that, in the early nineteenth century, threatened to set section against section.

"Handsome Harry" Clay

The man who stepped forward with a plan to avert such a division was himself a westerner, Henry Clay. Perhaps because he made his home in Kentucky, a state a generation older than Benton's Missouri, Henry Clay was concerned with welding the West to the old states, as well as with populating it. He wanted to see land in the hands of actual settlers. But he also wanted to see it used in an orderly fashion to integrate the economies of North, South, and West. He was a nationalist, common enough a type in American history. He was also a politician with a vision of the future beyond the next election day.

Born in Virginia in 1777, Henry Clay trained as a lawyer and settled in Lexington at 21 years of age. He prospered as a planter, a land speculator, and especially as a politician. Elected to the House of Representatives in 1810, Clay won notoriety as one of the most bellicose of the War Hawks who helped push President Madison into war in 1812. When the fighting bogged down in stalemate, Madison named Clay to represent the War Hawk element at the peace talks in Ghent in what is now Belgium.

Four engravings from O. Turner's History of the Holland Purchase *show how a New York farm was developed from wilderness over a 40-year period. The pattern held throughout the trans-Appalachian frontier as well.*

HOW THEY LIVED

How They Socialized

When Europeans traveled through newly opened parts of the United States, like much of Ohio during the 1810s and 1820s, they were impressed by the feats of labor necessary to make a home in raw wilderness. They invariably complained about the food of the frontier—greasy fried pork and cornmeal mush or fire-roasted cornbread. And they were shocked by the heavy drinking in which everyone seemed to indulge.

But most of all they shuddered at the isolation of those who were building a life in a new country. The Europeans who wrote books about their American experiences were sophisticated and literate; they were accustomed to a full and stimulating social life. So they were disturbed by the loneliness endured by American westerners, particularly the women whose daily chores centered around solitary cabins in the woods.

Mrs. Frances Trollope, an English woman who wrote a celebrated book, *The Domestic Manners of the Americans*, blamed the emotional excesses of western revivalist religion on the absence of any form of recreation, of release from daily toil and tedium, even in the comparatively large river port of Cincinnati. "It is thus," she wrote, in the shrieking, howling, and rolling about the floor she witnessed at churches, "that the ladies of Cincinnati amuse themselves; to attend the theatre is forbidden; to play cards is unlawful; but they work hard in their families and must have some relaxation."

Just a few miles outside of Cincinnati, Mrs. Trollope met a hard-bitten frontier woman who showed off her farm and boasted that it produced almost everything the household needed. Economically, the family was self-sufficient but for tea, sugar, and whiskey. Socially, the situation was somewhat different. When Mrs. Trollope prepared to leave, her hostess sighed and said, "'Tis strange for us to see company; I expect the sun may rise and set a hundred times before I shall see another *human* that does not belong to the family."

There is no distortion in this picture. Frontier life was extremely lonely for a great many pioneers. But not for all. During the 1820s, people in northern Ohio, an even newer region than the neighborhood of Cincinnati, managed to have a rich social life. William Cooper Howells, a printer who saw Ohio develop from wild forest into a populous industrial state, looked back on the parties of his youth with fond nostalgia. The point Howells made in his memoirs, *Recollections of Life in Ohio from 1813 to 1840*, was that Ohio pioneers combined amusement and diversion with work.

The raising of a family's log cabin or barn was done collectively by the people who lived within a

In Kentucky, in Europe, and in Washington, Clay had a taste for the good life. Keenly intelligent, famously handsome, graciously mannered, witty, ever-sociable, he charmed women and won the friendship and loyalty of men. He was equally at home sipping claret from crystal and sitting down to a game of faro that ended only when the whiskey was gone. Although he was a poor shot and killed no one,

Clay fought several duels, almost a prerequisite of success in western politics at the time.

But Clay's prominence—he hovered near the center of power in the United States for four decades—owed itself only incidentally to his style. Like Benton, he worked to build up the West. Transcending Benton and other westerners, Clay had a vision of a great and united nation that owed much to radius of a few miles. The host had cut all the logs in advance and brought them to the site; sometimes, though, this job too was done by means of a community "log-roll." The men who best handled an axe took charge of notching the logs at each end and raising them into position by hand. With a team for each of the four walls, the job went quickly. When the walls rose too high to reach from the ground, the logs were lifted by means of young, forked trees to men straddling the tops of the walls. "The men understood handling timber," Howells wrote, "and accidents seldom happened, unless the logs were icy or wet or the whisky had gone around too often." Howells himself, still quite a young man in Ohio's early years, took pride in taking on the job of "corner-man." While others built the walls, he "dressed up" the corners with an axe and guided the final logs into place. "It was a post of honor." The job was less laborious than that of raising the walls, but it took a head that "was steady when high up from the ground."

> When a gathering of men for such a purpose took place there was commonly some sort of mutual job laid out for women, such as quilting, sewing, or spinning up a lot of thread for some poor neighbor. This would bring together a mixed party, and it was usually arranged that after supper there should be a dance or at least plays which would occupy a good part of the night and wind up with the young fellows seeing the girls home in the short hours or, if they went home early, sitting with them by the fire in that kind of interesting chat known as sparking.

In addition to log-rolling and barn- and cabin-raisings, "grubbing out underbrush" and the tedious task of

processing flax (for linen and oil) were often done in conjunction with a community party. Other tasks—splitting logs into rails for fences, for example—were spiced up by holding a competition. Abraham Lincoln first ran for political office on his reputation as a virtuoso rail-splitter. But by far the most enjoyable kind of work party, remembered wistfully in practically every reminiscence of the frontier, was the husking bee. Not only was the job less laborious than the others and the occasion of a contest and a party, but husking bees took place in the autumn, when the harvest was done and the weather cool. It was the season when good food was most abundant and spirits were highest.

The ears of corn to be husked were divided into two piles. Two captains chose up sides, alternately selecting their teams from among the young men and boys and sometimes also from among the women and girls. Then the two parties fell to husking, all standing with the heap in front of them, and throwing the husked corn to a clear space over the heap, and the husks (for animal fodder) behind them. From the time they begin till the corn was all husked at one end, there would be steady work, each man husking all the corn he could, never stopping except to take a pull at the stone jug of inspiration that passed occasionally along the line.

When one team had finished husking, they let out a great shout (which was the signal to lay a community dinner on the table), briefly exchanged taunts for the excuses of the losers, and then finished the husking along with them. Another "rule of the game" that increased interest was the provision that a boy who husked a red ear could claim a kiss from one of the girls at the party. But Howells concluded: "I never knew it necessary to produce a red ear to secure a kiss when there was a disposition to give or take one."

Alexander Hamilton, while lacking Hamilton's undisguised contempt for ordinary folk.

The Open Road

Clay's special cause as a young politician was internal improvements, particularly the building of better roads to tie the far-flung sections of the United

States together—the costs of construction to be underwritten by the federal government. This was decidedly a western cause. Although the roads and highways of the eastern seaboard were wretched by the standards of western Europe, more than a century of population and development had resulted in a network of sorts. Beginning about 1790, the states and counties of the Northeast had graded and

Henry "Handsome Harry" Clay (1777–1852) in his thirties.

Federal Finance

Few entrepreneurs were willing to invest in even the cheapest road in the sparsely populated West. So-called roads there were usually nothing more than old Indian trails, footpaths widened to accommodate a wagon but, even then, often blocked by stumps. They guided the way to neighbors, church, or river town well enough, but they could not accommodate commerce.

Nor could the young western states afford to do much about the problem. They were caught in the vicious circle of needing good roads in order to attract population and move their products out, while lacking the population and, therefore, the tax base necessary to finance them.

The solution, in the view of westerners such as Henry Clay, was the federal government. As citizens of states that had been created by the Union, rather than states that were creators of it (to the end of his life, Thomas Jefferson referred to Virginia as "my country"), westerners were more apt to look to Congress and the president for aid than easterners were. Moreover, the construction of a highway system in the vast West was a massive project. As men like Clay saw it, only the federal government could bear the expense.

Clay worked tirelessly on behalf of the first federal construction project in the West—the national road that connected Cumberland, Maryland, on the Potomac River, with Wheeling on the Ohio River. It cost $13,000 per mile to build—an astronomical sum; the terrain was rugged—and was completed in 1818. Delighted by what this access to oceangoing commerce meant for Kentucky, Clay worked to have the national road extended to Vandalia, Illinois. He was always ready to listen when fellow westerners proposed new internal improvements.

Clay was uncommonly successful as a highway lobbyist, but he had formidable opponents. Many southerners, nationally minded before the War of 1812, began to worry about the cost of internal improvements—and the taxation needed to pay for laying crushed stone, dredging rivers, and the like. Some westerners, such as General Andrew Jackson, Clay's archrival for leadership of the section, feared that government finance of improvements was unconstitutional. Moreover, while Clay was blameless in the issue, many manipulators made fortunes on unnecessary or wasteful projects, generating opposition to Clay's free-spending.

graveled old trails. The Old Post Road between Boston and New York allowed year-round long-distance travel on that important route.

The Old Post Road was maintained by public monies. Other eastern highways were privately constructed toll roads known as turnpikes because entrances were blocked with a pole resembling a pike that was turned to allow access when the toll was paid. One of the most successful, the Lancaster Pike, connected the rich farm town of Lancaster, Pennsylvania, to Philadelphia, some 60 miles away.

By 1820, there were 4,000 miles of such toll roads in the United States. Some were surfaced with crushed rock, or macadam, a British import that was the forerunner of blacktop paving. A cheaper surfacing, more likely in the West, was made of planks laid parallel like railroad tracks, or even logs laid crosswise. For the obvious reason, the latter were called corduroy roads. The ride they provided was bumpy and shattered many hubs and axles, but they kept narrow, spoked wagon wheels out of the mud.

Until the 1820s, representatives of the New England states also inclined to oppose spending federal money on internal improvements. Their own road system was adequate, so little federal money would be spent in their backyards. However, as the richest section of the country, the Northeast would pick up the biggest part of the bill in taxes. Moreover, until the embargo and the War of 1812 disrupted the shipping business, New England's elite thought in terms of the Atlantic as the fount of their economic life.

Factory owners feared that an improved West would attract their own people.

The American System

To counter such sectional thinking, Clay revived Alexander Hamilton's gospel of "continentalism." He urged Americans to seek their future, first of all, on the North American continent. He called his program the American System.

RIVERS, ROADS, AND CANALS 1825–1860

First, Clay argued that northeastern industrialists had no reason to fear the consequences of internal improvements in the West. A populous West, connected to the Northeast by good roads, would provide a massive domestic market for the manufactured goods of New England and the Middle Atlantic states. He confronted the problem of taxes by compromising the Jeffersonian principle that western lands were to be disposed of as cheaply as possible. While not advocating extremely high prices—Clay supported graduation, for example—he proposed that revenues from land sales pay the greater part of the costs of internal improvements. He also appealed to manufacturing interests by advocating a high tariff that would protect northeastern factories from foreign competition.

To westerners, largely farmers who might otherwise oppose a high tariff, Clay pointed out that a flourishing industry would lead to large urban populations of workers who would buy western food products. Higher prices for manufactured goods—the consequence of the high tariff—were a small price to pay for such a bonanza. To complete the circular flow of products among the regions, the South would supply the mills of New England with cotton.

The capstone of Clay's nationalistic program was the Second Bank of the United States. Chartered in 1816, its role in the American System was to regulate the money supply needed to fuel the integrated economy.

The weak link in Clay's program was the South, to which it did not offer very much. Southerners needed no help in finding profitable markets for their cotton, and needed to make no concessions to sell it. The mills of Manchester, Leeds, and Bradford in England gobbled up all the fiber that southern planters could grow. With the exception of a few special interest groups like Louisiana sugar planters, who wanted tariff protection against West Indian competitors, southerners inclined to oppose Clay's program. To them, the American System meant bigger price tags on the manufactured goods that they, as agriculturists, had to buy.

THE TRANSPORTATION REVOLUTION

In the end, Clay had to be content with levering bits and pieces of his comprehensive program through Congress, not at all what he had in mind. Moreover,

many of his victories were temporary. His bills were repealed when his enemies, who were numerous, captured Congress and the White House. The American economy was to be integrated less by vision and legislation than by a revolution in transportation that conquered seasons, leveled mountains, and diverted the course of rivers.

The Erie Canal

New York led the way in what was a revolution in transportation. In 1817, after years of prodding and pointing by Governor De Witt Clinton to the miracles canals had wrought in England and France, the New York state legislature voted funds to dig a canal from the Hudson River to Lake Erie, from Albany to Buffalo. With picks, shovels, mules, and wagons, gangs of rough, muscular laborers, many of them immigrants from Ireland, excavated a ditch 4 feet deep, 40 feet wide, and, when it was completed in 1825, 364 miles long. (The canal was later enlarged to 7 feet deep and 70 feet wide.)

The Erie Canal was expensive—$7 million, or almost $20,000 per mile. Skeptics waited for the state of New York to buckle under its financial burden and declare bankruptcy. But when the ditch was finished, it opened up the Great Lakes basin to New York City's merchants and shippers by the cheapest means of transportation, water. Both city and state boomed. Linking the West with overseas commerce, New York quickly bypassed Philadelphia to become the country's biggest city.

Travel on the Erie Canal was slow. Mules on towpaths dragged the long, flat-bottomed canal boats at a lazy four miles an hour. But it tranformed the laborious adventure of emigrating to the West into an excursion. For a cent a mile, a pilgrim could put himself into Buffalo and the Great Lakes basin. For five cents a mile, a man with a taste for comfort could travel the Erie Canal first class. Far more important, it cost only $8 a ton to move factory goods west or western crops east. That was a 90 percent cut in the cost of overland transport!

The Canal Craze

Before the Erie Canal was dug, there were only about 100 miles of canal in the United States. (The longest one ran 28 miles.) Now those who had laughed at "Clinton's Folly" went berserk in their rush to imitate it. Many were fools, laying out canals where mules feared to tread.

The Erie Canal made possible the cheap transportation of goods.

One financial failure was the Mainline Canal in Pennsylvania. Smarting under the loss of business to New York City, Philadelphia merchants pressured the state legislature into pumping millions into this ill-advised venture. The Mainline Canal was shorter than the Erie. However, while the New York route rose only 650 feet above sea level at its highest point, and required 84 locks to control its muddy water, the Mainline Canal rose 2,200 feet and needed 174 locks. At the Allegheny ridge, the highest in the Pennsylvania Appalachians, boats had to be hauled out of the canal and over the mountain on rails laid on a fantastical inclined plane. Miraculously, the Mainline Canal was completed, but it was a bust: too slow, too expensive, too many bottlenecks crowded with swearing boatmen in the mountains—where no boatman belonged.

All in all, some 4,000 miles of ditch were dug in emulation of the Erie Canal. Another 7,000 miles were on the drawing boards when the bubble burst. While many of the canals were of inestimable use to locals, only a few made enough money to cover the money invested in them. So many states drained their treasuries to fund poorly advised projects that many politicians, including westerners, swore never again to finance internal improvements. As late as 1848, the constitution of the new state of Wisconsin forbade the expenditure of tax money on such ventures.

Railroads

The canal craze was also brought to an end by the appearance of a far better means of overland transportation, the railroad. As Pennsylvania's venture showed, canals were plausible only where the terrain was not theatrical and the supply of water plentiful and constant. Even the most successful canals, like the Erie, were out of commission during the winter months when they froze. The railroad never provided transportation as cheaply as canal boats. But railroads could run almost anywhere faster and, barring catastrophic blizzards, at any time of the year.

The first railroads in the United States were constructed in 1827, just two years after the first railroad in England proved workable. One line connected

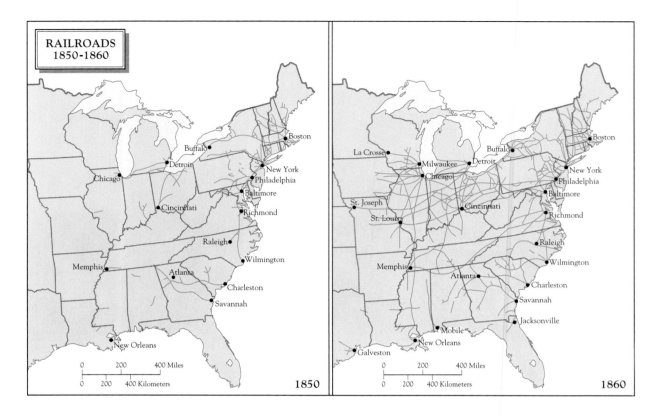

RAILROADS 1850-1860

1850

1860

the granite quarries of Quincy, Massachusetts, with the Neponset River. The other carried coal from Carbondale, Pennsylvania, to the Lehigh River. Both were only a few miles long and served single business enterprises, supplementing existing routes and means of transportation.

The potential of the railroad lay in using it, like the Erie Canal, as the trunk of a transportation system independent of traditional, natural routes. The first entrepreneurs to recognize this were Baltimoreans, merchants hoping to put their city back in the competition with New York for the trade of the West. In 1828, work began on America's first trunk line, the Baltimore and Ohio.

Construction of the B&O was repeatedly stalled by financial difficulties, but the line was finally completed to Wheeling on the Ohio River in 1853. In the meantime, dozens of less ambitious railroads were constructed. By 1848, there were more than 6,000 miles of railroad track in the United States, while fewer than 3,000 miles of track existed in all the rest of the world. In the railroad, America, not Britain, led the modernization movement. Before 1860, the Baldwin Locomotive Works of Philadelphia, just one of several manufacturers of steam engines, made 1,500 of them.

Triumphs and Limitations

The railroad conquered time, and with time the isolation of the West. At the end of the War of 1812, it took more than seven weeks to ship a cargo from Cincinnati to New York (by keelboat, wagon, and riverboat). In 1852, when the two cities were connected by rail, it took six to eight days.

The cost of constructing a railroad was immense. In addition to securing right of way and hiring armies of laborers, a railroad company had to buy its own rolling stock. (A canal or turnpike company simply collected tolls from users with their own boats and vehicles.) As a result, despite the total mileage of American railroads, few individual lines went very far. Indeed, competitive jealousies among the companies worked against true systems connecting distant points. Railway entrepreneurs built their lines in different gauges (the distance between the tracks), so that the cars of competing lines could not be used on them.

Most canals and railroads linked the West to the Northeast. However, the nation's great natural north-south artery, the Mississippi River, was not neglected during the revolution in transportation.

Although the railroad could not provide transportation as cheaply as canal boats did, it could go where canals could not. This early train is on one of the first lines to cross the Appalachian Mountains.

The New York and Erie Railroad

In order to offset the economic advantages that the Erie Canal had brought to the northern counties of New York State, the southern counties proposed to build a railroad between the Hudson River and Lake Erie. Chartered on April 24, 1832, the New York and Erie Railroad (later the Erie Railroad) covered 446 miles between Piermont on the Hudson (26 miles from New York City) and Dunkirk (instead of Buffalo) on Lake Erie.

By 1851, trains carried President Millard Fillmore and his cabinet to Dunkirk on the then longest continuous railroad line in the world. Secretary of State Daniel Webster set out on the jaunt, it was reported, "on a flat car, at his own request, a big easy rocking-chair being provided for him to sit on. He chose this manner of riding so that he could get a better view and enjoy the fine country through which the railroad passed."

"Old Man River"

It could not have been otherwise. With its great tributaries, the Ohio and the Missouri and dozens of smaller but navigable waterways, the "Father of Waters" tapped the central third of the continent. Westerners who lived on the Mississippi system could easily ship their corn or livestock to New Orleans on large log rafts that, broken up and sawed into lumber, were themselves a source of income.

The problem was in bringing goods back upstream. Sailing ships could not do the job. The Mississippi is a broad waterway but its current is powerful, and its channels narrow and shifting, the playthings of capricious sandbars. High riverbanks stole the wind from sails. Large sailing vessels could not buck the current much beyond New Orleans, while smaller boats carried too little to be worthwhile.

Some cargo was rowed upriver, some by poling small skiffs. Both were arduous tasks and extremely expensive. Savage keelboat men, such as the Ohio

River's legendary Mike Fink, literally pulled their vessels upstream. The keelboater lashed a heavy line to a tree on the riverbank and, from the deck of the craft, heaved the ropes in, repeating the process with another tree farther on.

It was no job for the languid, nor was it an efficient way to move bulk. It took about six weeks for a huge raft to float pleasantly downstream from Pittsburgh, where the Ohio River begins, to New Orleans. It took four to five months to bring a much smaller tonnage back, with even more raw-handed men drawing wages. It was more expensive to ship a cargo of English cloth or furniture from New Orleans to Illinois than to sail it from England to New Orleans.

Steamboat A-Coming

The marvel that resolved this dilemma was the flat-bottomed steamboat, which was a long time coming. James Watt, the Scotsman who first harnessed the power of steam pressure for the purpose of pumping water out of mines, regarded ships as the second most important application of his discovery. In 1787, a Connecticut Yankee named John Fitch succeeded in making a practical steamboat. During the summer of the Constitutional Convention in Philadelphia, with several delegates witnessing the spectacle, he ran his 45-foot steamer down and up the Delaware River.

The "Lord High Admiral of the Delaware," as Fitch commissioned himself, built several larger steamers and briefly provided regular service between Philadelphia and Burlington, New Jersey. But he was a star-crossed man, obstreperous and obnoxious with his most generous backers. Nor was his humor improved by the indifference of eastern capitalists who still thought in terms of the sea. They could not imagine how a vessel in which a good portion of the hold was committed to carrying fuel could compete with a sleek sailing ship drawing its energy from God's good sky.

In fact, the age of sail was far from over. For more than a century after the perfection of the steamship, clipper ships and great steel-hulled wind-jammers dominated many world trade routes, particularly the long ones around Cape Horn. But steamboats conquered the rivers. Robert Fulton understood this. In 1807, his *Clermont* wheezed and chugged up the Hudson River from New York City to Albany at five miles per hour. The *Clermont* was three times as long as John Fitch's boat, but the dimension that thoughtful people noticed was that it displaced only seven feet of water. The boat was able to clear obstacles that would have upended a sailing ship with less capacity.

Queens of the Mississippi

The steamboat paid its way on eastern rivers like the Hudson. (Fulton's success, in fact, helped to inspire the campaign to dig the Erie Canal.) But it was in the West that the great vessels found their natural home. In 1817, only ten years after the *Clermont*'s maiden voyage, there were 17 steamboats on the Mississippi. By 1830, there were 187 of them with new ones being constructed more quickly than old ones blew up.

Boiler explosions were no small problem. In order to minimize the weight of the boats, boilers were constructed more flimsily than experience and good sense prescribed. Nevertheless, Mississippi riverboat captains found it difficult to resist a race. As on the railroad, speed sold tickets and attracted shippers, so despite the opulence of some riverboats, a trip on one was a bit of a gamble. At the peak of the steamboat age, 500 people died in accidents each year.

Designers competed just as frantically to adapt boats to the western rivers. The greatest natural obstacles were the shifting sandbars of the Mississippi and Missouri, and snags, fallen trees that were to the river what icebergs were to the North Atlantic, quiet

Robert Fulton's Clermont *breasts the current of New York's Hudson River.*

predators capable of tearing a gaping hole in a wooden hull.

In 1841, the *Orphan Boy* was completed and eased onto the water. It could carry 40 tons of freight plus passengers. But even when fully loaded, it skimmed through water only two feet deep! The *Orphan Boy* was the ultimate, but a good many larger paddle-wheelers needed only three or four feet. Not only was this quality necessary to navigate the Father of Waters and the even trickier Missouri River, but it enabled the boats to tie up at almost any bank in order to take on the cordwood they burned in prodigious quantities.

Symbols of a New Era

The locomotive and the steamboat knit the far-flung reaches of the United States together as neither Alexander Hamilton nor the young Henry Clay had imagined possible. In the words of a Cincinnati booster, they brought "to the remotest villages of our streams, and to the very doors of our cabins, a little Paris, a section of Broadway, or a slice of Philadelphia to ferment in the minds of our young people." The moving machines belching acrid smoke symbolized a sense of nationality as surely as the person of George Washington had symbolized the common cause of independence and constitutional union.

When the steamboat was still in its infancy, however, and the first railroad a decade in the future, Americans were already drawing together in their hearts, or so it seemed. In the wake of the War of 1812, a sense of American nationhood seized on the imaginations of the people of West, North, and even—ever so briefly—the South.

CHRONOLOGY

1800–1820	Rapid growth of western population
1804	Land Act provides for sale of 160-acre parcels
1807	Robert Fulton's *Clermont* is successful
1817–1825	Construction of Erie Canal
1819	Financial panic
1827	First American railroads
1852	New York connected to Cincinnati by rail

FOR FURTHER READING

On the early American West, see Ray A. Billington, *America's Frontier Heritage*, 1967; R. S. Philbrick, *The Rise of the West, 1754–1830*, 1965; Dale Van Avery, *The Final Challenge: The American Frontier, 1804–1845*, 1964; Michael Williams, *Americans and Their Forests*, 1989; and Malcolm J. Rohrbough, *The Trans-Appalachian Frontier*, 1978. Every inquiry into the American West should look to the "founding father" of western history, Frederick Jackson Turner, in *The Frontier in American History*, 1920.

Important studies dealing with topics treated in this chapter include Richard D. Brown, *Modernization: The Transformation of American Life, 1600–1865*, 1976; W. Elliott Brownlee, *Dynamics of Ascent: A History of the American Economy*, 1979; Thomas C. Cochran, *Frontiers of Change: Early Industrialists in America*, 1981; Eugene S. Ferguson, *The Americanness of American Technology*, 1975; F. W. Gates, *The Farmer's Age: American Agriculture, 1815–1860*, 1960; Walter Havighurst, *Voices on the River: The Story of the Mississippi Waterways*, 1964; L. C. Hunter, *Steamboats on the Western Rivers*, 1949; Philip D. Jordan, *The National Road*, 1948; Douglass C. North, *The Economic Growth of the United States, 1790–1860*, 1951; R. M. Robbins, *Our Landed Heritage: The Public Domain*, 1942; Ronald E. Shaw, *Erie Water West: A History of the Erie Canal, 1792–1854*, 1966; George R. Taylor, *The Transportation Revolution, 1815–1860*, 1951; Richard C. Wade, *The Urban Frontier*, 1964; and Sam B. Warner, Jr., *The Urban Wilderness*, 1972. Two excellent newer works are Jeffrey S. Adler, *Yankee Merchants and the Making of the Urban West*, 1991; and Christopher Clark, *The Roots of Rural Capitalism*, 1990.

Pertinent biographies are William Chambers, *Old Bullion Benton: Senator from the New West*, 1970; and Glyndon D. Van Deusen, *The Life of Henry Clay*, 1937. For a different vantage point, see Russell David Edmunds, *Tecumseh and the Quest for Indian Leadership*, 1984.

The Fourth of July in 1818, a public observance that could be raucous.

14
CHAPTER

NATION AWAKENING

Political, Diplomatic, and Economic Developments

1815–1824

Our country! In her intercourse with foreign nations, may she always be in the right; but our country, right or wrong.

—Stephen Decatur

I can never join with my voice in the toast which I see in the papers attributed to one of our gallant naval heroes. I cannot ask of heaven success, even for my country, in a cause where she should be in the wrong. Let justice be done though the heavens fall. My toast would be, may our country be always successful, but whether successful or otherwise, always right.

—John Quincy Adams

enry Clay's vision of an integrated national economy, transcending states and sections, did not spring full-blown from ruminations in a quiet study. The idea of an American System was born in an era when a nationalistic sense permeated American society and culture. The era had its beginnings in 1815 with Andrew Jackson's victory at New Orleans and Stephen Decatur's punishment of the insolent Algerians. The news of both events was greeted with the discharging of muskets and pistols, flag-waving, shouting and singing, and patriotic oratory.

THE ERA OF GOOD FEELINGS

In the decade after the divisive War of 1812, Americans in every section of the country embraced an image of themselves as a new chosen people—unique and blessed on the face of the earth, unsullied by the corruptions of Europe, nurtured by their closeness to nature, committed in the marrow of their bones to liberty, democracy, and progress.

It was during this period that the Fourth of July became a day of raucous popular celebration. Formerly observed in religious services and decorous promenades of the social elite in city squares, the "Glorious Fourth" burst into prominence as a day when everyone paid homage to the nation with games, feasting, overdrinking, and boisterous gaiety.

Patriotic Culture

It was an era of patriotism in popular art. Woodcarvers and decorators trimmed canal boats, sailing ships, stagecoaches, and private homes with patriotic motifs: screaming eagles clutching braces of arrows; the idealized, vigilant female figure that represented liberty; and the flag, the only national ensign in the world that had progress sewn into it. Between 1816 and 1820, six new stars were added to Old Glory as six new states entered the Union.

The needlepoint samplers that girls made to display their skills began to depict patriotic themes as often as religious themes: the Stars and Stripes, or the saying of some national hero like Nathan Hale's "I regret that I have but one life to give for my country" or Decatur's "Our country right or wrong." Newspapers published exuberant verses that touted the glories of the United States. Songwriters churned out lyrics that celebrated American grandeur.

In 1817, William Wirt wrote a biography of Patrick Henry from which it might easily have been

Sing Me a Yankee-Doodle Song

One of the most joyously patriotic songs to come out of the War of 1812 was "The *Constitution and the Guerrière*," about a two-ship battle that ended in an American victory:

*It oft-times has been told
How the British seamen bold
Could flog the tars of France so neat and handy, O!
But they never found their match
Till the Yankees did them catch.
Oh the Yankee boys for fighting are the dandy, O!*

concluded that Virginians led the movement for independence and fought the war single-handedly. Annoyed patriots from other states looked for and dependably found patriotic demigods of their own.

Less controversial because of its singular subject was Mason Locke Weems's book, *The Life and Memorable Actions of George Washington*. Although originally published in 1800, Weems's unblushing study in hero worship peaked in popularity during the 1810s and 1820s, running through 59 editions. It was Weems who originated the story of the boy Washington chopping down the cherry tree and the tale of an older Washington throwing a silver dollar across the Rappahannock River. So noble was the father of his country that he could not fib; so far was he above other nations' leaders that even in physical strength he was a superman.

Another influential author of the time was Noah Webster, whose *American Spelling Book*, first published in 1783, sold more than 60 million copies. From the "blue-backed speller," schoolchildren learned that the American tongue was superior to British English because Webster had stripped it of Old World affectations. Many of the differences in spelling between American English and British English (labor, theater, curb, and jail as opposed to *labour, theatre, kerb,* and *gaol*) owe to Webster's linguistic patriotism.

He was also the father of that great event of the American elementary school, the spelling bee, for Webster believed in uniform spelling. He observed unhappily that even so great a national hero as William Clark, in his journals of the great expedition across the continent, spelled *mosquito* 19 different ways. Webster's *American Dictionary of the English*

The Fourth of July was an occasion for often rowdy celebrations.

Language, published in 1828, also distinguished American English by including hundreds of words adopted from Indian tongues.

James Monroe

The gentleman who presided over this outpouring of national pride was, like three of the four presidents who preceded him, a Virginian—James Monroe of Westmoreland County. His is a blurred figure in the history books; his facial features are soft, his personality has few hard edges. Even James Madison, with his less than scintillating presence, glows by comparison.

Monroe's achievements can be listed. He was one of Jefferson's most loyal (and most radical!) disciples, an excellent diplomat, a good administrator, and utterly incorruptible. "Turn his soul wrong side outwards," Jefferson said, "and there is not a speck on it." It can be noted that people thought his wife one of the most beautiful women in the country. Portraits reveal that the fifth president was eccentric in his dress; he wore the old-fashioned, skin-tight knee

breeches of the Revolutionary era, while his contemporaries were pulling on the utilitarian trousers of the nineteenth century.

But a two-dimensional oil painting is what James Monroe remains. Perhaps it is because he was so very

---

National Propriety

Noah Webster not only Americanized English, he was also very concerned that it be proper. He prepared an edition of the Bible in which he left out words "offensive to delicacy." Webster wrote:

Many words are offensive, especially for females, as to create a reluctance in young persons to attend Bible classes and schools, in which they are required to read passages which cannot be repeated without a blush; and containing words which on other occasions a child ought not to utter without rebuke.

HOW THEY LIVED

How They Navigated the Erie Canal

Thomas Jefferson inscribed his opinions on so many subjects that he may be excused for a few gaffes. Such as when he heard of New York's plan to connect the Hudson River to the Great Lakes by digging a great ditch. Jefferson wrote: "Talk of making a canal of three hundred and fifty miles through the wilderness—it is little short of madness."

The Erie Canal opened in November 1825, less than a year before Jefferson died. He had no opportunity to study the returns and recant his judgment: a fabulous excavation 4 feet deep and 40 feet wide, the breadth of a large state; a rise of 650 feet scaled by means of 84 locks; natural waterways traversed by aqueducts, the most dramatic features of any canal; travel time from Albany to Buffalo cut from 20 days to 8, later to 6; the cost of moving a ton of freight that distance slashed from $100 to $10, later to $5; the stupendous $7 million cost of digging the ditch repaid with interest in just 12 years; Ohio and Indiana growing faster than older Kentucky and Tennessee; New York City eclipsing Philadelphia as the nation's largest metropolis.

Then again, Jefferson might not have revised his opinion of the adventure. He had written in *Notes on Virginia*, "let our workshops remain in Europe," that "mobs" of workers who do not till the soil "add just so much to the support of pure government, as sores do to the strength of the human body." The 3,000 Irishmen who were lured to New York to dig the ditch and who were joined by thousands of others to maintain and "navigate" the canal when it was done comprised one of the "great cities" that Jefferson also thought quite mad, albeit a city of a very strange shape.

They were a primitive lot, the "canal boys," fresh off the wretched little potato patches from which the English landlords allowed them to feed themselves. Only a sense of history rare among peasants, a rich oral tradition, and their deep Roman Catholic piety raised them above barbarism. The cash wages they were paid to shovel and heave the dirt of upstate New York threatened to return them to it.

Sordid brothels, gambling dens, and prototypes of the American saloon followed the work crews. The drunken, eye-gouging, ear-biting "ructions" were prodigious. As portions of the canal were opened and work camps became towns and cities built around locks, depots for horses and mules, and junctures of feeder canals, the atmosphere hardly changed: it just moved from tents to clapboard and brick buildings. Canal boats moved around the clock. The canal towns roared around the clock.

The fact that the boisterous, brawling boatmen worked an economic miracle did not often enter into the reflections of the proper New Englanders who traveled the canal. The authors of many accounts seem to have trembled for their personal safety each of the 364 miles they were aboard one of the "queer-looking Noah's Ark boats."

Ironically, they were not only quite secure, they were enjoying a trip that was palpably more bearable than any alternative, rather comfortable for some, and elegant for those who could pay the fare on a first-class boat.

The most expensive way to travel on the canal was on the packets. At least 80 feet long and 15 wide, they maintained a schedule, whereas other boats

successful as president, calmly meeting and promptly dispatching the less than nation-shaking problems that rose to face him, and speaking in the pious generalities that a nation at peace with itself wanted to hear.

History, like the audience at a play, thrives on conflict. It grows torpid in times of stability. James Monroe had the political good luck, and the historical misfortune, of being president during an entr'acte, an interlude of calm between two times of crises. He could declare in his second inaugural address, and no

doubt believe it, that the United States "will soon attain the highest degree of perfection of which human institutions are capable."

Political Stability

The founding fathers' hopes for a government without political parties briefly came to pass under Monroe. The Federalists, revived during the War of 1812, collapsed when the shooting was over. After Jackson's victory at New Orleans, their opposition to the war,

moved when they were loaded. The packets were towed around the clock by three trotting horses, which were consequently changed often. Because the passengers' quarters on a packet were quite comfortable, horses that were resting were not brought aboard, as was done on second- and third-class boats. The big companies that ran packets—the Pilot, Telegraph, Merchant's, Washington, Citizen's, and Commercial—maintained large stables at intervals of ten to twelve miles.

For five cents a mile, a first-class passenger moved at between four and six miles per hour. The packets overtook slower boats by means of a procedure that was routine but, nonetheless, the occasion of some altercations. The slower boat slackened its line and the line of the quicker, horses straining, was passed over it. Requiring even more dexterity, when the towpath changed sides, the horses cleared a bridge and galloped up and over it. The best of the canal men took pride in negotiating this maneuver without so much as a tug on boat or horse-collar.

On a packet, men and women could sit on stuffed sofas in the saloon, which ran the length of the boat. Meals were served in the saloon. Allowing for the era's comparative disinterest in gourmandise, complaints about the cooking on the first-class boats were rare. At locks and stables, or when heavy traffic slowed the pace, passengers could walk the towpath ahead of the vessel.

At night, the saloon was efficiently divided into separate quarters for men and women. The sofas became beds. Upper bunks folded from the cabin walls. They were not roomy, scarcely more than five feet long with just enough room to roll over without unduly disturbing the passenger above.

If one was not apprehensive of the rough boatmen, nor interested in the often lovely scenery, the trip could be boring. Plenty of people played cards dawn to dusk, or idly bowed fiddles or played other instruments. As ever in America, there were preachers, clambering aboard when they were allowed, walking along the towpath shouting admonitions if they perceived a promising response among the travelers.

Second-class boats were usually smaller than a packet and carried their own horses and freight as well as passengers. They kept no schedule, but cast off when they were full.

The boat was towed into a lock (usually by a two-horse or mule team). The water was completely drained whence the boat sat on a scale. The toll was paid, and passengers in a hurry hoped that there would be no more interruptions "from Albany to Buffalo." Fare was one and a half cents a mile with food. In 1836, Jacob Schramm and a party of Germans made the trip on a second-class boat in seven days for only $8. They provided their own meals, easy enough to do with, by that year, towns lining the way.

Third-class boats, really freight scows willing to take an impecunious traveler aboard, cost even less, and delays could be interminable. Even then, the trip was safe and far easier than an overland trek. About the greatest danger on the Erie Canal was to fail to hear the boatman call, "Low bridge, everybody down," and to have one's head smartly rapped by a stone span while the boat traveled under it at four miles per hour.

particularly at the well-publicized Hartford Convention, seemed more like disloyalty than good sense.

The number of congressmen styling themselves Federalists declined from 68 during the war to 42 in 1817 and 25 in 1821 (compared with 158 Jeffersonian Republicans). By 1821, there were only four Federalists in a Senate of 48 members. Old John Adams, in retirement in Quincy, Massachusetts, took scant interest in the evaporation of the party that he helped to found. His son, John Quincy Adams, em-

braced the party of Thomas Jefferson and became Monroe's secretary of state.

During the 1810s, Republican congressmen and senators met in caucus to choose their presidential candidate and therefore, in effect, the president. Monroe handily defeated Federalist Rufus King in 1816. King won only the electoral votes of Delaware, Connecticut, and Massachusetts. The next year, when Monroe visited Boston, where Jefferson was loathed and Madison despised, he was received as a hero. A Boston newspaper congratulated him for inaugurating an "era of good feelings."

In 1820, Monroe was unopposed in the presidential election. (One member of the electoral college cast his vote for John Quincy Adams so that no president but Washington would have the distinction of being his country's unanimous choice, and to set up Adams as the party's nominee in 1824.) With only one political party, the United States had, in effect, no parties at all.

Smooth Sailing

There was another side to the consensus of the Era of Good Feelings: an indifference toward presidential politics. In 1816, William Crawford of Georgia could probably have won the Republican presidential nomination over Monroe, but Crawford did not think the prize worth a fight. His supporters simply did not attend the party caucus at which the candidate was to be named.

Nor was there much popular interest in general elections. In 1816, only 6 of 19 states chose presidential electors by statewide popular vote; in 1820, only 7 of 24 states did. In most of the others, the state legislatures made the choice, and they treated the task as though it were routine, like confirming the governor's proclamation of a Thanksgiving holiday. In 1820, the returns from Richmond, Virginia, a city of 12,000 people, revealed that only 17 men had bothered to vote.

There is nothing intrinsically wrong in a subdued presidency and popular indifference to politics, particularly according to the tenets of the Jeffersonian faith, to which James Monroe subscribed. Jefferson said that the government that governed least governed best. The absence of deeply divisive issues

---

Fortune Telling

In the early nineteenth century, some upper-class families amused themselves on a boy's fourth birthday by putting him in front of a pair of dice, a piece of fruit, a purse, and a silver knife. It was prophesied that if he picked up the knife, he would become a gentleman of leisure; the purse, a businessman; and the fruit, a farmer. If he picked up the dice, everyone had a good laugh.

---

during Monroe's tenure in office reflected the relative prosperity of the times and the American people's concern with westward expansion and economic growth. Moreover, if Monroe was neither a mover nor a shaker, movers and shakers often do a good deal of mischief. Monroe did none. He was a conscientious, competent, and hard-working executive. His administration was efficient and, without a popular clamor to distract them, he and his nationalistic secretary of state, John Quincy Adams, had an unbroken string of diplomatic successes.

Making Up with Mother England

In the Rush-Bagot Agreement of 1817, the United States and Britain agreed to limit the number of armed vessels on the Great Lakes. It was the first major concession that the former mother country made to the Americans since the Revolution. More important, the partial disarmament set the pattern for future policies that established the world's longest unfortified international boundary.

In 1818, Britain and the United States also established the southern boundary of British Canada at 49° north latitude, a line that now runs west from Lake Superior to Puget Sound. Although American claims in the Pacific Northwest were flimsy, and American interests there were next to nil, the British conceded Americans equal rights in what was called the Oregon country: present-day Oregon, Washington, the Idaho panhandle, and British Columbia.

Florida Is Secured

With Spain, Monroe-Adams diplomacy reaped even greater rewards. By 1819, the Spanish Empire was quaking. Rebellions broke out in practically every province, and rebel armies won most of the battles against demoralized loyalist troops. The leaders of the independence movement—Simón Bolívar, José de San Martín, and Bernardo O'Higgins—paid flattering homage to the example set for them by the United States. Their praises of the United States as the beacon light of their own freedom provided more fodder for the Americans' bumptious national pride.

The disintegration of the Spanish Empire also gave Florida to the United States. The peninsula never was a very valuable or secure part of the Spanish Empire. Thinly populated, Florida was held by the British for 20 years after 1763. In 1818, in pursuit of Indian enemies, Andrew Jackson brazenly crossed the border, ignored Spanish authority, and (on foreign soil) executed two British subjects for treason to the United States!

When the Spanish minister in Washington protested Jackson's incursion, Secretary of State Adams responded by offering to buy Florida. For $5 million, Spain agreed. Adams had only to confirm Spain's version of the disputed boundary between American Louisiana and Spanish Texas (at the present eastern border of the state of Texas), which was no concession at all. The United States had never seriously contested the Mexican boundary. In the Adams-Onís Treaty, the United States was guaranteed every acre to which the country had a reasonable claim.

The Monroe Doctrine

John Quincy Adams was also the author of the American policy statement that has immortalized Monroe's name. In December 1823, the president wrote in a message to Congress (and to Europe) that the United States was no longer to be considered an appendage of the Old World. With an "essentially different" destiny, the United States pledged not to dabble or intervene in European affairs. In return, Europe was to consider the Western Hemisphere closed to further colonization. Monroe said that any such attempts would be defined in Washington as "an unfriendly disposition." In other words, he threatened war.

The proclamation of the Monroe Doctrine (a name given it only years later) was prompted by two developments that disturbed the sensitive Adams. The first was expanded Russian exploration and fur trapping south of Alaska, which was Russian since 1741 by right of discovery. The Russians built an outpost, Fort Ross, provocatively close to Spanish San Francisco. In February 1821, the Czar ordered foreign ships to keep at least a hundred miles clear of Russian America's shores.

Much more important, Adams was troubled by rumblings in Austria and France. He feared those countries would send troops to the Western Hemisphere to help Spain regain control of its lost colonies.

Asserting American Identity

Neither threat amounted to anything. The Russians were interested in the plush pelts of the California sea otter, and by the 1820s, trappers had just about wiped out the animals in California's coves. In 1824, the Russians abandoned Fort Ross and withdrew to

Alaska. The French and Austrians had other problems more pressing than the fall of the Spanish Empire and the project was stillborn, which was just as well. In 1823, the United States was probably not up to dispatching an effective army to Mexico, let alone to South America. The popular uproar would have deafened the president who tried. If the Adams-Monroe closure of the New World to further colonization had any force, it was because the British, now utterly dominant on the Atlantic, wanted Hispanic America to be independent.

In fact, the British foreign minister, George Canning, proposed that Great Britain and the United States jointly proclaim the Americas closed to further colonization. Previously restricted in the extent of their trade in the rich markets of the old Spanish Empire, the British were the chief beneficiaries of Spanish-American independence.

Adams decided to act alone in asserting the different destiny of the Western Hemisphere so that the United States would not look like "a cock-boat in the wake of the British man-of-war." To nationalistic American sensibilities, British friendship could be as threatening as British antagonism.

Nationalism in the Courtroom

While Adams and Monroe proclaimed the national dignity of the American Republic to the world, Chief Justice John Marshall buttressed the constitutional primacy of the national government at home in a series of decisions that are still basic to American law.

This fabric, with its shields and stars and stripes, illustrates the patriotism of the early nineteenth century.

Marshall never again invalidated a law of Congress as he had done in *Marbury v. Madison*. Instead, while cultivating a reputation for physical laziness and squalid personal appearance, he dominated his fellow Supreme Court justices until 1835. In chambers by day, at the boardinghouse where several justices lived together by evening, over law books and tumblers brimming with whiskey, Marshall whittled away at the power of the states which, good Federalist to the end, he regarded as dangerous to the Union.

In *Fletcher v. Peck* (1810), the Marshall court declared a state law unconstitutional, thus establishing the right of the Supreme Court to act in matters that concerned one state alone. In *Martin v. Hunter's Lessee* (1816), Marshall established the court's authority to reverse the decision of a state court. In *McCulloch v. Maryland* (1819), Marshall prevented the state of Maryland (and all states) from taxing the nationally chartered Bank of the United States. "The power to tax is the power to destroy," the court declared. No state had the right to interfere with the national government's obligation to legislate on behalf of the common good, as the Constitution commissioned it to do.

In *McCulloch*, Marshall also propounded his views on the extent of governmental power. If the goal were legitimate and the law did not run counter to the Constitution, Congress and the president had the power to enact whatever legislation they chose to enact. It did not matter that the government in Washington was not specifically authorized by the Constitution to take a certain action (such as the establishment of a national bank). This was the issue that caused the first split between Hamilton and Jefferson. Now with Hamilton and his party both dead, John Marshall made "broad construction" of the Constitution the prevailing law of the land.

John Marshall served as chief justice during the administrations of six presidents, three of whom served two full terms. It would be difficult to argue that any of them contributed more to the shaping of American government than he. In 1833, the only Supreme Court justice of the Marshall era whose legal mind rivaled his own, Joseph Story, published *Commentaries on the Constitution of the United States*. Essentially, it was a commentary on fundamental law as John Marshall perceived it.

AMERICA'S INDUSTRIAL REVOLUTION

Another of Hamilton's dreams for the United States—and one of Jefferson's nightmares—also headed for fulfillment during the second and third decades of the nineteenth century. To some extent in the West, but particularly in New England and the Middle Atlantic states, manufacturing came to rival agriculture in economic importance, and population began a significant shift from farms and villages to the towns and cities where factories were centered. In this process, the people of the northeastern states were early participants in the Industrial Revolution.

What Industrialization Meant

Machine technology, the factory system for making goods, and the rapid growth of industrial cities were not revolutionary in the sense that people's lives were changed overnight. But the consequences of machines that made goods quickly and cheaply changed the terms of human existence far more profoundly than did any battle, or the beheading of any king or queen.

For example, in the United States today, less than 8 percent of the population lives on farms, and virtually no one produces more than a tiny fraction of the food they consume and the goods they use. They buy the commodities of life with money received for performing very specialized jobs. Even the typical farm family raises only one or two crops for

---

Rebecca Pennock Lukens

Women industrialists were rare but not unknown. One of the most successful was Rebecca Pennock Lukens, a Pennsylvania Quaker who managed the precursor of the Lukens Steel Corporation for a quarter century. Her father, Isaac Pennock, founded the Brandywine Iron Works, turning over management of the several factories to his son-in-law, Charles Lukens. When Lukens died in 1825, his only heirs were his young wife, Pennock's daughter, Rebecca, and her five small children. Rebecca was only thirty years of age. Nevertheless, she took her husband's place, became a well-respected ironmaster, and managed the works until 1849 when her son-in-law, her daughter's husband, succeeded her.

Modern urban areas such as Brooklyn were more like villages in the early nineteenth century, as this painting illustrates.

market, and purchases the same mass-produced necessities and luxuries that city dwellers buy.

Before industrialization, in colonial and early national America, the situation was reversed. Roughly 90 percent of the population (the proportion was constantly declining) lived on farms or in agricultural villages, and personally produced a sizable proportion of the food they ate and the goods they used. For most people, very little was purchased: shoes; some clothing; tools such as axes and guns; pottery and tin or pewter ware; some services such as milling flour, shoeing horses, and so on. As for other necessities, ordinary people improvised them from materials on hand.

The preindustrial farmer or shopkeeper had to be handy. A man with a door to hang often made the hinges himself. A woman who kept a tidy house made the broom with which she swept it. Heavy work, such as log-rolling and raising a roof beam on the frontier, husking corn, or cutting ice from a pond, was done cooperatively by neighbors. In all but the half dozen largest cities, townspeople of some means kept gar-

dens of an acre or so, often a dairy cow, commonly a brood sow. The Industrial Revolution changed that kind of unspecialized, largely self-sufficient life into the specialized, interdependent economy we know today.

It Started with Cloth

The first industrial machines were devised for the manufacture of textiles. This should not be surprising. Cloth is a universal necessity but making it by hand is tedious, difficult, and time-consuming.

In North America, as in much of the Western world, cloth making was largely woman's work, and the process took up much of the spare time of that half of the population. On poor and even middling American farms, cloth was made at home from scratch. Natural fiber from animals (wool) or plants (cotton and flax for linen) had to be gathered, cleaned, carded (untangled, combed), spun into thread or yarn, dyed, and then woven or knitted by hand into a fabric that could warm a body, cover a bed, protect a wagon load, or propel a ship.

Because the process took so much time and required hard-learned skills at every turn, fabric was expensive. The poor dressed in hand-me-downs often no better than rags. People of modest means made do with one set of clothing for work, another for "Sunday-go-to-meeting."

Cottage Industry

Well-to-do people dressed rather more handsomely, of course, and they did not card, spin, and weave. Cloth also had to be made in quantity for plantation slaves, soldiers, and sailors. Before industrialization, the needs

of such groups were met by cottage industry, or what was sometimes called "the putting-out system."

It worked like this. Farmwives and daughters contracted with a cloth dealer, sometimes called a factor, to receive fiber from him and spin it into yarn or thread in their homes. Working in odd, snatched moments, they were paid not by the hour but by the piece. They were, in the present-day term, independent contractors. The women and children (and sometimes men) in another family might weave cloth under the same system, again in their spare time.

This system of production did not significantly disturb traditional social structure and values. Households involved in cottage industry were able to participate in the money economy to the extent of what their women earned. Socially, however, these women remained farmwives, daughters, and spinsters (unmarried women in a household). They were not textile workers. Their values and the rhythm of their lives were essentially the same as those of their neighbors who were not part of "putting out."

In England in the middle of the eighteenth century, this system began to change. English inventors devised water-powered machines that spun thread and wove cloth at many times the speed that hand spinners and weavers could do it, and, as a result, at a fraction of the cost. With a monopoly on this technology, Britain prospered, supplying the world with cheap fabric. Not only were most women from Canada to Calcutta delighted to be spared the tedium of spinning and weaving, but the machine-made cloth was cheap enough for almost all to buy, and it was generally of better quality than homemade cloth. England found a market for its cheap cloth everywhere in the world. Comparable machines were rapidly developed for other forms of manufacture.

The Importance of Power

The key to exploiting the new machines was power—a fast-moving river, or somewhat later, the steam engine. A water wheel or mighty, hissing piston could turn hundreds of machines much faster than any foot-driven spinning wheel. Power is where it is found or made, however. The process of making cloth had to be centralized, brought under one roof; the machines had to be run for as long as there was light by which to see. Industrialization created the factory and a pace of labor governed by the clock, the tireless machines, and the capitalist's need to use his investment to the utmost.

Making Mittens

In the manufacture of goods that resisted mass machine production, the "putting-out" system flourished into the era of John D. Rockefeller and Standard Oil. In fact, Abby Condon, mother and schoolteacher of Penobscot, Maine, became an industrialist about the same time Rockefeller did.

In 1864, Mrs. Condon arranged with a mercantile house in Boston to take yarn home to Maine and return with mittens. The chief customer at the time was the Union Army. It was "government work," and Mrs. Condon was paid a munificent 25 cents for each pair of mittens she managed to have knitted.

The price plummeted to six cents a pair after the war, but Mrs. Condon simply increased production. She recruited at least 250 knitters, maybe more, among housewives and their daughters around Penobscot. Until 1882, it was entirely a cottage industry, knitting needles clicking in hundreds of homes. In that year, however, Mrs. Condon purchased four recently perfected knitting machines and built a small factory to house them. By the time of her death in 1906 at age 67, Mrs. Condon owned 150 knitting machines. Few were in factories, however. Most, in conservative rural Maine, she "put out" in private homes. Nevertheless, her old-fashioned business was consuming six tons of woolen yarn a year, producing about 96,000 pairs of mittens. Home manufacture of knitted goods remains common in New England in the twenty-first century.

Industrialization also created a class of workers who did nothing but tend machines. No longer was thread spun by a farmwife in odd moments. The industrial textile worker spent six days a week, from dawn to dusk, at the factory. Because she worked virtually all the daylight hours, she had to live close to the factory. The mill hand was a town dweller, no longer the farmer's daughter. A new social class emerged—the urban, industrial working class.

Early Factories

The British protected their monopoly of industrial technology as a magician guards his bag of tricks. It was, of course, illegal to export machinery and the plans for them. Indeed, engineers and mechanics expert in building or repairing textile machines were forbidden to leave the country.

One such engineer was Samuel Slater, 23 years old in 1790, and quite clever enough to know that the knowledge that provided comfort in England would make him rich abroad. Rather than risk being caught with plans for spinning machines, Slater committed to memory several long and intricate lists of specifications. He slipped away from his home and shipped off to America, where he struck a bargain with a Rhode Island merchant, Moses Brown, who had tried without success to build spinning machines.

Brown and a partner put up the money, and Slater contributed the expertise. In 1790, they opened a small water-powered spinning mill in Pawtucket, Rhode Island. The little factory housed only 72 spindles, a minor operation compared with what was to come. Still, they were the equivalent of 72 spinning wheels in 72 cottages, and each of the Slater devices turned many times faster and spun much longer than any farmwife could manage.

The capital investment was substantial but operating expenses small. The whole mill could be run by one supervisor and nine children between the ages of seven and twelve. Their labor cost Slater and Brown 33 to 60 cents per worker per week. Within a few years, both men were rich. Slater lived to be one of New England's leading industrialists, owning mills in three states.

There were other such acts of technological piracy. In 1793, two brothers from Yorkshire, John and Arthur Schofield, came to Byfield, Massachusetts, and established the first American woolens mill, and Francis Cabot Lowell smuggled plans for a power loom out of England. Throughout the nineteenth century, Englishmen would bring valuable technological advances in their sea trunks.

High Labor Costs

Once aroused, however, Americans proved more than able to advance the Industrial Revolution on their own. Alexander Hamilton had observed "a peculiar aptitude for mechanical improvements" in the American people. In the 1820s, a foreign observer marveled that "everything new is quickly introduced here. There is no clinging to old ways; the moment an American hears the word 'invention' he pricks up his ears."

One reason for the American infatuation with the machine was the labor shortage that vexed employers since the earliest colonial days. Land was abundant and cheap in the United States. Opportunities for an independent life were so ample that skilled artisans demanded and generally won premium pay. In the early nineteenth century, an American carpenter made about three times as much in real income as his European counterpart. Even unskilled workers in the United States could live considerably better than the day laborers of the Old World. What was sauce for the worker, however, was poison to the men who hired help. The machine, which did the job of many hand workers, was inevitably attractive to them.

Inventors Galore

Thus, Oliver Evans of Philadelphia earned a national reputation when he contrived a continuous operation flour mill. One man was needed to dump grain into one end of an ingenious complex of machinery. Without further human attention, the grain was weighed, cleaned, ground, and packed in barrels. Only at this point was a second man required to pound a lid on the keg. Evans saved millers half their payroll.

In 1800, Eli Whitney announced a system for casting small iron parts that promised to displace gunsmiths, one of the most skilled and best-remunerated of preindustrial craftsmen. Muskets and sidearms were expensive because the lock (firing device) was made up of a dozen or more moving parts, several of which were tiny and delicate. Each was individually fashioned by hand so that no two guns were the same; every one was custom-made. Not only was crafting a firearm time-consuming and expensive, but repairs required the attention of an artisan who was as skilled as the man who made the gun, for he had to fashion replacement parts from scratch.

Slater Mill, established in Rhode Island in 1790, was the first successful cotton spinning factory in the United States.

Whitney's innovation was to make the molds for the parts of a gun so precise that one component cast in them was enough like every other that they could be used interchangeably. He appeared before a congressional committee with ten functional muskets constructed (so he said) from interchangeable parts, took them apart, shuffled the components, and reassembled ten working muskets. His dramatic little (and possibly rigged) show won him a government contract to make 10,000 more.

Peter Cooper, learning that the Baltimore and Ohio needed a locomotive, boasted that "I'll knock an engine together in six weeks that will pull carriages at ten miles an hour." His locomotive actually went 18 miles per hour and set Cooper on the road to great riches. When Cooper constructed the Cooper Union, a building in New York City, he included a shaft for an elevator. None existed at the time, but Cooper, with his intense faith in American ingenuity, was sure one would soon be perfected.

Many cultures produce inventors, but the United States was unique in raising the inventor to the status of a hero, quite the equivalent of a conquering general or a great artist. Even bastions of tradition embraced practical science. In 1814, Harvard College instituted a course called "Elements of Technology." In 1825, Rensselaer Polytechnic Institute, a college devoted entirely to the new learning, was founded at Troy, New York. Others followed in quick succession, for Americans found nothing bizarre in teaching engineering side by side with Greek and Latin. Indeed, they were more likely to be suspicious of those who studied the classics.

A COUNTRY MADE FOR INDUSTRY

A cultural predilection to technology was only one of America's advantages in the Industrial Revolution. The United States was also blessed with the other

Machines replaced handwork even in specialized trades such as the manufacture of horseshoe nails.

prerequisites of an industrial society: resources necessary to feed the new machines; capital, surplus money to finance the building of factories; and labor, people to work them.

Resources

For a providentially minded people, it was as if the Creator had shaped the northern states with water-driven mills in mind. From New England to New Jersey, the country was traversed with fast-running streams that, dammed and channeled, provided power for factories. When steam power proved superior to water power, there were dense forests and rich deposits of coal to stoke the boilers. America's forests and strong agricultural base produced what raw materials the new industry required, from lumber to leather to hemp for rope. At the same time the textile industry was growing in New England, cotton cultivation ex-

panded throughout the South to provide enough of the snowy fiber for both England and America.

Capital

Money available for investment in industry came from the merchants and shippers of the Northeast. Ironically, many of these capitalists were practically forced to convert their wealth from ships into mills by the restrictions on trade that they thought would be the ruin of them. In 1800, at the beginning of the Napoleonic Wars, there were only seven mills in New England, with a total of 290 spindles. After Jefferson's Embargo, Madison's Non-Intercourse Acts, and the War of 1812 had disrupted shipping for 15 years, there were 130,000 spindles in 213 factories in Massachusetts, Connecticut, and Rhode Island alone. Aware of a good thing once they saw it, industrialists continued to expand. By 1840, there were 2 million spindles in the United States.

Banking Creates Money

Banks, a new phenomenon in the early nineteenth century, made it easier to channel capital where it was needed, though not everyone was pleased at the multiplication of lending institutions from 30 in 1801 to 88 in 1811. A bank issued more money in paper certificates than it actually had on hand in gold and silver. In 1809, anticipating the obsession of Thomas Hart Benton, John Adams growled that "every dollar of a bank bill that is issued beyond the quantity of gold and silver in the vaults represents nothing and is therefore a cheat upon somebody."

However, so long as the people who built a mill, supplied it with fiber, and worked the machines accepted the paper dollars lent by a bank to the mill owner, and so long as their grocers, landlords, and business associates accepted the paper money from them, it did not matter that the bank owned only $100,000 in gold and issued $1 million in paper. So long as the people who traded in the bills believed that they could present the paper to the bank and receive gold, capital was increased tenfold. So long as confidence and optimism were in rich supply, banks were a source of energy more powerful than the 32-foot falls of the Merrimack River.

Industry and Politics

With the increasing importance of industrial interests in the Northeast, the section's political interests shifted. Traditionally, New England ship owners were suspicious of a high tariff on imported goods. If taxes on imports were high, fewer Americans bought them and there was less business carrying manufactures across the ocean. Alexander Hamilton failed to get the tariff he wanted partly because New England merchants, strong Federalists on other issues, joined with farmers (who were consumers of manufactured goods and wanted the lowest prices possible) to defeat him.

As late as 1816, many New England congressmen voted against high tariffs. One of them was Daniel Webster, a 34-year-old representative from New Hampshire who numbered Portsmouth shipmasters among his legal clients. By 1823, when Webster returned to Congress, he had moved to Massachusetts and become counsel and confidant to several manufacturers. Now he was a strong and eloquent supporter of a high tariff. If infant industries were to grow, they had to be protected from competition

Ingenuity

The American fascination with gadgets and novel mechanical devices is almost as old as the republic. As foreign observers were to note, some wryly, some aghast, Americans seemed to leap into tinkering without planning. As one respected engineer liked to say, "Now, boys, we have got her done. Let's start her up and see why she doesn't work."

Between 1790 and 1800, Americans took out 306 patents. Between 1850 and 1860, the Patent Office cleared more than 28,000. Just a year earlier, in 1849, a young lawyer named Abraham Lincoln took out a patent for a device designed to float steamboats over shoals. He never learned if it worked because he did not start it up.

with the cheaper goods that the older and better developed British manufacturers could produce.

Labor

Industrialization eventually undercut and almost destroyed handicraft. Many people were needed to tend the machines in the new mills, and the United States lacked England's surplus of "sturdy beggars" roaming the countryside and overcrowding the cities. Few white Americans were desperately poor. Few men who could freely choose among farming profitably, moving west, or working in small independent shops, were attracted to low-paying, highly disciplined factory work.

The difficulty of recruiting labor from among traditional groups was reflected in the failure of the "Fall River system." In Fall River, Massachusetts, the mill owners attempted to hire whole families to work in the mills. It was an honest mistake. The family was the unit of production on the traditional farm and in the artisan's shop. But the system did not work very well in the factories. Family ties were too often at odds with the demands of employer on employee.

The Lowell Girls

Rather more successful, because it found a niche within the traditional social structure, was the system developed by Francis Cabot Lowell, who established several large mills at Waltham, Massachusetts, in

1813, and a whole town called Lowell in 1826. Lowell dispatched recruiters to roam rural New England. They persuaded farmers to send their young daughters to work in the mills. For 70 hours a week at the machines, the girls and young women earned $3, paying half of that for room and board at company-supervised lodging houses.

The long workweek put off no one. It was a normal enough regimen for a farm girl. The money was attractive, too. Farming the stony New England soil made no one rich, and Yankee farmers burdened with large families inevitably liked the idea of subtracting one diner from the table, especially if that diner was a daughter who, by going to Waltham or Lowell for a few years, could save a dowry large enough to attract a suitable husband. The Waltham system was successful precisely because it drew on a body of people for whom there were few other opportunities.

The trick was to persuade straitlaced New Englanders to allow girls of 14, 16, and 17 to leave home. Lowell worked it by providing a closely regulated life for his employees during off-hours as well as working hours. The Lowell girls lived in company-run dormitories, attended church services, and were kept busy (as if 70 hours at work were not enough!) with a variety of educational and cultural programs.

Most of the first American industrial workers were women—and children! In 1820, about half the factory hands in Massachusetts mills were under 16 years of age. A society of farmers in which everyone down to six years of age had assigned chores did not find this inhumane. And the pace of the early factory was far slower than the assembly line of the twentieth century. Operatives minding textile machines shut them down when they thought it necessary to do so. In some mills, girls were permitted to entertain (respectable) visitors while they watched their spindles. Most English visitors commented that American factories were idyllic compared with England's "dark, satanic mills."

In time, the American factory, too, would become a place of stultifying toil. But it is difficult to find many horrors in the first phase of American industrialization. Artists depicted mills as objects of beauty and town pride. By way of contrast with what later builders would create, those structures that have survived are regarded as architectural gems. Today, quite a few have been converted into up-scale shopping centers.

THE SOUTH AT THE CROSSROADS

While westerners tamed land, and northeasterners set about building a society dominated by mills and swelling cities, southerners reaffirmed their agrarian heritage. There were those who would have had it otherwise. In 1816, when Daniel Webster was still speaking for the shipping interests of old New England, John C. Calhoun of South Carolina dreamed of cotton factories in his own state.

But Calhoun's attraction to industrialization, like his War Hawk supernationalism during the War of 1812, was already doomed. His future lay in defending southern sectionalism, the plantation system, and the institution of slavery on which they rested. Ironically, this brilliant political theorist (and

Lowell Offering *(1845) was a literary magazine produced by women who worked in the Lowell, Massachusetts, mills.*

somewhat less able politician) was chained to such anachronistic institutions because of a machine which, if its technology was primitive, was profound in its dramatic consequences.

Slavery in Decline

When John C. Calhoun was born in 1782, African-American slavery appeared to be dying out. The northern states took steps to abolish human bondage during the last years of the eighteenth century. Slavery was never vital to the northern economy, so that northerners could afford to practice the revolution's principle of liberty.

Slavery was also declining in the South during the Revolutionary era. The world price of tobacco, one of the few crops for which slave labor was profitable, collapsed. On top of that, many of the old Chesapeake and Carolina tobacco fields were exhausted. Other slave-raised crops, such as South Carolina's rice and indigo, lost some luster when British subsidies were lost following independence (although South Carolinians remained the least apologetic defenders of slavery).

Southerners, as well as northerners, were moved by the ideals of the Declaration of Independence. Thomas Jefferson, its author, agonized throughout his life over the injustice of human bondage. In their wills, Jefferson, George Washington, and many other planters freed at least some of their slaves. Few spoke of slavery as anything better than a tragic social burden, a necessary evil. As late as 1808, only a few southerners objected when Congress (as the Constitution allowed) outlawed further importation of blacks from Africa. At the peace talks in Ghent in 1815, American and British commissioners discussed the possibility of cooperating in suppressing illegal traders. It is reasonable to suggest that the tragic institution would have been peacefully phased out in the United States (as it was in the British Empire) had it not been for the "absurdly simple contrivance" invented by Eli Whitney.

The Cotton Gin

In 1793, seven years before his demonstration of interchangeable parts, Eli Whitney visited a plantation near Savannah, Georgia. There he saw his first cotton plant and learned from a friend that it flourished everywhere in the upland South. Cotton fiber was worth 30 to 40 cents a pound—a fabulous price for

the by-product of a plant—but the upland cotton could not be exploited commercially because of the costs of separating the precious fiber from the plant's sticky green seeds. This job could be done only by hand, and the most nimble-fingered of people could process no more than a pound of fluff a day, hardly enough to justify hiring employees to do it, let alone setting an expensive slave to the job.

On the frost-free sea islands off the coast of South Carolina and Georgia, cotton had been cultivated profitably since 1786. But the variety planted there was long-staple cotton with shiny, smooth black seeds that could be popped out of the fiber by running the cotton bolls between two rollers. When this method was tried with the cotton of the uplands, the sticky green seeds were crushed, fouling the fiber with oil.

Whitney's device was so simple that a planter who had a decent collection of junk on the grounds could make a workable version. In fact, the ease of constructing the cotton gin (short for engine) denied Whitney the fortune he deserved for inventing it. His patents were ignored, and he was ground down into exhaustion in the courts.

Essentially, Whitney dumped the bolls into a box at the bottom of which were slots too small for the seeds to pass through. A drum studded with wire hooks revolved so that the hooks caught the fibers and pulled them through the slots, leaving behind the seeds without crushing them. Another drum, revolving in the opposite direction, brushed the fiber from the wire hooks.

It was a magnificent device. A single slave cranking a small gin could clean ten pounds of cotton a day ($3 to $4 at 1790 prices). A somewhat larger machine turned by a horse on a windlass could clean 50 pounds a day ($15 to $20!). Once steam-powered gins were introduced, the capacity for producing cotton was limited not by the processing problem but by the number of acres that a planter could cultivate.

The Revival of Slavery

Technology had come to the South, but not industry. The effects of Eli Whitney's machine were the revival of the South's traditional one-crop economy, the domination of southern society by large planters, and the reinvigoration of slavery. Like tobacco, cotton was well adapted to gang-cultivation. The crop required plenty of unskilled labor: plowing, planting, chopping (or weeding, an endless process in the

This celebration of Whitney's cotton gin left no doubt that the machine and slavery went hand in hand.

hot, wet, fertile South), ditch digging and cleaning, picking, ginning, baling, and shipping.

Moreover, the fertile upland black belt that extends from South Carolina and Georgia through eastern Texas was natural cotton country. Seduced by the same charms of riches that turned western farmers into speculators and doughty New England merchants into industrial capitalists, southerners streamed into the "Old Southwest" (Alabama, Mississippi, and northern Louisiana) and eventually into Arkansas across the Mississippi River. In 1800, excluding Indians, there were about 1,000 people in what is now Alabama. In 1810, there were 9,000; in 1820, 128,000! The growth of Mississippi was less dramatic but not lethargic: 1800, 8,000; 1810, 31,000; 1820, 75,000.

Nor was this an emigration of buckskin-clad frontiersmen with no more baggage than a long rifle and a frying pan. Wealthy planters from the old states made the trek, bringing their bondsmen and -women with them. In 1800, there were 4,000 blacks in Alabama and Mississippi. In 1810, there were 17,000 blacks,

virtually all of them slaves; in 1820, there were 75,000. Almost half the population of Mississippi was black and in bondage.

The price of slaves soared, doubling between 1795 and 1804. Blacks who were becoming financial burdens in Maryland and Virginia became valuable commodities in the new cotton South. The most humane masters found it difficult to resist the temptation of the high prices offered for their prime field hands, males between 18 and 30 years of age. Slave owners from as far north as New Jersey liquidated their human holdings to cotton planters.

The Missouri Crisis

There were still a few slaves in the North to be sold in 1819. Most states had adopted a gradualist approach to emancipation, by which no person born or brought into the state after a certain date could be enslaved. (There were a handful of aged slaves in New Jersey as late as the Civil War.)

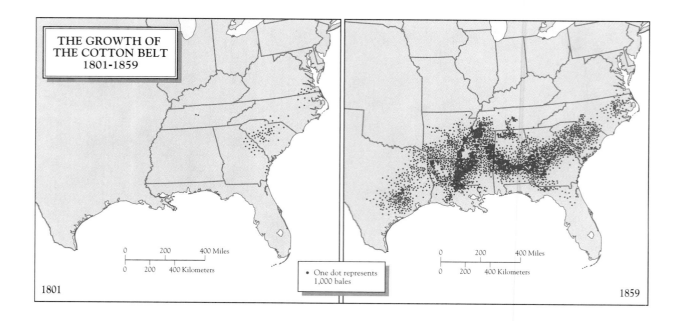

THE GROWTH OF
THE COTTON BELT
1801-1859

0   200   400 Miles
0   200   400 Kilometers

1801

• One dot represents
  1,000 bales

0   200   400 Miles
0   200   400 Kilometers

1859

But there was also, by 1819, a clear-cut line between slave states and free states. North of the Mason-Dixon line (the Maryland-Pennsylvania border) and the Ohio River, slavery was forbidden or in the process of abolition. South of it, the institution remained a vital part of society and economy. In 1819, quite in the middle of Monroe's "era of good feelings," the sectional character of the institution became, briefly, an explosive issue.

It was ignited by the application of the Missouri Territory to be admitted to the Union as a state. Although west of the Mississippi River, all but a tiny fraction of Missouri lay north of the Ohio River, the natural boundary between slave states and free states. Quite able to read a map and voicing moral objections to slavery, Congressman James Tallmadge of New York proposed that Missouri be admitted only after its state constitution was amended to forbid the further importation of slaves and to free all slaves within the state when they reached 25 years of age. In a word, Missouri would eliminate slavery gradually as the northern states had done or were doing.

Some northern representatives and senators leapt into the breach Tallmadge opened. One described slavery as "a sin which sits heavily on the soul of every one of us." On hearing of such rhetoric, old Thomas Jefferson wrote from Monticello that he was startled as though he had heard "a firebell in the night." John Quincy Adams expressed concern.

What worried both men was that once the morality of the discussants enters a debate, conflicts are not easily resolved by cutting a deal or trading quids for quos. Indeed, southern congressmen, particularly representatives of cotton states like Mississippi and Alabama, replied to their northern censors in fierce and furious language.

The Compromise

Ever unflappable, James Monroe was not unduly disturbed. A Virginian who was ambivalent as to the future of slavery, he encouraged compromise in Congress. The deal was actually devised, however, by another southerner who wanted no part of moral imprecations in discussions of slavery, Henry Clay.

Earning the nickname "The Great Compromiser" for his scheme, Clay proposed that Missouri be admitted to the Union as those who wrote its constitution wished, as a slave state. This smoothed southern feathers. In order to mollify northerners for whom slavery was an important issue, Clay proposed that the southern boundary of Missouri, 36° 30′ north latitude, be extended through the remainder of American territory—to the scarcely known crest of the Rocky Mountains. North of that line, slavery was forever prohibited. In territories south of 36° 30′, which meant only Arkansas Territory and recently acquired Florida, the citizens living there could decide whether the state would be slave or free.

Passions cooled, tempers eased. Congressmen who had glared at one another shook hands and turned to other business. But Jefferson's firebell continued, however muted, to echo in the distance and with a new timbre to its peal. For Clay's compromise also involved an informal institutionalization of a balance between free states and slave states. There were 22 states in the Union in 1819, 11 free, 11 slave. When Missouri was admitted, Congress also agreed to detach the Maine District from Massachusetts and admit it as a free state.

For 30 years, Congress would admit states virtually in pairs, preserving the balance. But because the Missouri Compromise forbade slavery in the major part of the Louisiana Purchase, it was inevitable that, sooner or later, a territory would seek admission to the Union as a free state with no slave state to balance it.

Indeed, the population of the free North was increasing much more quickly than the population of the South. Until 1810, the two sections grew at an uncannily similar rate. In 1820, however, despite the explosive growth of Mississippi and Alabama, there were nearly a million more people in the North than in the South, 5,219,000 to 4,419,000. As the disparity increased—and all signs said that it would—the good

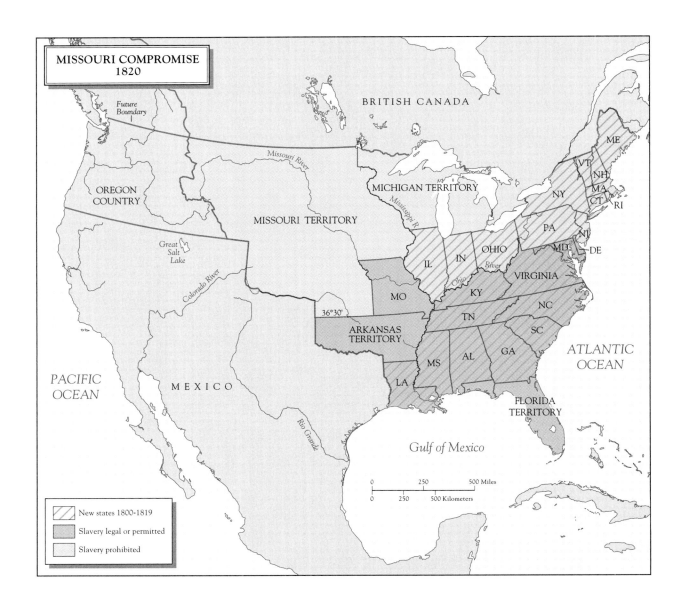

MISSOURI COMPROMISE
1820

New states 1800-1819

Slavery legal or permitted

Slavery prohibited

feelings that made James Monroe's presidency such a happy one were bound to be among the casualties.

CHRONOLOGY

1790	First American spinning mill, Pawtucket, R.I.
1793	Invention of cotton gin
1800	Eli Whitney proposes principle of interchangeable parts
1810–1819	Nationalistic decisions by Supreme Court
1810–1820	Parson Weems's biography of Washington published in 59 editions
1817	Rush-Bagot Agreement
1820	James Monroe reelected president without opposition Missouri Compromise
1823	Monroe Doctrine promulgated
1825	Rensselaer Polytechnic Institute founded
1825	Lowell, Massachusetts, founded
1828	Noah Webster's *American Dictionary of the English Language*

FOR FURTHER READING

Comprehensive histories of this era include the appropriate chapters of John R. Howe, *From the Revolution through the Age of Jackson*, 1973; Robert Heilbroner, *The Economic Transformation of America*, 1977; W. Elliott Brownlee, *Dynamics of Ascent: A History of the American Economy*, 1974; George Dangerfield, *The Era of Good Feelings*, 1952, and *The Awakening of American Nationalism*, 1815–1828, 1965. Research discoveries subsequent to Dangerfield's work have been incorporated in John Mayfield, *The New Nation, 1800–1845*, 1981. A fascinating social history, part of which covers these years, is Daniel Boorstin, *The Americans: The National Experience*, 1965.

The standard biography of the president of the Era of Good Feelings is William P. Cresson, *James Monroe*, 1971; and of his secretary of state, Samuel F. Bemis, *John Quincy Adams and the Foundation of American Foreign Policy*, 1949; although see also Leonard L. Richards, *The Life and Times of Congressman John Quincy Adams*, 1986; and William Earl Weeks, *John Quincy Adams and American Global Empire*, 1992. On a key policy, see Henry F. May, *The Making of the Monroe Doctrine*, 1975, and Dexter Perkins, *The Monroe Doctrine*, 1927. On the major political issue of the Monroe presidency, see Glover Moore, *The Missouri Controversy*, 1953, and Donald L. Robinson, *Slavery in the Structure of American Politics, 1765–1820*, 1979.

Early American industrialization has been a subject of lively inquiry in recent decades. Students should see Thomas Cochran, *Frontiers of Change: Early Industrialism in America*, 1981; Allan Dawley, *Class and Community in Lynn*, 1976; Thomas Dublin, *Women at Work: The Transformation of Work and Community in Lowell, Massachusetts, 1826–1860*, 1979; David J. Jeremy, *Transatlantic Industrial Revolution: The Diffusion of Textile Technologies between Britain and America*, 1981; Bruce Laurie, *The Working People of Philadelphia, 1800–1850*, 1980; and Leo Marx, *The Machine in the Garden: Technology and the Pastoral Ideal in America*, 1964. For economics and politics, see Ronald Schultz, *The Republic of Labor: Philadelphia Artisans and the Politics of Class, 1720–1830*, 1993; and Sean Wilentz, *Chants Democratic: New York City and the Rise of the American Working Class, 1788–1850*, 1983.

The grounds of the White House were opened to the public
for Andrew Jackson's inauguration in 1829.

15
CHAPTER

HERO OF THE PEOPLE

The Age of Andrew Jackson

1824–1830

His passions are terrible. When I was President of the Senate, he was senator, and he could never speak on account of the rashness of his feelings. I have seen him attempt it repeatedly, and as often choke with rage. His passions are, no doubt, cooler now; he has been much tried since
I knew him, but he is a dangerous man.

— *Thomas Jefferson*

Thou great democratic God!, . . . Thou who didst pick up Andrew Jackson from the pebbles; who didst hurl him upon a warhorse; who didst thunder him higher than a throne! Thou who, in all Thy mighty, earthly marchings, ever cullest Thy selected champions from the kingly commons.

— *Herman Melville*

Except an enormous fabric of executive power, the President has built up nothing. . . . He goes for destruction, universal destruction.

— *Henry Clay*

He has slain the Indians and flogged the British and therefore is the wisest and greatest man in the nation.

— *Democratic Party Voter*

The single-party system of the Monroe years had its virtues. At the top, at least, administration was efficient. In Congress debate was candid and eloquent, and usually carried out on a higher plane than in eras when partisanship has reigned. At its best, party loyalty is less edifying than loyalty to home, country, or principle. At worst, it is a poison that rewards tawdry, sycophantic hacks who prosper personally, their end in life, by mouthing the party line.

The national leaders of the "era of good feelings" were not hacks. They appreciated the ideals that underlay the founding fathers' dislike of party and faction. They believed it was the duty as well as the privilege of good men to govern.

But there were also many among them consumed by personal ambition, "a little insane" on the subject of high office, as Abraham Lincoln would say a generation later. A single-party organization could not accommodate the hunger for advancement of all of them. There were simply not enough nominations to go around.

So, by the end of 1824, as James Monroe prepared to pack up in the White House, Thomas Jefferson's Republican party went bust. By 1828, politically active Americans had aligned themselves into two camps that, within a few more years, coalesced into full-blown parties. With an eye on the Federalist-Jeffersonian competition of the first American party

system, historians describe the political reshuffling of the 1820s as the second-party system. Over this era loomed a giant of a man—some said a monster—Andrew Jackson of Tennessee.

THE SKEWED ELECTION OF 1824

During the quarter century the Jefferson Republicans dominated national politics, three traditions grew up around the presidency: King Caucus, the Virginia Dynasty, and an orderly succession to the White House by the secretary of state, who was appointed by his predecessor. In 1824, in part because the demands of each contradicted the other two, in part because so many politicians wanted to be president, two of these institutions were toppled and the third was discredited.

King, Dynasty, and Succession

The first to be dethroned was "King Caucus." This was the name given (by those who did not like it) for the method by which the Jeffersonians nominated their presidential and vice-presidential candidates between 1800 and 1824. In election years, Jefferson Republican members of Congress met in caucus (that is, as members of the party) and decided by vote whom they would support in the election. Until 1824, unsuccessful candidates accepted the decision of King Caucus; so did party members in the states.

In fact, fights within the caucus were without much spirit or lasting rancor. Monroe opposed Madison in 1808, lost, and three years later became his secretary of state. William Crawford opposed Monroe in 1816, lost narrowly because of his own half-hearted interest in the contest, and entered Monroe's cabinet. Partly by chance, but also because of the gentility with which caucus fights were fought, Madison and Monroe both stepped from the office of secretary of state into the White House. An orderly means of succession seemed to be established—presidents, like Roman emperors, adopting their heirs.

Americans spoke of a "Virginia Dynasty" in the presidency. All three of the Jefferson Republican presidents—Jefferson, Madison, and Monroe— were Virginians. Only one of the first five presidents, John Adams, was not from the Old Dominion. Until 1824, it was all quite tidy.

In Defense of Parties

Martin Van Buren had no apologies for his role in creating the Democratic party. He said that organizations dedicated to getting out the vote were inherently democratic; parties organized popular mandates for great causes. Van Buren also looked on parties as mechanisms for devising compromises among contending ideologies and interest groups, a problem that had worried the founding fathers. The most important signs of fissure in the America of the Age of Jackson had to do with sectionalism, the devotion of people to the interests of North, South, or West above the interests of the nation. Sectional animosities, which Henry Clay hoped to resolve with his "American System," Van Buren said would be healed by the creation of a great national party, the Democratic party.

In that year, however, the secretary of state was John Quincy Adams, so much a Massachusetts man that most southern Jeffersonians regarded him as a Federalist in disguise. They were suspicious of Adams's strident nationalism and disliked his belief that the national government should exercise extensive powers in shaping both economy and society. Most southern politicians hoped to make the secretary of the Treasury, William Crawford, the party's presidential nominee.

Crawford was from Georgia but, having been born in Nelson County, Virginia, he could qualify as the Virginia Dynasty's legitimate heir. Quite at odds with Adams, Crawford was an orthodox Jeffersonian who feared a powerful central government and favored strict construction of the Constitution. President Monroe supported his candidacy and Crawford was chosen by King Caucus. The trouble was, only Crawford supporters attended the party caucus in 1824. Others repaired to their own states where state legislatures named three additional candidates.

Candidate Stew

For a while it appeared that New York Governor De-Witt Clinton, the builder of the Erie Canal, and South Carolina Senator John C. Calhoun, would enter their names in the contest. Clinton dropped out when he excited few supporters and Calhoun set-

tled for second best, running as vice president with two other candidates.

One of them was John Quincy Adams. His supporters ignored the party caucus and rallied around the tradition that the secretary of state should succeed to the presidency. They also liked Adams because of his assertive and successful foreign policy, his support of a high tariff to protect young industries, and his belief that the federal government should take an active role in promoting economic prosperity, including a federally financed program of internal improvements. Adams was nominated by the Massachusetts state legislature.

Henry Clay, nominated by the legislature of Kentucky, shared most of Adams's views. The two men differed in little but their mutual aversion to one another's personal habits. When they were negotiators together at Ghent, the high-living Clay mocked the hard-working Adams as a prig. ("I have said the Lord's Prayer before retiring every night of my life. And I have never mumbled it once," Adams once said.) Adams, in turn, looked on Clay's drinking, gambling, and womanizing as dissolute and depraved. Now, in 1824, they divided the votes of those who favored their systematic, nationalistic economic program.

Unfortunately for Clay, he could not fully exploit his carefully cultivated image as a man of the growing progressive West. There was another westerner in the contest, Andrew Jackson of Tennessee, who was a military hero to boot. So magical was his name as the conqueror of the British and half a dozen Indian tribes that it did not matter that Jackson's political principles were something of a mystery, perhaps even to "the Ginral" himself. Only on the question of currency and banking was Jackson known to have taken a strong stand. Although rich—the wealthiest man in Tennessee, some said—Jackson detested banks and paper money. He was ruined in a financial panic in the 1790s and, as Americans were soon to learn, Andrew Jackson did not forget a grudge.

In 1824, Jackson's supporters did not allow voters to forget the Battle of New Orleans, or the fact that Jackson was a man of action who crossed the Appalachians poor, and by hook and crook and wiles and will—the American way—became a hero and the master of a plantation of imperial extent.

Who Won?

This appeal to sentiment and the support of Calhoun, who was also Jackson's vice-presidential candidate, was enough to win Jackson more popular and

---

Caucus

Caucus is an Americanism. In 1818, the witty editor of the *Edinburgh Review*, who did not like much about the United States, referred to it as "the cant word of the Americans," and British newspapers did not commonly use it—mis-use it, actually—until the end of the nineteenth century. However, it appears without self-consciousness in John Adams's diary as early as 1763, and others remembered its employment in New England in the early eighteenth century. Most plausibly, the word has an Algonkian origin. In his history of Virginia, Captain John Smith cites the word *ca-cawaassaugh*, meaning "one who advises." Early in the eighteenth century, New Englanders frequently adopted such Indian words as names of men's clubs.

electoral votes than Adams, Crawford, or Clay. He was also the only candidate to win at least one state in all three sections: Northeast, South, and West. But Jackson's totals fell short of a majority in the electoral college. Just as in the election of 1800, the responsibility of naming the president fell to the members of the House of Representatives, voting by the states.

Under the terms of the Twelfth Amendment to the Constitution (adopted in 1804), the House made its selection from among the top three finishers in the electoral college, which eliminated Clay. William Crawford also seemed to be out of the running. He had suffered a stroke that left him bedridden and unable to speak. Crawford's supporters insisted he would recover, and, in time, he did. But they were unable to arouse any enthusiasm outside the southern states that he carried in the general election.

Jackson's followers were confident of victory. As they saw it, the House of Representatives was morally bound to ratify the election of the man preferred by more voters than any other. It was a good argument—the democratic argument—but it did not carry the day. Instead, because of the political beliefs and personal ambitions of the influential Henry Clay, and perhaps the impulsive decision of Stephen

Van Rensselaer, an elderly congressman from New York, the second-place finisher in the election, John Quincy Adams, won the prize.

"Corrupt Bargain!"

Van Rensselaer, who cast the vote that threw the New York delegation and the election to John Quincy Adams, said that while he was praying for guidance, he glanced at the floor, saw a piece of paper on which was written "Adams," and took it as a sign from on high. Long before this providential moment, however, Clay had made his decision for Adams and, as Speaker of the House, he was in a position to reward congressmen who succumbed to his arguments. Clay favored Adams because, despite their personal distaste for one another, they agreed on most political issues. Jackson, on the other hand, was a sworn enemy of one of Clay's favorite projects, the Bank of the United States.

Moreover, Clay wanted to be president, and Jackson was surrounded by would-be successors: Calhoun of South Carolina (who easily won election as vice president); John Eaton of Tennessee; and Richard M. Johnson of Clay's own Kentucky. There was no room in the Jackson crowd for Harry Clay. Nor, indeed, could Clay imagine being a member of any crowd.

Adams, on the other hand, was a solitary and often cranky man with few close friends. Nor, because he had spent much of his life abroad as a diplomat, was Adams surrounded by and tied to a circle of political cronies, so Clay could reasonably hope to be his successor.

Clay and Adams did not sit down across a table and hammer out a tit-for-tat understanding. Clay was a man for a deal in a smoke-filled room. How else win the title, "Great Compromiser"? But Adams was too stubborn, too well-schooled in propriety, too self-righteous even, to "talk turkey." His distaste for the manual labor of politics that left the hands dirty would, soon enough, shatter his career as a national politician. Nevertheless, when Clay threw his influence in the House of Representatives behind Adams, and Adams later appointed Clay secretary of state, the losers of 1824 were sure that they were cheated by two cynical schemers.

John Randolph of Roanoke, a Crawford supporter, in an allusion from the novel *Tom Jones*, sneered at the union of "the puritan and the blackleg," an insult that led Clay to challenge him to a

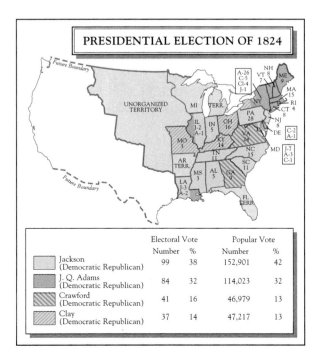

PRESIDENTIAL ELECTION OF 1824

	Electoral Vote		Popular Vote	
	Number	%	Number	%
Jackson (Democratic Republican)	99	38	152,901	42
J. Q. Adams (Democratic Republican)	84	32	114,023	32
Crawford (Democratic Republican)	41	16	46,979	13
Clay (Democratic Republican)	37	14	47,217	13

duel. (No one was hit.) The Jacksonians settled for shouting "corrupt bargain," obstructing the Adams presidency, and planning for revenge.

A New Party

Between 1824 and 1828, Jackson's alliance of supporters coalesced into a new political party. It included Jackson's western following and southerners led by John C. Calhoun, a formidable base. To ensure a national majority, however, the Jacksonians had to break the grip of the Adams-Clay forces in the populous Northeast. Toward this end, Martin Van Buren, an ambitious New Yorker, called on Jackson at his Tennessee mansion, the Hermitage, and put his influence in his native state at the general's service.

The South, the West, and New York—this was the consortium that allowed Jefferson and Aaron Burr to throw the first Adams out of office in 1800. Also, like the Jefferson Republicans of 1800, the Jacksonians appealed to the ordinary fellow—the common man—and depicted their opponents as the party of privilege.

This was mostly nonsense. The leaders of the Jackson party were of the same social class as the politicians surrounding Adams and Clay, and Andrew Jackson was no common man. But the Jacksonian appeal to democracy versus a conniving elite came naturally after the "corrupt bargain" controversy. "Let the people rule!," the Jacksonians cried even before Adams was inaugurated. Let them have the president that most of them chose in 1824. Seizing on the theme, the Jacksonians called themselves Democratic-Republicans, soon abbreviated as Democrats. It is with Jackson that the Democratic party we know took shape.

THE AGE OF THE COMMON MAN

Like his father, John Quincy Adams brought impressive credentials to the White House. On paper, no one—surely not the laconic General Jackson—was better qualified for the job. While Jackson could claim to have been slashed in the face by a British officer at the age of 14 (for refusing to shine the soldier's shoes), John Quincy Adams at that age was in high government service, as secretary to the American minister in Russia. He had been a diplomat in several European countries. He had also been sena-

tor from Massachusetts, and a secretary of state whose successes still rank him among the most able people to hold that post.

Another Unhappy Adams

Also like his father, Adams's qualifications ended with his achievements. Temperamentally, he was out of tune with his times, unable to provide what more and more Americans were demanding of their leader. In an age of electrifying political personalities—of Clay and Jackson and Calhoun—John Quincy Adams excited no one. Among a people beginning to prize equality above other political goals, and easy informality in society, Adams was standoffish, pompous, and sniffily self-conscious of his abilities, his learning, his ancestry, and his achievements, which he felt earned him the right to be president. He found it difficult to accept the point of view that high office should be awarded on any other basis than superior merit. He wrote in his diary, "whether I had the qualifications necessary for a President of the United States, was, to say the least, very doubtful to myself," but he was lying to himself. Adams did not doubt that he was the best that his generation had to offer.

Most damaging of all in an age when political horse-trading was frank, fast, and furious, John Quincy Adams tried to stand above partisan politics: "[That] I had no talents for obtaining the office [of president] by such means was perfectly clear." He allowed open enemies to hold office under him. To have removed them and filled the posts with his supporters, Adams felt, would have been to stoop to the shabby politics of which—unjustly in his opinion—he was accused in the "corrupt bargain" controversy.

Adams was also thin-skinned and short-tempered. He took criticism and sometimes mere suggestions as affronts to his office and his person. He cut himself off from possible allies who had honest, minor disagreements with him. By the end of his term, he had a smaller political base in Washington than any previous president, including his unhappy father.

A Democratic Upheaval

If Adams's personality was quirky, his social assumptions did not differ appreciably from those of his five predecessors. The staunchest Jeffersonians, despite their democratic talk, were self-conscious members of an elite of wealth, education, manners, and talent.

John Quincy Adams (1767–1848) was a well-qualified but unpopular president.

In the 1820s, however, it was outdated to think in terms of a "natural aristocracy" (or at least to speak of it in public). During the 1820s and 1830s, politics ceased to be largely the concern of the leisured, educated classes and came to preoccupy much of the white male population. The foremost foreign commentator on American attitudes, Alexis de Tocqueville, wrote that "almost the only pleasure which an American knows is to take part in government." A less sympathetic visitor to the United States, Mrs. Frances Trollope, was appalled that American men would rather talk politics than mend their fences and tend their crops. (In the last two years before statehood in 1820, Missouri Territory, with a population of 65,000 very common people, sent delegate John Scott a thousand petitions to be presented to Congress.)

In part, this great democratic upheaval was the fruit of half a century of democratic rhetoric. Though they saw themselves as natural aristocrats, the Jeffersonians said that the people should rule, and the idea caught up with them. The democratic upheaval of the 1820s and 1830s was also the consequence of the extraordinary growth and energy of the young republic. An increasingly prosperous people needed to struggle less in order to survive and had more time to think about public affairs. With issues like the tariff, land policy, and internal improvements bearing heavily on individual fortunes, ordinary folk had good reason to do so.

Finally, the wave of democratic spirit that swept Andrew Jackson on its crest had some peculiarly western sources. In attempting to attract population, the young western states extended the right to vote to all free, adult white males and enacted other laws designed to appeal to people of modest station. Kentucky, for example, abolished imprisonment for debt in 1821. No longer could a man or woman be jailed for financial misfortune.

Democratization was an eastern and urban movement, too. Fearful of losing population to the West, most eastern states responded to liberal western voting laws by adopting universal manhood suffrage. In 1824, about half the states still insisted on some property qualifications in order to vote. By 1830, only North Carolina, Virginia, and Rhode Island retained such laws on their books, and Rhode Island's conservatism in the matter was deceptive. Still governed under the state's seventeenth-century colonial charter, which could not be easily amended, Rhode Island was rocked by a brief violent uprising in 1842, Dorr's Rebellion, which resulted in extending the vote to all adult white males.

Interviewing the President

John Quincy Adams may have been aloof, but he was certainly more accessible than are presidents of the twentieth century. It was his custom to rise early, walk alone from the White House to the Potomac River, shed his clothes, and take a swim quite naked. A woman journalist, who had attempted for weeks to get an interview with the president, hit on the idea of following him on one of those expeditions. While he was in the water, she sat on his clothes and refused to budge until Adams answered all of her questions! He did, while treading water, and in a better humor than that in which he had held office hours while clad in frock coat and cravat.

In 1824, one state in four chose presidential electors in the state legislature. The others chose electors by popular vote in one form or another. By 1832, only planter-dominated South Carolina still clung to the less democratic method. Finally, given the right to vote, people did. In 1824, the first presidential election in which there was widespread participation, about one-quarter of the country's adult white males cast ballots. In 1828, one-half of the eligible voters voted and, in 1840, more than three-quarters of the electorate participated in the national election. If so many people voted today, it would be described as a revolution and probably would be just that.

"Workies"

Some of these new voters built parties around social issues. During the 1820s, a number of workingmen's parties sprang up in the eastern cities. Called the "Workies" and supported largely by skilled artisans who recently won the right to vote, these organizations pushed for a variety of reforms to protect mechanics, as skilled craftsmen were called: the abolition of imprisonment for debt, which hit the independent artisan hard; mechanics' lien laws, which prevented creditors from seizing a worker's tools and gave wage workers first crack at a bankrupt employer's assets; and free public education for all children. To the workingman of the Northeast, education was the equivalent of the westerner's free land, the key to moving up in the world.

The workingmen's parties had their local victories, especially in New York. But they dwindled when visionaries, such as Scottish-born reformer Frances Wright, tried to convert them to broader reforms. Wright, for example, fought for female equality and "free love," the freedom of all, unmarried and married, to enjoy sexual partners who were not their spouses.

Mainstream politicians of every persuasion had little interest in modifying the legal status of women, which meant challenging the supremacy of the male head of household. As for free love, mechanics and their wives were as likely as manufacturers and theirs to dally, but if anything, their publicly avowed sexual morals were more conservative than those of the elite. Artisans were conscious that their social status was superior to that of the urban underclass, which they associated with (among other things) promiscuity. Fanny Wright's preachments were titillating, but

they had little appeal and contributed to the drift of "Workie" voters to the Democrats.

The Anti-Masonic Party

Another expression of the democratic upheaval of the 1820s and 1830s was the Anti-Masonic party, which was founded in upstate New York when a bricklayer named William Morgan wrote an exposé of the Society of Freemasons. Morgan did not have so very much to say. Originally an association of free-thinkers who were skeptical of revealed religion (many of the founding fathers, including George Washington, had been members), the Freemasons became a social club for generally well-to-do men.

Most of Morgan's revelations had to do with rituals, secret handshakes, and other hocus-pocus. For example, he quoted the order's initiation ceremony, in which a new member swore "to keep all Masonic secrets under the penalty of having his throat cut, his tongue torn out, and his body buried in the ocean." This is not the sort of thing that, as a rule, post-adolescents take seriously. However, some Masons took it very seriously, or so it seemed. Morgan disappeared, and, a short time later, a corpse that may have been mutilated according to regulations was dragged out of the Niagara River.

The apparent murder inspired an extraordinary movement. According to politicians, who pointed out that Morgan was a workingman and that most Masons were prosperous farmers, merchants, bankers, and the like, the order was a conspiracy aimed at keeping the common man down. Secrecy, they added, had no place in a free, open society. It was through the handshakes, code words, and other signs exposed by Morgan that Masons recognized one another, favored brother Masons in business to the disadvantage of others, and schemed to control the economy and the government.

The Anti-Masons benefited from the traditional views about the sanctity of the family that Fanny Wright flouted. By maintaining that some secrets must be shared only with brother Masons, Anti-Masons said, the order was insinuating itself between husband and wife. If a husband were required to keep secrets from his own spouse, he was violating the marriage contract as surely as free lovers did.

The Anti-Masonic movement spread, especially in the Northeast. A number of leaders who would later play an important part in national politics first came to the fore as Anti-Masons: Thaddeus Stevens,

Thurlow Weed, William H. Seward, and Millard Fillmore. In 1832, the party's candidate for president, William Wirt, won 33,000 votes and carried the state of Vermont. In the same year, the party elected 53 candidates to Congress.

Andrew Jackson was a Mason. Consequently, while democratic in temper, the Anti-Masons were hostile to Jackson's Democratic party. Most of them remained in opposition to Jackson when their party's appeal faded, joining the Whig party.

Nominating Conventions

The Anti-Masonic episode was brief, a conjunction of class resentment and dollops of paranoia and political opportunism. (By no means did all the party's leaders believe that a conspiracy of handshaking Freemasons were on the verge of seizing control of the republic.)

During its heyday, however, the Anti-Masonic party made a lasting contribution to American politics. In Baltimore in 1831, the Anti-Masons were the first to hold a national party convention. With the caucus system of making presidential nominations dead, and nomination by state legislatures not firmly established, the major parties imitated the Anti-Masonic example. The Democrats first met in convention the next year, in 1832, nominating Andrew Jackson. The anti-Jackson Whigs followed suit a few years later.

The national convention, too, was seen as a democratic reform, bringing party activists from throughout the country together in one place.

Like the workingmen's parties, the Anti-Masonic party was short-lived. The principal beneficiary of the upheaval in democratic sentiments was the Democratic party, which formed around the person of Andrew Jackson. Between 1824 and 1828, Jackson's supporters perfected a nationwide organization whose sole purpose was to win the presidential election.

THE REVOLUTION OF 1828

Thomas Jefferson had called the election of 1800 the "Revolution of 1800." In 1800, however, there was not nearly so great a break with what had gone before as there was in Andrew Jackson's victory in the election of 1828. His election ended the era of sedate transfers of power from incumbent president to

secretary of state. Jackson was the first chief executive to come from a western state. (He was the first president who was not from Virginia or Massachusetts.) And the campaign that led to his election was noisier, harder fought, and "dirtier" than any the United States had experienced to date.

Slinging Mud

Personally, Jackson followed precedent by taking no part in the campaign of 1828. He sat in his Tennessee mansion, the Hermitage, while his supporters fired insulting salvos at President Adams. They depicted the incumbent as a usurper, an elitist, a man with effete European tastes who squandered money by filling the White House with elegant furniture and its cellar with European wines. The Democrats made a great fuss over Adams's purchase of a billiard table; billiards, by virtue of the high cost of the table, was a game of aristocrats. (In fact, Adams paid for his toy out of his own pocket.)

Alarmed by the effectiveness of these tactics, the Adams men replied that Jackson was a savage and a murderer. Calling themselves National-Republicans, they reminded voters that Jackson had executed two British subjects in Spanish Florida in 1818 (conveniently forgetting that Adams had supported Jackson after the fact). They printed broadsides that listed the men whom Jackson had killed in duels and the soldiers whom he had ordered shot.

But the assault that stung Jackson was the claim that he and his beloved wife, Rachel, had lived in sin. "Ought a convicted adultress and her paramour husband," wrote a Cincinnati editor, "be placed in the highest offices in this free and Christian land?" The circumstances surrounding the Jacksons' marriage were murky. At the least, Rachel Jackson's divorce was not final when the two wed, thus requiring them to go through a mortifying second ceremony, and they probably cohabited before the first wedding. Laxity in observing the demands of matrimony has never been rare in isolated places like the American frontier. Whatever Rachel Jackson's sexual habits as a young woman, however, by 1828 she was a prim and proper old lady, and she was tortured by the ugly gossip. When she died shortly after the election, Jackson blamed Adams and his supporters for his deeply felt loss.

In the meantime, Jackson's party responded in kind, digging up an old tale that, as minister to Russia, Adams had procured the sexual favors of a

Some Account of some of the Bloody Deeds
OF
GENERAL JACKSON.

Jacob Webb   David Morrow   John Harris   Henry Lewis   David Hunt   Edward Lindsey

A brief account of the Execution of the Six Militia Men.

The "Coffin Handbill," published by pro-Adams forces, presented Andrew Jackson's war deeds and duels as evidence of his barbarism.

young American girl for the dissolute czar. Then there were whispers of bizarre perversions in the Adams White House. Mudslinging had come to American politics with a vengeance. Everything was fair game.

The Symbol of His Age

But it was not mud that won the election of 1828 for Jackson. The party organization, put together by Jackson, Vice President Calhoun, and Martin Van Buren, turned that trick. Jackson swept to victory with 56 percent of a total vote that was more than three times as large as the vote in 1824 and 178 to 83 victory in the electoral college.

The upswing in popular participation carried over to Inauguration Day in 1829 when 10,000 people crowded the streets of Washington. They shocked genteel society with their drinking, coarse shouting, and boisterous invasion of the White House. Invited there by the new president, the mob muddied the carpets, broke crystal stemware, and stood on expensive upholstered sofas and chairs in order to catch a glimpse of their gaunt, white-haired hero.

The adoring mob was so unruly that Jackson's friends feared that he might be injured. They spirited him away through a window, and he spent his first night as president in a hotel. Back at the execu-

Don't Vote for Jackson

Among the campaign mud that found its way into print in 1821 was this aspersion to Andrew Jackson's lineage:

General Jackson's mother was a COMMON PROSTITUTE, brought to this country by the British soldiers! She afterwards married a Mulatto Man, with whom she had several children, one of which number GENERAL JACKSON IS ONE!

tive mansion, worried servants lured the mob outside to the broad lawn by setting up bowls of lemonade and whiskey punch and tables heaped with food.

The man whom these people worshiped was by no sensible definition a common man. Jackson's talents were exceptional, his will and integrity extraordinary. Nor was he the vicious desperado whom the Adams forces depicted. Jackson was a gracious gentleman whose manners, as more than one person announced with an air of surprise, were courtly.

It was also said of Jackson, however, that he was entirely comfortable sitting on a stump, chewing and spitting tobacco, and conversing with the crudest, most plain-spoken, and poorest frontiersmen. If he had become wealthy and ready to defend to the death every last cent and slave's straw hat that he owned, he never forgot his humble origins. Jackson was the first of the log-cabin presidents, the first to reap the rewards of his country's respect for self-made men.

Jackson thought well enough of himself, but he also believed that his success was due to the openness of American society. All people were not equally talented, but the good society provided everyone the opportunity to exploit his abilities and enjoy the fruits of his labor, unimpeded by artificial social and economic obstacles. Government's task was to preserve this opportunity by striking down obstacles to it, such as laws that benefited some and, therefore, handicapped others.

Jackson's view of government was, therefore, essentially negative. He believed that government should, as much as possible, leave people, society, and the economy alone so that natural social and economic forces could operate freely. The common term for this point of view is *laissez faire*, French for, roughly, "to leave alone."

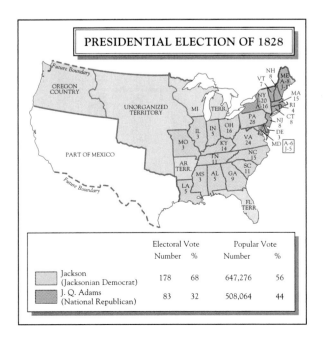

PRESIDENTIAL ELECTION OF 1828

	Electoral Vote		Popular Vote	
	Number	%	Number	%
Jackson (Jacksonian Democrat)	178	68	647,276	56
J. Q. Adams (National Republican)	83	32	508,064	44

Andrew Jackson (1767–1845), a portrait by Thomas Sully.

Attitudes of a Hero, Attitudes of a People

Jackson's vision of equal opportunity extended only to white males; but in this, too, as in his attitudes toward women, children, blacks, and Indians, he also represented the dominant opinion of his era.

Jackson believed that women lived in a different sphere than that of males. While menfolk struggled in an often brutal world, women guarded home and hearth. They were superior to men in religious and moral sensibility; indeed, it was because of these fine faculties that men had to shelter them from a public life that was hardening, at best, and often corrupting. Jackson and most Americans, including women, agreed with the clergyman who preached the "Gospel of Pure Womanhood." Woman's "chastity is her tower of strength, her modesty and gentleness are her charm, and her ability to meet the high claims of her family and dependents the noblest power she can exhibit to the world."

The reward due women for accepting their divinely decreed private, submissive role in the world was the sacred right to be treated with deference. Jackson himself was famous for his chivalry. Rough as the old soldier's life had been, he was prim and prudish in mixed company. Even in the absence of the ladies, he habitually referred to them as "the fair." Adding the word sex would have violated his sense of delicacy.

Toward children, visitors were amazed to discover, Jackson was indulgent. The man who aroused armies to bloodlust and slaughtered thousands without a wince, and the president who periodically exploded in rages that left him (and everyone else) trembling, beamed quietly as young children virtually destroyed rooms in the White House before his very eyes. The British minister wrote that he could not hear the president's conversation because the two men were surrounded by caterwauling children. Jackson smiled absent-mindedly and nodded all the while. At the table, the president fed children first, saying that they had the best appetites and the least patience.

Such indulgence was not universal in the United States. Many New Englanders tried to raise children in the old Puritan manner. But Europeans commented in horror that American children generally had the manners of "wild Indians." Some also noticed that American children were more self-reliant than European children because of the freedom that was allowed them. It was this quality—"standing on your own two feet"—that Jackson and his countrymen valued in their heirs. An unintended consequence of lax child rearing was to create adults who were unable to accept authority easily and to fall into a rage with anyone who contradicted them.

Democracy and Race

Toward Indians and blacks, Jackson also shared the prejudices of his age. Blacks were doomed to be subject to whites by Bible or Mother Nature or both. Blacks were slaves, and American blacks were fortunate to have such enlightened masters. Jackson did not trouble himself with the implications of the doctrine of equal rights—having lived with both the Declaration of Independence and human bondage for 50 years, most Americans found them quite compatible.

HOW THEY LIVED

How They Dueled . . . and Brawled

The duel—an arranged fight in cold blood between two men, in front of witnesses, and according to strict rules—originated in the medieval "wager of battle." A form of ordeal, the wager pitted a person accused of a crime against his accuser. If the accused won, he was declared innocent. Although condemned by religious leaders, the wager of battle survived in France until the 1500s. The duel rose in fashion to take its place.

A duel was not concerned with the guilt or innocence of a crime; it had no standing in the law. The issue in dueling was a gentleman's honor. A man who believed that he or a woman under his protection had been insulted, challenged the perceived villain to meet on the "field of honor." It was not necessary to fight to the death, as it was in the wager. Merely following the intricate code of manners that governed dueling established one's honor. A majority of duels ended when blood was drawn or, if by pistols, when each party discharged his weapon in the general direction of the other. The point was good manners. Only gentlemen dueled; the vulgar multitude brawled.

Although Edward Doty and Edward Leicester fought something on the order of a duel in Virginia in 1621, the custom was almost unknown in colonial America. Careful scholars have found records of but a dozen such fights before 1776. Then, during the Revolutionary War, French officers like Lafayette, Rochambeau, and de Grasse introduced the *Code Duello* to their American friends. A decade later, when French aristocrats fled the revolution in their country and settled in Louisiana, they made New Orleans the dueling capital of America. (On one Sunday in 1839, ten duels were fought in the Crescent City. A woman wrote that the young men of society kept score of their duels, as a young lady kept score of proposals of marriage.)

Dueling spread as rapidly as sudden wealth created self-made men (particularly southerners), who were in a hurry to prove their gentility. Timothy Flint, a northerner, wrote of Mississippi:

Many people without education and character, who were not gentlemen in the circles where they used to move, get accommodated here from the tailor with something of the externals of a gentleman, and at once set up in this newly assumed character. The shortest road to settle their pretensions is to fight a duel.

A *nouveaux* about whom Flint was writing put a better face on it: "A duel makes of every one of us a strong and independent power. . . . It grasps the sword of justice, which the laws have dropped, punishing what no code can chastise—contempt and insult." Librarian of Congress Daniel Boorstin has written that "of southern statesmen who rose to prominence after 1790, hardly one can be mentioned who was not involved in a duel."

It is only a slight exaggeration. Button Gwinnet, a signer of the Declaration of Independence from Georgia, was killed in a duel in 1777. James Madison fought a duel in 1797. Maryland-born Commodore Stephen Decatur fought one duel in 1801 and was killed in another in 1820. William H. Crawford, secretary of the Treasury under Monroe and presidential candidate in 1824, fought a duel. John Randolph of Roanoke fought two, the second in 1826 with Henry Clay of Kentucky, who also fought other men. Hero of the common man Senator Thomas Hart Benton of Missouri fought a number of duels and killed at least one of his opponents. Sam Houston of Texas fought a duel. A great many southerners who were prominent in the Confederacy were involved in duels; among them were William L. Yancey, Vice President Alexander H. Stephens, and General John C. Breckinridge. Confederate President Jefferson Davis was challenged to a duel by Judah P. Benjamin,

As a westerner, Jackson thought a great deal about Indians. He spent much of his life fighting Native Americans and seizing their land. More than any single person, he was responsible for crushing the military power of the great southeastern tribes—the Creeks, Choctaws, Cherokees, Chickasaws, and Seminoles.

Although he was ruthless in these wars, Jackson was not the simple-minded "Indian-hater" portrayed by his enemies (and by some historians today).

who later became a fast friend and served in three cabinet positions. Romantic legend has it that duels were fought over ladies. In fact, as implied in this list, many were fought over politics.

The most famous American duelist was Andrew Jackson, seventh president of the United States, who did fight over insults to his wife. Some of his enemies said that Jackson was involved in a hundred duels. That is unlikely. Even Old Hickory was not so tough or so lucky as to survive that many tests of honor and marksmanship.

However, the written terms of one of Jackson's duels have survived. In 1806, Jackson faced Charles Dickinson, a Nashville lawyer:

> It is agreed that the distance shall be 24 feet, the parties to stand facing each other, with their pistols drawn perpendicularly. When they are ready, the single word fire to be given at which they are to fire as soon as they please. Should either fire before the word is given, we [the seconds of both parties] pledge ourselves to shoot him down instantly. The person to give the word to be determined by lot, as also the choice of position.

Neither Dickinson nor Jackson fired before the word was given, but Dickinson fired first, gravely wounding but not felling Jackson. "Back to the mark, sir," Jackson said when Dickinson staggered in fear of what was to come. Then, according to Jackson's enemies, Jackson's pistol misfired, and in violation of the *Code Duello*, he pulled the hammer back and fired again. This breach of honor haunted Jackson for the rest of his life, for Dickinson died from the dubious shot.

Perhaps it was because of this slur on his character that when a man whom Jackson considered no gentleman challenged him some years later, Jackson refused to duel. But he offered to shoot it out in some "sequestered grove" as long as both parties understood that it was not an affair between social equals.

Actually, according to *The Code of Honor, or Rules . . . in Dueling*, written by a governor of South Carolina, a gentleman who was insulted by a social inferior was to cane him; that is, to flog the impudent lout about the head and shoulders with a walking stick. But Jackson's action points up the fact that in the West, dueling merged indetectably into plain brawling. An Alabama law of 1837 that outlawed dueling also forbade the carrying of the decidedly ungentlemanly weapons "known as Bowie knives or Arkansas Tooth-picks." The people who carried bowie knives were not likely to have read the "Twenty-eight Commandments of the Duel."

Of course, dueling was by no means an exclusively southern and western practice. Alexander Hamilton and Aaron Burr were not southerners. Benedict Arnold was from Connecticut; DeWitt Clinton, from New York; and Nathaniel Greene, from Rhode Island—they all fought duels. Moreover, the practice was just as illegal in the South as it was in the North. Killing a person in a duel was murder, punishable by death. South Carolina imposed a fine of $2,000 and a year in prison for seconds as well as duelists. Officeholders in Alabama were required to take an oath that they never had dueled or acted as seconds.

But Daniel Boorstin is certainly correct to say that the prevalence of dueling in the South up to the Civil War reflected the propensity of upper-class southerners to regard the unwritten laws of honor, manliness, decency, and courage as more important than the laws of legislatures. By the 1850s, the American South was the only part of the English-speaking world where dueling was still accepted in polite society. In the Senate that year, during an acrimonious sectional debate, Henry Foote of Mississippi drew a pistol on Thomas Hart Benton of Missouri.

He found much to admire in Native Americans, especially their closeness to nature and their courage in resisting their conquerors. There was an irrefutable tinge of tragic regret in Jackson's statement to Congress that the white and red races simply could not live side by side and, therefore, the Indians would simply die out. It was unfortunate; it was also the dictate of progress. Race, in Jackson's world, was a mighty force before which all sentiments must bow.

Government by Party

Attitudes are not policies, but President Jackson lost no time in establishing the latter. As the first president to represent a political party frankly and without apologies, he made it clear that he would replace those federal officeholders who had opposed him with his own supporters. One of Jackson's men, William Marcy of New York, phrased the practice of rewarding party members as "to the victor belong the spoils."

There were about 20,000 federal jobs in 1829, and Jackson eventually dismissed about one-fifth of the people in them. Even considering the fact that some federal officeholders supported him, that was by no means a clean sweep. In fact, John Quincy Adams, who never dismissed anyone, privately admitted that many of the people Jackson fired were incompetent.

As for those who were able, when Jackson's critics claimed that the men who were best qualified by education and training should hold government jobs, Jackson answered with quite another theory. He said that every government job should be designed so that any intelligent, freeborn American citizen could perform it adequately.

Attacks on the spoils system were noisy but short-lived. When the anti-Jackson forces eventually came to power in 1840, they carved up the spoils of office far more lustily than Jackson's men had done. The ruling party's patronage of its members became an established part of American politics.

Deliberative Assembly

The House of Representatives, the most democratic branch of the federal government, has rarely been honored as a deliberative assembly, and has been criticized in many eras for less than edifying characteristics. Perhaps never, however, was the House less admirable than during the Age of Jackson. In 1837, a reporter described the floor of the House as a "disgusting compound of tobacco juice, wafers, and sand." He continued, "Not all the soap and scrubbing-brushes in Christendom would make it fit for a peasant's hut." A British diplomat noted that, "judged from the Congress, one would suppose the nation to be the most blackguard society that was ever brought together."

ISSUES OF JACKSON'S FIRST TERM

When he became president, Jackson did not have particularly strong opinions on the questions of the tariff or internal improvements. In his first address to Congress, he called for a protective tariff, but he later drifted (again without passion) to the southern position of a tariff for revenue only.

Internal Improvements

As a westerner, Jackson understood the need for good roads and river channels free of snags and sandbars. As an advocate of laissez faire and of strict construction of the Constitution, however, he worried that it was not constitutional for the federal government to finance them. In 1830, when he vetoed a bill to construct a road between Maysville and Lexington, Kentucky, he told Congress that if the Constitution was amended to authorize such projects, he would approve them.

In the Maysville Road veto, Jackson seems to have been as interested in taking a slap at Henry Clay as in protecting constitutional niceties. The projected road would have been completely within Clay's home state of Kentucky, adding immeasurably to Clay's popularity there. Later, Jackson quietly approved other internal improvement bills when the expenditures promised to win votes for his own party.

On the rising constitutional issue of the day, the division of power between the federal government and the states, Jackson was again inconsistent according to how his personal sensibilities and party interests were involved. When the issue was Georgia's attempt to ignore the federally guaranteed rights of Indians, Jackson allowed the state to have its way. But when South Carolina attempted to defy his power as president, he moved quickly and decisively to crush the challenge—coming close to dusting off his old uniform, polishing his sword, and personally leading an army south.

Indian Removal

The rapid settlement of the trans-Appalachian West brought whites into close contact with large Indian tribes. Congress and Presidents Monroe and Adams agreed that this situation was unworkable. To resolve it, they advocated a policy of "Indian removal," the relocation of the tribes to an Indian Territory west of the Mississippi River that would be guaranteed to them "forever."

To implement removal meant scrapping old treaties that made the same promise. Various agreements gave the Indians lands east of the Mississippi "as long as the water runs and the grass grows." Nevertheless, burdened by demoralization and faced with a combination of inducements and threats, many trans-Appalachian tribes agreed to "removal" farther west.

Others rebelled. The Sac and the Fox of Illinois and Wisconsin rose up under Chief Black Hawk. They were defeated in a war in which a young Abraham Lincoln participated — his only military experience before his presidency. The Seminoles of Florida, their numbers augmented by runaway slaves, also fought back. They were never decisively defeated, but escaped into the swamplands, from where, between 1835 and 1842, they fought an effective holding action against the army.

The Cherokee Go to Court

Still other tribes, such as the Choctaws of the Old Southwest, were defrauded. Federal agents bribed renegade chiefs to sign removal treaties that were then enforced on the entire people. Another of the "civilized tribes," the Cherokees, seemed to win their fight to remain in their ancestral homeland.

Like the Creeks, Choctaws, and Chickasaws, the Cherokees adopted a good many white ways. They gave up their semi-nomadic hunting and gathering economy and farmed intensively, raising cash crops such as cotton, as well as crops for use. They kept black slaves and lived in houses that combined traditional and white American building techniques. In 1821, the tribe adopted an 86-character alphabet that a half-Cherokee silversmith named Sequoyah developed for their language. They printed newspapers and books and operated a school system, one of the best in the South.

According to their treaty with the United States government, the Cherokees were entitled to remain where they were. The tribe was recognized as a

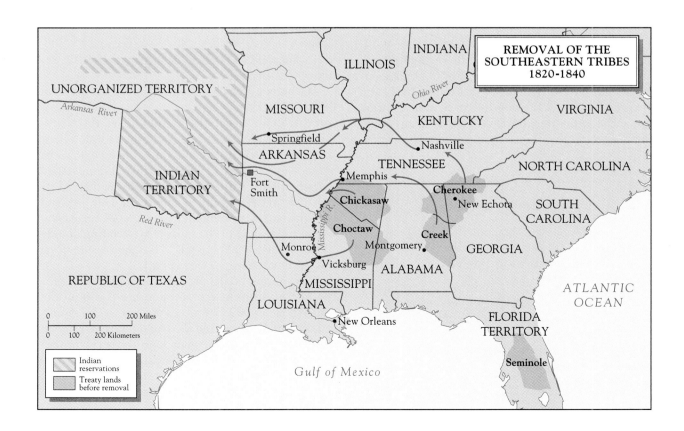

semi-sovereign nation within the United States. Therefore, they refused every attempt of the federal government to force them out.

The state of Georgia was more determined. Unlike in Congress, where the Cherokees had friends, the government of Georgia was dominated by people who wanted the Cherokee lands for whites and were willing to ignore federal treaties to get them. A Georgia court forced the issue by convicting a white missionary of a crime committed in Cherokee territory and, therefore, according to treaty, under tribal jurisdiction. The missionary and the Cherokee nation appealed the case of *Worcester v. Georgia* to the Supreme Court.

Chief Justice John Marshall had no more confidence in the ability of whites and Indians to live side by side than did Andrew Jackson. He had waffled on an earlier dispute between the Cherokees and Georgia. But Marshall was a staunch defender of the sanctity of a contract, which is precisely what the treaty with the Cherokees was. He ruled that the state of Georgia had no authority in Cherokee territory, threw out the conviction of Worcester, and made it clear that Georgia could not force the Cherokees to give up their land.

Sequoyah's invention of the Cherokee alphabet of 86 letters enabled thousands of Cherokees to read and write in their own language.

The Trail of Tears

Marshall's decision seemed to settle the matter, and the Cherokee nation celebrated. But Georgia gambled. The state had opted for Jackson in 1828, and the president was a lifelong Indian fighter. Georgia defied the Supreme Court, held on to its prisoner, engineered some dubious agreements with Cherokees who could be bought, and began the forcible removal of the tribe.

Georgia won its bet. "John Marshall has made his decision," Jackson was quoted as saying. "Let him enforce it." Thus began the Trail of Tears, the 1,200-mile trek of the Cherokees and other southeastern tribes to what is now Oklahoma. General John E. Wool, sent to supervise the forced march, commented distastefully of white Georgians who witnessed its start like "vultures ready to pounce on their prey and strip them of everything they have." A Georgian, who was to fight some of the most heart-rending bloody battles of the Civil War, said, "The Cherokee removal was the cruelest work I ever knew."

Two thousand people died in camps waiting for the migration to begin, and another 2,000 on the trail. About 15,000 Cherokees made it to Oklahoma, scarred and demoralized. It would take two or even three generations to recover, and the survivors remembered the betrayal of their constitutional principles by the white nation that robbed them of their homeland and whose ways they had embraced.

Appeal of the Cherokees

In 1835, its legal rights ignored, the Cherokee nation appealed to Congress on the basis of the values Americans ostensibly prized, values the Indians had adopted as their own.

In truth, our cause is your own. It is the cause of liberty and of justice. It is based on your own principles, which we have learned from yourselves. . . . On your kindness, on your humanity, on your compassions, on your benevolence, we rest our hopes.

16
CHAPTER

IN THE SHADOW
OF OLD HICKORY

Personalities and Politics

1830–1842

If there were two Henry Clays, one of them would make the other President of the United States.

—*Henry Clay*

He prefers the specious to the solid, and the plausible to the true. . . . I don't like Henry Clay. He is a bad man, an impostor, a creator of wicked schemes. I wouldn't speak to him, but by God, I love him.

—*John C. Calhoun*

[Calhoun is] a smart fellow, one of the first among second-rate men, but of lax political principles and a disordinate ambition not over-delicate in the means of satisfying itself.

—*Albert Gallatin*

John Quincy Adams has peculiar powers as an assailant, and almost always, even when attacked, gets himself into that attitude by making war on his accuser; and he has withal an instinct for the jugular and the carotid artery, as unerring as that of any carnivorous animal.

—*Rufus Choate*

Such is human nature in the gigantic intellect, the envious temper, the ravenous ambition, and the rotten heart of Daniel Webster.

—*John Quincy Adams*

Thank God. I—I also—am an American.

—*Daniel Webster*

When Andrew Jackson became president in 1829, few who knew him expected that he would serve for more than one term—if he lived to finish that. To his supporters around the country, Jackson was "Old Hickory"—a tough and timeless frontiersman who stood as straight as a long rifle. In person, he was a frail, 62-year-old wisp of a man who often looked to be a day away from death.

More than six feet tall, Jackson weighed only 145 pounds. No other president was as frequently ill as he. Jackson suffered from lead poisoning (he carried two bullets in his body), headaches, diarrhea, kidney disease, and edema (a painful swelling of the legs). He was beleaguered by coughing fits; during his White House years, he suffered two serious hemorrhages of the lungs.

VAN BUREN VERSUS CALHOUN

Jackson's choice of a vice president, therefore, was a matter of more than passing interest. In giving his approval to John C. Calhoun in 1828, Jackson was not simply pocketing South Carolina's electoral votes. He was naming his heir apparent as president and leader of the new Democratic party.

John C. Calhoun

Like Jackson, Calhoun was of Scotch-Irish background, the descendant of those eighteenth-century emigrants described, in practically every account of them, as quick-tempered and pugnacious. Calhoun was indeed, again like Jackson, a man of passion and stubborn, steely will. Portrait painters captured a piercing, burning gaze just an eyelash short of open rage, never the slightest hint of a smile, never a posture that would indicate that Calhoun knew even odd moments of peace of mind. Photographers, coming along later in his life, confirmed the painters' impressions. He was, in Harriet Martineau's words, "the cast-iron man, who looks as if he had never been born, and never could be extinguished."

Already by 1828, Calhoun was the captive of an obsession. He feared that the social institutions that were the backbone of his beloved South Carolina and much of the South—black slavery and the plantation aristocracy that owed its eminence and privileges to owning slaves—were mortally threatened by the rapid growth of population in the North, the increasing power of industrial capitalists, and what those developments meant for the policies of the national government in the not-too-distant future.

In this fear, Calhoun made a sharp break with his own youthful beliefs. The young Calhoun had been a nationalist and an exponent of industrialization. In 1815, he wanted to "bind the nation together with a perfect system of roads and canals." In 1816, he introduced the bill that chartered the Second Bank of the United States, arguing the desirability of centralizing the nation's financial power. Young man Calhoun urged South Carolinians to build steam-powered cotton mills amidst their fields, monopolizing the profits in their coveted crop from seed to bolt of cloth.

But when the South did not industrialize and the North did, thence demanding high protective tariffs that raised the prices of the manufactured goods that southern agriculturalists bought outside the section, Calhoun changed his tune. He became a defender of agrarian society and the plantation system. He opposed protective tariffs, was critical of internal improvements because of the taxes they meant, and even of the Bank of the United States he had helped

John C. Calhoun (1782–1850) as an old man: dignified, cheerless, unyielding, without optimism.

to found. When voices were raised about the morality of slavery, he became a vociferous exponent of that institution and a scourge of slavery's critics.

Jackson found few faults in such sentiments, but the two men differed about the relationship between the federal and state governments. The president believed the national government supreme. In *The South Carolina Exposition and Protest*, Calhoun proclaimed the state governments sovereign.

So fundamental a difference was quite enough to sour Jackson on his vice president. However, philosophical differences were exacerbated by a tempest on the Washington social scene which also served to create a rival to Calhoun as Jackson's heir.

Peggy O'Neill Eaton

The center of the storm was Peggy O'Neill, the once fetching daughter of a Washington hotel keeper. Peggy had been married to a sailor who, as seamen are inclined to be, was rarely at home. In his absence, Peggy found solace and several children in the arms of one of her father's boarders, Tennessee congressman John Eaton, whom Jackson made his secretary of war.

The affair was worth a whisper and a giggle, but not a good deal more. Such irregular conjunctions were by no means unheard-of in the capital. Washington was no longer the largely male city that it had been when Jefferson was president, but there was still a shortage of quarters suitable to families that lived well at home. Many congressmen continued to leave their wives behind and board at hotels. Inevitably, some found lady friends and, so long as they exercised minimal discretion, little was made

of it. Henry Clay was said to have been a roué, and Richard M. Johnson, vice president between 1837 and 1841, cohabited openly with a woman who was also his slave.

Still, Clay's affairs were quiet and Johnson left his mistress at home when he attended social functions. When Peggy O'Neill's husband died at sea and Eaton married her, he expected Washington society to receive her. Instead, there ensued a great hullabaloo. It was too much to expect women who had been faithful, lifelong, to the gospel of true womanhood, to sip tea with a fallen sister. Peggy O'Neill Eaton was roundly and brusquely snubbed.

The ringleader of the snubbers was Floride Calhoun, the sternly moralistic wife of the vice president. The wives of the cabinet members followed her example, and it aggravated Jackson. When his own niece, who served as his official hostess, refused to receive Peggy Eaton, Jackson told her to move out of the White House. Still mourning the death of his wife, which he blamed on sexual scandalmongers, Jackson also happened to be charmed by the vivacious Peggy. He actually summoned a cabinet meeting to discuss the subject (as he rarely did on political and economic issues), and pronounced her "as chaste as a virgin." He told his advisers to command their wives to receive her socially.

This was too big an order, even for "the Gin'ral." If women were excluded from politics and the professions, the rules of morality and social life were squarely within their sphere. Peggy Eaton continued to find little conversation at social functions. Only Secretary of State Martin Van Buren, who as a widower had no wife to oblige, dared to be seen admiring her gowns and fetching her refreshments.

The Rise of the Sly Fox

Charm and chitchat came naturally to Van Buren. His worst enemies conceded his grace and wit. His portraits, in contrast to Calhoun's, show a twinkle in the eye and a good-natured, intelligent smile.

But Martin Van Buren was much more than a jolly Dutchman. He was a devilishly clever politician, almost always several moves ahead of his rivals, particularly when they were impassioned true believers like Calhoun. Van Buren's wiles earned him the nickname "the Sly Fox of Kinderhook" (his hometown in New York).

He wrote no expositions, but he was the most successful—at least, the most modern—political organizer of his time. He owed his high position in

---

High Praise, Indeed

The testimony to Calhoun's brilliance was unanimous, and to his integrity scarcely less. He was praised by even two of the nation's great abolitionists, men sworn to destroy the institution Calhoun swore to preserve: slavery. William Lloyd Garrison called him "a man who means what he says and never blusters. He is no demagogue." Wendell Phillips spoke of "the pure, manly and uncompromising advocate of slavery; the Hector of a Troy fated to fall."

Jackson's cabinet to delivering most of New York's electoral votes in 1828. He understood that a political party, whatever its ideals, had first and foremost to be a vote-gathering machine; it had to win elections. Therefore, a political party must reward the activists who brought in the votes by appointing them to government positions.

Van Buren was also ambitious for himself. His sensitivity to the feelings of Peggy Eaton may have been quite sincere, but his actions also served to win Jackson's favor. He also offered the impulsive president a way out of the Eaton mess when the affair threatened to paralyze the administration and the leadership of the Democratic party.

Van Buren would resign as secretary of state, and Eaton would give up his post as secretary of war. The other members of the cabinet, whose wives were causing the president so much anxiety, would have no choice but to follow their example. Jackson would be rid of the lot, but no particular wing of the Democratic party could claim to have been wronged.

Jackson appreciated both the strategy and Van Buren's willingness to sacrifice his prestigious office in order to help him. He rewarded Van Buren by naming him minister to England, then, as now, the plum of the diplomatic service.

Calhoun Seals His Doom

The Sly Fox of Kinderhook was lucky, too. While he calculated each turning with an eye on a distant destination, as if he were in a steeplechase, Calhoun blundered and bumped into posts like a blind cart horse. When the Eaton business was still rankling Jackson, the president discovered in some old cabinet reports that, ten years earlier, Secretary of War Calhoun wanted to punish the general for his unauthorized invasion of Florida. Confronted with the evidence, Calhoun tried to explain his way out of his fix in a suspiciously long and convoluted monologue. The president cut him off by writing, "Understanding you now, no further communication with you on this subject is necessary."

Nor, it turned out, was there much further communication between Jackson and his vice president on any subject. In April 1830, Jackson and Calhoun attended a formal dinner during which more than 20 of Calhoun's cronies offered toasts in favor of states' rights and nullification. When it was the president's turn to lift a glass, he rose, stared at Calhoun, and toasted, "Our Union: It must be preserved." Calhoun

got the last word of the evening. He replied, "The Union, next to our liberty, the most dear." But Jackson took satisfaction from the fact that, as he told the story, Calhoun trembled as he spoke.

The old duelist delighted in such confrontations. Van Buren took pleasure in his enduring good luck, for he was in England during the nastiest period of the fight between Jackson and Calhoun, when even the slyest of foxes might have stumbled into a hound.

Then Calhoun blundered again, guaranteeing that Van Buren would succeed Jackson. Seeking personal revenge, Calhoun cast the deciding vote in the Senate's refusal to confirm Van Buren's diplomatic appointment. This brought the New Yorker back to the United States, but hardly in disgrace. Completely in Jackson's good graces by this time, Van Buren was named vice presidential candidate in the election of 1832, an assignment he might not have received had Calhoun left him in London.

THE WAR WITH THE BANK

Unlike his campaigns in 1824 and 1828, Jackson's bid for reelection in 1832 was fought over a serious issue—the future of the Second Bank of the United States. The Second B.U.S. was chartered in 1816 for a term of 20 years. After a shaky start (the Panic of 1819), it fell under the control of Nicholas Biddle, a courtly Philadelphian who administered its affairs cautiously, conservatively, profitably, and, so it seemed, to the benefit of the federal government and the national economy. The B.U.S. acted as the government's financial agent, providing vaults for its gold and silver, paying government bills out of its ac-

---

Rotation in Office

The lifelong Washington careers of Calhoun, Clay, Webster, and Benton belie the fact that a signal characteristic of the early American Congress was turnover. During the first forty years of the republic, 41 percent of the members of the House of Representatives dropped out after each election. Henry Clay's six years as speaker of the House was the longest tenure of any person in that post during the nineteenth century.

counts, investing deposits, and selling bonds (borrowing money for the government when it was needed).

The Powers of the Bank

Every cent that the government collected in excise taxes, tariffs, and from land sales went into the B.U.S., making it a large, fabulously rich, and powerful institution. Its 29 strategically located branches controlled about one-third of all bank deposits in the United States, and did some $70 million in transactions each year.

With such resources, the bank held immense power over the nation's money supply and, therefore, the economy. In a foolish but revealing moment, Nicholas Biddle told congressmen that the B.U.S. was capable of destroying any other bank in the country.

What he meant was that at any moment the B.U.S. was likely to have in its possession more paper money issued by a state bank than that state bank had specie (gold and silver) in its vaults. If the B.U.S. were to present this paper for redemption in specie, the issuing bank would be bankrupt and the investment in it wiped out.

On a day he was more tactful, Biddle said that his bank exercised "a mild and gentle but efficient control" over the economy. That is, simply because the state banks were aware of the sword that the B.U.S. held over them, they maintained larger reserves of gold and silver than they might otherwise have done. Rather than ruining banks, the B.U.S. ensured that they operated more responsibly.

A Private Institution

Biddle was as proud of the public service he rendered as of the bank's annual profits. Nevertheless, the fact remained that the bank was powerful because of its control of the money supply—a matter of profound public interest—but was itself a private institution. B.U.S. policies were made not by elected officials, nor by bureaucrats responsible to elected officials, but by a board of directors responsible to shareholders.

This was enough in itself to earn the animosity of a president who abhorred powerful special interests. Biddle therefore attempted to make a friend of the president by free-handed loans to key Jackson supporters, and he designed a plan to retire the national debt—a goal dear to Jackson's heart—timing the final installments to coincide with the anniversary of the Battle of New Orleans, but to no avail.

Jackson shook his head and explained to Biddle that it was not a matter of disliking the B.U.S. more than he disliked other banks; Jackson did not trust any of them. Like old Bullion Benton, he was a hard-money man. Faced with a stone wall in the White House, Biddle turned to Congress for friends.

The Enemies of the Bank

Biddle needed friends. The bank had many enemies who, except for their opposition to it, had little else in common.

First there was the growing financial community of New York City—the bankers and brokers who would soon be known collectively as "Wall Street." Grown wealthy from the Erie Canal and from New York's role as the nation's leading port, they were keen to challenge the Philadelphia financier's control of the nation's money supply. Second, the free-wheeling bankers of the West disliked Biddle's restraints. Caught up in the optimism of the growing region, these bankers wanted a free hand to take advantage of soaring land values. Oddly, the president, who hated all banks, had the support of a good many bankers in his hostility toward the B.U.S., and they were far from the most virtuous.

A third group that wanted to see the B.U.S. de-clawed was even more conservative in money matters than Biddle. Hard-money men like Jackson and Benton were opposed to the very idea of an institution that issued paper money in quantities greater than it had gold and silver on hand. Most eastern workingmen supported the hard-money position. They were sometimes paid in bank notes that, when they were presented to shopkeepers, were worth less than their face value because of the shakiness of the banks that issued them.

B.U.S. notes were "as good as gold." Nevertheless, the working-class wing of the Democratic party, called "Locofocos" in New York, lumped Biddle along with the rest and inveighed against his monopolistic powers.

The First Shot

For all his hostility toward the B.U.S., Jackson did not pick the fight that escalated into what was called "the Bank War." Henry Clay fired the first shot when, in January 1832, he was nominated for the presidency by supporters calling themselves National-Republicans. Although the bank's charter

A satirical "bank note" expressing the intense dislike of banks by "hard-money" Democrats.

did not expire for four more years, Clay persuaded Biddle to apply for a new charter immediately. A majority of both houses of Congress would support the bid, putting Jackson, as Clay saw it, on the spot.

That is, if Jackson gritted his teeth and signed the bank bill for fear of bucking a congressional majority, all well and good. The B.U.S. was one of the pillars of Clay's American System, as the first Bank of the United States was a pillar of Hamilton's design. If Jackson vetoed the bill, Clay would have an issue on which to wage his presidential campaign. Clay believed that, because the bank proved its value to the national economy, he would defeat Jackson by promising to rescue it.

Clay was not the last presidential nominee to believe that, presented with an issue, voters would decide on the basis of it rather than be dazzled by symbols. Jackson vetoed the bank bill, Clay ran on the issue, and went down resoundingly to defeat. Jackson was still a hero, still the reed vibrating in harmony with the popular mood. He won 55 percent of the popular vote and 219 electoral votes to Clay's 49. (Anti-Masonic candidate William Wirt won 7 electoral votes, and South Carolina gave its 11 votes to John Floyd.)

Financial Chaos

In September 1833, six months after his second inauguration, Jackson took the offensive. He ceased to deposit government monies in the bank, putting them instead into what were called his "pet banks," state-chartered institutions. The B.U.S., however, continued to pay the government's bills out of its account. Within three months, federal deposits in the B.U.S. sank from $10 million to $4 million. Biddle had no choice but to reduce the scope of the bank's operations. He also chose, no doubt in part to sting Jackson, to call in debts owed the bank by other financial institutions. The result was a wave of bank failures that wiped out the savings of thousands of people, just what Jackson had feared B.U.S. power might mean.

Under pressure from the business community, Biddle relented and reversed his policy, increasing the national supply of money by making loans to other banks. This action, alas, fed a new speculative boom. To Jackson's chagrin, many of the 89 pet banks to which he had entrusted federal deposits proved to be among the least responsible in using the money. They, too, fed the speculation.

In 1836, Henry Clay made his contribution to what would be the most serious American depression since the time of Jefferson's embargo. He convinced Congress to pass a distribution bill under the terms of which $37 million was distributed to the states for expenditure on internal improvements. Presented with such a windfall, the politicians reacted as politicians sitting on a bonanza usually do: they spent freely, crazily, backing the least worthy of projects and most questionable of promoters. Values in land, both in the undeveloped West and in eastern cities, soared. Federal land sales rose to $25 million in 1836. Seeking to get a share of the freely circulating cash, new banks were chartered at a dizzying rate. There had been 330 state banks in 1830; there were almost 800 in 1837.

And there was no Bank of the United States to cool things down gradually, for its national charter expired the previous year. Instead, action was left to Jackson, then in his last year of office, and he did the only thing within his power—he slammed a lid on the sale of federal land, the most volatile commodity in the boom. In July 1836, he issued the Specie Circular, which required that government lands be paid for in gold and silver coin; paper money was no longer acceptable.

Jackson's action stopped the runaway speculation, but with a heavy foot on the brake rather than the tug on the reins that the B.U.S. might have used. Western speculators who were unable to pay their debts to the government went bankrupt. Moreover, gold and silver were drained from the East, which contributed to a panic and depression there.

The Giant of His Age

Jackson's financial policy was a disaster built on ignorance and pigheadedness. It would have destroyed the career and reputation of a lesser man as, indeed, it did in the instance of Jackson's successor, Martin Van Buren. By the time the economy hit bottom, however, Jackson had retired to Tennessee. Seventy years old now, the man whom many thought would be lucky to live through one term, enjoying the easy and dignified retirement of a presidency that an old soldier deserved, had cut and chopped his way through eight pivotal years in the history of the nation.

Indeed, though aching and coughing and refusing to mellow (he said his biggest regret was not shooting Henry Clay and hanging John C. Calhoun), Jackson would live for nine more years, observing from his mansion home an era that unfolded in his shadow. He was never a wise man. His intelligence was limited; his education spotty; his prejudices often ugly. He was easily ruled by his passions and confused them with the interests of his country. His vision of America was pocked with more flaws than that of many of his contemporaries, including his enemies.

But for all this he was the symbol, the personification, of a democratic upheaval that changed the character of American politics. He presided over a

Andrew Jackson (1767–1845) became a symbol of a democratic upheaval that changed the character of American politics.

time of ferment in nearly every facet of American life. He set new patterns of presidential behavior by aggressively taking the initiative in making policy. He called upon the presidential veto power more often than had all his six predecessors put together.

Jackson also impressed his personality on a political party and an era that would end only when the slavery issue tore the entire country apart. Even the party that his enemies formed during his second term was held together, to a large extent, by hostility toward him and his memory. And his political foes managed to succeed only when they imitated the methods of the Jacksonian Democrats.

THE SECOND AMERICAN PARTY SYSTEM

By 1834, the realignment of politics resulting from Jackson's triumphs was complete. In the congressional elections that year, the old National-Republicans joined with former Jackson supporters who objected to one or another of his practices—his promiscuous use of the veto, his high-handed treatment of the Indians, his blow against South Carolina, and his war against the bank—and called themselves the Whigs.

Whigs versus Democrats

The word Whig was borrowed from English history. In Britain, the Whig party was traditionally the group inclined to reduce the power of the monarchy and increase the sway of Parliament. In the republican United States, the American Whigs said, the monarch to be reined in was "King Andrew I."

At least at first, the Whigs were held together by a negative impulse, their opposition to Jackson. They were, in fact, a disparate group. In the North, the Whig party included most men of education, means, and pretension to social status. There and in the West, supporters of the American System who believed that the federal government should take the initiative in shaping economic development were Whigs. In the South, high-tariff men, such as Louisiana sugar planters and Charleston financiers tended to be Whigs. Ironically, some strict states' rights advocates like John Tyler of Virginia and, for a short time, the great nullifier, John C. Calhoun, allied with the Whig party.

During the 1830s, Anti-Masons drifted into the party. Traditionalist New Englanders, suspicious of anything attractive to southerners, like the Democratic party, inclined to Whiggery. So did those few blacks who were permitted to vote, and the upper and middle classes of city and town who found the vulgarity of lower-class Democrats and the spoils system offensive to traditional American ideals. In 1834, this patchwork alliance was enough to win 98 seats in the House of Representatives and almost half the Senate, 25 seats to the Democrats' 27. Until the 1850s, while unlucky in presidential elections, the Whigs fought the Democrats on a basis of equality in House, Senate, and in the states.

To the Whigs, they were "the party of hope," the Democratic party "the party of fear," obsessively frightened by progress.

The Godlike Daniel

Except for Henry Clay, the most prominent Whig was Daniel Webster of Massachusetts. At the peak of his powers, he was idolized as a demigod in New England. The adoration owed mostly to his personal presence and his peerless oratorical powers. He was indeed a specimen of a statesman. With a great face that glowered darkly when he spoke, his eyes burned like "anthracite furnaces." A look from him, it was said, was enough to win most debates. Webster was described as "a steam engine in trousers" and "a small cathedral in himself." An admirer said he was "a living lie because no man on earth could be so great as he looked."

In fact, Webster was not a fraction so great as he looked. Although an able administrator and an effective diplomat, Webster possessed less than a shining character. Of humble origin, he took too zestfully to the high life available to the eminent. He dressed grandly, adored good food, and savored the company of the wealthy. He was also an alcoholic, often seen drunk. He invested his money as foolishly as he spent it and was constantly in debt. This tied him yet more closely to the New England industrialists who regularly sent him money. During the bank war, Webster indirectly threatened to end his services as legal counsel to the B.U.S. unless Nicholas Biddle paid him off. (Biddle did.)

Webster came to expect money in the mail after every speech on behalf of the tariff or even the ideal of the Union. As a result, while he remained popular in New England, his not-so-secret vices and venality provided an easy target for the Democrats and made him an object of suspicion among fellow Whigs who took personal integrity as seriously as they took public virtue.

Union and Liberty

And yet, it was this flawed man who gave glorious voice to the ideal that was to sustain the indisputably great Abraham Lincoln during the first years of the Civil War. In 1830, when Calhoun and Jackson were toasting the relative values of union versus liberty, Webster rose in the Senate to tell the nation that "Liberty and Union, now and for ever," were "one and inseparable."

He was replying to Robert Hayne of South Carolina, himself a fine orator who, when Calhoun was vice president, spoke Calhoun's lines on the floor. Hayne identified the doctrine of nullification with American liberty. Webster declared that, on the contrary, the Constitution was the wellspring of liberty in the United States, and the indissoluble union of the states was its greatest defense. "It is, Sir, the people's Constitution, the people's government, made for the people, made by the people, and answerable to the people." The liberty and union speech turned a political abstraction (the Union) into an object for which people would be willing to die. (It also provided three generations of schoolchildren with a memorization piece.)

1836: Whigs versus a Democrat

Differences within the Whig party prevented its convention of 1836 from agreeing on a platform. The delegates could not even agree on a compromise candidate to oppose Martin Van Buren, the Democratic nominee. Consequently, Whig leaders decided on the curious tactic of trying to throw the election into the House of Representatives, as had happened in 1824.

The Whigs named three candidates to run against Van Buren in those parts of the country where each was most popular. Webster ran in lower New England. Hugh Lawson White of Tennessee was the candidate in the South. In the Northwest and upper New England, the Whigs' man was William Henry Harrison, the hero of the Battle of Tippecanoe. Although the battle was a quarter of a century in the past, the party hoped that the memory was still strong among a people ever hungry for new lands.

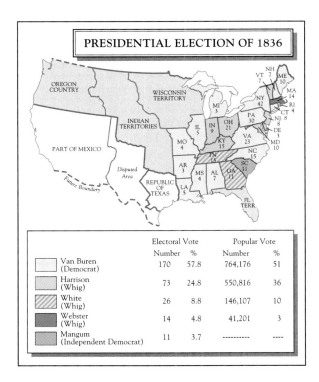

PRESIDENTIAL ELECTION OF 1836

	Electoral Vote		Popular Vote	
	Number	%	Number	%
Van Buren (Democrat)	170	57.8	764,176	51
Harrison (Whig)	73	24.8	550,816	36
White (Whig)	26	8.8	146,107	10
Webster (Whig)	14	4.8	41,201	3
Mangum (Independent Democrat)	11	3.7	----------	----

The strategy failed. While all three Whigs (and cantankerous South Carolina's Democratic candidate, Willie P. Mangum) won some electoral votes, Van Buren carried states in every section and a comfortable 170 to 124 majority in the electoral college. The Whigs held their own in Congress, still the minority but, with South Carolina unpredictable, in a strategic position to influence policy.

Depression

Election to the presidency was just about the last good thing that happened to Martin Van Buren. When his administration was just a few months old, the country reaped the whirlwind of runaway speculation and Jackson's Specie Circular. Drained of their gold and silver, several big New York banks announced in May that they would no longer redeem their notes in specie. Speculators and honest workingmen alike found themselves holding paper money that even the institutions that issued it would not accept as valid.

In 1838, the country sank into a depression. In 1841 alone, 28,000 people declared bankruptcy. Factories closed because their products did not sell. Several cities were unsettled by riots of unemployed workers. Eight western state governments defaulted on their debts.

Van Buren tried to meet the fiscal part of the crisis. A good Jacksonian, he attempted to divorce the government from the banks, which he blamed for the disaster. He established the subtreasury system, by which, in effect, the government would keep its funds in its own vaults. The Clay and Webster Whigs replied that what was needed was an infusion of money into the economy, not a withdrawal of it. But they could not carry the issue.

Van Buren also maintained the Jacksonian faith in laissez faire by refusing to take any measures to alleviate popular suffering. The founding fathers, he said (actually voicing Jefferson's and Jackson's sentiments), had "wisely judged that the less government interfered with private pursuits the better for the general prosperity."

Whatever the virtues of Van Buren's position—whatever the convictions of most Americans on the question of government intervention in the economy—it is difficult for any administration to survive a depression. The president, who reaps the credit for blessings that are none of his doing gets the blame when things go badly, however nebulous

Martin Van Buren (1782–1862) still looks the good-natured bon vivant in this daguerreotype of him as an elderly man.

his responsibility for the misfortune. By early 1840, the Whigs were sure that hard times would give their candidate the White House.

Whig Dilemma

But who was to be the candidate? In that year of likely victory, Henry Clay believed that he deserved the nomination. For 25 years, he had offered a coherent national economic policy that, for the most part, became Whig gospel. For half that time he led the fight against the Jacksonians. More than any other individual, he personified the Whig party.

But Clay's great career was also his weakness. In standing at the forefront for more than a quarter of a century, and a deal-maker by nature, Clay inevitably made mistakes and enemies, some of them bitter. His fellow Whig, Edmund Quincy, wrote of "the ineffable meanness of the lion turned spaniel in his fawnings on the masters whose hands he was licking for the sake of the dirty puddings they might have to toss him." Powerful language!

Victory-hungry young Whigs like Thurlow Weed of New York argued against nominating Clay. Better, he said, to choose a candidate who had no

political record, but who, like Jackson in 1824 and 1828, could be painted up as a symbol. The first and foremost object of a political party, Weed and others said, was to win elections. Only then could it accomplish anything. It was a sentiment worthy of the Sly Fox of Kinderhook.

"Tippecanoe and Tyler Too"

The ideal candidate for the Whigs was William Henry Harrison, an old western warhorse like Jackson, the victor of Tippecanoe, who had the added recommendation of descent from a distinguished Virginia family. (His father signed the Declaration of Independence.) Harrison ran better than any other Whig in the peculiar election of 1836 and he was associated with no controversial political position. Indeed, in 1836, his handlers admonished him to "say not one single word about his principles or his creed, let him say nothing, promise nothing. Let no [one] extract from him a single word about what he thinks. . . . Let use of pen and ink be wholly forbidden as if he were a mad poet in Bedlam."

Harrison was nominated in 1840 under pretty much the same conditions. To appeal to southerners, John Tyler of Virginia was nominated vice president: "Tippecanoe and Tyler Too!"

Marketing an Image

At first the Whigs planned to campaign simply by talking about Harrison's military record. Then a Democratic newspaper editor made a slip that opened up a whole new world in American politics. Trying to argue that Harrison was incompetent, the journalist sneered that the old man would be happy with an annual pension of $2,000, a jug of hard cider, and a bench on which to sit and doze at the door of his log cabin.

Such snobbery toward simple tastes and the humble life were ill-suited to a party that had come to power as the champion of the common man. The Whigs, who suffered Democratic taunts that they were the elitists, charged into the breach. They hauled out miniature log cabins at city rallies and at country bonfires. They bought and tapped thousands of barrels of hard cider. They sang raucous songs like

> Farewell, dear Van,
> You're not our man,
> To guide our ship,
> We'll try old Tip.

Stealing another leaf from the Jacksonian campaign book of 1828, the Whigs depicted Van Buren as an effeminate fop who sipped champagne, dined on fancy French food, perfumed his whiskers, and flounced about in silks and satins. Before he departed for Texas and his death at the Alamo, the colorful Whig politician Davy Crockett depicted Van Buren as "laced up in corsets such as women in a town wear, and if possible tighter than the best of them. It would be difficult to say from his personal appearance whether he was man or woman, but for his large red and gray whiskers."

It was all nonsense. Harrison lived in no log cabin but in a large and comfortable mansion. He was no simple country bumpkin but rather the opposite, a pedant given to tedious academic discourse on subjects of little interest to ordinary people. Van Buren, while indeed the dandy, was also an earthy man who subscribed to much more democratic ideas than did old Tip.

But nonsense worked (as it often has since). Although Van Buren won 47 percent of the popular vote, he was trounced in the electoral college by 60 to 234. Jacksonian chickens had come home to roost. Rarely again would a presidential election be contested without great fussing about irrelevancies and at least an attempt by the favorite to avoid concrete issues.

Moreover, with their successful appeal to the sentiments of the common man, the Whigs of 1840 demonstrated that the democratic upheaval of the preceding two decades was complete. Never again would there be political profit in appealing to the superior qualifications of "the better sort" in the egalitarian United States. What may be most notable about the election campaign of 1840 is that a political candidate was marketed like a commodity—packaged—long before the techniques of modern advertising had been conceived in the world of commerce.

Fate's Cruel Joke

Wherever William Henry Harrison stood on specific issues, he was fully in accord with one fundamental Whig principle—that Congress should make the laws and the president execute them. He was apparently quite willing to defer to the party professionals, particularly Clay, in framing policy. With large Whig majorities in both houses of Congress, the Great Compromiser had every reason to believe that, if not president in name, he would direct the

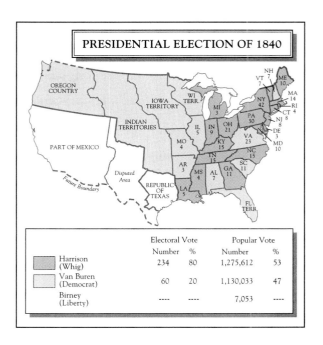

nation's affairs. Old Tip dutifully named four of Clay's lieutenants to the cabinet.

Harrison would have done well to defer to Daniel Webster in his field of expertise—oratory. Webster wrote an inaugural address for Harrison, but the president politely turned it down, having prepared his own. It was the longest, dullest inaugural address on record, a turgid treatise on Roman history and its relevance to the United States of America circa March 1841. Not even historians could have enjoyed it because it was delivered out of doors on a frigid, windy day. And Harrison caught a bad cold.

A Whig Marching Song

Let Van from his coolers of silver drink wine,
    And lounge on his cushioned settee;
Our man on his buckeye bench can recline,
    Content with hard cider is he.
Then a shout from each freeman—a shout
    from each State,
    To the plain, honest husbandman true,
And this to be our motto—the motto of Fate—
    "Hurrah for Old Tippecanoe!"

HOW THEY LIVED

How They Went to College

A university student today would have difficulty recognizing the colleges of the early nineteenth century. A student's life during the Jacksonian era more closely resembled college life in the Middle Ages than in the late twentieth century.

For example, all but a few colleges and universities were private institutions; as late as 1860, only 17 of the 246 colleges and universities in the United States were state-supported. Most were maintained by one or another Protestant denomination in order to train ministers and to indoctrinate other young men in their principles. They were funded by student tuition and by the subsidies that their affiliated churches granted them. This was particularly true of the colleges that were founded during the Jacksonian era, many of which were inspired by the evangelical commitment to reform society.

Colleges were all-male institutions. Higher education was still regarded as the final polishing of a cultivated man, the foundation for public life and for the practice of the professions, particularly the ministry. Women, whose social role most people perceived as domestic and private, had no need for formal learning.

This attitude was beginning to change, however. In 1833, Ohio's Oberlin College, a hotbed of reform, began to admit women students. A few colleges and universities followed suit, but the real expansion of educational opportunities for women came not with coeducation but with all-female institutions. The first of these were Georgia Female College in Macon (now Wesleyan College) and Mount Holyoke College in South Hadley, Massachusetts, founded by Mary Lyon in 1837.

College was not vocationally oriented, as it is today. That is, students were not taught the specific skills involved in the career they had selected. The young man who wanted to become an accountant, an engineer, an architect, or a businessman in the early nineteenth century apprenticed himself to someone skilled in those callings and learned "on the job." Women mastered skills thought proper to them at home. Although some universities had established medical and law schools, apprenticeship was also the most common means of preparing for those professions, too.

At college the curriculum remained much as it had been for centuries, a strictly prescribed course of study in the liberal arts and sciences (liberal in this case meaning "suitable to a free man"). Students learned the ancient languages (Latin, Greek, sometimes Hebrew), literature, natural science, mathematics, and political and moral philosophy—according to the beliefs of the church that supported the institution. Some colleges added modern languages and history by the Jacksonian period, but there were no "electives"; every student took the same courses.

The colleges were small. Except for the very oldest, such as Harvard and Yale universities, and for some public institutions, such as Thomas Jefferson's University of Virginia, the typical student body numbered only a few dozen and the typical faculty perhaps three or four professors and an equal number of tutors. Although faculty members and students came to know one another by sight and name, relations between them were not informal and chummy. On the contrary, professors erected a high wall of formality and ritual between themselves and those whom they taught, both out of the belief in the principle of hierarchy and out of the fear that too much friendliness would lead to a breakdown in discipline. Historian Joseph F. Kett has pointed out that stiff-necked behavior by instructors often owed to the fact that many of them were little older and sometimes even younger than most of their students. For example, Joseph

---

For weeks he suffered, half the time in bed, half the time receiving Whig office seekers as greedy as the Democrats of 1828. Then he took permanently to bed with pneumonia. On April 4, 1841, exactly one month after lecturing the country on republican virtue, he passed away.

John Tyler

At first the Whigs did not miss a stride. Clay lectured "Tyler Too" that he should consider himself an acting president, presiding over the formalities of government while a committee of Whigs chaired by

Caldwell became *president* of the University of North Carolina when he was only 24 years old.

Student behavior was regulated by long lists of detailed rules. Students were expected to toe the line not only in class but also in their private lives. Attendance at religious services was mandatory at most private institutions. Strict curfews determined when students living in dormitories turned out their lamps. Impoliteness might be punished by a fine or suspension, a practice that is seeing a revival in the "sensitive speech" policies of many contemporary universities. Students were expected to be deferential at all times.

This was the theory, at any rate. In practice, college students were at least as rambunctious as students of every era and more rebellious than any, save the generation of the 1960s. They defied their professors by day—the distinguished political philosopher Francis Lieber had to tackle students he wanted to discipline—and they taunted them by night. A favorite prank was stealing into the college chapel and ringing the college bell until dawn. Students threw snowballs and rocks through the windows of their tutors' quarters. They led the president's horse to the roof of three- and four-story buildings. Students at Dickinson College in Pennsylvania sent a note to authorities at Staunton, Virginia, where the college president was visiting, informing them that an escaped lunatic headed their way would probably claim to be a college president and should be returned under guard.

Other student actions were rebellions and not just pranks. Professors were attacked by mobs angry at strict rules or poor food. Professors sometimes were stoned, horsewhipped, and fired on with shotguns. At the University of Virginia in 1840, Professor Nathaniel Davis was murdered. Writing to his own son at college in 1843, Princeton Professor Samuel Miller warned against so much as sympathizing with potential rebels. Miller lived in fear of student uprisings, perhaps because one rebellion at Princeton was so serious that the faculty had to call in club-wielding townspeople to help put it down.

Why so much discontent? One reason is that the rules of college life were written at a time when most college students were 14 to 18 years old, while, by the early nineteenth century, college students were often in their mid-twenties. Adults simply were not inclined to conform to behavior appropriate to adolescents, and in a society that took pride in individual freedom, they were quite capable of reacting violently to constraint.

Moreover, many college students lived not in dormitories but in their own lodgings in nearby towns. They fraternized largely with other students and developed a kind of defiant camaraderie directed against all outsiders. Enjoying broad freedoms in their off-campus lives, they were unlikely to conform to strict rules of behavior when they were at the college.

Finally, while the rules were strict, enforcement was often inconsistent. "There were too many colleges," writes Joseph F. Kett, "and they needed students more than students needed them." Faculty members who were nervous for their jobs overlooked minor offenses until they led to greater ones, at which point, suddenly, they drew the line. Inconsistency, as ever, led to contempt for would-be authority.

Colleges might expel or suspend the entire student body for "great rebellion." However, financial pressures apparently resulted in their readmission for the price of a written apology. Samuel Miller described student rebels as "unworthy, profligate, degraded, and miserable villains," but if they had the tuition, there was always a place for them somewhere.

Clay made the real decisions. John Quincy Adams, now a Whig representative from Massachusetts, concurred. Tyler would have none of it. A nondescript man who had little imagination and a provincial view of national problems, Tyler insisted that the Constitution authorized him to exercise the same full presidential powers that he would have had if elected to the office.

Nevertheless, Tyler did his best to get along with Clay. He went along with the abolition of the subtreasury system, and, although a low-tariff man, he agreed to an increase of rates in 1842 as long as the

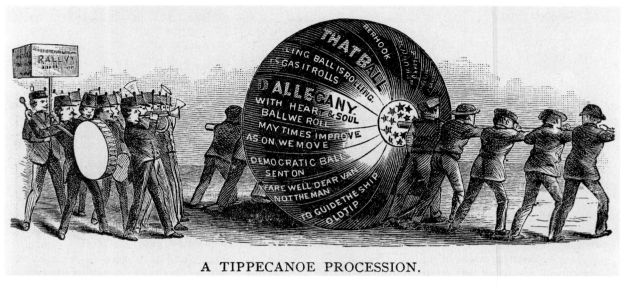

A TIPPECANOE PROCESSION.

During the campaign of 1840, the Whigs' great paper ball covered with slogans was rolled throughout the Midwest and Northeast to shouts of "Keep the ball rolling!"

rise was tied to ending federal finance of internal improvements. Tyler also supported Clay's attempt to woo western voters from the Democrats with his Preemption Act of 1841. This law provided that a family who squatted on up to 160 acres of public land could purchase it at the minimum price of $1.25 per acre without having to bid against others.

A President without a Party

But Tyler was not a real Whig. He had split with Jackson over King Andrew's arrogant use of presidential power. As a planter, his views on other issues were closer to those of John C. Calhoun (and Jackson!) than to those of the nationalistic northern and western Whigs. Most important, Tyler disliked the idea of a national bank and warned Clay not to try to force one on him.

Clay tried anyway, and Tyler vetoed one bank bill after another. Furious, the majority Whigs expelled the president from the party, and Tyler's cabinet resigned (except Secretary of State Webster, who wanted to complete some touchy negotiations with Great Britain). Clay left the Senate in order to prepare for the presidential campaign of 1844.

After the blow-up, Tyler's cabinet was made up of nominal southern Whigs much like Tyler himself. He hoped to piece together a new party of states' rights Whigs and Democrats for the contest of 1844.

Toward this end, he named John C. Calhoun secretary of state.

But party loyalty was too strong among both Whigs and Democrats for Tyler's scheme to work. Moreover, Calhoun had defied the Democrats too often to be in good graces with solid party men. In effect, Tyler served as a president without a party. The major political consequence of his presidency was the beginning of the deterioration of the Whig party in the South. States' righters like Tyler and Calhoun drifted back toward the Democratic party. In time, the great planters would not only return to the party of Jackson, but they would take it over.

British–American Friction

The major accomplishment of the Tyler administration was in the area of foreign affairs: solving a series of potentially dangerous disputes with Great Britain, and paving the way for the annexation of the Republic of Texas.

The first was a Whiggish goal that was engineered by Daniel Webster. One of the problems was a boundary dispute between Maine and New Brunswick. According to the Treaty of 1783, the line ran between the watersheds of the Atlantic and the St. Lawrence River. Both sides had agreed to the boundary as shown by a red line that Benjamin Franklin had drawn on a map.

The map disappeared, however, and in 1838, Canadian lumberjacks began cutting timber in the Aroostook Valley, which the United States claimed. A brief "war" between the Maine and New Brunswick militias ended with no deaths, and Van Buren managed to cool things down. But he could not resolve the boundary dispute.

The Canadian–American line immediately west of Lake Superior was also in question, and two other points of friction developed over American assistance to Canadian rebels and over the illegal slave trade in which some Americans were involved. The slavery issue waxed hotter late in 1841, when a group of blacks on the American brig *Creole* mutinied, killed the crew, and sailed to Nassau in the British Bahamas. The British hanged the leaders of the mutiny but freed the other slaves, enraging sensitive southerners.

The Webster–Ashburton Treaty

Neither England nor the United States wanted war, but old rancor and the British determination to build a road through the disputed Aroostook country repeatedly stalled a settlement. Fortuitously, Webster found a kindred spirit in the high-living British negotiator, Lord Ashburton, and over brandy they worked out a compromise. Webster made a big concession to the British, too big as far as many New Englanders were concerned. But never above a little chicanery, Webster actually forged Franklin's map to show a red line that gave Maine less territory than he had negotiated, and he warned that the United States had better take what it could get. (The real map surfaced some years later, and revealed that the United States was shorted.)

Ashburton was generous, too. He ceded a strip of territory in northern New York and Vermont to which the United States had no claim, and also about 6,500 square miles at the tip of Lake Superior. While wilderness at the time, the area around Lake Superior later became known as the Mesabi Range, one of the world's richest iron ore deposits.

When the Senate ratified the Webster-Ashburton Treaty in 1842, every outstanding issue between the United States and Britain was settled, except the two nations' joint occupation of Oregon on the Pacific coast. Webster had good reason to be pleased with himself, and he joined his fellow Whigs in leaving John Tyler's cabinet.

Pop Art

In 1834, when the hero of the common man still sat in the White House, Nathaniel Currier of New York democratized American art. He began to sell cheap prints featuring natural wonders, marvels of technology such as locomotives, battles, portraits of prominent people, and scenes of everyday life, both sentimental and comical.

Currier and James Ives (the partner arrived in 1852) sold their prints for as little as 25 cents for a small black and white print, to up to $4 for a hand-colored picture measuring 28 by 40 inches. They were cheap enough to be afforded by the poor, just expensive enough to be acceptable as a wall-hanging in a self-conscious, middle-class household.

More than 7,000 Currier and Ives prints were produced by a process that can only be called "industrial." Some experts specialized in backgrounds, others in machinery, others in individual faces, yet others in crowd scenes. By the late nineteenth century, it was a rare American who could not have identified "Currier & Ives" to an inquirer.

CHRONOLOGY

1829 Andrew Jackson sworn in as president, John C. Calhoun as vice president
Jackson learns that Calhoun is author of *The South Carolina Exposition and Protest* (1828) while Peggy O'Neill Eaton affair agitates Washington society

1830 Jackson and Calhoun openly hostile on issue of state sovereignty versus federal authority
Webster's "Reply to Hayne" identifies the Union with liberty

1832 Henry Clay spearheads early renewal of charter of Bank of United States as a presidential campaign issue
Jackson defeats Clay for presidency; Martin Van Buren elected vice president

1833 Jackson begins to deposit government money into "pet banks," many of which prove irresponsible

1834 National-Republicans and anti-Jackson Democrats form the Whig party

1836   Clay's Distribution Bill fuels wild speculation in western lands
In Specie Circular, Jackson abruptly halts speculation leading to destruction of many banks
In presidential election, Van Buren defeats three Whig candidates and one independent

1838   Serious depression begins

1840   Whigs nominate William Henry Harrison to oppose Van Buren in presidential election

Harrison elected in "Log Cabin and Cider" campaign

1841   Harrison dies after one month in office, first president to die while in office. He is succeeded by John Tyler, who soon clashes with Clay and other Whigs
Slaves on American brig *Creole* rebel and sail to Bahamas

1842   Webster-Ashburton Treaty resolves conflicts between United States and Great Britain

FOR FURTHER READING

For overviews, see Glyndon G. Van Deusen, *The Jacksonian Era, 1828–1848*, 1959; Edward Pessen, *Jacksonian America: Society, Personality, and Politics*, 1978; Robert Remini, *The Revolutionary Age of Andrew Jackson*, 1985; and, to appreciate the political and cultural values that informed Jackson's era, John W. Ward, *Andrew Jackson: Symbol for an Age*, 1955. The appropriate chapters of Richard Hofstadter, *The American Political Tradition and the Men Who Made It*, 1948, are still stimulating. Richard P. McCormick, *The Second American Party System*, 1966, is essential.

Martin Van Buren, if almost forgotten in popular culture, is the subject of three excellent biographical studies: D. B. Cole, *Martin Van Buren and the American Political System*, 1984; John Niven, *Martin Van Buren: The Romantic Age of American Politics*, 1983; and M. L. Wilson, *The Presidency of Martin Van Buren*, 1984. For his hapless nemesis, see Margaret Coit's now classic *John C. Calhoun: American Portrait*, 1950, and the more critical Richard N. Current, *John C. Calhoun*, 1966.

Dealing with the Bank War are Bray Hammond, *Banks and Politics in America*, 1957; Sean Wilentz, *Chants Democratic: New York City and the Rise of the American Working Class, 1788–1850*, 1983; Robert Remini, *Andrew Jackson and the Bank War*, 1967; and John McFaul, *The Politics of Jacksonian Finance*, 1972. Sympathetic to Biddle's position is Thomas P. Govan, *Nicholas Biddle: Nationalist and Public Banker*, 1959.

D. W. Howe, *The Political Culture of the American Whigs*, 1979, is a fine survey of a subject long neglected except in biographies. Among the best biographies of the Whigs are Glyndon Van Deusen, *The Life of Henry Clay*, 1937; Robert V. Remini, *Henry Clay: Statesman for the Union*, 1991; Richard N. Current, *Daniel Webster and the Rise of National Conservatism*, 1955; Sydney Nathan, *Daniel Webster and Jacksonian Democracy*, 1973; and M. G. Baxter, *One and Inseparable: Daniel Webster and the Union*, 1984. An important collective biography is Merrill D. Peterson, *The Great Triumvirate: Webster, Clay and Calhoun*, 1987. On the election of 1840 and its aftermath, see R. G. Gunderson, *The Log Cabin Campaign*, 1957.

An artist's rendition of New Harmony captured the sense of idyll the community's founders envisioned.

17

CHAPTER

SECTS, UTOPIAS, VISIONARIES, REFORMERS

Popular Culture in Antebellum America

God has found it necessary to take advantage of the excitability there is in mankind, to produce powerful excitements among them, before he can lead them to obey. Men are so spiritually sluggish, there are so many things to lead their minds off from religion, and to oppose the influence of the Gospel, that it is necessary to raise an excitement among them, till the tide rises so high as to sweep away the opposing obstacles.

—Charles G. Finney

To what extent can competence displace pauperism? How nearly can we free ourselves from the low-minded and the vicious, not by their expatriation, but by their elevation? To what extent can the resources and the powers of Nature be converted into human welfare, the peaceful arts of life advanced, and the vast treasures of human talent and genius be developed? How much of suffering, in all its forms, can be relieved? or what is better than relief, how much can be prevented? Cannot the classes of crimes be lessened, and the number of criminals in each class be diminished?

—Horace Mann

Before the Age of Jackson, literate Europeans thought of the United States as a cultural backwater, of little more interest to people of breeding than the Indians with whom the Americans fought and the Africans whom they enslaved.

Sidney Smith, a British wit, exquisitely lacerated American culture in 1820: "In the four quarters of the globe, who reads an American book? or goes to an American play? or looks at an American picture or statue? What does the world yet owe to American physicians or surgeons? What new substances have their chemists discovered? or what old ones have they analyzed? What new constellations have been discovered by the telescopes of Americans?—What have they done in the mathematics?"

Few of Smith's readers would have disagreed, including those Americans who imported his *Edinburgh Review*. Then, suddenly even, with the rise of Jacksonian democracy, American political practices and the everyday lives of the people pricked the interest of literate Europe and became something of a mania.

AS OTHERS SAW US

Before 1828, Europeans published some 40 books about the United States. After 1828, when Jackson's election seemed to roll in an era of the common man, the drollery of the notion enchanted educated Europeans. Hundreds of books about Americans were published in little more than a decade. Capitalizing on the curiosity of European readers, popular authors such as Frederick Marryat, Anthony Trollope, and Charles Dickens crossed the Atlantic to describe the scenery, explain the political institutions, and wonder over the manners, morals, quirks, and crotchets of the American people. The best of the books were by a French aristocrat, Alexis de Tocqueville and an English gentlewoman, Frances Trollope.

Best Sellers

In the first volume of *Democracy in America*, published in 1835, Tocqueville explained American political institutions, emphasizing their democratic character. He was intrigued by the implications of a people ruling themselves. In a second volume, published in 1840, Tocqueville commented on the social attitudes and customs of the democratic Americans.

Tocqueville found much to admire in the United States. Because he was a traditionalist, he was sur-

---

> ### *Book Learning*
>
> At the start of the nineteenth century, Great Britain, with a population of 18 million, published up to a thousand books per year. The United States, with a population of six million, published twenty.

---

prised to discover how well democratic government worked, and he admitted it. He had no trouble liking Americans as individuals. However, because Tocqueville believed that spiritual values and continuity in human relationships were essential to a healthy society, he was concerned that Americans seemed always on the move. Tocqueville was disturbed by the Americans' undiscriminating love of the new and contempt for the old, and most of all the relentless pursuit of money in Jacksonian America.

The subject of Mrs. Trollope's *Domestic Manners of the Americans*, published in 1832, was everyday life. With an eye as keen as an eagle's and a wit as sharp as talons, she swooped through American parlors, kitchens, drawing rooms, cabins, steamboats, theaters, churches, and houses of business—and liked very little of what she found there. Like Tocqueville, Mrs. Trollope was disturbed by the materialism, individualism, and instability of American society. On the former, she cited an English resident of the United States who told her "that in following, in meeting, or in overtaking, in the street, on the road, or in the field, at the theatre, the coffee house, or at home, he had never overheard Americans conversing without the word DOLLAR being pronounced between them."

Mrs. Trollope observed, as did others, that Americans rushed through hastily prepared meals. They trotted rather than walked down the street. (Frederick Marryat wrote that a New York businessman "always walks as if he had a good dinner before him and a bailiff after him.") Americans fidgeted when detained by some obligation lest they miss something in another part of town. When they did bring themselves to sit down they whittled wood, so unable were they to be still.

"The Very Houses Move"

More than one foreign observer remembered as a symbol of their American experience the spectacle of a team of sweating horses pulling a house on rollers from one site to another. Nothing in the United States was rooted, neither the homes nor the mighty oaks that westerners mowed down like hay, nor customs nor social relationships nor religious beliefs that had served humanity well for centuries.

Such instability was not without casualties, and dollar worship was not without its native critics. Many people failed through no fault of their own in the frantic decades of the early nineteenth century. The boom-and-bust financial cycle turned rich men into debtors and threw workers out of jobs that barely kept their families fed.

In the older agricultural regions of the Northeast, people whose forefathers were secure on small farms flirted with destitution as foodstuffs cheaper than those they produced flowed in from the West on newfangled canals and then railroads. Townspeople were disoriented by constant exposure to a more diverse and complicated world than their parents were confronted with in a lifetime: strangers passing through, some of them to pluck the locals as they went; immigrants from abroad coming to dig the ditches, gravel the roadbeds, and work in the new factories; promoters urging their

This idealized domestic scene is typical of what Mrs. Trollope might have seen during her visit to America.

children to strike for the West, where they would prosper and, of course, disappear.

Westerners were uprooted by definition. They were freed from old restraints, moral as well as economic, but also deprived of the comforts of family connections, tightly knit communities, and institutions that were not so mobile as they were. Small wonder that in addition to being a time of extraordinary economic growth, the Age of Jackson was also an era when people groped for explanations of topsy-turvy change and attempted, in their spiritual lives, to come to terms with it.

RELIGION IN THE EARLY NINETEENTH CENTURY

The end of the eighteenth century brought decline to organized religion in both the numbers of church members and influence. The Anglican church suffered because it was so closely tied to Great Britain. Congregationalists supported independence, but, in the 1790s, they bitterly opposed Thomas Jefferson. When he triumphed in 1800 and blood did not run in the gutters of Hartford and Portsmouth—as many

---

Unitarians

Unitarianism originated in 1785 when a Boston church struck from its services all references to the Trinity because the notion seemed idolatrous. The denomination spread rapidly throughout New England as the church of enlightened, generally well-to-do people. (A working-class equivalent of Unitarianism was Universalism.)

The Unitarian God was tailored to fit the worldly optimism of a comfortable people. He was not a distributor of justice and retribution but a kindly, well-wishing father. In the words of William Ellery Channing, the most famous early nineteenth-century Unitarian preacher, God had "a father's concern for his creatures, a father's desire for their improvement, a father's equity in proportioning his commands to their powers, a father's joy in their progress, a father's readiness to receive the penitent, and a father's justice for the incorrigible." He was not the God of John Winthrop and Jonathan Edwards.

---

ministers had predicted—Congregationalism lost its hold on many New Englanders. In the Jacksonian era, Massachusetts and Connecticut, the last states to pay ministers out of tax monies, ceased to do so.

Educated Americans abandoned old-time Calvinism because its overriding doctrine of predestination no longer accorded with the abundant, benign world they saw around them. Instead, they turned to rationalistic churches dedicated largely to ethics: Unitarianism and Universalism. Lyman Beecher, a Presbyterian and one of the giants among the clergymen of his era, commented on his arrival in Boston, "All the literary men of Massachusetts were Unitarians; all the trustees and professors of Harvard College were Unitarians; all the elite of wealth and fashion crowded Unitarian churches."

The Second Great Awakening

In fact, old-time religion did not disappear so much as it changed form, adapting to the democratic spirit of the new era. In the Second Great Awakening, eloquent preachers such as Charles Grandison Finney crisscrossed the Northeast with the message that, just as the Puritans had preached, human nature was tainted. Unlike the Puritans, Finney said that not just a few elect were saved through God's grace—God would bless everyone who repented and prayed for deliverance from his sinful nature.

A well-turned revivalist sermon began with an emotional description of the capacity of human beings for evil, of which sensible people have never needed proof. The second part of the sermon detailed the gruesome sufferings of hell, for which all sinners were destined. Like good politicians, however, the revivalists concluded on an optimistic note. Any person could be saved in the Christianity of equal opportunity if he or she repented and declared faith in Jesus Christ. Religion was voluntary, salvation a matter not of God's will, but of man's. "Don't wait!" Finney said, "Do it!, get saved!"

Tenting on the Old Camp Ground

Because few frontier settlements had buildings large enough to hold a big crowd, western revivalists held their meetings in openings in the forest sometimes cleared specifically for the purpose. Beginning in Kentucky at the turn of the century, people who lived isolated, lonely lives responded by the thousands to calls to come a-tenting, more than 20,000 in one instance. Camp meetings attracted would-be converts (and plenty of scoffers) from 200 miles away.

Such a concentration of humanity was itself exhilarating on the thinly populated frontier. But there was something else. The atmosphere of the camp meeting was electrifying. Dozens of preachers simultaneously harangued the crowd, some from well-constructed platforms, others from stumps. The meeting went on for a week or more. When the day's final pleas tailed off in the early morning hours, the moans of excited people could be heard from every direction.

Conversions were passionate. People fell to their hands and knees, weeping uncontrollably. Others scampered around on all fours, barking like dogs. A common manifestation was the "jerks." Caught up in the mass hysteria, people lurched about, their limbs jerking quite beyond their control. An oft-told tale was that a man who cursed God was seized by the jerks and broke his neck.

Small wonder that European tourists listed the camp meeting as one of the two peculiarly American sights that they "just must see." (The other was the slave auction.) Indeed, many Americans went just for the show and the chance to exploit the occasion with thieving, heckling, heavy drinking, and sexual opportunities.

Circuit Riders

The excesses of the camp meetings led inevitably to a reaction against them. Even the Methodists, who were among the earliest organizers of frontier revivals, drew back from what often became carnivals. Instead, they offered the circuit rider, a minister assigned to visit ten or twenty little western settlements that were too poor to support a resident parson. Intensely devoted, poorly paid, and usually unmarried, the circuit riders rode through slashes in the woods in all weather. They preached, performed marriages and baptisms, took their rest and meals in the cabins of the faithful, and rode on. The most famous of the circuit riders, Finis Ewing and Peter Cartwright, were rarely off their horses for more than three days at a time over more than three decades.

When towns grew to more than a dozen or so cabins, individualistic Americans were rarely able to agree on one denomination to serve the whole community. A town of a thousand might support half a dozen churches: Methodist (or Free Methodist, for the denominations divided and multiplied); Baptist (or Primitive Baptist or Free Will Baptist); Presbyterian; Disciples of Christ; and so on.

New denominations also sprouted and grew in Jacksonian America. Most of them withered and died with the first frost but others survive to this day. The two most durable homegrown religions of the period originated in a part of rural New York called the "burned-over district," because fiery revivals flared up there so often.

The Adventists

In 1831, a Baptist named William Miller began to preach that Christ's "Second Coming" to earth—the end of the world—would occur between March 21, 1843, and March 21, 1844. He convinced tens of thousands throughout the northeastern states with the complex mathematical formula by which he came to his unnerving conclusion.

At the beginning of the fateful year, a magnificent omen appeared in the sky for a month—it was Halley's comet—and converts flocked to join Miller's Adventists. (Advent means "coming" or "arrival.") Many sold their possessions and contributed the proceeds to the sect, which led critics to accuse Miller and his associate, Joshua V. Himes, of fraud.

On March 21, 1844, in order to be first to greet the Lord, several thousand people throughout New York and New England climbed hills in "Ascension Robes" (sold to them by Himes). When the sun set without incident, Miller discovered an error in his computations and set the date of the Second Coming at no later than October 22, 1844. Again some towns frothed with hysteria as the day approached. An even greater disappointment descended upon the land when, again, Christ did not appear. Miller himself was bewildered and broken. A disciple named Hiram Edson reorganized remnants of his followers around the more serviceable belief that the world would end soon. Because Edson observed the Jewish sabbath, Saturday, rather than Sunday, the new denomination became known as Seventh-Day Adventists.

The Mormons

The Church of Jesus Christ of the Latter-Day Saints, or Mormons, also originated in the burned-over district. The founder of the church was Joseph Smith, a daydreamer who preferred wandering the hills of the declining region to the tedious chores of farm life. When he was 20, Smith told his family and neighbors that, on one of his rambles, an angel, Moroni, showed him some gold plates bearing mysterious inscriptions which, using miraculous spectacles, Smith

Mormon Bitterness

Mormon Hosea Stout remembered welcoming the news of the Mexican War: "I confess that I was glad. . . . I hoped the war might never end until the States were entirely destroyed, for they had driven us into the wilderness, and now were laughing at our calamities."

was able to read. The story he translated was *The Book of Mormon*, a Bible of the New World telling of the descendants of the ancient Israelites in America, the Nephites, whom Christ had also visited.

Tales like Smith's had long circulated in the folklore of the burned-over district. To many Americans, told from childhood that their country was a new Eden, it was not preposterous that Christ should have visited the New World as well as Judea. To people unsettled by the frenzied pace of the Age of Jackson, it was not surprising that God should make his truth known in upstate New York. It was a time, as one of Smith's converts, Orson Pratt, wrote, when "wickedness keeps pace with the hurried revolutions of the age." Poet John Greenleaf Whittier, who was not a Mormon, wrote of the saints that "they speak a language of hope and promise to weak, heavy hearts, tossed and troubled, who have wandered from sect to sect, seeking in vain for the primal manifestation of divine power."

Persecution

Smith offered a way out of the era, but he was also his era's child. He extended the priesthood of his new religion to all white males, thus appealing to the Jacksonian yearning for equality, and he went west, taking his followers to Ohio, Missouri, and finally, in 1840, to Nauvoo, Illinois. The Mormons prospered. By 1844, Nauvoo was the largest city in the state.

Their prosperity as a group, and the Mormons' undisguised dislike of outsiders, whom they called "gentiles," begat envy and resentment, the same sort of dislike of secret, closed societies that produced the Anti-Masonic movement. Nevertheless, because the Mormons of Nauvoo voted as a bloc, they were courted by both Whig and Democratic politicians. Joseph Smith could probably have been elected to

high office in Illinois by trading Mormon votes for a major party nomination.

Instead, in 1844, he declared that he would be an independent candidate for the presidency. This news, added to fears of the well-armed Mormon militia of 2,000, the Nauvoo Legion, led to Smith's arrest. On June 27, with the complicity of officials, he and his brother were murdered in Carthage, Illinois.

Eden in the Desert

The Mormons might well have foundered had not an even more remarkable (and politically wiser) individual grappled his way to the top of the church hierarchy. Brigham Young also received revelations directly from God. The most important of these was the command that the Latter-Day Saints move beyond the boundaries of the sinful nation that oppressed them.

The Mormon migration was organized to the finest detail. Advance parties planted crops that would be ready for harvesting when the multitudes arrived on the trail. Nevertheless, the trek was harsh. Many Mormons actually walked, pulling heavy-laden carts as if they were oxen. It was a long walk. For his Zion, Young chose the most isolated and inhospitable region known to the explorers of the age, the basin of the Great Salt Lake.

"This is the place," he said, looking down from the Wasatch Mountains, and there the Mormons laid out a tidy city with broad avenues and irrigation ditches fed with water from the surrounding peaks. The desert bloomed. Within a few years more than 10,000 people lived in the Salt Lake basin.

At the same time the Mormons were constructing their Zion, American victory in war with Mexico brought them back under the American flag. Young did not fight the troops that arrived in Salt Lake, but he made it clear that real federal control of Utah, which the Mormons called Deseret, depended on cooperating with him. Prudently, the authorities named Young territorial governor.

Despite its large population, Utah was not admitted to the Union until 1896. Brigham Young had proclaimed polygamy official church doctrine in 1852 (Mormons had already been practicing it; Young himself had 27 wives and 56 children) and Congress refused to grant statehood until, in 1890, Young's successor received a revelation that polygamy was to be abandoned. Disputation on the issue among Mormon sects remains an issue in the Great Basin today.

Salt Lake City, the capital of the Mormon Zion, was as orderly as the Mormons were disciplined.

UTOPIAN COMMUNITIES

The Mormons lived in highly regulated communities in which individual rights and the freedom to accumulate private riches were subordinated to the good of the whole; indeed, the early Mormons practiced a form of communism. Similar social experiments held great appeal to people who were distressed by the poverty and moral misery that were, along with material progress, the fruits of a wide-open competitive economy. Some of the communities they founded were built on a religious foundation. Others were based on secular social theories.

The Shakers

Like the Mormons, the Shakers held property in common. They practiced celibacy because, like the Millerites, they believed that the Second Coming was imminent; therefore, it was unnecessary to perpetuate the human race. Founded and brought to the

United States by an English woman, Mother Ann Lee, the movement flourished as a refuge for people who sought stability in the tumultuous Jacksonian period. During the 1830s, the Shakers maintained

Whole Lot of Shakin' Goin' On

The true name of the Shakers was the United Society of Believers in Christ's Second Appearing. But outsiders began calling them "Shakers" because, among their other practices, they performed rhythmic dances (in groups, not men with women). They accepted this name despite its probably having been attached to them with derision. A century earlier, the Society of Friends had become known as Quakers in much the same way. Deriders had made fun of the admonition of the founder of the movement to "quake" on hearing the word of God.

more than 20 neat and comfortable communities in which men and women lived in separated quarters.

After their earliest years, the Shakers were not persecuted and ridicule of them was rarely malicious. Celibacy was peculiar, but it did not offend conventional morality, as did free love and polygamy. Indeed, as a group that needed converts in order to survive, the Shakers were unfailingly polite, cooperative, and fair in their dealings with outsiders. They lived simply, exciting no resentment of their prosperity. They had no secrets. In fact, the Shaker communities were popular tourist attractions because of the fine workmanship and elegant simplicity of their crafts, which they sold in order to support themselves.

Role Models

Religious communitarians like the Shakers withdrew from society in order to save their own souls. Other utopians, although not necessarily irreligious, were primarily interested in the social aspect of their communities, setting an example that others might follow. They had theories about what was wrong with the larger society (which almost always included its material preoccupations and commitment to private property), and sought to show the world, by the contentment of their alternative way of life, how the whole society should be organized.

New Harmony, Indiana, was founded in 1825 by Robert Owen, a British industrialist who, in an age of "dark, satanic mills," had created a model of paternalism at his textile mill in New Lanark, Scotland. About a thousand people responded to Owen's call to build a community at New Harmony in which all property was to be held in common, and life was to consist not of drudgery for the enrichment of some, but of joyous work for the good of all.

Unfortunately, the idealists at New Harmony were joined by many people who were interested only in the weekly philosophic discussions and, in between, an easy life financed by Owen. Believing deeply in the goodness of human nature, Owen was incapable of throwing out freeloaders. In 1827, disillusioned and a good deal poorer, he returned to Scotland. Within a short time, New Harmony broke up, and the old fields, orchards, and vineyards went to seed and weeds.

Fruitlands

Another star-crossed utopia was Fruitlands, the brainstorm of Bronson Alcott, a magnificent eccentric who is best remembered as the father of the author Louisa May Alcott. A lovable philosophizer, Alcott was incapable of coping with workaday life. He was, according to Louisa, "a man up in a balloon, with his family and friends holding the ropes which confine him to earth." Alcott inaugurated his communitarian lesson to the world by planting fruit trees within two feet of the front door of the community house, dropping his shovel, and returning to his meditations and endless colloquies with the collection of crackpots who gathered at Fruitlands.

One, whose name was Abram Wood, announced his defiance of worldly ways by deciding that his name was really Wood Abram. Another would not weed the garden because weeds had as much right to grow as did vegetables. Samuel Larned lived for one year on nothing but crackers (so he said) and the next on apples. A woman who could no longer tolerate the vegetarian diet at Fruitlands and ate a piece of meat at a neighboring farm was driven out as if she were a murderess. Another Fruitlander said that the way to break loose from empty social conventions was to greet people by saying, "Good morning, God damn you!" Everyone at Fruitlands agreed that cows were disgusting, but this doctrine was not enough to sustain the vitality of the community.

Through it all, Mrs. Alcott kept things afloat by doing most of the work. It is not clear if this sturdy, stoical, and resourceful woman ever took seriously a word her husband said.

Oneida: A Success Story

Most utopias were founded on the belief that private property was the source of injustice and human unhappiness. In this, they were rebelling against the most conspicuous phenomenon of the period—the helter-skelter competition for riches. In addition to private property, John Humphrey Noyes attacked the institution of marriage. Wedlock, he said, was itself a form of property: under American laws and customs, the husband effectively owned his wife. Hence, both were miserable.

Rejecting celibacy as an alternative, Noyes devised the concept of "complex marriage." In Oneida, New York, every man was married to every woman. Couples who chose to have sexual relations for pleasure (the initiative was the lady's) could do so, but not for the purpose of procreation. Noyes was an early exponent of what came to be called eugenics, improving the quality of the human race (and therefore society) by allowing only those superior in

Members of the Oneida community founded by John Humphrey Noyes believed that every man was married to every woman, a concept they called "complex marriage." They abandoned the concept in 1879.

health, constitution, and intellect to have children. (His method of birth control was male continence.)

Oneida's practice of free love, like the Mormons' polygamy, enraged the community's neighbors, and Noyes fled to Canada to escape arrest. Oneida, however, enjoyed a long life. The community prospered from its manufacture of silverware, silks, and a superior trap for fur-bearing animals. Finally abandoning complex marriage in 1879 and communal property in 1881, the surviving Oneidans reorganized as a corporation.

TRANSCENDENTALISM

Noyes was a Perfectionist. He believed that Christ's redemption of humanity was complete. Individuals had it within themselves to be perfect—that is, without sin—and therefore above rules that had been written for the imperfect. People had only to face up to their own potential for perfection, and it would be so.

Perfectionism was not so very far out of step with the popular spirit of the Jacksonian era. It was a time when, figuratively speaking, Americans believed that everything was within human competence. Noyes's error was to take the implications of his philosophy literally. When he put sinlessness into practice at Oneida by approving behavior that offended conventional morality, he was run out of the country.

Ralph Waldo Emerson, by way of contrast, became America's favorite philosopher by calling Perfectionism by another name—Transcendentalism—and by avoiding its implications in the way he led his life.

The Sage of Concord

Emerson was a Unitarian pastor in Boston whose assessment of human nature glowed with warmth and love. In 1832, despite his comfortable congregation's approval of his views, he announced that he could no longer accept the Unitarian practice of celebrating the Lord's Supper. He resigned and moved to Concord, Massachusetts, then well outside Boston.

"The profession is antiquated," Emerson said of preaching. But within a few years he was preaching again, albeit from a lectern rather than a pulpit. He shook his head sagely that people should cling to superstition, yet his own message was a welter of notions far more mystical than the Christianity of sophisticated Boston.

Transcendentalism defied criticism. Based on feelings rather than reason, Transcendentalism exalted a vague concept of nature's superiority to civilization, personal morality over laws, and the individual's capacity within himself to be happy, or sinless. When his ideas were criticized as fuzzy or contradictory, Emerson responded that his critics were not morally capable of understanding that the enlightened human being could dispose "very easily of the most disagreeable facts."

Transcend means "to go beyond, to rise above." As used by Emerson and his disciples, it meant to go above reason and beyond the material world. God was not a being, but a force. God was the oversoul, which was within all men and women because it was in nature. "Standing on the bare ground," Emerson wrote, "my head bathed by the blithe air and uplifted into infinite space—all mean egotism vanishes. I become a

Ralph Waldo Emerson (1803–1882) was America's popular philosopher.

"I'm OK, You're OK"

In February 1834, when he was 23 years of age, John Humphrey Noyes explained his doctrine of perfectionism to a classmate at Yale. "Noyes says he is perfect," his friend said. "Noyes is crazy." Noyes also wrote the good news in somewhat convoluted form to his mother: "The burden of Christian perfection accumulated upon my soul until I determined to give myself no rest while the possibility of the attainment of it remained doubtful." Polly Hayes Noyes, a no-nonsense Vermont farmwife, puzzled over the letter while she worked and said to her daughter, "Whatever does John mean?"

---

transparent eyeball; I am nothing; I see all; the currents of the Universal being circulate through me."

The writer Herman Melville, a contemporary of Emerson, called these teachings gibberish. But while Melville struggled to eke out a living with his writing—the great *Moby Dick* was a commercial failure— Emerson was lionized and able to make a good living. While Melville scrutinized the problem of evil in the world, Emerson ignored it along with other disagreeable phenomena.

Other Transcendentalists

Emerson's friend Henry David Thoreau was the introspective son of a Concord pencil manufacturer. Unlike the proper Emerson, Thoreau flaunted his eccentricity. In 1845, he constructed a small cabin in the woods near Walden Pond, just outside Concord. There he wrote *Walden* (1854), an account of his reflections while sitting by the pond.

Although *Walden* is the masterpiece of Transcendentalism, it is marred by the same dilettantism that robs Emerson's works of lasting value (except as masterpieces of style). Thoreau wrote as if he had seceded from civilization and struck off into the wilderness: "I wanted to live deep and suck out all the marrow of life, to live so sturdily and spartan, like as to put to rout all that was not life, to cut a broad swath and shave close, to drive life into a corner, and reduce it to its lowest terms."

But Walden was no Rocky Mountain fastness. It was a short walk to Concord, a walk that Thoreau took often when he felt like having a decent meal. Living deep and sucking the marrow out of life was rather like camping in the backyard.

Dissenters

Nathaniel Hawthorne and Margaret Fuller knew both Emerson and Thoreau, but they were never fully sympathetic with Transcendentalist euphoria. Both were romantics. But when Hawthorne looked into the human heart, he found evil rather than the divinity perceived by Emerson's transparent eyeball, and Fuller was impatient with the Transcendentalists' contentment to issue broad political pronouncements instead of cutting a broad swath and shaving close in real political action.

"The heart, the heart," Hawthorne wrote, "there was the little yet boundless sphere wherein existed the original wrong of which the crime and misery of the outward world were merely types." Guilt, sin, and moral decay were the themes of his many books, the lasting value of which is generally conceded. He and Melville were heretical soulfellows and good friends.

Margaret Fuller lived far more daringly than Thoreau. She took part in Giuseppe Garibaldi's rebellion in Italy, and died in a shipwreck while returning to the United States. Fuller was also a hard-headed thinker and a political activist. In 1845, three years before feminism emerged as a social and political movement, Fuller published *Woman in the Nineteenth Century*, a scathing indictment of the arguments against female equality. She died too soon to participate in the feminist movement, but Fuller was, in her writings, a bridge between the reflective thought of her age and its busy devotion to practical social action.

EVANGELICAL REFORMERS

Jacksonian America was a place of social tension. For a person inclined to see them, it was obvious that there were casualties as well as conquerors, and the latter whisked too quickly past the weak and unfortunate.

Some did not whisk by. Some Americans, mostly New Englanders, were moved by evangelical religious fervor to believe that society, like their souls, could be saved. Just as salvation was up to the individual, individuals could improve the lives of their fellow creatures. Indeed, the evangelicals believed it was their moral duty to bear witness against evils, social as well as personal.

Political activist Margaret Fuller (1810–1850) published a scathing indictment of the arguments against female equality in 1845, three years before the emergence of an organized feminist movement in America.

Gallaudet, Howe, and Bridgman

Thomas Gallaudet, an Episcopal clergyman, was grieved by deafness, and society's indifference to people without hearing. Traditionally, Americans regarded deafness, blindness, and other physical disabilities as punishment for sin, trials designed by God for the purpose of sanctification, or simply an unhappy circumstance visited on some by the roll of life's dice.

Building Self-Esteem

"Trust men," Ralph Waldo Emerson proclaimed, "and they will be true to you; treat them greatly and they will show themselves great." Herman Melville replied: "God help the poor fellow who squares his life according to this."

Whatever the case, physical handicaps were personal misfortunes under which the sufferer was to bear up, cared for by family or community. The individual who strove to overcome a handicap was of interest and edifying, but the problem was personal, not society's concern.

Gallaudet, a devoted evangelical, believed that the Christian was his brother's keeper, and the unique social isolation of the deaf troubled him. Learning in 1815 of techniques for teaching lip-reading and sign language developed in England, Gallaudet crossed the Atlantic where, he was disgusted to discover, the new methods were trade secrets, an article of commerce guarded as closely by the people who profited from them as a textile manufacturer guarded the plans for his weaving machines. To Gallaudet, tools for doing good were not to be bought and sold.

In France, he found a teacher of the deaf whose views accorded with his own. The men returned to the United States and, in 1817, founded the American Asylum, a free school for the deaf in Hartford, Connecticut. Gallaudet taught his techniques to every interested party and encouraged others to establish institutions like the American Asylum in other cities.

Samuel Gridley Howe organized the Perkins Institute for the Blind in Boston. Not only did he publicize his techniques, but, being a bit of a showman, Howe toured the country with a young girl named Laura Bridgman who was both deaf and blind. Howe had established communication with her, laying to rest the widespread assumption that such seriously handicapped people were helpless. Even overwhelming impediments to human fulfillment, Howe said, could be overcome if men and women were willing to do their moral duty.

Dorothea Dix

The plight of the insane aroused less sympathy than that of the physically handicapped. Traditionally, retarded people and harmless idiots were cared for by their families and communities and otherwise ignored or mocked. Dangerous lunatics were locked up at home or by legal authorities.

The line between violent insanity and criminality was blurred. Many a lunatic was hanged. Others were recognized as lacking moral responsibility but, nonetheless, confined in prisons or asylums where treatment consisted of little more than restraint. It was not uncommon for asylum guards to charge admission to visitors and goad the inmates into performing antics.

In 1841, Dorothea Dix, a teacher at a girls' school in Massachusetts, discovered that in the Cambridge House of Correction, the insane were locked in an unheated room, even in the depths of the Massachusetts winter. At 39, Dix had lived a genteel, sheltered life. She was pious and shy, and often ill. Her discovery of the evils in treatment of the insane galvanized her, and she became one of the most effective reformers of the century.

In 1843, she drafted a memorandum to the Massachusetts state legislature in which she made her case in the best evangelical terms:

> If I inflict pain upon you, and move you to horror, it is to acquaint you with sufferings which you have the power to alleviate, and make you hasten to the relief of the victims of legalized barbarity. . . . I proceed, gentlemen, to call your attention to the state of insane persons confined within this Commonwealth in *cages, closets, cellars, stalls, pens! Chained, naked, beaten with rods, and lashed* into obedience.

Dix's revelations did not square with New Englanders' image of themselves as the nation's most enlightened people. ("O New England," Noah Webster wrote, "how superior are thy inhabitants in morals, literature, civility, and industry!") The Massachusetts legislature immediately passed a bill to enlarge the state asylum and improve conditions elsewhere. Dix then carried her message throughout the nation and the world. She persuaded Congress to establish St. Elizabeth's Hospital for the Insane and 15 states to build humane asylums. She traveled to Europe, where she moved both Queen Victoria and the pope to improve treatment of the mentally deficient.

Crime and Punishment

Another institution that attracted the notice of reformers was the penitentiary. Large prisons for convicts serving long terms were new to the United States. Until the late eighteenth century, lawbreakers were rarely given long prison terms. The most serious crimes were punished by hanging: there were as many as 16 capital offenses in some states, including rape and homosexuality. Other felonies merited a flogging or physical mutilation. In Massachusetts, as late as 1805, counterfeiters, arsonists, wife beaters, and thieves were whipped or had their ears

Demented men and women were subjected to fantastical and often cruel "cures."

cropped or cheeks branded with a hot iron. Petty offenses—to be drunk and disorderly, disturbing the peace—were punished with fines or the humiliation of a dunking, the stocks, or the pillory.

During the 1790s, influenced by the Declaration of Independence and an Italian criminologist, Cesare Beccaria, most states reduced the number of capital offenses, abolished mutilation, and restricted the use of whipping. They turned instead to prison sentences as a means of punishing crime. However, conditions of confinement were execrable; for instance, Connecticut used an abandoned mine shaft as its penitentiary.

Prison Reform

It was generally agreed that the purposes of prison were punishment and the protection of society. As reformers pointed out, however, the security of society was not improved if prison transformed people into hardened criminals. In confining minor offend-

ers with habitual offenders, penitentiaries acted as schools of crime.

These observations led to the idea of the prison as a correctional institution, a place for moral and social rehabilitation. Theories as how best to accomplish this worthy goal differed. The Pennsylvania System, for example, kept its convicts in solitary confinement. The idea was that inmates would meditate on their crimes and leave prison determined not to offend again.

The flaws of the Pennsylvania System were twofold: individual cells were extremely expensive, and total isolation resulted in numerous cases of mental breakdown. The Auburn System, named after the town in which New York's state prison was located, addressed the problem of isolation by marching prisoners each day to large workrooms and a common dining hall. Conversation was forbidden, both to prevent education in crime and to keep order. Eventually, the Auburn System was adopted by other states, including Pennsylvania.

Another innovation of the period was the house of refuge, in which juveniles were kept isolated from adult criminals. By 1830, New York City, Philadelphia, and Boston maintained such facilities. Also after 1830, the practice of public executions declined. Reformers rejected the ancient belief that the sight of a man dangling from a rope provided a grim lesson for onlookers when as many as 10,000 people eagerly flocked to witness executions. It was obvious from the spectators' ribald behavior that they were there to enjoy a good show, not for the purposes of moral edification.

MORAL UPLIFT

Similarly undesirable behavior among the masses inspired a second kind of evangelical reform during the early nineteenth century. While Gallaudet, Howe, and Dix attended to injustices suffered by a few, other reformers addressed social problems that afflicted the entire society.

Demon Rum

For example, Americans drank heavily. They always had. In part, bibulousness was owed to the fact that grain was abundant and cheap in the United States. More was grown than was needed as food or could find ready markets abroad. English-style ales, cider, and rum were the everyday beverages of the East. In

NOTABLE PEOPLE

Notable Feminists

Elizabeth Cady Stanton (1815–1902) and Susan B. Anthony (1820–1906)

While individuals such as Fanny Wright and Margaret Fuller raised eloquent objections to the inequality of the sexes before 1848, that year marks the beginning of feminism as a social and political movement in the United States. Three of the four women who can be called the Founding Mothers of American Feminism were present in the little town of Seneca Falls, New York, during the second week of July 1848 when the "Declaration of Sentiments and Resolutions," a biting parody of the Declaration of Independence, was presented to the country.

Lucretia Coffin Mott (1793–1880) and Elizabeth Cady Stanton (1815–1902) had been friends for a number of years by virtue of their participation in the cause of abolition. In 1840, they tried to register as delegates to an international antislavery convention in London (it was Stanton's wedding trip), but they were refused admission because they were women. The injustice and the absurdity of it—people committed to the equal rights of the races defending the inequality of the sexes—rankled on them. But not until eight years later did they conclude that the rights of women deserved the same kind of fight as did the rights of blacks. Mott and Stanton were principal authors of the declaration "that all men and women are created equal" and the demand for "immediate admission of all to the rights and privileges which belong to them as citizens of the United States."

Both remained active in the long and mostly frustrating battle for female equality until their deaths at ripe ages. They were good-humored people—Stanton, a portly mother of seven, could be downright garrulous—living disproof of the sour-faced fanatics that enemies of the women's movement liked to depict feminists as being. However, they were not afraid to defy the powerful social convention that women should take no part in public life. In 1861, Stanton addressed the New York State legislature; she called for a reform of divorce laws, which, like those in other states, discriminated against and even sealed the social exorcism of divorced women.

Amelia Jenks Bloomer (1818–1894), by way of contrast, was a shy, retiring woman who was more comfortable alone with a pen than at the speaker's lectern. Ironically, her name was affixed to what was, at mid-century, considered the ultimate proof that the women's movement was ridiculous—the reform costume known as "bloomers."

Mrs. Bloomer attended the Seneca Falls convention but did not sign the declaration. Over the next several years, she drew closer to Stanton and increasingly devoted her temperance newspaper, *The Lily*, to questions of sexual inequality. In 1851, Bloomer

the West, the daily tonic was whiskey. Wine and brandy—most of it imported—were fixtures of middle- and upper-class life.

Few social occasions lacked alcohol. The hospitable family's first act upon receiving a guest was to uncork a bottle or to tap a barrel. Urban workingmen insisted that they needed liquor for strength, and employers of both craftsmen and unskilled laborers provided a ration, sometimes a big one, as part of the day's pay. As well, farmers were notorious for the little brown jugs that accompanied them in the fields.

By 1820, the annual consumption of spirits (not including beer, cider, and wine!) was more than 7.5 gallons for each American man, woman, and child. There were about 15,000 licensed distilleries in the country, and private stills were as common as chicken coops.

Temperance

Drunkenness was regarded as sinful and socially disruptive. During the 1780s, Dr. Benjamin Rush, a Philadelphia physician, described the physically de-

began to advocate reform in women's dress. Female fashion at the time consisted of tightly laced corsets, layers of petticoats, and floor-length dresses that had to be held up in the dusty, muddy, or garbage-strewn streets. The corset was dangerous — literally maiming vital organs — and a kind of shackle. It was difficult to do much of anything in the constrictive garb but to wear it.

The bloomer costume dispensed with the corset in favor of a loose bodice, substituted ankle-length pantaloons for the petticoats, and cut the outer skirt to above the knee. It was, in fact, not new in 1851, when Elizabeth Smith Miller, not Amelia Bloomer, dared to wear it in public. Women at the utopian colony of New Harmony had worn something like the reform costume, as had otherwise quite conventional women at lake and seaside resorts. But Miller and Bloomer wanted to make it standard wear. Because Mrs. Bloomer was its best-known exponent in the pages of the widely circulated *Lily* (and because her name suggested the billowing pantaloons), bloomers they came to be called.

Mrs. Bloomer wore the reform costume for about ten years. However, Stanton and her principal associate after 1852, Susan B. Anthony, gave up on it after only one year. Like many reformers before and since, they discovered that when they tried to emphasize issues that lay close to the heart of women's inferior status, enemies and journalists were more interested in the highly eccentric dress they wore.

As the century progressed, the most important feminist issue became the vote, woman suffrage, and the name of Susan B. Anthony (1820–1906) became synonymous with it. Ironically, like her friend Mrs. Stanton, Anthony considered the woman's plight as much broader than mere disenfranchisement. But as the vote alone was regarded by otherwise conservative women as a respectable demand they would support, Anthony went along for the sake of unity.

An unmarried woman, Susan B. Anthony was able to devote all her time to the movement. The other founding mothers, burdened with the duties of marriage and motherhood, were unable to do so. For more than half a century — from 1852, when she was refused permission to speak at a temperance convention, until her death in 1906 — she labored tirelessly for the cause that was still unfulfilled at the time of her death. Not until the Nineteenth Amendment to the Constitution was ratified in 1920 was the right of women to vote guaranteed.

All four of the founding mothers had connections with the Quakers, a sect that almost alone in the United States took the education of girls seriously. All but Bloomer had some formal schooling, which was very unusual in early nineteenth-century America. Every one of them was also interested in other reform movements: temperance, peace, costume, abolitionism (and some trivial quackeries). And all believed in principle that the emancipation of women depended on more than gaining the right to vote.

structive effects of excessive drinking. With the blossoming of the evangelical spirit during the 1830s, anti-alcohol reformers added two more arrows to the quiver.

First, they published statistics showing that a substantial number of crimes were committed by people who were drunk. Second, they drew a connection between poverty and drinking. A few said that the miseries of poverty led to drunkenness. Most, steeped in moralism and the evangelical sense of individual responsibility, believed that drunkenness was the reason for poverty.

The temperance movement then spread rapidly. By 1835, there were 5,000 temperance societies in the United States with a membership of more than a million. In 1840, six reformed sots founded a national organization, the Washington Temperance Society. Two years later, a more militant association, the Sons of Temperance, began to promote sobriety as a basic religious duty.

One of the Sons' most effective lecturers was John B. Gough, a former drunk who rallied audiences with the lurid language of the fire-and-brimstone revivalist: "Crawl from the slimy ooze, ye drowned drunkards, and with suffocation's blue and livid lips speak out against the drink." Wherever Gough preached, men and women tearfully swore off the bottle.

Prohibition

Anti-alcohol reformers, however, quarreled and split as promiscuously as the utopians. One line of division ran between the advocates of temperance in the use of alcohol and the complete abstainers. The former argued traditionally that drunkenness was the evil, not alcohol itself. They lodged no objection to the occasional sip of wine or restorative dram. The abstainers, observing that alcohol was addictive, concluded that it was inherently sinful. Moderation was not enough. It was necessary to swear off drink completely.

The Sons of Temperance was one of the largest and most effective organizations of the early anti-alcohol crusade.

> ### *Germans in America*
>
> Germans were so numerous in Texas in 1843 that the Texas Congress published the Lone Star Republic's laws in the German language. By 1860, there were 100,000 Germans in New York City. They supported 20 churches, 50 schools, 5 printers, and a theater.

A political dimension was added when the teetotalers divided between moral suasionists, who regarded abstinence from drink as an individual decision, and legal suasionists, who considered the prohibition of the manufacture and sale of liquor as a means of reforming society.

In 1838, Massachusetts experimented with a law designed to cut down alcohol consumption among the poor. The Fifteen Gallon Law prohibited the sale of whiskey or rum in quantities smaller than fifteen gallons. However, the temper of the Age of Jackson man ran against any device that provided privileges to the rich, who could afford to buy spirits in bulk. The Fifteen Gallon Law was repealed within two years.

In 1845, New York adopted a more democratic law, which authorized local governments to forbid the sale of alcohol within their jurisdictions. Within a few years, five-sixths of the state was dry. In 1846, the state of Maine, led by Neal Dow, a public-spirited Portland businessman, adopted the first statewide prohibition law. By 1860, 13 states had followed suit. But the custom of drinking was too much a part of the culture to be abolished by well-meaning ordinances. Prohibition laws were flagrantly violated and, by 1868, they were repealed in every state but Maine.

Temperance and prohibition were largely Protestant movements supported by evangelical reformers and directed toward native-born old-stock Americans. In the 1840s, however, the crusade against alcohol took on a new urgency because of the huge influx of immigrants who had (so far as reformers were concerned) an inordinate devotion to beer and whiskey.

The Stresses of Immigration

Only 8,400 Europeans came to the United States in 1820, hardly enough to excite notice. More than 23,000 arrived in 1830, however, and 84,000 in 1840.

In the midcentury year, at least 370,000 people stepped from immigrant ships onto wharves in the eastern seaports.

Not only were they numerous, but the immigrants of mid-century were, for the most part, people adhering to religious faiths little known in the United States and, in many cases, they spoke languages other than English.

Thirty-six hundred Irish came to the United States in 1820, many of them Protestant; 164,000 arrived in 1850, most of them Roman Catholic. Immigration authorities counted only 23 Scandinavian immigrants in 1820 and 1,600 in 1850, a number that would nearly triple within two years. In 1820, 968 Germans entered the United States; in 1850, 79,000 arrived.

Scandinavian and German immigrants inclined to cluster in sizable communities, retaining their languages and preserving Old World customs. Among these was the convivial beer garden, where families gathered to drink lager beer, first introduced to the United States in this era. To a teetotaler, the Irish were worse. They were notoriously given to gathering in saloons in cities and on construction sites, drinking whiskey. And they were Roman Catholic, as were about half of the German immigrants. Between 1830 and 1860, when the general population slightly more than doubled, the Roman Catholic population of the United States increased tenfold—from 300,000 to more than 3 million.

The "Whore of Babylon"

The growth of Catholicism in the United States was difficult for many Protestants to swallow. Since the days of the Puritans, they had been taught that the Church of Rome was the Bible's Whore of Babylon, not merely another Christian denomination but a fount of evil.

This prejudice took on new life in the second quarter of the nineteenth century because the pope, the spiritual leader of the world's Catholics, was also perceived as the political head of a reactionary and repressive state. In the papal states of central Italy, dissidents were jailed and, it was believed, tortured. The political principles of Catholicism seemed to be

The sudden flood of immigrants into the United States created a period of social turmoil, as reflected in this lithograph of an 1844 anti-Irish riot in Philadelphia.

the very antithesis of American traditions of democracy and liberty. Because of the intense devotion of most Irish immigrants to their faith and the authority of their priests, many Protestants feared that they were the shock troops of political reaction.

Moreover, the vast majority of the Irish immigrants were destitute. Landless in their native land, they were forced to emigrate because of extreme deprivation and, in the 1840s, because of the failure of the Emerald Isle's potato crop. Once in the United States, they were willing to accept work at almost any rate of pay, prompting Protestant workingmen to regard them as a threat to the traditionally high standard of living that at least skilled mechanics enjoyed. When economic unease combined with religious suspicion and the evangelical crusade against the new immigrants' apparently heavy drinking, the result was a social and political movement.

Anti-Catholicism and the Know-Nothings

The famous painter and inventor of the telegraph, Samuel F. B. Morse, wanted to cut off the immigration of Catholics. Anna Ella Carroll, in *The Great American Battle*, warned that Catholicism would "swallow up America." Street wars between Protestant and Irish Catholic workingmen regularly erupted in northeastern cities. In 1834, aroused by sermons that Catholic priests kept nuns for sexual purposes, murdering the infants born of these unions, a mob burned an Ursuline convent in Charlestown, Massachusetts. In Philadelphia in 1844, 20 people were killed and more than a hundred injured in anti-Catholic riots.

Anti-Catholicism took on political form with the founding, in 1850, of the Order of the Star-Spangled Banner, a secret organization dedicated to shutting off further immigration. Growing slowly at first, by 1855 there were 960 lodges of the order in New York State alone, and perhaps a million members nationwide. They were known as the "Know-Nothings," because, when asked by outsiders about the organization, they replied, "I know nothing."

In 1854, the order came above ground as the American party. Capitalizing on the disintegration of the Whigs and anxiety caused by the sectional hostility, the anti-Catholic, anti-immigrant movement swept to power in several states, including Massachusetts. At its peak, the American party elected 75 congressmen, eight governors, mayors in several major cities, and control of the legislatures in six states. A former president, Millard Fillmore, ran as its presidential nominee in 1856. Anti-Catholicism without cudgels was by no means a socially unacceptable bigotry.

Missionaries

Only a minority of Protestants believed in political action against Roman Catholics. The majority was indifferent to the faith of the newcomers, or stood by the guarantees of religious freedom in the First Amendment to the Constitution. Many of these people, however, approved of attempts by various missionary societies to convert Catholics and other peoples to Protestant denominations.

The American Tract Society and the American Bible Society distributed literature among the Catholic population. By 1836, the Tract Society estimated that it had sold or given away more then 3 million publications that explained Protestant beliefs. Another group concentrated on converting the few Jews in the United States. Most missionary activity, however, was directed overseas. Partly because the numerous denominational colleges of the United States turned out many more ministers than there were pulpits to fill, and partly because evangelicals felt responsible for the wrongs wreaked by Americans in other parts of the world, groups such as the American Board of Foreign Missions raised money to send zealous young men and women to preach the gospel far beyond the boundaries of the United States.

Blue Hawaii

American missionaries worked among the Indians of the West and traveled to Africa, India, and China. No part of the world, however, exerted a greater attraction to Americans than the Sandwich Islands, Hawaii.

The Pledge

Although it did not ease the fears of Protestant nativists, there was a temperance movement among Irish Catholics in the United States. In 1840, an Irish priest, Theobald Mathew, toured the United States and administered "The Pledge" to more than half a million Irish Catholic immigrants and their children, swearing them into the Teetotal Abstinence Society.

In 1819, a young Hawaiian Christian told graduates of Andover Theological Seminary of the harm done to his homeland by sailors and whalers, Americans prominent among them. The islands' location in the central Pacific made Hawaii an ideal site for whalers from New Bedford and Nantucket to stop in order to refit their vessels, replenish their provisions, and recover from scurvy on island fruits. Not incidentally, the seafarers introduced diseases unknown to Hawaiians that devastated the population. Between 1778 and 1804, the native population was halved, from about 300,000 to 150,000.

Because they also brought fascinating goods to a people who lived simply, the seafarers irrevocably corrupted Hawaiian culture. Back in New England, evangelicals found it easy to consider themselves obligated to set these wrongs right.

As early as 1820, young ministers and their wives, sisters, and mothers shipped out to Hawaii. Some Hawaiians resisted when the missionaries tried to force proper New England behavior on them. The most celebrated example of the missionaries' incapacity to distinguish religion from custom was their insistence that in the warm, humid climate of the islands, Christian girls and women dress in full-length calico and flannel "Mother Hubbard" dresses.

For the most part, however, the mission to Hawaii was an astonishing success. So disastrous to Hawaiian culture was contact with the West that traditional Hawaiian religious beliefs were entirely discredited. The missionaries brought the Bible into a void. By 1830, their schools enrolled 52,000 Hawaiians (40 percent of the population), teaching the indigenous language and evangelical religion in an alphabet the Americans introduced.

THE WOMEN'S MOVEMENT

Women were the backbone of the missionary movement. In part, this was a consequence of the westward movement back home. Because young men were freer than young women to break old ties and strike off on their own, New England was left with a surplus of women for whom there were no spouses. Evangelical reform, being within the realm of morality, was considered an acceptable outlet for their energies. Single women were prominent in every reform movement from temperance to abolitionism.

But there was more to the flowering of social activism among American women than demographics.

In consecrating their lives to the deaf, the poor, the missions, and other good works, ostensibly privileged and comfortable middle-class women were able to protest, however obliquely, the private, domestic, and dependent status that American society assigned them. This discontent found an outlet in the emergence of feminism as a social movement.

Seneca Falls Feminism

In the summer of 1848, a group of women called for a convention to be held at Seneca Falls, New York, to consider the "Declaration of Sentiments and Resolutions" they had drafted. The declaration was a deadly serious parody of the Declaration of Independence:

> When in the course of human events it becomes necessary for one portion of the family of man to assume among the people of the earth a position different from that which they have hitherto occupied, but one to which the laws of nature and nature's God entitle them, a decent respect to the opinions of mankind requires that they should declare the causes that impel them to such a course. . . .

The injustices suffered by women included the denial of the right to vote even when it was extended to "the most ignorant and degraded men"; the forfeiture by a married woman of control over her own property; the nearly absolute power of the husband over a wife's behavior, which "made her, morally, an irresponsible being"—a state utterly reprehensible to an evangelical; and the exclusion of women from the professions and other gainful employment.

Only 68 women and 32 men signed the document, but the Seneca Falls Declaration received national attention—sympathetic in reform newspapers, scornful and mocking in more conventional publications. Among the organizers of the conference were Lucretia Coffin Mott and Elizabeth Cady Stanton, who continued to play an important part in the feminist movement for a generation. Among the spectators was Amelia Jenks Bloomer, a temperance reformer who was soon to become famous as the advocate of a new style of dress that bore her name.

Stepping Aside

But the expectations of 1848—that equal rights for women was a demand whose time had come—were soon dashed to pieces. Americans, including most women, were not ready to think seriously about the civil equality of women. Even the vote, only one of the Seneca Falls demands, lay years in the future.

Evangelical reformers, while generally sympathetic to women's rights, urged the feminists to set their problems aside until a reform that they considered far more important was carried out. This was the abolition of slavery, a cause that was entering its final phase when the Seneca Falls convention was called. Stanton and Mott, who were abolitionists before they became feminists, tacitly agreed. They never silenced the call for women's rights, but they stepped to the side in the belief that when the slaves were freed, women would have their day.

CHRONOLOGY

1825 New Harmony founded in Indiana

1832 Trollope's *Domestic Manners of the Americans* published
Ralph Waldo Emrslon resigns pulpit

1835 Tocqueville's *Democracy in America* published

1841 Dorothea Dix launches career as reformer of insane asylums

1844 Adventists' "Great Disappointment"
Anti-Catholic riots
Joseph Smith murdered in Illinois

1845 Margaret Fuller's *Women in the 19th Century* published

1848 American Feminist movement begins at convention in Seneca Falls, New York

FOR FURTHER READING

For background and context, see Perry Miller, *The Life of the Mind in America from the Revolution to the Civil War*, 1966; I. H. Bartlett, *The American Mind in the Mid-Nineteenth Century*, 1967; Russell B. Nye, *Society and Culture in America, 1830-1860*, 1974; and Lewis Perry, *Intellectual Life in America*, 1984. S. E. Ahlstrom, *A Religious History of the American People*, 1972; and Martin E. Marty, *Righteous Empire: The Protestant Experience in America*, 1970, and *Pilgrims in Their Own Land: 500 Years of Religion in America*, 1984, are also valuable, as is Nathan O. Hatch, *The Democratization of American Christianity*, 1989.

Basic general studies of nineteenth-century reform include C. S. Griffin, *Thy Brother's Keepers: Moral Stewardship in the United States, 1800-1865*, 1960, and *The Ferment of Reform*, 1967; Arthur M. Schlesinger, Jr., *The American as Reformer*, 1960; Alice F. Tyler, *Freedom's Ferment: Phases of American Social History to 1860*, 1944; and R. G. Walters, *American Reformers: 1815-1860*, 1978.

An old but perennially delightful book with a somewhat jaundiced view of American enthusiasms of the era, particularly revivalism, is Gilbert Seldes, *The Stammering Century*, 1928. Also on revivalism, see Bernard R. Weisberger, *They Gathered at the River*, 1958, and C. A. Johnson, *The Frontier Camp Meeting*, 1955. Other titles dealing with religious and utopian sects in the nineteenth century include Marin Cardin, *Oneida*, 1969; Whitney R. Cross, *The Burned-Over District*, 1950; Robert O. Thomas, *The Man Who Would Be Perfect*, 1977; Carl J. Guarneri, *Utopian Alternative: Fourierism in Nineteenth Century America*, 1991; Stephen J. Stein, *The Shaker Experience in America*, 1992; and Leonard J. Arrington, *The Mormon Experience*, 1979.

On specific reforms, see Ray A. Billington, *The Protestant Crusade, 1800-1860*, 1938; F. L. Byme, *Prophet of Prohibition: Neal Dow and His Crusade*, 1961; M. E. Lender and J. K. Martin, *Drinking in America: A History*, 1982; H. E. Marshall, *Dorothea Dix: Forgotten Samaritan*, 1937; Blake McKelvey, *American Prisons: A Study in American Social History Prior to 1915*, 1936; W. G. Rorabaugh, *The Alcoholic Republic: An American Tradition*, 1979; David J. Rothman, *The Discovery of the Asylum*, 1970; I. R. Tyrrel, *Sobering Up: From Temperance to Prohibition*, 1979; and Carl Wittke, *The Irish in America*, 1956.

For feminism: Lois Banner, *Elizabeth Cady Stanton*, 1980; Carl M. Degler, *At Odds: Women and the Family in America from the Revolution to the Present*, 1980; Eleanor Flexner, *Century of Struggle: The Women's Rights Movement in the United States*, 1975; Gerda Lerner, *The Woman in American History*, 1970; Alma Lutz, *Susan B. Anthony*, 1979; William L. O'Neill, *Everyone Was Brave: The Rise and Fall of Feminism in America*, 1970; and Mary P. Ryan, *Womanhood in America*, 1975, and *Cradle of the Middle Class*, 1981.

For leading cultural figures of the era, see Perry Miller, ed., *The Transcendentalists*, 1950, a collection of their writings; and Paul F. Boller, *American Transcendentalism, 1830-1860*, 1974. See also the following biographical studies: Gay Wilson Allen, *Waldo Emerson: A Biography*, 1981; Paul Blanchard, *Margaret Fuller: From Transcendentalism to Revolution*, 1978; David P. Edgel, *William Ellery Channing: An Intellectual Portrait*, 1955; Walter Harding, *Thoreau: Man of Concord*, 1960; John McAleer, *Ralph Waldo Emerson: Days of Encounter*, 1984; and Joel Porte, *Representative Man: Ralph Waldo Emerson in His Time*, 1979. Differing views of cultural development are Ronald Story, *The Forging of an Aristocracy: Harvard and the Boston Upper Class*, 1980; and Ann Douglas, *The Feminization of American Culture*, 1983.

Alexis de Tocqueville, *Democracy in America*, particularly the second volume, is available in several editions, including abridgements, and is essential to every student of American history. See also Frances Trollope, *Domestic Manners of the Americans*, 1832.

This Currier and Ives depiction of a cotton plantation shows all the various activities of picking time but is highly idealized — designed to adorn the wall of a household in which slavery was regarded as a benevolent institution.

18
CHAPTER

A DIFFERENT COUNTRY

The South

Practised in the Arts of Despotism and Cruelty, we become callous to the Dictates of Humanity, & all the other finer feelings of the Soul. Taught to regard a part of our Species in the most abject and contemptible Degree below us, we lose that Idea of the Dignity of Man, which the hand of Nature had implanted in us. . . . Habituated from our Infancy to trample upon the Rights of human Nature, every generous, every liberal Sentiment, if not extinguished, is enfeebled in our Mind. And in such an infernal School are to be educated our future Legislators and Rulers.

— George Mason

There must doubtless be an unhappy influence on the manners of our people produced by the existence of slavery among us. The whole commerce between master and slave is a perpetual exercise of the most boisterous passions, the most unremitting despotism on the one part, and degrading submissions on the other. Our children see this and learn to imitate it. . . . The parent storms, the child looks on, catches the lineaments of wrath, puts on the same airs in the circle of smaller slaves, gives loose to the worst of passions and thus nursed, educated, and daily exercised in tyranny, cannot but be stamped by it with odious peculiarities.

—Thomas Jefferson

oodling at his desk one day, Thomas Jefferson drew up a list of character traits in which, he suggested, northerners and southerners differed. Northerners were cool and sober, he wrote, southerners were fiery and "voluptuary." Northerners were hard-working, self-interested, and chicaning (devious), southerners were lazy, generous, and candid. Northerners were "jealous of their own liberties, and just to those of others," southerners were "zealous for their own liberties, but trampling on those of others."

No doubt he had a point. Jefferson usually did, and it could not have been easy for him to tote up unattractive characteristics in his own people. (Never comfortably a nationalist, Jefferson referred to Virginia as "my country" until the day of his death.) Still, to fix upon the differences between the people of the North and the people of the South distorts the reality that they were much more alike than not. Southerners and northerners shared a common linguistic, religious, cultural, and political heritage. By 1826, the year of Jefferson's death, they also shared 50 years of national history.

Politically, North and South had inclined to line up on sectional lines. The Jefferson Republicans and Jackson's Democrats counted on a core of southern votes around which to build their majorities; the Federalists, National Republicans, and Whigs on their primacy in the New England states. Nevertheless, Jefferson and Jackson won the presidency only because they attracted many northern votes, too, while the Whigs competed with the Democrats as equals in the South until the 1850s. Zachary Taylor, one of only two Whigs elected president, was from Louisiana.

Despite the perturbation in South Carolina over the tariffs of 1828 and 1832, neither import duties, internal improvements, nor the question of a national bank seriously threatened the federal union.

SOUTHERN ANTISLAVERY

Until the 1830s, slavery was not a particularly divisive issue between the people of the two sections. The institution was abolished or in the process of elimination in the North, while it remained a buttress of southern society. Still, New Yorkers did not finally abandon the institution until 1827, and there were some slaves in New Jersey—all quite legal—as late as 1860. Except in a few states like Massachusetts and New Hampshire, where slavery was abolished at a blow in the Revolutionary Era, middle-aged northerners could tell the young firsthand of the days when there were slaves among them. Few northerners regretted doing away with the institution. Equally few found the fact that southerners clung to slavery to be intolerable.

Manumission and Race

In fact, until the 1830s, the future of slavery was an open question in the South. Many of the most powerful southerners, the very people who owed their wealth, leisure, and status to the forced labor of their human property, worried openly about the undesirable social, economic, and moral consequences of the institution. Thomas Jefferson agonized over slavery to the end of his life. It caused no disturbance when wealthy planters manumitted—freed—their slaves in their wills. George Washington was honored for doing so. George Wythe and Jefferson also freed some slaves in their wills. Less celebrated southerners frequently rewarded individual slaves with freedom for extraordinary services. In 1833, Virginian John Randolph freed 400 blacks with a stroke of his pen, the largest single manumission in American history.

The possibility of abolition—legal prohibition of slavery—arose several times in the states of the upper South. But, in the end, every state below the Mason-Dixon line and the Ohio River opted to preserve the institution. The decisive factors were the beliefs about race that were, simply, the assumption of the era. Most white southerners (and white northerners, for that matter) sincerely believed that blacks, as a people, were their innate inferiors in intelligence, initiative, and even moral fiber.

Jefferson's Bequest

Like many planters, Jefferson freed some slaves in his will. Sally Hemmings, whom Jefferson's enemies claimed was his mistress, was not among them. She was bequeathed to Jefferson's daughter, Patsy. Does this give the lie to the attacks on Jefferson? Some historians think not. They point out that Virginia required manumitted slaves to leave the state. To have freed Sally Hemmings, who was well along in years in 1826, would have forced her to leave her lifelong friends and children.

It was one thing for northerners holding such views to set blacks free. The black population was numerically insignificant in most northern states. In 1830, there were 125,000 blacks in the Northeast, amidst a total population of 5.54 million. There were but 42,000 blacks in the states of the Old Northwest, with 1.6 million people. So small a minority could be ignored, disdained, and pushed aside to root or die, as northern blacks were. There was no concern that their perceived undesirable traits would overwhelm the culture. The black population was not a social problem.

But blacks were the backbone of the agricultural workforce in the South, and a substantial part of the population, 2.16 million in 1830 as compared to 3.54 million whites. If such numbers, firmly under control as slaves, were suddenly or even gradually freed to compete with poor whites at the bottom of southern society, southerners who thought about the question usually concluded the result would be profound cultural decay, social dislocation, even chaos. The

Although this photograph was taken after the Civil War, the scene would have been much the same in 1830 or 1840.

How They Lived

The Republic of Porkdom

Today, a good many Americans would regard a tender corn-fed filet mignon as the *ne plus ultra* of fine eating. The ground-beef hamburger comes as close to being a national dish as is possible in a pluralistic society. Beef is unquestionably America's favorite meat; Americans consume almost two pounds of it to every pound of pork, including bacon and ham, that they eat.

Americans of the early nineteenth century prized beef too, but, while they ate quite as much meat per capita as we do, beef was far less common on their tables than pork. Indeed, according to a writer in *Godey's Lady's Book*—the combination *Ladies Home Journal, Ms.*, and *Vogue* of the era—put it,

> The United States of America might properly be called the great Hog-eating Confederacy, or the Republic of Porkdom. [In the] South and West . . . it is fat bacon and pork, fat bacon and pork only, and that continually morning, noon, and night, for all classes, sexes, ages, and conditions; and except the boiled bacon and collards at dinner, the meat is generally fried, and thus supersaturated with grease in the form of hog's lard.

Even slaves on well-managed plantations were provided with half a pound of salt pork a day.

Beef was less common, first of all, because it was relatively much more expensive than it is today. Cattle had to be transported on the hoof, which meant that cities could be supplied only from the near hinterland. Farmers on comparatively expensive real estate in the older states could generally do better cultivating their land than leaving it in pasture. Only with the development of the Great Plains after the Civil War did the price of beef decline. Even then, in 1900 Americans ate as much pork as beef.

Unlike cattle, hogs flourished on wasteland, multiplying their weight 150 times in eight months on nuts and roots in the woods, fallen orchard fruit unfit for consumption, harvested gardens and grain fields, and offal—garbage. They required next to no attention. Indeed, the "bony, snake-headed, hairy wild beasts," the American "razorback," needed no protection. (A farmer's fields and the farmer himself needed protection from them!)

Hogs were ideally suited to a nation where land was abundant and labor was scarce, and they thrived. As early as 1705, Robert Beverley wrote in his *History of Virginia* that "hogs swarm like Vermine upon the Earth, and are often accounted such. . . . When an Inventory of any considerable Man's Estate is taken, the Hogs are left out." In the southern states in 1850, there were two hogs for each human being.

Hogs had another recommendation over steers. They could be slaughtered where they were raised and cheaply preserved, butchered, and packed in salty brine in barrels to keep for a year or to be shipped to urban markets. Salt deposits were very important to early western pioneers because of the necessity of preserving pork. Cities on the Ohio and Mississippi Rivers, such as Cincinnati and St. Louis, owed much of their growth to their role as meat packers. Poor people owed their survival to salt pork. "I hold a family to be in a desperate way," a character in a James Fenimore Cooper novel put it, "when the mother can see the bottom of the pork barrel."

Scraping the bottom of the barrel is not the only catch phrase that survives in the language from the days of the Republic of Porkdom. We still use the term *pork barrel bill* to describe those congressional enactments, usually rushed through at the end of a session, that spend federal money in just about every district in which incumbents from the majority party are up for election—a highway improvement here, an agricultural station there, a defense installation somewhere else. The phrase conveys an image once familiar to every American—the none-too-pleasant appearance of chunks of pork bobbing about in a barrel of brine.

South's propertyless "po' white trash" was enough of a worry to thoughtful social conservatives; the idea of two million destitute free blacks caused them nightmares.

Before about 1830, there was little that was malicious or apocalyptic in southern statements along these lines. In fact, there was a melancholy sense of fatefulness in southern ruminations. In continuing to hold blacks as slaves, many planters of the late eighteenth and early nineteenth centuries believed, they were not so much preserving their own wealth and social standing as they were shouldering a tragic burden that was strapped to their backs by history. They were protecting the blacks from the hostility of poor whites; they were preserving their society from anarchy.

The Colonization Movement

The American Colonization Society, founded in 1817, tried to provide troubled southerners with an alternative to the "blot" of slavery on the one hand and chaos on the other. With the active support of such distinguished southerners as Bushrod Washington, Francis Scott Key, Presidents Madison and Monroe, John Marshall, and Henry Clay, the society proposed to raise money with which free blacks would be transported to West Africa. By ridding the South of free blacks, the advocates of colonization believed, they would avert racial conflict, encourage individual slave owners to free their human property, and prompt state legislatures to adopt laws abolishing the undesirable institution. Idealism was not the society's strong point; it described the free black population as "for the most part idle and useless, and too often vicious and mischievous."

Congress voted the Society $100,000 in seed money and, in 1820, it financed the emigration of a few former slaves to Sierra Leone, a colony estab-

lished by the British as a refuge for blacks freed from bondage within the British Empire. The society then purchased a stretch of African coastline south of Sierra Leone and helped establish the black Republic of Liberia, with its capital at Monrovia (named for President James Monroe). All told, about 11,000 American blacks settled in Liberia. They established a government patterned on the American model and, less happily, reduced the native people of the region to a kind of servitude with themselves on top.

Colonization proved an unrealistic program. There were 1.5 million slaves in the United States in 1820, and 2 million in 1830, far more people than could be colonized on a small strip of African seacoast. Moreover, few free blacks were interested in going to Africa. Most were generations removed from their African roots—which were rarely in Liberia in any case—and felt no attraction to an unknown land. Virginia, Georgia, and Arkansas may not have been hospitable homes, but homes they were. West Africa was not.

As for southern whites, the longer the price of cotton boomed on the world market, the less was heard about the antislavery aspects of colonization. When the Mississippi Colonization Society was founded in 1829, its pronounced purpose was to rid the state of free blacks. Its officers disassociated themselves from the old goal of encouraging planters to free their slaves. Even in the upper South, where little cotton was grown, the profitability of selling surplus slaves down the river dulled the appeal of

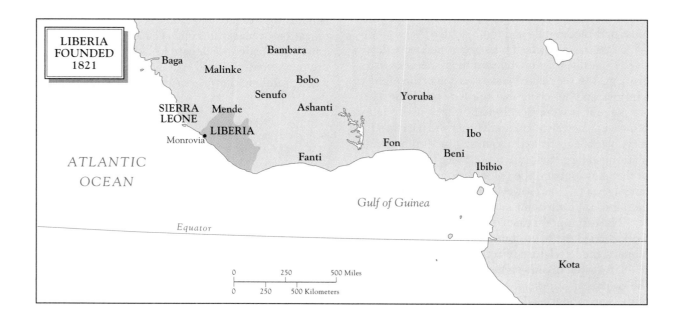

colonization. Except for one last debate, by 1830 the southern antislavery movement was dead.

The Last Debate

In December 1831, Governor John Floyd of Virginia asked the legislature to consider a plan to phase out slavery over a period of years. Slave owners were to be compensated for their losses; for the good of the state, taxpayers would accommodate those who lost property, just as if real estate were taken for the purposes of building a road. For three weeks in January 1832, the delegates discussed the proposal, for the most part moderately and intelligently.

Even the staunchest proslavery men were defensive. Typically, they introduced their speeches by regretting the fact that blacks were ever brought to Virginia, and by saying that the state would be a better place if it were developed by free white labor. However, they also concluded that the past was history; blacks constituted about half of Virginia's population; so large a population of free blacks was out of the question; and the colonization movement was obviously a failure. However tragic it was for the Old Dominion, Virginia must continue to be a slave state.

The assumption that a biracial society would not work carried the day—but just barely. At the end of January, the legislature rejected the Floyd plan by 73 to 58. A switch of only eight votes would have altered the course of American history, for the other states of the upper South—Delaware, Maryland, and Ken-

tucky—could not have ignored abolition in Virginia. Had those states phased slavery out, slavery would not have split the Union across the middle. It would have been the peculiar institution of a few, generally lightly populated states in the Deep South. As it was, once the Virginia debate was over, no powerful party of southern whites ever again considered the possibility of ridding themselves of the institution.

THREATS TO THE SOUTHERN ORDER

Both Floyd's proposal and the Virginia legislature's rejection of it were profoundly influenced by two events that electrified the South in 1831: the appearance in the North of a new kind of antislavery agitator, and an uprising of slaves in Southampton County, Virginia, under the leadership of Nat Turner.

Early Abolitionists

While the mainstream debate over slavery revolved around its political justice, economic wisdom, and social consequences, there had always been a few voices raised about the morality of human bondage. Some eighteenth-century Quakers, such as John Woolman of New Jersey and Anthony Benezet of Philadelphia, spoke publicly of the sinfulness of slavery. Benjamin Lay wrote a pamphlet called *All Slave-Keepers Apostates* and once kidnapped the child of a slave-owning Quaker for a day as an object lesson in what whites did to blacks. During the 1820s, Benjamin Lundy called for gradual abolition and the colonization of blacks in Haiti, Canada, or Texas (then a part of Mexico). Educated black people, notably the mathematician and astronomer Benjamin Banneker, published moral arguments against slavery and drew support from white religious groups and communities of free blacks in both North and South.

With few exceptions (like Benjamin Lay), these abolitionists treated the subject as one to be discussed calmly and moderately, in terms of one Christian concerned about the soul of another. Their fraternal attitude toward slave owners was typified by the Boston Unitarian William Ellery Channing, who told southerners, "We consider slavery your calamity and not your curse." None of them used language as harsh as had Virginians Thomas Jefferson or John Randolph in excoriating slavery.

David Walker and William Lloyd Garrison

In 1829, language and mood took on new forms. In that year, a free black dealer in cloth living in Boston, David Walker, published a pamphlet called *The Appeal*. After reviewing the traditional arguments about the immorality and injustice of slavery, Walker stated that unless whites abolished the institution, blacks had a moral duty to rise up in violent rebellion.

William Lloyd Garrison, a spare, intense young white man of 24, who was working for Benjamin Lundy in Baltimore, did not believe in violent rebellion. Among the many evangelical reform movements he supported was pacifism, or opposition to all wars. And yet, when Garrison founded his antislavery newspaper *The Liberator*, in Boston in January 1831, his language was belligerent and incendiary, and aimed not only at the institution of slavery—the sin—but at the sinners, slave owners. In the first issue of his paper Garrison wrote:

> I am aware that many object to the severity of my language; but is there not cause for severity? I will be as harsh as truth, and as uncompromising as justice. On this subject I do not wish to

The Philadelphia Anti-Slavery Society, 1851. Lucretia Coffin is seated second from the right.

The masthead of William Lloyd Garrison's antislavery newspaper.

think, or speak, or write, with moderation. No! No! Tell a man whose house is on fire to give a moderate alarm; tell him to moderately rescue his wife from the hands of the ravisher; tell the mother to gradually extricate her babe from the fire into which it has fallen;—but urge me not to use moderation in a cause like the present.

It was a declaration of war. To Garrison, the day of discourse and compromise was done. Slavery was evil, pure and simple; slave owners and those who accommodated them were doers of evil. Garrison described the slave owner's life as "one of unbridled lust, of filthy amalgamation, of swaggering braggadocio, of haughty domination, of cowardly ruffianism, of boundless dissipation, of matchless insolence, of infinite self-conceit, of unequaled oppression, of more than savage cruelty."

This sort of thing does not usually go down well with the subjects of it. Indeed, Garrison was even unpopular in the North. (He would have been wracked with doubt that the devil was in him had he been a mass hero.) Even in Boston, a center of antislavery sentiment, Garrison was hooted and pelted with stones when he spoke in public. On one occasion, a mob threw a noose around his neck and dragged him through the streets. He was rescued only when the aggressiveness of a group of abolitionist women momentarily shocked the mob. (Garrison was also a supporter of women's rights.)

In the South, Garrison was regarded as a monster. Not because he was against slavery, at least not at first: antislavery southerners loathed him as intensely as did proslavery southerners. Garrison and other extremist abolitionists were hated because they were believed to be inciting bloody slave rebellion. In 1831, the fear of slave rebellion in the South was no abstract speculation.

Nat Turner

Nat Turner, a slave of Southampton County, Virginia, was a queer amalgam of mystic dreamer and hardheaded realist. Literate—unusual among slaves—he pored over the Bible, drawing his own interpretations of its meaning. The rebellion he led in August and September 1831 was triggered by a solar eclipse that he took as a sign from God. And yet, Turner's revolt had a very practical goal—personal liberty—and Turner had a realistic conception of the

WANTED: Nat Turner

Five feet 6 or 8 inches high, weighs between 150 and 160 pounds, rather bright complexion, but not a mulatto. Broad shoulders, large flat nose, large eyes. Broad flat feet, rather knock-kneed, walks brisk and active. Hair on the top of the head very thin, no beard, except on the upper lip and at the top of the chin. A scar on one of his temples, also one at the back of his neck. A large knot on one of the bones of his right arm, near his wrist, produced [by] a blow.

odds that faced him. He planned with care, divulging his scheme to only a few trusted friends who swore with him to fight to the death. On the night of August 21, 1831, armed with little more than farm tools, the little group moved like lightning. They swept across Southampton County, killing 60 whites and recruiting more supporters from among the slaves.

The rising was over quickly, but before the rebels were rounded up after six weeks in hiding, there were 70 in their band. Forty, including Nat Turner, were hanged. Others, who were not directly responsible for spilling blood, were sold out of state. Undoubtedly, other blacks, including the innocent, were murdered by angry or frightened whites who did not bother to report the deaths. Law officers were not in a mood to work to rule.

The Fear of Rebellion

Turner's rebellion was not the first to throw a scare into white southerners. In 1800, a black man named Gabriel Prosser plotted an uprising in Richmond that may have passively involved as many as a thousand slaves. In 1822, a free black carpenter in Charleston, Denmark Vesey, tried to organize a conspiracy to murder whites, burn the city, and flee to Haiti. Also, runaway slaves in Georgia joined with Seminole Indians to raid outlying plantations and free the slaves there. At one time or another, planters in every part of the South suspected slaves of plotting rebellion.

No doubt many of the suspected plots were figments of overwrought imaginations; but there was nothing imaginary about Nat Turner, and a tremor of fear ran through the white South. In some parts of Louisiana, Mississippi, and South Carolina, blacks outnumbered whites by 20 to 1. Mary Boykin Chesnut, a South Carolinian of the planter class, was not observing a demographic curiosity when she described her family's plantation at Mulberry as "half a dozen whites and sixty or seventy Negroes, miles away from the rest of the world."

If many white southerners shared such anxieties, their belief in black inferiority meant that few were willing to admit that blacks, left to their own devices, were capable of mounting a rebellion. To white southerners, it was no coincidence that Turner's uprising followed the fiery first issue of *The Liberator* by only eight months. They took note of the fact that Turner knew how to read, and so they blamed antislavery propagandists like Garrison for the tragedy.

SOUTHERNERS CLOSE RANKS

Once Virginians decided that the Old Dominion would remain a slave state, the South stood almost alone in the western world. The northern states had abolished the institution. The Spanish-speaking republics of the Americas had done so, too. Great Britain was in the process of emancipating the slaves in its colonies. In the entire Christian world, slavery survived only in the Spanish colonies of Cuba and Puerto Rico and the independent Empire of Brazil.

After 1832, southerners faced up to the fact that American Negro slavery was a peculiar institution, a way of life almost unique to them, and they moved on three fronts to protect it. First, they insulated the South from outside ideas that threatened slavery, and they suppressed dissent at home. Second, white southerners ceased to apologize to themselves and others for slavery. Instead of calling it a historical tragedy or a necessary evil, they devised the argument that slavery was a positive good that benefited slave owner, slave, and society as a whole. Third, they reformed the state slave codes (the laws that governed the peculiar institution), both improving the material conditions under which slaves lived and instituting stricter controls over the black population.

Southern Anxieties

Both antislavery and proslavery southerners feared slave rebellion. The chief difference between them was in the tone in which they spoke of blacks.

Thomas Ritchie, an antislavery Virginian: "To attempt to excite discontent and revolt, or publish writings having this tendency, obstinately and perversely, among us, is outrageous—it ought not to be passed over with indifference. Our own safety—the good and happiness of our slaves, requires it."

Edward D. Holland, a proslavery South Carolinian: "Let it never be forgotten that our NEGROES are truly the *Jacobins* of the country; that they are the *anarchist*s and the *domestic enemy*, the *common enemy of civilized society*, and the barbarians who would, IF THEY COULD, become the DESTROYERS of our race."

Suppression of Dissent

Most southern states passed laws that forbade the distribution of abolitionist literature within their borders. Officials screened the federal mails and seized copies of *The Liberator*, other antislavery newspapers, and books. Georgia's legislature actually offered a reward of $5,000 to any person who would bring William Lloyd Garrison into the state to stand trial for inciting rebellion.

Even if the resolution were meant to be symbolic, a state legislature's willingness to sanction a felony illustrates the depth of bitterness in the South toward abolitionists. David Walker was murdered, found poisoned in his shop. In border states like Kentucky, abolitionists such as John Gregg Fee and the politician Cassius Marcellus Clay (a relative of Henry) were generally unmolested, but they were the exception. The expression of antislavery opinions was no longer acceptable below the Mason-Dixon line.

Nor even in Washington, beginning in 1836, southern congressmen annually nagged the House of Representatives to adopt a rule providing that every petition dealing with slavery that the House received be tabled, set aside with no discussion on the floor. Former President John Quincy Adams, now a member of Congress, argued that this gag rule violated the right to free speech. Adams was not an abolitionist. He considered crusaders like Walker and Garrison to be dangerous and irresponsible fanatics. But he insisted on the constitutional right of abolitionists to be heard, and because he criticized southerners for quashing the right of petition, the lifelong nationalist came to be lumped with the abolitionists as an enemy.

Positive Good

Shortly after Virginia's debate on the future of slavery, a professor of economics at the College of William and Mary, Thomas Roderick Dew, published a systematic defense of the slave system as a better way of organizing and controlling labor than the wage system of the North. By 1837, most southern political leaders were parroting and embroidering on Dew's theories. In the Senate, John C. Calhoun declared that compared with other systems by which racial and class relationships were governed,

Slaves beside their living quarters in South Carolina.

"the relation now existing in the slaveholding states is, instead of an evil, a good—a positive-good."

The proslavery argument included religious, historical, cultural, and social proofs of the justice and beneficence of the institution. The Bible, the positive-good propagandists argued, sanctioned slavery. Not only did the ancient Hebrews own slaves with God's blessing, but Christ had told a servant who wanted to follow him to return to his master and practice Christianity as a slave.

Dew and others pointed out that the great civilizations of antiquity, Greece and Rome, were slaveholding societies. Hardly barbaric in their eyes, slavery had served as the foundation of high culture since the beginning of recorded time. Slavery made possible the existence of a gracious and cultured upper class that, with its leisure, guarded the highest refinements of human achievement.

Southern planters took pride in the fact that, although elementary and secondary education in the South was inferior to that provided by the public school systems of the North, more upper-class southerners were college-educated than members of the northern elite. Even as late as 1860, there were more than 6,000 college students in Georgia, Alabama, and Mississippi and fewer than 4,000 in

the New England states, which were, altogether, more populous.

As an aristocracy, southerners said, the planters were closer to the tradition of the gentlemanly founding fathers than were the vulgar, money-grubbing capitalists of the North. Because gentlemen dominated politics in the South, the section was far better governed than was the North, where demagogues from the dregs of society could win election by playing on the whims of the mob. Some planters liked to think of themselves as descended from the cavaliers of seventeenth-century England. The South's favorite author was Sir Walter Scott, who spun tales of flowering knighthood and chivalry.

George Fitzhugh, Sociologist

But did all these proofs justify denying personal freedom to human beings? Yes, answered George Fitzhugh, a Virginia lawyer, in two influential books: *A Sociology for the South* (1854) and *Cannibals All!* (1857). He amassed statistics and other evidence with which he argued that the southern slave lived a better material and social life than did the northern wage worker or the European peasant.

Like Dew and Calhoun, Fitzhugh argued that someone had to perform the drudgery in every society. In the South, menial work was done by slaves who were cared for from cradle to grave. Not only did the slave owner feed, clothe, and house his workers, but he also supported slave children, the injured and the disabled, and the elderly—all of whom were nonproductive. Fitzhugh delighted to point out that by comparison, the northern wage worker was paid only as long as there was work to be done and the worker fit to do it. The wage worker who was injured was cut loose to fend for himself in an uncaring world. His children, the elderly, and the incompetent were no responsibility of capitalist employers.

Consequently, the North was plagued by social problems that were unknown in the South. The North teemed with obnoxious, nattering reformers. The lower classes were irreligious and, in their misery, tumultuous. The free working class was tempted by socialistic, communistic, and other doctrines that threatened the social order. By comparison, Fitzhugh claimed, southern slaves were contented, indeed happy. "A merrier being does not exist on the face of the globe," Fitzhugh wrote, "than the Negro slave of the United States."

Management

Fitzhugh equated happiness with the material conditions of slave life—housing, clothing, diet—and compared them favorably with the conditions under which the poorest wage workers of the North lived. By the 1850s, when he wrote, most southern state legislatures had defined minimum living standards as part of their slave codes, and magazines like the *Southern Agriculturalist* regularly featured exchanges among slave owners about how well they treated their people.

The most commonly stated reason for keeping slaves adequately housed, clothed, and fed was practical: a healthy slave worked more efficiently and was less likely to rebel or run away. Also underlying the trend toward improvement in the conditions of slave life after the 1830s was the South's determination to give the lie to the abolitionists' depiction of slavery as a life of unremitting horror. Planters who did provide decent accommodations for their slaves took pleasure in showing slave quarters to northern or foreign visitors. They reassured themselves that they were just the beneficent patriarchs that the positive-good writers described. Less likely to be trumpeted were the measures of control that were devised in the wake of the Turner rebellion.

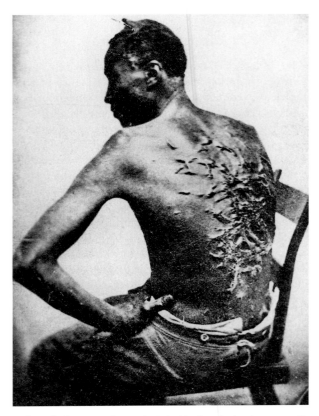

A slave displays scars from a brutal whipping. Such extreme cruelty was unusual, but many, perhaps most, slaves were whipped at one time or another.

Control

By 1840, the states of the Deep South had adopted laws that made it extremely difficult for a slave owner to free his slaves. Virginia required recently freed blacks to leave the state. (The law was impossible to enforce effectively.) It was also a crime in some southern states to teach a slave to read.

County governments were required to fund and maintain slave patrols. These mounted posses of armed whites policed the roads and plantations, particularly at night. They had the legal right to break into slave cabins or demand at gunpoint that any black (or white) account for himself or herself. Usually rough, hard-bitten men who were so poor that they sorely needed the undesirable job, the "paddyrollers" (patrollers) were brutal even with unoffending slaves and African Americans who were free. Black people hated and feared them. Their mere presence and arrogance cast a cloud of repression over the plantation regions that few outsiders failed to notice.

Blacks who were not under the direct supervision of their masters or overseers were required by law to carry written passes that gave them permission to be abroad, even just a mile or two from their cabins. Free blacks—there were about 250,000 in the South by 1860, 1 to every 15 slaves—also had to protect carefully the legal evidence of their status. Kidnappings of free blacks, and sale of them as slaves elsewhere in the South, were far from unknown.

The presence of free blacks presented a serious ideological problem for slave owners. One of the most effective means of controlling the slaves was to convince them that God and nature intended them to be slaves because of their race, and that they should be thankful to be under the care of their masters. But if slaves saw free blacks prospering, the argument flew to pieces. Slave owners also thought that free blacks were likely to stir up discontent among slaves, and they were probably right.

Religion could be an effective means of control, and careful masters paid close attention to the kind of preaching their property heard. Some owners took their slaves to their own churches where the minister was expected to deliver a sermon now and

then based on biblical stories such as that of Hagar: "The angel of the Lord said unto her, return to Thy mistress, and submit thyself under her hands." Other masters permitted the blacks, who preferred an emotional Christianity enhanced with vestiges of West African culture, to have preachers of their own race. But these often eloquent men were instructed—specifically or indirectly—to steer clear of any topics that might cast doubt on the justice of slavery. Some toed the line. Others conveyed their protest by placing heavy emphasis on the ancient Israelites' bondage in Egypt and Babylon—and their ultimate deliverance. The idealized institution of John C. Calhoun and George Fitzhugh bore only an accidental relationship to slavery as it actually existed.

CHRONOLOGY

1817 American Colonization Society Founded

1822 Colonization Society purchases Liberia

1829 David Walker's *Appeal* is published

1831 Virginia legislature debates abolishing slavery
The Liberator commences publication
Turner's rebellion in southern Virginia

1836 Congress begins voting "gag rule" forbidding consideration of petitions concerning slavery

1854 Publication of George Fitzhugh's *Sociology for the South*

FOR FURTHER READING

On the South and its distinctive characteristics, see Avery O. Craven, *The Growth of Southern Nationalism, 1848–1860*, 1953; Clement Eaton, *The Growth of Southern Civilization*, 1961, and *A History of the Old South*, 1975; I. A. Newby, *The American South*, 1979; and Charles S. Sydnor, *The Development of Southern Sectionalism, 1819–1848*, 1948. Few historians today would subscribe to the conclusions in Wilbur Cash, *The Mind of the South*, 1940, and yet it contains many perceptive insights. A contemporary "travel book" about the Old South well worth reading is Frederick Law Olmstead, *The Cotton Kingdom*, 1861. See also James Oakes, *Slavery and Freedom: An Interpretation of the Old South*, 1990.

Of more specific concern but vital to understanding the subject are Edward A. Ayers, *Vengeance and Justice: Crime and Punishment in the Nineteenth-Century American South*, 1984; Dickson D. Bruce, *Violence and Culture in the Antebellum South*, 1979; Victoria E. Bynum, *Unruly Women: The Politics of Social and Sexual Control in the Old South*, 1992; William J. Cooper, *The South and the Politics of Slavery, 1828–1856*, 1978; Elizabeth Fox-Genovese, *Within the Plantation Household*, 1988; John Hope Franklin, *The Militant South*, 1956; Eugene Genovese, *The Political Economy of Slavery*, 1962, and *The World the Slaveholders Made*, 1969; Patrick Gerster and William Cords, eds., *Myth and Image in Southern History*, 1974; Fred Bateman and Thomas Weiss, *A Deplorable Scarcity: The Failure of Industrialism in the Slave Economy*, 1981; Bertram Wyatt-Brown, *Southern Honor: Ethics and Behavior in the Old South*, 1982; James Oakes, *The Ruling Race: A History of American Slaveholders*, 1982; Frank Owsley, *Plain Folk of the Old South*, 1949; William R. Taylor, *Cavalier and Yankee: The Old South and American National Character*, 1961; and Gavin Wright, *The Political Economy of the Cotton South*, 1978.

A Ride for Liberty—The Fugitive Slaves, *painting by Eastman Johnson, ca. 1862.*

19
CHAPTER

THE PECULIAR INSTITUTION
Slavery as It Was Perceived and as It Was

Oppression has, at one stroke, deprived the descendants of the Africans of almost all the privileges of humanity. The Negro of the United States has lost all remembrance of his country; the language which his forefathers spoke is never heard around him; he abjured their religion and forgot their customs when he ceased to belong to Africa, without acquiring any European privileges. But he remains halfway between the two communities; sold by the one, repulsed by the other; finding not a spot in the universe to call by the name of country, except the faint image of a home which the shelter of his master's roof affords.

—Alexis de Tocqueville

O how accursed is that system, which entombs the godlike mind of man, defaces the divine image, reduces those who by creation were crowned with glory and honor to a level with four-footed beasts, and exalts the dealer in human flesh above all that is called God!

—William Lloyd Garrison

In December 1865, the Thirteenth Amendment to the Constitution was ratified and became a part of the basic law of the land. It is one of the shortest amendments, but in terms of what it did, it was the most momentous. In providing that "neither slavery nor involuntary servitude . . . shall exist within the United States," the Thirteenth wrote an end to the "great exception," a legal and social institution that flew in the face of the ideals that Americans believed gave their nation special meaning to the world, and to which they have been generally devoted: the freedom of the individual, impartial justice, equality of opportunity, and government by the people.

IMAGES OF SLAVERY

Since 1865, two images of slavery, one oozing romance, the other rife with horrors, have competed for possession of the American memory. Both visions actually took shape before 1865, when slavery was still a living institution. The seeds of the former were planted by the positive-good theorists with the assistance of a Pennsylvania-born songwriter who spent only a few months of his life in the South. The latter was cultivated in abundant detail by northern abolitionists who also, with the exception of a few African American activists, had little firsthand knowledge of the slave states.

Stephen Foster and the Sweet Magnolia

Stephen Foster was born in Pittsburgh in 1826. Musically inclined from youth, he was a pioneer of "pop music," one of the first Americans to support himself by composing songs that captured the fancy of a mass market. He wrote for traveling minstrel shows and sold sheet music, the songwriter's chief commodity before the invention of the player piano and the phonograph.

Foster's first successful song was "Oh! Susannah," a whimsical nonsense piece about the California gold rush of 1849 that is still popular in elementary school sing-alongs. Then, perhaps because the minstrel show was set in the South, with white (and sometimes black) performers rubbing burnt cork on their faces and joshing and singing in grotesquely exaggerated African American dialect, Foster turned to sentimental depictions of plantation life, often from

---

Devoted to Ol' Massa

Down in de cornfield
Hear dat mournful sound!
All de darkies am a-weeping
Massa's in de cold, cold ground.

Stephen Foster, 1852

---

the slave's perspective. In the world of "Swanee River" (1851), "Massa's in de Cold, Cold Ground" (1852), "My Old Kentucky Home" (1853), and "Old Black Joe" (1860), slaves were uncomplicated, loving creatures who enjoyed a simple but secure and satisfying life attached to a kindly old "Massa" who beamed kindly on his loyal "darkies."

Dancing, laughing blacks, grand houses, Spanish moss, the plunking of the banjo, the sweet scent of magnolia blossoms, and easygoing white folks were the ingredients of Foster's South, and it is well to remember that he was immensely popular in the heyday of the abolitionist movement. Within a generation of the Thirteenth Amendment, this vision of antebellum southern life was embraced by most white Americans, perhaps northerners above all. In the industrial age of the late nineteenth century—dirty, urban, and paced by the relentless drive of the machine, it was consol-

---

King Cotton

Southern politicians repeatedly lectured northerners that the South supported the national economy. That is, the money that cotton brought in from abroad provided most of the surplus capital that paid for the industrialization of the nation. This transaction was direct when protective tariffs on English-made goods forced southerners to buy American-made goods.

The politicians were right. Cotton did industrialize the United States before the Civil War. However, northern antislavery people had another way of considering this economic fact of life. Who, they asked, really produced the cotton? To a large extent, slaves did. And to that extent, the United States was industrialized by the forced labor of the blacks.

This romanticized depiction of slaves by Eastman Johnson presented just the picture defenders of slavery wanted the world to see: simple, comfortable, contented slaves.

ing to dream nostalgically of a South that had never been. The tradition culminated in Margaret Mitchell's novel of 1936, *Gone with the Wind*, and Hollywood's classic film based on the book (1939).

Theodore Dwight Weld and His Converts

Abolitionists depicted rather a different slavery. To these zealous black and white lecturers, journalists, and preachers who crisscrossed the northern states, the slave's world was a bawling hell of blacksnake whips, brutal slave catchers following packs of bloodhounds, children torn from their mothers' breasts to be sold down the river, squalor, disease, and near starvation under callous, arrogant masters, the sinister slavocrats.

William Lloyd Garrison was far from alone in presenting this message to northerners. Indeed, because of his rasping self-righteousness, he was probably less effective in the attack on slavery than people like Theodore Dwight Weld, a white evangelist, "as eloquent as an angel and powerful as thunder." Weld concentrated on converting prominent people to the antislavery cause. Two of his proselytes, Arthur and Lewis Tappan, were wealthy New York merchants who generously financed abolitionist institutions like Garrison's *Liberator*, Kenyon and Oberlin Colleges in Ohio, and the American Anti-Slavery Society, founded in 1833.

Another Weld convert was James G. Birney, an Alabama planter who freed his slaves and ran as the presidential candidate of the antislavery Liberty party in 1840 and 1844. Weld married yet another abolitionist

Most slaves were used as field hands and performed the heavy labor needed to raise such cash crops as cotton.

who had owned slaves, Angelina Grimké of a prominent South Carolina family. She and her sister Sarah instilled in him a perspective on the problem of slavery that was forever beyond Garrison, a consideration for the moral plight of the conscientious slave owner.

A Strange Species of Property

The slave's status as personal property worked only one way. That is, while the slave owner's rights over his slave were much the same as his rights over his cattle, slaves did not benefit from the exemptions other personal property enjoyed in the law. A cow, a hog, or a share of stock cannot commit a crime and be punished for doing so. Slaves could and, of course, were.

Black Abolitionists

While the abolitionist movement attracted white people, it was, unsurprisingly, most dependably supported by the free blacks of the North. Although generally poor, blacks provided a disproportionate share of the money needed to publish antislavery newspapers and send antislavery lecturers. Several prominent abolitionist crusaders were black.

Sojourner Truth was the name taken by a physical giant of a woman born as the slave Isabella in New York in 1797. Freed under the state emancipation law of 1827, she worked as a domestic servant for several years and then burst onto the abolitionist scene as one of the movement's most powerful orators. Sojourner Truth was illiterate to the end of her days — she died in 1893, at 96 years of age — but she transfixed audiences when she accompanied her speeches with songs she had written herself.

Sojourner Truth (ca. 1797–1883) was a freed slave who devoted herself to the abolition and women's rights movements.

The loudest single shot in this campaign was *Uncle Tom's Cabin, or Life among the Lowly*, written by Harriet Beecher Stowe, the daughter of Lyman Beecher, the Presbyterian minister who spearheaded the anti-Catholic agitations of the 1830s. Not only did Stowe's book sell an astonishing 3,000 copies the day it was published, and 300,000 copies within a year (roughly the equivalent of 3 million copies today), but it was adapted into a play that was performed by dozens of professional and amateur troupes in small towns and cities alike. So influential was Mrs. Stowe's tale of Uncle Tom, a submissive and loyal old slave, that when Abraham Lincoln was introduced to her during the Civil War, he is said to have remarked, "So you are the little woman who wrote the book that made this great war."

The most compelling of the black abolitionist orators was Frederick Douglass, who was born a slave in Maryland in 1817. Escaping to Massachusetts, he educated himself and, in 1845, wrote his autobiography, which, until the publication of *Uncle Tom's Cabin* in 1851 and 1852, was the most widely read antislavery document. Unlike most white abolitionists, Douglass could speak firsthand of life in a slave society and his message was no less troubling. For a while, because his former master was pursuing him, Douglass lived in England, where he furthered his education while friends back home purchased his freedom.

Harriet Beecher Stowe

The decisive antislavery argument was that it reduced human beings to the status of livestock, mere property. However, rather than dwell on a point that seemed abstract to many people, black and white abolitionists alike focused on the physical deprivations and cruelties suffered by slaves. Some antislavery lecturers traveled with runaway slaves whose backs had been disfigured from brutal beatings.

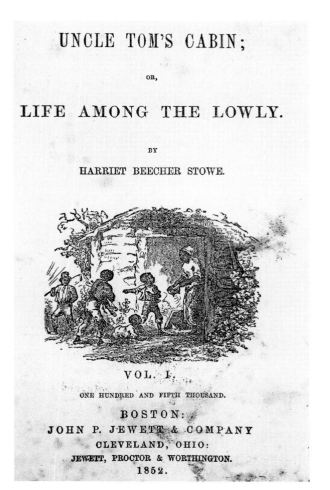

First published as a serial in 1851 and 1852, the book version of Uncle Tom's Cabin *was widely read, selling 300,000 copies within a year.*

NOTABLE PEOPLE

Frederick Douglass

Frederick Douglass was born in Talbot County, Maryland, about 1817. He did not know the actual day of his birth because he was born a slave. "By far the larger part of slaves," Douglass wrote, "know as little of their ages as horses know of theirs, and it is the wish of most masters within my knowledge to keep their slaves thus ignorant." Douglass met his mother, Harriett Bailey, only a few times. It was the custom in his part of the South to separate children from their mother when they were weaned, probably in order "to hinder the development of the child's affection toward its mother, and to blunt and destroy the natural affection of the mother for the child." Douglass did not know the identity of his father, only that he was white.

In 1838, about 21 years of age, Douglass escaped to Massachusetts, where he worked as a laborer and slowly emerged as the leading black abolitionist in the United States. He was both a stentorian orator and a superb pamphleteer. Taught the alphabet by the wife of one of his owners, he taught himself to read when his benefactress was ordered to stop educating him. His writing style was concrete and straightforward, devoid of the flowery extravagance favored in the mid-nineteenth century and all the more forceful for that. Indeed, when critics said Douglass lied about being a slave because no self-educated man could be so eloquent, he published a *Narrative* of his life in 1845. Although the book became the single most important document of the antislavery movement before *Uncle Tom's Cabin*, its publication put Douglass's freedom in jeopardy. He was still a fugitive under federal law and he named the names of his owners. To avoid arrest, Douglass fled to England where he amassed enough money to buy his freedom and return to the United States.

For the rest of his life, as orator, politician, editor, and author, Douglass was in the forefront of the American reform. Opposition to slavery preoccupied him until the Civil War. Then he turned his attention to civil rights for blacks, women's suffrage, and the cause of factory workers. With a Republican in the White House during most of the final 30 years of his life, he enjoyed the security of federal office, culminating in his appointment as minister to Haiti in 1889.

Douglass's importance to the antislavery movement rests in the fact that his intelligence and profound personal dignity had survived the degradations of slavery. His existence gave the lie to the proslavery argument that black people were racially incapable of citizenship. Moreover, while his personal experience of slavery included many horrors, which he did not hesitate to relate in lurid detail, Douglass emphasized the fact that the evil of slavery depended not on how slaves were actually treated, but lay in the nature of the institution. His theme was the dehumanization of both slave owner and slave. There has not been an indictment of slavery written since Douglass which cannot be found, usually well-developed, in his numerous writings.

He was as passionate an abolitionist as his white friend, William Lloyd Garrison, but far more humane a man. His hatred of slavery and other injustice was almost always accompanied by an attempt to understand those responsible for the institution. There was no racism in Frederick Douglass, which could not be said of others in the reform movement. When, in 1884, Douglass married a second time, to a white woman, many old abolitionist colleagues criticized him. Douglass shrugged with splendid insouciance that he was impartial: his first wife "was the color of my mother, and the second, the color of my father." He was the first in the line of the great spokesmen for African Americans that includes Booker T. Washington, Martin Luther King, Jr., and Malcolm X.

As a work of literature, *Uncle Tom's Cabin* is deficient, but its underlying theme is subtle: no matter how decent and well-intentioned the individual slave owner, he cannot help but do wrong by living with an inherently evil institution. In the story, Uncle Tom's original owner is the epitome of the paternalistic planter who genuinely loves his old slave—the proslavery argument's beau idéal. Nevertheless, when financial troubles make it necessary for him to raise money quickly, he is forced to sell his Tom. Heartbroken, the planter promises Tom that he will find him and buy him back as soon as he is able. Nevertheless, *he sells his beloved friend because he can; the law makes Tom a commodity!*

It was not, however, this insight into the peculiar institution that made *Uncle Tom's Cabin* so popular. Rather, the book's effectiveness owed to its graphic, lurid scenes of cruelty that Tom witnesses and suffers in the course of the story. Mrs. Stowe herself accepted this as the book's contribution. When southerners angrily complained that she had distorted the realities of slave life, she responded in 1853 with *A Key to Uncle Tom's Cabin*, which set out the documentary basis of most of her accusations, much of it quotations from southern newspapers.

Blacks never forgot this side of slavery, but with the ascendancy of the romantic version in the late nineteenth century, most white Americans did. Not until the civil rights movement of the 1950s and 1960s awakened the country to the tragic history of American blacks did the ugly face of the peculiar institution again impress itself on the popular consciousness.

WHAT SLAVERY WAS LIKE

Which image is correct? Both and neither. Although proslavery and antislavery partisans dealt with the peculiar institution as though it were monolithic, the same thing in Virginia and Texas, on cotton plantation and New Orleans river front, on sprawling plantation and gloomy frontier homestead, for field hand and big house butler, the reality of slavery was as diverse as the South itself.

Structure of the Institution: White Perspective

The census of 1860, the last census that was taken while slavery was legal, revealed that nearly 4 million people lived in bondage. They were equally divided between males and females. All but a handful lived in the 15 states south of the Mason-Dixon line and the Ohio River. West of the Mississippi River, Missouri, Arkansas, Louisiana, and Texas were slave states.

Only one white southern family in four owned slaves. Even when those whose living depended directly on the existence of the institution—overseers, slave traders, and patrollers—are added in, it is clear that only a minority of white southerners had a material stake in slavery.

Those who were very rich and politically powerful because they owned slaves were particularly few. In 1860, only 2,200 great planters, less than 1 percent of the southern population, owned 100 or more slaves. Only 254 persons owned 200 or more. Nathaniel Heyward of South Carolina was at the top of this dubious pyramid; he owned 2,000 slaves on 17 plantations.

More typical of the southern slave owner was Jacob Eaton of neighboring North Carolina. On his 160-acre farm he worked side by side with the slave family he owned. Eaton's yeoman class—small independent farmers who owned one to nine slaves—was the backbone of both the South and the slavery system. About 74 percent of southern slave owners fell into this category. Another 16 percent of slave owners fell into the middle category of those who owned between 10 and 20 people. A mere 10 percent of slave owners owned more than 20 slaves.

Structure of the Institution: Black Perspective

If the big plantation was rare from a white perspective, life in the shadow of the big house was more common in the eyes of the blacks. By 1860, more than half the slaves lived on what we would think of as a plantation rather than a farm. Perhaps half a million belonged to members of the great planter class.

There were a few black slave owners. The census of 1830 revealed 3,775 free African Americans in possession of 12,760 black slaves. One of the most bizarre cases was that of Dilsey Pope, a free black woman of Columbus, Georgia, who owned her husband. There was a fierce quarrel and Mrs. Pope sold him to a white neighbor. When the couple reconciled, the new owner refused to sell the husband back to Mrs. Pope. (Their marriage had no standing in the law.)

There were even some great planters who were black. Andrew Durnford of New Orleans owned 77 slaves. When questioned about this, Durnford said frankly that his ownership of other blacks was self-interest. Owning slaves was the way to wealth in the South. Although he contributed to the American Colonization Society, Durnford freed only four slaves during his lifetime, another in his will.

First Light to Sundown

Few blacks enjoyed the material advantages of living—better food, clothing, sanitation, sometimes living quarters—as domestic servants. Cooks, maids, butlers, valets, and footmen made life more pleasant

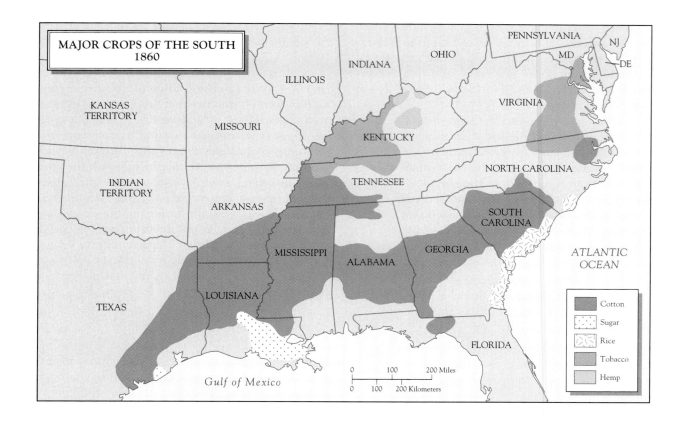

for the great planters who could afford them, but they did not make money for their masters. The vast majority of slaves were field hands who raised a cash crop by means of heavy labor from first light to sundown almost year-round. For a slave owner to justify investing capital in a labor force rather than hiring free laborers and putting his capital elsewhere, it was necessary to keep the property hopping.

Cotton was by far the most important southern product (the most important *American* product!). During the 1850s, an average annual crop of 4 million bales brought more than $190 million into the American economy from abroad. Cotton represented two-thirds of the nation's total exports and (in 1850) fully 1.8 million slaves out of 3.2 million worked it. Other cash crops that slaves raised were tobacco (350,000 slaves), sugar (150,000), rice (125,000), and hemp, from which rope was manufactured (60,000).

Southern farmers and planters strove to be self-sufficient. Therefore, slaves raised corn, vegetables, and hogs for food, and hay for fodder, as well as their cash crop. There was plenty of work to be done on farm or plantation year-round. The calendar of a cotton plantation was packed with jobs, major and odd, except for a short period around Christmas, to which the slaves looked forward as "laying-by time."

Curiously, because slaves were expensive—up to $2,000 for a first-rate field hand, a healthy man in the prime of life—planters preferred to hire free black or Irish workers to perform some unhealthy and dangerous tasks. Few risked their costly human property on draining swamps or working at the bottom of chutes down which 600-pound bales of cotton came hurtling at high speeds, sometimes flipping end over end.

The Rhythms of Labor

By the 1850s, a slave produced from $80 to $120 in value each year and cost between $30 and $50 to feed, clothe, and shelter. The margin of profit was not large enough to allow the small-scale slave owner to live without working in the fields along with his slaves.

Planters who owned 10 to 20 slaves were less likely to perform menial tasks. But because slaves rarely worked any more than they were forced to do (their share of the fruits of their labor was quite firmly fixed) the owner had to supervise them—constantly bribing, cajoling, threatening, or whipping them to

Washington the Slave Owner

At the time of his death in 1799, George Washington owned 300 slaves at Mount Vernon and four additional plantations. The father-of-his-country's record as a patriarch was mixed. On the one hand, according to a visitor from Poland, the slaves' houses at Washington's River Farm were "more miserable than the most miserable cottages of our peasants." Washington himself expressed embarrassment over living conditions at River Farm.

On the other hand, Washington was deeply concerned to respect his slaves' family and marriage relationships. Children remained with their mothers until age 14. Slave husbands and wives were separated when one but not the other was needed elsewhere, and some of Washington's slaves were married to the slaves of other planters or to free blacks. However, Washington meticulously recorded who was tied to whom, and he refused to sell costly surplus slaves "because they could not be disposed of in families . . . and to disperse the families I have an aversion."

Moreover, Washington's plantations were within four miles of one another and "nightwalking," conjugal visits, were a constant problem of which he complained but did little. In his will, Washington provided that his slaves be freed only after his wife's death because they had intermarried with Martha Washington's "Dower Negroes" and it "would excite the most painful sensations" if they were to be separated.

slipshod labor as their workers rushed through their tasks to get to their own chores or recreation.

Under the gang system, slaves worked from sunrise to sundown in groups under a white overseer or black driver. It is impossible to know how frequently they felt the sting of the blacksnake. The lash was always in evidence, however, in black hand as well as white. Frederick Douglass wryly remarked that "everybody in the South wants the privilege of whipping someone else."

The Slave Trade

Slaves were defined in law as chattel property, personal movable possessions legally much the same as cattle, hogs, a cotton gin, a chair, or a share of stock. They could be bought, sold, bartered, willed, or given away as a present. In practice in the volatile cotton economy, the commerce in slaves was brisk and potentially quite profitable.

The slave trade was the ugliest face of slavery. Even strident defenders of the institution admitted it. The general flow of the commerce was down the river—the Mississippi—from the older tobacco states to the cotton states of the Deep South. Professional slave traders bought blacks in Virginia and Maryland, and shipped them or marched them in coffles (groups chained together in a line) to New Orleans, where as many as 200 companies were in the business.

The slave auction was in many ways like a livestock auction. Foreigners, northerners, and many southerners were simultaneously disgusted and fascinated by them, much as American tourists in Mexico or Spain today react to bullfights. Prospective buyers crowded around the auction block, examining the teeth of the slaves in which they were interested, as they would examine those of horses; running them around to test their wind; wiping handkerchiefs over their bodies to determine if the auctioneer had dyed gray hairs black or rubbed oil into aged dry skin; and then raucously entering their bids.

Some abolitionists claimed that slaves were methodically bred like animals. Indeed, women were rewarded for bearing children, thus increasing their owners' wealth, and were sometimes described in auction advertisements as good breeders. In Maryland, census takers discovered plantations on which the workforce consisted of one adult male, half a dozen young women, and perhaps twice that many small children—not a group likely to get a lot done if agriculture was the idea. However, the gospel of

move along. With more than 20 slaves, a planter could afford to hire a professional overseer or to put a straw boss or slave driver (himself a slave) in charge of supervision. On the very large plantations, masters had little direct contact with their field hands. They could cultivate a genuine ignorance of how overseers and straw bosses mistreated their "people."

Slaves on larger plantations worked according to the task system or the gang system. Under the task system, a specific job was assigned each day. When it was done, the slave's time was his or her own. For some planters this was the most efficient form of organization because, when provided with an incentive, however meager, the slaves worked harder. Others complained that the result of the task system was

Slaves were kept in these cells in Alexandria, Virginia, until they were sold by slave traders.

the positive-good required slave owners who took it seriously to abhor such immorality, and slave breeding as a business was undoubtedly rare.

Masters aspiring to be patriarchs disapproved of everything about the slave trade, describing slave traders as base, crude, unworthy men. Nevertheless, as Harriet Beecher Stowe and others pointed out, without the slave trade there could be no slavery. If some humans were to be property, others had to have the right to buy and sell them. Where there is trade, there must be brokers.

The Foreign Slave Trade

After 1808, it was a violation of federal law to import slaves. But when the price of slaves was high, some buccaneers were willing to try to bring in blacks from West Africa or Cuba.

It was a risky business. The Royal Navy patrolled African waters, and American naval vessels cruised the Atlantic and Gulf coasts. Nevertheless, an estimated 50,000 to 55,000 Africans and black Cubans were smuggled into the United States between 1808 and 1861. During the 1850s, several travelers in the South reported seeing a number of black men and women with filed teeth, tattoos, and ritual mutilations that were practiced only in Africa. On the very eve of the Civil War, a slave vessel successfully made its way into the Charleston harbor.

In the late 1850s, the price of slaves soared beyond the reach of all but the very wealthy. A group of southern politicians met at Vicksburg, Mississippi, and formally demanded the reopening of the African slave trade. Such a law would never have passed Congress, but the Vicksburg Convention alarmed many northerners and contributed to the hardening of sectional hostilities that contributed to the Civil War.

LIFE IN THE QUARTERS

The slave codes of most southern states provided that slaves had no civil rights. They could not own property under the law; therefore, they could not legally buy and sell anything. They could not make contracts. They could not marry legally. They could not testify in court against any white person (nor could free blacks in most southern states). They could not even leave the plantation without their owners' written permission.

It was a crime for a slave to strike a white person under any circumstances, even self-defense. Slaves could not carry firearms. They could not congregate in more than small groups except at religious services under white supervision. They could not be abroad at night. And in most southern states, it was a crime for a white or another black to teach a slave to read.

The slaves' rights were those to life and, under most slave codes, a minimum standard of food, clothing, and shelter.

Humans without Human Rights

The actual experience of slave life had little to do with the letter of the slave codes; for example, it was not accounted murder when a master killed a slave during "moderate" or "reasonable" punishment, words difficult to define in courts. Whipping was the most common means of corporal punishment, and 50 lashes—quite enough to kill a man—was not an uncommon sentence. In the end, the slaves' only guarantee against death or brutal mistreatment at the hands of their masters was the gospel of patriarchy, social pressure, public opinion, religious scruples, and the cash value of the slaves.

There are few better guarantees than a man's self-esteem and his money, but neither was foolproof. Struggling slave owners had little time for their genteel neighbors' opinions of their moral sense. Slave owners and overseers did fly into uncontrolled rages and kill slaves. Because their property rights in their slaves inevitably took precedence over the slaves' few human rights, owners were rarely punished. After an incident of hideous torture in Virginia in 1858, with the slave victim dying after 24 hours of beating and burning, the law punished the sadistic master by imprisoning him. But he was not required to forfeit ownership of several other blacks.

A Diverse Institution

If the laws protecting slaves were not effective, it was also true that many slave owners were moved by personal decency and by their determination to live up to the ideal of the benevolent patriarch to care for their slaves far better than the law required, and sometimes in violation of the slave codes.

A family that owned only one or two slaves occasionally developed a relationship much like partnership with them. White owners and black slaves ate the same food, slept in the same cabin, and worked together intimately. On the whole, however, the slave on a large plantation was more likely to be better off, simply because of the poverty of the struggling small farmer.

After about 1840, large-scale slave owners generally provided simple but adequate rations. It was common to allow slaves to keep their own vegetable plots and even chickens; masters sometimes did not keep their own gardens and coops but bought vegetables and eggs from their slaves. Here and there was a master who allowed the blacks to raise hogs for their own use, but the master could not always be sure if the pork chop on the slave's table was the slave's own or stolen from him.

Some slaves were permitted to buy and sell outside the boundaries of the plantation and to keep the money they earned. Along the Mississippi River, task system slaves working on their own time cut wood for the steamboats. Some sold chickens and eggs in nearby towns, and some slaves even kept shotguns for hunting. One remarkable character was Simon Gray, a skilled flatboatman who was paid $8 a month to haul lumber to New Orleans. Gray commanded crews of up to 20 men, including free whites, and kept detailed accounts for his owner. He eventually bought his own freedom.

A few masters permitted their slaves to save money in order to purchase their own, their spouse's, or their children's freedom. In at least one instance, a Kentucky judge actually enforced an agreement on

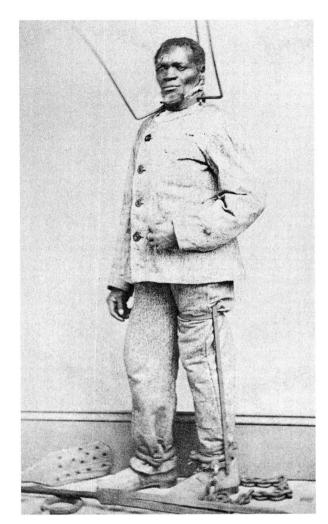

This photograph of an African American with instruments of punishment was widely distributed to raise money "for the benefit of colored people."

a purchase price between a master and slave as a valid contract.

Another example of open violation of the slave code was on the model plantation of Joseph Davis, brother of Jefferson Davis, the future president of the Confederate States of America. Ignoring a Mississippi state law forbidding the education of blacks, Joseph Davis maintained a school and teacher for the children of the quarters.

It is important to recall, however, that for every master like Joseph Davis there was another who kept his slaves just sound enough to work and who agreed with the man who wrote without embarrassment to a magazine that "Africans are nothing but brutes,

Freedom Song

When Israel was in Egypt land
Let my people go
Oppressed so hard they could not stand
Let my people go.
Go down, Moses,
Way down in Egypt land
Tell old Pharaoh
To let my people go.

and they will love you better for whipping, whether they deserve it or not."

MODES OF PROTEST

Whether their master was kindly or cruel, their material circumstances adequate or execrable, the blacks hated their lot in life. While some were deeply and sincerely attached to their masters, and while rebellion was rare after Nat Turner, the blacks resisted slavery in other ways. When freedom became a realistic possibility during the Civil War, slaves deserted their homes by the thousands to flee to Union lines and, in the case of the young men, to enlist in the Union Army. As a South Carolina planter wrote candidly after the war, "I believed these people were content, happy, and attached to their masters." That, he concluded sadly, was a delusion.

Malingering and Thieving

This honest man might have been spared his disappointment had he given deeper consideration to white people's stereotypes of the blacks under slavery. It was commonly held that blacks were inherently lazy, irresponsible, and would not work except under close supervision. In fact, free blacks generally worked quite hard, and the same slaves whose laziness was a constant aggravation in the cotton fields, toiled in their own gardens from dawn to dusk on Sundays and often, by moonlight, during the week. In slavery, the only incentive to work hard for the master was negative—the threat of punishment—and that incentive was often not enough to cause men and women to ignore the blazing southern sun. When the overseer or driver was over the hill, it was nap time.

Theft was so common on plantations that whites believed blacks to be congenital thieves. Again, the only incentive not to steal a chicken, a suckling pig, or a berry pie from the big-house kitchen was fear of punishment. If a slave was not caught, he had no reason to believe he had done wrong. One chicken thief who was caught in the act of eating his prize explained this point trenchantly to his master: if the chicken was master's property and he was master's property, then master had not lost anything because the chicken was in his belly instead of scratching around the hen yard. It is not known if this meditation saved the philosopher from a whipping.

Running Away

The most direct testimony of slave discontent was the prevalence of runaways. Only blacks who lived in the states that bordered the free states—Delaware, Maryland, Kentucky—had a reasonable chance of escaping

Uncle Remus Explains

Many historians of slavery believe that because violent resistance by blacks was suicidal, many slaves (and post–Civil War southern blacks) devised the technique of "playing Uncle Tom," that is, playing a docile role in front of whites in order to survive. Uncle Remus describes this behavior in "Why Br'er Possum Loves Peace." Mr. Dog attacks Br'er Coon and Br'er Possum. Br'er Coon fights back and drives Mr. Dog away, but at the price of taking some damage himself. In the meantime, Br'er Possum plays possum, plays dead.

Later, representing blacks who want to fight back, Br'er Coon berates Br'er Possum for cowardice. "'I ain't runnin' wid cowards deze days,' sez Br'er Coon." Br'er Possum replies that just because he did not fight does not mean that he is a coward:

I want no mo' skeer'd dan you is right now . . . but I'm de most ticklish chap w'at you ever laid eyes on, en no sooner did Mr. Dog put his nose down yer 'mong my ribs dan I got ter laffin. . . . I don't mine fightin', Br'er Coon, no mo' dan you duz . . . but I declar' ter grashus ef I kin stan' ticklin.

Wit, not violence, was the way to deal with vicious whites. Note that it is Mr. Dog, not Br'er—Brother.

to permanent freedom. A great many were successful "riding" what they called the "underground railway," rushing at night from hiding places in one abolitionist's home to another. Because the railway was not so well organized as legend has it, most runaways who succeeded probably did so on their own devices, or by depending on African American "conductors." Harriet Tubman, who escaped from her master in 1849, returned to the South 19 times to lead other blacks to freedom. (During the Civil War, Tubman was a Union spy behind Confederate lines.)

In calling for a stricter Fugitive Slave Act in 1850 (a law that gave the federal government the responsibility of returning slaves), southerners estimated that as many as 100,000 blacks escaped to the free states. Several times that number tried and failed.

Common throughout the South was running away in the full knowledge that capture and punishment were inevitable. Nevertheless, the appeal of a few days or weeks of freedom, or the chance to visit a spouse or a friend on another plantation, was worth the risk to so many blacks that runaway slaves were a vexation to masters from Maryland to Mississippi.

Runaways in hiding relied on other blacks to conceal and feed them. The fact that they were hidden and fed at risk to their benefactors of corporal punishment reveals the existence of a sense of solidarity among the slaves that can never be fully understood by historians because the slaves kept no written records. But some indication of the quality of life in the slave quarters from sundown to first light can be conjectured from what is known of black religion and folklore.

Let My People Go

By the 1850s, most slaves had warmly embraced an emotional brand of Protestant Christianity that was basically Baptist and Methodist in temper. Religious services were replete with animated sermons by unlettered but charismatic preachers and exuberant rhythmic singing, the Negro spirituals loved by whites as well as by blacks.

In the sermons and spirituals, hymns that combined biblical themes with African musical forms, the slaves explicitly identified with the ancient Hebrews. While in bondage in Babylon and Egypt, the Hebrews had been, in their simplicity and poverty, God's chosen people. In the afterlife, all human beings would be equal and happy.

Harriet Tubman (left; ca. 1820–1913) stands with a group of slaves she helped escape to freedom.

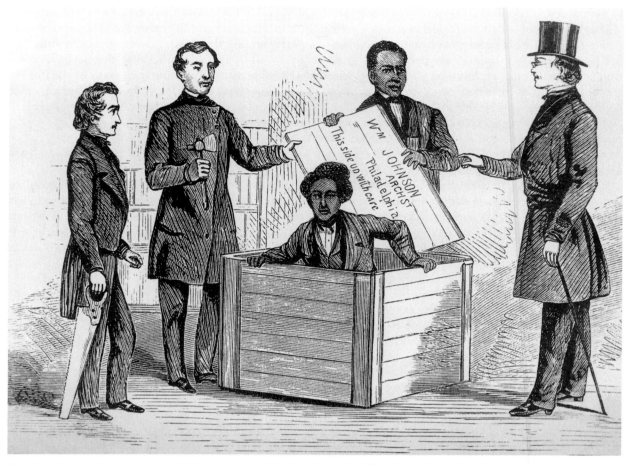

Henry Brown's escape from slavery in a shipping crate earned him the nickname "Box" for the remainder of his life.

This cry of protest was not lost on the whites. But as long as they believed that slaves associated freedom with the next life, there was no reason to stifle the cry. However, there was also a worldly facet of slave religion. Biblical characters who were delivered in life, such as Joshua, Jonah, and Daniel, were heroes in African American hagiography. One kind of spiritual, such as "Ride on, King Jesus," depicted Christ as a warrior messiah. The implications were obvious.

"Bred en Bawn in a Brier-Patch"

Another thinly masked form of protest was the folk tales for which black storytellers became famous, particularly the Br'er Rabbit stories that were collected after the Civil War as *Uncle Remus: His Songs and Sayings* by Georgia journalist Joel Chandler Harris. In these yarns, elements of which have been traced back to West African folklore, the rabbit, a weak victim of stronger animals and unable to defend himself by force, survives and flourishes through the use of trickery and complex deceits.

In the most famous of the Uncle Remus stories, "How Mr. Rabbit Was Too Sharp for Mr. Fox," Br'er Fox has the rabbit in his hands and is debating with himself whether to barbecue him, hang him, drown him, or skin him. Br'er Rabbit assures the fox that he will be happy with any of these fates as long as the fox does not fling him into a nearby brier-patch, which he fears more than anything. Of course, that is exactly what Br'er Fox does, whence Br'er Rabbit is home free. "Bred en bawn in a brier-patch, Br'er Fox," Br'er Rabbit shouts back tauntingly, "bred en bawn in a brier-patch." The slaves, unable to taunt their masters so bluntly, satisfied themselves with quiet trickery and coded tales about it.

It is worth noting that in the Uncle Remus stories, Br'er Rabbit now and then outsmarts himself and suffers for it. As in all social commentary of substance, the slaves were as sensitive to their own foibles as to those of their masters.

The Slave Community

Like Br'er Rabbit, slaves presented a different face to whites than among their own people. Often, individuals reinforced white beliefs in their inferiority by playing the lazy, dimwitted, comical "Sambo," quite devoted to "Ol' Marse" and patently incapable of taking care of themselves. Some observant whites noticed that Sambo was quick-witted enough when surprised while talking to other slaves, or that he literally slaved in his own garden and only slept in the cotton fields.

For the most part, however, the vitality of black culture and the slave community remained concealed from whites. It can be read only in the folktales and sermons and recollections of slavery gathered after emancipation. Perhaps the most striking demonstration of the resourcefulness of the blacks in sticking together for mutual support lies in the fact that family connections were powerful and productive. By 1865, when slavery was abolished, there were ten times as many slaves in the United States as had been imported from Africa and the West Indies. The American slave population was the only one in the Western Hemisphere to increase as a result of natural reproduction. Only after the blacks of South and Central America were freed from bondage did their numbers grow naturally.

Against all odds, the nuclear family was a strong institution among slaves and remained so after emancipation, as this photo of Virginia peanut farmers implies.

CHRONOLOGY

1818   African slave trade abolished

1851–1860   Stephen Foster's sentimental songs of
            an idyllic South are published

1840, 1844 James G. Birney is presidential candi-
            date for abolitionist Liberty party

1845   Publication of Frederick Douglass's
            Autobiography

1850   Strict and effective Fugitive Slave
            Law enacted
            Slave trade abolished in Washington

1851   Publication of Harriet Beecher
            Stowe's *Uncle Tom's Cabin*

1936   Publication of Margaret Mitchell's
            Gone with the Wind (film in 1939)

FOR FURTHER READING

Ulrich B. Phillips, *American Negro Slavery*, 1919, and *Life and Labor in the Old South*, 1929, present sometimes romanticized, almost sympathetic portraits of slavery, and yet, despite the bias of the books, they contain much valuable information and are congenially written. Kenneth Stampp, *The Peculiar Institution*, 1956, was an explicit response to Phillips and is equally valuable.

Since the 1960s, slavery has been studied exhaustively in virtually all its aspects. Just a few of the hundreds of titles include Ira Berlin, *Slaves without Masters*, 1975; John Blassingame, *The Slave Community*, 1972, and *Slave Testimony*, 1977; Carl N. Degler, *Neither Black nor White: Slavery and Race Relations in Brazil and the United States*, 1971; Stanley Elkins, *Slavery*, 1968; Robert Fogel and Stanley Engermann, *Time on the Cross*, 1974—the findings of which are attacked in Herbert Gutman and Richard Sutch, *Slavery and the Numbers Game*, 1975; Paul A. David, et al., *Reckoning with Slavery*, 1976; and Michael Tadman, *Speculators and Slaves: Traders and Slaves in the Old South*, 1989.

See also George M. Frederickson, *The Black Image in the White Mind*, 1971; Eugene Genovese, *The Political Economy of Slavery*, 1962, and *Roll Jordan Roll*, 1975; Herbert G. Gutman, *The Black Family in Slavery and Freedom, 1750–1925*, 1976; Lawrence W. Levine, *Black Culture and Black Consciousness: Afro-American Folk Thought from Slavery to Freedom*, 1977; Gilbert Osofsky, *Puttin' on Ol' Massa*, 1969; Harold

Rawick, *From Sundown to Sunup*, 1967; Robert Starobin, *Industrial Slavery in the Old South*, 1970; Stephen B. Oates, *The Fires of Jubilee: Nat Turner's Fierce Rebellion*, 1975; and Jacqueline Jones, *Labor of Love, Labor of Sorrow: Black Women, Work, and the Family from Slavery to the Present*, 1985.

Useful books on abolitionism include Ronald Abzug, *Passionate Liberator: Theodore Dwight Weld and the Dilemma of Reform*, 1980; William McFeely, *Frederick Douglass*, 1991; M. L. Dillon, *The Abolitionists: The Growth of a Dissenting Minority*, 1974; Aileen S. Kraditor, *Means and Ends in American Abolitionism: Garrison and His Critics on Strategy and Tactics, 1834–50*, 1967; Gerda Lerner, *The Grimké Sisters from South Carolina: Rebels against Slavery*, 1967; Jean Fagan Yellin, *Women and Sisters: The Antislavery Feminists in American Culture*, 1989; Walter M. Merrill, *Against Wind and Tide: A Biography of William Lloyd Garrison*, 1963; Benjamin Quarles, *Black Abolitionists*, 1969; Gerald Sorin, *Abolitionism: A New Perspective*, 1972; J. B. Stewart, *Holy Warriors: The Abolitionists and American Slavery*, 1976; and B. P. Thomas, *Theodore Dwight Weld: Crusader for Freedom*, 1950.

On the pro-slavery argument, see George M. Frederickson, *The Black Image in the White Mind*, 1971; W. S. Jenkins, *Pro-Slavery Thought in the Old South*, 1935; William Stanton, *The Leopard's Spots: Scientific Attitudes toward Race in America, 1815–1859*, 1960; and Harvey Wish, *George Fitzhugh: Propagandist of the Old South*, 1943.

A family bound overland brims with pioneer strength and determination.

20
CHAPTER

FROM SEA TO SHINING SEA

American Expansion

1820–1848

Our manifest destiny is to overspread the continent allotted by Providence for the free development of our yearly multiplying millions.

— *John Louis O'Sullivan*

If I were a Mexican, I would tell you, "Have you not room in your own country to bury your dead men? If you come into mine, we will greet you with bloody hands, and welcome you to hospitable graves."

— *Thomas Corwin*

After the purchase of Louisiana in 1803, the national boundaries of the United States appeared to be complete. Thomas Jefferson believed that the land he acquired from France would provide farms for the sons and daughters of his beloved yeomanry for centuries. After Lewis and Clark returned with the news that there was no easy route across the North American continent to the Pacific, thus killing hopes of an easy trade with the Far East, there seemed little point in looking farther west.

The Atlantic Ocean and the Mississippi River were America's outlets to the rest of the world. The Rocky Mountains, imagined more than known, provided a pronounced natural boundary in the West. To some, indeed, the eastern slope of the Rockies seemed to be a natural boundary. Rainfall was so sparse on the plains rolling eastward from the Rockies that the grasslands were practically treeless. The country was thought of as a void fit for only the bison that wandered them and the mounted Indians who followed the great herds.

In the Southwest, there was desirable land beyond the Sabine River, the boundary between Louisiana and Mexican Texas agreed to in 1819 by John Quincy Adams. Eastern Texas was fertile and well-watered. But the early leaders of the Mexican Republic were cordial toward the *norteamericanos*, whose war for independence and constitution had inspired them. During the 1820s, conflict between Mexico and the United States was difficult to imagine.

Things change. Within a few decades, the Mexican president Porfirio Díaz would lament of his country, "Poor Mexico, so far from God and so close to the United States."

MEXICO: SO CLOSE TO THE UNITED STATES

Even after Cortés and the conquistadores looted the riches of the native Mexican cultures, the viceroyalty of New Spain remained the jewel of the Spanish Empire. Spanish-born *gachupines* and Mexican-born white *criollos* monopolized the best lands and lived fat off the labor and skills of the Indians and mixed-blood mestizos. Mexico was home to the greatest of the indigenous New World civilizations, an amalgam of Spanish and Indian cultures. When the English settlers at Jamestown were surviving on roots and oysters grubbed from tidal waters, 300 poets competed for a prize in Mexico City. In 1609, Spanish adventurers established Santa Fe in the Sangre de Cristo Mountains of present-day New Mexico, deep in the North American continent. When Sydney Smith was mocking the absence of culture in the United States, an intellectual and literary life rivaling that of the lesser capitals of Europe flourished in Mexico City.

Mexico Expands North

Indeed, while Anglo-Americans were just beginning to penetrate the Appalachians, Spanish adventurers and friars were planting colonies in what is now the United States. The rivers of Texas, especially the Rio Bravo of the North, or the Rio Grande, were dotted with presidios (military bases) and missions far more numerous than the old French trading posts along the Mississippi.

During the first years of American independence, a Franciscan priest, Junípero Serra, established a string of missions in California, the northernmost at Sonoma northeast of San Francisco. His plan, eventually fulfilled, made it possible for a foot traveler along the *camino real* (royal highway) to spend every night in a secure, hospitable mission compound. As in New Mexico, a gracious but simple way of life evolved among the small numbers of *californios* who lived in the most distant Mexican province.

The Santa Fe Trade

In 1821, newly independent Mexico abandoned the old Spanish restrictions on trade with the United States. William Becknell, an alert and enterprising businessman in Independence, Missouri, immediately set off with pack animals laden with American manufactures: cloth, shoes, tools, and some luxury items. Feeling his way by compass, with an eye for animal paths, and by dead reckoning across what is now Kansas, he blazed an 800-mile trail to Santa Fe. To his surprise and delight, the route was suitable for wagons and the 7,000 inhabitants of the mountain community were so remote from the centers of Mexican population—it took a year and a half for trains of wagons, each drawn by a twenty-mule team, to make the round trip between Mexico City and Santa Fe—that they were starved both for imports and a market for their own produce. Becknell pocketed a fine profit selling the furs and gold that he brought back to Missouri.

Annually for 14 years, convoys of heavy wagons retraced Becknell's tracks. Only a few Missourians, such as the famous scout Kit Carson, actually settled in Santa Fe or nearby Taos, an Indian village, and those who did were happy to adapt to the gracious Spanish-Indian culture of the region. Nevertheless, the presence of even a few *sajones* (Saxons) in northernmost Mexico forged a link between an attractive country and the United States that was—no matter the flag that flew—stronger than the link between Santa Fe and Mexico City.

The Great American Desert

As for the American territory that the Santa Fe traders crossed, where the Stars and Stripes did fly, most Americans believed it was worthless. In what is now central Nebraska and Kansas, at about 100° west lon-

gitude, the land begins a gradual rise from an elevation of about 2,000 feet to, at the base of the Rockies, 5,000 to 7,000 feet. These high plains lie in the rain shadow of the Rockies. Before the winds from the West reach the plains, the moisture in them is scooped out by the great mountains. Save for next-to-useless cottonwoods along the rivers, few trees grew on the great plains. The vastness of the landscape unnerved people who were accustomed to forests.

When Americans gazed over the windblown buffalo grass on the rolling plains, they thought not of farmland but of the ocean. The Santa Fe traders called their wagons prairie schooners. Less romantic military map makers labeled the country "the Great American Desert." Many travelers observed that the

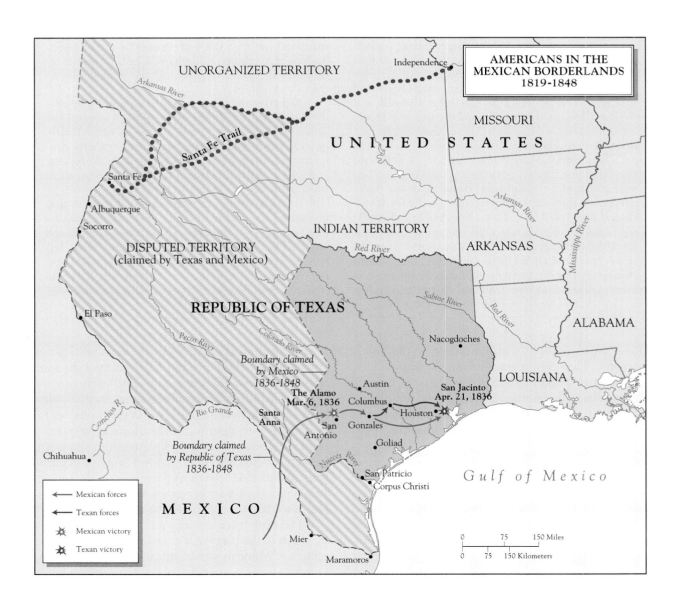

HOW THEY LIVED

Zorro and the Californios

Alta California—Upper California—was thinly populated when the United States seized it in the Mexican War, but it was far from an empty land. Indians were more numerous in California's mild climate than in any region of North America except the Eastern Woodlands a century and more earlier. And thousands of Mexicans had followed Spain's mission fathers north in the late eighteenth and early nineteenth centuries. Some of these *californios,* as they called themselves, clustered around small mercantile towns and *presidios* (military bases) such as San Diego, Los Angeles, Monterey, Yerba Buena (San Francisco), and Sonoma. Most, however, were ranchers living in isolation on vast government land grants. A few Americans, like John Bidwell and William Ide, as well as Europeans like the Dane, Peter Lassen, and the Swiss, John Augustus Sutter, had taken out grants.

They and the *californios* were rich in acres but they lived just a notch or two above subsistence. The only commodities California produced for the international market were hides and tallow, the fat of cattle and sheep cooked down for use in soap and candle manufacture. Neither brought in much money and few ships called at remote California ports. Even the richest *californios* lived in adobe homes, rarely more than one story high and rarely large. Furniture and most manufactures were made on the scene by Indian

craftsmen. Diet was ample (plenty of beef!) and *californio* cuisine, while ingenious, was inelegant.

Nevertheless, the *californios* were proud of their independence and self-sufficiency and keenly conscious of their social status at the top of California's rather simple pyramid. Most of the grandees were of modest background but, just as the great planters of eighteenth-century Virginia took their values and mores from the English gentry, elite *californios* considered themselves *hidalgos,* Spanish noblemen, rightful rulers but also the benefactors of their lessers, both poor Mexicans and Indians. The top families intermarried, carefully planning the genealogies of their descendants.

Tight-knit as it was, the *californio* community was divided down the middle by the American invasion. Some, feeling little commitment to old Mexico, quickly made their peace with their gringo conquerors and salvaged at least some of their property and social position. Others resisted and won a few small battles before being overcome.

It was less the American victory, however, that inundated the *californios* (and non-Hispanic *hidalgos* like Sutter), than the great gold rushes of 1849 and 1850. The Spanish-speaking ranchers were left behind or literally overrun by the flood of gold seekers. Among those who were ruined was Salomón María Simeón Pico, the son of a soldier who had been

grass that nourished 10 million bison would fatten cattle too. However, it was difficult to imagine how hypothetical steers might be transported to eastern markets. All agreed that the Indians of the plains, who were satisfied to trade with or charge tolls to the Santa Fe traders, were welcome to what they had.

The Texans

To the south, the Great Plains extended into Texas, then part of the Mexican state of Coahuila. There cattle could be grazed within easy driving distance of the Gulf of Mexico and shipped by water to New Orleans. As early as 1819, a Connecticut Yankee named

Moses Austin was attracted by the possibilities of a grazing economy there, and he also noted the suitability of eastern Texas to cotton cultivation.

He died before he was able to implement his idea, but in 1821, his son Stephen Austin concluded his father's agreement with the Mexican government. Austin was licensed to settle 300 American families in Texas, each household to receive 177 acres of farmland and/or 1,428 acres of pasture land. In return, Austin promised that the settlers would abide by Mexican law and observe the Roman Catholic religion.

The earliest settlers may well have meant to keep their part of the bargain, but Texas was so far from the centers of Mexican power and culture, and the immi-

granted 11 Spanish leagues (48,829 acres, 19,756 hectares) between the Tuolumne and Stanislaus Rivers, two of the richest gold-bearing streams. According to legend, Pico not only lost his herds and land, but his wife was raped and beaten, dying soon thereafter.

It is not easy to separate legend from fact in Pico's subsequent career. It is clear that he became a masked highwayman on the old *camino real* between Santa María and Santa Barbara, and cut an ear off each of his mostly gringo victims to leave no doubt as to the identity of the perpetrator. (Pico strung his trophies and carried them on his saddle horn like a lariat.) It is less likely that he gave his cash earnings to impoverished *californio* families, but he was something of a popular hero among them even during his lifetime. Pico moved about California with impunity for eight years, aided no doubt by the fact that two brothers were mayors of San Luis Obispo and San Jose.

His most famous scrape with the law came in November 1851, when he shot the hat off the head of Los Angeles Judge Benjamin Hayes, who was presiding over the trial of three *californios* charged with murder. Although himself wounded, Pico escaped, helped by another *californio* who held off a pursuing sheriff with a sword. In 1857, Pico moved to Baja California. Three years later, he was arrested by Mexican authorities and summarily executed.

In the twentieth century, as "Zorro"—the Fox—a name Pico never used, the anti-American bandit became a popular culture hero in the United States. In 1919, writer Johnston McCulley collected the many Pico legends, deftly adapted them to appeal to an American readership, and published them as *The Curse of Capistrano*. Pico's fictional name was Don Diego Vega and he lived not in California's American era but earlier, when California was a Mexican province. His enemies were not gringos but corrupt Mexican authorities.

Unlike Pico the highwayman, Don Diego was a gracious *hidalgo* by day who donned a mask not for the purpose of robbery but to fight for justice and something much like what was called "the American Way." So admirable a gentleman could not be amputating ears and stringing them on rawhide, of course. Instead, McCulley's Zorro left his trademark by cutting a "Z" on his victims' cheeks.

Even that was too nasty for television. In the 1950s, when Zorro came into American living rooms on the small screen, he contented himself to cut "Z" into the bark of trees, on the sides of buildings, or, bloodlessly on the clothing of his adversaries. Rather more remarkably, the television Zorro devoted a good deal of his time to protecting decent and well-meaning gringos from venal Mexicans.

---

grants were so numerous (20,000 whites and 2,000 blacks, mostly slaves, by 1834), that Texas was inevitably American in culture and customs. Even so, because the province was prosperous and produced some tax revenues, there might have been no trouble. Then in 1831, Mexico abolished slavery, and in 1833, General Antonio López de Santa Anna seized power in the capital. By this time, slavery was vital to the Texas economy and Santa Anna proved to be less accommodating a Mexican president than his predecessors.

Above all, Santa Anna wanted to put an end to the squabbling that had plagued Mexican politics since independence, to promote a sense of Mexican nationality. He centralized the powers of govern-

ment in the constitution he promulgated in 1835 and canceled American trading rights in Santa Fe. His reforms meant an end to the considerable autonomy the Texans had enjoyed and jeopardized their economic and cultural connections to the United States.

A small number of both Anglo and Hispanic Texans rebelled and seized the only military garrison in Texas, at San Antonio. At first, like the Americans of 1775, most of the rebels claimed that they were fighting only for the rights they had traditionally exercised as Mexican citizens. However, having far less in common with their mother country than the revolutionaries of 1775 had with Great Britain, some spoke of independence from the outset.

The Alamo and San Jacinto

Like King George III, Santa Anna had no intention of negotiating with his troublesome subjects. Rather, he welcomed the Texas uprising as an opportunity to rally the divided Mexican people around a national cause. In early 1836, he led an army of 6,000 to San Antonio, where he calculated that he could easily defeat the 200 Texans (and a few Americans) who were holed up in the former mission compound, the Alamo.

Among the defenders were men already famous in the United States. The garrison was commanded by William Travis, one of the most prominent Texans, and James Bowie, inventor of the large skinning (and brawling) knife that many westerners carried and that now bears his name. Best known was the Whig politician and humorist, David Crockett of Tennessee.

Santa Anna could have passed the Alamo by, leaving a small detachment to contain the garrison. The real threat lay farther east, where Sam Houston, an old crony of Andrew Jackson, was frantically trying to raise an army among frontier farmers. But Houston was having his troubles. Not every Texan supported him. Others were uneasy about confronting a professional army. By moving quickly, Santa Anna might easily have snuffed out the insurrection.

Instead, he sat in San Antonio for ten days, unable to comprehend why the defenders of the Alamo,

---

Santa Anna's Gift

Santa Anna's first presidency was ruined by Americans in Texas. However, he bore little animosity to the American people. In exile in Staten Island, New York, in 1869, Santa Anna and a photographer acquaintance, Thomas Adams, imported a ton of chicle, sap from the sapodilla tree, which the two men thought might be a substitute for rubber. That project went nowhere, but Adams, now on his own, heard a girl order "paraffin wax candy" at a drugstore, not to eat but to chew. Recalling that Santa Anna chewed chicle, Adams marketed the substance as an alternative to chewing tobacco, a ubiquitous habit thought filthy in polite society. Adams made a decent living from "chewing gum," but it made a high school dropout, William Wrigley, Jr., rich when, in 1893, he hit on the idea of sweetening and flavoring the chicle, calling it "Juicy Fruit."

The San Patricios

The San Patricios—the St. Patricks—were mostly Irish-Americans who volunteered to fight on the Mexican side in the war with the United States. Some were impelled by the fact that the Mexicans were, like them, Roman Catholics. Others were motivated, like other Americans, by the fact that they regarded the aggression of the United States as unjust. Some were abolitionists, opposed to the expansion of slavery the Mexican War meant. Although most San Patricios were Irish, there were also Germans, Poles, and *esclavos negros*, black slaves, in the unit.

The San Patricios fought well and are honored in Mexico to this day for their services. To American troops, however, they were traitors and those captured after the Battle of Chapultepec were hanged.

---

whose cause was hopeless, would not surrender. When he realized that they were buying time for Sam Houston, he attacked at tremendous cost to his army and ordered all prisoners executed. Under an ancient, if controversial rule of war, he had a right to do so: soldiers defending a palpably hopeless position lost their right to quarter. But exercising so antiquated a right, Santa Anna became the author of an atrocity. The executions (only a few women were spared) rallied virtually all Texans, including many of Mexican origin and culture, to the fight against the general-president.

On the banks of the Rio San Jacinto on April 21, Sam Houston routed the Mexican army and captured Santa Anna. In order to secure his release, Santa Anna agreed to the independence of Texas with a southern boundary at the Rio Grande rather than at the Rio Nueces, which had been the boundary between Texas and Coahuila proper. As soon as he was free, Santa Anna repudiated the agreement and refused to recognize the Republic of Texas. But the demoralized Mexican army was in no condition to mount another campaign, and the Texans discreetly remained north of the Nueces.

The Lone Star Republic

In October 1836, Sam Houston was inaugurated president of a republic patterned on that of the United States. Texas legalized slavery and dispatched an envoy to Washington. Houston hoped that his old

A dramatic depiction of the last moments of The Battle of the Alamo.

friend Andrew Jackson would favor annexation. In his nationalistic heart, Jackson liked the idea of sewing the Lone Star of the Texas republic on the American flag. However, Congress was then embroiled in a nasty debate in which the question of slavery was being bandied about. Jackson did not want to complicate matters by proposing the admission of a new slave state. In order to spare his successor a problem, he even delayed diplomatic recognition of the Republic of Texas until his last day in office.

Martin Van Buren opposed the annexation of Texas, and he was spared a debate on admission when the depression of the late 1830s distracted Americans from territorial questions. The Texans, disappointed and ever worried about Mexico, looked to Europe for an ally.

The British were happy to oblige. The British coveted Texas cotton and welcomed any opportunity to contain the growth of American power. Had it not been for the Texans' commitment to slavery, an institution which the British had recently abolished in the empire, there might have been more than a commercial connection between the old monarchy and the new republic.

THE OREGON COUNTRY

The American government was uneasy about British influence in Texas. Britons and Americans also stepped warily around one another on the western coast of North America in what was known as the Oregon Country. This land of prosperous Indians, sheltered harbors, spruce and fir forests, and rich valley farmlands was not considered the property of any single nation. This situation came about when the two empires with claims to it had withdrawn, one to the south and one to the north.

A Distant Land

Spain's claim to Oregon was never more than nominal. Spanish and Mexican influence ended at the mission town of Sonoma just north of San Francisco. So after 1819, when the boundary of Spanish America was set at 42° north latitude (the present southern line of the state of Oregon), the claim was itself overreaching.

The Russians had established a string of forts, timbering camps, and fur-trapping stations on the Pacific coast from present-day Alaska to Fort Ross, less than a hundred miles from San Francisco Bay. However, the czars had difficulty populating Siberia on the Russian mainland. Few Russians were interested in removing to permanent settlements even farther from Europe. Moreover, by the 1820s, the trappers had looted the coastal waters of the sea otters whose lush, warm furs brought them there. Rather than get involved in a competition for territory that they could not defend, the Russians withdrew northward in 1825 and set the boundary of Russian America at 54° 40′ north latitude, the present southern boundary of the state of Alaska.

Between 42° and 54° 40′ lay the Oregon Country into which Britons, Canadians, and Americans trickled. Because Oregon was far from their centers of power, the British and Americans agreed to what they called a joint occupation, which was in truth very little occupation at all, but more of an announcement that other nations were unwelcome.

The Mountain Men

The Americans, British, and Canadians in Oregon were few in number and not the sort to put down roots. Most were fur trappers scouring the chill creeks of the West in search of the pelt of the North American beaver. Furriers in New York, London,

and Paris paid good prices for beaver; they sewed the pelts into plush coats for the wealthy, and chopped, steamed, and pressed the fur into felt, a versatile fabric with a worldwide market.

Even before William Becknell set out for Santa Fe, American and Canadian veterans of the War of 1812 were disappearing into the northern Rockies with large-bore rifles, iron traps, and a sense of relief at leaving civilization behind for 11 months a year. These mountain men never numbered more than a few hundred at any one time. They took Indian wives; they learned Indian lore calculated to foster survival in remote, rugged wilderness; and they sometimes lived with, sometimes battled against, the tribes of the region. Other whites who dealt with the mountain men minded their manners, considering them to be savages themselves.

Jeremiah "Liver-Eatin'" Johnson waged a ten-year vendetta with the Crow tribe. He earned his colorful nickname when, to let the Crow know that it was he who killed one of their warriors, he cut out and ate the livers of his victims. (Toward the end, Johnson later said, he just cut them out.) Jim Beckwourth, the son of a slave woman and a free white man, discovered the pass through the Sierra Nevada that rose to the lowest elevation, while New York–born Jedediah Smith opened South Pass in Wyoming, the route that would be followed by most overland emigrants. And Jim Bridger explored almost every nook of the Rockies. He was the first non-Indian to lay eyes on the Great Salt Lake.

Each year, in late summer or early fall, the trappers brought their furs to prearranged locations on the Platte, Sweetwater, or Big Horn rivers. For a few weeks, buyers from the British Hudson's Bay Company and John Jacob Astor's American Fur Trading Company, mountain men, and Indians of various tribes traded goods, drank whiskey, and enjoyed a riotous orgy, and now and then bit off the ear of an old pal. Of more lasting significance was the knowledge of western geography they imparted to the folks back home, particularly the fact that while it was a long, hard trip, it was possible to cross overland to Oregon, even with wagons.

The Oregon Trail

Among the first to make the six-month journey for the purpose of settling in Oregon were missionaries. In 1834, the Methodists sent Jason Lee to preach the gospel to the Indians of Oregon. In 1835, four Flathead Indians visited the American Board of Foreign Missions and, so the board reported, persuaded them that Presbyterianism was the gospel that they really wanted to hear. In 1836, Marcus and Narcissa Whitman carried it to them on foot. A few years later, the Catholic University at St. Louis sent Father Pierre-Jean de Smet to the Oregon Country.

The trek usually began at Independence, Missouri. It was also there in 1843 that the first great wagon train was organized. A thousand Oregon-or-Busters outfitted and provisioned themselves, often packing oddly chosen mementos of home: cumbersome furniture and fragile china gewgaws. They swore to observe strict rules of behavior and cooper-ation for the duration of the crossing, and hired mountain men as guides.

The Oregon Trail crossed Kansas to the Platte River and followed that broad, shallow course to Fort Laramie, the westernmost army outpost. The emigrants and their famous covered wagons then crossed the Continental Divide at South Pass and struggled through the Rockies to near the source of the Snake River, which flows into the great Columbia and the Pacific.

A wagon train made up to 20 miles a day (or as few as none at all) depending on the terrain and the weather. At night, exhausted by the tremendous labor of moving a hundred wagons and several hundred

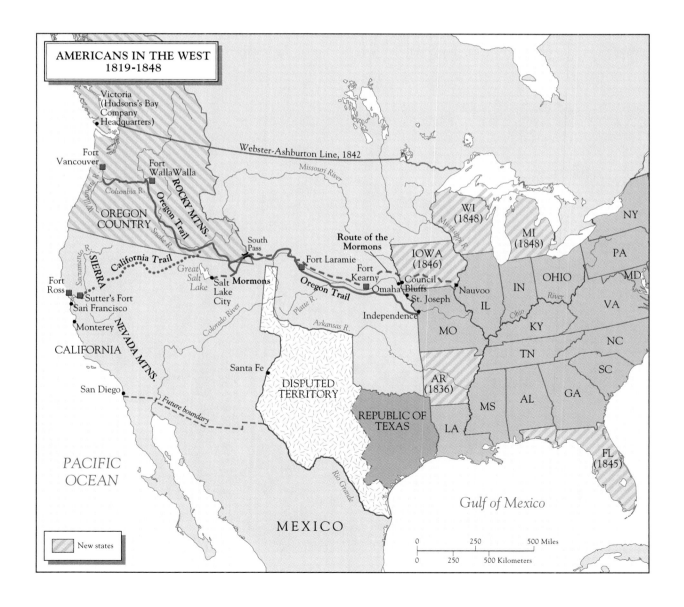

head of cattle, horses, and mules, the emigrants drew their prairie schooners into a hollow square or circle.

The Indians of the plains and mountains did not threaten large, well-organized expeditions. While the Indians were hardly delighted to see large numbers of strangers crossing their ancestral lands (3,000 in 1845 alone), the whites were, at least, crossing it. They disappeared into the sunset. Although they warred constantly with one another, the tribes had few firearms and were, therefore, no match for the emigrants. The Oregon-bound travelers worried less about Indian attack than about theft. Indians made a game of stealing horses that strayed too far from the caravans. They also traded with the whites and picked up the discarded goods that littered the trail. Even before the stream of wagons wore deep ruts into the sod and rock—which can be seen today here and there—the Oregon Trail was clearly marked with broken furniture, empty barrels, incapacitated wagons, the skeletons of worn-out cattle and horses, and simple grave markers that signaled the end of someone's dream. Death from accident or disease, particularly cholera, was common, but it was impossible to lose the way.

Joint Occupation

By 1845, the American population of the Columbia and Willamette valleys had grown to 7,000 and the British-Canadian Hudson's Bay Company prudently moved its headquarters from the mouth of the Columbia to Vancouver Island. What is now the state of Washington served as a buffer zone between British and American population centers. Still, occasional clashes threatened the device of joint occupa-

A rare photograph of two wagon trains moving west. One, probably bound for Oregon, leaves the other, bound for California.

tion that Daniel Webster and Lord Ashburton had worked out as recently as 1842.

The Americans wanted to end the joint occupation and annex the Oregon Country to the United States. In July 1843, a group met at Champoeg and established a provisional territorial government under the American flag. A few politicians back east supported them. The idea of territorial expansion, previously something of a dirty concept because it involved seizing land that belonged to someone else, had taken on positive dignity. Expansion became a sacred duty for some Americans; they came to believe that they had an obligation to increase the domain over which democracy and liberty held sway.

The Push to the Pacific

This was the doctrine of Manifest Destiny. Dazzled by the nation's energy and progress, politicians and newspaper editors, mostly Democratic and largely southern and western, began to speak of the right, even the duty of Americans to take control of lands that lay wasted by savage aborigines and backward Mexicans or were corrupted by the decadent British.

Legal claims, however universally recognized, were less important to such people than the sacred mission of the United States to plant free, democratic institutions in Oregon and in thinly populated parts of Mexico. It remained for a New York journalist, John O'Sullivan, to coin a phrase. It was, he said, the "manifest destiny" of the United States to expand from sea to sea. God and nature intended Americans to possess the North American continent.

The Texas Debate

In 1843, expansion became a matter of earnest debate. The Texans renewed their request for annexation, and won the support of a number of prominent Americans. Many northern Democrats, such as Lewis Cass of Michigan, James Buchanan of Pennsylvania, and Stephen Douglas of Illinois, were enraptured by the idea of territorial expansion. They feared that until Texas was incorporated within the United States, it would be a standing temptation to the expansive British. Southern Democrats, such as Calhoun and President John Tyler, had an additional reason for favoring annexation. Slavery was legal in Texas. If Texas were brought into the Union, the power of the proslavery bloc in Congress would be increased.

For the same reason, many political and cultural leaders of New England strenuously opposed annexation. Northern Whigs and some northern Democrats were determined that slavery should not expand beyond the states where it was already legal. Less hostile toward England than people of other sections, New Englanders did not object to the possibility of Great Britain's taking Texas. The British, at least, would abolish slavery there. Finally, the anti-Texas forces pointed out that admitting Texas would almost certainly lead to a war with Mexico in which the Mexicans, not the Americans, would be in the right.

Clay and Van Buren

Both of the likely presidential nominees of 1844 were unhappy to see Texas annexation shaping up as the principal issue of the campaign. Henry Clay knew that his Whig party, already strained by the slavery issues, could split in two over the issue. His likely opponent, Martin Van Buren, who commanded a safe majority of delegates to the Democratic nominating convention, had the same problem. The Democrats were torn between proslavery and antislavery factions. If the two old rogues took opposite stances on the question, the campaign would throw both parties into disarray. Therefore, they met quietly and agreed that both would oppose annexation, thus eliminating Texas as an election issue.

Their bargain presented lame-duck President Tyler with an opportunity. He would be a third candidate favoring the annexation of Texas. Tyler had

---

Five States of Texas?

Texas is not unique among the states because it was an independent nation before it became a state. Hawaii also claims that distinction. (After a fashion, California was briefly a republic, too.) However, by the joint resolution of the American and Texan congresses that brought Texas into the Union, Texas reserved the right to divide into five states without further congressional approval. The advisability of splitting arose periodically in Texas politics because collectively, the states carved out of Texas would have ten United States senators rather than two.

Nonviolent Civil Disobedience

Henry David Thoreau's preachment that a person was morally obligated to disobey an immoral law was given effective political form in the twentieth century by the leader of the Indian independence movement, Mohandas Gandhi, and by the leader of the American civil-rights movement, Martin Luther King, Jr. Both insisted on defying unjust laws. With those who said that their principle would lead to anarchy if everyone accepted it, Gandhi and King disagreed. Because they would not use violence and they would passively accept the punishment that the established government inflicted on them—in other words, go to jail—the majority of people would recognize the justice of their cause and change the law.

no party organization behind him, so his announcement did not unduly disturb either Clay or Van Buren. Then occurred one of those unlikely events that change the course of history. Manifest Destiny Democrats revived a neglected party rule that a presidential nominee receive the support of two-thirds instead of a simple majority of the delegates to the convention. With his anti-Texas pledge, Van Buren was stymied. Pro-annexation Democrats numbered far more than a third of the delegates.

After eight ballots ended in no decision, the convention turned to a dark-horse candidate, that is, a candidate who was not considered a contender at the beginning of the race. He was James Knox Polk of Tennessee, a protégé of Jackson not yet 50 years old. (He was called "Young Hickory.") Polk had been a Van Buren supporter who favored annexation, a perfect compromise candidate.

The Election of 1844

"Who is Polk?" the Whigs asked scornfully when they learned who was running against their hero, Clay. The snideness was misplaced. Polk had been Tennessee's governor and served in the House of Representatives for 14 years, several of those as speaker. But his stature was midget indeed when his career and personality were set beside those of Henry Clay. Polk was a frail man with a look of melancholy and timidity about him. He was priggish; he disapproved of alcohol, dancing, and card playing.

At first, Henry Clay was overjoyed to be running against a political nobody. After three attempts, he would be president at last! The unpopular Tyler and the obscure Polk would divide the pro-Texas vote. The anti-Texas vote, including the antislavery Democrats who would have voted for Van Buren, were his.

Then a piece of the sky fell. Tyler withdrew from the race, and every dispatch seemed to say that Manifest Destiny was carrying the day. Clay began to waffle on the expansion issue, and his equivocation alienated enough anti-Texas Whigs to cost him the election. In New York State, which Polk carried by a scant 5,000 votes (and with New York, the election), long dependable Whig districts gave 16,000 votes to James G. Birney's abolitionist Liberty party. Antislavery voters cost Clay his last chance to be president.

Encouraged by the result of the election and egged on by Secretary of State Calhoun, Tyler moved on the Texas question. He could not muster the two-thirds vote in the Senate that a treaty required, but he had a simple majority of both houses of Congress behind him. Three days before Polk's inauguration, Congress approved a joint resolution annexing Texas. A few months later, the Texas Congress concurred and Texas became the twenty-eighth state.

He Did What He Said He'd Do

The apparently mousy Polk proved to be a master politician, a shrewd diplomat, and, in terms of accomplishing what he set out to do, one of the most

"Dark Horse"

The first president to be described as a "dark horse," that is, a candidate whom no one much thought about before the campaign actually began, was James K. Polk. The phrase came from a novel published in England by Benjamin Disraeli, a future prime minister, in 1832: "A dark horse which never had been thought of, and which the careless St. James had never even observed in the list, rushed past the grandstand in sweeping triumph." Other "dark horses" elected president were James A. Garfield (1880) and Warren G. Harding (1920). Dark-horse candidates who lost the general election were William Jennings Bryan (1896) and Wendell Willkie (1940).

Austin, the capital of the Lone Star Republic, Texas, in 1840, five years after independence.

successful of presidents. When he took his oath of office, Polk announced he would serve just one term and during those four years he would secure Texas to the Union, acquire New Mexico and California from Mexico, and annex as much of the Oregon Country as circumstances permitted.

Texas statehood was in the bag by Inauguration Day. The hardworking president immediately went to work on Oregon. Taking his cue from a chauvinistic slogan, "Fifty-four Forty or Fight!" (seizing all of Oregon for the United States up to the southern boundary of Russian America at 54° 40′ north latitude) Polk alarmed the British by hinting at a war neither nation wanted. Having bluffed, his diplomats presented it as a concession that Polk would settle for an extension of the Webster-Ashburton line, at 49° north latitude, as the northern boundary of American Oregon. The Oregon country would be cut in half, with England retaining all of Vancouver Island.

In fact, the British got no more than they occupied and the Americans got no less than they could reasonably defend. Except for a minor adjustment of the line in the Strait of Juan de Fuca, worked out in 1872, the American-Canadian boundary was final in 1846.

Polk was candid about his designs on California and New Mexico. The United States had no legal claim in either province. Nor could Polk claim that, as in Texas and Oregon, California and New Mexico were already peopled by Americans. Unassimilated gringos were few in New Mexico, and there were only about 700 Americans in California compared with 6,000 *californios*. In 1842, an American naval officer, Thomas Catesby Jones, somehow got it into his head that the United States was at war with Mexico, and he seized the provincial capital of California at Monterey. When he learned that he was mistaken, he had to run down the flag and sail off a little foolishly. But, embarrassed as Jones might have been, he was merely a few years ahead of his time. When Mexico turned down Polk's offer to buy California and New Mexico for $30 million, he decided to take them by force.

War with Mexico

The luckless Santa Anna was back in power in Mexico City when Polk became president. This time, however, while he refused to discuss the sale of California and New Mexico, he moved cautiously, ordering Mexican troops in the north not to provoke the Americans. To no avail: Polk was determined to have war. He drew up an address asking Congress for a declaration on the basis of the Mexican government's debts with some American banks. In the meantime, he ordered General Zachary Taylor of Louisiana to

Showtime

During the middle years of the nineteenth century, the traveling panorama was a cheap and popular diversion in urban and rural areas alike. On sheets of canvas sewn end to end, painters depicted historical events or natural wonders, along which paying customers walked, sometimes with printed explanations, sometimes listening to guides. Biblical scenes, Revolutionary War battles, portraits and deeds of notable Americans, and Indian massacres (and retribution) were particularly popular.

The largest was John Banvard's PANORAMA OF THE MISSISSIPPI, first unfurled in 1846. On canvas twelve feet high and three miles long (a mile-and-a-half walk), Banvard showed 1,200 miles of Mississippi River from the mouth of the Missouri to New Orleans. Panoramas gradually ceased to draw viewers in the late nineteenth century although Banvard's was updated by the insertion of Civil War battles and had a longer life than most.

take 1,500 men from the Nueces River in Texas to the Rio Grande. In April 1846, 16 American soldiers were killed in a skirmish between Mexican and American patrols in the disputed region.

Feigning moral outrage, Polk rewrote his speech and declared that because of Mexican aggression, a state of war between the two nations already existed. Constitutionally, this was nonsense; Congress alone has the power to declare war. Americans had fought battles with the British and French at sea and sent punitive expeditions into the Barbary states and Florida, and the conflicts had not been called wars. But patriotic danders were up; both houses of Congress approved Polk's action.

The Mexican army was actually larger than the American but the Mexican troops were ill-equipped, demoralized by endless civil war, and commanded by officers who owed their commissions to social status rather than merit. In less than two years, the Americans conquered most of the country.

In the summer of 1846, Stephen W. Kearny occupied Santa Fe without resistance. Then he marched his troops to California, where he found that the Americans and a few *californio* allies already had won a nearly bloodless revolution and established the Bear Flag Republic. Kearny had only to

raise the American flag and mop up a few scattered Mexican garrisons.

In September, Zachary Taylor took the offensive in northern Mexico, occupying Matamoros and defeating the Mexican army at Nuevo León (also known as Monterrey). Although "Old Rough and Ready," as his men called him, showed shrewd tactical judgment, the Nuevo León garrison escaped. Polk, who disliked Taylor, used this mistake as an excuse to divert some of Taylor's troops to a command under General Winfield Scott. Nevertheless, in February 1847, Taylor became a national hero when, with his shrunken army, he was attacked at Buena Vista by Santa Anna himself and won a total victory.

The next month, March 1847, General Winfield Scott landed at Vera Cruz and fought his way toward Mexico City along the ancient route of Hernán Cortés. He won a great victory at Cerro Gordo and an even bigger one at Chapultepec, where he captured 3,000 men and eight generals. On September 14, 1847, Scott donned one of the gaudy uniforms he loved (his men called him "Old Fuss and Feathers") and occupied Mexico City, "the Halls of Montezuma."

By refusing to negotiate after the disaster at Cerro Gordo, the obstinate Santa Anna almost destroyed Mexico itself. Scott's subsequent destruction of the remnants of the Mexican army encouraged some prominent Americans, including members of Polk's cabinet, to call for annexation of the entire country. Polk recalled Nicholas Trist, who was attempting to negotiate a less extreme treaty in Mexico, because of Trist's moderation. Fortunately for Mexico and the United States, Trist ignored Polk's frantic messages long enough to sign the Treaty of Guadalupe Hidalgo in February 1848.

The treaty was harsh enough. Mexico ceded to the United States the Rio Grande boundary, California, and the province of New Mexico, which included the Mormon Zion in Utah and the present states of Arizona and Nevada. The United States paid Mexico $15 million and assumed responsibility for about $3 million that the Mexican government owed Americans.

Mexico was dismembered like a carcass of beef. One-third of its territory was taken largely because the United States was strong enough to do so. While the ineptitude of the Mexican military leadership played a part in the national disaster, the partition of the country could not help but leave a bitterness in the historical memory of the Mexican people.

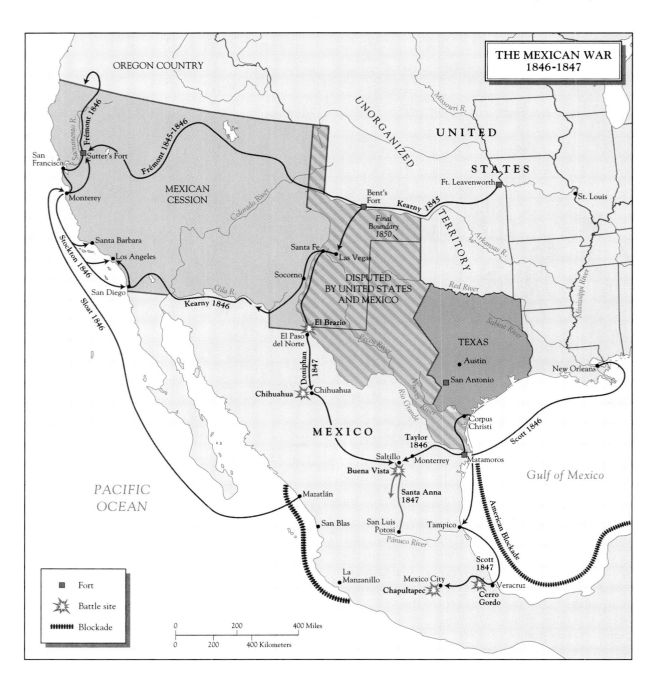

THE MEXICAN WAR
1846-1847

OREGON COUNTRY

UNITED

STATES

UNORGANIZED

TERRITORY

Frémont 1846

Sacramento R.

Missouri R.

San Francisco

Sutter's Fort

Frémont 1845-1846

Ft. Leavenworth

St. Louis

Monterey

MEXICAN
CESSION

Colorado River

Bent's Fort

Kearny 1845

Arkansas R.

Stockton 1846

Santa Barbara

Los Angeles

Santa Fe

Final
Boundary
1850

Las Vegas

San Diego

Socorno

Gila R.

Kearny 1846

DISPUTED
BY UNITED STATES
AND MEXICO

Red River

Sabine River

Mississippi River

Sloat 1846

El Brazio

El Paso
del Norte

Pecos River

TEXAS

Doniphan
1847

Chihuahua

Chihuahua

Austin

New Orleans

Rio Grande

Nueces River

San Antonio

MEXICO

Taylor
1846

Corpus
Christi

Scott 1846

PACIFIC
OCEAN

Mazatlán

Saltillo

Monterrey

Matamoros

Gulf of Mexico

Buena Vista

Santa Anna
1847

American Blockade

San Blas

San Luis
Potosi

Tampico

Pánuco River

Scott
1847

La
Manzanillo

Mexico City

Chapultepec

Veracruz

Cerro
Gordo

■ Fort

✸ Battle site

▬▬▬ Blockade

0   200   400 Miles

0   200   400 Kilometers

The Opposition

The Mexican War was generally popular in the United States. The army could accept only a fraction of the young men who volunteered to fight it. It was an easy fight; only 1,700 died in battle (although 11,000 soldiers succumbed to disease).

Nevertheless, the war had many vociferous critics. Many Whigs, including a young politician from Illinois named Abraham Lincoln, voted against the declaration. In New England, a number of prominent politicians and clergymen condemned the war from platform and pulpit. Ralph Waldo Emerson and much of the Massachusetts intellectual establishment opposed it. Henry David Thoreau went to jail rather than pay a tax that he believed would help pay for adding new slave states to the Union. "Why are you in here, Henry?" asked Emerson, arriving to bail

Known as "Old Fuss and Feathers" because of his love of pomp and splendid uniforms, General Winfield Scott must have loved this depiction of his entry into Mexico City.

Thoreau out. "Why are you out there, Waldo?" Thoreau replied; he regarded it as a moral duty to obstruct the cynical war, even if just symbolically.

Not even the army was unanimously keen on the fight. Years later in his autobiography, then Captain Ulysses S. Grant remembered, "I was bitterly opposed to the measure, and to this day regard the war . . . as one of the most unjust ever waged by a stronger against a weaker nation. . . . Even if the annexation itself could be justified, the manner in which the . . . war was forced upon Mexico cannot."

The vote in the Senate ratifying the Treaty of Guadalupe Hidalgo was only 38 to 14. Had four senators changed their votes, the treaty would not have been approved.

Expansion Run Amok

Cynical as the Mexican acquisition was, it was moderate compared with the suggestion to seize the entire country. Even after Guadalupe Hidalgo was

signed, and a rebellion broke out in the Yucatán Peninsula, Polk asked Congress to authorize the army, which was still in Mexico, to take over the tropical province. Curiously, some antislavery northerners were sympathetic. Because slavery was illegal in Mexico and the Mexicans were opposed to the institution, they believed new American states carved from the country would come into the Union as free states.

The president also had designs on Cuba, where 350,000 slaves had long excited the imagination of proslavery southerners. Polk wanted to present the Spanish government there with a choice between selling the rich sugar island or running the risk of a rebellion fomented by the United States, followed by military intervention.

This was the most bizarre suggestion concocted in the flush of victory, but not the most grandiose. J. D. B. De Bow, an influential southern editor and publisher, wrote that it was the American destiny to absorb not only all of Mexico, but also the West

Indies, Canada, and Hawaii. That was for appetizers. De Bow continued:

> The gates of the Chinese empire must be thrown down by the men from the Sacramento and the Oregon, and the haughty Japanese tramplers upon the cross be enlightened in the doctrines of republicanism and the ballot box. The eagle of the republic shall poise itself over the field of Waterloo, after tracing its flight among the gorges of the Himalaya or the Ural mountains, and a successor of Washington ascend the chair of universal empire.

No such golden age of empire followed the Mexican War. Indeed, the acquisition from Mexico, modest as it was by De Bow's standards, proved to be more than the old Union, just 60 years of age when the war ended, could digest.

CHRONOLOGY

1819–1821	Moses and Stephen Austin negotiate settlement of Americans in Mexican Texas
1821	Santa Fe opened to American trade
1831	Mexico abolishes slavery, including in Texas
1834	First American missionaries in Oregon Country
1835	López de Santa Anna centralizes Mexican government
1836	Santa Anna captures Alamo but is defeated by Texans at San Jacinto Sam Houston elected president of Mexico
1843	First crossing of Oregon Trail
1844	James K. Polk elected president on an expansionist platform
1845	Oregon Country divided between Great Britain and United States
1846–1848	Mexican War
1847	Scott occupies Mexico City
1848	Treaty of Guadalupe Hidalgo

FOR FURTHER READING

Ray A. Billington was the dean of western history writers during the later years of his life. See his *The Far Western Frontier, 1830–1860*, 1956, and *Westward Expansion*, 1974, for overviews. Also essential is Frederick Merk, *History of the Westward Movement*, 1978. More "literary," a writer of classics, in fact, is Bernard DeVoto; see his *Across the Wide Missouri*, 1947, and *The Year of Decision, 1846*, 1943. See Nelson Limerick, *Legacy of Conquest*, 1987, for a view emphasizing government policies and cultural differences.

Other important works on mid-nineteenth-century expansion include John Mack Faragher, *Women and Men on the Oregon Trail*, 1979; Norman A. Graebner, *Empire on the Pacific: A Study in American Continental Expansion*, 1955; Thomas R. Hietala, *Manifest Design: Anxious Aggrandizement in Late Jacksonian America*, 1985; D. M. Pletcher, *The Diplomacy of Annexation: Texas, Oregon, and the Mexican War*, 1973; John D. Unruh, *The Plains Across: The Overland Emigrants and the Trans-Mississippi West, 1840–1860*, 1978; and Albert K. Weinberg, *Manifest Destiny*, 1936.

On Oregon, see the contemporary Francis Parkman, *The Oregon Trail*, 1849; Frederick Merk, *The Oregon Question*, 1967; and Malcom Clark, Jr., *The Eden-Seekers: The Settlement of Oregon, 1812–1862*, 1981. L. R. Duffus, *The Santa Fe Trail*, 1930, is still the standard work on that subject. On fur trappers and traders, see D. L. Morgan, *Jedediah Smith and the Opening of the West*, 1953; P. C. Phillips, *The Fur Trade*, 1961; and D. J. Wishart, *The Fur Trade of the American West, 1807–1840*, 1979.

On Texas: E. C. Marker, *Mexico and Texas, 1821–1835*, 1928; W. C. Brinkley, *The Texas Revolution*, 1952; Frederick Merk, *Slavery and the Annexation of Texas*, 1972; and Arnoldo De Leon, *They Called Them Greasers: Anglo Attitudes Toward Mexicans in Texas, 1821–1900*, 1983. The best biography of President Polk is Charles Seller, *James K. Polk: Continentalist*, 1966; but see also Paul H. Bergeron, *The Presidency of James K. Polk*, 1987.

On the Mexican War: K. Jack Bauer, *The Mexican–American War, 1846–1848*, 1974; John S. D. Eisenhower, *So Far from God: The U.S. War with Mexico*, 1989; Robert W. Johansen, *To the Halls of Montezuma: The Mexican War in the American Imagination*, 1985; and John H. Schroeder, *Mr. Polk's War: American Opposition and Dissent*, 1973.

Hopeful placer miners at Spanish Flat, California, 1832.

21
CHAPTER

APPLES OF DISCORD

The Poisoned Fruits of Expansion

1844–1854

I was born an American; I will live an American; I shall die an American.

— *Daniel Webster*

I have heard something said about allegiance to the South. I know no South, no North, no East, no West, to which I owe any allegiance. The Union, sir, is my country.

— *Henry Clay*

The Union cannot . . . be saved by eulogies on the Union, however splendid or numerous.
The cry of "Union, Union, the glorious Union!" can no more prevent disunion than the cry of "Health, health, glorious health!" on the part of the physician can save a patient lying dangerously ill.

— *John C. Calhoun*

American soldiers in Mexico suffered terribly from disease; a disproportionately large number of men in uniform died during the Mexican War. But the invasion force was small and the fighting was, as battles go, short, easy, and decisive. The army suffered no serious defeat and won several improbable victories. The news from every front—California, Santa Fe, beyond the Rio Grande, and from the "Halls of Montezuma" in the heart of Mexico—could not help but be thrilling back home. Americans lionized Generals Zachary Taylor and Winfield Scott. Both would run for president.

Still, the victory celebration was short-lived. The fruits of the conquest, vast new lands extending from the Rockies to the Pacific Ocean, proved to be apples of discord. They divided Americans on political and sectional lines even before the Treaty of Guadalupe Hidalgo officially transferred title to them to the United States. The ever flammable question of slavery was the cause of the trouble.

THE SECTIONAL SPLIT TAKES SHAPE

Slavery was the subject of acrimonious debate before the Mexican War. Since the 1830s, abolitionists had hurled anathemas from pulpit, platform, and press at southern slave owners. Proslavery Americans had vilified abolitionists as incendiaries who were determined to inspire blacks to rebellion and massacre. The rhetoric on both sides was antagonistic, often ugly, and sometimes vicious.

Before the annexation of Texas and the Mexican War, however, the slavery debate lay at the periphery of national politics. Presidents and congressional leaders who recognized the issue as dangerous and divisive—a clear majority of the generation of Jackson, Benton, Clay, and Webster—found it advisable to avoid political debates in which the peculiar institution raised its head, to rush through them, or to quash them at the start.

A Dead Letter

The question of slavery came up all too often in Washington. Abolitionists and proslavery zealots in Congress could and did deliver impassioned sermons about good and evil, sinners and saints. Thomas Hart Benton became so disgusted by gratuitous injections of the slavery issue into discussions of other questions that he compared Congress's plight to the biblical visitation of plagues on Pharaoh's Egypt:

> You could not look on the table but there were frogs. You could not sit down at the banquet table but there were frogs, you could not go to the bridal couch and lift the sheets but there were frogs! We can see nothing, touch nothing, have no measures proposed, without having this pestilence thrust before us.

Benton was himself a slave owner, although by no means a proslavery extremist. His daughter was to marry a prominent antislavery politician, John C. Frémont. He was disgusted because, a practical politician, he knew there were few points at which Congress had authority to touch the institution of slavery. The Constitution unambivalently defined slavery as a domestic institution of the states. Short of a constitutional amendment abolishing slavery, the state governments alone had the power to decide whether or not citizens were permitted to own human property.

A constitutional amendment abolishing slavery was out of the question. Three-fourths of the states must agree to any change in the Constitution and, in the early nineteenth century, slave states were equal in number to free states. In fact, when war was declared on Mexico in May 1846, 15 of the 28 states were slave states. Stridently defending the peculiar institution at home, southern state legislatures were not apt to consider nationwide abolition. It was this

---

Riders

In the process of lawmaking, a *rider* is a clause, usually dealing with an unrelated matter, that is attached to a bill already under consideration in Congress or in a state assembly. The strategy of those who propose riders is to turn them into law despite considerable opposition. Opponents will so badly want the bill under consideration that they will pass it even with the objectionable rider. Thus Wilmot tried to attach his antislavery measure to an appropriations bill that was desperately needed. Only because the anti-Wilmot forces in the Senate were strong enough to vote it down did the Wilmot Proviso not cause a major crisis.

sanctioning of slavery that prompted William Lloyd Garrison to call the Constitution "a covenant with hell," but neither he nor other abolitionists could provide a workable way around it. They were moral crusaders, not politicians.

Nibbling at the Edges

The Constitution did empower Congress "to exercise exclusive legislation in all cases whatsoever" over the District of Columbia. So, abolitionist congressmen regularly called for the prohibition of slaveholding in Washington or, at least, a ban on the slave trade, the buying and selling of slaves, in the capital.

Congress also had the power to legislate concerning slaves who ran away from their masters and crossed state lines. The Fugitive Slave Act of 1793 provided that such runaways be returned to their owners. (The law was frequently ignored or obstructed by antislavery northerners, including some federal officials.) Some antislavery northern congressmen wanted to use the interstate commerce clause of the Constitution to prohibit the sale of slaves from any one state to another as a means of hobbling the institution. Southern hotheads proposed reopening the African slave trade, which Congress also had the authority to do.

All of these issues aroused the passions of the extremists and vexed the moderates who wanted to keep the slavery issue off center stage. To a large extent they succeeded. The question that was to engage moderates in the slavery debate, and eventually to divide the United States in half, was the status of the peculiar institution in the western territories.

The Wilmot Proviso

All agreed that Congress had authority to legislate regarding slavery in the federal territories, possessions that had not yet been admitted to the Union as states. The Confederation Congress did just that in the Northwest Ordinance of 1787 when it forbade slavery north of the Ohio River. Under the Constitution, Congress decided the question of slavery in the Louisiana Purchase lands in the Missouri Compromise of 1820.

Indeed, the Missouri Compromise was the salvation of those moderate politicians who wanted to keep the subject of slavery off the floor of Congress. It seemed to have settled the question for all time by permitting slavery in U.S. territories south of 36° 30′

The Berrien Proviso

Another "rider" of the era of the Mexican War, proposed in February 1847 by Senator John M. Berrien, was even less successful than David Wilmot's. The Berrien Proviso proposed that "the true intent of Congress in making this appropriation [for the army is] that the war with Mexico ought not to be prosecuted by this Government with any view to the dismemberment of that republic." Even in the northern states, Berrien's ideals were unacceptable.

---

north latitude, and prohibiting it to the north. Once Arkansas was admitted as a slave state in 1836, the only western land in which slavery was legal was Oklahoma, then known as Indian Territory. In all other parts of the Louisiana Purchase, slavery was "forever prohibited" by a congressional act that assumed an attitude of finality second only to that of the Constitution.

The annexation of Texas and the acquisition of new lands from Mexico upset the Missouri settlement. Many antislavery northerners opposed annexing Texas because it added a slave state in violation of the spirit of the law of 1820. Proslavery southerners supported the war with Mexico so exuberantly because they looked forward to annexing lands into which, because they were not subject to the Missouri Compromise, slavery could legally expand.

Determined to prevent this, Congressman David Wilmot of Pennsylvania attached a rider to several bills appropriating money to the army during the war. The Wilmot Proviso declared that slavery would be forbidden in any lands taken from Mexico. It passed the House of Representatives in both 1846 and 1847. Every northern Whig and all but four northern Democrats voted for it. Every northern state legislature but New Jersey's endorsed it. A majority of northerners stated quite clearly that they opposed the expansion of slavery anywhere. In the Senate, however, slave states held the edge and, with the help of a few northern senators, the Wilmot Proviso was voted down.

John C. Calhoun led the argument against it. He said that the Constitution guaranteed to the citizens of all states who emigrated to the territories the same rights they enjoyed at home in the states. The citizens of some states had the legal right to own slaves.

Therefore, Calhoun said, they had the right to take their slaves with them when they went west.

The Free Soil Party

When President Polk endorsed Calhoun's reasoning, a large number of northern Democrats bolted and organized the Free Soil party. Some of them were abolitionists, but by no means all. As a party, the Free Soilers allowed that the people of the southern states had every constitutional right to preserve slavery at home. In fact, most Free Soilers cared little about the plight of the blacks. There was a streak of racism in the rhetoric of many of them; a few wanted to ban free blacks, as well as slaves and slave owners, from the western territories. As late as 1857, an Oregon law prohibited (ineffectively) the emigration of free blacks into the state.

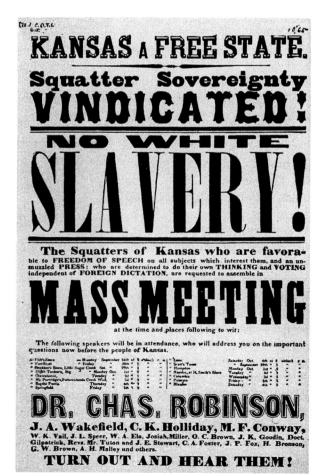

The Free Soilers were heirs of the ideals of Thomas Jefferson. They believed that small family farmers were the backbone of the nation. The Mexican Acquisition, therefore, should be dedicated to the promotion and prosperity of such people, just as Jefferson had reserved the Northwest Territory for them in 1787. Slavery must be kept out of the West because, where there were slaves, there were slave owners; and slave owners, as the example of the southern states amply demonstrated, used their economic edge over small farmers to stifle true democracy. "Free Soil! Free Speech! Free Men!" was their cry.

The Election of 1848

Polk did not run for reelection in 1848. A hard worker, he literally wore himself out expanding the nation and died less than four months after leaving Washington, at only 54 years of age. In his place, the Democrats nominated one of his northern supporters, the competent but gloriously dull Lewis Cass of Michigan, one of the few northern congressmen to vote against the Wilmot Proviso.

The Whigs, having lost once again with their elder statesman Clay in 1844, returned to the winning formula of 1840—a popular general. They nominated the hero of the Battle of Buena Vista, Zachary Taylor of Louisiana. Because Taylor was a slave owner as well as a southerner, Whig strategists hoped that he would carry southern states that would otherwise be lost to the Democrats on the Wilmot issue.

In fact, Taylor was a most remarkable presidential candidate. "He really is a most simple-minded old man," said Whig educator Horace Mann. "Few men have ever had more contempt for learning," wrote General Winfield Scott. "He doesn't know himself from a side of sole leather in the way of statesmanship," wrote Horace Greeley. A coarse, cranky, and blunt-spoken old geezer of 64 years, Taylor allowed proudly that he had never bothered to cast a vote in his life. When the letter from the Whig party announcing his nomination arrived, he refused to pay the postage owing on it. When the news of the honor finally broke through, he responded diffidently: "I will not say I will not serve if the good people were imprudent enough to elect me."

The Free Soilers were able to put up a more distinguished and able candidate than either the Democrats or the Whigs, former president Martin Van Buren. Sixty-six years of age, he had come out stridently against the expansion of slavery. (There was

The volatility of politics in Kansas Territory is expressed in this poster announcing an antislavery meeting.

probably a whiff of Old Kinderhook opportunism in his stand; later, Van Buren had no difficulty supporting Democrats who favored expansion.)

Little Van did not have a chance, but his name on the ballot was decisive in his home state of New York. He won more votes there than Lewis Cass, throwing New York's 36 electoral votes to the Whig Taylor. Along with New York, as so many times earlier and since, went the election of 1848.

CALIFORNIA, HERE I COME

Moderates hoped that the Whig victory would cool the sectional passions aroused by the Wilmot Proviso and the rise of the Free Soilers. Although Taylor was himself a southerner, and carried more than half the southern states, he represented a party traditionally dedicated to compromise between North and South. He was, in fact, the victor in every New England state except New Hampshire.

But Old Rough and Ready was to know little harmony as president. Far from it: events in far-off California, unfolding even as he was nominated and elected, caused a crisis that almost split the North and South into warring parties in 1850.

Gold!

On the evening of January 24, 1848, a carpenter from New Jersey, James Marshall, took a walk along the American River where it tumbled through the foothills of California's Sierra Nevada. Marshall was an employee of John Augustus Sutter, a Swiss adventurer who had turned a vast Mexican land grant into a kind of feudal domain. Sutter's castle was an adobe

fort on the Sacramento River, defended by cannon he had purchased from the Russians when they abandoned Fort Ross.

Marshall was building a sawmill for Sutter. He was inspecting the tail race—the ditch that returned rushing water to the river after it turned the wheel that drove the sawmill—when he picked up a curious, heavy metallic stone. It was a nugget. Returning to his crew, he said, "Boys, I think I have found a gold mine."

Indeed he had, and it meant the end of Sutter's mill. Sutter's workers dropped hewing timbers to shovel gravel from the bed of the American and other streams, separating the sand and silt from what proved to be plenty of gold dust and nuggets. For a moment, Marshall's discovery was the end of San Francisco. A foggy town of 500 souls, San Francisco was depopulated when its inhabitants, including most of the recently posted American military garrison, headed for the golden hills.

The next year—1849—80,000 people descended on California in the great gold rush that, as a mass emigration of zealous, single-minded souls, has been compared to the Crusades of the Middle Ages. By the end of the year, the population of California was about 100,000, more than in the states of Delaware and Florida. The Forty-Niners were producing $10 million annually in gold. Californians believed that their population and value to the nation merited immediate statehood. When Congress convened in December, California had already submitted a provisional constitution that prohibited slavery.

A contemporary engraving captured the grandeur of the California landscape and the ruggedness of the miner's life.

Trauma

The stunning rapidity of these events lay at the heart of the crisis that ensued. President Polk and proslavery southerners wanted Mexican lands, California most of all, to provide an outlet for the expansion of slavery. They assumed, with good reason, that much of the Mexican Acquisition would be peopled slowly by emigrants from the adjacent southern states who, thanks to the defeat of the Wilmot Proviso, could take their slaves with them. In time, new slave states would emerge in Mexico's lost provinces.

But the Treaty of Guadalupe-Hidalgo that gave California to the United States had not even been signed when James Marshall took his famous stroll. When the Forty-Niners demanded statehood, California had not yet been organized as a territory. Legally, it was still a conquered province, ostensibly under the control of the military. Proslavery southerners saw their well-laid and well-executed plans to create a slave state on the Pacific pulverized like the rocks in California's streams.

Worst of all, if California were admitted to the Union as a free state, the South would lose its equality with the North in the United States Senate. Southerners were already a minority in the House of Representatives, where seats are apportioned according to population. In 1849, there were about 9 million people in the South and 14 million in the North, and only three-fifths of the South's slaves were counted in apportioning House seats.

The Senate, therefore, where each state is represented by two members regardless of population, had assumed special significance to southern sectionalists like Calhoun. In 1849, there were 15 slave states and 15 free states, a comforting equality. However, with no potential slave state on the horizon, and with two embryonic free states in Oregon and Minnesota Territories, California statehood looked like nothing less than a calamity.

A majority of southern congressmen arrived in Washington in December 1849, declaring their opposition to the admission of California. The North's toleration of abolitionists, they said, made it impossible for the South to trust the goodwill of any free-state senators. Southerners needed equality in the Senate in order to protect their interests.

Clay's Last Stand

The southern intransigents soon discovered that President Taylor was not on their side. The owner of more than 100 slaves did not mind saying that he would take up arms to protect his right to keep them. But Old Rough and Ready was a nationalist. For reasons of national pride, prosperity, and security, he insisted that California be admitted immediately. If it must be as a free state, too bad, but so be it. He further angered southern congressmen when he decided that a boundary dispute between Texas and what was slated to become New Mexico Territory be resolved in favor of New Mexico.

Tempers were boiling when Congress convened. The election of a Speaker of the House of Representatives, usually a formality, took 63 ballots. In the Senate the next month, Henry Clay, a frail and weary 72 years old now and beyond all hopes of becoming president, attempted to cap his career as the Great Compromiser by proposing a permanent solution to the slavery question.

Clay's Omnibus Bill was a compromise in the old tradition; it required both sides to make significant concessions in the interests of the common good, the preservation of the Union. The bill provided that California be admitted as a free state and that the rest of the Mexican Acquisition be organized as territories with no reference to the status of slavery there. Thus, proslavery southerners could hold out the possibility of future slave states in what is now Utah, Nevada, New Mexico, and Arizona.

The Texas land dispute was resolved in favor of the federal government but with face-saving concessions to Texas, including Congress's assumption of the large debt of the former Republic of Texas.

Clay ignored abolitionist demands that slavery be banned in the District of Columbia. The South had a strong constitutional point on that matter, and the mere suggestion of abolition angered those southern moderates whom Clay was counting on to push through his Omnibus Bill. (Many of them brought their slave maids, cooks, and grooms to

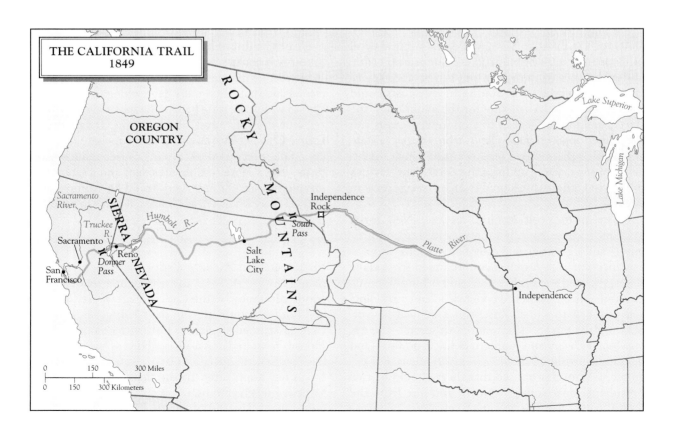

THE CALIFORNIA TRAIL
1849

Washington.) However, he tried to mollify northern sensibilities by proposing the abolition of the slave trade in the national capital. At their best, slave auctions were ugly affairs. To many moderate southerners like Clay, it was wretched public relations to shine a spotlight on the commerce.

To compensate slave owners for this symbolic rebuff, Clay included a new, stronger Fugitive Slave Act in his package. Until 1850, it was not difficult for antislavery northerners, including state and local officials, to protect runaway slaves within their jurisdiction. Clay's bill allowed special federal commissioners to circumvent local courts, arrest fugitive slaves in the North, and return them to their owners.

Failure

Not too many years earlier, the Omnibus Bill would have sailed through Congress amidst cheers, tossed hats, and invitations to share a bottle of whiskey after adjournment. But Texas, the war, and California had changed the times and soured tempers. Extremists from both sections, and some congressmen who were regarded as moderates, refused to accept the Omnibus Bill because it contained concessions they regarded as morally reprehensible.

A majority of northerners, not just abolitionists, abhorred the Fugitive Slave Act. By allowing federal officials to arrest people who committed no crime under the laws of their own states, it made slavery quasi-legal everywhere. Southern extremists could not bring themselves to vote for the abolition of the slave trade in the District of Columbia. Texans and their allies opposed taking lands from that slave state and putting them into a territory into which the legality of slavery was up for grabs. President Taylor's friends in Congress resented compensating Texas in any way.

The spirit of compromise was dead. New York's William H. Seward called the very idea of compromise "radically wrong and essentially vicious." Southern "fire-eaters," younger congressmen from slave states, pledged themselves to yield nothing. John C. Calhoun, once a master of cool reason and cold logic, was reduced to the sophistry of a cynical lawyer, defining the purposes he wanted to serve—the expansion of slavery and southern political power—and devising convoluted theories to justify them. For example, Calhoun proposed that there should be two presidents, one from the North and one from the South, each with the power of veto over congres-

sional acts. The old man spent his last days, dying painfully of throat cancer, surrounded by a gaggle of romantic young disciples with, in the whole bunch, half his brains.

Henry Clay, almost as decrepit, plugged away unsuccessfully among those who thought they were moderates. His cause was boosted when Daniel Webster delivered one of his greatest orations in support of the compromise. Webster announced that in order to save the Union, he would vote even for the fugitive slave provisions of the Omnibus Bill. He was vilified for his speech in New England. Perhaps nothing better illustrates the growth of extremism in the North than the fact that prominent New Englanders who had winked at Webster's personal dissoluteness and panhandling of bankers and industrialists for 30 years denounced him for taking the middle ground on a debate that was tearing the Union apart. "The word 'honor' in the mouth of Mr. Webster," wrote Ralph Waldo Emerson, "is like the word 'love' in the mouth of a whore."

THE COMPROMISE OF 1850

Even if the Omnibus Bill had passed Congress, President Taylor would have vetoed it. He was too stubborn and willful to be a politician and his mind was set on two matters the Omnibus Bill defied. He insisted that California be admitted with no strings attached and that Texas must get nothing for giving up land to which the state had, in Taylor's view, no claim.

But the bill never reached him. It failed and Henry Clay left Washington. In the meantime, however, fate intervened to save his cause, and to bring to the fore a more flexible president and a senator of unique resourcefulness who would be as important in the Senate of his era as Henry Clay was in his own.

Death of a Soldier

First, truculent Zachary Taylor was swept from the scene. On July 4, 1850, the president attended a patriotic ceremony on the Capitol mall where, for several hours, he sat hatless in the blazing sun listening to long-winded speeches. Returning to the White House, he wolfed down a large bowl of sliced cucumbers and several quarts of iced milk.

A few hours later the old man took to bed with severe stomach cramps, not surprising under the circumstances. Instead of leaving him alone, his doctors bled him and administered one powerful medicine after another—ipecac to make him vomit, quinine for his fever, calomel as a laxative, and opium for the pain they were causing him. Old Rough and Ready was murder on Mexicans and Texans, but he could not handle the pharmacopoeia of the nineteenth century. On July 9, he died and was succeeded by Vice President Millard Fillmore.

Fillmore is remembered as our least memorable president, a joke repeated so often as to be worn bare. He had flirted with radical politics early in his career, and would do so again. But in 1850 he was firmly within the moderate Whig camp of Clay and Webster, and sensitive to how close the Union was to a breakup. Although he did not declare publicly for compromise, it was generally assumed he favored it.

The "Little Giant"

The senator who succeeded in putting together a compromise was Stephen A. Douglas of Illinois. Barely over five feet in height, Douglas was known as the "Little Giant" because of his success as a lawyer, his oratorical powers, and his role as tactical mastermind of the Illinois Democratic party. Only three years a senator in 1850, Douglas nevertheless had mobilized the contacts and the guile to devise an ingenious strategy for shimming Clay's compromise into the law books.

Instead of presenting the sharply divided House and Senate with a single Omnibus Bill, parts of which offended nearly everyone, Douglas separated Clay's package into six component parts. These he maneuvered individually through Congress by patching together a different majority for each bill.

Thus, Douglas could count on northern senators and representatives to support California statehood and the abolition of the slave trade in the District of Columbia. To these votes he managed to add those of just enough southern moderates from the border states to slip the bills through. He could count on a solid southern bloc for the Fugitive Slave Act and the Texas bill. To this group he added just enough northern moderates to make a majority.

The "Compromise of 1850" was not really a compromise in the sense that both sides gave a little, took a little. A majority of both northern and southern congressmen refused to yield an inch. Only 4 of 60 senators voted for all of Douglas's bills, and only 11 voted for 5 of the 6. (Even Douglas was absent

Stephen Douglas (1813–1861), the "Little Giant," as a young man.

from the vote on the Fugitive Slave Act.) Only 28 of 240 representatives voted for all of the bills.

Douglas's manipulations were brilliant; he made extremely controversial bills into laws when a mere handful of his colleagues were committed to the spirit of compromise. His success also proved popular in the nation at large, where moderation on sectional questions was probably stronger than it was under the Capitol dome. But Douglas did nothing to extinguish the fires of hostility that were smoldering in Congress.

Exit the Old Guard

In the thirty-first Congress of 1849–1851, the nation's second generation of leaders, those who had governed the country since the passing of the founding fathers, rubbed elbows with the third generation, a new and very different breed. Andrew Jackson was already gone, dead at last in 1845. Henry Clay and Daniel Webster both passed on in 1852. Thomas Hart Benton survived until 1858, but only to

HOW THEY LIVED

How They Mined the Gold

Very few of the forty-niners knew even the rudiments of how gold was mined. Only the Mexicans, who generally were called Sonorans in California after the Mexican state from which many came, and the Cornish from southwestern England had been miners before they came to the gold fields.

However, technological innocence was no great handicap in California in 1849 and the early 1850s because placer mining—recovering pure gold from the sands and gravels of creek beds—required very little expertise. What placer mining called for was backbreaking toil, which the forty-niners were prepared to invest.

Placer mining is a mechanical process. In order to ascertain whether there was gold in a creek, a miner "panned" it. That is, he scooped up a pound or so of silt, sand, and pebbles in a sturdy, shallow pan; removed the stones by hand (making certain he did not discard any nuggets, chunks of gold); and then agitated the finer contents, constantly replenishing the water in the pan so that the lighter mud and sand washed over the sides while the heavier gold remained.

When miners (who usually worked in partnerships of two, three, or more) discovered enough "color" in a pan to warrant systematic mining of a placer, they staked a claim and built a "rocker" or a "long tom," two easily constructed devices that performed the washing process on a larger scale.

The rocker was a watertight wooden box, three to five feet long and a foot or so across, that was built on a base like that of a rocking chair so that it could be tipped from side to side. On the bottom were a series of riffles made of wood or in the form of corrugated metal, and sometimes a sheet of fine wire mesh. These simulated the crevices in a creek bed, where the gold naturally collected. Into the rocker, by means of a sluice, ran a constant stream of water. While one "pard" shoveled gravel and sand into the box, another rocked it and agitated the contents with a spade or a pitchfork. As with panning, the lighter worthless mineral washed out (stones, again, were manually discarded), and the gold remained at the bottom to be retrieved at the end of the day, weighed, divided, and cached.

The long tom took more time to build but was easier to work and more productive. In effect, the water-bearing sluice was extended into a long, high-sided, watertight box with a series of riffles built into the bottom. Using the long tom, all the partners could shovel gravel almost continuously. It was not necessary to agitate the contents. The long tom was also better adapted to "dry mining" than was the rocker. That is, in order to wash gold anywhere but in a creek, it was necessary to transport water to the site by means of a sluice.

---

discover that the new era had no place for him. Because he refused to defend slavery as a positive good, and like Webster placed the Union above sectional prejudices, he lost his Senate seat in 1850, was defeated in a race for the House of Representatives from Missouri in 1856, and then lost again when he ran for governor of the state.

John C. Calhoun would have won election after election had he lived to be a hundred. Alone of the giants of the age of Jackson, he made the transition—he led the transition!—from commitment to Union to extreme southern sectionalism. But Calhoun did not survive to see the results of his unhappy career. On March 4, 1850, too ill to deliver his last speech to the Senate, an uncompromising attack on the North, he had to listen while it was read for him, his glazed eyes burning with defiance and hatred. Less than a month later he was dead.

Fire-Eaters and Abolitionists

Shortly before his death, Calhoun croaked to one of his disciples that it was up to the young to save "the South, the poor South." With each year of the 1850s,

Slavery in the Territories

The Missouri Compromise provided that slavery was "forever forbidden" in the *territories* of the Louisiana Purchase lands north of 36° 30′, but did it also mean that states evolving out of those territories were also forbidden to legalize slavery? Probably not. Before he signed the Missouri Compromise, President Monroe consulted with his advisors and all of them, including John Quincy Adams, said that, no, once a territory had become a state, its domestic institutions were its own business. That was surely true. Had the people of the state of Maine chosen to legalize slavery as late as 1864, they were constitutionally free to do so. However, forbidding slavery in the territories meant that, in reality, states developing there would inevitably be free states. There would be no slave owners at the new state's constitutional convention and, as the examples of the Free Soil and Republican parties show, where there were no slave owners there was precious little interest in legalizing slavery.

War, an ambitious Democrat had to be a doughface in order to win his party's presidential nomination. The Democratic party needed a northern candidate to have a hope of winning. However, because of the party's two-thirds rule—a nominee needed two of three convention delegates—only a northerner acceptable to the South, that is, friendly to southern interests in the matter of slavery, could be nominated. Lewis Cass of Michigan, the nominee in 1848, was a doughface; so was Franklin Pierce of New Hampshire and the Democratic nominee in 1856, James Buchanan of Pennsylvania.

The Republican Party

The Kansas-Nebraska Act killed the Whig party. When southern Whigs voted for it along with the southern Democrats, the Whigs of the North bade them farewell. Already, many northern Whigs were abolitionists. Those who were not, like Abraham Lincoln of Illinois, regarded the Missouri Compromise as a great achievement. Willing to tolerate slavery in the South, unwilling to accept its expansion, the northern Whigs joined with the Free Soilers to form the new Republican party.

So spontaneous was the explosion of anti-Kansas-Nebraska Act sentiment that the Republican party really had no single birthplace. The Republicans of Ripon, Wisconsin, later insisted that they were the first to use the name but boosters in other towns also had plausible claims. The fact is, the Republican party combusted all over the North and then coalesced as a national institution or, rather, for there was no Republican party in the South, a *sectional* institution. Rather more striking, the Republican demand that the Kansas-Nebraska Act be repealed was so popular that the infant party actually captured the House of Representatives in the midterm election of 1854.

At first, the Republicans were a single-issue party of protest, not much different than the Free Soilers. But their leaders were experienced and cagey politicians who soon worked out a comprehensive program. The Republicans stole Douglas's thunder on the railroad question by insisting that the transcontinental be built on the central route. They appealed to farmers who might be indifferent to the question of slavery in the territories by advocating a Homestead Act giving western lands to families who would actually settle and farm it.

From the Whigs, the Republicans inherited the demand for a high protective tariff, thus winning some manufacturing interests to their side. Also appealing to industrial capitalists was the Republican

Public Relations

Although few said so publicly, many southern leaders privately admitted that they were glad to see the slave trade abolished in Washington, D.C. It was not a major market town, and everyone admitted that the auction block was slavery's ugliest face. With a large foreign population, which inclined to be antislavery, in the national capital at all times, the disappearance of the auction block in Washington could be considered a kind of public-relations measure, hiding an unpleasant reality from visitors.

The ending of the slave trade in Washington did not have that effect, however. There were slave auctions in both Arlington and Alexandria, Virginia, across the Potomac River, and diplomats and tourists found it quite easy to cross over to see them.

JNº C. FREMONT.   Wᵐ L. DAYTON.
THE CHAMPIONS OF FREEDOM.

A celebrated explorer, John C. Frémont (on left) was the first Republican candidate for the presidency.

demand for a liberal immigration policy, which would attract cheap European labor to the United States.

Also from the Whigs, Republicans inherited a disdain for Democrats as vulgar, self-serving, and ignorant. As poet Walt Whitman put it in a diatribe not to be topped, the Democrats of Washington were

the meanest kind of bawling and blowing office-holders, office-seekers, pimps, malignants, conspirators, murderers, fancy-men, custom-house clerks, contractors, kept-editors, spaniels well-train'd to carry and fetch, jobbers, infidels, disunionists, terrorists, mail-riflers, slave-catchers, pushers of slavery, creatures of the President, creatures of would-be Presidents, spies, bribers, compromisers, lobbyers, sponges, ruin'd sports, expell'd gamblers, policy-backers, monte-dealers, duellists, carriers of conceal'd weapons, deaf men, pimpled men, scarr'd inside with vile disease, gaudy outside with gold chains made from the people's money and harlot's money twisted together; crawling serpentine men, the lousy combinings and born freedom-settlers of the earth.

Because the Republicans were not a national party as the Whigs had been, their hopes of national victory lay in a sweep of the free states, which would be enough to win the presidency. In that hope, government by a party frankly representing only one section of the country, lay a threat to the unity of the nation.

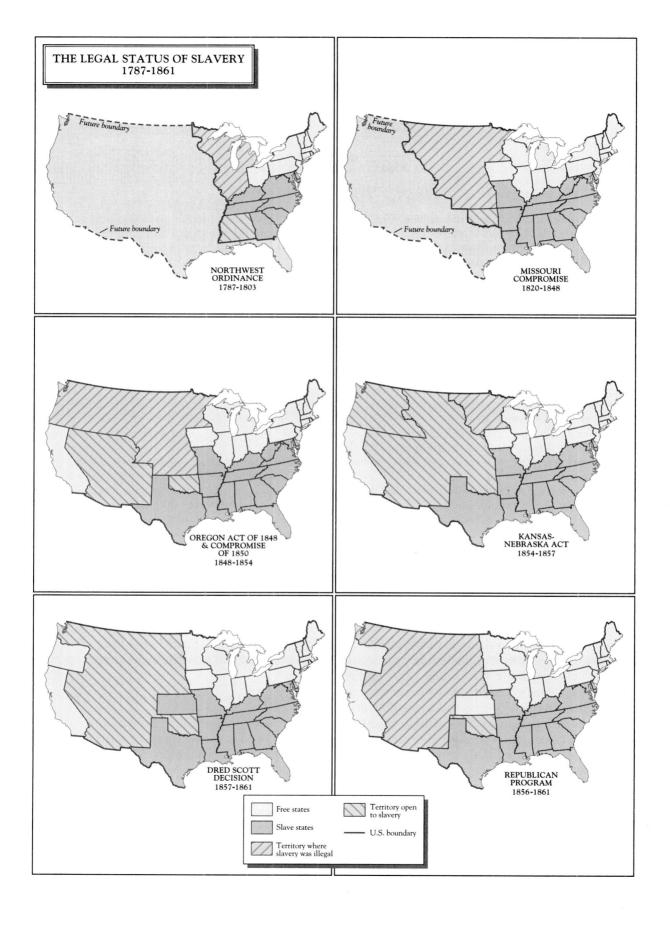

THE LEGAL STATUS OF SLAVERY
1787-1861

NORTHWEST
ORDINANCE
1787-1803

MISSOURI
COMPROMISE
1820-1848

OREGON ACT OF 1848
& COMPROMISE
OF 1850
1848-1854

KANSAS-
NEBRASKA ACT
1854-1857

DRED SCOTT
DECISION
1857-1861

REPUBLICAN
PROGRAM
1856-1861

Free states

Slave states

Territory where
slavery was illegal

Territory open
to slavery

U.S. boundary

Future boundary

HOW THEY LIVED

Rapping from the Great Beyond

In 1847, John and Margaret Fox moved with their two youngest daughters, 14-year-old Margaret and Cathy, 11, to the small town of Hydesdale, New York, about 20 miles from Rochester. They were denizens of the "Burned-over District," a declining rural region of New York State so buffeted by social dislocation for decades that it had sent tens of thousands of desperate emigrants west, and been scorched by repeated waves of torrid religious enthusiasms. Thus: "the Burned-over District." Rural New York was the birthplace of moral reform movements such as feminism, new religions like Mormonism and Adventism, and a flourishing revivalism among the old denominations there. Indeed, the Foxes were described as "sober, respectable Methodists"; inasmuch as John Fox was a reformed drunkard who had abandoned his family for several years, the Foxes may well have been recently saved.

Their cottage in Hydesdale was haunted. It was said there had been a murder in its precincts and the soul of the victim occasionally made its presence known. In March 1848, Margaret and Cathy announced that such a spirit from beyond had communicated with them by means of a series of raps and

knocks. They demonstrated their discovery to neighbors, asking questions that could be answered by a number of audible raps agreed upon between the sisters and the spirit.

Rural New Yorkers may have had a reputation for spiritual eccentricity, but several visitors to the Fox home scoffed that the girls were making the rapping sounds themselves by "cracking" their knuckles or some other joint safely covered by the floor-length skirts of the era. Almost immediately, however, an older sister, Leah, rushed the girls off to Rochester where large audiences, at 25 cents a person, could witness the communications on their "spiritual telegraph." The girls, and Leah now too, were examined in private rooms by women who stripped them, looking for rap-making devices.

They found none. Nevertheless, it was observed that when the girls' legs were tightly bound, fewer spirits spoke. Still, people flocked to the séances (as they were soon known), especially people grieving over a lost parent, spouse, or child, who always responded reassuringly of a spirit world much like the material one but without unhappiness, illness, and evil.

the raid in Lawrence, in an act that he announced was retribution, a fanatical abolitionist named John Brown swooped down on a small settlement on the banks of Pottawatomie Creek and ordered five proslavery Kansans executed with a farmer's scythe.

Southern politicians, who had treated the proslavery violence in Kansas as something of a joke, screamed in humanitarian anguish. Northern abolitionists who had wrung their hands over the barbarism of the border ruffians were suddenly silent.

That a ritual murderer should be praised by people who were inclined to parade their moral rectitude indicates the extremity to which the hatred between antislavery northerners and proslavery southerners had reached. Activists on both sides no longer spoke and acted according to rational principles;

they were in favor of any act done in the name of "the South, the poor South" or of the godly cause of striking the chains from the bondsmen.

Charles Sumner and Preston Brooks

Congress itself provided the stage for another bloody debacle in May 1856. Senator Charles Sumner of Massachusetts, an abolitionist who found no contradiction between his pacifism and his gift for vituperative oratory, delivered a speech on the floor of the Senate called "The Crime against Kansas."

Sumner described the persecution of free-state settlers and blamed the violence on his southern colleagues. All was pretty standard fare until Sumner added some gratuitous personal insults to an elderly

"Spiritualism" became a mania. By 1850 there were almost 100 mediums (people who mediated between the material and spiritual worlds) in the prison town of Auburn. Some mediums specialized in rapping, others in mirror writing. Tables were levitated. Some séances were accompanied by music.

The Fox sisters moved to New York City where they appeared before celebrities such as Horace Greeley, William Cullen Bryant, George Bancroft, and James Fenimore Cooper. Some were amused, some were believers. The Foxes's most sensational "spiritual telegram" came from recently deceased John C. Calhoun, who announced that, since his passing, he had become an abolitionist. In fact, spiritualists generally supported such reform movements as abolition and women's suffrage, and preached tolerance of all religious denominations. It became a fixture in a "stammering century" that also embraced phrenology and mesmerism.

The sensational success of spiritualism's early years has an even broader context than a social inclination to embrace unscientific -isms. The similar ideas of the great Swedish polymath, Emmanuel Swedenborg, had commanded disciples in several Protestant denominations for a century. Swedenborg saw the material world as a mere "laboratory" for the perfection of the human soul. Just a few years before the Fox sisters broke on the scene, a less-celebrated preacher, Andrew Jackson Davis, had described a reachable spirit world throughout the northern states. Charles Dickens's *A Christmas Carol*, which was structured around the visits of spirits to the home of Ebeneezer Scrooge, was published in 1843 and was one of the most popular books of the decade. Samuel F. B. Morse's telegraph, sending messages over long distances in something very much like raps, was itself still a novelty that indubitably worked yet remained as mysterious and implausible to uneducated people as the Fox sisters' communications.

The Civil War revived belief in spiritualism when hundreds of thousands of Americans grieved for sons, husbands, brothers, and fathers snuffed out in their youth. It suffered a setback in the 1880s when Margaret Fox, who had become a Roman Catholic, rather excessively denounced spiritualism as "the most wicked blasphemy known to the world," demonstrating how she had created raps with a double-jointed big toe. Nevertheless, the possibility of communicating with the world of spirits remains a widespread belief today.

---

senator from South Carolina, Andrew Butler. Butler suffered from a physical defect that caused him to drool when he spoke, and Sumner made some coarse allusions to slobbering in connection with the less-than-human qualities of slave owners.

Two days later, Butler's nephew, a congressman named Preston Brooks, walked into the Senate chamber to stand behind Sumner, who was seated at his desk writing. Brooks proceeded to beat the senator senseless with a heavy cane. Brooks said that he was merely putting into practice the chivalric Code Duello, which held that a gentleman avenge the personal insult of an equal by challenging him to a duel, but that one caned a social inferior.

In fact, Brooks's action made a mockery of chivalry. He had approached Sumner from behind.

(Sumner, a big man, might well have floored Brooks had they met face to face.) Then, instead of merely humiliating Sumner with a few sharp raps, Brooks bludgeoned the senator to within an inch of death while Sumner, his legs tangled in his fallen desk, lay helpless to defend himself.

Instead of disowning Brooks as a bully and coward, southerners feted him at banquets and made him gifts of dozens of gold-headed canes to replace the one that he broke on Sumner's head. The House voted against expelling him and, when Brooks resigned, his district resoundingly reelected him. At the same time, northerners forgot that Sumner had stepped far beyond the bounds of common decency in his description of Senator Butler, and made him a martyr. While Sumner recovered — it would be

Fervent abolitionist John Brown (1800–1859) directed the execution of five proslavery Kansans.

several years before he returned to the Senate—Massachusetts reelected him so that his empty desk would stand as a rebuke to the South.

A HARDENING OF LINES

In normal times, politicians who argue violently in Congress socialize quite cordially outside the Capitol. Even Andrew Jackson and Nicholas Biddle were capable of pleasantries at parties and balls. By 1856, this ceased to be true. Both northerners and southerners carried firearms into the congressional chambers and ceased to speak with one another even on informal occasions. Against this foreboding backdrop was held the presidential election of 1856.

The Election of 1856

Inevitably, the Democrats chose a doughface, but he was not Stephen A. Douglas. The Little Giant, a hero in the South in 1854 when he opened the territories to slavery, lost his appeal after events in Kansas indicated that the opportunity he created was largely theoretical. Indeed, Douglas himself told northerners not to worry about the Kansas-Nebraska Act. The concession to slavery, he said, was symbolic, a gesture of goodwill to southerners. In the end, Douglas said, Kansas would be a free state because of the greater population of the North and the unsuitability of Kansas to plantation agriculture. After the success of the New England Emigrant Aid Society in dispatching antislavery settlers to Kansas, his reasoning rang loudly and unpleasantly in southern ears.

Instead of Douglas, the Democrats nominated James Buchanan of Pennsylvania, a man of long political experience, but pedestrian talent and, apparently, effete manner. (Andrew Jackson called him "Miss Nancy" behind his back.) Politically, Buchanan was profoundly lucky. He was out of the country serving as minister to Great Britain between 1853 and 1856 and was, therefore, not closely associated with the Kansas controversy. However, he won plaudits from southern extremists when he was a party to a statement known as the Ostend Manifesto, a call for the United States to purchase Cuba from Spain. Some southerners envisioned Cuba as a sixteenth slave state.

The Republicans chose John C. Frémont, famous as "the Pathfinder," the dashing leader of two exploration parties that helped map the way to Oregon and California. Frémont was no giant of character or intellect. His greatest recommendation was his wife, Jessie Benton, the beautiful, willful, and intelligent daughter of Old Bullion. In the mood of 1856, however, Frémont was a logical choice for the Republicans: he believed that the western lands should be reserved for family farmers.

The Pathfinder suffered from two serious handicaps: he had abolitionist leanings, which scared off moderate northerners, and he was a bastard at a time when illegitimacy still carried a stain of shame.

Despite these burdens and despite being unlisted on the ballot in every slave state, Frémont won a third of the popular vote. He might actually have defeated Buchanan had not former President Millard Fillmore been in the race on the Know-Nothing ticket. Anti-Catholicism, the bete noire of the

Know-Nothings, was riding a wave as more and more Catholic Germans and Irish immigrated to the United States. Fillmore actually outpolled Frémont in California and probably took enough votes from him in Pennsylvania and Illinois to throw those states and the election to Buchanan.

Dred Scott

Buchanan's presidency began with a bang. In his inaugural address he hinted that the issue of slavery in the territories would shortly be settled for all time. Two days later, on March 6, 1857, Americans learned what he meant when the Supreme Court handed down its decision in the case of *Dred Scott* v. *Sandford*.

Dred Scott had been a slave in Missouri. Most of his life he was the valet of an army officer. In 1834, Scott accompanied his master to Illinois, where slavery was prohibited under the Northwest Ordinance of 1787. Briefly, he lived in a part of the Louisiana Purchase where slavery was then illegal under the Missouri Compromise. For four years, in other words, Scott lived on free soil before returning to Missouri.

By 1846, he became the property of an abolitionist who, rather than manumit him right away, saw an opportunity to strike a blow against the institution of slavery. With financial and legal help, Scott sued his master for his freedom on the grounds that for part of his life he was held as a slave in territory where Congress had prohibited slavery—a contradiction.

Ironically, Missouri courts had released slave plaintiffs with cases similar to Scott's, but that was before sectional animosity cut so broadly through the political fabric of the nation. In the Missouri courts, Scott lost his case on the grounds that whatever his status may have been in Illinois in 1834, he became quite legally a slave again when he was returned to Missouri.

Chief Justice Taney: The Final Solution

Although every Supreme Court justice commented individually on Scott's appeal, Chief Justice Roger B. Taney, an old Jackson henchman from Maryland, spoke for the majority when he declared that because he was black, Scott was not a citizen of the state of Missouri, which restricted citizenship to people of

Dred Scott (1795?–1858) went to the Supreme Court to win freedom and lost.

the white race. Therefore, Scott could not sue in the state courts.

Instead of leaving the decision at that, which would have been unpopular in the North, but judicially proper, Taney continued. He believed that he had discovered the constitutional solution to the question that was tearing the country apart. In fact, the doctrine Taney propounded was pure John C. Calhoun, the extreme southern constitutional argument on the question of slavery in the territories.

Taney declared that the Missouri Compromise was unconstitutional in prohibiting slavery in the territories because Congress was forbidden to discriminate against the citizens of any of the states. State legislatures could outlaw slavery, to be sure. But territorial legislatures could not do so because they were the creatures of Congress. They were, therefore, subject to the Constitution's restraints on Congress.

Republican Panic

Republicans, including moderates who urged accommodating the South in some way, were enraged. They saw the history of the question of slavery in the

The Race Issue

Because few American whites believed in racial equality, it was to the interest of northern Democrats to accuse the Republicans of advocating race mixture. "I am opposed to Negro equality," Stephen A. Douglas said in his debate with Abraham Lincoln in Chicago. "I am in favor of preserving, not only the purity of the blood, but the purity of the government from any mixture or amalgamation with inferior races."

The Democrats' line forced Republicans to reassure their constituents that opposition to slavery did not necessarily mean a belief in the equality of the races. Lincoln replied to Douglas: "I protest, now and forever, against that counterfeit logic which presumes that because I do not want a Negro woman for a slave, I necessarily want her for a wife.... As God made us separate, we can leave one another alone, and do one another much good thereby."

Lincoln shrewdly took the debate back to the territorial question by saying, "Why, Judge, if we do not let them get together in the Territories, they won't mix there."

territories as a step-by-step whittling away of the power of the federal government to prevent the expansion of slavery.

That is, between 1820 and 1854, under the Missouri Compromise, slavery was illegal in all territories north of 36° 30′. With the Kansas-Nebraska Act of 1854, slavery could be legalized in those territories if the settlers there chose to do so. With the Dred Scott decision of 1857, there was no way that the settlers in a territory could prohibit a slave owner from moving there along with his human property. According to *Dred Scott* v. *Sandford,* popular sovereignty was as unconstitutional as the Missouri Compromise was because a territorial legislature had no more authority than Congress did.

Republicans began to speak of a slavocratic conspiracy, now involving the Supreme Court, which was determined to thwart the will of a majority of the American people. Their fury was fanned in October 1857 when proslavery settlers in Kansas, augmented by a good many Missouri residents, sent to Congress the Lecompton Constitution, which called for admission of Kansas as a slave state. Although the

Lecompton Constitution obviously did not represent the sentiments of a majority of Kansans, President Buchanan urged Congress to accept it.

Republicans were also enraged by the zest with which, under Buchanan, the federal government enforced the Fugitive Slave Act of 1850, seizing runaway slaves in free states and returning them to their masters in the South. In one case, a fugitive was pursued and caught at the cost of $40,000—an expensive bond servant indeed. In Milwaukee, an antislavery mob stormed a jail where a runaway slave was taken by federal marshals and set him free.

Other abolitionists, particularly free blacks in the North, organized the underground railroad. This was a shifting network of households commencing at the Ohio River and Mason-Dixon line. By hiding runaway slaves by day, "conductors" on the line helped them move by night to Canada—out of the country—the only place where they would be free of the slavocracy.

Probably, the underground railroad was less systematic than, in later years, its romanticizers claimed it was. More likely, runaway slaves following "the drinking gourd"—the Big Dipper and the North Star to Canada—were much on their own in finding food and friends who would shelter them. Nevertheless, there were "conductors" who made a profession of helping slaves escape. Harriet Tubman, herself a former slave, returned to the South at the risk of her freedom, even her life, to lead hundreds of blacks out of bondage.

Lincoln and Douglas: Two Northern Answers

Stephen A. Douglas did not take Taney's rebuke of popular sovereignty lying down. In a series of debates in Illinois in 1858, Douglas and a Springfield Republican who wanted his seat in the Senate, Abraham Lincoln, proposed two northern solutions to the question of slavery in the territories.

"A house divided against itself cannot stand," Lincoln said in June 1858. "I believe that this government cannot endure half-slave and half-free." He meant that southerners would not be satisfied with keeping slavery where it already existed. Since they had insisted in the Dred Scott decision and in the Fugitive Slave Act on imposing the institution on people who did not want it, the southerners were forcing a showdown that, in the long run, would result in sectional conflict.

Douglas argued that popular sovereignty was still alive and kicking, and still the best solution to the problem. When Lincoln reminded him that the Supreme Court had ruled it unconstitutional in the Dred Scott decision, Douglas replied at Freeport, Illinois, in August 1858 that, Roger B. Taney notwithstanding, a territorial legislature could keep slavery out of a territory simply by failing to enact a slave code. No slave owner would dare take his valuable human property to a place where there were no laws to protect his power over his slaves. The Supreme Court might be able to overturn a territorial law, Douglas pointed out, but the Court could not force a territorial legislature to enact one it did not choose to enact.

The Freeport Doctrine was diabolically ingenious, and Douglas won reelection to the Senate, very narrowly. But events proved that Lincoln was also correct about the intentions of the southern extremists. When they were presented with the logic of the Freeport Doctrine, which did not favor their cause, they went on the offensive again, demanding that Congress pass a national slave code that would affirmatively protect slavery in all the territories.

John Brown: Yet Another Solution

John Brown had dropped out of sight after the murders on Pottawatomie Creek. But he was busy. Moving about New England behind a newly grown beard, Brown persuaded several well-to-do abolitionists who had abandoned pacifism that the time had come to strike violently at slavery. With their financial support, he organized a band of 22 insurrectionists, including some blacks and several of his own sons, at an isolated farm in Maryland. Just across the Potomac River, at the mouth of the Shenandoah, was Harpers Ferry, Virginia, site of one of the federal government's two major arsenals. Brown's plan was to seize the arsenal, capture guns and ammunition, and escape into the Appalachians, which rose steeply around the town.

From the mountains, he argued, his guerrilla army would swoop down on plantations, free a few slaves at a time, and enlarge the corps. Soon, Brown predicted, black rebellions would erupt all over the South, resolving for all time the great moral and political problem of slavery.

Brown's critics later said that the scheme proved that the old man was out of his mind. He may well

John Brown's Mountains

In the Appalachians, to which John Brown planned (but did not succeed) to escape, were nearly impenetrable places. During the Civil War, gangs of Confederate draft dodgers and deserters roamed them without fear of the authorities. So isolated are some hollows in the Appalachians that patterns of speech and folk ballads of Elizabethan England and Scotland survived there unchanged into the twentieth century, while they had long since disappeared elsewhere in the English-speaking world.

have been insane—he was certainly not the sort one invited to a favorite daughter's wedding—but there was nothing crazy about John Brown's military thinking. His plan prefigured in many ways the theory of guerrilla warfare that twentieth-century national liberation movements put into practice with great success: operate from a remote and shifting base; avoid big battles in which conventional military forces have the overwhelming advantage; fight only small surprise actions when the odds favor the freewheeling guerrillas; and win the friendship and support of the ordinary people, in Brown's case the slaves. The odds were never with him, but they were not prohibitive.

The Raid and the Reaction

Brown's most obvious mistake was to depart from his plan almost as soon as he got started. On October 16, 1859, his little band hit and easily captured the arsenal. Then, however, he either lost his nerve or fooled himself into believing that the slaves nearby

John Brown as Martyr

John Brown understood that while he was doomed, his death would ultimately serve the antislavery cause. Shortly before his execution, he wrote to his wife, "I have been whipped but am sure I can recover all the lost capital occasioned by that disaster; by only hanging a few minutes by the neck."

Border Ruffians

The western counties of Missouri would have been breeding grounds for violence even if, after 1856, the slavery issue had not been injected to agitate the settlers there. Western Missouri was still raw frontier, an extremely poor farming and grazing country where reigned the lawless instability of America's move west. With the slavery issue added to this dangerous mix, the border counties produced a disproportionate number of dubious characters in the years immediately before, during, and after the Civil War. In addition to the sacking of Lawrence, Kansas, and John Brown's action on Pottawatomie Creek, western Missouri was prime recruiting ground for William C. Quantrill's notorious raiders, a Civil War unit given more to terroristic attacks on civilians than to fighting the Union Army. Quantrill's right-hand man, Bloody Bill Anderson, scalped the northerners whom he killed. Future outlaws Jesse and Frank James and the Younger brothers came from this country, as did the "bandit queen," Myre Belle Shirley, or Belle Starr.

were on the verge of joining him. Forgetting what Frederick Douglass had told him, that Harpers Ferry was "a perfect steel trap," he holed up in the roundhouse of the arsenal, where he was promptly surrounded by United States Marines under the command of Colonel Robert E. Lee. In two days Lee's professionals killed ten of Brown's followers and captured Brown. He was promptly tried for treason against the state of Virginia, found guilty, and hanged in December.

Most northerners responded to the incident as southerners did. They were shocked by the raid, and grimly approved the speedy trial and execution of the old man. However, many prominent abolitionists were ominously silent, and a few openly praised Brown as a hero and a martyr. Ralph Waldo Emerson said that Brown's death made the gallows as holy as the Christian cross.

There was just enough of this kind of palaver to arouse the southern fire-eaters to a new pitch of hysteria. Brown's raid revived deep fears of slave rebellion, and here were prominent northerners praising a lunatic who tried to start one. Southern editors and politicians wondered how they could continue to

remain under the same government as people who encouraged their massacre.

It was true that the federal government had moved quickly and efficiently to crush Brown. Southerners had few complaints with the presidency in 1859. But 1860 was an election year. What was to happen if the Republicans won the White House, thus taking control of the federal police powers? Could the South then depend on protection against John Browns, Nat Turners, Harriet Tubmans, and Ralph Waldo Emersons?

THE ELECTION OF 1860

The southern extremists declared that if the Republicans won the presidential election of 1860, the southern states would secede from the Union; the Yankees should be aware of that possibility before they voted. Then, having threatened northern voters, the same extremists guaranteed a Republican victory. They split the Democratic party that had served southern interests so well along sectional lines.

The Democrats Split

The Democratic party was the last important national institution in the United States. The Whigs were gone, buried by the slavery issue. The large Protestant churches had broken into northern and southern branches. So had most fraternal lodges and commercial associations. The Republican party, of course, had an exclusively northern membership. Only within the Democratic party did men from

Lee's Loyalty to Virginia

Robert E. Lee, perhaps the most respected active soldier in the army in 1861, was asked what he would do if there was a civil war. Would he support the North or the South? In effect, Lee replied neither; he would support his native state, Virginia:

If Virginia stands by the old Union, so will I. But if she secedes (though I do not believe in secession as a constitutional right, nor that there is sufficient cause for revolution) then I will follow my native state with my sword and, if need be, with my life.

both sections still come together to try to settle their differences.

In April 1860, with the excitement of the Brown affair still hanging in the air, the Democratic convention met in Charleston. The majority of the delegates, including some southern moderates, supported the nomination of Stephen A. Douglas. But the southern extremists withheld their votes. The delegations of eight southern states announced that they would support Douglas only if he repudiated the Freeport Doctrine and supported their demand for a federal slave code.

The Douglas forces pointed out that to do this would be to drive northern Democrats into the Republican party. Unmoved by this reasoning, the eight hard-line delegations walked out of the convention. The Douglas forces recessed without nominating their leader, hoping to talk sense into the minority.

When the Democrats reassembled in Baltimore in June, the southern extremists still refused to budge. Disgusted by what they considered political suicide, the regular Democrats nominated Douglas for president and chose a southern moderate, Herschel V. Johnson of Georgia, as his running mate. The southern Democrats then nominated John C. Breckinridge of Kentucky to represent them in the election. In an attempt to give the ticket a semblance of national support, the southerners chose a doughface from Oregon, Joseph Lane, as their vice presidential candidate.

Republican Opportunity

Meanwhile, the Republicans met in Chicago. They were optimistic but cautious. With the Democrats split, they smelled victory. But they also knew that if they ran on too extreme an antislavery candidate—like Frémont in 1856—many northern voters would scurry back to the moderate Douglas. Even worse would be winning on too radical a platform: Southerners would make good on their threat to secede, which none but a few extremist abolitionists wanted to see.

Consequently, the Republican convention retreated from the rhetoric of previous years and rejected party stalwarts such as William H. Seward and Salmon P. Chase. Both men were on the record with inflammatory antisouthern statements. Seward had spoken of "a higher law than the Constitution" in condemning slavery and of an "irrepressible conflict" between North and South, precisely the sort of words that the Republicans of 1860 wished to avoid.

Chase had been a militant abolitionist in Ohio politics for more than a decade.

Instead, the Republicans picked a comparatively obscure midwesterner, Abraham Lincoln of Illinois. Lincoln was rock solid on the fundamental Republican principle: slavery must be banned from the territories. But he was no abolitionist; he had steered clear of the Know-Nothings, thus maintaining a good relationship with German voters; and he was moderate, humane, and ingratiating in his manner. In his famous debates with Douglas in 1858 and in a speech introducing himself to eastern Republicans in New York City in February 1860, he struck a note of humility and caution. Not only was slavery protected by the Constitution in those states where it existed, he said, but northerners ought to sympathize with slave owners rather than attack them. Lincoln himself was born in Kentucky, a slave state. He knew that a quirk of fate would have made him a slave owner, so he found it easy to preach the golden rule. By choosing him, the Republicans accommodated southern sensibilities as far as they could without giving up their own principles.

The Republicans adopted a comprehensive platform: a high protective tariff; a liberal immigration policy; the construction of a transcontinental railway; and a homestead act. In part, this platform was designed to win the votes of rather different economic groups: eastern industrial capitalists and workers, and midwestern farmers. In addition, by avoiding a single-issue campaign, the Republicans hoped to signal the South that they were not, as a party, antislavery fanatics. They also named a vice-presidential candidate who was a Democrat as late as 1857, Hannibal Hamlin of Maine.

The Old Man's Party

A fourth party entered the race, drawing its strength from the states of the upper South: Maryland, Virginia, Kentucky, and Tennessee. Henry Clay's conciliatory brand of Whiggery—an inclination toward compromise and a deep attachment to the Union—was still strong in the border states. The platform of the Constitutional Union party consisted, in effect, of stalling: it was a mistake to force any kind of sectional confrontation while tempers were up; put off the difficult problem of slavery in the territories to a later, calmer day.

For president the Constitutional Unionists nominated John Bell of Tennessee, a protégé of Clay, and

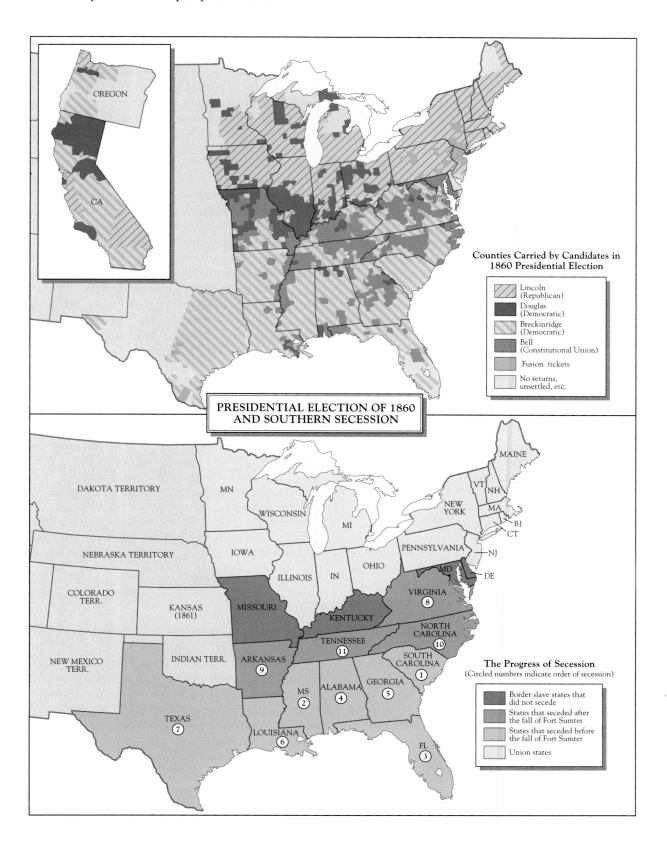

OREGON

CA

Counties Carried by Candidates in 1860 Presidential Election

- Lincoln (Republican)
- Douglas (Democratic)
- Breckinridge (Democratic)
- Bell (Constitutional Union)
- Fusion tickets
- No returns, unsettled, etc.

PRESIDENTIAL ELECTION OF 1860 AND SOUTHERN SECESSION

MAINE

DAKOTA TERRITORY · MN · WISCONSIN · MI · VT · NH · NEW YORK · MA · RI · CT

NEBRASKA TERRITORY · IOWA · PENNSYLVANIA · NJ

COLORADO TERR. · KANSAS (1861) · ILLINOIS · IN · OHIO · MD · DE

MISSOURI · KENTUCKY · VIRGINIA ⑧ · NORTH CAROLINA ⑩

NEW MEXICO TERR. · INDIAN TERR. · ARKANSAS ⑨ · TENNESSEE ⑪ · SOUTH CAROLINA ①

MS ② · ALABAMA ④ · GEORGIA ⑤

TEXAS ⑦ · LOUISIANA ⑥ · FL ③

The Progress of Secession
(Circled numbers indicate order of secession)

- Border slave states that did not secede
- States that seceded after the fall of Fort Sumter
- States that seceded before the fall of Fort Sumter
- Union states

for vice president they chose the distinguished Whig orator Edward Everett of Massachusetts. But they found only minority support outside of the border states. Republicans and both northern and southern Democrats sneered at them as "the old man's party."

Republican Victory

Abraham Lincoln won 40 percent of the popular vote, not much more than Frémont had drawn in 1856. But he carried every free state except New Jersey, which he split with Douglas. He also won a clear majority in the electoral college. Breckinridge was the overwhelming choice of the South. He won a plurality in 11 of the 15 slave states but a popular vote nationally of only 18 percent. Still, a majority of voters preferred the candidates who appealed to strong sectional feelings and rejected the candidates who appealed to a spirit of nationalism, Douglas and Bell.

A photograph of Abraham Lincoln (1809–1865), taken about the time he became the Republican candidate for president.

But not by much. Douglas won a mere 12 electoral votes (Missouri's nine and three from New Jersey), but he ran second to Lincoln in some northern states and to Breckinridge in some states in the South. John Bell carried three of the border states and was strong almost everywhere. Even if the Douglas and the Bell votes (the "moderate" votes) had been combined, however, Lincoln would have won. Nevertheless, inasmuch as many Lincoln and some Breckinridge supporters were more interested in making a noise than fighting, it seems clear that most of the American people preferred some kind of settlement to the breakup of the Union.

South Carolina Leads the Way

They did not get their wish. Having announced that Lincoln's election would lead to secession, the fire-eaters of South Carolina (where there was no popular vote for presidential electors) called a convention that, on December 20, 1860, unanimously declared that "the union now subsisting between South Carolina and the other States, under the name of the 'United States of America,' is hereby dissolved."

During January 1861, the six other states of the Deep South followed suit, declaring that a Republican administration threatened their domestic institutions. Then came a glimmer of hope. The secession movement stalled when none of the other southern states approved secession ordinances. At the same time they rejected secession, however, conventions in several border states declared their opposition to any attempt by the federal government to use force against the states that had seceded. By rebuffing the big talkers on both sides, the leaders of the border states hoped to force a compromise.

The outgoing president, James Buchanan, was not the man to engineer such a compromise. No one had much respect for Old Buck, including his own advisers, mostly southerners, who now betrayed him. His secretary of war, John Floyd of Virginia, transferred tons of war materiel to states that either had left the Union or were on the verge of leaving it. Floyd's act skirted close to treason, but Buchanan did nothing.

Other Buchanan allies resigned their offices and left Washington, hardly pausing to remember the president who had worked so hard to accommodate them. The first bachelor ever to occupy the White House was quite alone, and he knew it. After a hand-wringing message sent to Congress in which he declared that while secession was illegal, he as president was powerless to do anything about it, Buchanan sat back to wait for the day he could go home.

HOW THE UNION BROKE

As Buchanan slumped, Senator John J. Crittenden stood up. Like many Kentuckians, Crittenden made a career of mediating between the North and the Deep South. Now he proposed that rather than divide the Union, divide the territories. Extend the Missouri Compromise line to the California border; guarantee slavery to the south of it, and forbid slavery to the north.

The Compromisers Fail

Because of the Dred Scott decision, Crittenden's plan could not be put into effect by congressional action; it was necessary to divide the territories by constitutional amendment. Crittenden hoped that the specter of civil war, now chillingly real, with military companies drilling in both North and South, would prompt both northern and southern state legislatures to act in haste.

With some encouragement they might have done so. There was a flurry of enthusiasm for Crittenden's compromise on both sides of the Mason-Dixon line. But before the southern extremists were forced to take a stand, President-elect Lincoln quashed the plan. His reasons were political but nonetheless compelling. His Republican party was a diverse alliance of people who disagreed with one another on many issues. The one adhesive that bound them together was the principle that slavery must not expand into the territories. If Lincoln gave in on this point, he would take office with half his party sniping at him.

Lincoln also discouraged a second attempt at compromise, a peace conference held in Washington in February 1861. It was a distinguished assembly, chaired by former President John Tyler. Tyler had been a southern extremist, and, a few months later, he would support the secession of Virginia. But he worked hard for a settlement in February, proposing a series of constitutional amendments along the same lines as Crittenden's.

Once again, Lincoln drew the line on allowing slavery in the southern territories. Instead, he endorsed

an amendment, passed by both houses of Congress, that would forever guarantee slavery in the states where it already existed. As he well knew, this was a purely symbolic gesture that granted nothing the South did not already possess—and could be overturned by constitutional amendment at a later date. By February, in fact, the secessionists had lost interest in preserving the Union. They were caught up in the excitement of creating a new nation.

The Confederate States of America

According to secessionist theory, the seven states that left the Union were now independent republics. However, no southern leader intended his state to go it alone. Although they were disappointed that eight of the fifteen slave states still refused to join them, they met in Montgomery, Alabama, shortly before Lincoln's inauguration, and established their own confederacy.

The government that the southerners created differed little from the one that they had rejected. The Confederates declared that all United States laws were to remain in effect until amended or

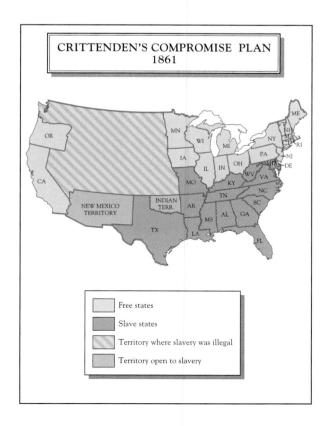

Fort Sumter in the Harbor of Charleston, where the Civil War began.

repealed, and they copied the Constitution of 1787 almost word for word. The few changes they made reflected the South's obsession with slavery and with Calhoun's political theories, and resulted in several curious contradictions.

Thus, the Confederates defined the states as sovereign and independent but called their new government permanent. Even more oddly, the Confederates declared that individual states might not interfere with slavery, a restriction on states' rights that no prominent Republican had ever suggested.

The Confederates also modified the presidency. The chief executive was to be elected for a term of six years rather than four, but he was not permitted to run for a second term. While this seemed to weaken the office, the Confederates allowed the president to veto parts of congressional bills rather than, as in the Union, requiring the president to accept all or nothing.

Jefferson Davis

As their first president, the Confederates selected Jefferson Davis. On the face of it, he was a good choice. His bearing was regal, he wore his dignity easily, and he was the model slave owner, the sort that southerners liked to pretend was typical of the institution. Davis also seemed to be a wise choice because he was not closely associated with the secessionist movement. Indeed, Davis asked his fellow Mississippians to delay secession until Lincoln had a chance to prove himself. When his state overruled him, Davis delivered a moderate, eloquent, and affectionate farewell speech in the

Senate. By choosing such a man, rather than a fire-eater, the Confederates demonstrated their willingness to work with southerners who opposed secession, who were numerous. With Davis, the Confederacy could also appeal to the eight slave states that remained within the Union.

In other ways, the choice of Jefferson Davis was ill-advised. It was not so much the coldness of his personality; George Washington had been icier. Davis's weakness was that despite his bearing, he lacked self-confidence and was, consequently, easily irritated and inflexible. He proved incapable of co-operating with critics, even those who differed with him on minor points. He seemed to need yes-men in order to function, and, as a result, he denied his administration the services of some of the South's ablest statesmen.

Worse, Davis was a dabbler. Instead of delegating authority and presiding over the government, he repeatedly interfered in the pettiest details of administration—peering over his subordinates' shoulders,

Jefferson Davis (1808–1889), president of the Confederacy.

arousing personal resentments among even those who were devoted to him. He had been a good senator; he was not qualified to be the "Father of His Country."

Abe Lincoln

By comparison, Abraham Lincoln knew the value of unity and competent assistants. Rather than shun his rivals within the Republican party, he named them to his cabinet. Seward became secretary of state; Salmon P. Chase was Lincoln's secretary of treasury. After a brief misadventure with an incompetent secretary of war, Simon Cameron, Lincoln appointed a Democrat, Edwin Stanton, to that post because his talents were obvious. Lincoln wanted able aides, not pals or toadies. Within their departments, Lincoln's cabinet officers were free to do anything that did not conflict with general policy. As a result, a cantankerous and headstrong group of men never seriously challenged his control of basic policy.

Lincoln differed from Davis in other ways. Far from regal, he was an awkward, plain, even ugly man. Tall and gangling, with oversize hands and feet, he impressed those who met him for the first time as a frontier oaf. His enemies called him "the baboon." Some of his supporters snickered at his clumsiness and were appalled by his fondness for dirty jokes.

But both friends and enemies soon discovered that the president was no yokel. Lincoln had honed a sharp native intelligence on a stone of lifelong study, and proved to be one of the three or four most eloquent chief executives. And yet, behind his brilliance was a humility born of modest background that can be found in no other American president.

Lincoln needed all his abilities. On March 4, 1861, when he was sworn in before a glum Washington crowd, the Union was in tatters. During the previous two months, the Stars and Stripes had been hauled down from every flagstaff in the South except for one at Fort Pickens in Pensacola, Florida, and another at Fort Sumter, a rocky island in the harbor of Charleston, South Carolina.

A War of Nerves

Neither of the forts threatened the security of the Confederacy. They were old installations designed for defense and were manned by token garrisons. But symbols take on profound importance in uneasy

A crowd gathered in front of the unfinished Capitol Building to hear Abraham Lincoln's first inaugural address on March 4, 1861.

times, and the southern fire-eaters, itching for a fight, ranted about the insulting occupation of their country by a foreign power.

Davis was willing to live with the Union forts for the time being. Unlike the hotheads, he understood that the Confederacy could not survive as long as only seven states adhered to it. His policy was to delay a confrontation with the North until he could make a foreign alliance or induce the eight slave states that remained in the Union to join the Confederacy. He feared that if he fired the first shot, the states of the upper South might support the Union.

The extremists disagreed. They believed that a battle, no matter who started it, would bring the other slave states to their side. Nevertheless, when the commander at Sumter announced that he would soon have to surrender the fort for lack of provisions, Davis had his way.

Within limits, Lincoln also favored delaying a confrontation. He believed that the longer the states of the upper South postponed a decision to secede,

the less likely they were to go. Moreover, the leaders of Virginia, Kentucky, Tennessee, and Arkansas formally warned him against using force against the Confederacy. If the Union fired the first shot, they would secede.

Finally, Lincoln did not have the people of the North solidly behind him. Northern Democrats would not support an act of aggression and Winfield Scott, Lincoln's chief military adviser, told him that the army was not up to a war of conquest. Some abolitionists who were also pacifists, such as Horace Greeley and William Lloyd Garrison, urged the president to "let the wayward sisters depart in peace."

Lincoln had no intention of doing that. He was determined to save the Union by peaceful means if possible, by force if necessary. He reasoned that if the Confederates fired the first shot, the border states might secede anyway, but at least the act of rebellion would unite northerners behind him. If he delayed a confrontation indefinitely, he still might lose the border states and have a divided, uncertain North.

This was the reasoning behind Lincoln's decision to resupply Fort Sumter. He announced that he would not use force against the state of South Carolina, and repeated his wish that the crisis be resolved peacefully; but he insisted on his presidential obligation to maintain the government's authority in Charleston harbor.

And so the war came. When the relief ship approached the sandbar that guarded Charleston harbor, the Confederacy attacked. On the morning of April 12, 1861, artillery under the command of General P. G. T. Beauregard opened up. The next day, Sumter surrendered. Davis was reluctant until the end. In a way, he lost control of South Carolina. His inability to control the Confederate states would haunt his administration for four years.

The Border States Take Sides

In a way, the Battle of Fort Sumter served both Confederate and Union purposes. While Lincoln was able to call for 75,000 volunteers and to get them, his call pushed four more states into the Confederacy. Virginia, North Carolina, Tennessee, and Arkansas seceded from the Union, and in deference to Virginia's importance, the capital of the new nation was moved from Montgomery to Richmond.

Secessionist feeling was also strong in the slave states of Maryland, Kentucky, and Missouri. Lincoln was able to prevent them from seceding by a combination of shrewd political maneuvers and the tactful deployment of troops. Delaware, the fifteenth slave state, never seriously considered secession.

Then, in the contest for the border states, the North won a bonus. The mountainous western part of Virginia was peopled by farmers who owned few slaves and who traditionally resented the planter aristocracy that dominated Virginia politics and was now in favor of secession. The westerners had no interest in fighting and dying to protect the human property of the rich. In effect, the 50 western counties of Virginia seceded from the Old Dominion. By an irregular constitutional process, the Republicans provided the means for West Virginia to become a Union state in June 1863.

For the border states, the Civil War was literally a war between brothers. Henry Clay's grandsons fought on both sides. Several of President Lincoln's brothers-in-law fought for the South, and Jefferson Davis had cousins in the Union Army. The most poignant case was that of Senator Crittenden of Kentucky, who had tried to head off war with a compromise. One of his sons became a general in the Union Army and another a general in the Confederate Army.

The Irony of Secession

However much as the people of the border states disliked secession, they were not opposed to slavery. In order to reassure them, Lincoln issued several pronouncements that the purpose of the war was to preserve the Union and not to abolish slavery. In emphasizing this war aim, he pointed up the irony of secession. While southerners claimed that they had gone their own way in order to protect their peculiar institution, they actually had thrown away the legal and constitutional guarantees that they had had as U.S. citizens.

Under the Fugitive Slave Act, slaves who ran away to the northern states were returned to their owners. In order to escape, slaves had to get to Canada, out of the country. With secession, out of the country was hundreds of miles closer—over the Tennessee-Kentucky or the Virginia-Maryland line. This fact was dramatized early in the war when several Union generals declared that slaves who had fled to Union lines were contraband of war, subject to confiscation and therefore free. At first Lincoln countermanded these orders so as not to antagonize

A recruiting poster calling for volunteers to fight for the Union.

the loyal border states, especially Kentucky. But it was obvious that the South had made it easier for slaves to get away than it had been before secession.

In leaving the Union as individual states, the southerners had waived all legal rights to the territories, which were federal property. Their action was the most effective guarantee, short of a constitutional amendment, that slavery would be banned from the territories.

Some southerners had no intention of giving up the territories, of course. The Indians of Oklahoma, for example, were generally pro-Confederate. But to win the Indian lands and, perhaps, New Mexico meant launching the very war that Davis hoped to avoid. Secession was less a rational political act than it was the fruit of passion, suspicion, and sectional hatred blinding the southern extremists to reality.

CHRONOLOGY

1856   Raid on Lawrence, Kansas, by proslavery "jayhawkers"
John Brown murders proslavery settlers in Kansas
Charles Sumner assaulted in Senate

1857   James Buchanan becomes president
Dred Scott decision

1858   Lincoln–Douglas debates in Illinois

1859   John Brown's raid on Harpers Ferry

1860   Republican Abraham Lincoln wins in four-way presidential election
South Carolina secedes from Union

FOR FURTHER READING

Most of the books cited here also deal with events treated in Chapter 23, particularly Avery O. Craven, *The Growth of Southern Nationalism, 1848–1860*, 1953, and *The Coming of the Civil War*, 1957; James McPherson, *Battle Cry of Freedom*, 1988; Alan Nevins, *Ordeal of the Union*, 1947; and David Potter, *The Impending Crisis, 1848–1861*, 1976. Also see Eric Foner, *Politics and Ideology in the Age of the Civil War*, 1980; and Stephen B. Oates, *The Approaching Fury: Voices of the Storm, 1820–1861*, 1997.

The events that promoted sectional bitterness in North and South during the 1850s are treated in Stanley W. Campbell, *The Slave-Catchers: Enforcement of the Fugitive Slave Law, 1840–1860*, 1968; James C. Malin, *John Brown and the Legend of Fifty-Six*, 1970; Truman Nelson, *The Old Man: John Brown at Harpers Ferry*, 1973; Stephen Oates, *To Purge This Land with Blood: A Biography of John Brown*, 1970; Don E. Fehrenbacher, *The Dred Scott Case: Its Significance in American Law and Politics*, 1978; C. B. Swisher, *Roger B. Taney*, 1935; Thomas Gossett, *Uncle Tom's Cabin and American Culture*, 1985; Tyler Anbinder, *Nativism and Slavery: The Northern Know-Nothings and the Politics of the 1850s*, 1992; R. W. Johansen, *The Lincoln–Douglas Debates*, 1965; and William Gienapp, *The Origins of the Republican Party*, 1987.

On the secession crisis, the standard works are Kenneth M. Stampp, *And the War Came: The North and the Secession Crisis, 1860–1861*, 1950, and W. L. Barney, *The Road to Secession*, 1972. See also Stephen A. Channing, *Crisis of Fear: Secession in South Carolina*, 1970, and R. A. Wooster, *The Secession Conventions of the South*, 1962. Don Fehrenbacher, *Prelude to Greatness: Lincoln in the 1850s*, 1962, is essential; Richard N. Current, *Lincoln and the First Shot*, 1963, and *The Lincoln Nobody Knows*, 1958, deal with the president's actions in 1861. For his predecessor, see P. S. Klein, *President James Buchanan*, 1962; for his southern opposite number, Clement Eaton, *Jefferson Davis*, 1977. See also Stephen B. Oates, *With Malice toward None*, 1979.

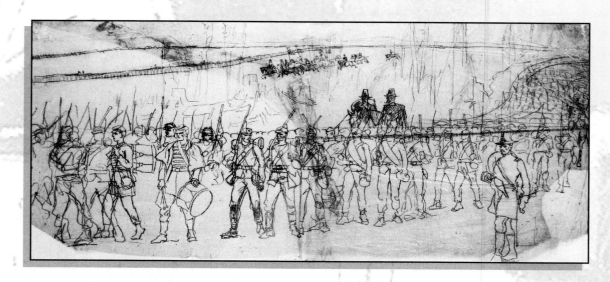

A soldier's sketch of troops on the move.

23

CHAPTER

TIDY PLANS, UGLY REALITIES

The Civil War: 1861–1862

The first blast of civil war is the death warrant of your institution.

— Benjamin Wade

Had slavery been kept out of the fight, the Union would have gone down. But the enemies of the country were so misguided as to rest their cause upon it, and that was the destruction of it and of them.

— Joshua Lawrence Chamberlain

The attack on Fort Sumter answered the first big question: there would be a shooting war. When Lincoln called for volunteers to preserve the Union, and Jefferson Davis summoned the young men of the South to defend the honor and independence of the South, both were flooded with enthusiastic recruits. By the summer of 1861, the Union had 186,000 soldiers in uniform, the Confederacy 112,000.

But what kind of war would it be? What would battle be like? Nowhere in the world had armies of such size clashed since the Napoleonic Wars in Europe half a century earlier. During the Mexican War, the United States had fielded no more than 10,000 men at a time. Now, just 15 years later, two American forces were faced with the challenge of feeding, clothing, sheltering, transporting, and controlling a mass of humanity ten and twenty times that size.

The significance of numbers was not lost on European military men. Several nations dispatched high-ranking officers to the United States to observe how the Americans managed their problem. The lessons they took back with them would inform military thinking for 50 years.

THE ART AND SCIENCE OF WAR

The American Civil War took up where Napoleon and Wellington left off. American military men were trained in a theory of battle devised by a Swiss officer who had served in both the French and the Russian armies, Antoine-Henri Jomini. A textbook based on Jomini's *Art of War* was the standard authority on tactics at West Point, where virtually all the major commanders of the Civil War learned their craft.

Position, Maneuver, and Concentration

Jomini emphasized position and maneuver as the keys to winning battles or, better yet, in making battle unnecessary by persuading the enemy of the futility of fighting. The goal of the commanding general was to occupy high ground, and, when a battle threatened, ascertain the weakest point in the enemy's lines and concentrate power there. The commander who prepared more thoroughly, better exploited the terrain, and moved his troops more skillfully than his opponent would break through the opposing line and force the enemy from the field. The object then was to capture and occupy cities important in trade and government, forcing the enemy's capitulation. The idea was that, lacking what we would call a national infrastructure, the enemy had nothing for which to fight. Napoleon defeated his enemies in Europe (except for Russia) when he occupied their major cities.

Jomini reduced battle situations to 12 models. Therefore, commanders trained in his school, and with a brain in their heads, knew pretty much what their adversaries had in mind at all times—or should have. So long as both sides observed the rules, there would be no long casualty lists. The general who was outfoxed knew that his duty was to disengage so that his men would be able to fight on another day under more favorable circumstances. Retreat, far from being an occasion of shame, was among the most vital of maneuvers because it preserved an army as a functioning machine.

The Armies

The armies of the Civil War were divided into cavalry, artillery, and infantry, with support units such as the Corps of Engineers (which constructed fortifications) and the Quartermaster Corps (entrusted with supply).

The cavalry's principal task was reconnaissance. Horse soldiers were the eyes of an army; battle plans were based on the information they brought back from sometimes spectacular rides completely around the enemy forces. Because of their mobility and speed, cavalry units were also used for raids, plunging deep into hostile territory, burning and destroying what they found in their path, sometimes seizing useful military booty, and then hightailing it out before they could be confronted by big guns and masses of infantry.

In the age of big guns, the decisive cavalry charge was a dead issue; that had been shown a decade earlier in the Crimean War when the famous "Light Brigade" was slaughtered in attacking artillery head-on. In a pitched battle by the time of the Civil War, cavalry was used to reinforce weak points in the lines and, if enemy troops retreated, to pursue, harass, and scatter them. But cavalrymen were lightly armed by definition; for all the dash and flash, cavalry played a subsidiary role in pitched battle. Nevertheless, it remained the glamorous service: the horses and shades of the days of chivalry!

The artillery was slow to move and, with its toil, noise, and grime, notoriously unglamorous. But, as

Napoleon had shown, big guns were critical to both attack and defense. Before an attacking army moved, its artillery slugged away at enemy positions with exploding shells, "softening them up." In defense, the artillery greeted attacking infantry with grapeshot (a charge of small iron balls). Examinations of dead soldiers after Civil War battles revealed that an attacking army suffered far more from cannon than from small arms fire. Indeed, soldiers in the field estimated that they fired a man's weight in lead and iron for each enemy they killed. A Union expert found that calculation conservative; he said that 240 pounds of gunpowder and 900 pounds of lead were required to bring one Confederate soldier down.

As always before the Nuclear Age, the infantry was the backbone of the army. The cavalry might worry the enemy, and the artillery weaken him, but it was the foot soldiers who slugged it out face to face, took the casualties, and won and lost the battles. The commander of infantry was the commander of battle.

Battle

Infantry was organized into companies (ideally 100 men), regiments (ten companies) and the brigade of three or more regiments, 2,000 to 3,000 men. Under the command of a brigadier general, the soldiers formed double lines in defense or advanced over a front of about a thousand yards. During the first campaigns of the Civil War, captains in the front lines tried to march the men in step in two ranks, as had been the practice in the Napoleonic Era. But with the greater firepower available by the 1860s, so formal a structure was sensibly abandoned. It was enough that the men continued to run, trot, or simply walk into oncoming grapeshot, minié balls (conical bullets), noise like a thunderstorm in hell, and a haze of black, sulfurous smoke. Junior officers led the charge, thus the ranks of lieutenant and captain suffered high casualties. Other officers walked behind the lines in order to discourage stragglers. They sometimes shot men who panicked and broke ranks.

If the advancing army was not forced to turn back, and the defenders did not abandon their position in a panic, the final phase of battle was hand-to-hand combat. The attackers clambered over the enemy's fortifications of earth and timber. Attackers and defenders swung their muskets at one another like the baseball bats they played with in their spare time until the defenders broke and ran or the attackers were killed or captured. The men had bayonets,

Wilhelmina and Joanna

Women fought in the Civil War, too, posing as men, of course. Official records list 127 female soldiers; one historian suggests the number was 400. Among them were Jennie Hodges, who fought for an Illinois regiment as Albert Cashier. Sarah Emma Edmonds was Franklin Thompson in the Second Michigan.

but during the Civil War neither side succeeded in training soldiers to use them very well. The importance of mastering this difficult and deadly skill was one lesson that the European observers took home with them (as well as the opinion that Americans were afraid of cold steel).

There was plenty of shooting but not a great deal of aiming. Except for special units of sharpshooters, foot soldiers were not marksmen. There was little sense in taking on the big and expensive job of training large numbers of men in the skill of hitting small targets at great distances. With a few important exceptions (Shiloh, Antietam, Gettysburg), Civil War battles were not fought in open country. The men confronted one another in dense woods on terrain broken by hills, stone fences, and ditches. In several battles, attackers had to clamber up rugged Appalachian cliffs. Often, opposing soldiers could not see one another until they were on the verge of touching.

Even in open country, hundreds of cannon and tens of thousands of muskets filled the air with a dense, acrid smog that, on a windless day, shrouded the battlefield. (Smokeless powder was still in the future.) Even if a soldier could shoot well, there was little he could aim at in order to prove it.

Billy Yank and Johnny Reb

As in all wars, the men who fought the Civil War were young, most between the ages of 17 and 25 with drummer boys of but 12. They came from every state and social class, although when both sides adopted draft laws (the Confederacy in April 1862, the Union in March 1863), the burden fell more heavily on poorer farmers and working people than on the middle and upper classes.

This was because the draft laws included significant exemptions favoring the well-to-do. The

The Union battery at Fredericksburg and photographer Timothy O'Sullivan were under fire by Confederate artillery when this photograph was taken.

Confederate law exempted men who owned 20 or more slaves. It was sorely resented by Johnny Reb, the common soldier, who rarely owned any slaves. Both the Confederate and Union draft laws allowed a man who was called to service to pay for a substitute at a price that was beyond the means of the ordinary fellow. In the North, a draftee could hire another to take his place or simply pay the government $300 for an exemption. In July 1863, working-class resentment of the law led to a week-long riot in New York City. Mobs of mostly Irish workingmen sacked draft offices, attacked rich men, and harassed and lynched blacks, whom they considered the cause of the war and a threat to their jobs. Some 60,000 people were involved; at least 400 were killed; and some $5 million in property was destroyed.

In the South, resistance to the draft was less dramatic. Nevertheless, thousands of draft dodgers headed west or into the Appalachians and the Ozarks, where some organized outlaw gangs, raided farms, and occasionally skirmished with Confederate troops. Most southern opposition to the war centered in poor mountain counties.

Both Union and Confederate armies were plagued by a high desertion rate, about 10 percent through most of the war. Some individuals specialized in desertion, the bounty jumpers. Because some states and cities paid cash bonuses, or bounties, to men who signed up, a few made a lucrative, if risky business of enlisting, skipping out at first opportunity, and looking for another unit offering bounties. In March 1865, Union military police arrested one John O'Connor. He confessed to enlisting, collecting a bounty, and deserting 32 times. Surely he was the champion in his profession.

Shirking was not typical of either side, however. Over the course of the war, 1.5 million young men served in the Union Army, and more than 1 million, from a much smaller population, with the Confederate. Whatever their resentments, ordinary people thought they had something at stake in the conflict. Despite their exemption, southern slave owners served in proportion to their numbers.

Army Life

The war they knew was not much like the war presented to the folks back home. In artists' paintings and engravings in newspapers, masses of men in tidy blue and gray uniforms moved in order across open fields amidst waving flags and cloud-like puffs of white smoke. In reality, battle was a tiny part of military experience. Mostly, the war involved waiting, digging trenches, building breastworks, marching, and being carted from one place to another in crowded trains.

The war meant poor food and shelter. In the South, supply was rarely efficient. Even when the Confederacy had enough uniforms, shoes, and food—which was not always—there were problems in getting them to the soldiers. In the North, the inevitable profiteers sold the government tainted beef and shoddy blankets that fell apart in the rain. On both sides, physicians were unprepared to cope with so many patients; dysentery, typhoid, influenza, and other epidemic illnesses killed more soldiers than did enemy guns.

THE SOBERING CAMPAIGN OF 1861

Army life also involved drilling, day in and day out. But those who rallied to the colors in the spring of 1861 thought of the war as an adventure, a vacation from the plow and hog trough, that would be over too soon. They trimmed themselves in gaudy uniforms. Some, influenced by pictures of Turkish soldiers in the recently concluded Crimean War, called themselves "Zouaves" and donned Turkish fezzes and baggy pantaloons. Other units adopted names that would have been more appropriate to a boys' club. One Confederate regiment was called "The Lincoln Killers."

On to Richmond

Abraham Lincoln shared the illusion that the war would be short and painless. He waved off Winfield Scott's professional warning that it would take three years and 300,000 men to crush the rebellion. Lincoln asked the first volunteers, mostly members of state militias, to enlist for only 90 days. That would be enough. Southerners too spoke of "our battle summer." The soldiers and civilians on the two sides disagreed only as to who would be celebrating when the leaves fell in the autumn of 1861.

These pleasant illusions were blown away on a fine July day about 20 miles outside Washington. Believing that his volunteers could take Richmond before their short enlistments expired, Lincoln sent General Irvin McDowell, who had never commanded more than a dozen men in the field, march-

ing directly toward the Confederate capital with 30,000 troops. Laughing and joking as they went, sometimes shooting at targets, the boys from Ohio and Massachusetts were accompanied by a parade of carriages filled with congressmen, socialites, newspaper reporters, and curiosity seekers. The crowd carried picnic lunches and bickered as to where in Richmond they would enjoy a late supper.

Weary from their 30-mile march, and short of water, they were met by a Confederate force of about 22,000 under the command of General Beauregard, recently arrived from Fort Sumter. The rebels had hastily dug in on high ground behind a creek called Bull Run, near a railroad crossing named Manassas Junction. McDowell attacked immediately, guessing the Confederate left flank to be the weakest point in the line. He was right about that. Although his troops were shocked by the ferocity of the musket fire that greeted them, they almost cracked the southern line.

Had it cracked, the war would likely have been over in the upper South. To the rear of Beauregard's line, the road to Richmond lay open. At the critical moment, however, 9,000 Virginians commanded by Joseph E. Johnston arrived on the field after a frantic train ride from the Shenandoah Valley. A brigade under the command of Thomas J. Jackson, a 37-year-old mathematics instructor at Virginia Military Academy, shored up the sagging Confederate left. The Union soldiers fell back and then broke in hysteria, fleeing for Washington along with the panicked spectators.

Celebrations and Recriminations

The South had a victory and a hero. At the peak of the battle for the left flank, a South Carolinian rallied his men by shouting, "There stands Jackson like a stone wall." The name stuck, for it seemed appropriate to more than Thomas J. Jackson's performance on the battlefield. He was introspective and humorless, an object of some behind-the-hand mockery to his students before the war, a stern Scots-Irish Presbyterian who lacked the human touch and was never loved by his troops, as some generals are.

But his men stood in awe of him because Jackson came to life when the bullets whistled. He never yielded a line to the enemy, and he was a genius at maneuvering troops. For two years Jackson would do what the South needed done, inserting his men in critical positions and standing like a stone wall against Union assaults.

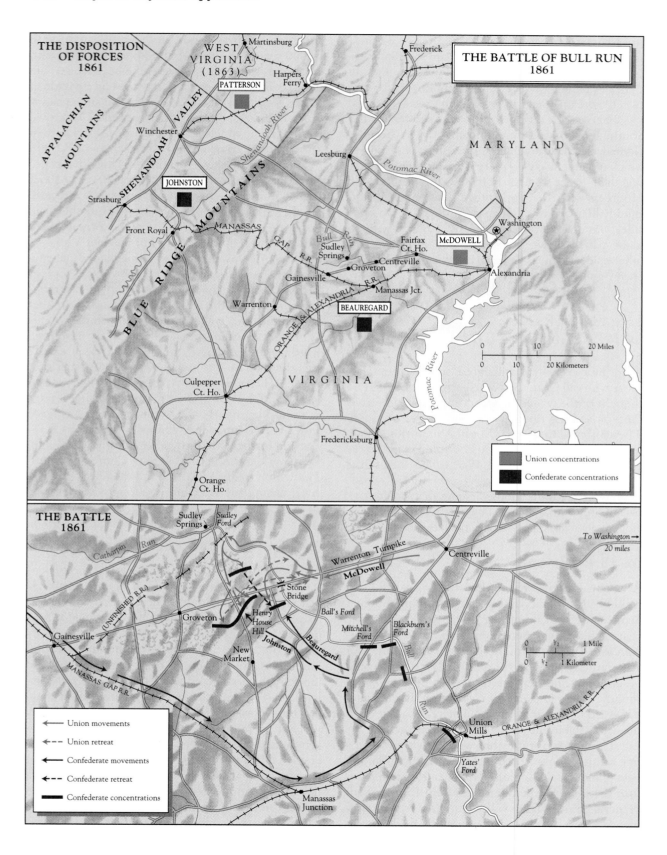

THE DISPOSITION OF FORCES 1861

THE BATTLE OF BULL RUN 1861

WEST VIRGINIA (1863)

Martinsburg

Frederick

APPALACHIAN MOUNTAINS

PATTERSON

Harpers Ferry

Winchester

SHENANDOAH VALLEY

Shenandoah River

Leesburg

MARYLAND

Potomac River

JOHNSTON

BLUE RIDGE MOUNTAINS

Strasburg

Washington

Front Royal

MANASSAS GAP R.R.

Bull Run

Sudley Springs

Fairfax Ct. Ho.

McDOWELL

Centreville

Alexandria

Gainesville

Groveton

ORANGE & ALEXANDRIA R.R.

Manassas Jct.

Warrenton

BEAUREGARD

Culpepper Ct. Ho.

VIRGINIA

Potomac River

0   10   20 Miles
0   10   20 Kilometers

Fredericksburg

Orange Ct. Ho.

Union concentrations

Confederate concentrations

THE BATTLE 1861

Sudley Springs

Sudley Ford

Warrenton Turnpike

Centreville

To Washington →
20 miles

Catharpin Run

McDowell

Stone Bridge

(UNFINISHED R.R.)

Groveton

Henry House Hill

Ball's Ford

Mitchell's Ford

Blackburn's Ford

Gainesville

Johnston

Beauregard

New Market

0   ½   1 Mile
0   ½   1 Kilometer

MANASSAS GAP R.R.

Bull Run

Union Mills

ORANGE & ALEXANDRIA R.R.

Yates' Ford

Manassas Junction

← Union movements

◄-- Union retreat

← Confederate movements

◄-- Confederate retreat

▬ Confederate concentrations

Fed Up in Dixie

By no means did all white southerners rally to the "Stars and Bars," as the Confederate flag was nicknamed. In the up-country South, the foothills on both sides of the Appalachian Ridge, few people owned slaves and many of them opposed secession as the project of the great planters, whose political and economic domination they resented. Western Virginia and eastern Tennessee voted against secession and provided thousands of soldiers for the *Union* army. So did many counties in western North Carolina and northern Alabama. Once the war was underway, the Confederate government's practice of expropriating crops and livestock to feed its armies aggravated the situation. When food became expensive and scarce in cities like Richmond and even in the countryside, southern women rioted in protest against the war.

By way of contrast, General Beauregard's reputation suffered at Bull Run because he failed to follow up his victory by marching on Washington. Within a few months he was replaced as Confederate commander in Virginia by Joseph E. Johnston, who brought the troops and Stonewall Jackson from the Shenandoah Valley.

Johnston was a superior field commander, but neither Beauregard nor anyone else was to blame for the South's failure to capture Washington. As Johnston himself put it, "The Confederate Army was more disorganized by victory than that of the United States by defeat"; and a disorganized army is no army at all. All the better generals at Bull Run, plus deskmen like Robert E. Lee, who was President Davis's military adviser, emphasized the need for regrouping and hard training.

Summer Lull

President Davis agreed, and he cautioned Richmond society that there was more fighting to come. But few seemed to listen. The common soldiers were cocky and overconfident as a result of their victory and minor casualties. Southern politicians spoke as though the war were over. Volunteer officers nagged their tailors to finish sewing gold braid on dress uniforms, so that they could show them off once or twice before

the Union capitulated. And then they bickered. At a round of gala parties in Richmond, old personal jealousies erupted as blustering colonels and generals blamed one another for blunders real and imaginary.

In the North, however, the defeat at Manassas taught a sorely needed lesson. The spectacle of McDowell's troops throwing down their guns and trotting wild-eyed into Washington, where they lay down to sleep in doorways and on the sidewalks, alarmed Lincoln and brought him around to Winfield Scott's way of thinking. The war would be no summer's pastime but a long, hard fight. Now, when Lincoln asked Congress for troops, he wanted 300,000 men under three-year enlistments.

He also relieved Irvin McDowell from command of what was now called the Army of the Potomac, replacing him with George B. McClellan. The former president of the Illinois Central Railroad (for which Lincoln had been a lawyer), McClellan had a reputation as an organizer and administrator. In November 1861, Winfield Scott retired, and McClellan also took charge of the Union armies that were being drilled throughout the Midwest.

Northern Strategy

Though Scott was gone, a three-part strategy that he outlined to Lincoln before the fighting began was now adopted. First, it was necessary to defend Washington with the Army of the Potomac and to maintain constant pressure on Richmond in the hope of capturing the city. This was important because Richmond was less than 100 miles from Washington, the seat of the Confederate government, a railroad hub, and a major industrial center, home of the Tredregar Iron Works, which was to sustain Virginia's fighting machine during the war.

Second, because Lincoln and his advisers believed that the Ohio-Mississippi waterway was vital to the economic life of the midwestern states, Union armies would strike down the great valley. Their object was to gain complete control of the Mississippi as soon as possible in order to permit western farmers to resume the export of foodstuffs, by which they lived, and to split the Confederacy in two. Then the trans-Mississippi front (Arkansas and Texas) could be neglected while the Union concentrated its force in the East.

Third, the Union would use its overwhelming naval superiority to blockade the South, strangling its export economy. If the Confederates were unable to sell cotton abroad, they could not buy the

"Brother against brother" was not just a romantic contrivance. The phenomenon was by no means uncommon. At the Union assault on Hilton Head, Naval Commander Percival Drayton (right) commanded the U.S.S. Pocahontas, *one of the vessels attacking Confederate troops under Brigadier General Thomas F. Drayton (left), his brother. Both were South Carolinians.*

Fast Track

George Armstrong Custer, better known for his Indian fighting after the war, graduated from West Point in 1861, last in his class. Nevertheless, a stunningly brave soldier and battle leader, he rose to the rank of general within two years. Custer was not, however, the youngest Civil War general. Galusha Pennypacker was named a brigadier general at 21 and a major general before the age of 22.

manufactures, particularly the munitions, that were essential in a lengthy war. Scott called this strategy the Anaconda Plan after the South American snake that slowly crushes its prey. The powerful Union would asphyxiate its foe.

On the face of it, an effective blockade was out of the question. The Confederate Atlantic and Gulf coastlines were labyrinths of inlets, sheltered channels, coves, bays, bayous, salt marshes, and lonely broad beaches. It was quite impossible to prevent every vessel from reaching shore or from making a break for the high seas. Nevertheless, an effective national commerce could not be rowed through the surf or unloaded in swamps, and the commanders of the Union Navy felt confident that with time their ships could bottle up the Confederate ports.

Dixie's Challenge

Southern strategy had a simpler design but a flimsier foundation. In order to attain its basic goal—independence—the Confederacy needed only to turn back Union advances until Britain or France, both of which nations expressed some sympathy for the southern cause, came to the rescue, or until the people of the

North grew weary of fighting and forced Lincoln to negotiate. In the broadest sense, the story of the Civil War tells how these hopes were dashed and how, although long frustrated and delayed, the Union strategy succeeded.

The Confederacy's hope of foreign intervention died first. In the case of France, it may have been doomed from the beginning by the personality of the French emperor, Napoleon III. On one day a scheming power politician who recognized that an independent Confederacy might be molded into a valuable French protectorate, Napoleon III was, on the next, a flighty romantic.

At first, while leading the southerners on, he delayed when the more prudent British dithered. (Napoleon did not want to intervene in the war without British approval.) Then, when he was approached by a group of Mexican aristocrats who, in order to defeat a revolution of Indians and mestizo peasants, offered to make an emperor of his nephew, Maximilian of Austria, Napoleon III saw a grander opportunity in America's tragedy. While the United States at peace might have resisted European interference in Mexico—it was not so long since expansionists had spoken of annexing the whole country themselves—the United States tearing itself apart was helpless to take action. Anyway, what self-respecting emperor wanted a dependency of quarrelsome, headstrong cotton planters when he could tread in the footsteps of Cortés? Not Napoleon III. By the end of 1862, he was sidestepping the southern diplomats who continued to court him.

The pro-Confederate sentiments of the British government were more solidly founded. The South was the principal source of cotton for the British textile industry and British industrialists generally supported Henry Lord Palmerston's Liberal government. Moreover, many English aristocrats looked upon the southern planters as their rough-cut kinsmen, flattering them in their anglophilia and imitation of the British upper classes. Finally, a great many British politicians relished the opportunity to shatter the growing power of the American upstart.

However, supporting a country in which slavery was legal was a touchy matter in antislavery Britain. The British government was not willing to take that chance until the Confederates demonstrated that they had a real chance of winning. A combination of southern blunders in export policy, bad luck, Union diplomatic skill, and a key Union victory at the Confederacy's brightest hour dashed the Confederate dream (and British hopes) of redrawing the map of North America.

King Cotton Dethroned

The first Confederate blunder was Jefferson Davis's notion to blackmail Britain into coming to the aid of the South. In the excited solidarity of the Confederacy's first days, he prevailed on cotton shippers to keep the crop of 1860 at home, storing it on wharves and in warehouses. The idea was to put the pinch on British mill owners so that they would set up a cry for a war that would liberate the coveted fiber.

"Cotton diplomacy" did not work. English mill owners had a huge stockpile of cotton reserves thanks to a bumper crop in 1859. By the time these and other supplies ran out in 1862 the price of cotton tripled, inducing Egyptian and Middle Eastern farmers to plant the crop. Within a year, they were filling much of the gap created by the American war. To make matters worse, Union troops captured enough southern cotton to keep the mills of New England humming and even to sell some to Great Britain. The northern cause was also aided by the antislavery sentiments of the English working class, including laborers in the cotton mill towns.

As the war lengthened, cotton diplomacy was completely scuttled by two successive poor-grain crops in western Europe. Fearing food shortages, monarchist England discovered that Union wheat was more royal than Confederate cotton. Blessed with bumper crops, northern farmers shipped unprecedented tonnages of grain to Europe at both financial and diplomatic profit.

The Diplomatic War

In November 1861, a zealous Union naval officer almost ruined the northern effort to keep England neutral. The captain of the U.S.S. *San Jacinto* boarded a British steamer, the *Trent*, and seized two Confederate diplomats who were aboard, James M. Mason and John Slidell. Northern public opinion was delighted. It was refreshing to hear for a change of an American warship bullying a British vessel. But Lincoln took a dimmer view of the incident. The British minister came close to threatening war. To the president, Mason and Slidell were two hot potatoes, and he took advantage of the first lull in the public celebrations to hasten them aboard a British warship. "One war at a time," he remarked to his cabinet.

No harm was done. In France, Slidell was frustrated by Napoleon III's Mexican ambitions and, in England, Mason proved no match for the Union minister, Charles Francis Adams, in the delicate game of diplomacy. Mason did manage to see two commerce-raiders, the *Florida* and the *Alabama*, constructed for the Confederacy and put to sea. But Adams cajoled and threatened the British government into preventing a sister ship and several Confederate rams from leaving port. He moved with great skill and energy through the salons of London, and kept Great Britain out of the war until the North turned the tide in its direction.

1862 AND STALEMATE

As Confederate hopes of bringing England in dimmed, the South increasingly looked to northern sympathizers and defeatists to aid their cause. Some northerners frankly favored the South. Former President Franklin Pierce openly said so. Pro-southern sentiment was strongest in the Union slave states of Delaware, Maryland, Kentucky, and Missouri, of course, but also in the lower counties of Ohio, Indiana, and Illinois, a region with a strong southern heritage. However, these "copperheads," as northerners who sympathized with the South were called (after the poisonous snake that strikes without warning), were never able to mount a decisive threat to the Union war effort. They were a minority, and Lincoln played free with their civil liberties in order to silence them.

Lincoln and the Copperheads

One of the president's most controversial moves against the opponents of the war was his suspension of the ancient legal right of *habeas corpus*, a protection against arbitrary arrest that is basic to both English and American law. At one time or another, 13,000 people were jailed, almost always briefly, because of alleged antiwar activity. Lincoln also used his control of the post office to harass and even suppress antiadministration newspapers.

The most prominent copperhead was Clement L. Vallandigham, a popular Democratic congressman from Ohio. His attacks on the war effort were so unsettling that, after General Ambrose Burnside jailed him, Lincoln feared he would be honored as a martyr. The president solved the problem by handing Vallandigham over to the Confederates as if he

The Union supply depot at City Point, Virginia. Providing for a huge army was one aspect of warfare in which the North's matériel superiority was decisive.

were a southern agent. Identifying Vallandigham with treason was unfair but shrewd; in 1863, he was forced to run for governor of Ohio from exile in Canada. At home, he might have won. But *in absentia* he was defeated, and when he returned to the United States the next year, he was harmless enough that Lincoln was able to ignore him.

More worrisome than the copperheads was defeatism, the belief that the war was not worth the expense in blood and money. Each time Union armies lost a battle, more northerners wondered if it would not be wiser to let the southern states go. Or, they asked, was it really impossible to negotiate? Was Lincoln's Republican administration, rather than the southern states, the obstacle to a compromise peace?

It was in fact impossible for Lincoln to secure reunion on any other basis than military victory. Even at the bitter end of the war, when the Confederacy was not only defeated but devastated, Jefferson Davis insisted on southern independence as a condition of peace. As long as the South was winning the battles, any kind of negotiation on the part of the North was out of the question.

And the South did win most of the battles in 1861 and 1862. The show belonged to Stonewall Jackson and General Robert E. Lee, who was to succeed Joseph E. Johnston as commander of the Army of Northern Virginia when, at the Battle of the Seven Pines on May 31, 1862, Johnston was seriously wounded. Time after time, Lee and Jackson halted or drubbed the Army of the Potomac. Nevertheless, even in his most triumphant hour in the summer of 1862, Lee revealed that his military genius was limited by his supreme virtue, his self-conscious image of himself as a Virginia gentleman, the scion of a distinguished old family.

Lee's cause was not so much the Confederacy as the dignity of "Old Virginny." He did not like slavery, the obsession of the southern hotheads. He may never have owned a slave himself, and had freed his wife's slaves in 1857 when he served as executor for her father's will. He did not much like the hotheads of the Deep South, regarding them as vulgar parvenus. And he opposed Virginia's secession until it was a fact. Consequently, Lee never fully appreciated the fact that while he was defending the Old Dominion with such mastery, the southern cause was being slowly throttled at sea, in the dozens of coastal enclaves Union troops occupied, and in the Mississippi Valley.

The Campaign in the West

Lincoln, although no military man and the author of several Civil War blunders, understood this. "We must have Kentucky," Lincoln told his cabinet. Without Kentucky—the southern bank of the Ohio River—he feared the war would be lost. Even before the army recovered from the defeat at Manassas, Lincoln approved moving a large force into the state under the command of Generals Henry Halleck and Ulysses S. Grant. In early 1862, Grant thrust into Tennessee, quickly capturing two important forts, Henry and Donelson. These guarded the mouths of the Tennessee and Cumberland Rivers, two waterways of far greater strategic value than muddy Bull Run. Moving on, however, General Grant fought the battle that taught both sides that they were not playing chess.

Moving up the Tennessee River unopposed, Grant intended to attack Corinth, Mississippi, in the northern part of the state. He knew that Confederate General Albert Sidney Johnston planned to defend the town, but had no idea that Johnston was also prepared to attack. On April 6, 1862, while camped near a church named Shiloh at Pittsburg Landing, Tennessee, Grant's armies were caught in their bedrolls by 40,000 rebels. Many were killed before they awoke. The others held on, but just barely. Only when Union reinforcements under General Don Carlos Buell ar-

rived that night, joining with Grant's men the next day, did the Confederates withdraw.

Albert Sydney Johnston, regarded by some military historians as one of the Confederacy's best field commanders, was killed at Shiloh Church. Other southern losses numbered 11,000 of 40,000 troops engaged. The Union lost 13,000 of 60,000 men. Bodies were stacked like cordwood while massive graves were dug. Acres of ground were reddened with blood, and the stench of death sickened the survivors at their grisly job of cleaning up. Compared with the minor casualties at Bull Run—compared with the losses in most battles in any war to that date—Shiloh was a horror.

Grant was discredited, accused of having been drunk on the morning of the attack. Soldiers of the two armies fraternized less often between battles, as they had done in the woods of Tennessee, where Confederate and Union guards conversed in the night, traded tobacco for coffee, and, on at least one occasion, played a Sunday baseball game. Bull Run showed that there would be a long war; Shiloh showed that it would be bloody. Not even the success of naval officer David G. Farragut a short time after Shiloh, which put the Union in control of New Orleans, could cure the sense of melancholy that followed on the great battle.

The War at Sea

Confederate seamen on the commerce-raiders *Florida*, *Alabama*, and *Shenandoah* got to see the world. These fast, heavily armed ships destroyed or captured more than 250 northern merchantmen ($15 million in ships and cargo) in every corner of the seas. For

---

Indians in Gray and Blue

While blacks were a mainstay of the Union army, most Native Americans sat out the war, perhaps somewhat heartened that, for once, the whites were fighting among themselves. Some tribes formed units, however, particularly those from Indian Territory, where slavery was legal. About 5,500 Native Americans fought on the Confederate side, about 4,000 for the North. An Iroquois officer served on General Grant's staff. When Lee met him at Appomattox, he briefly took him for an African American and stared in shocked disbelief.

the Union sailors assigned to the blockade, by way of contrast, days were long and boring, spent slowly patrolling the waters outside southern ports in scorching sun and winter winds.

The Confederates threatened the blockade in March 1862. Out to the mouth of the Chesapeake steamed an old warship, the *Merrimack*, in brand-new clothes (and renamed the *Virginia*). She had been covered over with iron plates forming the shape of a tent. The *Merrimack* was a ram, outfitted on its prow with an iron blade like a plowshare that could slice through a wooden hull. Cannonballs bounced off the sloping armor as though they were made of rubber. Within a few hours of her debut, the *Merrimack* sank several Union warships.

Left unopposed for a few weeks, this single ship might have broken the blockade of the Chesapeake. But the *Merrimack* did not have even a few days. The Union had an experimental vessel of its own, the even odder-looking *Monitor*. It too was ironclad, but resembled a cake tin on a platter skimming the waves. For five hours on March 9, 1862, the two ships had at one another, then disengaged. The battle was technically a draw, but strategically an important Union victory. The *Merrimack* had to retreat for repairs. In May, the Confederates destroyed the vessel so that it would not fall into Union hands. The *Monitor* proved to be just a prototype for a flotilla of others like it.

McClellan and the "Slows"

In creating the Army of the Potomac, George McClellan made an invaluable contribution to the Union cause. Not only were his men better trained than most southern troops, but they usually were better armed. While the Confederates had to import or capture most of their guns, McClellan and his successors had a limitless supply of munitions and constantly improved firearms. The Springfield repeating rifle, introduced toward the end of the war, allowed Union soldiers to fire six times a minute instead of once or twice.

The trouble with McClellan was that he would not exploit the tremendous edge he created. He was a man of contradictions. On the one hand, he loved

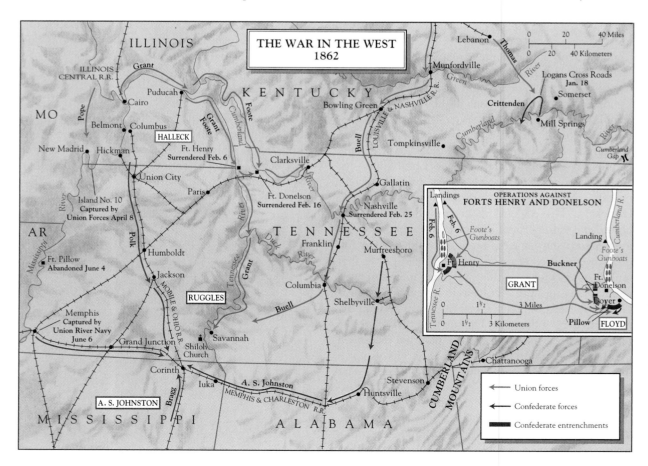

to pose, strut, and issue bombastic proclamations to his men in the style of Napoleon and Wellington. On the other, when it came time to fight, he froze as though he were one of their statues. His problem was not entirely a matter of personality. McClellan was a Democrat. He did not want to crush the South. He believed that merely by creating an awesome military force, he could persuade the Confederates to give in without a bloody battle.

Moreover, McClellan was sincerely devoted to his soldiers. He could not bring himself to fight a battle in which the dead bodies would pile up as they had at Shiloh. Finally, he was a traditionalist. If there had to be a battle, he wanted overwhelming superiority. He could never get enough men to suit his conservative nature.

To Lincoln, who disliked McClellan (the feeling was mutual), it was a simpler matter. Lincoln said that McClellan was ill; he had a bad case of "the slows."

The Peninsula Campaign

When McClellan finally did move in April 1862, he did not drive directly on Richmond. Instead, he moved by sea to historic Yorktown on the peninsula between the York and James Rivers. After a month he had 110,000 troops poised to take Richmond from the south, bypassing the city's fortifications.

It could have worked. The Confederate Army of Northern Virginia was outnumbered and caught by surprise. On the last day of May, Joseph Johnston was seriously wounded and Robert E. Lee hastily took charge. Instead of pouncing, however, McClellan sat and fiddled. He overestimated the size of the Confederate force that faced him and demanded reinforcements from Lincoln. But Lincoln refused when Lee fooled him into thinking that Washington was in danger of attack.

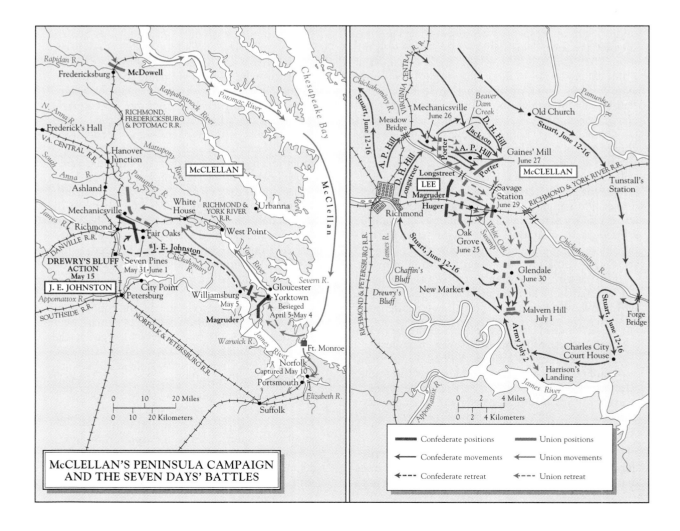

McCLELLAN'S PENINSULA CAMPAIGN AND THE SEVEN DAYS' BATTLES

HOW THEY LIVED

How They Fought

The Civil War battle experience was much the same whether the soldiers wore Union blue or Confederate gray—except that the troops of the North were almost always better supplied with shelter, clothing, shoes, medicines, food, and arms and ammunition. It is difficult to say how much this meant to the final outcome of the war. Cold, wet, tired, and ill soldiers are surely less effective than well-equipped ones, and Confederate troops without shoes—not an uncommon sight—were usually, but not always, exempt from charging enemy lines, a further depletion of the outnumbered southern force.

Nevertheless, Johnny Reb, the Confederate foot soldier, won the respect of both his officers and his enemies as a formidable fighting man. As early as the second Battle of Bull Run in 1862, the commander of a unit called Toombs's Georgians told of leading so many barefoot men against the Yankees that they "left bloody footprints among the thorns and briars." Nevertheless, they followed him. Johnny Reb and his Union counterpart, Billy Yank, knew when they were going to fight. In only a few large-scale battles was an army caught by surprise. Jomini's "rules" were well-known by the generals on both sides, and preparations for massive attack were so extensive that getting caught napping, as Grant's men were at Shiloh, was rarely repeated. In fact, the men who would be *defending* a position were generally prepared for battle with extra rations and ammunition earlier than the attackers, who knew when they would be moving.

Two or three days' supply of food was distributed before a battle. A historian of the common soldier, Bell I. Wiley, suggests that in the Confederate ranks

> this judicious measure generally fell short of its object because of Johnny Reb's own characteristics: he was always hungry, he had a definite prejudice against baggage, and he was the soul of improvidence. Sometimes, the whole of the extra rations would be consumed as soon as it was cooked, and rarely did any part of it last for the full period intended.

This carelessness could have serious consequences because fighting was heavy toil; tales of units that were incapacitated by hunger at the end of a day's battle were common. Wiley points out that after Bull Run in the East and Shiloh in the West, however, few soldiers took other than close care of their canteens. Waiting, marching, and running in the heat, cold, and rain, and the grime and dust of battle made everyone intolerably thirsty. "I must have swallowed whole spoonfuls of gunpowder in my haste at biting the cartridges," wrote Samuel Byers, an Iowan at the Battle of Corinth. "I had thirst beyond description. My canteen was full of water, too, but who could stop then to take a drink!"

As short a time as possible before the ensuing battle, each infantryman was given 40 to 60 rounds of ammunition to stash in the cartridge box he wore on a strap slung over a shoulder. (Soldiers rarely carried more than a few rounds of ammunition at other times because the powder got damp without meticulous care.) The Spencer repeating rifles took a round that looked like any modern cartridge. The muzzle-loading musket—which was used by all the Confederates and most of the Yankees—took a round that consisted of a ball and a charge of powder wrapped together in a piece of paper that was twisted closed at the powder end. To load the musket, a soldier bit off the twist so that the powder was exposed, pushed the cartridge into the muzzle of his gun, inserted the paper he held in his teeth to keep the ball from rolling out, and rammed a rod (fixed to his gun) into the barrel to the breech. Each time he fired, he had to reload. That moment, and when men were retreating, were considered far more dangerous than when troops were advancing.

When a battle was to be joined, the commanding general addressed his troops either personally or in written orations read by line officers. George McClellan was noted among Union commanders for his stirring orations in the tradition of Napoleon and Wellington. Confederate General Albert Sidney Johnston also took the high road in his speech before Shiloh:

> The eyes and the hope of eight millions of people rest upon you. You are expected to show yourselves worthy of your race and lineage; worthy of the women of the South, whose noble devotion in this war has never been exceeded in

A soldier's amateurish sketch, drawn whilst under fire, captures the confusion of Civil War battle as no professional painting did.

any time. With such incentives to brave deeds and with the trust that God is with us, your general will lead you confidently to the combat, assured of success.

Because the Confederate cause was defense of a homeland, it could easily be put in such noble terms. The Union Army, however, had something of a morale problem during the early stages of the war because "the Union" was so abstract and Billy Yank was, after all, invading someone else's land.

After the Emancipation Proclamation, the morale of the Union soldiers improved, while that of the Confederates declined. Now, Billy Yank was fighting "to make men free"—a line from the favorite Union song—while some southern commanders were reduced to appealing to base instincts. For example, General T. C. Hindman exhorted in December 1862:

> Remember that the enemy you engage has no feeling of mercy. His ranks are made up of Pin Indians, Free Negroes, Southern Tories, Kansas Jayhawkers, and hired Dutch cutthroats. These bloody ruffians have invaded your country, stolen and destroyed your property, murdered your neighbors, outraged your women, driven

your children from their homes, and defiled the graves of your kindred.

Bell I. Wiley points out that toward the end of the war, Confederate soldiers fought most grimly and intensely when they were up against a black detachment on the Union line.

Grimness was lacking before the earliest battles. The men were high spirited on both sides. As the war ground on, the experienced soldiers tended to grow quiet and reflective before the fighting started. Some read their Bibles. Others—but not many, it seems—took a few quick pulls of whiskey. Friends made and remade promises to look for one another when the battle was over, to help those too seriously wounded to move, and to gather personal belongings to return to a friend's family if he was killed. During the final, brutal battles before Richmond, soldiers wrote their names and addresses on pieces of paper that they pinned to their clothing on the assumption that there would be no friends alive to care for their bodies. The waiting was usually over about dawn. The command to charge was given. And with a shout, the repeated "hoorays" of the Union troops, and the eerie "rebel yell" of the Confederates, the simultaneous excitement and dread of battle began.

Lee had set one of the traps that flummoxed northern commanders time and again. He had sent Stonewall Jackson on a diversionary mission, feigning an assault on Washington that Jackson did not have the strength to bring off. The ruse was successful, and Jackson then sped east to reinforce the Confederate armies that were defending Richmond. By the time McClellan gave in to the president's impatient demand for action, Johnston, Lee, and Jackson had 85,000 men to hold him.

Seven days of nearly constant battle followed between June 26 and July 2, 1862. Again overly cautious and outsmarted on the field, McClellan was fought to a standstill. Even then he held a favorable position. His supply lines were intact; Confederate morale was badly shaken by the 25 percent casualties the South had suffered; and Richmond was only a few miles away, nearly within range of bombardment. A massive Union push in the summer of 1862 might have carried the day and ended the war.

But it was Lincoln's turn to make a mistake. He called off the Peninsula Campaign. He ordered the Army of the Potomac back to Washington by ship, and replaced McClellan with General John Pope, who proposed to take the Manassas route to Richmond.

Pope had won several victories in the West and was a favorite with the abolitionists in Congress because of his opposition to slavery. But he was an unimaginative general, no match for the wily Lee and Jackson. At the end of August, Lee met him on the same ground as the first Battle of Manassas and beat him back with much more ease than the Confederates had defeated McDowell.

Junior staff officers relax during the Peninsula Campaign. The young man reclining in the right foreground is Captain George Armstrong Custer, soon to be one of the war's youngest generals. A decade later he rode to immortality at the Battle of the Little Bighorn.

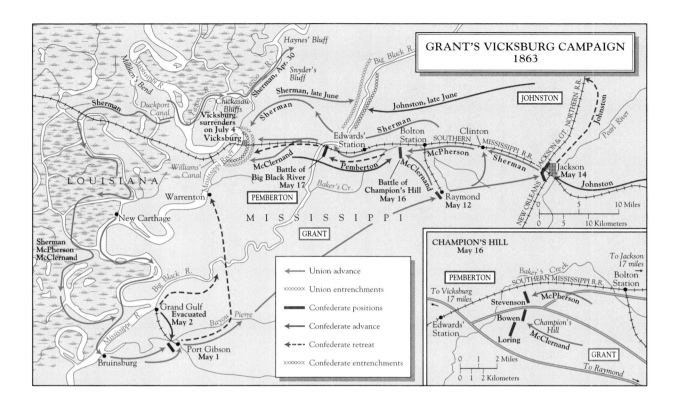

dinary Joshua Lawrence Chamberlain of Maine still held a steep bulbous knoll called Little Round Top. It was a valuable position. The troops that occupied Little Round Top could enfilade the open fields that separated the two armies. That is, they could shoot into an advancing army from the side, thus increasing the odds of finding a target.

That night, Lee's imagination failed him. Although badly outnumbered now, he decided on a mass frontal attack against the Union center. One of his generals, James Longstreet, argued long and loudly against a move that violated Jomini's cautions and was chillingly reminiscent of Burnside's charge into a powerful position at Fredericksburg. Longstreet pointed out that after two days in which to dig in, the Union troops would be well entrenched on Cemetery Ridge. Better, he said, that the Confederates sit tight and force Meade to make the next move. In the war to that date, the advantage always rested with the defensive position.

Pickett's Charge

Stonewall Jackson might have persuaded Lee to defend or, alternatively, to try to turn the Union's right flank again. James Longstreet could not. But he was

Confederate General Robert E. Lee.

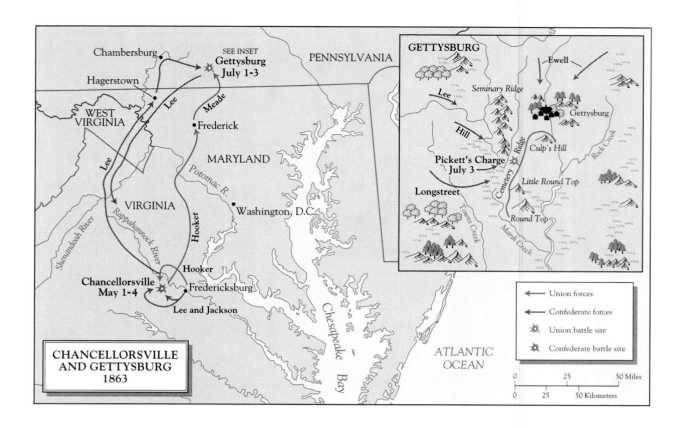

dead right. Just a few miles away, General Meade was betting on an assault to his center and he was ready for it. He concentrated his strength there, and, on the afternoon of July 3, he had the satisfaction of seeing his decision pay off. Between one and two o'clock, howling the eerie rebel yell, 15,000 men in gray uniforms began to trot across the no-man's-land. This was Pickett's Charge, somewhat of a misnomer because the angry Longstreet was actually in command of it. The attack was a nightmare. The

men were slaughtered first by artillery and then by minié balls. The worst of the fire came from Little Round Top, which was reinforced the previous night.

About a hundred Virginians actually reached the Union lines. There was a split second of glory, but it lasted no longer than that. The attackers were immediately surrounded by a thousand Union soldiers and killed or captured.

Pickett's Charge lasted less than an hour. When the Confederate survivors dragged themselves back to Seminary Ridge, 10,000 men were dead, wounded, or missing. Five of twenty regimental commanders involved in the massive assault were wounded. The other fifteen were dead. So were two Confederate brigadier generals.

On July 4, a somber Robert E. Lee, with 28,000 fewer rebels than he had led into Pennsylvania, waited for the Union counterattack. It never came. Meade was still ruminating over Pickett's Charge. He would not expose his men to the horrors of crossing an open field into the mouths of cannon. By nightfall, a drizzle became a downpour, making the Potomac impassable and setting up Lee's army for plucking. Defeated and huddled together, the

Unsung Confederate Hero

Joseph Reid Anderson is only occasionally mentioned in the histories of the Civil War, but he was a major contributor to the Confederate war effort. Anderson was the owner and manager of the Tredregar Iron Works of Richmond, Virginia, and he kept the huge factory running until April 1865, when the Confederacy itself fell.

Confederates were in a worse position than they were after Antietam. But the rain also discouraged Meade from launching an attack. When Lincoln got the news he fumed: "We had them within our grasp. We had only to stretch forth our hands and they were ours. And nothing I could say or do could make the Army move."

High Tide

For all Lincoln's disappointment, Gettysburg was an important victory. It ravaged southern morale: intelligent Confederates understood that their armies would never again be capable of an offensive campaign. Lincoln was still without the decisive, relentless general who would take advantage of the Union's numerical superiority. But that too was to change. Not long after the news of Gettysburg arrived in Washington, a spate of telegrams from the West informed the president that the long siege of Vicksburg had also ended on July 4, 1863.

Literally starving after having stripped the streets of pets and the cellars of rats, the people of the city had surrendered to Ulysses S. Grant. Five days later, Port Hudson, Louisiana, the last Confederate outpost on the Mississippi, gave up without a battle. Union General Nathaniel Banks took 30,000 prisoners there. Within a week, the Confederacy lost several times more men than the rebels had put into the field at the first Battle of Bull Run.

The Tennessee Campaign

Worse followed bad. In September, a previously cautious Union general, William S. Rosecrans, attacked the one remaining Confederate Army in the West. Rosecrans pushed Braxton Bragg out of Tennessee and into northern Georgia. Union troops then occupied Chattanooga, an important railroad center on the Tennessee River.

Like Grant at Shiloh, however, Rosecrans was surprised by a counterattack. On September 19, reinforced by grim Confederate veterans of Gettysburg, Bragg hit him at Chickamauga Creek. It was one of the few battles of the war in which the Confederates had the larger army, 70,000 to Rosecrans's 56,000, and numbers told. The rebels smashed through the Union right, scattering the defenders and making Chickamauga one of the bloodiest battles of the war. It would have been a total rout

but for the stand on the Union left flank led by a Virginian who remained loyal to the Union, George H. Thomas, the "Rock of Chickamauga." Thanks to Thomas's stand, the Union troops were able to retire in good order to the fortifications of Chattanooga.

Wisely, Bragg decided to besiege the city rather than attack it. But unlike Grant at Vicksburg, Bragg had enemies other than the army trapped inside the town. Grant himself marched his men to Chattanooga and brought 23,000 troops from the East by rail. Late in November, he drove Bragg's Confederates from their strongholds on Missionary Ridge and Lookout Mountain and back into Georgia.

The long campaign for Tennessee was over. It took two years longer than Lincoln expected but at last the Confederacy was severed in two. Finally, the stage was set for the final Union offensive. After Vicksburg and Chattanooga, there was no doubt about who was the man to lead it. Early in 1864,

The Battle of the Crater

Early in the siege of Petersburg, one of the war's most bizarre battles occurred. Miners from Pennsylvania dug a tunnel under a salient in the Confederate lines and planted four tons of gunpowder beneath a critical point in the fortifications. The plan was to detonate the charge and send a massive assault force led by a crack unit of black troops.

At almost the last moment, the selected shock troops were replaced by a less experienced white unit. Some said the reason for the change was the staff's apprehension that the Union command would be accused of treating black troops as cannon fodder. (The charge had been levied before.) Others said that the change was to deny blacks the opportunity of leading an attack that could end the war immediately, as indeed a breakthrough at "the crater" might very well have done.

In any case, victory was not the issue of the battle. Instead of leading the charge around the massive 170-foot-long, 60-foot-wide, 30-foot-deep crater, the first wave incredibly massed into it and others followed. They were easy targets for the Confederate counterattack that restored the defenders' lines at a cost of 4,000 Union losses.

HOW THEY LIVED

Marching Through Georgia

In the fall of 1865, General William Tecumseh Sherman, with a battle-tempered army of 60,000, occupied Atlanta, Georgia, the most important city of the heart of the Confederacy. In order to win the prize, Sherman's men had fought a series of ugly actions, including some victories that had been very close calls.

But Atlanta was an insecure prize. The civilian population was fiercely hostile. A strong Confederate army, its whereabouts not precisely known, menaced Sherman's position. The Yankee line of supply, a jugular vein for so large an army, was fragile, 100 miles of easily raided railroad to Chattanooga, Tennessee. Sherman had reason to be apprehensive of a massive set-piece battle.

Instead, he proposed, he would evacuate Atlanta, burning it so that the city would be useless to the Confederates. "Let us . . . make it a desolation," he urged as early as August 10th. Sherman would then "astonish" the Confederates by marching without supply lines across Georgia, "smashing things generally," and rendezvous with a naval relief force at Savannah. His men would "eat out" the country.

Sherman had more in mind than the delicacy of his isolated position. He meant to savage southern society and the economy of rural Georgia, punishing the staunch Confederates of the region for sustaining four years of costly rebellion. After some hesitation, President Lincoln approved the plan and Sherman's superior, Ulysses S. Grant, telegraphed the go-ahead.

On November 11th, Sherman's men officially evacuated the burning city. So as to move quickly—essential!; the army simply could not afford a battle—the men marched in four parallel columns, cutting a swath 30 miles, sometimes 60 miles wide through the rich Georgia countryside. Each column usually stretched out for five miles when, after 15 miles of marching, it paused for the night's rest.

Sherman charged his men to "discriminate" against the rich in seizing the food, mules, horses, oxen, and hogs they needed in order to keep moving. He told his officers to leave enough at every farm for the people who lived there to survive. Rape was to be punished as an outrage and "Soldiers must not enter the dwellings of the inhabitants, or trespass."

How stern Sherman meant to be in enforcing these strictures cannot be known. However, they were immediately and widely ignored and the general shrugged off accusations of brutal behavior with

Lincoln promoted U. S. Grant to the rank of lieutenant general and gave him command of all Union forces.

TOTAL WAR

Grant proved that he could be a daring tactician of the old school. At Vicksburg, with dash and flair, he outsmarted and outmaneuvered the enemy. Then he demonstrated his understanding that the nature of war had changed. He informed Lincoln that his object was not the capture of Confederate flags, commanders, cities, and territory, but the total destruction of the enemy's ability to fight.

The Union's superiority in numbers was overwhelming, and Grant intended to put his edge to work. He would force the Confederates to fight constant bloody battles on all fronts, trading casualties that the North could afford and the South could not. At the same time, he would destroy the Confederacy's capacity to feed, shod, clothe, and arm its soldiers. He would complete on land what the naval blockade had begun. He would strangle the southern economy.

Grant called off what was left of the gentleman's war. His kind of fighting was not chivalrous. It involved making war not only on soldiers but on a society. It was left to Grant's best general and good friend, the blunt-spoken William Tecumseh Sherman, to give it a name. "War is hell," Sherman said. He was a no-nonsense man, even unpleasant in his refusal to dress up dirty work with fuss, feathers, and pretty words.

the observation that his men had suffered grievously at the hands of the rebels.

In fact, crime against persons was not wholesale. Only six rapes were documented, a remarkable figure. Indeed, Georgians in Sherman's path knew that women were generally safe. Frequently, when Sherman's army was close, the men of plantation and farm hid, leaving their women behind to plead for mercy. One Confederate soldier wrote that "the Federal army generally behaved very well. . . . I don't think there was ever an army in the world that would have behaved better, on a similar expedition. . . . Our army certainly wouldn't."

This was a rare southern voice. Almost every other witness of the March, Union as well as Confederate, quavered in description of the damage Sherman's army did. The typical farm or village was not hit just once but several times, first by foraging parties ("pioneers") seizing food and livestock, then by the column itself, the first comers looting, the rear guard burning or shooting the animals that were still alive. An estimated 15,000 horses, 20,000 cattle, and 100,000 hogs were seized, eaten, or simply destroyed. Half a million bushels of corn disappeared, and 100,000 bushels of just-harvested sweet potatoes.

There was little armed conflict. The Confederate army under bold but ineffective General John Hood never caught up with Sherman. The 60,000 Union soldiers were confronted only by tiny bands of guerrillas able to raid and run, nothing more.

The March Through Georgia was burned into the southern psyche as an atrocity for more than a century. At the time, many northern voices were raised in protest. For the most part, however, Sherman's vengeance filled a deep-felt need in the hearts of northerners. They believed the war should have been ended before Sherman's men left Atlanta. General Robert E. Lee, in Virginia, was finished by the fall of 1864. By preparing for another campaign in the spring, he seemed to be the cause of yet more thousands of casualties that were entirely unnecessary. The Confederate case was dead. Sherman's terrible rampage was emotional compensation for frustration in the Union. Indeed, Sherman's partisans said it was his March Through Georgia, more than any other factor, that compelled Lee to give up before the campaign of 1865 had to be fought.

Sherman's assignment was to move from his base in Chattanooga toward Atlanta, laying waste the rich agricultural production of the black belt. Grant, with General Meade as his field commander, would personally direct the onslaught against Richmond.

Grant before Richmond

The war of attrition—the war of grinding down the Confederacy—began in May 1864. With 100,000 men, Grant marched into the Wilderness, wooded country near Fredericksburg where Burnside was defeated. There Grant discovered that Lee was cuts above any commander he had yet faced. Although outnumbered, Lee outmaneuvered Grant and actually attacked. While Grant's men suffered almost twice as many casualties as the southerners, replacements rushed to the Union front. On the southern side, Lee just counted his dead and sent his wounded men home.

Now it was Lee's turn to discover that he too was up against a new kind of rival. Instead of withdrawing to Washington where his men could lick their wounds and regroup as the book said he should do, and as all previous Union commanders had done, Grant shifted his men to the south and attacked again, at Spotsylvania Court House. For five days, spearheaded in places by African American troops, the Army of the Potomac assaulted the southern trenches. Grant lost 12,000 men, again almost twice Lee's casualties. Northern congressmen and editors howled. The man was a butcher! But Grant was unmoved. He sent a curt message to Washington that he intended "to fight it out on this line if it takes all summer."

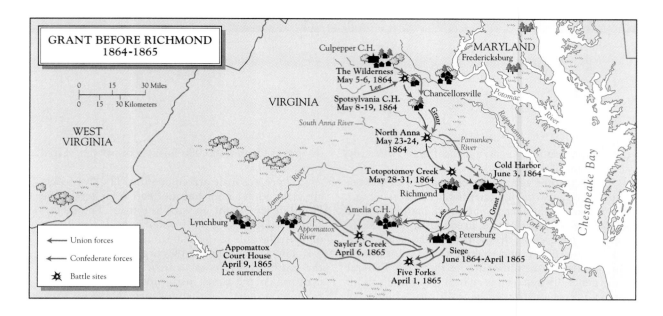

It took even longer. Time after time, Lee rallied his shrinking army and somehow managed to scratch together enough munitions and provisions to keep his men in the field. Time after time, he threw Grant back. At Cold Harbor, south of Spotsylvania, the two fought another gory battle. Before they charged, Union troops wrote their names on scraps of paper and pinned the tags to their uniforms. They expected to die.

Petersburg and the Shenandoah

Still Grant came on, always swinging to the south. On June 18, he attempted to capture Petersburg, a rail center that was the key to Richmond's survival. He might have succeeded immediately but for the failure of General Benjamin Butler, a political general in charge of 30,000 reinforcements, to join him in time. This time, Grant was as shaken by his casualties as his critics were. Some 55,000 had been lost in the campaign, more men than Lee had under arms at the end of the year. One unit from Maine attacked with 850 soldiers and returned to the lines with 218. Grant finally paused and sat down to besiege Petersburg. The siege would last ten months, through the harshest winter of the war.

In the meantime, in July, Lee tried a trick that earlier had worked. He sent General Jubal Early on a cavalry raid toward Washington designed to force Grant into weakening his besieging army. Early was remarkably successful. His men actually rode to within sight of the Capitol dome and some tough-talking politicians began to stutter. But Early's raid was the Confederacy's last hurrah. Grant did not panic, and, this time, neither did Lincoln. The men stayed at Petersburg and raised Lee's bet. Grant sent a Union cavalry commander, Philip Sheridan, to intercept Early, preventing him from rejoining Lee.

Sheridan chased Early into the Shenandoah Valley, the fertile country to the west of Richmond that served as a Confederate sanctuary and as Richmond's breadbasket for three years. Sheridan defeated Early three times. More important, he laid waste to the valley that had fed the Army of Northern Virginia, burning houses, barns, and crops, and slaughtering what livestock his men did not eat. He reported that when he was done, a crow flying over the Shenandoah Valley would have to carry its own provisions.

Sherman in Georgia

General Sherman was even more thoroughgoing in scouring Georgia. He moved into the state at the same time that Grant entered the Wilderness. At first he met brilliant harassing action by Joseph E. Johnston. Then an impatient Jefferson Davis, unaware that Johnston's army was not up to a major battle, replaced him with the courageous but foolish John B. Hood, whom Sherman defeated. On September 2, 1864, Union troops occupied Atlanta. The loss of this major rail center was a devastating blow to Confederate commerce and morale.

A Union wagon train crosses a temporary bridge on the Rapidan River on its way to the Wilderness Campaign.

Sherman's position was delicate. His supply lines ran to Chattanooga, more than 100 miles away over an easily raided, mostly single-track railroad. A bold move by the Confederates would have isolated him in the middle of hostile territory where—with Grant committed to Petersburg—he could not be relieved. Once again, the new Union leadership turned difficulty into triumph. Sherman ordered the people of Atlanta to evacuate the city, and he put it to the torch. He then set out to the southeast, moving quickly in order to avoid a set battle that he could not afford to fight. His men were instructed to destroy everything of use to the Confederacy in a swath 60 miles wide. They not only tore up the railroad between Atlanta and Savannah, but they burned the ties and twisted the iron rails around telegraph poles. "Sherman bow ties," they called them.

Sherman's purpose was twofold. First, he wanted to make it difficult for the southern army (under Johnston's command once again) to feed itself. Second, he wanted to punish the people of Georgia. Those who caused and supported the war would suffer for it. This was total war carried into the realm of social responsibility.

Sherman reached Savannah on December 10 and captured it two weeks later. Resupplied from the sea, Sherman then turned north to join Grant. He expected the two of them together would fight the final battle of the war at Petersburg.

The Sudden End

That final battle was never fought. In February 1865, Jefferson Davis tried to make peace by sending the Confederate vice president, Alexander H. Stephens, and two other emissaries to meet with Lincoln and Secretary of State Seward on a ship off Hampton Roads, Virginia. The South was reeling, but, absurdly, Davis insisted on Confederate independence as a condition of peace. It is difficult to imagine what he was thinking. There was very little Confederacy left. The conference broke up.

Late in March, Lee tried to draw Grant into a battle in open country. By this time he had 54,000 men to Grant's 115,000, and he was easily pushed back. On April 2, knowing that his 37-mile lines were too long for his shrunken army to man, Lee abandoned Petersburg (and therefore Richmond) and made a dash west. He had a notion to turn south,

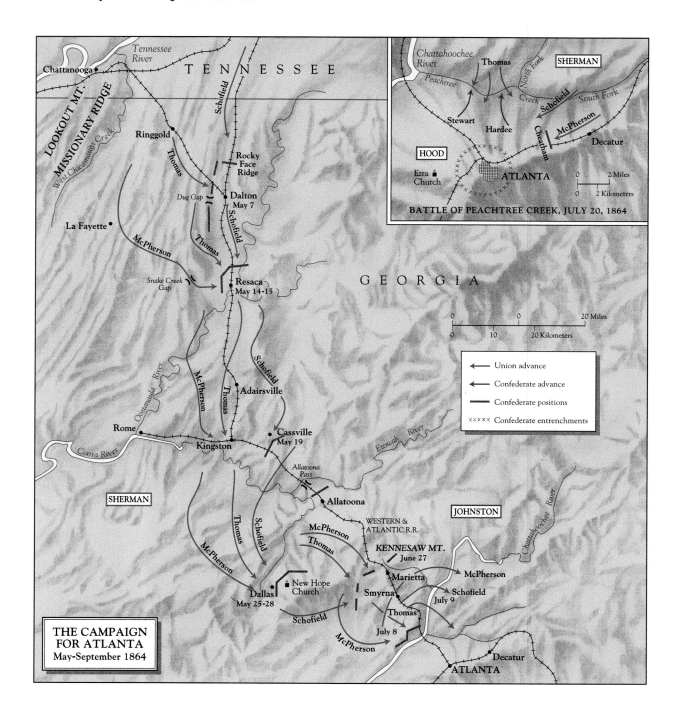

BATTLE OF PEACHTREE CREEK, JULY 20, 1864

Union advance
Confederate advance
Confederate positions
×××× Confederate entrenchments

THE CAMPAIGN FOR ATLANTA
May–September 1864

resupply in untouched North Carolina, and link up with Johnston for a last stand.

With help from Sheridan, Grant cut him off. Desertions had reduced Lee's proud army to 30,000 men, and some of them were shoeless. On April 7, Grant called for a surrender, and, two days later, he met Lee at Appomattox Court House in Virginia. The terms were simple and generous. The Confederates surrendered all equipment and arms except for the officers' revolvers and swords. Grant permitted both officers and enlisted men to keep their horses for plowing. After taking an oath of loyalty to the Union, the southern troops could go home.

This ruined stretch of railway near Atlanta was destroyed by Sherman's troops on their way to Savannah. In other places they made bonfires of the ties and melted the rails over them.

Jefferson Davis, who seemed to have lost his sense of reality, ordered Johnston to fight on. The veteran soldier, who had not fared well by Davis's whims, knew better than to obey. On April 18, he surrendered to Sherman at Durham, North Carolina. The ragged remnants of two other Confederate armies gave up over the next several weeks.

THE AMERICAN TRAGEDY

The United States had never fought a more destructive war. More than one-third of the men who served in the opposing armies died in action or of disease, were wounded, maimed permanently, or captured by the enemy. In some southern states, more than one-quarter of all the men of military age lay in cemeteries. The depth of the gore can best be understood by comparing the 620,000 dead (360,000 Union,

260,000 Confederate) with the population of the United States in 1860, about 30 million. Considering that half the population was female and 7 or 8 million males were either too old or too young for military service, more than one out of every twenty-five men who were eligible to die in the war did lose their lives. Until the Vietnam War of the 1960s and 1970s added its dead to the total, more Americans were killed in the Civil War than in all other American wars combined.

Assassination

There was one more casualty to be counted. On April 14, Good Friday, just a few days after the fall of Richmond, President Lincoln, his wife, and a few friends attended a play at Ford's Theater in Washington. Shortly after ten o'clock, Lincoln was shot point-blank in the head by a zealous pro-Confederate, John Wilkes Booth. Lincoln died early the next morning.

Booth was one of those unbalanced characters who pop up periodically to remind us of the significance of the irrational in history. An actor with delusions of grandeur, Booth organized a cabal including at least one mental defective to avenge the Confederacy by wiping out the leading officials of the Union government. Only he succeeded in his mission, although one of his coconspirators seriously wounded Secretary of State Seward with a knife.

As he escaped, Booth shouted, *"Sic semper tyrannis!"* which means "Thus always to tyrants" and was the motto of the state of Virginia. Booth fled into Virginia; on April 26, he was cornered and killed at Bowling Green. In July, four others were hanged for Lincoln's murder, including a woman, Mary Surratt, in whose boardinghouse the plot was hatched. But vengeance did not bring the president back, and his loss proved to be inestimable, perhaps more for the South than for the North.

Father Abraham

To this day, Lincoln remains a central figure of American history. More books have been written about him than about any other American. He was the epitome of the American Dream. He rose from modest frontier origins to become the leader of the nation in its greatest crisis.

Lincoln was not overwhelmingly popular as a president. The radicals of his own party assailed him because of his reluctance to make war on slavery early in the war, and his opposition to punishing the South when the war neared its end. Northern Democrats vilified him because the war dragged on and the casualties mounted to no avail. People of all points of view mocked his ungainly appearance and bemoaned his lack of dignity. As late as September 1864, with the casualties before Petersburg at horrible levels, Lincoln expected to lose his bid for re-election to the Democratic party candidate, General George McClellan.

Lincoln weathered McClellan's threat thanks in part to political machinations; he made Nevada a state, although it consisted of little more than half a dozen mining camps of uncertain future. By pushing through admission, he gained three electoral votes for his party. He also directed his generals to put Republican troops on furlough on election day so that

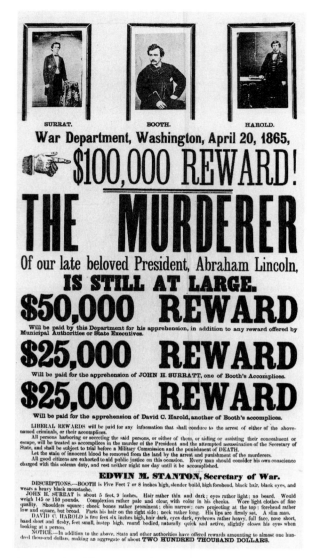

A poster advertising a reward for the capture of Lincoln's assassin, John Wilkes Booth, and his accomplices.

they could vote for him, while he kept units that were favorable to McClellan on isolated duty. Lincoln also appealed to pro-war Democrats by dropping the name "Republican" and calling himself the Union party candidate. For vice president he chose a Democrat from Tennessee, Andrew Johnson.

But Lincoln did not win the election of 1864 because of political ploys. He won because he had quietly gained the respect of the majority of the people of the North by the example of his dogged will, personal humility, and eloquent humanitarianism. In

The Lincoln conspirators on the gallows about to be executed.

a speech dedicating a national cemetery at Gettysburg in November 1863, he stated American ideals more beautifully (and succinctly) than anyone had done since Jefferson's preamble to the Declaration of Independence. His second inaugural address, delivered in Washington a month before Lee's surrender, was simultaneously a literary masterpiece, a signal to southerners that they could lay down their arms without fear of retribution, and a plea to northerners for a compassionate settlement of the national trauma. "With malice toward none," he concluded, "with charity for all; with firmness in the right, as God gives us to see the right, let us strive on to finish the work we are in."

Union and Nation

Before 1861, "United States" was grammatically a plural; since 1865, it has been a singular. That is, before the Civil War, one said, "The United States are . . ." Since, we have said, "The United States is . . ."

Lincoln quietly charted the transformation in his speeches. In his First Inaugural Address (March 1861), he used the word *Union* 20 times, *nation* not once. In his First Message to Congress (July 1861), he said *Union* 49 times and *nation* thrice. In the Gettysburg Address, Lincoln never said *Union* but referred to *nation* five times.

CONSEQUENCES OF THE CIVIL WAR

The military triumph of the Union guaranteed several fundamental changes in the nature of the American republic. Once and for all, the constitutional unity of the states was defined beyond argument. The states' rights theories of John C. Calhoun, so compelling in the abstract, were buried without honor at Appomattox. The United States was not a federation of independent and sovereign states. It was a nation, one and indivisible. Politicians have described themselves as states' righters since the Civil War. To a small extent, the line between state and national jurisdiction remains unsettled to this day. But never again after 1865 would anyone suggest that a state could leave the Union if its people disapproved of some national policy.

A New Political Majority

The political dominance of the South was destroyed by the Civil War. Since the founding of the republic, southerners played a role in the government of the country out of all proportion to their numbers. Eight of the fifteen presidents who preceded Lincoln came from slave states. At least two of the seven northerners who had held the office — Pierce and Buchanan — were frankly prosouthern in their policies. After Lincoln and Andrew Johnson, no resident of a former Confederate state would occupy the White House until Lyndon B. Johnson in 1963, and he was more westerner than southerner. Only in 1976, with the election of Jimmy Carter of Georgia, was an unambivalent southerner accepted by the American people as their leader.

Since the time of Andrew Jackson, southerners had dominated Congress through a combination of political skill, agrarian alliance with western farmers, and threat of secession. In making good on its threat to secede, the southern bloc destroyed this alliance. The Democratic party remained a major force in New York and the agricultural states of the North. But the Republicans held the edge above the Mason-Dixon line, and never again would a coalition of farmers dominate the government in Washington.

In its place, northeastern industrial and financial interests came to the fore. Businessmen had been late in joining the antislavery coalition. To bankers, great

> ### Don't Swap Horses
>
> Until the end of the nineteenth century, candidates for the presidency did not actively campaign. They did, however, urge on their supporters. In the wartime election of 1864, Lincoln himself provided his party's slogan by telling a leading supporter the story of the Dutch farmer who said he never swapped horses in the middle of a stream. Indeed, Americans never have changed presidents voluntarily during a war. Even during the unpopular war in Vietnam, it took the retirement of Lyndon B. Johnson in 1968 to put Republican Richard M. Nixon in the White House. With the war still on in 1972, Nixon won reelection by a landslide.

merchants, and factory owners, the Republican party was of interest more because of its economic policies than because of its hostility to slavery. With the war concluded, however, these forces held a strong position and could exploit the sentimental attachment of many voters to the "Grand Old Party."

New Economic Policies

During the war, the Republican Congress passed a number of bills that would have been defeated had southerners been in their seats and voting. In July 1862, about the time of Antietam, both houses approved the Pacific Railways Act. As modified later in the war, this act gave 6,400 square miles of the public domain to two private companies, the Union Pacific and the Central Pacific railroads. These corporations were authorized to sell the land and use the proceeds to construct a transcontinental railway, the ultimate internal improvement. In 1864, while Grant slogged it out with Lee before Richmond, Congress gave the Northern Pacific Railroad an even more generous subsidy. These acts revolutionized the traditional relationship between private enterprise and the federal government.

The tariff was another issue on which southern agricultural interests had repeatedly frustrated the manufacturers of the Northeast. Since 1832, with few exceptions, the Democratic party drove the taxes on imported goods ever downward. The last tariff before the war, passed in 1857 with the support of southern congressmen, set rates lower than they were since the War of 1812.

In March 1861, even before secession was complete, the Republican Congress rushed through the Morrill Tariff, which pushed up the taxes. In 1862 and 1864, rates went even higher. By 1867, the average tax on imported goods stood at 47 percent, about the same as it was under the act of 1828 that the southerners had called the Tariff of Abominations and that Calhoun called fit grounds for secession.

The South had long frustrated the desire of northern financial interests for a centralized banking system. Hostility to a national bank was one of the foundation stones of the old Democratic party. During the war, with no southern congressmen in Washington and with the necessity of financing the Union Army looming over Congress, New York's bankers finally got their way.

Financing the War

The Union financed the war in three ways: by heavy taxation, by printing paper money, and by borrowing, that is, selling bonds abroad and to private investors within the United States. The principal taxes were the tariff, an excise tax on luxury goods, and an income tax. By the end of the war, the income tax provided about 20 percent of the government's revenue.

The government authorized the printing of $450 million in paper money. These bills were not redeemable in gold. Popularly known as "greenbacks" because they were printed on one side in a distinctive green ink, they had value only because the federal government declared they must be accepted in the payment of debts. When the fighting went badly for the North, they were traded at a discount. By 1865, a greenback with a face value of $1 was worth only 67 cents in gold. This inflation was minuscule compared with that in the Confederacy, where government printing presses ran amok. By 1864, a citizen of Richmond paid $25 for a pound of butter and $50 for a breakfast. By 1865, prices were even higher, and some southern merchants would accept only gold or Union currency, including greenbacks!

The banking interests of the North were uncomfortable with the greenbacks. However, they profited nicely from the government's large-scale borrowing. By the end of the war, the federal government owed its own citizens and some foreigners almost $3 billion, about $75 for every person in the country. Much of this debt was held by the banks. Moreover, big financial houses like Jay Cooke's in Philadelphia reaped huge profits in commissions for their part in selling the bonds.

Free Land

Another momentous innovation of the Civil War years was the Homestead Act. Before the war, southern fear of encouraging the formation of more free states in the territories effectively paralyzed any attempt to liberalize the means by which the federal government disposed of its western lands. In May 1862, the system was overhauled. The Homestead Act provided that every head of family who was a citizen or who intended to become a citizen could receive 160 acres of public domain. There was a small filing fee, and homesteaders were required to live for five years on the land that the government gave them. Or, after six months on the land, they could buy it outright for $1.25 per acre.

A few months after approving the Homestead Act, Congress passed the Morrill Act. This law granted each loyal state 30,000 acres for each member whom that state sent to Congress. The states were to use the money that they made from the sale of these lands to found agricultural and mechanical colleges. In subsequent years, the founding of 69 land-grant colleges greatly expanded educational opportunities, particularly in the West.

Again, it was a free-spending policy, which parsimonious southern politicians would never have accepted, and the revolutionary infusion of government wealth into the economy spawned an age of unduplicated expansion—and corruption.

Free People

No consequence of the Civil War was so basic as the final and irrevocable abolition of slavery in the United States. In a sense, the peculiar institution was doomed when the first shell exploded over Fort Sumter. As Congressman Ben Wade of Ohio told southerners in 1861, "the first blast of civil war is the death warrant of your institution." Slavery was not only an immoral institution; by the middle of the nineteenth century, it was hopelessly archaic. It is the ultimate irony of wars that are fought to preserve outdated institutions that war itself is one of the most

African-American soldiers served in most military capacities, but always in segregated units.

powerful of revolutionary forces. Precariously balanced institutions such as slavery rarely survive the disruptions of armed conflict.

Once hundreds of thousands of blacks had left their masters to flee to Union lines, once virtually all the slaves had learned of the war, it was ridiculous to imagine returning to the old ways. Even if the South had eked out a negotiated peace, even if the North had not elected to make emancipation one of its war aims, slavery would have been dead within a decade.

And yet, many southerners refused to recognize this reality until the end. Several times the Confederate Congress turned down suggestions, including one from General Lee, that slaves be granted their freedom if they enlisted in the Confederate Army. Only during the last two months of the conflict did any blacks don Confederate uniforms, and those few never saw action.

On the other side of the lines, 150,000 blacks, most of them runaway slaves, served in the Union Army. They were less interested in preserving the

"Dixie" and "The Battle Hymn"

The unofficial anthems of the Confederate and Union soldiers, "Dixie" and "The Battle Hymn of the Republic," were each stolen from the other side. "Dixie" was written for a minstrel show by Dan Emmett, the Ohio-born son of an abolitionist. The music to "The Battle Hymn of the Republic" (and its predecessor, "John Brown's Body") was a southern gospel song by an unknown composer. It was heard in Charleston, South Carolina, during the 1850s.

> ### *Family Circle*
>
> In Washington, D.C., slavery was abolished by congressional action, with slave owners compensated for their financial losses. One of the largest and surely the oddest payment under this enactment was to Robert Gunnell, himself an African American who received $300 each for his wife, children, and grandchildren—18 people in all. Gunnell had owned them as slaves, believing it was the safest status for members of his family.

Union than in freeing slaves. Their bravery won the admiration of a great many northerners. President Lincoln, for example, confessed that he was surprised that blacks made such excellent soldiers, and he seems to have been revising the racist views that he formerly shared with most white Americans.

For a time, at least, so did many Union soldiers. Fighting to free human beings, a positive goal, was better for morale than fighting to prevent secession, a negative aim at best. By 1864, as they marched into battle, Union regiments sang "John Brown's Body," an abolitionist hymn, and Julia Ward Howe's more poetic "Battle Hymn of the Republic":

As He died to make men holy,
Let us die to make men free.

Because the Emancipation Proclamation did not free all slaves, in February 1865 Radical Republicans in Congress proposed, with Lincoln's support, the Thirteenth Amendment to the Constitution. It provided that "neither slavery nor involuntary servitude, except as a punishment for crime . . . shall exist within the United States." Most of the northern states ratified it within a few months. Once the peculiar institution was destroyed in the United States, only Brazil, some Moslem countries, and undeveloped parts of the world continued to condone the holding of human beings in bondage.

CHRONOLOGY

1863	Battle of Chancellorsville
	Grant surrounds Vicksburg
	Battle of Gettysburg
	Vicksburg surrenders
	Battles for Chattanooga
1864	Grant repeatedly attacks Richmond
	Sherman occupies Atlanta, crosses Georgia
1865	Lee surrenders at Appomattox
	Lincoln is assassinated

FOR FURTHER READING

The works listed in "For Further Reading" in Chapter 23 are relevant to this chapter as well. See also Maris Vinovskis, *Toward a Social History of the American Civil War*, 1990; Joseph T. Glatthaar, *Forged in Battle: The Civil War Alliance of Black Soldiers and White Officers*, 1990; Emory Thomas, *The Confederacy as a Revolutionary Experience*, 1971; Paul D. Gates, *Agriculture and the Civil War*, 1965; Leon F. Litwack, *Been in the Storm So Long*, 1979; Robert P. Sharkey, *Money, Class, and Party*, 1959; Hans A. Trefousse, *The Radical Republicans*, 1968; and Bell Wiley, *Southern Negroes, 1861–1865*, 1938, and *The Plain People of the Confederacy*, 1943.

Useful biographical studies include James M. McPherson, *Abraham Lincoln and the Second American Revolution*, 1990; Garry Wills, *Lincoln at Gettysburg: The Words That Remade America*, 1992; William McFeely, *Grant: A Biography*, 1981; and Charles Royster, *The Destructive War: William Tecumseh Sherman, Stonewall Jackson, and the Americans*, 1991.

Freedmen pose for a photographer in Richmond, Virginia, in 1865.

25
CHAPTER

RECONSTRUCTION

Rebuilding the Shattered Union: 1863–1877

No State shall make or enforce any law which shall abridge the privileges or immunities of citizens of the United States; nor shall any State deprive any person of life, liberty, or property, without due process of law.

— *Fourteenth Amendment to the Constitution*

Oh, I'm a good old rebel, that's what I am,
And for this land of freedom, I don't give a damn,
I'm glad I fought ag'in her, I only wish we'd won,
And I don't axe any pardon for anything I've done.

— *Reconstruction Era Doggerel*

Republicans gave the ballot to men without homes, money, education, or security, and then told them to use it to protect themselves. It was cheap patriotism, cheap philanthropy, cheap success.

—*Albion W. Tourgée*

When the guns fell silent in 1865, the people of the South looked about them to see a society, an economy, and a land in tatters. Some southern cities, such as Vicksburg, Atlanta, Columbia, and Richmond, were flattened, eerie wastelands of charred timbers, rubble, and free-standing chimneys. Few of the South's railroads could be operated for more than a few miles. Bridges were gone. River-borne commerce, the lifeblood of the states beyond the Appalachians, had dwindled to a trickle. Old commercial ties with Europe and the North had been snapped. After four years of printing paper money valued in hope alone, the South's banks were ruined.

Even the cultivation of the soil was disrupted. The small farms of the men who served in the ranks lay fallow by the thousands, many of them never to be claimed by their former owners. Great planters who abandoned their fields to advancing Union armies discovered that weeds and scrub pine were more destructive conquerors than vengeful Yankees. The people who had toiled in the great fields, the former slaves, were often gone, looking elsewhere for a place to start new lives as free men and women. Many of those who remained in their lifelong homes also made it clear they wanted nothing of the past. When a Union soldier told recently freed women in South Carolina he would bring their former master back to them, they shouted, "Don't bring him here."

"But what shall we do with him?"

"Do what you please."

"Shall we hang him?"

"If you want. . . ."

"But shall we bring him *here* and hang him?"

". . . No, no, don't fetch him here, we no want to see him nebber more again."

THE RECONSTRUCTION DEBATE

In view of the desolation and social dislocation, *reconstruction* would seem to be an appropriate description of the 12-year period following the Civil War. But the word does not refer to the literal rebuilding of the South, the laying of bricks, the spanning of streams, the reclaiming of the land, and only secondarily to the rebuilding of a society.

Reconstruction refers to the political process by which the 11 rebel states were restored to a normal constitutional relationship with the 25 loyal states and their national government. It was the Union,

that great abstraction over which so many had died, that was reconstructed.

Blood was shed during Reconstruction too, but little glory was won. Few political reputations—northern or southern, white or black, Republican or Democratic—emerged from the era without blemish. It may well be that Abraham Lincoln comes down to us as a heroic and sainted figure only because he did not survive the war. Indeed, the Reconstruction policy Lincoln proposed as early as 1863 was repudiated by members of his own party, who would surely have fought the Emancipator as they fought his successor, Andrew Johnson. Lincoln anticipated the problems he did not live to face. He described as pernicious the constitutional issues with which both sides in the bitter Reconstruction debate masked their true motives and goals.

Lincoln's Plan to Restore the Union

By the end of 1863, Union armies controlled large parts of the Confederacy, and ultimate victory, while not in the bag, was reasonable to assume. To provide for a rapid reconciliation of North and South, Lincoln declared on December 8, 1863, that as soon as 10 percent of the voters in any Confederate state took an oath of allegiance to the Union, the people of that state could organize a government and elect representatives to Congress. Moving quickly, enough voters in occupied Tennessee, Arkansas, and Louisiana complied.

Congress Checks the President

Congress, however, refused to recognize the new governments, leaving the three states under the command of the military. Motives for checking Lincoln's plan varied as marvelously as the cut of the chin whiskers that politicians were now sporting, but two were repeatedly voiced. First, almost all Republican congressmen were alarmed by the broad expansion of presidential powers during the war. No president since Andrew Jackson (still an arch-villain to those Republicans who had been Whigs) had assumed as much authority as Lincoln had—at the expense of Congress. Few congressmen wished to see this trend continue during peacetime, as Lincoln's plan for Reconstruction promised to ensure.

Second, Radical Republicans, abolitionists who were at odds with Lincoln over his foot-dragging in moving against slavery, objected that the president's

Congressman Robert Elliot of South Carolina argues in the House of Representatives for a civil rights bill.

plan made no allowances whatsoever for the status of the freedmen, as the former slaves were called. These Radicals took the lead in framing the Wade-Davis Bill of July 1864, which provided that only after 50 percent of the white male citizens of a state swore an oath of loyalty to the Union could the Reconstruction process begin. Then, the Wade-Davis Bill insisted, Congress and not the president would decide when the process was complete. Wade-Davis promised to slow down a process Lincoln wanted to speed along (the 50 percent requirement) and to seize control of the process from the president.

Lincoln responded with a pocket veto and, over the following months—the last of his life—he hinted that he was ready for compromise. He said he would be glad to accept any former rebel states which opted to reenter the Union under the congressional plan and he let it be known he had no objection to giving the right to vote to blacks who were "very intelligent and those who have fought gallantly in our ranks." He urged the military governor of Louisiana to extend the suffrage to some blacks.

Stubborn Andy Johnson

Lincoln's lifelong assumption that blacks were inferior to whites and his determination to win back quickly the loyalty of southern whites prevented him from accepting the full citizenship of African Americans without reservation. However, he was willing to be flexible. "Saying that reconstruction will be accepted if presented in a specified way," he said, "it is not said that it will never be accepted in any other way." The man who succeeded him was not so accommodating.

Like Lincoln, Andrew Johnson of Tennessee grew up in stultifying frontier poverty. Unlike Lincoln, who taught himself to read as a boy and was ambitious from the start, Johnson grew to adulthood illiterate. He was working as a tailor when he swallowed his pride and asked a schoolteacher in Greenville, Tennessee, to teach him to read and write. She did, and later married him, encouraging Johnson to pursue a political career. Andrew Johnson had more political experience than Lincoln or, for that matter, than most presidents have had. Johnson held elective office on every level, from town councilman to congressman to senator and, during the war, as governor of occupied Tennessee.

Experience, alas, is rarely a substitute for natural aptitude. Whereas Lincoln was an instinctively coy politician who was sensitive to the realities of what he could and could not accomplish, Johnson was unsubtle, insensitive, willful, and stubborn.

Johnson was ill with a bad cold when he was sworn in as vice president. He bolted several glasses of brandy for strength, and took the oath of office a little drunk and thick-tongued. The incident was jested about, but Vice President Johnson had the goodwill of the Radicals because he had several times called for the harsh punishment of high-ranking Confederates. (He said he wanted to hang Jefferson Davis as a traitor.) However, after narrowly escaping death in the plot that felled Lincoln, Johnson lost the Radicals' backing in no time when, like Lincoln, he insisted that he, the president, possessed the authority to decide when rebel states were reconstructed. Thus ensued the debate over what Lincoln had called "a pernicious abstraction."

Johnson: They Are Already States

Johnson based his case for presidential supervision on the assumption that the southern states had never left the Union because it was constitutionally forbidden to do so: the Union was one and inviolable, as Daniel Webster said; it could not be dissolved. Johnson and the entire Republican party and most northern Democrats held to that principle in 1861. He stuck by it in 1865.

There had indeed been a war and an entity known as the Confederate States of America. But individuals fought the one and created the other, according to Johnson; the states had not. Punish the rebels, Johnson said—he approved several confiscations of rebel-owned lands—but not Virginia, Alabama, and the rest. They were still states, inalienable components of the United States of America. Seating their duly elected representatives in the Congress was a purely administrative affair. Therefore, the president, the nation's chief administrator, would decide how and when to do it.

Logic versus Horse Sense

There was nothing wrong with Johnson's logic; he was an excellent constitutionalist. The president's problem was his inability or refusal to see beyond constitutional tidiness to the world of human feelings, hatreds, resentments, and flesh and blood—especially blood.

Obstinate, often vulgar, Andrew Johnson was a self-taught student of the Constitution. Rigorous adherence to it, as he read it, and a reflexive distaste for the idea of black citizenship doomed his early friendly relationship with the Radical Republicans.

The fact was, virtually every senator and representative from the rebel states—Johnson was an exception—had left their seats in the winter and spring of 1861, and Congress and president had functioned as the Union through four years of war. More than half a million people were killed and a majority of northerners blamed these tragedies on arrogant, antagonistic, rich southern slave owners who, when Johnson announced that he would adopt Lincoln's plan of Reconstruction (with some changes), began to assume the leadership in their states that, as slavocrats, they had always held.

Nor did Johnson's reputation as a man who wanted to punish individual rebels hold up. By the end of 1865 he pardoned 13,000 Confederate leaders, thus making them eligible to hold public office under his plan for Reconstruction. In elections held in the fall under Johnson's plan, southern voters sent many of these rebels to Congress, including four Confederate generals, six members of Jefferson Davis's cabinet, and as senator from Georgia, former Confederate Vice President Alexander H. Stephens.

The Radicals: They Have Forfeited Their Rights

Thaddeus Stevens, Radical leader in the House of Representatives, replied to Johnson's argument that the former Confederate states had committed state suicide when they seceded. They were not states. Therefore, it was within the power of Congress, and Congress alone, to admit "Alabama," "Arkansas," and the rest. Senator Charles Sumner came to the same conclusion by arguing that the southern states were conquered provinces and therefore had the same status as the federal territories of the West.

These theories suited the mood of most northerners very well, but they were constitutionally indefensible. A rather obscure Republican, Samuel Shellabarger of Ohio, came up with the formula that appealed to angry, war-weary northerners and made constitutional sense: the rebel states had forfeited their rights as states. Congress's Joint Committee on Reconstruction found that "the States lately in rebellion were, at the close of the war, disorganized communities, without civil government, and without constitutions or other forms, by virtue of which political relations could legally exist between them and the federal government." Such a state of affairs meant that only Congress could decide when the 11 former Confederate states might once again function as members of the Union.

The Radicals

Congress refused to seat the senators and representatives who came to Washington under the Johnson Reconstruction plan. The leaders of the resistance were Radical Republicans who, whatever constitutional arguments they put forward, were determined to crush the southern planter class they had hated for so long and, with varying degrees of idealism, wanted to help the black freedmen who had, for so long, been exploited by slave owners.

Some Radicals, like Stevens and Sumner and Benjamin "Bluff Ben" Wade of Ohio, believed in racial equality. George W. Julian of Indiana proposed to confiscate the land of the planters and divide it, in 40-acre farms, among the freedmen. With economic independence they could guarantee their civil freedom and political rights. Other Radicals wanted to grant the freedmen citizenship, including the vote, for frankly political purposes. Black voters would provide the backbone for a Republican party in the South, which did not exist before the war, and was unlikely to be more than a splinter group if only southern whites voted.

The Radicals were a minority within the Republican party. However, they were able to win the support of party moderates because of Johnson's repeated blunders and a series of events in the conquered South that persuaded a majority of northern voters that Lincolnian generosity would

---

Discouraging Rebellion

Among other provisions of the Fourteenth Amendment, the former Confederate states were forbidden to repay "any debt or obligation incurred in aid of insurrection or rebellion against the United States." By stinging foreign and domestic individuals and banks that had lent money to the rebel states, the amendment was putting future supporters of rebellion on notice of the consequences of their actions.

mean squandering the Union's military victory and making a mockery of the cause for which so many young men died.

THE CRITICAL YEAR

The reaction of most blacks to the news of their freedom was to test it by leaving the plantations and farms on which they had lived as slaves.

Many flocked to cities, which they associated with free blacks. Others, after a period of wandering, gathered in ramshackle camps in the countryside, eagerly discussing the rumor that each household would soon be allotted 40 acres and a mule. Without a means of making a living in a stricken land, these congregations were potentially, and in some cases in fact, dens of hunger, disease, crime, and disorder.

The Freedmen's Bureau

In order to prevent chaos in conquered territory, Congress created the Bureau of Refugees, Freedmen, and Abandoned Lands, popularly known as the Freedmen's Bureau. Administered by the army under the command of General O. O. Howard, the bureau provided relief for the freedmen (and some whites) in the form of food, clothing, and shelter; attempted to find jobs for them; set up hospitals and schools run by idealistic black and white women from the northern states, sometimes at the risk of their lives; and otherwise tried to ease the transition from slavery to freedom.

When the Freedmen's Bureau bill was first enacted, Congress assumed that properly established state governments would be able to assume responsibility for these services within a year after the end of the hostilities. The Bureau was scheduled to close its doors, its job accomplished, in March 1866.

In February 1866, however, the process of Reconstruction was at a standstill. Congress refused to recognize Johnson's state governments but had not created any to its own liking. The former Confederacy was, in effect, still under military occupation. So Congress passed a bill extending the life of the bureau.

Johnson vetoed it and, a month later, he vetoed another congressional act that granted citizenship to the freedmen. Once again, his constitutional reasoning was sound. The Constitution gave the states the power to rule on the terms of citizenship within their borders, and Johnson continued to insist that the state governments he had set up were legitimate.

He might have won his argument. Americans took their constitutional fine points seriously in those days and Radical demands for black civil equality ran against the grain of white racism, which was widespread. However, the actions of the Johnson government toward blacks, and the apparent refusal of many southern whites to acknowledge their defeat in the war, nullified every point Johnson scored.

The Black Codes

Because blacks as slaves were the backbone of the southern labor force, the southern legislatures naturally expected the blacks to continue to bring in the crops after the war. The freedmen wanted the work. Far from providing farms for them, however, the Johnsonian state governments did not even establish a system of employment that treated the blacks as free men and women. On the contrary, the black codes defined a form of second-class citizenship that looked to blacks and many whites like a step or two back into slavery.

In some states, blacks were permitted to work only as domestic servants or in agriculture, just what they did as slaves. Other states made it illegal for blacks to live in towns and cities.

In no state were blacks allowed to vote or to bear arms. In fact, few of the civil liberties listed in the Bill of Rights were accorded them.

South Carolina said that African Americans could not sell goods! Mississippi required freedmen to sign 12-month labor contracts before January 10 of each year. Those who failed to do so could be arrested, and their labor sold to the highest bidder in a manner that (to say the least) was strongly reminiscent of the detested slave auction. Dependent children could be forced to work. Blacks who reneged on their contracts were not to be paid for the work that they had already performed.

The extremism of the black codes alienated many northerners who might have accepted a milder form of second-class citizenship for the freedmen. (Only a few northern states allowed African Americans full civil equality.) Northerners were also disturbed when whites in Memphis, New Orleans, and smaller southern towns rioted, killing and injuring blacks, while the Johnson state governments sat passively by.

Freedmen pose with their reading books in front of their log schoolhouse.

The Fourteenth Amendment

Perceiving the shift in mood, in June 1866, Radical and Moderate Republicans drew up a constitutional amendment on which to base congressional Reconstruction policy. The long and complex (and later controversial) Fourteenth Amendment banned from holding high federal or state office all high-ranking Confederates unless they were pardoned by Congress. This struck directly at many of the leaders of the Johnson governments in the South. The amendment also guaranteed that all "citizens of the United States and of the State wherein they reside" were to receive fully equal treatment under the laws of the states.

If ratified, the Fourteenth Amendment would preclude southern states from passing any more laws like the black codes. However, it also promised to cancel northern state laws that forbade blacks to vote, and in that aspect of the amendment Johnson saw an opportunity. Calculating that many northerners, particularly in the Midwest, would rather have ex-Confederates in the government than grant full civil equality to blacks, Johnson decided to campaign against the Radicals on the amendment issue in the congressional election of 1866.

The Radical Triumph

The first step was the formal organization of a political party. Johnson, conservative Republican allies such as Secretary of State Seward and a few senators, and some Democrats therefore called a convention of the National Union party in Philadelphia. The message of the convention was sectional reconciliation. To symbolize it, the meeting was opened by a procession of northern and southern Johnson supporters in which couples made up of one southerner and one northerner marched arm in arm down the center aisle of the hall.

Unhappily for Johnson, the first couple on the floor was South Carolina Governor James L. Orr, a huge, fleshy man, and Massachusetts Governor John A. Andrew, a little fellow with a way of looking intimidated. When Orr seemed to drag the mousy Andrew down the length of the hall, Radical politicians and cartoonists had a field day. Johnson's National Union movement, they said, was dominated by rebels and preached in the North by obsequious stooges.

In the fall, Johnson sealed his doom. He toured the Midwest seeking support—he called it his "swing around the circle"—and from the start discredited himself. Johnson learned his oratorical skills in the rough-and-tumble, stump-speaking tradition of eastern Tennessee. There, voters liked a red-hot debate between politicians who scorched each other and the hecklers that challenged them.

Midwesterners also liked that kind of ruckus, but not, it turned out, from their president. When Radical hecklers taunted Johnson and he responded gibe for gibe, Radicals shook their heads sadly that a man of so little dignity should be sitting in the seat of Washington and Lincoln. Drunk again, they supposed.

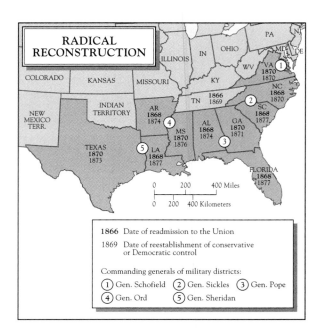

RADICAL RECONSTRUCTION

1866 Date of readmission to the Union

1869 Date of reestablishment of conservative or Democratic control

Commanding generals of military districts:
① Gen. Schofield ② Gen. Sickles ③ Gen. Pope
④ Gen. Ord ⑤ Gen. Sheridan

The result was a landslide. Most of Johnson's candidates were defeated. The Republican party, now led by the Radicals, controlled more than two-thirds of the seats in both houses of Congress, enough to override every veto that Johnson dared to make.

RECONSTRUCTION REALITIES AND MYTHS

The Radical Reconstruction program was adopted in a series of laws passed by the Fortieth Congress in 1867. These dissolved the southern state governments that were organized under Johnson and partitioned the Confederacy into five military provinces, each commanded by a major general. The army would maintain order while voters were registered: blacks and those whites who were not specifically disenfranchised under the terms of the Fourteenth Amendment. The constitutional conventions that these voters elected were required to abolish slavery, give the vote to adult black males, and ratify the Thirteenth and Fourteenth Amendments. After examination of their work by Congress, the reconstructed states would be admitted to the Union, and their senators and representatives could take their seats in the Capitol. The Radicals assumed that at least some of these congressmen would be Republicans.

Old Thad Stevens

Few Radical Republicans were as sincerely committed to racial equality as Thaddeus Stevens of Pennsylvania. In his will he insisted on being buried in a black cemetery because blacks were banned from the one where he normally would have been interred.

Nevertheless, even Stevens came to terms with the racism of those northern whites who refused the vote to blacks in their own states. In order to win their support for black suffrage in the South, Stevens argued that the situation was different in the South because blacks made up the majority of loyal Union men there. "I am for negro suffrage in every rebel state," he said. "If it be just, it should not be denied; if it be necessary, it should be adopted; if it be a punishment to traitors, they deserve it."

Readmission of the Southern States

Tennessee complied immediately with these terms and was never really affected by the Radical experiment in remaking the South. Ironically, it was Andrew Johnson, military governor of Tennessee during the war, and a good one, who laid the basis for a stable government in the Volunteer State.

In 1868, largely as a result of the black vote, six more states were readmitted. Alabama, Arkansas, Florida, Louisiana, North Carolina, and South Carolina sent Republican delegations, including some blacks, to Washington. In the remaining four states—Georgia, Mississippi, Texas, and Virginia—because some whites obstructed every attempt to set up a government in which blacks would participate, the military continued to govern until 1870.

In the meantime, with Congress more firmly under Radical control, Thaddeus Stevens, Charles Sumner, and other Radicals attempted to establish the supremacy of the legislative over the judicial and executive branches of the government. With the Supreme Court they were immediately successful. By threatening to reduce the size of the court or even to try to abolish it, the Radicals intimidated the justices. Chief Justice Salmon P. Chase decided to ride out the difficult era by ignoring all cases that dealt with Reconstruction issues, just what the Radicals wanted.

As for the presidency, Congress took partial control of the army away from Johnson and then struck at his right to choose his own cabinet. The Tenure of Office Act forbade the president to remove any appointed official who was confirmed by the Senate without first getting the Senate's approval of the dismissal.

The Impeachment of Andrew Johnson

Although Johnson attempted to delay and obstruct congressional Reconstruction by urging southern whites not to cooperate, the strict constitutionalist in him had come to terms with the fact of the Radicals' control of the government. He executed the duties assigned him under the Reconstruction acts. However, because of the same constitutional scruples, he decided to defy the Tenure of Office Act. To allow Congress to decide if and when a president could fire a member of his own cabinet was a clear infringement of the independence of the executive branch of the government. In February 1868, Johnson dismissed the single Radical in his cabinet, Secretary of War Edwin Stanton.

Strictly speaking, the Tenure of Office Act did not apply to Stanton's dismissal because he was appointed by Lincoln, not by Johnson. Nevertheless, the House of Representatives drew up articles of impeachment, passed them, and appointed a committee to serve as Johnson's prosecutors. The Senate acted as the jury in the trial, and the Chief Justice presided.

President on Trial

All but two of the eleven articles of impeachment dealt with the Tenure of Office Act. As expected, Johnson's defenders in the Senate argued that it did not apply to the Stanton case, and, in any event, its constitutionality was highly dubious. The other two articles condemned Johnson for disrespect of Congress. There was no doubt about this. Johnson had spared few bitter words in describing the Radical Republicans. The president was capable of civility, but not when his temper was up. However, Johnson's defenders argued with timeless merit that sharp and vulgar language did not approach being the "high crimes and misdemeanors" that the Constitution stipulates as the reason for impeachment.

The flimsiness of the charges did not matter, as they often do not when politics are on the table. The Radicals had determined to humiliate Johnson, and most moderate Republicans, sensing a turn to Radicalism in the public mood, did what successful politicians who like their jobs always do: they went along.

Conviction of an impeached federal official—removal of that person from office—requires a two-thirds majority of the Senate. In 1868, that

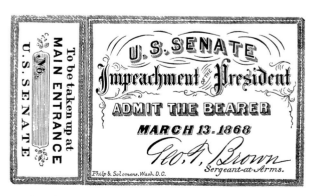

A ticket of admission to the Senate gallery to witness the impeachment of Andrew Johnson.

Was Johnson Impeached?

Andrew Johnson *was* impeached, the first American president to be so. *Impeachment* is not removal from office but the bringing of charges, the equivalent of indictment in a criminal trial. The official who is found guilty of the articles of impeachment is *convicted* and removed from office (and may be sent to prison or otherwise penalized if convicted in a subsequent criminal trial). Johnson was *not* convicted of the charges brought against him. Nor was President William Jefferson Clinton, after he was caught lying in a sex scandal in 1998. However, like Johnson, he was impeached. The House of Representatives brought charges against him and, in his case, he was fined in July 1999 by a federal judge for his dishonesty under oath.

meant 36 senators had to vote for conviction, no more than 18 for acquittal. The actual vote in Johnson's case was 35 to 19. He remained in office by a single vote.

Actually, it was not so close. Six Moderate Republican senators agreed privately that if their vote was needed for acquittal, they would vote for acquittal. They did not accept the validity of the Articles of Impeachment and they did not believe that the president should be removed from office simply because he was at odds with Congress. Moreover, if Johnson were removed from office, his successor would have been Ben Wade of Ohio, a Radical of such dubious deportment—he had a fouler mouth than Johnson—that by comparison the president was as courtly as George Washington. Finally, the sobersided among them argued, 1868 was an election year: an already weakened Andy Johnson's days were numbered. The immensely popular Ulysses S. Grant would be the Republican nominee in November and victory in November was a sure thing.

In the end, of the six, only Senator Edward Ross of Kansas joined Democrats and a handful of conservative Republicans to vote for Johnson's acquittal. To him went the historical glory of choosing principle but also, as he had been threatened by the Radicals, political death The Kansas legislature turned him out of office at the next election.

The Fifteenth Amendment

Grant easily defeated New York Governor Horatio Seymour in the electoral college by a vote of 214 to 80. However, the popular vote was much closer, a hair's breadth in some states. Nationwide, Grant won by 300,000 votes, and, some rudimentary arithmetic showed, he got 500,000 black votes in the southern states. Grant lost New York, the largest state, by a very thin margin. Had blacks been able to vote in New York (they were not), Grant would have carried the state easily. In Indiana, Grant won by a razor-thin margin. Had African Americans been able to vote in that northern state (they were not), it would not have been close.

In other words, the future of the Republican party seemed to depend on the black man's right to vote in the northern as well as the southern states. Consequently, the Moderates in Congress supported Radicals in drafting a third Civil War amendment. The Fifteenth forbade states to deny the vote to any person on the basis of "race, color, or previous condition of servitude." Because Republican governments favorable to blacks still controlled most of the southern states, the amendment was easily ratified. The Radical Reconstruction program was complete.

Legends

By the end of the nineteenth century and increasingly after 1900, a legend of Reconstruction took form in American popular consciousness. Most white people came to believe that Reconstruction was a time of degradation and humiliation for white southerners. Omnipresent northern (and African American) soldiers bullied them for a decade. They languished under the political domination of ignorant former slaves who were incapable of good citizenship, carpetbaggers (northerners who went south in order to exploit the tragedy of defeat), and scalawags (white southerners of low caste who cooperated with blacks and Yankees).

The "Black Reconstruction" governments, the legend continued, were hopelessly corrupt as well as unjust. The blacks, carpetbaggers, and scalawags looted the treasuries and demeaned the honor of the southern states. Only by heroic efforts did decent white people, through the Democratic party, redeem the southern states once they had retaken control of them. Some versions of the legend glamorized the role of secret terrorist organizations, such as the Ku Klux Klan, in redeeming the South.

The Kernel of Truth

As in most legends, there was a kernel of truth in this vision of Reconstruction. The Radical governments did spend freely. There was plenty of corruption in southern government; for example, the Republican governor of Louisiana, Henry C. Warmoth, banked $100,000 during a year when his salary was $8,000. In 1869, the state of Florida spent as much on its printing bill (a notorious budget line in which to hide thievery) as was spent on every function of state government in 1860.

Sometimes the theft was open and ludicrous. Former slaves in control of South Carolina's lower house voted a payment of $1,000 to one of their number who lost that amount in a bet on a horse race. Self-serving carpetbaggers were numerous, as were vindictive scalawags and incompetent black officials.

The Legend in Perspective

No doubt, some soldiers were rough with former rebels, especially during the first years of reconstruction. But Radical Reconstruction did not rest on military rule. There were just 15,000 Union troops in the South in 1867, only 6,600 in 1870, and a mere 3,000 in 1876. This was not the stuff of which military dictatorships are made.

As for political corruption, large governmental expenditures were unavoidable in the postwar South. Southern society was being rebuilt almost from scratch—an expensive proposition. It was the lot of the Radical state governments to provide social services—for whites as well as blacks—that had simply been ignored in the southern states before the Civil War. Statewide public school systems were not founded in the South until Reconstruction. Programs for the relief of the destitute and the handicapped were likewise nearly unknown before Republicans came to power.

Corrupt politicians are inevitable in times of massive government spending, no matter who is in charge; shady deals were not unique to southern Republican governments during the 1860s and 1870s. The most flagrant theft of public treasuries during the period was the work of Democrats in New York, strong supporters of white southerners who wanted to reduce the blacks to peonage. (New York's Tweed

---

Birth of a Legend

The legend of a South "prostrate in the dust" during Reconstruction had its origins during the Reconstruction era. In 1874, journalist James S. Pike wrote of "the spectacle of a society suddenly turned bottomside up. . . . In the place of this old aristocratic society stands the rude form of the most ignorant democracy that mankind ever saw, invested with the functions of government. It is the dregs of the population habilitated in the robes of their intelligent predecessors, and asserting over them the rule of ignorance and corruption, through the inexorable machinery of a majority of numbers. It is barbarism overwhelming civilization by physical force."

Ring also spent fabulous sums on "printing.") In fact, the champion southern thieves of the era were not Radicals but white Democrats hostile to black participation in government. After a Republican administration in Mississippi ran a clean, nearly corruption-free regime, the first post-Reconstruction treasurer of the state absconded with $415,000. This paled compared to the swag usurped by E. A. Burke, the first post-Reconstruction treasurer of Louisiana, who took $1,777,000 with him to Honduras in 1890.

As for the carpetbaggers, many of them brought much-needed capital to the South. They were hot to make money, to be sure, but in the process of developing the South, not as mere exploiters. Many of the scalawags were by no means unlettered "poor white trash," as the legend had it, but southern Whigs who disapproved of secession and who, after the war, drifted naturally, if briefly, into the Republican party that their northern fellow Whigs had joined.

Blacks in Government

The blacks who rose to high office in the Reconstruction governments were rarely ignorant former field hands. Most, at the upper level, were well-educated, refined, even rather conservative men. Moreover, whatever the malfeasances of Radical Reconstruction, the blacks could not be blamed; they never controlled the government of any southern state. For a short time, they were the majority in the legislatures of South Carolina (where blacks were the

NOTABLE PEOPLE

Blacks in Congress

Better a white crook than a black crook; better a white grafter than a black of stature and probity. Such was the view of the "Redeemers," white Democrats who wrested control of southern state governments from the Republican party during Reconstruction. They depicted black officials as incompetent, corrupt, and uninterested in the welfare of the South as a whole. With most southern whites contemptuous of the recently freed slaves, it was an effective appeal. Other issues paled into near invisibility in what seemed the blinding urgency in asserting "white supremacy."

At low levels, many black officeholders were incompetent and self-serving. A few high in state administrations were venal grafters. That their Redeemer challengers were rarely better and often worse did not, however, lend a reflective bent to southern voting behavior. Rather, race was all.

Hiram Revels (left) and Blanche K. Bruce (right), both of Mississippi, were elected to the United States Congress during Reconstruction.

While none of the blacks who sat in Congress in the wake of the Civil War may be said to have been statesmen of the first order, as a group they were as able and worthy a lot as the era's other "ethnic delegations" in the Capitol, any random selection of farmer-congressmen or businessmen-congressmen, any northern or western state delegation of either party, any random selection of 22 Redeemers.

Between 1869 and 1901, 20 blacks served in the House, two in the Senate. South Carolina, where blacks outnumbered whites, sent eight; North Carolina four; Alabama three; and Virginia, Georgia, Florida, Louisiana, and Mississippi one each. Both black senators, Hiram K. Revels and Blanche K. Bruce, represented Mississippi, where potential black voters also outnumbered whites.

Thirteen of the twenty-two had been slaves before the Civil War, the others were lifelong free blacks. Their educational attainment compared well

with that of Congress as a whole. Ten of the black congressmen had gone to college, five had graduated. Six were lawyers (rather less than among all congressmen—nothing for which to apologize); three were preachers; four farmers. Most of the others were skilled artisans, by no means "the dregs of society" as the Redeemers ritually portrayed them.

Hiram Revels was a Methodist pastor. He was born in North Carolina in 1822 but, as a free black, prudently removed to Indiana and Ohio where, during the Civil War, he organized a black regiment. The end of the war found him in Natchez where a cultivated and conservative demeanor (and a willingness to defer to white Republicans) made him an attractive candidate for the Senate.

Blanche K. Bruce was born a slave in 1841, but he was well educated: his owner leased him to a printer. In 1861, he escaped from his apparently lackadaisical master and, in the wake of the Union troops, moved to Mississippi. His record in the Senate was conservative and quiet.

The most durable of the black congressmen was J. H. Rainey of South Carolina. He sat in Congress between 1869 and 1879, winning his last election in the year of the Hayes-Tilden debacle. In most of his district, blacks outnumbered whites by 6 to 1 and 8 to 1. He was retired in the election of 1878 only as a consequence of widespread economic reprisals against black voters and some little violence.

Rainey's parents had bought their freedom long before the Civil War but, in 1862, he was drafted to work on the fortifications in Charleston harbor, a condition that was tantamount to enslavement. However, Rainey escaped to the West Indies and worked his way to the North, returning to his home state early during Reconstruction.

Rainey was indeed vindictive toward the white South, exploiting racial hostilities as nastily as any Redeemer on the other side. Most of the black congressmen were, unsurprisingly, preoccupied with civil rights issues. No doubt, had South Carolina's blacks retained the franchise, Rainey would have exploited racial hostility as destructively as his opponents.

However, Rainey was by no means oblivious to other questions. By the end of the 1870s, he used his modest seniority to work for southern economic interests that transcended the color line. He defended the rights of Chinese in California on conservative "pro-business" Republican, as well as racial, grounds and attempted to improve relations with the black republic of Haiti.

George H. White was the last black to sit in Congress from a southern state before the passage of the Civil Rights Act of 1965. Born a slave in 1852, he attended Howard University in Washington (then a black institution) and practiced law in North Carolina.

In 1896, he won election to the House of Representatives by adding a number of white Populist votes to a black Republican bloc. At the time, some southern Populists, like Thomas Watson of Georgia, preached interracial political cooperation in an attempt to build a solid agrarian front to the "Bourbons" into which the Redeemers had been transformed. Unlike the northern Populists, who fastened on the Republican party as their chief enemy, southern Populists sometimes saw allies in black Republican voters. Their issues were agrarian: almost all southern blacks tilled the soil.

This put black politicians like White in an impossible situation. Preferment in the national Republican party required him to adhere to a line that, under President William McKinley, also elected in 1896, became conservative and imperialistic. White spoke out on behalf of a high tariff—albeit on the grounds that it favored the workingman: "the ox that pulls the plow ought to have a chance to eat the fodder"—and favored the Spanish-American War.

Inevitably, his positions alienated those whites who had helped elect him. Moreover, southern Populism was undergoing a momentous transformation during the late 1890s. Shrewd Democratic party politicians like Benjamin "Pitchfork Ben" Tillman combined a populist appeal to poor whites with an incendiary hatred of blacks.

Racial hatred was the staple of demagogues like Tillman (and, soon enough, Tom Watson in Georgia). However, they also hammered on the fact that southern blacks voted overwhelmingly Republican and that meant a "plutocratic" federal government.

Conservatives like White were easy targets and, in 1898, the North Carolina Populists switched sides, supporting the Democratic candidate and almost ousting White after only one term.

He knew his political future was doomed and compensated for "an organization man's" first term by speaking out loudly during his second about what was happening in the South (while most white Republicans merely shrugged). Only after 1898 did he fasten almost exclusively on civil rights issues, describing himself as "the representative on this floor of 9,000,000 of the population of these United States."

By 1900, black voters in White's district had been reduced to a fragment. He did not even bother to stand for reelection and sure humiliation. Instead, in his farewell speech in 1901, he delivered his finest oration, an eloquent speech that served as the coda to Reconstruction's failure to integrate blacks into the American polity:

These parting words are in behalf of an outraged, heartbroken, bruised and bleeding, but God-fearing people, faithful, industrial, loyal people, rising people, full of potential force. The only apology that I have to make for the earnestness with which I have spoken is that I am pleading for the life, the liberty, the future happiness, and manhood suffrage for one-eighth of the entire population of the United States.

majority of the population) and precisely one-half of the legislature of Louisiana. Only two blacks served as United States senators, Blanche K. Bruce and Hiram Revels, both cultivated men from Mississippi. No black ever served as a governor, although Lieutenant Governor P. B. S. Pinchback of Louisiana briefly acted in that capacity when the white governor was out of the state. Whatever Reconstruction was, its color was not black.

Redemption

The crime of Reconstruction in the eyes of most southern whites was that it allowed blacks the opportunity to participate in government. The experiment failed because black voters were denied an economic foundation on which to build their civil equality, and because northerners soon lost interest in the ideals of the Civil War.

Because few of them owned land, the blacks of the South were dependent on white landowners for their sustenance. When southern landowners concluded that it was to their interest to eliminate the blacks from political life, they could do so by threatening unemployment.

Unprotected former slaves could not command the respect of poorer whites, who provided most of the members of terrorist organizations like the Ku Klux Klan, which was founded in 1866 by former slave trader and Confederate general Nathan Bedford Forrest. These nightriders, identities concealed under hoods, frightened, beat, and even murdered blacks who insisted on voting. Congress outlawed and, within a few years, the army effectively suppressed the Klan and similar organizations like the Knights of the White Camellia, but, in the meantime, many blacks were terrorized into staying home on election day.

Congress was unable to counter the conviction of increasing numbers of white southerners that only through "white supremacy," the slogan of the southern Democratic parties, could the South be redeemed. In most southern states, where whites were the majority, an overwhelming white vote on this issue alone was enough to install legislators and governors who promptly found effective ways to disenfranchise the blacks.

In the North and West, each year that passed saw the deterioration of interest in the rights of southern blacks. At no time had more than a minority of northern whites truly believed blacks to be

their equals. As an era of unprecedented economic expansion unfolded in the wake of the Civil War, and unprecedented scandals rocked the administration of Ulysses S. Grant, to whom the protection of black civil rights was entrusted, support for Reconstruction dwindled. Albion W. Tourgée, a white northerner who fought for black civil equality in North Carolina, wrote that trying to enforce the Fourteenth and Fifteenth Amendments without federal support was "a fool's errand."

THE GRANT ADMINISTRATION

Ulysses S. Grant was the youngest man to be president up to his time, only 46 years of age when he took the oath of office in 1869. In some ways, his appearance remained as unimpressive as when reporters caught him whittling sticks on the battlefield. Stoop-shouldered and taciturn in public, Grant has a peculiar frightened look in his eye in most of the photographs of him, as though he suspected he had risen above his capabilities.

In fact, Grant disliked the duties and power of the presidency. It was the perquisites of living in the White House that he fancied. He took with relish to eating caviar and tournedos sauce béarnaise and sipping the best French wines and cognac. The earthy general whose uniform had looked like that of a slovenly sergeant developed a fondness for expensive, finely tailored clothing.

Indeed, the elegant broadcloth on his back was the emblem of Grant's failure as president. Money and fame came too suddenly to a man who spent his life struggling to get by. Both he and his wife were overwhelmed by the adulation heaped on him. When towns and counties took his name, and when cities made gifts of valuable property and even cash—$100,000 from New York City alone—Grant accepted them with a few mumbled words of thanks. He never fully understood that political gift-givers were actually paying in advance for future favors. Or, if he did understand, he saw nothing wrong in returning kindness with the resources at his disposal. Among the lesser of his errors, he gave federal jobs to any of his and his wife's relatives who asked and they were not bashful about asking. Worse, Grant remained as loyal to them as he was loyal to junior officers in the army. In the military, backing up subordinates when they slip up is a virtue, essential to morale. Grant never quite learned that in politics backing up subordinates who steal is less than admirable.

Black Friday

Grant's friends, old and new, wasted no time in stealing. Unlucky in business himself, the president luxuriated in the flattery lavished on him by wealthy men. In 1869, two unscrupulous speculators, Jay Gould and Jim Fisk, made it a point to be seen in public with the president, schemed secretly with Grant's brother-in-law, Abel R. Corbin, and hatched a plot to corner the nation's gold supply.

Having won Corbin's assurance that he would keep Grant from selling government gold, Gould and Fisk bought up as much gold and gold futures (commitments to buy gold at a future date at a low price) as they could. Their apparent control of the gold market caused the price of the precious metal to soar. In September 1869, gold was bringing $162 an ounce. Gould and Fisk's plan was to dump their holdings and score a killing.

Finally grasping that he was an accomplice to a scam, on Friday, September 24, Grant dumped $4 million in government gold on the market and the price collapsed, but Gould and Fisk suffered very little. Jim Fisk simply refused to honor his commitments to buy at higher than the market price and hired thugs to threaten those who insisted. (High finance could be highly exercising during the Grant years.) But businessmen who needed gold to pay debts and wages were ruined by the hundreds, and thousands of workingmen lost their jobs. The luster of a great general's reputation was tarnished before he was president for a year.

Other Scandals

During the construction of the Union Pacific Railway in the years following the Civil War, the directors of the UP set up a dummy corporation called the Crédit Mobilier. This company charged the UP some $5 million for work that actually cost about $3 million. The difference went into the pockets of Union Pacific executives. Because the UP was heavily subsidized by the federal government, and therefore under close scrutiny, key members of Congress were cut in on the deal. Among the beneficiaries was Schuyler Colfax, who was Grant's vice president. Speaker of the House James A. Garfield also accepted a stipend.

Three of Grant's cabinet appointees were involved in corruption. Carriers under contract to the Post Office Department paid kickbacks in return for exorbitant payments for their services. The secretary of war, William W. Belknap, took bribes from companies that operated trading posts on Indian reservations under his authority. He and his subordinates shut their eyes while the companies defrauded the tribes of goods that they were due under the terms of federal treaties. Grant insisted that Belknap leave his post, but since Belknap was Grant's old crony, the president refused to punish him on behalf of cheated Indians.

Nor did Grant punish his secretary of the treasury, Benjamin Bristow, or his personal secretary, Orville E. Babcock, when he learned that they sold excise stamps to whiskey distillers in St. Louis. Whenever the president came close to losing his patience (which was considerable), Roscoe Conkling or another stalwart reminded him of the importance of party loyalty. Better a few scoundrels escape than party morale be damaged and the Democrats take over.

The Liberal Republicans

Although the full odor of the Grant scandals was loosed only later, enough scent hung in the air in 1872 that a number of prominent Republicans broke openly with the president. Charles Sumner of Massachusetts, a senator since 1851 and chairman of the Senate Foreign Relations Committee, split with the president over Grant's determination to annex the island nation of Santo Domingo to the United States.

Carl Schurz of Missouri and the British-born editor of *The Nation* magazine, E. L. Godkin, were appalled by the steamy atmosphere of corruption in Washington and the treatment of public office as a way of making a living rather than as performing a public service. Schurz and Godkin (although not Sumner) had also given up on Reconstruction, which, whatever his personal sentiments, Grant enforced. Although not necessarily convinced that blacks were inferior to whites, they concluded that ensuring civil rights for blacks was not worth the instability of government in the South, nor the continued presence of troops in the southern states. Better to allow the white redeemers to return to power.

An anti-Reconstruction cartoon depicts the South burdened by military oppression and an evil-looking Grant.

The Election of 1872

This was also the position of the man whom the Liberal Republicans named to run for president in 1872, the editor of the *New York Tribune*, Horace Greeley. He described southern blacks as "simple, credulous, ignorant men," and the carpetbaggers he once encouraged to go south "as stealing and plucking, many of them with both arms around negroes, and their hands in their rear pockets, seeing as they cannot pick a paltry dollar out of them." The freedmen, Greeley and other Liberal Republicans believed, needed the guidance of enlightened gentlemen like himself, or, better than no one, responsible southern whites.

An exciting journalist, Greeley was a terrible choice as a presidential nominee. He was a lifelong eccentric, one of the century's great "nuts." Throughout his 61 years, Greeley clambered aboard almost every reform or fad from abolitionism and women's rights to vegetarianism, spiritualism (communicating with the dead), and phrenology (reading a person's character in the bumps on his or her head).

Even in his appearance, Greeley invited ridicule. He looked like a crackpot with his round, pink face exaggerated by close-set, beady eyes and a wispy fringe of white chin whiskers. He wore an ankle-length overcoat on the hottest days, and carried a brightly colored umbrella on the driest. Sharp-eyed Republican cartoonists like Thomas Nast had an easy time making fun of Greeley.

To make matters worse, Greeley needed the support of the Democrats to make a race of it against Grant, and he proposed to "clasp hands across the bloody chasm." This was asking too much of Republican party regulars. Voters who disapproved of Grant disapproved much more of southern Democrats.

Moreover, throughout his editorial career, Greeley had printed just about every printable vilification of Democrats that the English language offered, especially of southerners. The Democrats did give him their nomination, but southern whites found it difficult to support a lifelong foe. A large black vote for Grant in seven southern states helped give the president a 286-to-66 victory in the electoral college.

Horace Greeley's (1811–1872) eccentric chin whiskers were ridiculed even in an age of fanciful beards.

THE TWILIGHT OF RECONSTRUCTION

The Liberals returned to the Republican party. For all their loathing of the unhappy Grant, upon whom the scandals piled during his second term, the Liberals found their flirtation with the Democrats humiliating. Among them, only Charles Sumner remained true to the cause of the southern blacks. His Civil Rights Act of 1875 (passed a year after his death) guaranteed equal accommodations for blacks in public facilities such as hotels and theaters and forbade the exclusion of blacks from juries. Congress quietly dropped another provision forbidding segregated schools.

The Act of 1875 was the last significant federal attempt to enforce equal rights for the races for 80 years. Not only had northerners lost interest in Civil War idealism, but southern white Democrats had redeemed most of the former Confederacy. By the end of 1875, only three states remained Republican: South Carolina, Florida, and Louisiana.

The Disputed Election

The Democratic candidate in 1876, New York Governor Samuel J. Tilden, called for the removal of troops from these three states, which would bring the white supremacy Democrats to power. The Republican candidate, Governor Rutherford B. Hayes of Ohio, ran on a platform that guaranteed black rights in the South, but Hayes was known to be skeptical of black capabilities and a personal friend of a number of white southern politicians.

When the votes were counted, Hayes's opinions seemed to be beside the point. Tilden won a close popular vote, and he appeared to sweep the electoral college by a vote of 204 to 165. However, Tilden's margin of victory included the electoral votes of South Carolina, Florida, and Louisiana, where Republicans still controlled the state governments. After receiving telegrams from party leaders in New York, officials there declared that in reality Hayes had carried their states. According to these returns, Hayes eked out a 185-to-184 electoral vote victory.

It was not that easy. When official returns reached Washington, there were two sets from each of the three disputed states—one set for Tilden, and one for Hayes. Because the Constitution did not provide for such an occurrence, a special commission was established to decide which set of returns was valid. Five members of each house of Congress and five members of the Supreme Court sat on this panel. Seven of them were Republicans; seven were Democrats; and one, David Davis of Illinois, a Supreme Court justice and once Abraham Lincoln's law partner, was known as an independent. Because no one was interested in determining the case on its merits, each commissioner fully intending to vote for his party's candidate, the burden of naming the next president of the United States fell on Davis's shoulders.

He did not like it. No matter how honestly he came to his decision, half the voters in the country would call for his scalp because he voted down their candidate. Davis prevailed on friends in Illinois to get him off the hook by naming him to a Senate seat then vacant. He resigned from the court and, therefore, the special commission. His replacement was a Republican, and the stage was set for the Republicans to steal the election.

The Compromise of 1877

The commission voted on strict party lines, eight to seven, to accept the Hayes returns from Louisiana, Florida, and South Carolina—thus giving Rutherford B. Hayes the presidency by a single electoral vote. Had that been all there was to it, there might have been further trouble. At a series of meetings, however, a group of prominent northern and southern politicians and businessmen came to an informal agreement that was satisfactory to the political leaders of both sections.

The Compromise of 1877 involved several commitments, not all of them honored, for northern investment in the South. Also not honored was a vague agreement on the part of some conservative southerners to build a lily-white Republican party in the South based on economic and social views that they shared with northern conservatives.

As to the disputed election, Hayes would be permitted to move into the White House without resistance by either northern or southern Democrats. In return, he would withdraw the last troops from South Carolina, Florida, and Louisiana, thus allowing the Democratic party in those states to oust the Republicans and destroy the political power of the blacks.

Despite the proclamations before Inauguration Day that Democrats would fight if Tilden were not elected, there was no trouble. This was not because the men who hammered out the Compromise of 1877 were so very powerful. It merely reflected the growing disinterest of Americans in the issues of the Civil War and Reconstruction and their increasing preoccupation with the fabulous economic growth of the country. Southern blacks, of course, were the casualties of this watershed year, but since the price they paid was suppression, few whites heard their complaints and fewer were interested.

CHRONOLOGY

1863	Lincoln announces his plan for reconstruction
1864	Congress enacts Wade-Davis Bill, its reconstruction plan. Lincoln pocket-vetoes Wade-Davis Bill
1865	Lincoln assassinated; Andrew Johnson is president
1865–1866	Black codes enacted in former slave states; race riots in several southern cities
1866	Johnson vetoes renewal of Freedmen's Bureau Radical Republicans draw up Fourteenth Amendment National Union party formed Republicans win overwhelming victory in congressional elections
1866–1867	Congress draws up and effects reconstruction plan over presidential veto
1868	Johnson impeached and acquitted Grant elected president
1872	Grant easily reelected over Horace Greeley
1876	Uncertain results in presidential election
1877	Rutherford B. Hayes named president by special commission Reconstruction ended in last three states under Republican control

FOR FURTHER READING

James McPherson, *Ordeal by Fire: The Civil War and Reconstruction*, 1982, is the best one-volume account of Reconstruction. Also see Eric Foner, *Reconstruction: America's Unfinished Revolution*, 1988. See William A. Dunning, *Reconstruction: Political and Economic*, 1907, for the old, harshly critical view of the era's policies that dominated American historical thinking for half a century. For a rejoinder, see W. E. B. Du Bois, *Black Reconstruction*, 1935. John Hope Franklin, *Reconstruction after the Civil War*, 1961, provides a more brief, objective account, as does Herman Belz, *Reconstructing the Union*, 1969. A splendid account of the reaction of blacks to freedom is Leon F. Litwack, *Been in the Storm So Long*, 1979. Also valuable are Joel Williamson, *The Crucible of Race: Black-White Relations in the American South Since Emancipation*, 1984; and Michael Perman, *Emancipation and Reconstruction, 1862–1879*, 1987.

Valuable studies of special topics include Richard N. Current, *Three Carpetbag Governors*, 1967; Stanley Kutler, *Judicial Power and Reconstruction Politics*, 1968; George C. Rable, *But There Was No Peace: The Role of Violence in the Politics of Reconstruction*, 1984; Robert C. Morris, *Reading, 'Riting, and Reconstruction: The Education of Freedmen in the South, 1861–1870*, 1981; Willie Lee Rose, *Rehearsal for Reconstruction*, 1964; Hans A. Trefousse, *The Radical Republicans*, 1969; A. W. Trelease, *KKK: The Ku Klux Klan Conspiracy and Southern Reconstruction*, 1971; C. Vann Woodward, *Reunion and Reaction: The Compromise of 1877 and the End of Reconstruction*, 1951; and Gaines M. Foster, *Ghosts of the Confederacy: Defeat, the Lost Cause, and the Emergence of the New South*, 1987.

APPENDIX

The Declaration of Independence

*The Constitution of the
United States of America*

Admission of States

Population of the United States

Presidential Elections

*Presidents, Vice Presidents,
and Cabinet Members*

Justices of the U.S. Supreme Court

*Political Party Affiliations
in Congress and the Presidency*

 Harcourt Online Documents

The Declaration of Independence

THE UNANIMOUS DECLARATION OF THE THIRTEEN UNITED STATES OF AMERICA,

When in the Course of human events it becomes necessary for one people to dissolve the political bands which have connected them with another, and to assume among the Powers of the earth, the separate and equal station to which the Laws of Nature and of Nature's God entitle them, a decent respect to the opinions of mankind requires that they should declare the causes which impel them to the separation.

We hold these truths to be self-evident, that all men are created equal, that they are endowed by their Creator with certain unalienable Rights, that among these are Life, Liberty and the pursuit of Happiness. That to secure these rights, Governments are instituted among Men, deriving their just Powers from the consent of the governed. That whenever any Form of Government becomes destructive of these ends, it is the Right of the People to alter or to abolish it, and to institute new Government, laying its foundation on such principles and organizing its Powers in such form, as to them shall seem most likely to effect their Safety and Happiness. Prudence, indeed, will dictate that Governments long established should not be changed for light and transient causes; and accordingly all experience hath shewn, that mankind are more disposed to suffer, while evils are sufferable, than to right themselves by abolishing the forms to which they are accustomed. But when a long train of abuses and usurpations, pursuing invariably the same Object evinces a design to reduce them under absolute Despotism, it is their right, it is their duty, to throw off such Government, and to provide new Guards for their future security. Such has been the patient sufferance of these Colonies; and such is now the necessity which constrains them to alter their former Systems of Government. The history of the present King of Great Britain is a history of repeated injuries and usurpations, all having in direct object the establishment of an absolute Tyranny over these States. To prove this, let Facts be submitted to a candid world.

He has refused his Assent to Laws, the most wholesome and necessary for the public good.

He has forbidden his Governors to pass Laws of immediate and pressing importance, unless suspended in their operation till his Assent should be obtained; and when so suspended, he has utterly neglected to attend to them.

He has refused to pass other Laws for the accommodation of large districts of people, unless those people would relinquish the right of Representation in the Legislature, a right inestimable to them and formidable to tyrants only.

He has called together legislative bodies at places unusual, uncomfortable, and distant from the depository of their Public Records, for the sole Purpose of fatiguing them into compliance with his measures.

He has dissolved Representative Houses repeatedly, for opposing with manly firmness his invasions on the rights of the People.

He has refused for a long time, after such dissolutions, to cause others to be elected; whereby the Legislative Powers, incapable of Annihilation, have returned to the People at large for their exercise; the State remaining in the mean time exposed to all the dangers of invasion from without, and convulsions within.

He has endeavoured to prevent the Population of these States; for that purpose obstructing the Laws for Naturalization of Foreigners; refusing to pass others to encourage their migrations hither, and raising the conditions of new Appropriations of Lands.

He has obstructed the Administration of Justice, by refusing his Assent to Laws for establishing Judiciary Powers.

He has made Judges dependent on his Will alone, for the tenure of their offices, and the amount and payment of their salaries.

He has erected a multitude of New Offices, and sent hither swarms of Officers to harass our People, and eat out their substance.

He has kept among us, in times of peace, Standing Armies without the Consent of our legislatures.

He has affected to render the Military independent of and superior to the Civil Power.

He has combined with others to subject us to a jurisdiction foreign to our constitution, and unacknowledged by our laws; giving his Assent to their Acts of pretended Legislation:

Text is reprinted from the facsimile of the engrossed copy in the National Archives. The original spelling, capitalization, and punctuation have been retained. Paragraphing has been added.

For Quartering large bodies of armed troops among us:

For protecting them, by a mock Trial, from Punishment for any Murders which they should commit on the Inhabitants of these States:

For cutting off our Trade with all parts of the world:

For imposing Taxes on us without our Consent:

For depriving us in many cases, of the benefits of Trial by Jury:

For transporting us beyond Seas to be tried for pretended offences:

For abolishing the free System of English Laws in a neighbouring Province, establishing therein an Arbitrary government, and enlarging its Boundaries so as to render it at once an example and fit instrument for introducing the same absolute rule into these Colonies:

For taking away our Charters, abolishing our most valuable Laws, and altering fundamentally the Forms of our Governments:

For suspending our own Legislatures, and declaring themselves invested with Power to legislate for us in all cases whatsoever.

He has abdicated Government here, by declaring us out of his Protection, and waging War against us.

He has plundered our seas, ravaged our Coasts, burnt our towns, and destroyed the lives of our people.

He is at this time transporting large Armies of foreign Mercenaries to compleat the works of death, desolation and tyranny, already begun with circumstances of Cruelty and perfidy scarcely paralleled in the most barbarous ages, and totally unworthy the Head of a civilized nation.

He has constrained our fellow Citizens taken Captive on the high Seas to bear Arms against their Country, to become the executioners of their friends and Brethren, or to fall themselves by their Hands.

He has excited domestic insurrections amongst us, and has endeavoured to bring on the inhabitants of our frontiers, the merciless Indian Savages, whose known rule of warfare, is an undistinguished destruction of all ages, sexes and conditions.

In every stage of these Oppressions We have Petitioned for Redress in the most humble terms: Our repeated Petitions have been answered only by repeated injury. A Prince, whose character is thus marked by every act which may define a Tyrant, is unfit to be the ruler of a free People.

Nor have We been wanting in attentions to our British brethren. We have warned them from time to time of attempts by their legislature to extend an unwarrantable jurisdiction over us. We have reminded them of the circumstances of our emigration and settlement here. We have appealed to their native justice and magnanimity, and we have conjured them by the ties of our common kindred to disavow these usurpations, which, would inevitably interrupt our connections and correspondence. They too have been deaf to the voice of justice and of consanguinity. We must, therefore, acquiesce in the necessity, which denounces our Separation, and hold them, as we hold the rest of mankind, Enemies in War, in Peace Friends.

WE, THEREFORE, the Representatives of the UNITED STATES OF AMERICA, in General Congress, Assembled, appealing to the Supreme Judge of the world for the rectitude of our intentions, do, in the Name, and by Authority of the good People of these Colonies, solemnly publish and declare, That these United Colonies are, and of Right ought to be FREE AND INDEPENDENT STATES; that they are Absolved from all Allegiance to the British Crown, and that all political connection between them and the State of Great Britain, is and ought to be totally dissolved; and that, as Free and Independent States, they have full Power to levy War, conclude Peace, contract Alliances, establish Commerce, and to do all other Acts and Things which Independent States may of right do. And for the support of this Declaration, with a firm reliance on the protection of divine Providence, we mutually pledge to each other our Lives, our Fortunes and our sacred Honor.

The Constitution of the United States of America

We the People of the United States, in Order to form a more perfect Union, establish Justice, insure domestic Tranquility, provide for the common defence, promote the general Welfare, and secure the Blessings of Liberty to ourselves and our Posterity, do ordain and establish this Constitution for the United States of America.

Article. I.

Section. 1. All legislative Powers herein granted shall be vested in a Congress of the United States, which shall consist of a Senate and House of Representatives.

Section. 2. The House of Representatives shall be composed of Members chosen every second Year by the People of the several States, and the Electors in each State shall have the Qualifications requisite for Electors of the most numerous Branch of the State Legislature.

No Person shall be a Representative who shall not have attained to the Age of twenty five Years, and been seven Years a Citizen of the United States, and who shall not, when elected, be an Inhabitant of that State in which he shall be chosen.

Representatives and direct Taxes[1] shall be apportioned among the several States which may be included within this Union, according to their respective Numbers, which shall be determined by adding to the whole Number of free Persons, including those bound to Service for a Term of Years, and excluding Indians not taxed, three fifths of all other Persons.[2] The actual Enumeration shall be made within three Years after the first Meeting of the Congress of the United States, and within every subsequent Term of ten Years, in such Manner as they shall by Law direct. The Number of Representatives shall not exceed one for every thirty Thousand, but each State shall have at Least one Representative; and until such enumeration shall be made, the State of New Hampshire shall be entitled to chuse three; Massachusetts eight; Rhode Island and Providence Plantations one; Connecticut five; New York six; New Jersey four; Pennsylvania eight; Delaware one; Maryland six; Virginia ten; North Carolina five; South Carolina five; and Georgia three.

When vacancies happen in the Representation from any State, the Executive Authority thereof shall issue Writs of Election to fill such Vacancies.

The House of Representatives shall chuse their Speaker and other Officers; and shall have the sole Power of Impeachment.

Section. 3. The Senate of the United States shall be composed of two Senators from each State, chosen by the Legislature thereof, for six Years; and each Senator shall have one Vote.[3]

Immediately after they shall be assembled in Consequence of the first Election, they shall be divided as equally as may be into three Classes. The Seats of the Senators of the first Class shall be vacated at the Expiration of the second Year, of the second Class at the Expiration of the fourth Year, and of the third Class at the Expiration of the sixth Year, so that one third may be chosen every second Year; and if Vacancies happen by Resignation, or otherwise, during the Recess of the Legislature of any State, the Executive thereof may make temporary Appointments until the next Meeting of the Legislature, which shall then fill such Vacancies.[4]

No Person shall be a Senator who shall not have attained to the Age of thirty Years, and been nine Years a Citizen of the United States, and who shall not, when elected, be an Inhabitant of that State for which he shall be chosen.

The Vice President of the United States shall be President of the Senate, but shall have no Vote, unless they be equally divided.

The Senate shall chuse their other Officers, and also a President pro tempore, in the Absence of the Vice President, or when he shall exercise the Office of President of the United States.

The Senate shall have the sole Power to try all Impeachments. When sitting for that Purpose, they shall be on Oath or Affirmation. When the President of the United States is tried, the Chief Justice shall preside:

Text is from the engrossed copy in the National Archives. Original spelling, capitalization, and punctuation have been retained.

[1]Modified by the Sixteenth Amendment.

[2]Replaced by the Fourteenth Amendment.

[3]Superseded by the Seventeenth Amendment.

[4]Modified by the Seventeenth Amendment.

And no Person shall be convicted without the Concurrence of two thirds of the Members present.

Judgment in Cases of Impeachment shall not extend further than to removal from Office, and disqualification to hold and enjoy any Office of honor, Trust or Profit under the United States: but the Party convicted shall nevertheless be liable and subject to Indictment, Trial, Judgment and Punishment, according to Law.
Section. 4. The Times, Places and Manner of holding Elections for Senators and Representatives, shall be prescribed in each State by the Legislature thereof, but the Congress may at any time by Law make or alter such Regulation, except as to the Places of chusing Senators.

The Congress shall assemble at least once in every Year, and such Meeting shall be on the first Monday in December, unless they shall by Law appoint a different Day.[5]
Section. 5. Each House shall be the Judge of the Elections, Returns and Qualifications of its own Members, and a Majority of each shall constitute a Quorum to do Business; but a smaller Number may adjourn from day to day, and may be authorized to compel the Attendance of absent Members, in such Manner, and under such Penalties as each House may provide.

Each House may determine the Rules of its Proceedings, punish its Members for disorderly Behaviour, and, with the Concurrence of two thirds, expel a Member.

Each House shall keep a Journal of its Proceedings, and from time to time publish the same, excepting such Parts as may in their Judgment require Secrecy; and the Yeas and Nays of the Members of either House on any question shall, at the Desire of one fifth of those Present, be entered on the Journal.

Neither House, during the Session of Congress, shall, without the Consent of the other, adjourn for more than three days, nor to any other Place than that in which the two Houses shall be sitting.
Section. 6. The Senators and Representatives shall receive a Compensation for their Services, to be ascertained by Law, and paid out of the Treasury of the United States. They shall in all Cases, except Treason, Felony and Breach of the Peace, be privileged from Arrest during their Attendance at the Session of their respective Houses, and in going to and returning from the same; and for any Speech or Debate in either House, they shall not be questioned in any other Place.

No Senator or Representative shall, during the Time for which he was elected, be appointed to any civil Office under the Authority of the United States, which shall have been created, or the Emoluments whereof shall have been encreased during such time; and no Person holding any Office under the United States, shall be a Member of either House during his Continuance in Office.
Section. 7. All Bills for raising Revenue shall originate in the House of Representatives; but the Senate may propose or concur with Amendments as on other Bills.

Every Bill which shall have passed the House of Representatives and the Senate shall, before it become a Law, be presented to the President of the United States; If he approve he shall sign it, but if not he shall return it, with his Objections to that House in which it shall have originated, who shall enter the Objections at large on their Journal, and proceed to reconsider it. If after such Reconsideration two thirds of that House shall agree to pass the Bill, it shall be sent, together with the Objections, to the other House, by which it shall likewise be reconsidered, and if approved by two thirds of that House, it shall become a Law. But in all such Cases the Votes of both Houses shall be determined by yeas and Nays, and the Names of the Persons voting for and against the Bill shall be entered on the Journal of each House respectively. If any Bill shall not be returned by the President within ten Days (Sundays excepted) after it shall have been presented to him, the Same shall be a Law, in like Manner as if he had signed it, unless the Congress by their Adjournment prevent its Return, in which Case it shall not be a Law.

Every Order, Resolution, or Vote to which the Concurrence of the Senate and House of Representatives may be necessary (except on a question of Adjournment) shall be presented to the President of the United States; and before the Same shall take Effect, shall be approved by him, or being disapproved by him shall be repassed by two thirds of the Senate and House of Representatives, according to the Rules and Limitations prescribed in the Case of a Bill.
Section. 8. The Congress shall have power To lay and collect Taxes, Duties, Imposts and Excises, to pay the Debts and provide for the common Defence and general Welfare of the United States; but all Duties, Imposts and Excises shall be uniform throughout the United States;

To borrow Money on the credit of the United States;

To regulate Commerce with foreign Nations, and among the several States, and with the Indian Tribes;

To establish an uniform Rule of Naturalization, and uniform Laws on the subject of Bankruptcies throughout the United States;

---

[5]Superseded by the Twentieth Amendment.

To coin Money, regulate the Value thereof, and of foreign Coin, and fix the Standard of Weights and Measures;

To provide for the Punishment of counterfeiting the Securities and current Coin of the United States;

To establish Post Offices and post Roads;

To promote the Progress of Science and useful Arts, by securing for limited Times to Authors and Inventors the exclusive Right to their respective Writings and Discoveries;

To constitute Tribunals inferior to the Supreme Court;

To define and punish Piracies and Felonies committed on the high Seas, and Offences against the Law of Nations;

To declare War, grant Letters of Marque and Reprisal, and make Rules concerning Captures on Land and Water;

To raise and support Armies, but no Appropriation of Money to that Use shall be for a longer Term than two Years;

To provide and maintain a Navy;

To make Rules for the Government and Regulation of the land and naval Forces;

To provide for calling forth the Militia to execute the Laws of the Union, suppress Insurrections and repel Invasions;

To provide for organizing, arming, and disciplining, the Militia, and for governing such Part of them as may be employed in the Service of the United States, reserving to the States respectively, the Appointment of the Officers, and the Authority of training the Militia according to the discipline prescribed by Congress;

To exercise exclusive Legislation in all Cases whatsoever, over such District (not exceeding ten Miles square) as may, by Cession of particular States, and the Acceptance of Congress, become the Seat of the Government of the United States, and to exercise like Authority over all Places purchased by the Consent of the Legislature of the State in which the Same shall be, for the Erection of Forts, Magazines, Arsenals, dock-Yards, and other needful Buildings;—And

To make all Laws which shall be necessary and proper for carrying into Execution the foregoing Powers, and all other Powers vested by this Constitution in the Government of the United States, or in any Department or Officer thereof.

Section. 9. The Migration or Importation of such Persons as any of the States now existing shall think proper to admit, shall not be prohibited by the Congress prior to the Year one thousand eight hundred and eight, but a Tax or duty may be imposed on such Importation, not exceeding ten dollars for each Person.

The Privilege of the Writ of Habeas Corpus shall not be suspended, unless when in Cases of Rebellion or Invasion the public Safety may require it.

No Bill of Attainder or ex post facto Law shall be passed.

No Capitation, or other direct, Tax shall be laid, unless in Proportion to the Census or Enumeration herein before directed to be taken.

No Tax or Duty shall be laid on Articles exported from any State.

No Preference shall be given by any Regulation of Commerce or Revenue to the Ports of one State over those of another: nor shall Vessels bound to, or from, one State, be obliged to enter, clear, or pay Duties in another.

No Money shall be drawn from the Treasury, but in Consequence of Appropriations made by Law, and a regular Statement and Account of the Receipts and Expenditures of all public Money shall be published from time to time.

No Title of Nobility shall be granted by the United States: And no Person holding any Office of Profit or Trust under them, shall, without the Consent of the Congress, accept of any present, Emolument, Office, or Title, of any kind whatever, from any King, Prince, or foreign State.

Section. 10. No State shall enter into any Treaty, Alliance, or Confederation; grant Letters of Marque and Reprisal; coin Money; emit Bills of Credit; make any Thing but gold and silver Coin a Tender in Payment of Debts; pass any Bill of Attainder, ex post facto Law, or Law impairing the Obligation of Contracts, or grant any Title of Nobility.

No State shall, without the Consent of the Congress, lay any Imposts or Duties on Imports or Exports, except what may be absolutely necessary for executing its inspection Laws: and the net Produce of all Duties and Imposts, laid by any State on Imports or Exports, shall be for the Use of the Treasury of the United States; and all such Laws shall be subject to the Revision and Controul of the Congress.

No State shall, without the Consent of Congress, lay any Duty of Tonnage, keep Troops, or Ships of War in time of Peace, enter into any Agreement or Compact with another State, or with a foreign Power, or engage in War, unless actually invaded, or in such imminent Danger as will not admit of delay.

Article. II.

Section. 1. The executive Power shall be vested in a President of the United States of America. He shall hold his Office during the Term of four Years, and, together with the Vice President, chosen for the same Term, be elected, as follows:

Each State shall appoint, in such Manner as the Legislature thereof may direct, a Number of Electors, equal to the whole Number of Senators and Representatives to which the State may be entitled in the Congress: but no Senator or Representative, or Person holding an Office of Trust or Profit under the United States, shall be appointed an Elector.

The Electors shall meet in their respective States, and vote by Ballot for two Persons, of whom one at least shall not be an Inhabitant of the same State with themselves. And they shall make a List of all the Persons voted for, and of the Number of Votes for each; which List they shall sign and certify, and transmit sealed to the Seat of the Government of the United States, directed to the President of the Senate. The President of the Senate shall, in the Presence of the Senate and House of Representatives, open all the Certificates, and the Votes shall then be counted. The Person having the greatest Number of Votes shall be the President, if such Number be a Majority of the whole Number of Electors appointed; and if there be more than one who have such Majority, and have an equal Number of Votes, then the House of Representatives shall immediately chuse by Ballot one of them for President; and if no Person have a Majority, then from the five highest on the List the said House shall in like Manner chuse the President. But in chusing the President, the Votes shall be taken by States, the Representation from each State having one Vote; A quorum for this Purpose shall consist of a Member or Members from two thirds of the States, and a Majority of all the States shall be necessary to a Choice. In every Case, after the Choice of the President, the Person having the greatest Number of Votes of the Electors shall be the Vice President. But if there should remain two or more who have equal Votes, the Senate shall chuse from them by Ballot the Vice President.[6]

The Congress may determine the Time of chusing the Electors, and the Day on which they shall give their Votes; which Day shall be the same throughout the United States.

No Person except a natural born Citizen, or a Citizen of the United States, at the time of the Adoption of this Constitution, shall be eligible to the Office of President, neither shall any Person be eligible to that Office who shall not have attained to the Age of thirty five Years, and been fourteen Years a Resident within the United States.

In Case of the Removal of the President from Office, or of his Death, Resignation, or Inability to discharge the Powers and Duties of the said Office, the Same shall devolve on the Vice President, and the Congress may by Law provide for the Case of Removal, Death, Resignation or Inability, both of the President and Vice President, declaring what Officer shall then act as President, and such Officer shall act accordingly, until the Disability be removed, or a President shall be elected.[7]

The President shall, at stated Times, receive for his Services, a Compensation, which shall neither be encreased nor diminished during the Period for which he shall have been elected, and he shall not receive within that Period any other Emolument from the United States, or any of them.

Before he enter on the Execution of his Office, he shall take the following Oath or Affirmation:—"I do solemnly swear (or affirm) that I will faithfully execute the Office of President of the United States, and will to the best of my Ability, preserve, protect and defend the Constitution of the United States."

Section. 2. The President shall be Commander in Chief of the Army and Navy of the United States, and of the Militia of the several States, when called into the actual Service of the United States; he may require the Opinion, in writing, of the principal Officer in each of the executive Departments, upon any Subject relating to the Duties of their respective Offices, and he shall have Power to grant Reprieves and Pardons for Offences against the United States, except in Cases of Impeachment.

He shall have Power, by and with the Advice and Consent of the Senate, to make Treaties, provided two thirds of the Senators present concur; and he shall nominate, and by and with the Advice and Consent of the Senate, shall appoint Ambassadors, other public Ministers and Consuls, Judges of the supreme Court, and all other Officers of the United States, whose Appointments are not herein otherwise provided for, and which shall be established by Law; but the Congress may by Law vest the Appointment of such inferior Officers, as they think proper, in the President alone, in the Courts of Law, or in the Heads of Departments.

The President shall have Power to fill up all Vacancies that may happen during the Recess of the Senate, by granting Commissions which shall expire at the End of their next Session.

Section. 3. He shall from time to time give the Congress Information of the State of the Union, and recommend to their Consideration such Measures as he

---

[6]Superseded by the Twelfth Amendment.

[7]Modified by the Twenty-fifth Amendment.

shall judge necessary and expedient; he may, on extraordinary Occasions, convene both Houses, or either of them, and in Case of Disagreement between them, with Respect to the Time of Adjournment, he may adjourn them to such Time as he shall think proper; he shall receive Ambassadors and other public Ministers; he shall take Care that the Laws be faithfully executed, and shall Commission all the Officers of the United States.

Section. 4. The President, Vice President and all civil Officers of the United States, shall be removed from Office on Impeachment for, and Conviction of, Treason, Bribery, or other high Crimes and Misdemeanors.

Article. III.

Section. 1. The judicial Power of the United States, shall be vested in one supreme Court, and in such inferior Courts as the Congress may from time to time ordain and establish. The Judges, both of the supreme and inferior Courts, shall hold their Offices during good Behaviour, and shall, at stated Times, receive for their Services, a Compensation, which shall not be diminished during their Continuance in Office.

Section. 2. The judicial Power shall extend to all Cases, in Law and Equity, arising under this Constitution, the Laws of the United States, and Treaties made, or which shall be made, under their Authority;—to all Cases affecting Ambassadors, other public Ministers and Consuls;—to all Cases of admiralty and maritime Jurisdiction;—to Controversies to which the United States shall be a Party;—to Controversies between two or more States;—between a State and Citizens of another State;[8]—between Citizens of different States,—between Citizens of the same State claiming Lands under Grants of different States, and between a State, or the Citizens thereof, and foreign States, Citizens or Subjects.

In all Cases affecting Ambassadors, other public Ministers and Consuls, and those in which a State shall be Party, the supreme Court shall have original Jurisdiction. In all the other Cases before mentioned, the supreme Court shall have appellate Jurisdiction, both as to Law and Fact, with such Exceptions, and under such Regulations as the Congress shall make.

The Trial of all Crimes, except in Cases of Impeachment, shall be by Jury; and such Trial shall be held in the State where the said Crimes shall have been committed; but when not committed within any State, the Trial shall be at such Place or Places as the Congress may by Law have directed.

Section. 3. Treason against the United States, shall consist only in levying War against them, or in adhering to their Enemies, giving them Aid and Comfort. No Person shall be convicted of Treason unless on the Testimony of two Witnesses to the same overt Act, or on Confession in open Court.

The Congress shall have Power to declare the Punishment of Treason, but no Attainder of Treason shall work Corruption of Blood, or Forfeiture except during the Life of the Person attainted.

Article. IV.

Section. 1. Full Faith and Credit shall be given in each State to the public Acts, Records, and judicial Proceedings of every other State. And the Congress may by general Laws prescribe the Manner in which such Acts, Records and Proceedings shall be proved, and the Effect thereof.

Section. 2. The Citizens of each State shall be entitled to all Privileges and Immunities of Citizens in the several States.

A Person charged in any State with Treason, Felony, or other Crime, who shall flee from Justice, and be found in another State, shall on Demand of the executive Authority of the State from which he fled, be delivered up, to be removed to the State having Jurisdiction of the Crime.

No Person held to Service or Labour in one State, under the Laws thereof, escaping into another, shall, in Consequence of any Law or Regulation therein, be discharged from such Service or Labour, but shall be delivered up on Claim of the Party to whom such Service or Labour may be due.

Section. 3. New States may be admitted by the Congress into this Union; but no new State shall be formed or erected within the Jurisdiction of any other State, nor any State be formed by the Junction of two or more States, or Parts of States, without the Consent of the Legislatures of the States concerned as well as of the Congress.

The Congress shall have Power to dispose of and make all needful Rules and Regulations respecting the Territory or other Property belonging to the United States; and nothing in this Constitution shall be so construed as to Prejudice any Claims of the United States, or of any particular State.

Section. 4. The United States shall guarantee to every State in this Union a Republican Form of Government, and shall protect each of them against Invasion; and on Application of the Legislature, or of the Executive (when the Legislature cannot be convened) against domestic Violence.

---

[8]Modified by the Eleventh Amendment.

Article. V.

The Congress, whenever two thirds of both Houses shall deem it necessary, shall propose Amendments to this Constitution, or, on the Application of the Legislatures of two thirds of the several States, shall call a Convention for proposing Amendments, which, in either Case, shall be valid to all Intents and Purposes, as Part of this Constitution, when ratified by the Legislatures of three fourths of the several States, or by Conventions in three fourths thereof, as the one or the other Mode of Ratification may be proposed by the Congress; Provided that no Amendment which may be made prior to the Year One thousand eight hundred and eight shall in any Manner affect the first and fourth Clauses in the Ninth Section of the first Article; and that no State, without its Consent, shall be deprived of its equal Suffrage in the Senate.

Article. VI.

All Debts contracted and Engagements entered into, before the Adoption of this Constitution, shall be as valid against the United States under this Constitution, as under the Confederation.

This Constitution, and the Laws of the United States which shall be made in Pursuance thereof; and all Treaties made, or which shall be made, under the Authority of the United States, shall be the supreme Law of the Land; and the Judges in every State shall be bound thereby, any Thing in the Constitution or Laws of any State to the Contrary notwithstanding.

The Senators and Representatives before mentioned, and the Members of the several State Legislatures, and all executive and judicial Officers, both of the United States and of the several States, shall be bound by Oath or Affirmation, to support this Constitution; but no religious Test shall ever be required as a Qualification to any Office or public Trust under the United States.

Article. VII.

The Ratification of the Conventions of nine States, shall be sufficient for the Establishment of this Constitution between the States so ratifying the Same.
Done in Convention by the Unanimous Consent of the States present the Seventeenth Day of September in the Year of our Lord one thousand seven hundred and Eighty seven and of the Independence of the United States of America the Twelfth. **In witness** whereof We have hereunto subscribed our Names,

Articles in Addition to, and Amendment of, the Constitution of the United States of America, Proposed by Congress, and Ratified by the Legislatures of the Several States, Pursuant to the Fifth Article of the Original Constitution.

Amendment I[9]

Congress shall make no law respecting an establishment of religion, or prohibiting the free exercise thereof; or abridging the freedom of speech, or of the press; or the right of the people peaceably to assemble, and to petition the Government for a redress of grievances.

Amendment II

A well regulated Militia, being necessary to the security of a free State, the right of the people to keep and bear Arms shall not be infringed.

Amendment III

No Soldier shall, in time of peace, be quartered in any house, without the consent of the Owner, nor in time of war, but in a manner to be prescribed by law.

Amendment IV

The right of the people to be secure in their persons, houses, papers, and effects, against unreasonable searches and seizures, shall not be violated, and no Warrants shall issue, but upon probable cause, supported by Oath or affirmation, and particularly describing the place to be searched, and the persons or things to be seized.

Amendment V

No person shall be held to answer for a capital or otherwise infamous crime, unless on a presentment or indictment of a Grand Jury, except in cases arising in the land or naval forces, or in the Militia, when in actual service in time of War or public danger; nor shall any person be subject for the same offence to be twice put in jeopardy of life or limb; nor shall be compelled in any criminal case to be a witness against himself, nor be deprived of life, liberty, or property, without due process of law; nor shall private property be taken for public use, without just compensation.

---

[9] The first ten amendments were passed by Congress September 25, 1789. They were ratified by three-fourths of the states December 15, 1791.

Amendment VI

In all criminal prosecutions, the accused shall enjoy the right to a speedy and public trial, by an impartial jury of the State and district wherein the crime shall have been committed, which district shall have been previously ascertained by law, and to be informed of the nature and cause of the accusation; to be confronted with the witnesses against him; to have compulsory process for obtaining witnesses in his favor, and to have the Assistance of Counsel for his defence.

Amendment VII

In suits at common law, where the value in controversy shall exceed twenty dollars, the right of trial by jury shall be preserved, and no fact tried by a jury, shall be otherwise reexamined in any Court of the United States, than according to the rules of the common law.

Amendment VIII

Excessive bail shall not be required, nor excessive fines imposed, nor cruel and unusual punishments inflicted.

Amendment IX

The enumeration in the Constitution, of certain rights, shall not be construed to deny or disparage others retained by the people.

Amendment X

The powers not delegated to the United States by the Constitution; nor prohibited by it to the States, are reserved to the States respectively, or to the people.

Amendment XI[10]

The Judicial power of the United States shall not be construed to extend to any suit in law or equity, commenced or prosecuted against one of the United States by Citizens of another State, or by Citizens or Subjects of any Foreign State.

Amendment XII[11]

The Electors shall meet in their respective States and vote by ballot for President and Vice-President, one of whom, at least, shall not be an inhabitant of the same State with themselves; they shall name in their ballots the person voted for as President, and in distinct ballots the person voted for as Vice-President, and they shall make distinct lists of all persons voted for as President, and of all persons voted for as Vice-President, and of the number of votes for each, which lists they shall sign and certify, and transmit sealed to the seat of the government of the United States, directed to the President of the Senate;—The President of the Senate shall, in the presence of the Senate and House of Representatives, open all the certificates and the votes shall then be counted;—The person having the greatest number of votes for President, shall be the President, if such number be a majority of the whole number of Electors appointed; and if no person have such majority, then from the persons having the highest numbers not exceeding three on the list of those voted for as President, the House of Representatives shall choose immediately, by ballot, the President. But in choosing the President, the votes shall be taken by states, the representation from each state having one vote; a quorum for this purpose shall consist of a member or members from two-thirds of the states, and a majority of all the states shall be necessary to a choice. And if the House of Representatives shall not choose a President whenever the right of choice shall devolve upon them, before the fourth day of March next following, then the Vice-President shall act as President, as in the case of the death or other constitutional disability of the President.—The person having the greatest number of votes as Vice-President, shall be the Vice-President, if such number be a majority of the whole number of Electors appointed, and if no person have a majority, then from the two highest numbers on the list, the Senate shall choose the Vice-President; a quorum for the purpose shall consist of two-thirds of the whole number of Senators, and a majority of the whole number shall be necessary to a choice. But no person constitutionally ineligible to the office of President shall be eligible to that of Vice-President of the United States.

Amendment XIII[12]

SECTION 1. Neither slavery nor involuntary servitude, except as a punishment for crime whereof the party shall have been duly convicted, shall exist within the United States, or any place subject to their jurisdiction.

---

[10]Passed March 4, 1794. Ratified January 23, 1795.

[11]Passed December 9, 1803. Ratified June 15, 1804.

[12]Passed January 31, 1865. Ratified December 6, 1865.

SECTION 2. Congress shall have power to enforce this article by appropriate legislation.

Amendment XIV[13]

SECTION 1. All persons born or naturalized in the United States, and subject to the jurisdiction thereof, are citizens of the United States and of the State wherein they reside. No State shall make or enforce any law which shall abridge the privileges or immunities of citizens of the United States; nor shall any State deprive any person of life, liberty, or property, without due process of law; nor deny to any person within its jurisdiction the equal protection of the laws.

SECTION 2. Representatives shall be apportioned among the several States according to their respective numbers, counting the whole number of persons in each State, excluding Indians not taxed. But when the right to vote at any election for the choice of electors for President and Vice-President of the United States, Representatives in Congress, the Executive and Judicial officers of a State, or the members of the Legislature thereof, is denied to any of the male inhabitants of such State, being twenty-one years of age, and citizens of the United States, or in any way abridged, except for participation in rebellion, or other crime, the basis of representation therein shall be reduced in the proportion which the number of such male citizens shall bear to the whole number of male citizens twenty-one years of age in such State.

SECTION 3. No person shall be a Senator or Representative in Congress, or elector of President and Vice-President, or hold any office, civil or military, under the United States, or under any State, who, having previously taken an oath, as a member of Congress, or as an officer of the United States, or as a member of any State legislature, or as an executive or judicial officer of any State, to support the Constitution of the United States, shall have engaged in insurrection or rebellion against the same, or given aid or comfort to the enemies thereof. But Congress may by a vote of two-thirds of each House, remove such disability.

SECTION 4. The validity of the public debt of the United States, authorized by law, including debts incurred for payment of pensions and bounties for services in suppressing insurrection or rebellion, shall not be questioned. But neither the United States nor any State shall assume or pay any debt or obligation incurred in aid of insurrection or rebellion against the United States, or any claim for the loss or emancipation of any slave; but all such debts, obligations, and claims shall be held illegal and void.

SECTION 5. The Congress shall have the power to enforce, by appropriate legislation, the provisions of this article.

Amendment XV[14]

SECTION 1. The right of citizens of the United States to vote shall not be denied or abridged by the United States or by any State on account of race, color, or previous conditions of servitude—

SECTION 2. The Congress shall have power to enforce this article by appropriate legislation.

Amendment XVI

The Congress shall have power to lay and collect taxes on incomes, from whatever source derived, without apportionment among the several States, and without regard to any census or enumeration.

Amendment XVII[15]

The Senate of the United States shall be composed of two Senators from each State, elected by the people thereof, for six years; and each Senator shall have one vote. The electors in each State shall have the qualifications requisite for electors of the most numerous branch of the State legislatures.

When vacancies happen in the representation of any State in the Senate, the executive authority of such State shall issue writs of election to fill such vacancies: *Provided*, That the legislature of any State may empower the executive thereof to make temporary appointments until the people fill the vacancies by election as the legislature may direct.

This amendment shall not be so construed as to affect the election or term of any Senator chosen before it becomes valid as part of the Constitution.

Amendment XVIII[16]

SECTION 1. After one year from the ratification of this article the manufacture, sale, or transportation of intoxicating liquors within, the importation thereof into, or the exportation thereof from the United States and all territory subject to the jurisdiction thereof for beverage purposes is hereby prohibited.

---

[13]Passed June 13, 1866. Ratified July 9, 1868.

[14]Passed February 26, 1869. Ratified February 2, 1870.

[15]Passed May 13, 1912. Ratified April 8, 1913.

[16]Passed December 18, 1917. Ratified January 16, 1919.

SECTION 2. The Congress and the several States shall have concurrent power to enforce this article by appropriate legislation.

SECTION 3. This article shall be inoperative unless it shall have been ratified as an amendment to the Constitution by the legislatures of the several States, as provided in the Constitution, within seven years from the date of the submission hereof to the States by the Congress.

Amendment XIX[17]

The right of citizens of the United States to vote shall not be denied or abridged by the United States or by any State on account of sex.

Congress shall have power to enforce this article by appropriate legislation.

Amendment XX[18]

SECTION 1. The terms of the President and Vice-President shall end at noon on the 20th day of January, and the terms of Senators and Representatives at noon on the 3d day of January, of the years in which such terms would have ended if this article had not been ratified; and the terms of their successors shall then begin.

SECTION 2. The Congress shall assemble at least once in every year, and such meeting shall begin at noon on the 3d day of January, unless they shall by law appoint a different day.

SECTION 3. If, at the time fixed for the beginning of the term of the President, the President elect shall have died, the Vice-President elect shall become President. If a President shall not have been chosen before the time fixed for the beginning of his term, or if the President elect shall have failed to qualify, then the Vice-President elect shall act as President until a President shall have qualified; and the Congress may by law provide for the case wherein neither a President elect nor a Vice-President elect shall have qualified, declaring who shall then act as President, or the manner in which one who is to act shall be selected, and such person shall act accordingly until a President or Vice-President shall have qualified.

SECTION 4. The Congress may by law provide for the case of the death of any of the persons from whom the House of Representatives may choose a President whenever the right of choice shall have devolved upon them, and for the case of the death of any of the persons from whom the Senate may choose a Vice-President whenever the right of choice shall have devolved upon them.

SECTION 5. Sections 1 and 2 shall take effect on the 15th day of October following the ratification of this article.

SECTION 6. This article shall be inoperative unless it shall have been ratified as an amendment to the Constitution by the legislatures of three-fourths of the several States within seven years from the date of its submission.

Amendment XXI[19]

SECTION 1. The eighteenth article of amendment to the Constitution of the United States is hereby repealed.

SECTION 2. The transportation or importation into any State, Territory, or possession of the United States for delivery or use therein of intoxicating liquors, in violation of the laws thereof, is hereby prohibited.

SECTION 3. This article shall be inoperative unless it shall have been ratified as an amendment to the Constitution by conventions in the several States, as provided in the Constitution, within seven years from the date of the submission hereof to the States by the Congress.

Amendment XXII[20]

No person shall be elected to the office of the President more than twice, and no person who has held the office of President, or acted as President, for more than two years of a term to which some other person was elected President shall be elected to the office of the President more than once.

But this Article shall not apply to any person holding the office of President when this Article was proposed by the Congress, and shall not prevent any person who may be holding the office of President, or acting as President, during the term within which this Article becomes operative from holding the office of President or acting as President during the remainder of such term.

Amendment XXIII[21]

SECTION 1. The District constituting the seat of Government of the United States shall appoint in such manner as the Congress may direct:

---

[17] Passed June 4, 1919. Ratified August 18, 1920.

[18] Passed March 2, 1932. Ratified January 23, 1933.

[19] Passed February 20, 1933. Ratified December 5, 1933.

[20] Passed March 12, 1947. Ratified March 1, 1951.

[21] Passed June 16, 1960. Ratified April 3, 1961.

A number of electors of President and Vice President equal to the whole number of Senators and Representatives in Congress to which the District would be entitled if it were a State, but in no event more than the least populous State; they shall be in addition to those appointed by the States, but they shall be considered, for the purposes of the election of President and Vice President, to be electors appointed by the State; and they shall meet in the District and perform such duties as provided by the twelfth article of amendment.

SECTION 2. The Congress shall have power to enforce this article by appropriate legislation.

Amendment XXIV[22]

SECTION 1. The right of citizens of the United States to vote in any primary or other election for President or Vice President, or for Senator or Representative in Congress, shall not be denied or abridged by the United States or any State by reason of failure to pay any poll tax or other tax.

SECTION 2. The Congress shall have power to enforce this article by appropriate legislation.

Amendment XXV[23]

SECTION 1. In case of the removal of the President from office or of his death or resignation, the Vice President shall become President.

SECTION 2. Whenever there is a vacancy in the office of the Vice President, the President shall nominate a Vice President who shall take office upon confirmation by a majority vote of both Houses of Congress.

SECTION 3. Whenever the President transmits to the President pro tempore of the Senate and the Speaker of the House of Representatives his written declaration that he is unable to discharge the powers and duties of his office, and until he transmits them a written declaration to the contrary, such powers and duties shall be discharged by the Vice President as Acting President.

SECTION 4. Whenever the Vice President and a majority of either the principal officers of the executive department or of such other body as Congress may by law provide, transmit to the President pro tempore of the Senate and the Speaker of the House of Representatives their written declaration that the President is unable to discharge the powers and duties of his office, the Vice President shall immediately assume the powers and duties of the office of Acting President.

Thereafter, when the President transmits to the President pro tempore of the Senate and the Speaker of the House of Representatives his written declaration that no inability exists, he shall resume the powers and duties of his office unless the Vice President and a majority of either the principal officers of the executive department or of such other body as Congress may by law provide, transmit within four days to the President pro tempore of the Senate and the Speaker of the House of Representatives their written declaration that the President is unable to discharge the powers and duties of his office. Thereupon Congress shall decide the issue, assembling within forty-eight hours for that purpose if not in session. If the Congress, within twenty-one days after receipt of the latter written declaration, or, if Congress is not in session, within twenty-one days after Congress is required to assemble, determines by two-thirds vote of both Houses that the President is unable to discharge the powers and duties of his office, the Vice President shall continue to discharge the same as Acting President; otherwise, the President shall resume the powers and duties of his office.

Amendment XXVI[24]

SECTION 1. The right of citizens of the United States, who are eighteen years of age or older, to vote shall not be denied or abridged by the United States or by any State on account of age.

SECTION 2. The Congress shall have power to enforce this article by appropriate legislation.

Amendment XXVII[25]

No law, varying the compensation for the service of the Senators and Representatives, shall take effect, until an election of Representatives shall have intervened.

---

[22]Passed August 27, 1962. Ratified January 23, 1964.

[23]Passed July 6, 1965. Ratified February 11, 1967.

[24]Passed March 23, 1971. Ratified July 5, 1971.

[25]Passed September 25, 1989. Ratified May 7, 1992.

Admission of States

Order of admission	State	Date of admission	Order of admission	State	Date of admission
1	Delaware	December 7, 1787	26	Michigan	January 26, 1837
2	Pennsylvania	December 12, 1787	27	Florida	March 3, 1845
3	New Jersey	December 18, 1787	28	Texas	December 29, 1845
4	Georgia	January 2, 1788	29	Iowa	December 28, 1846
5	Connecticut	January 9, 1788	30	Wisconsin	May 29, 1848
6	Massachusetts	February 6, 1788	31	California	September 9, 1850
7	Maryland	April 28, 1788	32	Minnesota	May 11, 1858
8	South Carolina	May 23, 1788	33	Oregon	February 14, 1859
9	New Hampshire	June 21, 1788	34	Kansas	January 29, 1861
10	Virginia	June 25, 1788	35	West Virginia	June 20, 1863
11	New York	July 26, 1788	36	Nevada	October 31, 1864
12	North Carolina	November 21, 1789	37	Nebraska	March 1, 1867
13	Rhode Island	May 29, 1790	38	Colorado	August 1, 1876
14	Vermont	March 4, 1791	39	North Dakota	November 2, 1889
15	Kentucky	June 1, 1792	40	South Dakota	November 2, 1889
16	Tennessee	June 1, 1796	41	Montana	November 8, 1889
17	Ohio	March 1, 1803	42	Washington	November 11, 1889
18	Louisiana	April 30, 1812	43	Idaho	July 3, 1890
19	Indiana	December 11, 1816	44	Wyoming	July 10, 1890
20	Mississippi	December 10, 1817	45	Utah	January 4, 1896
21	Illinois	December 3, 1818	46	Oklahoma	November 16, 1907
22	Alabama	December 14, 1819	47	New Mexico	January 6, 1912
23	Maine	March 15, 1820	48	Arizona	February 14, 1912
24	Missouri	August 10, 1821	49	Alaska	January 3, 1959
25	Arkansas	June 15, 1836	50	Hawaii	August 21, 1959

Population of the United States
(1790–1996)

Year	Total population (in thousands)	Number per square mile of land area (continental United States)	Year	Total population (in thousands)	Number per square mile of land area (continental United States)
1790	3,929	4.5	1829	12,565	
1791	4,056		1830	12,901	7.4
1792	4,194		1831	13,321	
1793	4,332		1832	13,742	
1794	4,469		1833	14,162	
1795	4,607		1834	14,582	
1796	4,745		1835	15,003	
1797	4,883		1836	15,423	
1798	5,021		1837	15,843	
1799	5,159		1838	16,264	
1800	5,297	6.1	1839	16,684	
1801	5,486		1840	17,120	9.8
1802	5,679		1841	17,733	
1803	5,872		1842	18,345	
1804	5,065		1843	18,957	
1805	6,258		1844	19,569	
1806	6,451		1845	20,182	
1807	6,644		1846	20,794	
1808	6,838		1847	21,406	
1809	7,031		1848	22,018	
1810	7,224	4.3	1849	22,631	
1811	7,460		1850	23,261	7.9
1812	7,700		1851	24,086	
1813	7,939		1852	24,911	
1814	8,179		1853	25,736	
1815	8,419		1854	26,561	
1816	8,659		1855	27,386	
1817	8,899		1856	28,212	
1818	9,139		1857	29,037	
1819	9,379		1858	29,862	
1820	9,618	5.6	1859	30,687	
1821	9,939		1860	31,513	10.6
1822	10,268		1861	32,351	
1823	10,596		1862	33,188	
1824	10,924		1863	34,026	
1825	11,252		1864	34,863	
1826	11,580		1865	35,701	
1827	11,909		1866	36,538	
1828	12,237		1867	37,376	

Figures are from *Historical Statistics of the United States, Colonial Times to 1957* (1961), pp. 7, 8; *Statistical Abstract of the United States: 1974*, p. 5, Census Bureau for 1974 and 1975; and *Statistical Abstract of the United States: 1988*, p. 7.

(continued)

Population of the United States (continued)
(1790–1996)

Year	Total population (in thousands)	Number per square mile of land area (continental United States)	Year	Total population (in thousands)[1]	Number per square mile of land area (continental United States)
1868	38,213		1907	87,000	
1869	39,051		1908	88,709	
1870	39,905	13.4	1909	90,492	
1871	40,938		1910	92,407	31.0
1872	41,972		1911	93,868	
1873	43,006		1912	95,331	
1874	44,040		1913	97,227	
1875	45,073		1914	99,118	
1876	46,107		1915	100,549	
1877	47,141		1916	101,966	
1878	48,174		1917	103,414	
1879	49,208		1918	104,550	
1880	50,262	16.9	1919	105,063	
1881	51,542		1920	106,466	35.6
1882	52,821		1921	108,541	
1883	54,100		1922	110,055	
1884	55,379		1923	111,950	
1885	56,658		1924	114,113	
1886	57,938		1925	115,832	
1887	59,217		1926	117,399	
1888	60,496		1927	119,038	
1889	61,775		1928	120,501	
1890	63,056	21.2	1929	121,700	
1891	64,361		1930	122,775	41.2
1892	65,666		1931	124,040	
1893	66,970		1932	124,840	
1894	68,275		1933	125,579	
1895	69,580		1934	126,374	
1896	70,885		1935	127,250	
1897	72,189		1936	128,053	
1898	73,494		1937	128,825	
1899	74,799		1938	129,825	
1900	76,094	25.6	1939	130,880	
1901	77,585		1940	131,669	44.2
1902	79,160		1941	133,894	
1903	80,632		1942	135,361	
1904	82,165		1943	137,250	
1905	83,820		1944	138,916	
1906	85,437		1945	140,468	

[1]Figures after 1940 represent total population including armed forces abroad, except in official census years.

Year	Total population (in thousands)[1]	Number per square mile of land area (continental United States)	Year	Total population (in thousands)[1]	Number per square mile of land area (continental United States)
1946	141,936		1972	209,896	
1947	144,698		1973	211,909	
1948	147,208		1974	213,854	
1949	149,767		1975	215,973	
1950	150,697	50.7	1976	218,035	
1951	154,878		1977	220,239	
1952	157,553		1978	222,585	
1953	160,184		1979	225,055	
1954	163,026		1980	227,225	64.0
1955	165,931		1981	229,466	
1956	168,903		1982	232,520	
1957	171,984		1983	234,799	
1958	174,882		1984	237,001	
1959	177,830[2]		1985	239,283	
1960	180,671	60.1	1986	241,596	
1961	183,691		1987	234,773	
1962	186,538		1988	245,051	
1963	189,242		1989	247,350	
1964	191,889		1990	250,122	
1965	194,303		1991	254,521	
1966	196,560		1992	245,908	
1967	198,712		1993	257,908	
1968	200,706		1994	261,875	
1969	202,677		1995	263,434	
1970	205,052	57.5	1996	266,096	
1971	207,661		1997	267,744	
			1998	270,299	
			1999	274,114	

[1]Figures after 1940 represent total population including armed forces abroad, except in official census years.

[2]Figures after 1959 include Alaska and Hawaii.

Presidential Elections
(1789–1832)

Year	Number of states	Candidates[1]	Parties	Popular vote	Electoral vote	Percentage of popular vote[2]
1789	11	**George Washington***	**No party designations**		69	
		John Adams			34	
		Minor Candidates			35	
1792	15	**George Washington**	**No party designations**		132	
		John Adams			77	
		George Clinton			50	
		Minor Candidates			5	
1796	16	**John Adams**	**Federalist**		71	
		Thomas Jefferson	Democratic-Republican		68	
		Thomas Pinckney	Federalist		59	
		Aaron Burr	Democratic-Republican		30	
		Minor Candidates			48	
1800	16	**Thomas Jefferson**	**Democratic-Republican**		73	
		Aaron Burr	Democratic-Republican		73	
		John Adams	Federalist		65	
		Charles C. Pinckney	Federalist		64	
		John Jay	Federalist		1	
1804	17	**Thomas Jefferson**	**Democratic-Republican**		162	
		Charles C. Pinckney	Federalist		14	
1808	17	**James Madison**	**Democratic-Republican**		122	
		Charles C. Pinckney	Federalist		47	
		George Clinton	Democratic-Republican		6	
1812	18	**James Madison**	**Democratic-Republican**		128	
		DeWitt Clinton	Federalist		89	
1816	19	**James Monroe**	**Democratic-Republican**		183	
		Rufus King	Federalist		34	
1820	24	**James Monroe**	**Democratic-Republican**		231	
		John Quincy Adams	Independent Republican		1	
1824	24	**John Quincy Adams**	**Democratic-Republican**	108,740	84	30.5
		Andrew Jackson	Democratic-Republican	153,544	99	43.1
		William H. Crawford	Democratic-Republican	46,618	41	13.1
		Henry Clay	Democratic-Republican	47,136	37	13.2
1828	24	**Andrew Jackson**	**Democratic**	647,286	178	56.0
		John Quincy Adams	National Republican	508,064	83	44.0
1832	24	**Andrew Jackson**	**Democratic**	687,502	219	55.0
		Henry Clay	National Republican	530,189	49	42.4
		William Wirt	Anti-Masonic	33,108	7	2.6
		John Floyd	National Republican		11	

[1]Before the passage of the Twelfth Amendment in 1804, the Electoral College voted for two presidential candidates; the runner-up became vice president. Figures are from *Historical Statistics of the United States, Colonial Times to 1957* (1961), pp. 682–83; and the U.S. Department of Justice.

[2]Candidates receiving less than 1 percent of the popular vote have been omitted. For that reason the percentage of popular vote given for any election year may not total 100 percent.

*Note: Boldface indicates the winner of each election.

Presidential Elections (1836–1888)

Year	Number of states	Candidates	Parties	Popular vote	Electoral vote	Percentage of popular vote[1]
1836	26	**Martin Van Buren**	**Democratic**	**765,483**	**170**	**50.9**
		William H. Harrison	Whig		73	
		Hugh L. White	Whig	739,795	26	
		Daniel Webster	Whig		14	
		W. P. Mangum	Independent		11	
1840	26	**William H. Harrison**	**Whig**	**1,274,624**	**234**	**53.1**
		Martin Van Buren	Democratic	1,127,781	60	46.9
1844	26	**James K. Polk**	**Democratic**	**1,338,464**	**170**	**49.6**
		Henry Clay	Whig	1,300,097	105	48.1
		James G. Birney	Liberty	62,300		2.3
1848	30	**Zachary Taylor**	**Whig**	**1,360,967**	**163**	**47.4**
		Lewis Cass	Democratic	1,222,342	127	42.5
		Martin Van Buren	Free Soil	291,263		10.1
1852	31	**Franklin Pierce**	**Democratic**	**1,601,117**	**254**	**50.9**
		Winfield Scott	Whig	1,385,453	42	44.1
		John P. Hale	Free Soil	155,825		5.0
1856	31	**James Buchanan**	**Democratic**	**1,832,955**	**174**	**45.3**
		John C. Frémont	Republican	1,339,932	114	33.1
		Millard Fillmore	American	871,731	8	21.6
1860	33	**Abraham Lincoln**	**Republican**	**1,865,593**	**180**	**39.8**
		Stephen A. Douglas	Democratic	1,382,713	12	29.5
		John C. Breckinridge	Democratic	848,356	72	18.1
		John Bell	Constitutional Union	592,906	39	12.6
1864	36	**Abraham Lincoln**	**Republican**	**2,206,938**	**212**	**55.0**
		George B. McClellan	Democratic	1,803,787	21	45.0
1868	37	**Ulysses S. Grant**	**Republican**	**3,013,421**	**214**	**52.7**
		Horatio Seymour	Democratic	2,706,829	80	47.3
1872	37	**Ulysses S. Grant**	**Republican**	**3,596,745**	**286**	**55.6**
		Horace Greeley	Democratic	2,843,446	2	43.9
1876	38	**Rutherford B. Hayes**	**Republican**	**4,036,572**	**185**	**48.0**
		Samuel J. Tilden	Democratic	4,284,020	184	51.0
1880	38	**James A. Garfield**	**Republican**	**4,453,295**	**214**	**48.5**
		Winfield S. Hancock	Democratic	4,414,082	155	48.1
		James B. Weaver	Greenback-Labor	308,578		3.4
1884	38	**Grover Cleveland**	**Democratic**	**4,879,507**	**219**	**48.5**
		James G. Blaine	Republican	4,850,293	182	48.2
		Benjamin F. Butler	Greenback-Labor	175,370		1.8
		John P. St. John	Prohibition	150,369		1.5
1888	38	**Benjamin Harrison**	**Republican**	**5,477,129**	**233**	**47.9**
		Grover Cleveland	Democratic	5,537,857	168	48.6
		Clinton B. Fisk	Prohibition	249,506		2.2
		Anson J. Streeter	Union Labor	146,935		1.3

[1]Candidates receiving less than 1 percent of the popular vote have been omitted. For that reason the percentage of popular vote given for any election year may not total 100 percent.

[2]Greeley died shortly after the election; the electors supporting him then divided their votes among minor candidates.

Presidential Elections
(1896–1932)

Year	Number of states	Candidates	Parties	Popular vote	Electoral vote	Percentage of popular vote[1]
1892	44	**Grover Cleveland**	**Democratic**	**5,555,426**	277	**46.1**
		Benjamin Harrison	Republican	5,182,690	145	43.0
		James B. Weaver	People's	1,029,846	22	8.5
		John Bidwell	Prohibition	264,133		2.2
1896	45	**William McKinley**	**Republican**	**7,102,246**	271	**51.1**
		William J. Bryan	Democratic	6,492,559	176	47.7
1900	45	**William McKinley**	**Republican**	**7,218,491**	292	**51.7**
		William J. Bryan	Democratic; Populist	6,356,734	155	45.5
		John C. Wooley	Prohibition	208,914		1.5
1904	45	**Theodore Roosevelt**	**Republican**	**7,628,461**	336	**57.4**
		Alton B. Parker	Democratic	5,084,223	140	37.6
		Eugene V. Debs	Socialist	402,283		3.0
		Silas C. Swallow	Prohibition	258,536		1.9
1908	46	**William H. Taft**	**Republican**	**7,675,320**	321	**51.6**
		William J. Bryan	Democratic	6,412,294	162	43.1
		Eugene V. Debs	Socialist	420,793		2.8
		Eugene W. Chafin	Prohibition	253,840		1.7
1912	48	**Woodrow Wilson**	**Democratic**	**6,296,547**	435	**41.9**
		Theodore Roosevelt	Progressive	4,118,571	88	27.4
		William H. Taft	Republican	3,486,720	8	23.2
		Eugene V. Debs	Socialist	900,672		6.0
		Eugene W. Chafin	Prohibition	206,275		1.4
1916	48	**Woodrow Wilson**	**Democratic**	**9,127,695**	277	**49.4**
		Charles E. Hughes	Republican	8,533,507	254	46.2
		A. L. Benson	Socialist	585,113		3.2
		J. Frank Hanly	Prohibition	220,506		1.2
1920	48	**Warren G. Harding**	**Republican**	**16,143,407**	404	**60.4**
		James N. Cox	Democratic	9,130,328	127	34.2
		Eugene V. Debs	Socialist	919,799		3.4
		P. P. Christensen	Farmer-Labor	265,411		1.0
1924	48	**Calvin Coolidge**	**Republican**	**15,718,211**	382	**54.0**
		John W. Davis	Democratic	8,385,283	136	28.8
		Robert M. La Follette	Progressive	4,831,289	13	16.6
1928	48	**Herbert C. Hoover**	**Republican**	**21,391,993**	444	**58.2**
		Alfred E. Smith	Democratic	15,016,169	87	40.9
1932	48	**Franklin D. Roosevelt**	**Democratic**	**22,809,638**	472	**57.4**
		Herbert C. Hoover	Republican	15,758,901	59	39.7
		Norman Thomas	Socialist	881,951		2.2

[1]Candidates receiving less than 1 percent of the popular vote have been omitted. For that reason the percentage of popular vote given for any election year may not total 100 percent.

Presidential Elections
(1936–1992)

Year	Number of states	Candidates	Parties	Popular vote	Electoral vote	Percentage of popular vote[1]
1936	48	**Franklin D. Roosevelt**	**Democratic**	**27,752,869**	**523**	**60.8**
		Alfred M. Landon	Republican	16,674,665	8	36.5
		William Lemke	Union	882,479		1.9
1940	48	**Franklin D. Roosevelt**	**Democratic**	**27,307,819**	**449**	**54.8**
		Wendell L. Willkie	Republican	22,321,018	82	44.8
1944	48	**Franklin D. Roosevelt**	**Democratic**	**25,606,585**	**432**	**53.5**
		Thomas E. Dewey	Republican	22,014,745	99	46.0
1948	48	**Harry S Truman**	**Democratic**	**24,105,812**	**303**	**49.5**
		Thomas E. Dewey	Republican	21,970,065	189	45.1
		J. Strom Thurmond	States' Rights	1,169,063	39	2.4
		Henry A. Wallace	Progressive	1,157,172		2.4
1952	48	**Dwight D. Eisenhower**	**Republican**	**33,936,234**	**442**	**55.1**
		Adlai E. Stevenson	Democratic	27,314,992	89	44.4
1956	48	**Dwight D. Eisenhower**	**Republican**	**35,590,472**	**457**	**57.6**
		Adlai E. Stevenson	Democratic	26,022,752	73	42.1
1960	50	**John F. Kennedy**	**Democratic**	**34,227,096**	**303**	**49.9**
		Richard M. Nixon	Republican	34,108,546	219	49.6
1964	50	**Lyndon B. Johnson**	**Democratic**	**43,126,506**	**486**	**61.1**
		Barry M. Goldwater	Republican	27,176,799	52	38.5
1968	50	**Richard M. Nixon**	**Republican**	**31,785,480**	**301**	**43.4**
		Hubert H. Humphrey	Democratic	31,275,165	191	42.7
		George C. Wallace	American Independent	9,906,473	46	13.5
1972	50	**Richard M. Nixon**	**Republican**	**47,169,911**	**520**	**60.7**
		George S. McGovern	Democratic	29,170,383	17	37.5
1976	50	**Jimmy Carter**	**Democratic**	**40,827,394**	**297**	**50.0**
		Gerald R. Ford	Republican	39,145,977	240	47.9
1980	50	**Ronald W. Reagan**	**Republican**	**43,899,248**	**489**	**50.8**
		Jimmy Carter	Democratic	35,481,435	49	41.0
		John B. Anderson	Independent	5,719,437		6.6
		Ed Clark	Libertarian	920,859		1.0
1984	50	**Ronald W. Reagan**	**Republican**	**54,281,858**	**525**	**59.2**
		Walter F. Mondale	Democratic	37,457,215	13	40.8
1988	50	**George H. Bush**	**Republican**	**47,917,341**	**426**	**54**
		Michael Dukakis	Democratic	41,013,030	112	46
1992	50	**William J. Clinton**	**Democratic**	**44,908,254**	**370**	**43.0**
		George H. Bush	Republican	39,102,343	168	37.4
		H. Ross Perot	Independent	19,741,065		18.9
1996	50	**William J. Clinton**	**Democratic**	**47,402,357**	**379**	**49**
		Robert J. Dole	Republican	39,198,755	159	41
		H. Ross Perot	Reform	8,085,402		8

[1]Candidates receiving less than 1 percent of the popular vote have been omitted. For that reason the percentage of popular vote given for any election year may not total 100 percent.

Presidents, Vice Presidents, and Cabinet Members

President	Vice President	Secretary of State	Secretary of Treasury	Secretary of War	Secretary of Navy
George Washington 1789–1797	John Adams 1789–1797	Thomas Jefferson 1789–1794	Alexander Hamilton 1789–1795	Henry Knox 1789–1795	
		Edmund Randolph 1794–1795 Timothy Pickering 1795–1797	Oliver Wolcott 1795–1797	Timothy Pickering 1795–1796 James McHenry 1796–1797	
John Adams 1797–1801	Thomas Jefferson 1797–1801	Timothy Pickering 1797–1800 John Marshall 1800–1801	Oliver Wolcott 1797–1801 Samuel Dexter 1801	James McHenry 1797–1800 Samuel Dexter 1800–1801	Benjamin Stoddert 1798–1801
Thomas Jefferson 1801–1809	Aaron Burr 1801–1805 George Clinton 1805–1809	James Madison 1801–1809	Samuel Dexter 1801 Albert Gallatin 1801–1809	Henry Dearborn 1801–1809	Benjamin Stoddert 1801 Robert Smith 1801–1809
James Madison 1809–1817	George Clinton 1809–1813 Elbridge Gerry 1813–1817	Robert Smith 1809–1811 James Monroe 1811–1817	Albert Gallatin 1809–1814 George Campbell 1814 Alexander Dallas 1814–1816 William Crawford 1816–1817	William Eustis 1809–1813 John Armstrong 1813–1814 James Monroe 1814–1815 William Crawford 1815–1817	Paul Hamilton 1809–1813 William Jones 1813–1814 Benjamin Crowninshield 1814–1817
James Monroe 1817–1825	Daniel D. Tompkins 1817–1825	John Quincy Adams 1817–1825	William Crawford 1817–1825	George Graham 1817 John C. Calhoun 1817–1825	Benjamin Crowninshield 1817–1818 Smith Thompson 1818–1823 Samuel Southard 1823–1825
John Quincy Adams 1825–1829	John C. Calhoun 1825–1829	Henry Clay 1825–1829	Richard Rush 1825–1829	James Barbour 1825–1828 Peter B. Porter 1828–1829	Samuel Southard 1825–1829

Postmaster General	Attorney General
Samuel Osgood 1789–1791	Edmund Randolph 1789–1794
Timothy Pickering 1791–1795	William Bradford 1794–1795
Joseph Habersham 1795–1797	Charles Lee 1795–1797
Joseph Habersham 1797–1801	Charles Lee 1797–1801
Joseph Habersham 1801 Gideon Granger 1801–1809	Levi Lincoln 1801–1805 John Breckinridge 1805–1807 Caesar Rodney 1807–1809
Gideon Granger 1809–1814 Return Meigs 1814–1817	Caesar Rodney 1809–1811 William Pinkney 1811–1814 Richard Rush 1814–1817
Return Meigs 1817–1823 John McLean 1823–1825	Richard Rush 1817 William Wirt 1817–1825
John McLean 1825–1829	William Wirt 1825–1829

(continued)

Presidents, Vice Presidents, and Cabinet Members *(continued)*

President	Vice President	Secretary of State	Secretary of Treasury	Secretary of War	Secretary of Navy	Postmaster General
Andrew Jackson 1829–1837	John C. Calhoun 1829–1833 Martin Van Buren 1833–1837	Martin Van Buren 1829–1831 Edward Livingston 1831–1833 Louis McLane 1833–1834 John Forsyth 1834–1837	Samuel Ingham 1829–1831 Louis McLane 1831–1833 William Duane 1833 Roger B. Taney 1833–1834 Levi Woodbury 1834–1837	John H. Eaton 1829–1831 Lewis Cass 1831–1837 Benjamin Butler 1837	John Branch 1829–1831 Levi Woodbury 1831–1834 Mahlon Dickerson 1834–1837	William Barry 1829–1835 Amos Kendall 1835–1837
Martin Van Buren 1837–1841	Richard M. Johnson 1837–1841	John Forsyth 1837–1841	Levi Woodbury 1837–1841	Joel R. Poinsett 1837–1841	Mahlon Dickerson 1837–1838 James K. Paulding 1838–1841	Amos Kendall 1837–1840 John M. Niles 1840–1841
William H. Harrison 1841	John Tyler 1841	Daniel Webster 1841	Thomas Ewing 1841	John Bell 1841	George E. Badger 1841	Francis Granger 1841
John Tyler 1841–1845		Daniel Webster 1841–1843 Hugh S. Legaré 1843 Abel P. Upshur 1843–1844 John C. Calhoun 1844–1845	Thomas Ewing 1841 Walter Forward 1841–1843 John C. Spencer 1843–1844 George M. Bibb 1844–1845	John Bell 1841 John C. Spencer 1841–1843 James M. Porter 1843–1844 William Wilkins 1844–1845	George E. Badger 1841 Abel P. Upshur 1841–1843 David Henshaw 1843–1844 Thomas Gilmer 1844 John Y. Mason 1844–1845	Francis Granger 1841 Charles A. Wickliffe 1841–1845
James K. Polk 1845–1849	George M. Dallas 1845–1849	James Buchanan 1845–1849	Robert J. Walker 1845–1849	William L. Marcy 1845–1849	George Bancroft 1845–1846 John Y. Mason 1846–1849	Cave Johnson 1845–1849
Zachary Taylor 1849–1850	Millard Fillmore 1849–1850	John M. Clayton 1849–1850	William M. Meredith 1849–1850	George W. Crawford 1849–1850	William B. Preston 1849–1850	Jacob Collamer 1849–1850
Millard Fillmore 1850–1853		Daniel Webster 1850–1852 Edward Everett 1852–1853	Thomas Corwin 1850–1853	Charles M. Conrad 1850–1853	William A. Graham 1850–1852 John P. Kennedy 1852–1853	Nathan K. Hall 1850–1852 Sam D. Hubbard 1852–1853
Franklin Pierce 1853–1857	William R. King 1853–1857	William L. Marcy 1853–1857	James Guthrie 1853–1857	Jefferson Davis 1853–1857	James C. Dobbin 1853–1857	James Campbell 1853–1857

Attorney General	Secretary of Interior
John M. Berrien 1829–1831 Roger B. Taney 1831–1833 Benjamin Butler 1833–1837	
Benjamin Butler 1837–1838 Felix Grundy 1838–1840 Henry D. Gilpin 1840–1841 John J. Crittenden 1841	
John J. Crittenden 1841 Hugh S. Legaré 1841–1843 John Nelson 1843–1845	
John Y. Mason 1845–1846 Nathan Clifford 1846–1848 Isaac Toucey 1848–1849	
Reverdy Johnson 1849–1850	Thomas Ewing 1849–1850
John J. Crittenden 1850–1853	Thomas McKennan 1850 A. H. H. Stuart 1850–1853
Caleb Cushing 1853–1857	Robert McClelland 1853–1857

(continued)

Presidents, Vice Presidents, and Cabinet Members *(continued)*

President	Vice President	Secretary of State	Secretary of Treasury	Secretary of War	Secretary of Navy	Postmaster General
James Buchanan 1857–1861	John C. Breckinridge 1857–1861	Lewis Cass 1857–1860 Jeremiah S. Black 1860–1861	Howell Cobb 1857–1860 Philip F. Thomas 1860–1861 John A. Dix 1861	John B. Floyd 1857–1861 Joseph Holt 1861	Isaac Toucey 1857–1861	Aaron V. Brown 1857–1859 Joseph Holt 1859–1861 Horatio King 1861
Abraham Lincoln 1861–1865	Hannibal Hamlin 1861–1865 Andrew Johnson 1865	William H. Seward 1861–1865	Salmon P. Chase 1861–1864 William P. Fessenden 1864–1865 Hugh McCulloch 1865	Simon Cameron 1861–1862 Edwin M. Stanton 1862–1865	Gideon Welles 1861–1865	Horatio King 1861 Montgomery Blair 1861–1864 William Dennison 1864–1865
Andrew Johnson 1865–1869		William H. Seward 1865–1869	Hugh McCulloch 1865–1869	Edwin M. Stanton 1865–1867 Ulysses S. Grant 1867–1868 John M. Schofield 1868–1869	Gideon Welles 1865–1869	William Dennison 1865–1866 Alexander Randall 1866–1869 William M. Evarts 1868–1869
Ulysses S. Grant 1869–1877	Schuyler Colfax 1869–1873 Henry Wilson 1873–1877	Elihu B. Washburne 1869 Hamilton Fish 1869–1877	George S. Boutwell 1869–1873 William A. Richardson 1873–1874 Benjamin H. Bristow 1874–1876 Lot M. Morrill 1876–1877	John A. Rawlins 1869 William T. Sherman 1869 William W. Belknap 1869–1876 Alphonso Taft 1876 James D. Cameron 1876–1877	Adolph E. Borie 1869 George M. Robeson 1869–1877	John A. J. Creswell 1869–1874 James W. Marshall 1874 Marshall Jewell 1874–1876 James N. Tyner 1876–1877
Rutherford B. Hayes 1877–1881	William A. Wheeler 1877–1881	William M. Evarts 1877–1881	John Sherman 1877–1881	George W. McCrary 1877–1879 Alexander Ramsey 1879–1881	R. W. Thompson 1877–1881 Nathan Goff, Jr. 1881	David M. Key 1877–1880 Horace Maynard 1880–1881
James A. Garfield 1881	Chester A. Arthur 1881	James G. Blaine 1881	William Windom 1881	Robert T. Lincoln 1881	William H. Hunt 1881	Thomas L. James 1881
Chester A. Arthur 1881–1885		F. T. Frelinghuysen 1881–1885	Charles J. Folger 1881–1884 Walter Q. Gresham 1884 Hugh McCulloch 1884–1885	Robert T. Lincoln 1881–1885	William E. Chandler 1881–1885	Thomas L. James 1881 Timothy O. Howe 1881–1883 Walter Q. Gresham 1883–1884 Frank Hatton 1884–1885

Attorney General	Secretary of Interior
Jeremiah S. Black 1857–1860 Edwin M. Stanton 1860–1861	Jacob Thompson 1857–1861
Edward Bates 1861–1864 James Speed 1864–1865	Caleb B. Smith 1861–1863 John P. Usher 1863–1865
James Speed 1865–1866 Henry Stanbery 1866–1868 O. H. Browning 1866–1869	John P. Usher 1865 James Harlan 1865–1866
Ebenezer R. Hoar 1869–1870 Amos T. Akerman 1870–1871 G. H. Williams 1871–1875 Edwards Pierrepont 1875–1876 Alphonso Taft 1876–1877	Jacob D. Cox 1869–1870 Columbus Delano 1870–1875 Zachariah Chandler 1875–1877
Charles Devens 1877–1881	Carl Schurz 1877–1881
Wayne MacVeagh 1881	S. J. Kirkwood 1881
B. H. Brewster 1881–1885	Henry M. Teller 1881–1885

(continued)

Presidents, Vice Presidents, and Cabinet Members *(continued)*

President	Vice President	Secretary of State	Secretary of Treasury	Secretary of War	Secretary of Navy	Postmaster General
Grover Cleveland 1885–1889	T. A. Hendricks 1885	Thomas F. Bayard 1885–1889	Daniel Manning 1885–1887 Charles S. Fairchild 1887–1889	William C. Endicott 1885–1889	William C. Whitney 1885–1889	William F. Vilas 1885–1888 Don M. Dickinson 1888–1889
Benjamin Harrison 1889–1893	Levi P. Morton 1889–1893	James G. Blaine 1889–1892 John W. Foster 1892–1893	William Windom 1889–1891 Charles Foster 1892–1893	Redfield Procter 1889–1891 Stephen B. Elkins 1891–1893	Benjamin F. Tracy 1889–1893	John Wanamaker 1889–1893
Grover Cleveland 1893–1897	Adlai E. Stevenson 1893–1897	Walter Q. Gresham 1893–1895 Richard Olney 1895–1897	John G. Carlisle 1893–1897	Daniel S. Lamont 1893–1897	Hilary A. Herbert 1893–1897	Wilson S. Bissel 1893–1895 William L. Wilson 1895–1897
William McKinley 1897–1901	Garret A. Hobart 1897–1899 Theodore Roosevelt 1901	John Sherman 1897–1898 William R. Day 1898 John Hay 1898–1901	Lyman J. Gage 1897–1901	Russell A. Alger 1897–1899 Elihu Root 1899–1901	John D. Long 1897–1901	James A. Gary 1897–1898 Charles E. Smith 1898–1901
Theodore Roosevelt 1901–1909	Charles Fairbanks 1905–1909	John Hay 1901–1905 Elihu Root 1905–1909 Robert Bacon 1909	Lyman J. Gage 1901–1902 Leslie M. Shaw 1902–1907 George B. Cortelyou 1907–1909	Elihu Root 1901–1904 William H. Taft 1904–1908 Luke E. Wright 1908–1909	John D. Long 1901–1902 William H. Moody 1902–1904 Paul Morton 1904–1905 Charles J. Bonaparte 1905–1906 Victor H. Metcalf 1906–1908 T. H. Newberry 1908–1909	Charles E. Smith 1901–1902 Henry C. Payne 1902–1904 Robert J. Wynne 1904–1905 George B. Cortelyou 1905–1907 George von L. Meyer 1907–1909
William H. Taft 1909–1913	James S. Sherman 1909–1913	Philander C. Knox 1909–1913	Franklin MacVeagh 1909–1913	Jacob M. Dickinson 1909–1911 Henry L. Stimson 1911–1913	George von L. Meyer 1909–1913	Frank H. Hitchcock 1909–1913
Woodrow Wilson 1913–1921	Thomas R. Marshall 1913–1921	William J. Bryan 1913–1915 Robert Lansing 1915–1920 Bainbridge Colby 1920–1921	William G. McAdoo 1913–1918 Carter Glass 1918–1920 David F. Houston 1920–1921	Lindley M. Garrison 1913–1916 Newton D. Baker 1916–1921	Josephus Daniels 1913–1921	Albert S. Burleson 1913–1921

Attorney General	Secretary of Interior	Secretary of Agriculture	Secretary of Commerce and Labor		
A. H. Garland 1885–1889	L. Q. C. Lamar 1885–1888 William F. Vilas 1888–1889	Norman J. Colman 1889			
W. H. H. Miller 1889–1893	John W. Noble 1889–1893	Jeremiah M. Rusk 1889–1893			
Richard Olney 1893–1895 Judson Harmon 1895–1897	Hoke Smith 1893–1896 David R. Francis 1895–1897	J. Sterling Morton 1893–1897			
Joseph McKenna 1897–1898 John W. Griggs 1898–1901 Philander C. Knox 1901	Cornelius N. Bliss 1897–1898 E. A. Hitchcock 1898–1901	James Wilson 1897–1901			
Philander C. Knox 1901–1904 William H. Moody 1904–1906 Charles J. Bonaparte 1906–1909	E. A. Hitchcock 1901–1907 James R. Garfield 1907–1909	James Wilson 1901–1909	George B. Cortelyou 1903–1904 Victor H. Metcalf 1904–1906 Oscar S. Straus 1906–1909		
G. W. Wickersham 1909–1913	R. A. Ballinger 1909–1911 Walter L. Fisher 1911–1913	James Wilson 1909–1913	Charles Nagel 1909–1913		

				Secretary of Commerce	Secretary of Labor
J. C. McReynolds 1913–1914 T. W. Gregory 1914–1919 A. Mitchell Palmer 1919–1921	Franklin K. Lane 1913–1920 John B. Payne 1920–1921	David F. Houston 1913–1920 E. T. Meredith 1920–1921		W. C. Redfield 1913–1919 J. W. Alexander 1919–1921	William B. Wilson 1913–1921

(continued)

Presidents, Vice Presidents, and Cabinet Members *(continued)*

President	Vice President	Secretary of State	Secretary of Treasury	Secretary of War	Secretary of Navy	Postmaster General
Warren G. Harding 1921–1923	Calvin Coolidge 1921–1923	Charles E. Hughes 1921–1923	Andrew W. Mellon 1921–1923	John W. Weeks 1921–1923	Edwin Denby 1921–1923	Will H. Hays 1921–1922 Hubert Work 1922–1923 Harry S. New 1923
Calvin Coolidge 1923–1929	Charles G. Dawes 1925–1929	Charles E. Hughes 1923–1925 Frank B. Kellogg 1925–1929	Andrew W. Mellon 1923–1929	John W. Weeks 1923–1925 Dwight F. Davis 1925–1929	Edwin Denby 1923–1924 Curtis D. Wilbur 1924–1929	Harry S. New 1923–1929
Herbert C. Hoover 1929–1933	Charles Curtis 1929–1933	Henry L. Stimson 1929–1933	Andrew W. Mellon 1929–1932 Ogden L. Mills 1932–1933	James W. Good 1929 Patrick J. Hurley 1929–1933	Charles F. Adams 1929–1933	Walter F. Brown 1929–1933
Franklin Delano Roosevelt 1933–1945	John Nance Garner 1933–1941 Henry A. Wallace 1941–1945 Harry S Truman 1945	Cordell Hull 1933–1944 E. R. Stettinius, Jr. 1944–1945	William H. Woodin 1933–1934 Henry Morgenthau, Jr. 1934–1945	George H. Dern 1933–1936 Harry H. Woodring 1936–1940 Henry L. Stimson 1940–1945	Claude A. Swanson 1933–1940 Charles Edison 1940 Frank Knox 1940–1944 James V. Forrestal 1944–1945	James A. Farley 1933–1940 Frank C. Walker 1940–1945
Harry S Truman 1945–1953	Alben W. Barkley 1949–1953	James F. Byrnes 1945–1947 George C. Marshall 1947–1949 Dean G. Acheson 1949–1953	Fred M. Vinson 1945–1946 John W. Snyder 1946–1953	Robert P. Patterson 1945–1947 Kenneth C. Royall 1947	James V. Forrestal 1945–1947	R. E. Hannegan 1945–1947 Jesse M. Donaldson 1947–1953
				Secretary of Defense		
				James V. Forrestal 1947–1949 Louis A. Johnson 1949–1950 George C. Marshall 1950–1951 Robert A. Lovett 1951–1953		
Dwight D. Eisenhower 1953–1961	Richard M. Nixon 1953–1961	John Foster Dulles 1953–1959 Christian A. Herter 1957–1961	George M. Humphrey 1953–1957 Robert B. Anderson 1957–1961	Charles E. Wilson 1953–1957 Neil H. McElroy 1957–1961 Thomas S. Gates 1959–1961		A. E. Summerfield 1953–1961

Attorney General	Secretary of Interior	Secretary of Agriculture	Secretary of Commerce	Secretary of Labor	Secretary of Health, Education, and Welfare
H. M. Daugherty 1921–1923	Albert B. Fall 1921–1923 Hubert Work 1923	Henry C. Wallace 1921–1923	Herbert C. Hoover	James J. Davis 1921–1923	
H. M. Daugherty 1923–1924 Harlan F. Stone 1924–1925 John G. Sargent 1925–1929	Hubert Work 1923–1928 Roy O. West 1928–1929	Henry C. Wallace 1923–1924 Howard M. Gore 1924–1925 W. J. Jardine 1925–1929	Herbert C. Hoover 1923–1928 William F. Whiting 1928–1929	James J. Davis 1923–1929	
J. D. Mitchell 1929–1933	Ray L. Wilbur 1929–1933	Arthur M. Hyde 1929–1933 Roy D. Chapin 1932–1933	Robert P. Lamont 1929–1932 William N. Doak 1930–1933	James J. Davis 1929–1930	
H. S. Cummings 1933–1939 Frank Murphy 1939–1940 Robert Jackson 1940–1941 Francis Biddel 1941–1945	Harold L. Ickes 1933–1945	Henry A. Wallace 1933–1940 Claude R. Wickard 1940–1945	Daniel C. Roper 1933–1939 Harry L. Hopkins 1939–1940 Jesse Jones 1940–1945 Henry A. Wallace 1945	Frances Perkins 1933–1945	
Tom C. Clark 1945–1949 J. H. McGrath 1949–1952 James P. McGranery 1952–1953	Harold L. Ickes 1945–1946 Julius A. Krug 1946–1949 Oscar L. Chapman 1949–1953	C. P. Anderson 1945–1948 C. F. Brannan 1948–1953	W. A. Harriman 1946–1948 Charles Sawyer 1948–1953	L. B. Schwellenbach 1945–1948 Maurice J. Tobin 1948–1953	
H. Brownell, Jr. 1953–1957 William P. Rogers 1957–1961	Douglas McKay 1953–1956 Fred Seaton 1956–1961	Ezra T. Benson 1953–1961	Sinclair Weeks 1953–1958 Lewis L. Strauss 1958–1961	Martin P. Durkin 1953 James P. Mitchell 1953–1961	Oveta Culp Hobby 1953–1955 Marion B. Folsom 1955–1958 Arthur S. Flemming 1958–1961

(continued)

Presidents, Vice Presidents, and Cabinet Members *(continued)*

President	Vice President	Secretary of State	Secretary of Treasury	Secretary of Defense	Postmaster General[1]	Attorney General
John F. Kennedy 1961–1963	Lyndon B. Johnson 1961–1963	Dean Rusk 1961–1963	C. Douglas Dillon 1961–1963	Robert S. McNamara 1961–1963	J. Edward Day 1961–1963 John A. Gronouski 1961–1963	Robert F. Kennedy 1961–1963
Lyndon B. Johnson 1963–1969	Hubert H. Humphrey 1965–1969	Dean Rusk 1963–1969	C. Douglas Dillon 1963–1965 Henry H. Fowler 1965–1968 Joseph W. Barr 1968–1969	Robert S. McNamara 1963–1968 Clark M. Clifford 1968–1969	John A. Gronouski 1963–1965 Lawrence F. O'Brien 1965–1968 W. Marvin Watson 1968–1969	Robert F. Kennedy 1963–1965 N. deB. Katzenbach 1965–1967 Ramsey Clark 1967–1969
Richard M. Nixon 1969–1974	Spiro T. Agnew 1969–1973 Gerald R. Ford 1973–1974	William P. Rogers 1969–1973 Henry A. Kissinger 1973–1974	David M. Kennedy 1969–1970 John B. Connally 1970–1972 George P. Schultz 1972–1974 William E. Simon 1974	Melvin R. Laird 1969–1973 Elliot L. Richardson 1973 James R. Schlesinger 1973–1974	Winton M. Blount 1969–1971	John M. Mitchell 1969–1972 Richard G. Kleindienst 1972–1973 Elliot L. Richardson 1973 William B. Saxbe 1974
Gerald R. Ford 1974–1977	Nelson A. Rockefeller 1974–1977	Henry A. Kissinger 1974–1977	William E. Simon 1974–1977	James R. Schlesinger 1974–1975 Donald H. Rumsfeld 1975–1977		William B. Saxbe 1974–1975 Edward H. Levi 1975–1977

[1]On July 1, 1971, the Post Office became an independent agency. After that date, the Postmaster General was no longer a member of the Cabinet.

Secretary of Interior	Secretary of Agriculture	Secretary of Commerce	Secretary of Labor	Secretary of Health, Education, and Welfare	Secretary of Housing and Urban Development	Secretary of Transportation
Stewart L. Udall 1961–1963	Orville L. Freeman 1961–1963	Luther H. Hodges 1961–1963	Arthur J. Goldberg 1961–1963 W. Willard Wirtz 1962–1963	A. H. Ribicoff 1961–1963 Anthony J. Celebrezze 1962–1963		
Stewart L. Udall 1963–1969	Orville L. Freeman 1963–1969	Luther H. Hodges 1963–1965 John T. Connor 1965–1967 Alexander B. Trowbridge 1967–1968 C. R. Smith 1968–1969	W. Willard Wirtz 1963–1969	Anthony J. Celebrezze 1963–1965 John W. Gardner 1965–1968 Wilbur J. Cohen 1968–1969	Robert C. Weaver 1966–1968 Robert C. Wood 1968–1969	Alan S. Boyd 1966–1969
Walter J. Hickel 1969–1971 Rogers C. B. Morton 1971–1974	Clifford M. Hardin 1969–1971 Earl L. Butz 1971–1974	Maurice H. Stans 1969–1972 Peter G. Peterson 1972 Frederick B. Dent 1972–1974	George P. Shultz 1969–1970 James D. Hodgson 1970–1973 Peter J. Brennan 1973–1974	Robert H. Finch 1969–1970 Elliot L. Richardson 1970–1973 Caspar W. Weinberger 1973–1974	George W. Romney 1969–1973 James T. Lynn 1973–1974	John A. Volpe 1969–1973 Claude S. Brinegar 1973–1974
Rogers C. B. Morton 1974–1975 Stanley K. Hathaway 1975 Thomas D. Kleppe 1975–1977	Earl L. Butz 1974–1976	Frederick B. Dent 1974–1975 Rogers C. B. Morton 1975 Elliot L. Richardson 1975–1977	Peter J. Brennan 1974–1975 John T. Dunlop 1975–1976 W. J. Usery 1976–1977	Caspar W. Weinberger 1974–1975 Forrest D. Matthews 1975–1977	James T. Lynn 1974–1975 Carla A. Hills 1975–1977	Claude S. Brinegar 1974–1975 William T. Coleman 1975–1977

(continued)

Presidents, Vice Presidents, and Cabinet Members *(continued)*

President	Vice President	Secretary of State	Secretary of Treasury	Secretary of Defense	Attorney General	Secretary of Interior	Secretary of Agriculture
Jimmy Carter 1977–1981	Walter F. Mondale 1977–1981	Cyrus R. Vance 1977–1980 Edmund S. Muskie 1980–1981	W. Michael Blumenthal 1977–1979 G. William Miller 1979–1981	Harold Brown 1977–1981	Griffin Bell 1977–1979 Benjamin R. Civiletti 1979–1981	Cecil D. Andrus 1977–1981	Robert Bergland 1977–1981
Ronald W. Reagan 1981–1989	George H. Bush 1981–1989	Alexander M. Haig, Jr. 1981–1982 George P. Shultz 1982–1989	Donald T. Regan 1981–1985 James A. Baker 1985–1988 Nicholas F. Brady 1988–1989	Caspar W. Weinberger 1981–1987 Frank C. Carlucci 1987–1989	William French Smith 1981–1985 Edwin Meese 1985–1988 Richard Thornburgh 1988–1989	James G. Watt 1981–1983 William P. Clark 1983–1985 Donald P. Hodel 1985–1989	John R. Block 1981–1986 Richard E. Lyng 1986–1989
George H. Bush 1989–1992	J. Danforth Quayle 1989–1992	James A. Baker 1989–1992 Lawrence S. Eagleburger 1992	Nicholas F. Brady 1989–1992	Richard Cheney 1989–1992	Richard Thornburgh 1989–1990 William Barr 1990–1992	Manuel Lujan 1989–1992	Clayton Yeutter 1989–1990 Edward Madigan 1990–1992
William Clinton 1993–	Albert Gore 1993–	Warren M. Christopher 1993–1996 Madeleine K Albright 1997–	Lloyd Bentsen 1993–1994 Robert E. Rubin 1994–1999 Lawrence H. Summers 1999–	Les Aspin 1993–1994 William J. Perry 1994–1996 William S. Cohen 1997–	Janet Reno 1993–	Bruce Babbitt 1993–	Mike Espy 1993–1994 Dan Glickman 1994–

Secretary of Commerce	Secretary of Labor	Secretary of Health, Education, and Welfare	Secretary of Housing and Urban Development	Secretary of Transportation	Secretary of Energy	Secretary of Veterans' Affairs
Juanita Kreps 1977–1981	F. Ray Marshall 1977–1981	Joseph Califano 1977–1979 Patricia Roberts Harris 1979–1980	Patricia Roberts Harris 1977–1979 Moon Landrieu 1979–1981	Brock Adams 1977–1979 Neil E. Goldschmidt 1979–1981	James R. Schlesinger 1977–1979 Charles W. Duncan, Jr. 1979–1981	

		Secretary of Health and Human Services	Secretary of Education			
		Patricia Roberts Harris 1980–1981	Shirley M. Hufstedler 1980–1981			

Secretary of Commerce	Secretary of Labor	Secretary of Health and Human Services	Secretary of Education	Secretary of Housing and Urban Development	Secretary of Transportation	Secretary of Energy	Secretary of Veterans' Affairs
Malcolm Baldridge 1981–1987 C. William Verity, Jr. 1987–1989	Raymond J. Donovan 1981–1985 William E. Brock 1985–1987 Ann Dore McLaughlin 1987–1989	Richard S. Schweiker 1981–1983 Margaret M. Heckler 1983–1985 Otis R. Bowen 1985–1989	Terrell H. Bell 1981–1985 William J. Bennett 1985–1988 Lauro Fred Cavazos 1988–1989	Samuel R. Pierce, Jr. 1981–1989	Drew Lewis 1981–1983 Elizabeth H. Dole 1983–1987 James H. Burnley 1987–1989	James B. Edwards 1981–1982 Donald P. Hodel 1982–1985 John S. Harrington 1985–1989	
Robert Mosbacher 1989–1991 Barbara Franklin 1991–1992	Elizabeth H. Dole 1989–1992 Lynn Martin 1992	Louis Sullivan 1989–1992	Lamar Alexander 1990–1992	Jack Kemp 1989–1992 1990–1992	Samuel Skinner 1989–1990 Andrew Card	James Watkins 1989–1992	Edward J. Derwinski 1989–1992
Ronald H. Brown 1993–1996 Mickey Kantor 1996–1997 William M. Daley 1997–	Robert B. Reich 1993–1997 Alexis M. Herman 1997–	Donna E. Shalala 1993–	Richard W. Riley 1993–	Henry G. Cisneros 1993–1997 Andrew M. Cuomo 1997–	Frederico F. Peña 1993–1997 Rodney Slater 1997–	Hazel O'Leary 1993–1997 Frederico F. Peña 1997–1998 Bill I. Richardson 1998–	Jesse Brown 1993–1998 Togo D. West, Jr. 1998–

Justices of the U.S. Supreme Court

Chief Justices appear in bold type

	Term of Service	Years of Service	Appointed by
John Jay	1789–1795	5	Washington
John Rutledge	1789–1791	1	Washington
William Cushing	1789–1810	20	Washington
James Wilson	1789–1798	8	Washington
John Blair	1789–1796	6	Washington
Robert H. Harrison	1789–1790	—	Washington
James Iredell	1790–1799	9	Washington
Thomas Johnson	1791–1793	1	Washington
William Paterson	1793–1806	13	Washington
John Rutledge[1]	1795	—	Washington
Samuel Chase	1796–1811	15	Washington
Oliver Ellsworth	1796–1800	4	Washington
Bushrod Washington	1798–1829	31	J. Adams
Alfred Moore	1799–1804	4	J. Adams
John Marshall	1801–1835	34	J. Adams
William Johnson	1804–1834	30	Jefferson
H. Brockholst Livingston	1806–1823	16	Jefferson
Thomas Todd	1807–1826	18	Jefferson
Joseph Story	1811–1845	33	Madison
Gabriel Duval	1811–1835	24	Madison
Smith Thompson	1823–1843	20	Monroe
Robert Trimble	1826–1828	2	J. Q. Adams
John McLean	1829–1861	32	Jackson
Henry Baldwin	1830–1844	14	Jackson
James M. Wayne	1835–1867	32	Jackson
Roger B. Taney	1836–1864	28	Jackson
Philip P. Barbour	1836–1841	4	Jackson
John Catron	1837–1865	28	Van Buren
John McKinley	1837–1852	15	Van Buren
Peter V. Daniel	1841–1860	19	Van Buren
Samuel Nelson	1845–1872	27	Tyler
Levi Woodbury	1845–1851	5	Polk
Robert C. Grier	1846–1870	23	Polk
Benjamin R. Curtis	1851–1857	6	Fillmore
John A. Campbell	1853–1861	8	Pierce
Nathan Clifford	1858–1881	23	Buchanan
Noah H. Swayne	1862–1881	18	Lincoln
Samuel F. Miller	1862–1890	28	Lincoln
David Davis	1862–1877	14	Lincoln
Stephen J. Field	1863–1897	34	Lincoln
Salmon P. Chase	1864–1873	8	Lincoln
William Strong	1870–1880	10	Grant
Joseph P. Bradley	1870–1892	22	Grant
Ward Hunt	1873–1882	9	Grant

[1]Acting Chief Justice; Senate refused to confirm appointment.

Chief Justices appear in bold type

	Term of Service	Years of Service	Appointed by
Morrison R. Waite	1874–1888	14	Grant
John M. Harlan	1877–1911	34	Hayes
William B. Woods	1880–1887	7	Hayes
Stanley Matthews	1881–1889	7	Garfield
Horace Gray	1882–1902	20	Arthur
Samuel Blatchford	1882–1893	11	Arthur
Lucius Q. C. Lamar	1888–1893	5	Cleveland
Melville W. Fuller	1888–1910	21	Cleveland
David J. Brewer	1890–1910	20	B. Harrison
Henry B. Brown	1890–1906	16	B. Harrison
George Shiras, Jr.	1892–1903	10	B. Harrison
Howell E. Jackson	1893–1895	2	B. Harrison
Edward D. White	1894–1910	16	Cleveland
Rufus W. Peckham	1895–1909	14	Cleveland
Joseph McKenna	1898–1925	26	McKinley
Oliver W. Holmes, Jr.	1902–1932	30	T. Roosevelt
William R. Day	1903–1922	19	T. Roosevelt
William H. Moody	1906–1910	3	T. Roosevelt
Horace H. Lurton	1910–1914	4	Taft
Charles E. Hughes	1910–1916	5	Taft
Willis Van Devanter	1911–1937	26	Taft
Joseph R. Lamar	1911–1916	5	Taft
Edward D. White	1910–1921	11	Taft
Mahlon Pitney	1912–1922	10	Taft
James C. McReynolds	1914–1941	26	Wilson
Louis D. Brandeis	1916–1939	22	Wilson
John H. Clarke	1916–1922	6	Wilson
William H. Taft	1921–1930	8	Harding
George Sutherland	1922–1938	15	Harding
Pierce Butler	1922–1939	16	Harding
Edward T. Sanford	1923–1930	7	Harding
Harlan F. Stone	1925–1941	16	Coolidge
Charles E. Hughes	1930–1941	11	Hoover
Owen J. Roberts	1930–1945	15	Hoover
Benjamin N. Cardozo	1932–1938	6	Hoover
Hugo L. Black	1937–1971	34	F. Roosevelt
Stanley F. Reed	1938–1957	19	F. Roosevelt
Felix Frankfurter	1939–1962	23	F. Roosevelt
William O. Douglas	1939–1975	36	F. Roosevelt
Frank Murphy	1940–1949	9	F. Roosevelt
Harlan F. Stone	1941–1946	5	F. Roosevelt
James F. Byrnes	1941–1942	1	F. Roosevelt
Robert H. Jackson	1941–1954	13	F. Roosevelt
Wiley B. Rutledge	1943–1949	6	F. Roosevelt

(continued)

Justices of the U.S. Supreme Court *(continued)*

Chief Justices appear in bold type

	Term of Service	Years of Service	Appointed by
Harold H. Burton	1945–1958	13	Truman
Fred M. Vinson	1946–1953	7	Truman
Tom C. Clark	1949–1967	18	Truman
Sherman Minton	1949–1956	7	Truman
Earl Warren	1953–1969	16	Eisenhower
John Marshall Harlan	1955–1971	16	Eisenhower
William J. Brennan, Jr.	1956–1990	34	Eisenhower
Charles E. Whittaker	1957–1962	5	Eisenhower
Potter Stewart	1958–1981	23	Eisenhower
Byron R. White	1962–1993	31	Kennedy
Arthur J. Goldberg	1962–1965	3	Kennedy
Abe Fortas	1965–1969	4	Johnson
Thurgood Marshall	1967–1991	24	Johnson
Warren E. Burger	1969–1986	18	Nixon
Harry A. Blackmun	1970–1994	24	Nixon
Lewis F. Powell, Jr.	1971–1987	15	Nixon
William H. Rehnquist[2]	1971–	—	Nixon
John P. Stevens III	1975–	—	Ford
Sandra Day O'Connor	1981–	—	Reagan
Antonin Scalia	1986–	—	Reagan
Anthony M. Kennedy	1988–	—	Reagan
David Souter	1990–	—	Bush
Clarence Thomas	1991–	—	Bush
Ruth Bader Ginsburg	1993–	—	Clinton
Stephen G. Breyer	1994–	—	Clinton

[2]Chief Justice from 1986 (Reagan administration).

Political Party Affiliations in Congress and the Presidency, 1789–1995*

Congress	Year	House* Majority Party	House* Principal Minority Party	House* Other (except Vacancies)	Senate* Majority Party	Senate* Principal Minority Party	Senate* Other (except Vacancies)	President and Party
1st	1789–1791	Ad-38	Op-26	—	Ad-17	Op-9	—	F (Washington)
2nd	1791–1793	F-37	DR-33	—	F-16	DR-13	—	F (Washington)
3rd	1793–1795	DR-57	F-48	—	F-17	DR-13	—	F (Washington)
4th	1795–1797	F-54	DR-52	—	F-19	DR-13	—	F (Washington)
5th	1797–1799	F-58	DR-48	—	F-20	DR-12	—	F (John Adams)
6th	1799–1801	F-64	DR-42	—	F-19	DR-13	—	F (John Adams)
7th	1801–1803	DR-69	F-36	—	DR-18	F-13	—	DR (Jefferson)
8th	1803–1805	DR-102	F-39	—	DR-25	F-9	—	DR (Jefferson)
9th	1805–1807	DR-116	F-25	—	DR-27	F-7	—	DR (Jefferson)
10th	1807–1809	DR-118	F-24	—	DR-28	F-6	—	DR (Jefferson)
11th	1809–1811	DR-94	F-48	—	DR-28	F-6	—	DR (Madison)
12th	1811–1813	DR-108	F-36	—	DR-30	F-6	—	DR (Madison)
13th	1813–1815	DR-112	F-68	—	DR-27	F-9	—	DR (Madison)
14th	1815–1817	DR-117	F-65	—	DR-25	F-11	—	DR (Madison)
15th	1817–1819	DR-141	F-42	—	DR-34	F-10	—	DR (Monroe)
16th	1819–1821	DR-156	F-27	—	DR-35	F-7	—	DR (Monroe)
17th	1821–1823	DR-158	F-25	—	DR-44	F-4	—	DR (Monroe)
18th	1823–1825	DR-187	F-26	—	DR-44	F-4	—	DR (Monroe)
19th	1825–1827	Ad-105	J-97	—	Ad-26	J-20	—	C (J. Q. Adams)
20th	1827–1829	J-119	Ad-94	—	J-28	Ad-20	—	C (J. Q. Adams)
21st	1829–1831	D-139	NR-74	—	D-26	NR-22	—	D (Jackson)
22nd	1831–1833	D-141	NR-58	14	D-25	NR-21	2	D (Jackson)
23rd	1833–1835	D-147	AM-53	60	D-20	NR-20	8	D (Jackson)
24th	1835–1837	D-145	W-98	—	D-27	W-25	—	D (Jackson)
25th	1837–1839	D-108	W-107	24	D-30	W-18	4	D (Van Buren)
26th	1839–1841	D-124	W-118	—	D-28	W-22	—	D (Van Buren)
27th	1841–1843	W-133	D-102	6	W-28	D-22	2	W (Harrison) W (Tyler)
28th	1843–1845	D-142	W-79	1	W-28	D-25	1	W (Tyler)
29th	1845–1847	D-143	W-77	6	D-31	W-25	—	D (Polk)
30th	1847–1849	W-115	D-108	4	D-36	W-21	1	D (Polk)
31st	1849–1851	D-112	W-109	9	D-35	W-25	2	W (Taylor) W (Fillmore)
32nd	1851–1853	D-140	W-88	5	D-35	W-24	3	W (Fillmore)
33rd	1853–1855	D-159	W-71	4	D-38	W-22	2	D (Pierce)
34th	1855–1857	R-108	D-83	43	D-40	R-15	5	D (Pierce)
35th	1857–1859	D-118	R-92	26	D-36	R-20	8	D (Buchanan)
36th	1859–1861	R-114	D-92	31	D-36	R-26	4	D (Buchanan)
37th	1861–1863	R-105	D-43	30	R-31	D-10	8	R (Lincoln)
38th	1863–1865	R-102	D-75	9	R-36	D-9	5	R (Lincoln)
39th	1865–1867	U-149	D-42	—	U-42	D-10	—	R (Lincoln) R (Johnson)
40th	1867–1869	R-143	D-49	—	R-42	D-11	—	R (Johnson)
41st	1869–1871	R-149	D-63	—	R-56	D-11	—	R (Grant)
42nd	1871–1873	R-134	D-104	5	R-52	D-17	5	R (Grant)
43rd	1873–1875	R-194	D-92	14	R-49	D-19	5	R (Grant)
44th	1875–1877	D-169	R-109	14	R-45	D-29	2	R (Grant)
45th	1877–1879	D-153	R-140	—	R-39	D-36	1	R (Hayes)
46th	1879–1881	D-149	R-130	14	D-42	R-33	1	R (Hayes)
47th	1881–1883	R-147	D-135	11	R-37	D-37	1	R (Garfield) R (Arthur)
48th	1883–1885	D-197	R-118	10	R-38	D-36	2	R (Arthur)

*Letter symbols for political parties. Ad—Administration; AM—Anti-Masonic; C—Coalition; D—Democratic; DR—Democratic-Republican; F—Federalist; J—Jacksonian; NR—National-Republican; Op—Opposition; R—Republican; U—Unionist; W—Whig.

Source: *Historical Statistics of the United States: Colonial Times to the Present*, Various eds. Washington, D.C.: GOP.

Political Party Affiliations in Congress and the Presidency, 1789–1995 *(continued)*

Congress	Year	House* Majority Party	House* Principal Minority Party	House* Other (except Vacancies)	Senate* Majority Party	Senate* Principal Minority Party	Senate* Other (except Vacancies)	President and Party
49th	1885–1887	D-183	R-140	2	R-43	D-34	—	D (Cleveland)
50th	1887–1889	D-169	R-152	4	R-39	D-37	—	D (Cleveland)
51st	1889–1891	R-166	D-159	—	R-39	D-37	—	R (B. Harrison)
52nd	1891–1893	D-235	R-88	9	R-47	D-39	2	R (B. Harrison)
53rd	1893–1895	D-218	R-127	11	D-44	R-38	3	D (Cleveland)
54th	1895–1897	R-244	D-105	7	R-43	D-39	6	D (Cleveland)
55th	1897–1899	R-204	D-113	40	R-47	D-34	7	R (McKinley)
56th	1899–1901	R-185	D-163	9	R-53	D-26	8	R (McKinley)
57th	1901–1903	R-197	D-151	9	R-55	D-31	4	R (McKinley) R (T. Roosevelt)
58th	1903–1905	R-208	D-178	—	R-57	D-33	—	R (T. Roosevelt)
59th	1905–1907	R-250	D-136	—	R-57	D-33	—	R (T. Roosevelt)
60th	1907–1909	R-222	D-164	—	R-61	D-31	—	R (T. Roosevelt)
61st	1909–1911	R-219	D-172	—	R-61	D-32	—	R (Taft)
62nd	1911–1913	D-228	R-161	1	R-51	D-41	—	R (Taft)
63rd	1913–1915	D-291	R-127	17	D-51	R-44	1	D (Wilson)
64th	1915–1917	D-230	R-196	9	D-56	R-40	—	D (Wilson)
65th	1917–1919	D-216	R-210	6	D-53	R-42	—	D (Wilson)
66th	1919–1921	R-240	D-190	3	R-49	D-47	—	D (Wilson)
67th	1921–1923	R-301	D-131	1	R-59	D-37	—	R (Harding)
68th	1923–1925	R-225	D-205	5	R-51	D-43	2	R (Coolidge)
69th	1925–1927	R-247	D-183	4	R-56	D-39	1	R (Coolidge)
70th	1927–1929	R-237	D-195	3	R-49	D-46	1	R (Coolidge)
71st	1929–1931	R-267	D-167	1	R-56	D-39	1	R (Hoover)
72nd	1931–1933	D-220	R-214	1	R-48	D-47	1	R (Hoover)
73rd	1933–1935	D-310	R-117	5	D-60	R-35	1	D (F. Roosevelt)
74th	1935–1937	D-319	R-103	10	D-69	R-25	2	D (F. Roosevelt)
75th	1937–1939	D-331	R-89	13	D-76	R-16	4	D (F. Roosevelt)
76th	1939–1941	D-261	R-164	4	D-69	R-23	4	D (F. Roosevelt)
77th	1941–1943	D-268	R-162	5	D-66	R-28	2	D (F. Roosevelt)
78th	1943–1945	D-218	R-208	4	D-58	R-37	1	D (F. Roosevelt)
79th	1945–1947	D-242	R-190	2	D-56	R-38	1	D (Truman)
80th	1947–1949	R-245	D-188	1	R-51	D-45	—	D (Truman)
81st	1949–1951	D-263	R-171	1	D-54	R-42	—	D (Truman)
82nd	1951–1953	D-243	R-199	1	D-49	R-47	—	D (Truman)
83rd	1953–1955	R-221	D-211	1	R-48	D-47	1	R (Eisenhower)
84th	1955–1957	D-232	R-203	—	D-48	R-47	1	R (Eisenhower)
85th	1957–1959	D-233	R-200	—	D-49	R-47	—	R (Eisenhower)
86th	1959–1961	D-283	R-153	—	D-64	R-34	—	R (Eisenhower)
87th	1961–1963	D-263	R-174	—	D-65	R-35	—	D (Kennedy)
88th	1963–1965	D-258	R-177	—	D-67	R-33	—	D (Kennedy) D (Johnson)
89th	1965–1967	D-295	R-140	—	D-68	R-32	—	D (Johnson)
90th	1967–1969	D-247	R-187	1	D-64	R-36	—	D (Johnson)
91st	1969–1971	D-243	R-192	—	D-58	R-42	—	R (Nixon)
92nd	1971–1973	D-255	R-180	—	D-54	R-44	2	R (Nixon)
93rd	1973–1975	D-242	R-192	1	D-56	R-42	2	R (Nixon, Ford)
94th	1975–1977	D-291	R-144	—	D-61	R-37	2	R (Ford)
95th	1977–1979	D-292	R-143	—	D-61	R-38	1	D (Carter)
96th	1979–1981	D-277	R-158	—	D-58	R-41	1	D (Carter)
97th	1981–1983	D-242	R-192	—	R-54	D-45	1	R (Reagan)
98th	1983–1985	D-266	R-167	2	R-55	D-45	—	R (Reagan)
99th	1985–1987	D-252	R-183	—	R-53	D-47	—	R (Reagan)
100th	1987–1989	D-258	R-177	—	D-55	R-45	—	R (Reagan)
101st	1989–1991	D-262	R-173	—	D-57	R-43	—	R (Bush)
102nd	1991–1993	D-267	R-167	1	D-57	R-43	—	R (Bush)
103rd	1993–1995	D-256	R-178	1	D-56	R-44	—	D (Clinton)
104th	1995–1997	R-230	D-204	1	R-52	D-48	—	D (Clinton)
105th	1997–1999	R-228	D-206	1	R-55	D-45	—	D (Clinton)
106th	1999–2001	R-223	D-211	1	R-55	D-45	—	D (Clinton)

CREDITS

INDEX

Indigo, 58, 73, 109, 282
Industrial Revolution, 274–281
Industrialization
 banking and, 280
 capital for, 279–280
 cottage industry, 276
 in early nineteenth century, 274–281
 in England, 276, 277
 inventions and, 277–278
 labor and, 280–281
 Lowell girls and, 280–281
 politics and, 280
 power for, 276–277
 "putting out" system, 276
 resources for, 279
 technological piracy and, 277
Infantry in Civil War, 439
Influenzas, 20
Inquisition, 24
Insane, treatment of, 338, *339*
Inter Caetera, 13, 24
Internal improvements. *See* Transportation
Intolerable Acts, 148–149, 151, 171
Inventions
 cotton gin, 282
 industrialization and, 277–278
 of Jefferson, 224
Ireland, Catholicism in, 125
Irish immigrants, 343–344
Iroquois, 39, 84, 87, 89–90, 92–93, *92*, 105, 128–129, 163, 447
Irving, Washington, 237
Isabella of Castille, Queen, 8, 12, 13, 19
Isthmus of Panama, 12
Italy, 9

Jackson, Andrew
 in Battle of New Orleans, 241–242, 268
 on Buchanan, 422
 Burr and, 233
 death of, 407
 Democratic party and, 293
 duels and, 301
 Peggy Eaton and, *308*, 311
 Florida expedition of, 272–273, 296, 312
 on government, 298
 Hermitage home of, 293, 296
 illness of, 310
 Indians and, 300–304
 internal improvements and, 258
 as log cabin president, 298
 as Mason, 296
 as "Old Hickory," 310
 opinions of, 289
 physical appearance of, 310
 portrait of, *299, 315*
 presidency of, 237, 302–306, 310–315, 387
 in presidential election of 1824, 291–292
 in presidential election of 1828, 296–298, *298*
 presidential inauguration of, *288*, 298
 and Second Bank of the United States, 312–315
 significance of, 315
 on slavery, 299
 social life of, 422
 spoils system and, 302
 Whigs' opposition to, 316
 on women and children, 299
Jackson, Rachel, 296
Jackson, Thomas J. "Stonewall," 441, 443, 446–447, 452, 458, 460
Jacobins, 207–208
Jamaica, 60
James, Jesse and Frank, 426
James I, King of England, 31, 34, 36, 37, 44, 46, 54, 106
James II, King of England, 56, 76
Jamestown, Va., 35–38, *35*, 44, 96
Jay, John, 179, 198, 210, 215
Jay's Treaty, 210, *211*, 214, 215, 216
Jefferson, Thomas
 achievements of, 223–225
 Banneker and, 153
 Burr's trial and, 234

on character traits of northerners and southerners, 350
 compared with Madison, 192
 Congregationalists' opposition to, 330
 and Constitution of U.S., 191
 and Declaration of Independence, 156–157, 162, 224
 and disestablishment of Anglican Church, 181
 on Erie Canal, 270
 French Revolution and, 207, 208
 on government, 272
 and Hamilton's financial policies, 205
 on human nature, 195, 224
 inventions of, 224
 on Jackson, 289
 and Kentucky and Virginia resolutions of 1798, 193, 218–219, 225, 227, 305, 306
 Louisiana Purchase and, 228–234, *231*, 382
 as minister to France, 192, 224
 on Monroe, 269
 Monticello home of, *222*, 224
 Northwest Ordinances and, 188
 presidency of, 225–236, 237
 in presidential election of 1796, 215–216
 in presidential election of 1800, 219, 296
 in presidential election of 1804, 233
 relationship with Sally Hemmings, 225, 350
 as secretary of state, 203, 208, 224
 as slaveowner, 153, 182, 225, 282, 350
 on slavery, 284, 349
 social life of, 227
 on Society of Cincinnati, 165
 and "strict construction" of U.S. Constitution, 205, 231
 University of Virginia and, 224, 320
 as vice president, 216, 224
 Washington and, 177, 201
 writings by, 224
Jeffersonian Republicans, 208, 214–220, 225–226, 238, 271–272, 290–291
Jenkins, Robert, 117
Jenkins' Ear, War of, 117
Jerez, Rodrigo de, 36
Jews
 after American Revolution, 181
 in colonial America, 55, 78, 79
 in Confederation period, *182*
 Spanish Inquisition against, 24
Jogues, Isaac, 56
"John Brown's Body," 474, 475
John I, King of Portugal, 10
John II, King of Portugal, 11
Johnson, Andrew, 470, 472, 479–486, *480*
Johnson, Anthony, 96
Johnson, Herschel V., 427
Johnson, Jeremiah "Liver-Eatin'," 388
Johnson, Lyndon B., presidency of, 472
Johnson, Richard M., 311
Johnson, Samuel, 103, 128, 152, 182
Johnston, Albert Sidney, 447, *448*, 450–451
Johnston, Joseph E., 441, 443, 446, 449, *449*, 460, 466–469
Joliet, Louis, 90–91
Jomini, Antoine-Henri, 438, 450
Jones, John Paul, 172
Jones, Thomas Catesby, 393
Judicial review principle, 227
Judiciary Act of 1789, 227
Julian, George W., 481
Jury trial, 130–131
Juvenile justice, 339

Kalb, Johann, 173
Kalm, Peter, 124
Kansas Territory
 Bleeding Kansas, 418–422
 geography of, 383–384
 Kansas-Nebraska Act and, 411–413, 418, *419*, 422, 424
 slavery in, *402*, 411, 418–422
Kansas-Nebraska Act, 411–413, 418, *419*, 422, 424
Karlsefni, Thorfinn, 8
Kearny, Stephen W., 394
Keelboats, 263–264

Kendall, Larcum, 71
Kennedy, John F., on Jefferson, 224
Kentucky, 166–167, 211, 233, 250, 302, 330–331
Kentucky Resolutions of 1798, 193, 218–219, 225, 227, 305, 306
Kenyon College, 365
Kett, Joseph F., 320–321
Key, Francis Scott, 238, 353
King, Martin Luther, Jr., 368, 392
King, Rufus, 271
"King Caucus," 290–291
King George's War, 117
King Philip's War, 89
King William's War, 110–111
King's College (Columbia), 116
King's Mountain, battle of, 164
Kiowa, 83
Knights of the White Camellia, 490
Know-Nothings, 344, 422–423
Knox, Henry, 164, 203
Kosciusko, Thaddeus, 173
Ku Klux Klan, 490

La Salle, Robert Cavelier, Sieur de, 91
Labor
 industrialization and, 280–281
 workingmen's parties in 1820s, 295
Ladonnière, René Goulaine de, 39
Lafayette, Marie Joseph, Marquis de, 172, 173, 177, 207, 300
Lafitte, Jean, 241
Laissez faire, 298, 317
Lake Champlain, Battle of, 240
Lake Erie, 239, 263
Lake Superior, 323
Land Act of 1804, 251–252
Land-grant colleges, 473
Land survey, rectangular system of, 187–188
Lane, Joseph, 427
Languages
 of Indians, 83, 85, 233
 of New Guinea, 85
 Webster's spelling book and dictionary, 268–269
Larned, Samuel, 334
Las Casas, Bartolomé de, 18–19, 93
Lassen, Peter, 384
Latin America. *See also* specific countries
 British colonies in, 60
 Meso-American civilization, 5–8, 14–16, 24
Latter-Day Saints. *See* Mormons
Lawrence, Kan., raid, 418, 420
Laws
 in Massachusetts Bay colony, 49–50
 property laws in colonial America, 107
 riders on bills, 400
 slave codes, 372–373
Lawson, Hugh, 317
Lay, Benjamin, 354, 355
Leclerc, Charles, 230
Lecompton Constitution, 424
Lee, Mother Ann, 333
Lee, Henry, 201
Lee, Jason, 388
Lee, Richard Henry, 133, 156
Lee, Robert E.
 as Civil War commander, 446–447, *449*, 452–453, 455, 458, 460–463, 465–468, 474
 as Davis's military adviser, 443
 and Harpers Ferry raid by John Brown, 426
 loyalty of, to Virginia, 426, 447
 portrait of, *461*
Leicester, Edward, 300
Leisler, Jacob, 76
Leisler's Rebellion, 78
Leopard, 236
Levant traders, 9
Lewis, Meriwether, 230–233, 382
Lewis and Clark Expedition, 230–233, *231*, 382
Lexington, 250
Lexington, battle of, 151, *154*
Liberator, 355–356, *356*, 357, 358, 365
Liberia, 353, *353*
Liberty party, 365